THE LIBRARY
W9-ANJ-133

After Tylor

After Tylor

British Social Anthropology
1888–1951

George W. Stocking, Jr.

The University of Wisconsin Press

The University of Wisconsin Press
114 North Murray Street
Madison, Wisconsin 53715

2 4 6 8 10 9 7 5 3 1

Printed in the United States of America

Publication of this book was assisted by a grant from the
Publication Program of the National Endowment for the Humanities,
an independent federal agency.

Library of Congress Cataloging-in-Publication Data
Stocking, George W., 1928–
After Tylor: British social anthropology, 1888–1951 /
George W. Stocking, Jr.
590 pp. cm.
Includes bibliographical references and index.
ISBN 0-299-14580-8
1. Ethnology—Great Britain—History—19th century.
2. Ethnology—Great Britain—History—20th century.
3. Social evolution—Great Britain—History.
I. Title.
GN308.3.G7S74 1995
306'.0941—dc20 95-6365

This book is dedicated to Elizabeth Steinberg, long-time colleague in the publication of histories of anthropology, for her commitment to the crafting of books and her tolerance of authorial idiosyncrasy.

Contents

Illustrations

Preface

Like *Victorian Anthropology*—to which it is a sequel—*After Tylor* has been long in the making. The bulk of the primary research, including work in British manuscript archives and interviews with senior British social anthropologists—was done in 1969 and 1973, during two six-month periods in England. A number of the chapters were drafted in the early 1970s as lectures for graduate courses, and during the 1980s I published several essays in the *History of Anthropology* series drawing on those lectures and on the research they had incorporated. Although I have of course kept up with (and often reviewed) the relevant literature, and have done considerable further research, most of this earlier material—rethought, restructured, reworked, and augmented—has found its way into the present book.[1] It represents the second and third volumes of what was originally conceived of as a trilogy, the first part of which became *Victorian Anthropology*.

Given the common genesis of these volumes, many of the orienting remarks I might offer about *After Tylor* would repeat those in the preface of *Victorian Anthropology*. Instead, I refer interested readers to those pages, and will comment here on ways this book differs from its predecessor, beginning with the matter of title. One might expect a sequel to *Victorian Anthropology* to be called "Edwardian Anthropology." That would hardly do, however, for the time span here covered, most of which might better be called "Georgian," were that appellation not preempted by an earlier historical period. After toying with some other possibilities, I decided in the end on *After Tylor*, with an added substantive and temporal qualifier. In doing so, I implicitly acknowledged certain characteristics of its argument.

Although longer than *Victorian Anthropology*, *After Tylor* has a narrower focus. There is nothing here comparable to what some might regard as the centerpiece of the earlier volume: "Victorian Cultural Ideology and the Image of Savagery (1780–1870)." In part, this lack reflects a difference in organizing historiographic principle. In contrast to *Victorian Anthropology*, with its successive circles of context, all concentric to the period 1850 to 1870, *After Tylor* moves in a straight chronological line from 1888 to 1951 (albeit with several backtracks imposed by its reiterative biographical structure). While I have tried to keep in mind a broad range of contexts for the developments I recount, *After Tylor* is not envisioned as an exercise in "multiple contextualization." I have not attempted here to present the emergence of British social anthropology in relation to contemporary British cultural ideology or social and political history. There is, for instance, no note made of the perhaps significant conjunction of Radcliffe-Brown's turn to synchronic functionalism between 1910 and 1914 and the contemporary social tumult recounted by George Dangerfield in *The Strange Death of Liberal England*. But one is struck immediately by the resonance of the major political-cultural issues of that account—the "worker's rebellion", the "women's rebellion" and the threat of civil war in Ireland—to agenda issues of present historical interpretation: class, gender, ethnicity (or as Edwardian rhetoric would have had it, "race"). That the "doctrine of survivals" should have been succeeded at this historical moment by an interest in what Radcliffe-Brown called the "social function of conservatism" seems an historical problem worth more systematic exploration.

Tylor's conception of anthropology as a liberal "reformer's science" purging Victorian culture of the unexamined "survivals" of traditional "superstition" took for granted its own unexamined utilitarian assumption: that conservatism, political or cultural, could have no positive "social function" (though were the issue posed to him, Tylor might have acknowledged its utility in preserving "respectability"). Had my book been more narrowly focussed chronologically—had it been "Edwardian Anthropology"—these and other themes that appear now in bits and snatches might have been given a structuring role in its narrative. One thinks, for instance, of Frazer's image of the "volcano" beneath "the smooth surface of cultured society" and Marett's preoccupation with "mobbish" psychology, or contrastively, of Radcliffe-Brown's anarchism and Haddon's socialistic urban sociological interests—not to mention the latter pair's links to Havelock Ellis, or the unconventional sexual identities of several of their anthropological confreres. Brought together in the light of Radcliffe-Brown's reference to the "social function of conservatism," these might form part of a more systematically contextualized view of a post-Victorian moment in the longer durée of British social anthropology. What has sometimes been understood in terms of a compatibility of theoretical orientation ("functionalism") and administrative policy ("indirect rule") in the mature colonialism of the interwar period (below, 368) might also (if not alternatively) be seen in relation to an earlier moment of domestic political and cultural crisis.

Far from feeling such broader contexts irrelevant, I encourage anyone so inclined to pursue this particular lead, along with others suggested by hints of detail or gestures of direction given in the present text—as well as issues unacknowledged even indirectly. However, I do feel that—quite aside from historiographic predilection, or constraints of form, or research exhaustion, or limits of space—there is a certain intellectual justification for the narrower focus of the present book. This has to do with the boundaries of anthropology in a certain phase of its development. The structure of the previous volume reflected the fact that the sources of Victorian anthropology were diverse, its ambitions global, its institutionalization limited, its professionalization barely begun, its tradition of intradisciplinary discourse undeveloped, and its boundaries therefore very permeable. This is not to imply that any scientific or scholarly discipline—perhaps least of all anthropology—can be impermeable to formative (or constraining) forces that, far from being simply "external," operate inside the minds and within the institutions of any organized community of disciplined inquirers.[2] But it is to suggest that as anthropological inquiry became institutionalized and professionalized, discourse within the disciplinary community became somewhat more endogenous. Anthropological discourse continued to reflect such generalized human concerns as origin, difference, religion, sexuality, kinship, work—and such more specifically Eurocentric concerns as the relationships between those called "savages" and an expansive European civilization. But discussion of these topics tended increasingly to be constrained by prior discourse within the same disciplinary community, or by issues raised within closely related disciplinary communities, and in the process less accessible to outsiders and less directly affected by exogenous influences. Without limiting my account to the development of "method and theory," my primary focus has been on the development of anthropology as a form of disciplined inquiry. Even in treating the ineluctable relation of anthropology and colonialism, the emphasis has been on the way in which colonial concerns contributed to the institutionalization of a particular movement within British anthropology.

Here, then, is another narrowing implicit in the telos of my title: this is a book about the emergence of a particular subdiscipline or form of anthropology which in Britain came to be called social anthropology. As others have more recently argued—and as was clearly evident in my treatment of its Victorian phase—British anthropology for most of the period covered by this book was a somewhat more diverse and embracive inquiry than it came to be among the followers of Malinowski and Radcliffe-Brown. If the linguistic anthropology that became part of the "four fields" in the American anthropological tradition was underdeveloped in Britain, the fact remains that anthropology in the British evolutionary and ethnological traditions was a quite wide-ranging inquiry.[3] It encompassed prehistoric archeology, material culture, and physical anthropology, and had close relationships with folklore and with classical studies. This greater range of inquiry is surely evident here, insofar as the emergence of functionalism in its "pure" Malinowskian or "hybrid" Radcliffe-Brownian form is presented in relation to prior paradigms of evolutionism and diffusionist ethnology, and other connections have also been suggested (notably with psychology, psychoanalysis, sociology, and philosophy). In contrast to accounts which see social anthropology as suddenly emergent in 1922, or localized in the work of a particular school, *After Tylor* does attempt to cover a fairly broad range of anthropological activity over an extended period. The emphasis, however, has not been on recapturing a broader unity of anthropology that may once have existed, but rather on tracing the process by which a narrower inquiry emerged.

There are of course losses as well as gains in such a narrowing of focus. Among them is the critique of "race," which came later in Britain than in the United States, and did not play the same role in the development of anthropological theory—and which is treated here only in several footnotes.[4] More generally, there were many people who published on anthropological topics and were active in anthropological institutions in the period from 1888 to 1951 who here receive only slight notice or go unmentioned—as well as others, briefly resurrected, who may well merit more extensive treatment. Rather than representing cohorts, the argument here follows a certain group of characters, who interacted with one another around certain central issues of debate throughout a longer period of time. Even for these anthropologists, I am acutely conscious that much has been scanted or excluded. Quite aside from archives that I could not consult or published sources that I may have overlooked, there are any number (several iceberg-tips) of notes and photocopies in my files that are not reflected in my account. And while a number of those treated at length (including Fison and Codrington, Lang and Marett, Elliot Smith and Perry, as well as Hocart) are not customarily included in the genealogy of British social anthropology, my narrative is presented in what are, speaking loosely, lineage terms.

Lineage, of course, was one of the central concepts of British social anthropology,[5] and consistent also with the structure of British university life: on one of the two occasions when I interviewed him, Evans-Pritchard spoke of his position at Oxford in terms of a rather short lineage connecting him ("my chair") through Radcliffe-Brown and Marett directly to Edward Tylor. While I would like to think that the intellectual lineage constructed in this book is more complex than such reminiscence suggests, it does include most of the usual suspects, starting with Tylor and culminating in Radcliffe-Brown—although without dealing more than incidentally with the interwar cohort of their students.

While *After Tylor* is not in any systematic way a comparative study, there is a thread of contrastive allusion to the work of Franz Boas and his students in the United States—a contrast which plays a role in the formal structuring of the book. In making these trans-Atlantic connections, however, I am not simply referencing what for many years has been the other major focus of my own historical research.[6] I also follow the lead of many of my historical actors, for whom the Boasian tradition was a quite frequent reference point. With several exceptions, my allusions come in the context of direct interchange between the two traditions, which for some purposes may be regarded as variants of a single hegemonic anglophone anthropology.

After Tylor does not explore all aspects of theoretical or methodological issues that might interest present anthropologists, and it refers only occasionally to the very considerable later literature in which the work of earlier anthropologists is subject to explication, elaboration, evaluation, or critique. Most notable in this regard are the two culminating figures, Malinowski and Radcliffe-Brown, whose work has been the subject of extensive discussion, much of it critical. So critical, indeed, that one may be tempted to ask, "How could so many presumably intelligent anthropologists have been so easily infected by such ostensibly sterile and/or derivative viewpoints?" Without accepting the terms of this query, and acknowledging the limits of my own contextualization, I hope that the present narrative may help us to understand how anthropological viewpoints since criticized or rejected might once have seemed reasonable to reasonable men and women.

This need not imply that the assumptions, the forms, and the boundaries of inquiry established in the years before 1950 may not appropriately be called into question (as many of them have been), or that they might not be recontextualized from a more systematically critical point of view. My own approach, however, is still motivated by the "historicist" spirit which I hope has characterized my work over the last four decades. Although my understanding of the limits of historicism has evolved since I wrote the essay on "The Limits of Presentism and Historicism" in 1966, and although I feel that deconstruction and defamiliarization may contribute to historical understanding, I construe my role as historian more in terms of reconstruction and refamiliarization.[7] My goal is that of representation rather than critique. Like an anthropologist, I seek to understand the contexts and modes of thought, expression, and action of people who lived in worlds which, though continuous with, were rather different from my own. Although I may be critical of features of their world—and especially of those that have been constitutive of features that I reject in my own—I have chosen as historian rather to represent than to criticize them. To this end, I rely heavily on the actual words of my actors, as preserved in printed or written form, within the limits of my transcriptive abilities.* As an incidental consequence, I note here that the spelling of native words and the terminology of ethnic identification may at points be incorrect by present standards; by the same token, where my actors have used masculinist or racialist rhetoric, I have not attempted to correct them.

But if *After Tylor* attempts to recreate past anthropological worlds in a narrative mode, it is nevertheless intended to be analytical rather than anecdotal. There is, of course, a great deal of analysis involved in the construction of an effective narrative argument. And aside from that which is explicitly argued, there is also a great deal here that is, as it were, "written between the lines"—a phrase I use to describe a narrative argument composed of details selected precisely because they suggest or illustrate larger interpretive points that may not be elaborated as such. All this, to the end of creating a thickly textured and variously contextured historical tapestry that seeks (albeit uncertainly) to represent in verisimilar narrative fashion the emergence of British social anthropology. To the extent that I have been successful, then others, with assumptions (epistemological and ideological) and agendas (deconstructive or reconstitutive) different from my own, may find this book both interesting and useful, for a while to come.

*It should be noted that, from the mid-1920s on, there has survived (at the ever-moving margin of memory) a body of oral tradition surrounding the history of British social anthropology—as indeed, of anthropology generally. A colleague of mine once told me (at second hand, from those who had been there) that in the 1950s certain elder social anthropologists used to take fledglings on rural outings, on which they would indoctrinate them in the authorized version of the discipline's mythistory. My files (and memories) include a number of such stories, as well as more systematic notes on conversations, interviews, or reminiscent seminar presentations with or by the figures of this narrative (below, 533). In a general way, the latter have informed my historical understanding, and I have occasionally referred to them for specific information which seemed important for my account and consistent with other sources. It is historiographically appropriate to note, however, that just as oral tradition runs the risk of mythicization, so the exclusion (and eventual loss) of anecdote involves, at the very least, a certain dessication. But despite the urging of anthropological colleagues to rely more on oral evidence (for them, a traditionally privileged mode), my account is based almost entirely on written sources, both published and unpublished.

Acknowledgments

In the long course of working on this book, I have accumulated a large number of scholarly debts—intellectual, institutional, funding, and otherwise. Of the many previously acknowledged in *Victorian Anthropology,* I will refer only to several here, along with many new ones. These include the archivists and other staff members of the various repositories listed below under Manuscript Sources who graciously guided me to and allowed me to read and copy correspondence and other materials relating to this project, as well the librarians at other institutions at which I pursued it. Early in the research process, I was based for a time at King's College, Cambridge (1969), and subsequently for several months in the Department of Anthropology of the London School of Economics (1973). Three other institutions later provided support, financial and otherwise, for extended periods during which the bulk of the writing was done: the Center for Advanced Study in the Behavioral Sciences in Stanford, California (1976–1977), the Getty Center for the History of Art and the Humanities in Santa Monica, California (1988–1989), and the Institute for Advanced Study, Princeton, New Jersey (1992–1993); at the first and third of those places my work was supported by the National Endowment for the Humanities. Throughout the period of research and writing, the Department of Anthropology at the University of Chicago has provided a uniquely supportive milieu, as well as occasional financial assistance from the Adolph and Marian Lichtstern Fund for Anthropological Research. The Wenner-Gren Foundation for Anthropological Research gave support for closely related projects. There are also a large number of debts to individuals—more, I am sure, than memory and notes enable me to recall. I am, of course, especially grateful to Helena Wayne, daughter of Bronislaw Malinowski, and Cynthia Pike, daughter of A. R. Radcliffe-Brown, who have been helpful in various ways. Among colleagues in the United States I think especially of Bob Richards, who has long-sufferingly served as my computer guru. Others who have offered advice or assistance, bibliographical or otherwise, include Andrew Apter, Ralph Austen, Barney Cohn, John Comaroff, Ray Fogelson, Dell Hymes, Robert Alun Jones, Marshall Sahlins, Hal Scheffler, David Schneider, Michael Silverstein, Raymond Smith, and Joan

Vincent. I am particularly grateful to those (listed below, under Oral Sources) who gave me the benefit of their more direct personal knowledge and experience of the later phases of this history, including several who over more extended periods responded to queries offered by mail or in conversation: Sir Raymond Firth, and the late Fred Eggan, Meyer Fortes, and Sol Tax. I owe thanks also to British anthropologists of the more recent period who answered postal queries, including Anne Akeroyd, Jonathan Benthall, Maurice Bloch, Mary Douglas, Roy Ellen, Tim Ingold, Peter Lawrence, Ioan Lewis, John Middleton, Rodney Needham, John Peel, Peter Rivière, Andrew Strathern, Marilyn Strathern, and James Urry. In addition, there are a number of people in Britain and commonwealth countries who assisted my attempts to find suitable illustrations—among them John Davis, Deborah James, David Phillipson, Pamela Reynolds, and Christopher Wright. At various points along the way, the research and preparation of the text have been assisted by Matti Bunzl, Lawrence Carucci, Mark Francillon, Gabrielle Lyon, Edward Martinek, Marcia Tucker, Bill Young, and Miklós Vörös (who prepared a preliminary index of proper names)—as well as by students in seminars and courses devoted to topics herein treated. Chapter One was presented in more or less its present form in a seminar at the Institute for Advanced Study and to the Morris Fishbein Workshop in the History of the Human Sciences at the University of Chicago. To all who assisted, I offer my thanks. However, since no one but myself and my editor, Elizabeth Steinberg, has read the final version of this manuscript, and since her careful attention to detail is matched by an openness to my occasional resistances, I have no one but myself to blame for any errors, weaknesses, or inadequacies that remain. Finally, as always, there is my wife Carol Bowman Stocking, who as usual resists acknowledgment, but who gives me great freedom to do my own scholarly thing.

After Tylor

Prologue
Tylor and the Reformation of Anthropology

In November 1888, Edward Burnett Tylor, then near the peak of his reputation and influence as the leading British anthropologist of the nineteenth century, read a paper to a meeting of the Anthropological Institute of Great Britain and Ireland "On a Method of Investigating the Development of Institutions; Applied to Laws of Marriage and Descent." By this time, Tylor's great period of anthropological achievement lay behind him. His magnum opus, *Primitive Culture,* had been in print for nearly twenty years; the last of his four book-length works, a brief general treatise on the science of anthropology, had appeared seven years previously, at the time he became Reader in Anthropology at Oxford University. In neither work was Tylor primarily concerned with the topics that were later to be central to British social anthropology: kinship and social organization. Although he had published several essays on matters of "Primitive Sociology," for the most part he relegated such problems to John McLennan and other practitioners of what he called "the Comparative Jurisprudence of the lower races," while he attended to the evolutionary study of culture, with emphasis on language, myth, religion, and material culture. However, his first major anthropological work, *Researches into the Early History of Mankind,* had contained a chapter on the geographical distribution of "some remarkable customs"—including marriage prohibitions, avoidance, and the couvade—and from that time on Tylor seems to have collected systematic information on these and other sociological matters. Twenty-three years later, in what was surely the most important contribution of his later years, he presented the results of an analysis of data on some 350 different peoples, first in a public lecture at Oxford and then to his anthropological confreres in London.[1]

Because it contains in compressed form all the major methodological and conceptual assumptions of evolutionary anthropology, the argument of Tylor's paper is worthy of some "unpacking." His explicitly stated concern was the improvement of anthropological method, a matter to which he devoted attention at various points throughout his career, and his goal was classically positivistic: to overcome "a certain not unkindly hesitancy on the part of men engaged in the precise operations of mathematics, physics, chemistry, [and] biology to admit that the problems of anthropology are amenable to scientific treatment." Specifically, Tylor wanted to establish the central methodological principle of social evolutionism—the comparative method—on a sounder basis "of tabulation and classification." In doing so, he appealed to the authority of the leading German anthropologist, Adolf Bastian, who was "never weary of repeating that in statistical investigation the future of anthropology lies." Although Tylor argued in terms of "adhesions" rather than "correlations," it is likely also that he had in mind the work of the leading British statistician, Francis Galton, who as president of the Anthropological Institute chaired the meeting at which Tylor gave his paper—and who one month later himself gave the paper in which he first used the term we now associate with his name. And as Galton reminded the audience, Tylor's enterprise was much in the spirit of Herbert Spencer, who "went to great cost . . . to obtain a collection of the customs of all available nations, savage and civilised, arranged in a uniform and orderly manner for purposes of intercomparison."[2]

While Tylor's statistical method looked explicitly to the future of anthropological inquiry, the substance of his paper dealt with what for two decades had been a central issue of theoretical concern among social evolutionary writers: "the formation of laws of marriage and descent." In approaching this problem, Tylor proceeded like the artist who began a large battle scene with the bayonet of a single soldier, starting "in one corner of the field" with the particular custom of "avoidance"—the "barbaric etiquette" by which marriage partners might not look at, speak to, or even mention the names of their immediate affinal relatives. "Absurd as the custom may seem to Europeans," Tylor had found it among 66 of his 350 peoples—in 45 cases between the husband and the wife's relatives; in 13, between the wife and the husband's relatives; and in 8, mutually. The next step in painting the larger picture was to examine the "adhesions" of this "quaint and somewhat comic custom," by "showing which peoples have the same custom, and what other customs accompany it or lie apart from it."[3]

Pursuing this tack, Tylor looked next at "customs of the world as to residence after marriage," which he grouped in three categories: 65 cases of the husband's permanent residence in the wife's family abode; 76 more in which after a temporary stay there, the married couple removed themselves to the husband's home; and 141 in which the wife moved immediately to the home of the husband. The "adhesion" of the residence and avoidance rules was evident from the fact that their coincidences were more than might be expected "following the ordinary law of chance distribution." Among the cases of what would now be called matrilocal residence there were 14 in which there was ceremonial avoidance between the husband and the wife's relatives, whereas a chance association would have predicted only 9. To "find a reason" for these connections, Tylor recalled the analogous English "social rite" of "cutting," appealing to the similarity of the working "of the human mind in all stages of civilisation" as a ground for suggesting that what was involved was a refusal, in the English idiom, to "recognize" the intruding relative.[4]

From here, Tylor moved to another custom no less "quaint-seeming" to the European mind: "the practice of naming the parent from the child"—for which he coined the term "teknonymy." Illustrating his argument with three overlapping circles, Tylor noted that the adhesions of teknonymy with avoidance and with maternal residence were each more than chance would have predicted. Even more significantly, there were eleven instances in which all three customs occurred together, which should have happened "between once and twice"—suggesting "their common causation by the heavy odds of six to one." To account for "the origin" of the three customs, it was "not necessary to invent a hypothesis"; the "luminous instance" of the Cree Indians was enough to suggest that the father was "ceremonially treated as a stranger till his child, being born a member of the family, gives him a status as father of a member of the family, whereupon they consistently leave off the farce of not recognizing him." That Tylor in fact conflated "cause" and "origin" with the notion of "rational motive" is evident in his comments on those cases in which the husband avoided his wife's relatives despite the fact that he did not live with them: this apparently "motiveless proceeding" became intelligible on the assumption that it was "a survival from a time when he would have lived with them"—a possibility which Tylor documented with ethnographic data provided by his Australian correspondent A. W. Howitt.[5]

Having thus introduced a temporal dimension into his causal picture, Tylor offered a second graphic representation, in which horizontal lines separated the three residence patterns, and the avoidance cases were represented by vertically rectilinear figures indicating the proportion in each of the three residence sectors—which Tylor now began to call "periods" or "stages." From the fact that cases of mutual avoidance or avoidance of the husband's family by the wife were missing from the lower sector, Tylor argued that residence on the wife's side must have been earliest, since, if the chart were turned upside down, "avoidance between the husband and the wife's family would be represented as arising in the stage when the husband lived away from it, while avoidance between the wife and the husband's family, which ought on this supposition to continue by survival into the stage of residence on the wife's side, is not found there."[6]

With the pattern of his argument established, Tylor broadened his canvas to encompass "the great division of society into matriarchal and patriarchal"—classifications which he immediately proceeded to refine, first by distinguishing the specific features of descent, authority, succession, and inheritance, and then by substituting the more "appropriate" terms "maternal" and "paternal" (with "maternal-paternal" for his intermediate "stage"). He then went on to look at customs that he felt could be "used as indicators" to determine "the direction in which mankind has tended to move from one of the stages to another." The first of these was the levirate (the rule governing remarriage of a widow to her husband's brother or another affinal kinsman), which Tylor suggested was "sufficiently accounted for as a custom of substitution, belonging to the period when marriage is a compact not so much between two individuals as between two families"—and which, in the transitional stage, began to be replaced by the principle of "filial succession." Turning then to the couvade, a "farcical proceeding" in which the father "makes a ceremonial pretense of being the mother," Tylor followed Johann Bachofen's "great treatise" (*Das Mutterrecht*) in arguing that this "apparently absurd custom, which for twenty centuries has been the laughing-stock of mankind, proves to be not merely incidentally an indicator of the tendency of society from maternal to paternal, but the very sign and record of that vast change."[7]

In all of this, the concept of survivals was the linch-pin of Tylor's reasoning, which he described in geological terms: "Just as the forms of life . . . of the Carboniferous formation may be traced on into the Permian, but Permian types and fossils are absent from the Carboniferous strata formed before they came into existence, so here widow-inheritance and couvade, which, if the maternal system had been later than the paternal, would have lasted on into it, prove by their absence the priority of the maternal." Generalizing his argument, Tylor spoke of it as a culmination of the social evolutionary tradition that had emerged in the 1860s: "Thus the present method confirms on an enlarged and firm basis the inference as to the antiquity of the maternal system arrived at by the pioneers of the investigation, Bachofen and McLennan, and supported by the later research of a generation of able investigators—Morgan, Lubbock, Bastian, Giraud-Teulon, Fison, Howitt, Wilken, Post, Lippert and others."[8]

With "the great social transformation" previously delineated by the major social evolutionary anthropologists thus reconfirmed, Tylor went on to incorporate into the picture several customs that had been matters of sharp controversy among them. On the one hand, there were "marriage by capture" and "exogamy," the significance of which had been debated since McLennan first advanced a theory of the evolution of "primitive marriage" in 1865; on the other, there was the "classificatory system of relationships"—the grouping of both lineal and collateral relatives within the same category of kinship terminology—which the dean of American evolutionary anthropologists, Lewis Henry Morgan, had interpreted in terms of an interrelated series of stages in the evolution of marriage forms and kinship systems, culminating in the monogamic "descriptive system" of the Aryan and Semitic "races."[9]

After using the distribution of different forms of "marriage by capture" to demonstrate "the breaking up of the maternal system," Tylor offered an extended discussion of "exogamy," in the context of the "classificatory system of relationships"—the two customs being, he suggested, "in fact two sides of one institution." Recent ethnographic evidence had shown that, contrary to McLennan's usage, exogamy had to do not with "the capture of wives in war between alien nations, but rather with the regulation of marriages within groups of clans or tribes who have connubium"—so that a tribe as a whole might be endogamous at the same time that its component clans practiced exogamy. Tylor focussed especially on a group of twenty-one peoples who would not allow the marriage of the children of brothers, or the children of sisters, but did allow the child of a brother to marry the child of a sister, a practice to which he gave the name "cross-cousin marriage." Recalling R. H. Codrington's description of marriage classes among Melanesians, and the Australian data of A. W. Howitt and Lorimer Fison, which Fison had used to explain the origin of Morgan's Turanian system of relationships, Tylor suggested that the simplest systems of exogamy, those which were "dual in their nature, that is consisting of two classes or groups of classes, stand in direct connection with cross-cousin marriage and classificatory relationship." Examining his data for adhesions between exogamy and the classificatory system, Tylor found thirty-three cases where chance would have predicted twelve—which suggested to him that there was "a close causal connexion between the two institutions." Thus McLennan and Morgan, who had engaged in "sharp discussion" over the former's allegation that the classificatory system was "a mere system of addresses" without sociological significance, were in fact "all the while allies pushing forward the same doctrine from different sides."[10]

Having resolved to his satisfaction the sharpest theoretical controversy within the social evolutionary school, Tylor moved finally to address its most important unresolved conundrum: the meaning and origin of exogamy. Restating his objections to McLennan's explanation in terms of marriage by capture, Tylor recalled how, back in 1865 (i.e., before McLennan had given the custom its name) he himself had suggested that "marrying out" might reflect "the wish to bind different tribes together in friendship by intermarriage." Drawing now on further ethnographic data, Tylor suggested that there had been "a period in the growth of society" when the distinction between endogamy and exogamy would have been "a political question of the first importance." So long as "small hordes" wandering over unpopulated areas could find "abundant food," endogamous units could persist and if necessary divide without coming into conflict. But when growing populations pressed against one another, the "policy of isolation" would no longer suffice. In this new situation, exogamy, "by enabling a growing tribe to keep itself compact by constant unions between its spreading clans," would give those tribes practicing it an overriding advantage: "again and again in the world's history, savage tribes must have had plainly before their minds the simple practical alternative between marrying out and being killed out." Whatever the problematic relation between exogamy and totemism (an issue recently broached by William Robertson Smith) the adaptive function of exogamy itself was clear enough: resisting "the tendency of uncultured populations to disintegrate," it cemented them "into nations capable of living together in peace and holding together in war, till they reach the period of higher military and political organisation."[11]

Ostensibly, Tylor was more interested in his innovative method than in the substance of his argument. And he was not unaware of certain of its limitations. Thus he cautioned his audience that, in postulating a reason for any empirically determined "causal connexion between two groups of phenomena," the investigator was on "less solid ground," since the presumed reason "may be only analogous to the real reason, or only indirectly corresponding with it, or only partly expressing it, as its correlation with other connexions may eventually show"—and suggested that this methodological reservation was "to be taken as understood through the rest of this enquiry." But as his opening analogy of the artist painting the battle scene suggested, Tylor's methodological brush, starting from a single custom, had swept across a very broad evolutionary canvas. As soon as the method of "adhesions" was "systematically applied, principles of social development become visible":

> Even the diagrams of this paper may suffice to show that the institutions of man are as distinctively stratified as the earth on which he lives. They succeed each other in series substantially uniform over the globe, independent of what seem the comparatively superficial differences of race and language, but shaped by similar human nature acting through successively changed conditions in savage, barbaric and civilised life.[12]

Edward Burnett Tylor, c. 1900, at his desk, inscribing global evolutionary comparison. (Courtesy of the Pitt Rivers Museum, University of Oxford)

As this climactic quotation suggests, Tylor's paper was in fact a powerfully condensed summary representation of twenty-five years of social evolutionary argument. All of the evolutionary principles were there: the psychic unity of mankind, the uniform stages of development, the doctrine of survivals, and, of course, the comparative method, which was the primary focus of the paper. All the major evolutionary writers were not only referred to but brought together within a single interpretive frame. And throughout there was the characteristic tone of tolerantly patronizing ethnocentrism: savage customs might be farcical, but viewed in evolutionary context, they were rational, and they could be made the subject of systematic scientific investigation. If one were to choose a single paper to exemplify the paradigm of social evolutionary argument, one would be hard put to find a better one than this. The difficulty—clear now, though it could not have been to Tylor—was that it was not the prospective exemplar of an ascendant paradigm, but the retrospective exemplar of a paradigm about to enter a period of decline.[13]

This is not to say that Tylor's paper was without influence on later anthropology. Quite the contrary: it was one of the most important single papers in the history of the discipline, widely influential at the turn of the century, and continuing to be widely cited and several times reprinted on into the second half of the twentieth century. But the paper—and the discussion it provoked—can as well be read as the beginning of a period of questioning of the assumptions of "classical evolutionism," a period of criticism, doubt, recantation, and conversion which over the next several decades was to lead to what has been called "the revolution in anthropology."[14]

Even on the very evening that Tylor spoke, serious questions were raised about his methodological innovation—questions which, although posed in rather narrow terms, in fact threatened to undercut a basic assumption of evolutionary anthropology. Francis Galton, whose racially oriented biometric work did not preclude a critical interest in methodological issues in what would now be called cultural anthropology, expressed concern about "the degree in which the customs of the tribes and races which are compared together are independent." If it happened that "some of the tribes had derived [these customs] from a common source, so that they were duplicate copies of the same original," then they could not be treated as separate cases of adhesions. Similarly, W. H. Flower, of the British Museum, after congratulating Tylor on the "application of a rigid statistical method of research," cautioned that "the value of such a method depended entirely upon the units of comparison being of equivalent value." In response to the suggestion that "some of the concurrences might result from transmission from a common source," Tylor noted that this was "a difficulty ever present in such investigations." But he insisted that "when a community or group of communities follows a law of marriage and descent substantially similar, this may be taken as a unit, notwithstanding historical connection and the consequent partial correspondence which may exist between it and other unit systems." Assuming the role of disciplinary patriarch, he went on to reassure his colleagues that "correspondences brought about by historical connexion tend to set off against [i.e., balance] one another, leaving the results of general human action more or less clear."[15]

Despite Tylor's casual dismissal of what was later to go into the literature as "Galton's problem,"[16] some rather serious methodological and conceptual issues had in fact been broached—issues that Galton and Flower were not themselves fully aware of. In asking whether certain customs might not have "a common source," Galton as a statistical methodologist was concerned with what would count as a unit for quantitative comparative purposes. But when Tylor in response spoke of this as a difficulty "ever present in such investigations," he was in fact referring to a more general problem that had concerned him since the beginning of his anthropological career: whether the occurence of similar cultural phenomena in two human groups was to be explained as the result of "the like working of men's minds under like conditions," or "as proof of blood relationship or of intercourse, direct or indirect, between the races among whom it is found." Reduced to the alternative of "independent invention" or "diffusion" (intercourse and racial inheritance being two different manifestations of a common historical source), this issue serves as a marker of several major transitions in the history of anthropology. The first was the transition from diffusionary "ethnology" to evolutionary "anthropology" in the 1860s, in which Tylor emerged as the preeminent British anthropologist of the later nineteenth century; the second was the reaction against evolutionism and the international reassertion of diffusionary ethnology in the early twentieth century, first in the United States, and later in Germany and England, as Tylor faded from the scene.[17] From this point of view, "Galton's problem" may be taken as foreshadowing this later development—though as a lifelong convert to the evolutionary views his cousin Darwin advanced in 1858, Galton would scarcely have intended this.

Similarly, the matter of defining "units of comparison of equivalent value" raised, if only by implication, the further problem of the definition of cultural categories: whether, when classifying two apparently similar cultural practices among two different groups, the armchair anthropologist was dealing with two instances of one phenomenon or separate examples of two quite different phenomena. For Galton, Flower, and Tylor, who were still secure in their epistemological ethnocentrism, this issue did not arise; but in the context of an emerging tradition of academically trained ethnographic fieldworkers, it was to become a troublesome one for some anthropologists in the next generation.

In 1888 it was already troubling the young German émigré ethnographer Franz Boas, who the year before had raised the question of whether cultural artifacts that American evolutionary anthropologists had classified into "genera" and "species" were not instead superficially similar instances of phenomena with quite different cultural meanings. And during the very month in which Tylor delivered his paper, Boas had in process an essay "On Alternating Sounds" in which he argued that sounds in non-European languages which European observers had heard as varying renditions of a sound in their own language were rather, from the native point of view, two quite different sounds that European observers had difficulty assimilating to one of their own taken-for-granted sound categories. As was gradually to emerge in the more general critique of evolutionism Boas was then beginning to develop, the broader problem was whether the cultural practices of savages were to be treated as imperfect approximations of those of European civilization, or rather as quite differently constituted cultural categorizations that were at best problematically commensurable to a Eurocentric evolutionary standard.[18]

When Tylor presented his paper to the Anthropological Institute, Boas was already serving as field ethnographer for a committee the British Association for the Advancement of Science had established to investigate the Indians of the Northwest Coast of Canada; within a few weeks, Tylor, who chaired the committee, had sent him a copy. Having been trained in physics and having worked under Bastian at the Berlin Ethnographic Museum, Boas was more open than most young anthropologists might have been to the possibilities of such a statistical approach. According to one later recollection, for a time he felt that "everything could be solved by methods" implicit in Tylor's paper. Boas, however, applied his version of Tylor's method of adhesions not to a worldwide comparison of social customs, but to a study of the regional distribution of folklore elements, and his goal was from the beginning explicitly diffusionary. He wanted to "reconstruct the original myths of each people, and to trace the migration of myths," in order to see how borrowed elements were "modified by preexisting ideas." Boas felt that this procedure would cast light on a fundamental issue of evolutionary anthropology: the "independent origin of ideas and inventions" in different tribes—which, as we have noted, may be glossed as a variant of "Galton's problem."[19]

In 1888, Boas himself still accepted the notion of the evolutionary priority of matrifocal forms. But by 1896, his distribution studies of folktale elements and other aspects of Northwest Coast culture, in the context of a systematic critique of evolutionary racial assumptions, had led him to a general critique of evolutionary anthropology. In "The Limitations of the Comparative Method of Anthropology," Boas still affirmed the ultimate goal of deriving "general laws" of human development, but he insisted that comparison was only legitimate when preceded by historical study, since apparently like phenomena might in fact be the result of quite different historical processes—which may be glossed as a transformation of "Galton's problem."[20]

By that time, Tylor himself had come to doubt the evolutionary priority of "the matriarchal family system." And in a letter acknowledging Boas' paper, he suggested that Boas' work pointed toward "a most necessary reformation" in anthropology, in which "the logical screw" would have to be "very much tightened up." Tylor himself, however, did not attempt the tightening; much of his work in the period after 1888 is better interpreted as an attempt to shore up some of the basic assumptions of evolutionary anthropology—notably, the defense of animism and the equation of antipodal peoples with paleolithic man. And despite Tylor's private appreciation of the power of Boas' critique, the reformation in anthropology followed a rather different course and led to a different outcome in Great Britain than it did in the United States.[21]

Three-quarters of a century later, Meyer Fortes was inclined to savor the somewhat misleading paradox of an exchange of founding fathers in the nursery of modern anthropology—Tylor, who (putatively) offered the first anthropological definition of "culture," being the founder of American cultural anthropology, and Morgan, who discovered "the key significance of kinship systems in human social organization," the founder of British social anthropology. Fortes' paradox depended in part on an inadequate appreciation of the limitations of Tylor's evolutionary conception of culture and the role of Franz Boas in the development of the modern anthropological concept.[22] It also reflected the limitations of the historiography of modern British social anthropology.

Since then, a number of works (including Fortes') have appeared which have dealt with aspects of twentieth-century British anthropology. But there is still a tendency to think of the emergence of social anthropology in somewhat discontinuous terms. Despite its critical stance toward Fortes, and its substantial grounding in documentary sources, the most systematic monographic study may be read as an extended elaboration of Fortes' notion that Rivers' "rediscovery" of Morgan was "the beginning of a method and theory of research which took deep root in British anthropology." Alternatively, the "revolution in anthropology" has been seen in archetypal terms as the oedipal slaying of James G. Frazer, the inheritor of Tylor's mantle as armchair evolutionary theorist, by Bronislaw Malinowski, the self-proclaimed inventor of modern fieldwork. In contrast, the most comprehensive general study of British social anthropology, after the briefest prefatory reference to Rivers and Frazer, began with the *annus mirabilis* of 1922, which saw the publication of the first major works of both Malinowski and Radcliffe-Brown. And while there has recently been work on the institutional and social context of British anthropology in the turn-of-the-century period, the intellectual history of British anthropology between its two "classical" moments (social evolutionism and structural functionalism) still tends to be a rather shadowy if not actually dark age.[23] Without attempting to illuminate every still-shadowed cranny, the essays that follow are intended to cast further light on the major phases of the emergence of modern British social anthropology in the six decades after 1888.

ONE

Center and Periphery

Armchair Anthropology, Missionary Ethnography, and Evolutionary Theory

During his lifetime, Tylor had several direct experiences with ethnographic "otherness": his early travels in Mexico and the United States, his subsequent attendance at London seances with a view to their anthropological significance, and a visit to the Zuni pueblo during his American trip of 1884. But for the most part, his anthropology was very much in the "armchair" tradition. He read widely in classical sources, in travel literature, and in accounts of exploration and missionary activity—in most of the published sources, ancient and modern, that might provide information about the variety of human customs and belief. And he read critically. If the role of the armchair anthropologist was to derive general laws of cultural development by comparing the customs and beliefs of peoples of all races, all regions, and all stages of culture, it was essential that such information be as reliable as possible.[1]

As his "adhesions" paper suggests, from an early point Tylor was interested in the improvement of ethnographic data. In 1874 he played the dominant intellectual role in the formulation of the British Association's *Notes and Queries on Anthropology, for the Use of Travellers and Residents in Uncivilized Lands.* Although its questions about religion and mythology were clearly structured by the categories of Tylor's *Primitive Culture,* the emphasis was on detailed and careful observation, and the prefaces to each section were clearly intended to counteract the effects of monotheistic ethnocentrism—to enable observers reared in the Christian tradition to recognize animistic religion where otherwise they might simply have reported some form of degenerate "devil worship," or even that their particular "savage" group had no religion at all.[2]

The first and most important of the limited surviving fruits of the first edition of *Notes and Queries* was the information "On the Aboriginal

Inhabitants of the Andaman Islands" provided by E. H. Man, the son of the director of the penal settlement established on an archipelago in the Bay of Bengal to incarcerate Sepoy rebels of the "Indian Mutiny." Long feared as cannibals, the diminutive Andamanese were one of a handful of peoples competing for the dubious honor of utmost primitivity; in the comparative categorization of second-hand ethnographic data compiled for Herbert Spencer by his assistant David Duncan, they were grouped with the Tasmanians and the Australians as "types" of "lowest" and "Negrito" races. Man was himself director of the Andaman Homes—encampments for the "pacification" and "civilization" of "a people hitherto living in a perfectly barbarous state, replete with treachery, murder, and every other savageness." He was thus in an unusually good position to collect information on a group of considerable interest to evolutionary theoreticians. Published in three installments in the *Journal of the Anthropological Institute* and then as a monograph, Man's ethnographic data followed the categories of *Notes and Queries* in their numbered order, going beyond them only to offer comments on Andaman religion from a traditional Christian degenerationist point of view that clashed somewhat with the assumptions of Tylorian evolutionary theory.[3]

The schedule of questions forwarded from the anthropological center was not, however, the only link between the armchair and the ethnographic periphery. Another previously unappreciated form was what may be called "epistolary ethnography." Like several other armchair anthropologists, Tylor established postal contact with various "men on the spot" who seemed particularly well-situated and competent observers, often with an interest in the general issues that were the focus of his theoretical concern. Although communication could take months, some of these people became active participants in the ethnographic process, answering queries, volunteering information, sometimes writing papers which Tylor shepherded into print. A number of the most active and sophisticated were in fact missionaries, many of whom had extended experience with particular native peoples, but only a few of whom were able to respond to native religion in a relatively unethnocentric way.[4]

In proposing "cross-cousin marriage" as a solution to the dispute between McLennan and Morgan, Tylor appealed specifically to the ethnographic work of two missionaries who were almost his exact contemporaries: the Wesleyan Methodist Lorimer Fison and the High Church Anglican Robert Henry Codrington.[5] The two may be taken also as representatives of two distinct styles of "missionary ethnography," with somewhat differing relationships to evolutionary theory. When at the end of the century other armchair anthropologists began to call into question a number of the assumptions of evolutionism, the ethnographic data collected by Fison and Codrington in Australia and Melanesia played an important role in the debate.

Lorimer Fison and the Search for Primitive Promiscuity

Lorimer Fison was born in 1832 in the little village of Barningham, Suffolk, where his father "ruled supreme" as the area's largest landowner. Although apparently of Quaker background, the elder Fison brought up his family "in the Evangelical school of the Church of England," and the young Fison's earliest education took place at home under the affectionate supervision of his mother, the well-educated daughter of a clergyman-scholar. After a time in school in Sheffield, Fison enrolled in Caius College, Cambridge, in 1855, with the intention of studying mathematics, but within two terms was "sent down" for a student prank. As the thirteenth of twenty children whose paternal estate had suffered from the repeal of the Corn Laws, young Fison found prospects at home not too bright. But the 1850s were a decade when a young man could seek his fortune at the ends of the earth, and Fison sailed from England in 1856 to join the gold rush that had begun in Australia four years previously—and which by the end of the decade had tripled Australia's European population.[6]

After several years in the gold fields, Fison received news of his father's death in England, which affected him profoundly. In the depths of his sorrow he attended a camp meeting, underwent a conversion experience of the archetypical sort, and left the gold fields to resume university training in Melbourne. There he joined the Wesleyan Methodists, volunteered for service as a missionary in the Fiji Islands, was ordained a minister, and in 1863 set sail with his wife for "Cannibal Feejee." During his early years in Fiji, Fison displayed the aggressive ethnocentrism characteristic of so many of his Methodist missionary confreres. Letters he published in the *Wesleyan Missionary Notices* spoke of the "hundred thousand men, women and children who still worship false gods, and practice all the abominations of Fijian heathenism" recently documented in Thomas Williams' *Fiji and the Fijians*—among them a cannibal feast at which "fifty-five bodies were shared out and cooked." In his private correspondence Fison quite despaired of the success of missionary endeavor. Granting that the Fijians were capable of "moral improvement" that would fit them for heaven, he nevertheless considered them incapable of the "social and political improvement" that would fit them for earth. "It is useless to say that such as they *are,* our fathers *were;* they are made of different stuff." They lived now "in a different mind-world, out of which it seems utterly impossible to bring them," and Fison was certain that they "must perish from the face of the earth." He envied the immigrant English cotton planters who, "combining to face manfully the difficulties of their position," banded together to preserve "peace, and law, and order"; and he looked forward to the day when "the Anglo-Saxon Jacob has fully supplanted the foolish Fijian Esau."[7]

In anticipation of that eventuality—and perhaps to compensate for the disappointment of his missionary hopes—Fison began about 1866 to collect "folktales and sagas" from native informants. Transmitted by a sister in Oxford, these came to the attention of England's leading comparative philologist, Friedrich Max Müller, who spoke approvingly of Fison's efforts "in giving this people a literature." That same sister married a close friend of Goldwin Smith, the Regius Professor of Modern History, who in 1868 emigrated to Cornell University in upstate New York. There Smith became acquainted with the leading American anthropologist Lewis Henry Morgan, who was then at work on his *Systems of Consanguinity and Affinity of the Human Family*. When Morgan mentioned to Smith that he had not yet been able to collect any data from Fiji and Tonga, Smith suggested that he send some of his kinship schedules to Fison, who was able to get the completed schedules back just in time for inclusion in a special appendix to Morgan's volume. For Fison, this was the beginning of what he later called "a second life running side by side and subordinate" to his missionary vocation.[8]

The intellectual lifeline of that second existence was the correspondence Fison maintained over the next two decades with the two leading figures of evolutionary anthropology. Given Fison's initially rather traditional Christian degenerationist view of the Fijians, it might have been more consistent intellectually had that line extended to Müller, who was at the center of a philologically focussed network of overseas correspondents, and whose work provides a kind of anti-positivist counterpoint to the dominant social evolutionism of the later nineteenth century. However, Morgan's interest in kinship had itself originally developed in relation to issues of pre-evolutionary philological ethnology, in specific opposition to polygenist ethnologists of the 1850s. In this context, the fact that a "classificatory system" of consanguinity (or kinship terminology) was shared by all American Indians and widely distributed throughout Asia and Oceania was presumed by Morgan to demonstrate the unity of the American race, its derivation from groups in the Old World, and, ultimately, the unity of mankind.[9]

By the time his kinship schedules reached Fison, however, Morgan had recast the "classificatory system" into the social evolutionary framework in which Tylor later discussed it. From an initial state of "promiscuous intercourse" there had arisen, in sequence, the "Communal Family" (founded on the intermarriage of brothers and sisters); the "Barbarian Family" ("supervening upon the communal after the Tribal organization came in and broke up the intermarriage of brothers and sisters"—but allowing "the old licence" beyond that relationship); the "Patriarchal Family" (founded on the marriage of one man to several wives); and the "Civilized Family" (founded on the fully developed idea of property, and its transmission to one's own children, which required "marriage between single pairs," with "exclusive cohabitation," to ensure "certainty of parentage" and "decrease the number of heirs"). Linked to this sequence, and in fact essential to its reconstruction, was a series of "systems of consanguinity": the Malayan, the Turanian, and Ganowanian forms of the "classificatory system," followed (after the "overthrow" of that system with the emergence of the "Civilized Family") by three forms of the "descriptive" system: the Uralian, the Semitic, and the Aryan. It was to the documentation of this scheme (which was slightly modified in later formulations) that Fison was to devote his "second life." [10]

For an active missionary and believing Christian, the project was not without a certain intellectual and emotional tension and ambivalence. Although Morgan's developmental scheme of marriage stages had been defined in a non-Darwinian context, and Morgan himself was cautious in relating it to Darwinian assumptions, it was (with some conceptual stress) easily subsumed within the framework of evolutionary discourse. Fison himself was convinced that Morgan was "a thorough Darwinian," and in the beginning was disturbed that the inquiry seemed to run against his own deeply held belief that man could not progress on his own power, but only with the help of God. After some soul-searching, Fison agreed "to work on until we find out all the links in the chain before beginning to quarrel about the question as to who made it." [11]

Although Morgan originally hoped that Fison would be able to take over kinship investigations throughout the oceanic area from Polynesia to Madagascar, Fison's second life focussed on Australia, to which he returned in 1871 for a four-year respite from the rigors of missionary life. At Morgan's request, Fison "ransacked the public library" for information concerning Australian kinship systems, which, as Morgan later suggested, were just "a step from promiscuity" and afforded "the first direct evidence of a state of society which had previously [only] been deduced, as extremely probable, from systems of consanguinity and affinity." Fison, however, soon gave up on the kinship terms themselves, because the variation in their usage made a "complete schedule of all the various degrees of relationship . . . a hopeless puzzle." Instead, he decided to concentrate on the class and totem divisions which were a distinguishing feature of Australian Aboriginal society. Working through a missionary intermediary, he was "the first to find out the combination of Class names and Totems among the Kamilaroi-speaking tribes," and eventually came to the conclusion that from these "the whole system of relationship could be deduced . . . with the certainty of a mathematical demonstration." Over the next several years, Fison made further attempts to involve others in the work, distributing circulars modelled on Morgan's, and writing to several leading Australian newspapers inviting readers to cooperate in the collection of information. Most of the answers he received were perfunctory listings of kin terms; one person alone appreciated "the logic of the system," and had actually figured out "the principle of Morgan's hypothesis before he became acquainted with it as Mr. Morgan's." That person was Alfred William Howitt, whose name was from then on linked with Fison's in the study of Australian social organization.[12]

Two years older than Fison, Howitt was the son of two well-known early Victorian writers, friends and followers of William Wordsworth, who were drawn also to German romantic literature, and who took their five children to Germany for several years in the early 1840s. After study at University College, London, young Alfred accompanied his father to Australia in 1852, where they tried their luck in the gold rush. After two years of "toilsome digging and wandering" in the wilderness, the father returned to England to publish a book on his experiences. Alfred, however, elected to stay on, first as a farmer on land belonging to his uncle, and then as a cattle driver. After 1859, Howitt—by then an experienced bushman—was sent on exploring expeditions, under both private and governmental auspices, into the central Australian desert and the then still almost unknown region of Gippsland in southeastern Australia. As a reward for his governmental services, he was appointed Police Magistrate and Warden of the Goldfields in Gippsland, a post he held from 1863 to 1889.[13]

Riding on horseback every year over hundreds of miles of wild and mountainous country, Howitt became interested in natural history and geology. By the late 1860s, he had read Darwin, whose picture he is said to have kept over his bed. Further inspired by a copy of John Lubbock's *Prehistoric Times* his sister sent to him from England, Howitt began to collect ethnographic information. Although his early contacts with the local Aborigines inclined him to regard them as "an idle, incorrigibly treacherous, lying race," greater familiarity led to a more sympathetic paternalism; eventually, he came to be regarded as a fully initiated member of the Kurnai tribe.[14]

In the partnership that developed, it was the mathematically inclined Fison who (despite his religious reservations) played the primary role of evolutionary theoretician. Howitt, who developed an ingenious

Lorimer Fison (seated) talking with A. W. Howitt, when they met, after long correspondence, at Howitt's home in Sale, Australia, 1882. (Courtesy of E. A. Walker, Bombala, N.S.W.)

method for collecting kin terms by arranging sticks on the ground in a family tree, was above all the ethnographer—although he, too, contributed evolutionary interpretations, sometimes with a Darwinian irreverence Fison found upsetting. Before Fison returned to Fiji in 1875 (where he served until 1884 as principal of a training school for native teachers), he and Howitt developed a new questionnaire, which included Howitt's instructions for the arrangement of kin terms in a "Genealogical Table" and Fison's for the collection of "Classnames and Totems." With the assistance of R. Brough Smyth, secretary of both the Department of Mines and the Board for the Protection of Aborigines—who hoped to draw on the results for his own book on "The Aborigines of Victoria"—the questionnaire was forwarded to "all sorts and conditions of people, Right Reverend Roman Catholic dignitaries, squatters, pound keepers, government officials in all the colonies." At first, the results were disappointing; Howitt complained to Morgan in 1877 that for every hundred circulars there were only five responses, only one of which was usable. Nevertheless, by 1881 Howitt was "in communication with over fifty correspondents . . . who are more or less successfully working for me and under my direction." Beyond this, there was of course Howitt's own work with the Aborigines of Gippsland.[15]

By this time, the Kurnai had already been literally decimated by the inroads of "civilization," the population having fallen from an estimated 1500 in 1839 to 140 in 1877. Most of those remaining had been at least nominally converted to Christianity, spoke some English, and had settled near missions, where "the force of their old customs" was greatly attenuated. Howitt, who apparently had an imperfect knowledge of the language, got much of his information from a single informant, from whose "numerous fragments" he was able to piece together "an incomplete fabric" that would "show dimly what is the domestic and social life of a savage tribe. . . ." But through his "official position in the district" and his unusual personal style, which led him to be regarded "almost as one of themselves," Howitt could also draw on the group as a whole, even calling them together, "in his character of 'The Great Gomera,' " to recreate ceremonies that had not been practiced for a quarter-century. At a later point, he told Tylor that he could not send him a large new turndun (or bullroarer) that he had had made because "I may yet require it to gather the Wolgal and Woradjeri people" for a "Bora meeting" he was planning, though he could not be sure "until the arrival here of the Wolgal headman who will probably act as my messenger." [16]

Something of the flavor of Howitt's ethnological work is evident in a grim "anecdote" he sent to Morgan in 1876. A married Aboriginal woman in Gippsland ran off with a man called Charly; when she was later returned, her husband ran his *ierrumbuddy* (a large wooden spear) through her back so that it came out her side, proclaiming: "I have done with her—you can keep her." For the next few days, during which the woman's insides kept coming out of the gaping wound, "all the men had her in common." To Howitt, this bloody episode was "clear" evidence of the "Pairing System"—which would have placed the Aborigines higher in the evolutionary scale than Morgan had predicted—because various of Morgan's criteria were implied in the incident: cohabitation was "during the pleasure of the husband," who claimed "fidelity under penalties," but did not "admit reciprocal obligations," reserving to himself the right of polygamy.[17] By the time the Gippsland material was incorporated into a general explanatory framework, however, it was interpreted by Fison as a special transitional case.

Before that happened, Morgan's views had been subject to sharp criticism by several British evolutionary writers—criticism that was also to shape the arguments of Fison and his co-worker. Although Morgan had been courteously treated by Lubbock and McLennan when he visited England on his European tour of 1870, and in fact conceived his magnum opus *Ancient Society* as a synthesis of his own and British evolutionary arguments, his work was not well received in Britain. For McLennan, who (mistakenly) felt that Morgan had leaned heavily on his own *Primitive Marriage* without acknowledging it, a major issue was the use of kinship terms as a means of reconstructing earlier forms of marriage—McLennan arguing that the whole classificatory system was "a system of mutual salutations only," rather than a system of kinship based on actual blood ties implying real "rights and obligations." McLennan and Lubbock tended to dismiss Morgan's work as "utterly unscientific"; even Tylor, who was more friendly, felt that Morgan had "built up a structure of theory wider and heavier than his foundations of fact will bear." There was in this more than a touch of national and class condescension; Tylor allowed himself the gentle mockery of suggesting that Morgan had traced the evolution of man from "a gregarious mute . . . to a cultured republican."[18]

In contrast, Fison and Howitt, like Morgan's ancestors, were emigrant Englishmen, and like him, more than a bit republican. Fison wrote to Morgan that he felt "a malicious delight in tracing back aristocratic notions to the ways of savages and showing that they were mere unreasonable survivals of savage notions which were perfectly reasonable in their day" (although he also asked Morgan if he could get him an honorary M.A. at an American university, because he felt "ashamed of going into print without the letters to my name"). Beyond this, both men felt a strong personal tie to the man who had started them in anthropology; as Fison put it: "I am proud to look upon myself as a member of your *gens*"—"strike the *gens* anywhere and every member starts up in arms against the striker."[19]

As their contribution to the defense of their clan elder, Fison and Howitt by early in 1879 had sent to Morgan a 200-page manuscript with the hope that, like his *Systems*, it might be published by the Smithsonian Institution. But although Morgan wrote a laudatory preface, the Smithsonian could not promise immediate publication; and when Fison received an inquiry from Tylor about their work, they began to reconsider: "it is known that [Tylor] is collecting materials for a work on the natives, and he seems to consider that he has a heaven born right to the use of other peoples' brains and labours." On the grounds that "secret piracy necessitates immediate publishing," they decided to publish in Australia.[20]

Although given its title from the groups on which each of its authors specialized, the theoretical significance of *Kamilaroi and Kurnai* was suggested by the subtitle: *Group Marriage and Relationship, and Marriage by Elopement*. Its purpose was to document and elaborate Morgan's evolutionary scheme at several of its most problematic points, and at the same time to rebut the views of his British critics, with Howitt's "marriage by elopement" (which Fison saw as "a grand fact of no mere local occurrence") playing a role similar to that played by "marriage by capture" in McLennan's system.[21]

The first of the book's five memoirs was Fison's attempt to "trace the origin and development" of Morgan's Turanian system of kinship through a study of the "class divisions" of the tribes speaking the Kamilaroi language. Fison's first concern was simply to show that the division into marriage classes was very widespread in Australia. However, the basic division into two classes had in some cases developed, by a process of segmentation, into a division into four, and in general the classes were further divided into "gentes distinguished by totems." As Fison suggested in a letter to Tylor: "We have traced the classes from the extreme west . . . to the extreme south . . . through New South Wales and Queensland up to Port Darwin in the north, and turning aside to a telegraph station almost in the centre of the continent." Nearly everywhere "among those tribes the classes have the same arrangements, though the words used to designate them are widely different. . . ."[22]

To begin with, Fison argued that marriage between the classes was governed by four rules: it was "theoretically communal" (i.e., "based upon the marriage of all the males in one division of a tribe to all of the females of the same generation in another division"); it was exogamous (i.e., forbidden within every such division); the wife remained in her own division rather than joining the husband's; and descent was reckoned through the mother. Fison then went on to argue that, on the basis of these four rules, all of the terms of kinship of the Turanian system were "the logical outcome of the Australian classes." The argument was organized as a series of fourteen propositions (e.g., "All my mother's sisters, own and collateral, are my mothers"), each "demonstrated" by the diagrammed subdivisions of the Mount Gambier tribe (Kumite, Kroki, Kumitigor, Krokigor), from each of which a series of deductions were made: If ego be Kumite . . . Then his children will be Kroki B . . . But . . . Therefore . . . "Q. E. D."[23]

In the second memoir, "On Group Marriage and Relationship," Fison turned from the static analysis of the logic of marriage rules and kinship relations to more dynamic problems, attempting to articulate the Australian data with Morgan's developmental sequence, and defending that sequence against its British critics. According to Fison, Morgan's theory required "the former prevalence of what he calls the Malayan [kinship] system with the consanguine family," or as Fison sometimes called it, the "undivided commune." It was in the transition from the undivided commune to the division into two marriage classes (generalized by a later generation of anthropologists as "the dual organization") that exogamy had originated. Morgan had argued that this was the result of a conscious "reformatory movement" to limit the marriage of blood brothers and sisters; McLennan and Lubbock saw it as the incidental result of infanticide or marriage by capture. By this time, it seems that

Fison's hesitation to accept the "undivided commune" was due less to his own religious scruples than to his feeling that such "promiscuity" would be "terribly shocking to many of my best friends among our ministers." But he was willing to argue that "given a state of society such as that indicated by the Dieri legend of the Murdu," then "the division of the community into two exogamous intermarrying classes, like Kumite and Kroki, would have precisely the reformatory effect which Mr. Morgan's theory requires."[24]

Fison felt he was on firmer ground in attacking the views of Lubbock and McLennan. Lubbock's arguments were not to be taken too seriously, he suggested to Morgan, since a work such as *The Origin of Civilisation* could "be compiled by anybody who could afford to give an ordinary clerk a pound a week to make extracts from works on Savage Tribes in any good library"—which was probably close to the mark in the case of Lubbock, and in fact exactly described the way Herbert Spencer collected his data. Fison (and Howitt) took McLennan more seriously, once a copy of his book finally reached them in 1879, and they no longer had to deal with his arguments at second hand: if he had better data, "his logical mind would have inevitably led him to somewhat different conclusions." Acknowledging McLennan's authorship of the "convenient" terms "endogamy" and "exogamy," they insisted that many groups that were exogamous at the level of the class division were in fact endogamous at the level of the tribe, a position which undercut much of McLennan's argument about the origin of exogamy by infanticide. And on the crucial issue of the meaning of kinship terms—whether they were "mere" terms of address, or whether they embodied "real relationships to the native mind"—Fison was sharply critical.[25]

If Australians found it so abhorrent for a man to take a wife from a group with a certain classificatory relationship to him that they would punish the act by death, the term for that relationship could hardly be a "mere" form of address. "The group relationships seem unreal to us only because we look at them from our own point of view." But they were as real to the "savage" as our own were to us, and they brought "the rights, the duties, and the prohibitions which ours bring to us." Although those who judged morality by European standards might not appreciate it, the tribe was in fact punishing incest as it conceived of it. McLennan's difficulty was that he assumed that savages worked out their understanding of kinship inductively like good empiricists, starting from the tie of child and mother and gradually extending it. In opposition to this, Fison developed an argument which in some respects anticipates the later Durkheimian tradition.[26]

Although it was "a great mistake to say that savages do not reason," their reasoning proceeded by deduction rather than induction. They did not put together a number of separate facts and draw from them a general conclusion; rather, "some large fact, involving a general principle, fills their minds, and they accept its logical consequences, clinging to them long after they have ceased to be able to carry them out in everyday life, with a persistence which is often ludicrous, and sometimes even pathetic." From this perspective, "the group relationships arising from the marriage of the exogamous divisions are precisely what the savage would perceive and adopt, while Mr. McLennan's process of reasoning would be altogether foreign to his mind." The savage did not piece together his system "out of the various degrees of relationship as he perceived them one by one." "Paradoxical as it might sound," it was his system of relationships "which gave him his degrees of relationship." However, their psychological reality was not in any sense reduced by the fact that they were arrived at deductively rather than inductively. On the contrary, as Howitt suggested, "if Mr. M'Lennan had had as much personal acquaintance with savages as we have had, he would have seen, as clearly as we see, that the classificatory system is to them as truly a system of 'blood ties'—that is, of kinships—as our own descriptive system is to us."[27]

In making his argument, Fison insisted that it could only be understood if "we dismiss from our minds our own notions of relationship": "we must bear in mind that to the savage *the group is the individual*." This was hard for those enculturated in the traditions of atomistic individualism to appreciate, and McLennan, Lubbock, and Tylor, as well as Morgan himself, all evinced some difficulty on this point. As Fison suggested to Morgan, the problem was what one took as the basic unit of discussion. The unit "with which I begin is the unit at this end of the line—the unit which I find in myself"; but if one followed that line back, the individual unit was soon "swallowed up by the gens, the gens by the phratria, the phratria by the old commune." Discussing with Morgan the difficulty Tylor had in accepting their point of view, Fison suggested that Tylor's objections "have arisen chiefly on account of his putting into such words as 'wife,' 'marriage,' etc. the full meaning which they bear with regard to our own system." Tylor had apparently suggested to Fison that in the Australian context "spouse" meant "a woman of the class one may marry into"; against this, Fison suggested "a woman of the class to which mine was born married," so that "spouse" in fact referred to that "class which is 'spouse' to the husband-class.' "[28]

As Fison put the matter in *Kamilaroi and Kurnai*, "the idea of marriage under the classificatory system of kinship is founded on the rights neither of the woman nor of the man," but on "the rights of the tribe, or rather of the classes into which the tribe is divided." Echoing Henry Maine's *Ancient Law*, with its distinction between societies founded on status and on contract, Fison argued that "class marriage is not a contract entered into by two parties" but "a natural state into which both parties are born." Again, one notes the anticipatory Durkheimian resonances: in the beginning, the individual has "no independent existence" and "in the tribal divisions and subdivisions we see what appears to be a steady progress towards the *individualizing of the individual.*" Originally "the whole tribe, in its corporate capacity may perhaps have been the individual holding all rights vested in itself." But whether or not that had been true in the past, the Kamilaroi provided a clear present instance of a tribe "separated into two corporate bodies with partially independent rights." And from there we could "follow the process of segmentation throughout the minor subdivisions, until at length we come to the civilized man with his personal rights and possessions, and his gospel of political economy teaching him that self-seeking on the part of the individual must result in the greatest good of the greatest number." In this argument, Fison went beyond Morgan: one of the issues in their correspondence was whether the phratry was the product of an aggregation of separate gentes, as Morgan argued, or whether it was the outcome of Fison's segmenting process.[29]

The upward march of social evolution was primarily manifest in *Kamilaroi and Kurnai,* however, in relation to Howitt's Gippsland groups, which were treated in an extensive ethnographic account that formed the volume's third memoir. In it, Howitt—along lines suggested in the spearing anecdote—argued that the Kurnai, unlike the Kamilaroi, had advanced to the stage of Morgan's Pairing (or Syndyasmian) Family. Following upon Howitt's account, Fison attempted to explain the "theory of the Kurnai system." Unlike the Kamilaroi, Kurnai class divisions did not each include both sexes, and descent was always along sexual lines. Marriage was a matter of contract rather than status, insofar as women had the power of choice (in the sense that marriage was by elopement over the opposition of her kinfolk). Once established, marriage was no longer in any sense communal: all marital rights were vested exclusively in the husband. Finally, each division or gens could marry anywhere beyond its own limits, rather than only within specified subdivisions. All this Fison explained—in the context of Howitt's argument for the geographical isolation of the Kurnai—in terms of the following "theory": "The Kurnai are the descendants of an isolated division of a tribe which formerly consisted of two exogamous intermarrying divisions . . . [and] their regulations as to marriage and descent are such as would arise from an endeavour to follow the regulations of such divisions under circumstances of peculiar difficulty." Thus, if a single exogamous division of a Kamilaroi tribe found itself separated permanently from the rest of the tribe, it would be forced to depart from the old marriage rule of class exogamy, since all of its children would be of one class. In doing so, however, it would try to preserve the letter if not the spirit of the law by simply pretending that the young men were of their father's rather than their mother's class, thus legitimizing their marriage to the young women of the division, who would continue to follow the mother. Elopement was simply a further elaboration of the fiction—the parents wanting no part of the whole process, and in fact putting up great resistance to every marriage, even to the point of beating the lovers within an inch of their lives.[30]

As evidence that the Kurnai system had developed from the Kamilaroi, Fison referred his readers to "Mr. Howitt's Latin note" on page 202, the point of which Fison later conveyed to Tylor: in the Kurnai tribe, where marriage took place by elopement, "the man must give previous notice to those males who are his *pares* . . . and they must meet the woman in the bush, and use her as their wife, before he can elope with her." For Fison, the "survival" of this practice was evidence for the former existence of the sexual communism characteristic of Kamilaroi class marriages: before a Kurnai man could exercise complete control over his wife's sexual behavior, his assertion of individual right must be expiated by an acknowledgment of the vestigial right of the class as a whole.[31]*

Fison concluded his argument by pointing out the tremendous significance of Howitt's Kurnai data, not only as an illustration (albeit in exceptional circumstances) of the general sequence of the development of marriage forms, but as actually offering an instance of a tribe currently "*in process* of change" from female to male descent. What his "theory" did was to transform the "apparent anomaly" presented by the Kurnai into evidence for what, within the social evolutionary paradigm, was

*References to sexual topics presented a problem for serious anthropologists in the Victorian era. There was, of course, a previous (and continuing) tradition of erotic anthropology, manifest in such works as Richard Knight's *Discourse on the Worship of Priapus*—originally issued to a scandalized public in 1786 and privately reprinted, with a supplementary essay by the antiquarian folklorist Thomas Wright, in 1865. The controversial Anthropological Society of London, in which Richard Burton played an important role, excluded women so that such topics might be discussed (Stocking 1987b:253). The leading social evolutionists, however, were thoroughly "respectable" men—hence Howitt's Latin footnote. In correspondence with Morgan, Fison found some customs "indescribably filthy," and in the case of an incident of "torture inflicted on the offending organ" (subincision?), asked "But how is one to publish descriptions of these things?" Latin, he felt, was "almost a childish device," when "both *virgo* and *puer* of the present day know Latin enough to understand them" (Fison to Morgan 4/17/81, 3/18/81, in Stern 1930:439–40, 437). Although such issues are only touched on here and there in the present volume, the history of British social anthropology might be written in terms of its relationship to changing views of sexual prudery and pornography. (For hints or gestures toward such a general interpretation, see Leach 1985:218, 235; Lyons & Lyons 1986; Tuzin 1994.)

the absolutely critical transition in the evolution of the family. The argument depended, however, on taken-for-granted assumptions about the direction of change: for the Kamilaroi to have developed from the Kurnai would have been "a retrogressive movement," a "reversal" of the "known" or "natural order."[32] It also depended heavily on the argument from "survival."

Throughout the book, Fison and Howitt continually distinguished between the "theoretical" and the "actual" marriage practices of the Australians. At one point, Howitt in fact stated that "I am not aware that any tribes having the typical communal structure still exist in Australia at the present time," although it was "premature to say positively that they do not until full information has been collected as to all the aboriginal communities." As far as the actual practice of communism was concerned, the main evidence lay in Howitt's "thousand miles of wives," which Fison called "the most extensive system of communal marriage the world has ever known" and described to Tylor in the following terms: "say that A and B are two intermarrying classes; then if a Kamilaroi native from the Darling River, belonging to class A, visited a tribe at Port Darwin, he would be provided with a woman from class B in that tribe, as his temporary wife." On the basis of such practices as these, and accepting that "the social condition, as shown by actual customs, is always in advance of the theoretical social condition to be inferred from class rules and the kinship terms," it was possible to arrange the Australian data in a "gradually progressive series, commencing at a society nearly approaching to the divided exogamous commune, and extending upwards to a society based upon individual marriage." But the "survivals" which made it possible to infer a prior "theoretical" state, like the progressive series thus documented, were heavily dependent on prior assumption. Against McLennan's argument that the levirate was a survival of polyandry, Fison suggested that "there is no need for us to look upon it as a survival of anything at all"—and in any case, "it would serve very well as a survival of group marriage." But if the acceptance of a given survival depended thus on which particular variant of evolutionary theory one happened to favor, late-nineteenth-century social evolutionism as a paradigm could not survive without the argument from survivals; and its adherents were not usually inclined to subject their own use of the concept to serious scrutiny.[33]

Although Fison suggested to Morgan in 1881 that he and Howitt were "gradually tending towards Germany and America," where science was "followed for its own sake and not in the interests of a clique," in fact their later anthropological careers were oriented very much toward England. Morgan's death in 1881 cut them off from American science, and McLennan's death the same year removed their most effective British antagonist. By that time, they had already found Tylor, then president of the Anthropological Institute, very much interested in their data and by no means unreceptive to their argument; noting their work favorably in his presidential address of 1880, Tylor helped arrange for the presentation and publication of two joint theoretical papers and a number of ethnographic papers by Howitt over the next several years. In the meantime, Fison had returned to Australia from Fiji in 1884 to settle in Victoria, where after 1888 he edited a Methodist newspaper. Continuing as police magistrate until 1889, Howitt then became Secretary of Mines for Victoria, holding various governmental positions until 1901, when he retired to live in Melbourne until he died in 1906, a year before Fison. Both men returned to England for visits: Fison, at Tylor's invitation in 1894, to address the British Association for the Advancement of Science, Howitt, in 1904 to see through the press the only full-length anthropological work that either produced after *Kamilaroi and Kurnai*, an ethnographic account entitled *The Native Tribes of South-East Australia*.[34]

During much of this period, the three men remained in correspondence about matters anthropological; the letters of Fison to Tylor are especially revealing of the later history of social evolutionism. They confirm, for instance, that in the heyday of classical evolutionism there was still a continuing interest in problems more characteristic of a prior paradigmatic alternative: the diffusionary philological ethnology epitomized by James Cowles Prichard, which social evolutionism displaced in the 1860s, and which, transformed, was to reemerge in the early twentieth century. Thus a recurrent sub-theme in the correspondence was the possibility of an ethnic relationship between the Fijians and certain African tribes on the basis of linguistic similarities (such as the occurrence of the word *Tanganyika* in Fiji).[35] But for present purposes the letters are even more suggestive in relation to the fate of evolutionary argument itself.

After the completion of *Kamilaroi and Kurnai*, Fison had visions of a second volume systematically pursuing the evolution of social organization up the scale from Australia, a project in which Fiji was to figure centrally. Writing to Howitt, he proposed an evolutionary sequence in which the Kamilaroi stood for communal marriage with maternal descent, the Kurnai (Howitt's "Missing Link") represented the "beginning of kinship through the father," and the Fijians would provide the link upward to the social organization described in William Hearn's *Aryan Household*. Henry Maine, Fustel de Coulanges, and Hearn had "most ably followed the trail downwards from the Aryan Household"; in contrast, Fison and Howitt would "follow it upwards." While Morgan began "at the Headwaters," and Hearn and his fellows just "below the fork," it was "between Morgan and Hearn our Country lies."[36]

As it happened, however, the second volume was never to be written, and it is in fact possible to trace in Fison's correspondence a certain creeping tone of disillusion with evolutionary theory. Significantly, the focal issue was that of "primitive promiscuity," which in fact occupied a critical position at the base of the social evolutionary paradigm. Despite his reluctance as a Christian missionary, Fison had been "forced" to "look to the old undivided commune for the beginning," and very early in his correspondence with Tylor he reported that "the evidence for an absolute communism behind these [class divisions] is becoming stronger and stronger." Fison was particularly impressed by a Fijian ceremony he had asked several intermediaries to investigate for him.[37]

In relying on others to gather information, Fison took some care to assure that the evidence would be reliable. After more than a decade in the field, he had become quite sensitive to the practical problems of ethnography, especially as carried on by missionaries: "there are many things the native won't tell to any white man, but there are still more which he won't tell to his missionary," who was "apt to look upon all heathen customs as necessarily devil-inspired, and so to condemn customs which are innocent in themselves, because they suppose them to have a meaning which the natives themselves most certainly do not attach to them." The more Fison learned of "savage customs," the more he saw "the necessity of unlearning our own notions as a preliminary to understanding the working of the native's mind." Indeed, it was scarcely possible "even to state their customs without conveying an incorrect impression, for our words are not coterminous with theirs in their meanings" and almost inevitably suggested "to an Englishman's mind something different from that which is in the mind of the savage. . . ." To solve the problem, Fison had accustomed himself "to think in Fijian in order more fully to acquire the language," with the "disastrous" consequence upon his removal to Australia that he had to translate his own thoughts into English as he went along, and once "startled a congregation by commencing the opening prayer in Fijian instead of English"—a "very curious" experience which "suggested several interesting points of inquiry."[38]

In this context, Fison took precautions in preparing his intermediary ethnographer, Mr. Heffernan, "carefully abstaining from giving him the particulars I had heard from my native informants" in order to "avoid the danger of his making special inquiry as to anything he might hear from me, and which the natives might not tell him of their own accord"—because, if one put the question in a form that seems to seek an affirmative answer, "the polite savage is too apt to return the answer which he thinks his questioner wants." Nor was Fison willing to rely on Heffernan alone: "I *never* accept an account of any custom, even from a native, without further investigation made either by myself or by some trustworthy persons." Confident that the account of the ceremonies at Nandi could "be depended on," Fison reported to Tylor that on the fourth day, there had been general sexual license. In the words of the natives, there were "no owners of pigs or women" and "while it is going on we do exactly as the pigs do"—"whoever wishes to take a woman does so, and the owner of the pig or woman is not angry." Heffernan was assured by the natives that "the communism is absolute, not excluding own brothers and sisters, although these relatives may not even look at one another at other times." Fison felt that this ceremony, and another he recounted in the same letter, were "two clear instances of a temporary return to communism as an expiatory measure."[39]

Although Fison was still not certain of the existence of primitive promiscuity, he felt that "if we deny that communism was ever the absolute rule for everyday life, we must find some other explanation for this well-established practice" of communism as expiation. And he was much impressed when his missionary friend Robert Codrington observed that the linguistic forms for husband and wife among the Banks Islanders were always plural, which a native informant explained by the former practice of wives being held in common by a group of brothers—evidence that was all the more valuable because Codrington had been "a doubter if not a positive unbeliever" in primitive promiscuity.[40]

Ten years later, Fison reported to Tylor on his discussions with a man who was studying in Assam—"a real worker, not a theorist": "if he has made no mistake about the *pali* in which the girls and boys sleep together, we have got at something which takes us a step farther back than the Australians have taken us." His friend's facts clearly suggested that "this notion came in upon an older licence, and it is just what the facts of occasional promiscuity, ceremonial promiscuity—which I sent you some years ago—would lead us to expect to find." Fison had urged his informant to "make a special inquiry as to whether there were any prohibitions at all among these young people," for "if we can get a clear case of a village in which all the boys and girls sleep together *indiscriminately*, there is certainly a case of promiscuity, for in that case not even own brothers and sisters [of which Fison himself had so many] could be excluded."[41]

"If we can get a clear case . . ." Coming twenty-five years after primitive promiscuity had been hypothesized as the starting point of the evolution of human marriage, the phrasing suggests a certain paradigmatic ennui. And in fact the empirical documentation of that theoretical will-o'-the-wisp was not to be. Indeed, its theoretical significance was from the beginning evidence of a discontinuity between the paradigms of social and biological evolutionism: Darwin himself had felt that primitive promiscuity was belied by the possessive sexuality of male apes. By

1890, the concept was coming under attack among some younger social evolutionary writers, such as Edward Westermarck. And Tylor—an armchair anthropologist, but a cautious one—did not in fact incorporate it into the argument of his 1888 paper.[42]

Fison's response to that paper was a bit less enthusiastic than Tylor might have hoped, given the prominent place that his and Howitt's evidence had in its argument. Although Fison commented that "most of your conclusions are the right ones," he disagreed with Tylor's interpretation at a number of points, especially regarding his theory of the origin of exogamy. Reflecting on his own work (and unknowingly projecting the fate of social evolutionism itself), he told Tylor that he no longer troubled himself with "speculations as to *how things came to be*": "It is quite enough to find out *what they are*." Although Fison continued to defend Morgan on various issues, and was still in fact worrying the origin of exogamy as late as 1895, the tone of the argument was by this time quite tired. Referring to an article that he had just published, Fison said, "I think it will finally settle the question as to the origin of the Classificatory terms; but as to the origin of the exogamous intermarrying divisions out of which they came, that is another question." He could not shut his eyes to "the evidence of a prior promiscuity," or at least could not "account for the facts in my possession on any other theory." But as he had told Tylor in Oxford on his recent visit to England, he had "left off making theories." That "most beautiful one of mine—the theory of the Kurnai system—has finally cured me": "it accounts for all the facts, but it is wrong in spite of that." Two years before, Fison had publicly made the same disavowal, although unfortunately without explication or documentation: his "beautiful" theory accounted for Kurnai marriage rules "so completely and so satisfactorily that the Kurnai ought to be ashamed of themselves for having been perverse enough to arrive at their system by a different road, which further inquiry showed us most conclusively that they did."[43]

At the end of Fison's career, there were signs of a regression from the more relativistic anthropological understanding implied in some of his letters to Tylor. Several years before his death, he published the *Tales from Old Fiji* that he had collected in the 1860s. While the introduction shows no specific sign of the "preconceived notions as to idolatry, Satanic agency, and so forth" that Fison had once felt forestalled an effective missionary ethnography, it is full of comments on the horrendous practices of the Fijians. Rather than arguing the virtues of long residence in giving a more kindly view of the natives, Fison here ended by arguing exactly the opposite: "travellers, after spending a short time among friendly savages, have sometimes given us an account of them more favourable than that which a fuller acquaintance has elicited; but the testimony of competent observers, who have been enabled to look below the surface, is unanimous to the effect that beneath this simple and childlike exterior there is too often a horror of cruelty and filth"—which only a "thorough knowledge of their tongue" would reveal. Unfortunately, "the most significant words of this class" were "so shocking in their horror, and so revolting in their filth," that it was "impossible to quote them."[44] Although his rhetoric may have reflected the presumed tastes of a more popular audience, Fison seems here once again back in the ethnocentric missionary posture of his early years in "cannibal Feejee," before his "second life" began.

Robert Henry Codrington: Melanesian Mana and Evolutionary Categories

There was, however, another type of missionary in the later nineteenth century, and another style of missionary ethnography. Although the contrast has sometimes been made by posing Roman Catholic missionaries against Protestant, it has also been posed, in temporal terms, within the Protestant missionary tradition itself. In the earlier nineteenth century, missionaries were characteristically self-educated artisan mechanics, for whom missions (like the emigration of their less spiritual confreres) were a form of upward mobility; aggressively ethnocentric, they sometimes found realization of their upward social drive in the establishment of theocratic regimes in which they exercised not only spiritual but political leadership. In the 1850s, the example of David Livingstone signalled and stimulated a shift in the social origin of missionaries, who were now more often recruited from university men higher up in the class hierarchy, for whom missionary activity had a different social meaning, and who were perhaps inclined toward a more empathetic view of the religious and cultural practices of those whom they sought to convert. If Fison—a Methodist, but no mechanic—was in these terms something of a hybrid, Robert Henry Codrington was clearly of the second type.[45]

Bearer of a family name of considerable distinction, Codrington was the second son of an Anglican clergyman, and was educated at Charterhouse before he came to Wadham College, Oxford, in 1849—where, in the college debating society, he argued that "the eighteenth century was the most degraded in English history." Although ill-health and a breakdown just before the examination "spoiled his honors degree," Codrington became a Fellow of the college in 1855, the year in which he was ordained and began to serve as curate in an Oxford church. His High Church Anglo-Catholic persuasion was evidenced in a pilgrimage he made in 1859 to Rome, where he was presented to the Pope, who talked with "such dignity and kindness that one felt disposed to plump down and kiss his toe." On the same trip, Codrington's lifelong interest in linguistic difference was stimulated by an encounter with an American "philologer" named Haldeman, who demonstrated for him a sound like that produced by "a smart separation of soapy hands," which formed "the concluding syllable of some [American] Indian words"; Codrington thought it remarkable that a man who thought so much about pronunciation should talk "the vilest nasalist Yankee conceivable."[46]

In 1860, when the vicar to whom he was curate was appointed Bishop of Christ Church, New Zealand, Codrington gave up excellent prospects for ecclesiastical promotion at home to venture into the South Seas. There, too, he declined advancement, rejecting the bishopric of Otago in 1863 in order to have direct experience with mission work. Instead, he accompanied Bishop John Coleridge Patteson of the Melanesian Mission on the voyage of the mission ship *Southern Cross* to the various island mission stations. After returning to England to consider the matter, in 1867 he joined the Melanesian Mission as Patteson's right-hand man.[47]

The Melanesian Mission was a mission of a somewhat unusual type, with a distinct form and spirit. The basic plan of this peripatetic Christianizing venture, developed previously by Bishop George Selwyn as an accommodation to the number of islands and the climatic problems they were believed to pose for Europeans, was to bring Melanesians to a central place, give them the Anglo-Catholic faith "clothed in Melanesian forms," and send them back to the islands as mission teachers. In the year that Codrington arrived, the summer base was moved from New Zealand, which had proven too cold for Melanesians, to Norfolk Island, half way between New Zealand and the southernmost portion of Melanesia. That compromise was consistent with the mission's desire to interfere as little as possible with Melanesian customs; as Patteson later suggested, too often "we seek to denationalize these races," whereas "we ought surely to change as little as possible—only what is incompatible with the simplest form of Christian teaching and practice." In a similar fashion, the Melanesian Mission was, relatively speaking, strikingly egalitarian. According to Codrington, Patteson felt for Melanesians "neither the contempt which calls them 'niggers' . . . nor that even more galling condescension which calls them a 'child race' "; he was instead a strong believer "in the principle of the equality of black and white in missionary work." Mission members and native students shared the day-to-day work, and although there was some differentiation according to skills, for a long time Codrington was the cook; all ate together; while there was a High Table as in an English college, it seated both whites and blacks. All of this was in sharp contrast to other missions (Fison's included) in which menial service was required from native scholars as a matter of course. Codrington had seen native teachers "on their way to be missionary pioneers on savage islands where their English teachers dare not land, living between the decks on the London Mission ship with the cows." In contrast, the Melanesian Mission sought to work on the basis of "perfect equality as to race"; if "in the working of the system" the European gained a certain superiority, at least one Melanesian was in fact in a position of authority, and none were required to be servants to the English.[48]

The colonial world around, however, was systematically racist, and increasingly it impinged on the activities of the Melanesian Mission. The shutting-off of American cotton for British textile mills during the Civil War gave a great boost to cotton production in two areas near Melanesia—Fiji and Queensland—and especially in the latter a solution was found in "contract" labor from Melanesia. By 1870, Codrington's letters expressed concern over the methods of labor recruiters: contracts made through interpreters with men who had no idea what they were agreeing to, and were often deceived as to the terms; young men "bought" from parents for hatchets and knives, or simply kidnapped at gunpoint; people deliberately killed so that their heads might be traded with headhunting tribes in other areas; sham messages sent from Bishop Patteson, who was then later forced to swim ashore on islands where he had previously been welcomed.[49]

In 1871, a crisis point was reached when Patteson landed on Nukapu, an island in the Santa Cruz group that had previously been victimized by a "blackbirder." As was his custom in "questionable places," Patteson went ashore alone, only to be assaulted by natives, who split his head open with a stone adze. Codrington and his colleagues attributed the tragedy to the practices of blackbirders, and his next report to the Society for the Propagation of the Gospel incorporated an appeal to British public opinion, which was referred to Prime Minister Gladstone. As a result of the general furor, laws controlling the labor trade were passed the following year, although it was not finally abolished until after 1900.[50]

Despite his opposition to blackbirding, which he likened to the African slave trade, Codrington granted the planters' need for labor—although when he went to Queensland in 1872 to investigate at first hand, he had difficulty accepting his bishop's injunction not to offend people by "strong language": "strong language is very much what is wanted in this Colony." However, he was ambivalent about native retaliations: while he felt that "the remembrance of one hundred kidnapped and eighteen killed for their heads by the white traders must be allowed for" in understanding the massacre of the crew of the ship *Sandfly*, he nevertheless thought that the natives involved had been mostly motivated by the desire for plunder. When the British navy retaliated, he was much upset that "all those people whose homes were burnt, canoes smashed, pigs shot, trees cut down, were as completely innocent of the massacre of the Sandfly's men as if they had been on another island; five people did it, and five alone"; nevertheless, he concluded that nothing but "heavy punishment" would "stop such outrages." As for the future of the islands in the long run, he believed that their "natural destiny" was Chinese: after the labor trade had destroyed "our people," the Chinese would come in as labor and stay as permanent populations—and "it might be worse."[51]

But if he seems to have accepted as inevitable the onrushing dynamic of imperial expansion, Codrington had great reservations about the impact of the "civilization" into which the Melanesian laborers were being introduced. With so many of the productive males removed, the island food supply was depleted, and there was a general demoralization, heightened by the pillaging carried on by deracinated laborers who returned to the islands armed with guns. "In these seas, at least," commerce was "a propaganda of irreligion and uncivilization." Unfortunately, all over the world "civilization in its modern form presents itself to savages always with its worst side first": "the greatest blackguards are on the edge of civilization everywhere." Indeed, "the low class of so-called civilized people are really much farther behind in many essentials of civilization than pure savages as far as I have seen." Thakombau—one of the more notorious chiefs of "cannibal Feejee," who had converted to Christianity in 1854 and who came to visit at Norfolk Island in 1875—was "more of a gentleman than most white men in these dominions." Whatever happened, Codrington was resolved never to allow himself to become a "colonial"—and in the event, he avoided that fate by returning to live out the last thirty years of his long life in England, where he served as prebendary of the Chichester Cathedral.[52]

Assured of his own status as an English gentleman, Codrington saw himself in a kind of united front with gentlemen savages against "colonial loafers." And like some other upper-class Englishmen overseas (and many anthropologists as well) he had a bias in favor of untouched savages, before "the traders got at them." The "most wonderful thing about heathen savages is that they are so extremely like other people, when one gets used to the color, which is the best wear for the climate"; they were certainly "no dirtier than our laborers," and their lives were not disfigured by "any grinding miseries and wants." Once they had abandoned cannibalism and warfare and polygamy, and put on a minimum of clothes, Codrington was not sure what civilization had to offer them besides Christianity—"and supposing them all to be Christianized, what in the world are they to find to do?" The best thing was to prevent contact insofar as it could be prevented, which the mission tried to do by convincing the natives not to sell their children to blackbirders or to accept employment overseas themselves.[53]

Given the considerable contrast between their missionary situations and styles, it is perhaps not surprising that there was a considerable difference also in the anthropological styles of Fison and Codrington. Codrington's was firmly rooted in, and never transplanted from, the pre-evolutionary tradition of linguistic ethnology. Bishop Patteson had met Max Müller in Germany in the 1840s, and was close to him at Oxford in the early 1850s, when Müller began lecturing there on comparative philology. When Müller sent him a copy of his *Outline Dictionary for the Use of Missionaries* after its publication in 1856, Patteson responded with copies of the Lord's Prayer and the Apostles' Creed in the several island languages he knew. Nine years later, when Patteson sent Müller eleven skeleton grammars he had compiled, it was hoped that the study of the extreme dialectical variation of savage languages might ultimately bear on the question of the monogenesis or polygenesis of language—which, in its more general form of the ultimate racial unity of mankind, was the paradigm question of pre-evolutionary ethnology. At this time, Müller sent on to Patteson (and through him, to Codrington as well) Tylor's *Researches into the Early History of Mankind* and Maine's *Ancient Law*. But Patteson's anthropological interests remained focussed on philological questions, although his death cut short any hope that his work might be systematized.[54]

While he lacked Patteson's natural linguistic gifts, and took some time to pick up Motu, which had become the lingua franca of the Norfolk Island school, Codrington carried on Patteson's work, and very much in the same "ethnological" tradition. In 1874, he drew on Patteson's materials to respond to the German anthropologist Georg Gerland, who had sent him a copy of the South Seas volume of his continuation of Theodor Waitz's staunchly monogenist *Anthropologie der Naturvölker*. Arguing the essential unity of all the peoples in the area between Madagascar and Hawaii, Codrington suggested that just as the Irish were a mixture of Celts and Teutons, who were both in turn from the same Indo-Germanic stock, so were the Papuans and the Polynesians both descendants of the single stock Gerland had inappropriately named Malay. If European anthropologists refused to recognize this, it was because Melanesians had "the misfortune to be black," and it was simply presumed that their language could not be of the same family as that of the brown-skinned Malays or Polynesians.[55]

Although his early anthropological connections were primarily to Max Müller's network of missionary philologists, Codrington (like Fison, and in fact through him) also established ties to evolutionary anthropology. The natives whose kidnapping from Nukapu had precipitated Patteson's murder had been taken to work on cotton plantations in Fiji; and Codrington, in following up the tragedy, began a correspondence with Fison in 1872, which, despite an occasional hint of friction between High Church Anglicanism and Methodist Dissent, was to continue until 1890.[56]

After a desultory beginning, the interchange accelerated in the later 1870s, as Fison's work on *Kamilaroi and Kurnai* intensified. The anthropological initiative seems to have come largely from Fison, with Codrington providing comparative Melanesian data within categories defined by Fison and Howitt's evolutionary enterprise, although there was also some discussion of Codrington's migrational ethnological concerns. In 1879, Fison saw to the publication of Codrington's "Notes on the Customs of Mota, Banks Islands"—suggesting an evolutionary framework in which Codrington's straightforwardly descriptive material took on broader significance, and offering comparisons to the Fijians, who he thought represented the next higher evolutionary stage. Thus Fison noted that the dual exogamous intermarrying divisions Codrington described as something more than families and less than tribes represented a step from uterine toward agnatic inheritance; he also suggested that certain apparent deviations from the regular evolutionary line were in fact due to the anomalous introduction of currency, which prevented the development of hereditary ranks.[57]

Remarking on Codrington's "wonderful insight" into island languages, Fison encouraged him to publish a general comparative treatment of Melanesian languages. He had "learned a hundred-fold more" about the structure of the Fijian language from Codrington than from his own "long and intimate intercourse with the people." After Fison forwarded some of Codrington's linguistic and ethnological information to Tylor in 1881, Codrington himself came into direct contact with the evolutionary center. When he returned to England in 1883 to work up his linguistic materials, he attended the first series of lectures that Tylor gave as Reader in Anthropology at Oxford.[58] But unlike Fison, Codrington never really became a convert to evolutionism. He accepted a generalized sequence of social development and the priority of maternal to paternal forms, and he tried, sometimes with negative results, to relate his work to evolutionary categories. But the particular attitudes toward savagery he had developed out of his missionary experience, in the context of what may be called his ethnographic fieldwork—though the two were really inseparable—left him always somewhat dubious of certain evolutionary assumptions.

Codrington's "fieldwork" was limited by the fact that he stayed mostly at Norfolk Island. He refused the bishopric after Patteson's death because severe seasickness made the island circuit in the *Southern Cross* extremely difficult for him and because he had trouble digesting native food. He did, however, make the "island voyage" five times, his longest single stop being six weeks on Mota in 1869. Beyond this, he depended on his contact with the natives brought from the various islands to Norfolk Island, where he lived in close contact with them for fifteen years or more. Although that contact was directed toward the modification of their traditional culture, Codrington shared Patteson's conviction that it should be modified only as much as necessary to establish Christianity, which should be propagated as much as possible on the basis of native belief. Because he assumed that there would be many correspondences between the old religion and the new, Codrington thought it useful pedagogically to get natives to tell him about their old beliefs. He worked closely with Christianized and literate natives at Norfolk Island who often provided him with written texts or more systematic accounts either of their own cultures or those of islands to which they had gone as teachers.[59] The effect of this experience was twofold: on the one hand, to convince him of the inadequacies of past observation, of the difficulties of penetration, of the problems of translation; on the other, to lead him to a rather simple view of the possibilities of understanding other cultures from within.

The limitations of previous ethnographic knowledge were egregiously manifest in the works of armchair anthropologists back at home, of whom for Codrington (as for Fison) the most flagrant example was John Lubbock. "Many of our anthropologists' books are full of such statements, and the more I read of these books the more I am persuaded either that the Melanesians, at all events, are not savages, or that traveller's stories about savages are very untrustworthy." They "put into the natives' minds and mouths either what they expect will be there, or what is in their own thoughts." Savages were often reported as being unable to count beyond four, simply because they counted down from the index finger, and when the European inquirer got to five and they had no more fingers to count, they became nonplussed. Giving their own sense to adopted English words, they might say of a tabooed place that there were "plenty devil up there," and "in the next edition of some anthropological work these sayings are made to prove something of which the natives had never the slightest notion." Because Europeans always asked the word for something by pointing their finger at a specific object, natives always gave answers by reference to the object specified, attaching to it the appropriate pronominal particle (e.g., "my head"), thus "confirming" the charge that they were incapable of "abstraction," when in fact their language had many "class words." Inasmuch as "scientific people" did not "allow moral feelings to savages," Codrington could not believe "that these are savages according to the scientific descriptions." It was "quite enough for my purpose if lying, stealing, etc. are called bad, and truth, obedience to parents, and kindness to the sick are called good"; and if they used "the same word for a good action and a good axe," then he felt that he was quite "as savage myself as they are."[60]

Codrington was very sensitive to the difficulties of ethnographic observation, especially in matters relating to religion—which embraced "a very wide range of beliefs and practices, the limits of which it would be very difficult to define." It was "equally difficult to ascertain with precision" what these beliefs were, because the natives were "not accustomed to present them in any systematic form among themselves," and because of the difficulty of working through pidgin or a lingua franca, which might be adequate for the ordinary purposes of life, but not for conveying "the real meaning of those expressions which his informants must needs use in his own tongue, because he knows no equivalent for them in the common language which is employed." Missionaries had further difficulties because they usually worked with the young, who were not fully initiated; because "converts are disposed to blacken generally and indiscriminately their own former state"; and because "natives who are still heathen will speak with reserve of what still retains with them a sacred character." Furthermore, a "considerate missionary" would respect that reserve; if he did not, the native was likely "to amuse himself" at the missionary's expense. Those missionaries who did make "systematic enquiries" about native religion were likely to do so "too soon, and for the whole of their after-career make whatever they observe fit into their early scheme"; others so managed it "that neither they nor the first generation of their converts" really knew what the old religion was. Resident traders, though "free from some of a missionary's difficulties," had others of their own, notably those associated with the use of "pigeon English," which carried "its own deceits." And regardless of his calling, every European outsider carried "with him some preconceived ideas; he expects to see idols, and he sees them," so that "images are labelled idols in museums whose makers carved them for amusement." These preconceptions affected the questions asked, and "the native, with very vague beliefs floating in cloudy solution in his mind," found in them "a thread on which these [beliefs] will precipitate themselves"; "without any intention to deceive, he avails himself of the opportunity to clear his own mind while he satisfies the questioner."[61]

In Codrington's personal solution to the problems of observation, a critical factor would seem to have been time, not simply because it took time to learn another system of belief, but because the passage of time helped to give one the humility that such learning required. In the preface to his general ethnography, *The Melanesians,* he quoted his friend Fison (to whom he was "indebted for much instruction"): "When a European has been living for two or three years among savages he is sure to be fully convinced that he knows all about them; when he has been ten years or so amongst them, if he be an observant man, he finds that he knows very little about them, and so begins to learn." What Codrington had sought to learn in the several decades since he first visited the islands in 1863 was "the native view": "I have endeavoured as far as possible to give the natives' account of themselves by giving what I took down from their lips and translating what they wrote themselves." Although written by a missionary, his book was "not meant to have what is generally understood to be a missionary character." Rather, it was intended to accomplish what he felt was "one of the first duties of a missionary": to "try to understand the people among whom he works." Granting that it was likely that in an inquiry so conducted, "the worst side of native life may be out of sight, and the view given seem generally more favourable than might be expected," Codrington simply said that "if it be so, I shall not regret it."[62]

Although Codrington began, he said, "with his full share of the prejudices and predilections belonging to missionaries," they were in fact somewhat different from those of many missionaries. In the classic degenerationist view of missionary Christianity, savages were doubly fallen humans; in addition to their common human share in the sin of Adam's fall, their savagery was itself the product of a second fall: the loss of sacred knowledge and the descent into idolatry and devil worship as they were pushed through hostile environments to the corners of the earth. But rather than finding evidence of a lost primitive monotheism in surviving traces of Jewish ritual, and beyond searching for cultural and linguistic similarities that would reestablish ethnological connections between present "racial" groups, Codrington was interested in looking behind what others despised as superstition to find a grounding of religious belief that was shared by all humankind: "to find the common foundation, if such there be, which lies in human nature itself ready for the superstructure of the Gospel."[63]

Evolutionary anthropologists, too, had sought such a common foundation. For Tylor, the essential core of all religion was "animism" (or "the belief in Spiritual Beings"): the idea that the human body (and by extension, other beings of the natural world, both animate and inanimate) was animated by "a thin unsubstantial human image," the "cause of life or thought in the individual it animates," capable of "leaving the body far behind" and "continuing to exist and appear to men" after its death; from this basic idea had evolved all known religious beliefs and rituals, up to and including those of the Church of England. Codrington

Robert Henry Codrington, while living in retirement at Chichester, 1895. (Courtesy of the Pitt Rivers Museum, University of Oxford)

never explicitly rejected the doctrine of animism, but he did by implication call it into question at a number of points. Thus in 1881, before he attended Tylor's lectures, Codrington doubted that the belief in souls was based, as Tylor's doctrine would have had it, upon the experience of dreams and visions. Nor did direct contact with Tylor eliminate all doubt. In his general Melanesian ethnography of 1891, Codrington could find no evidence "anywhere in Melanesia [of] a belief in a spirit which animates any natural object, a tree, a waterfall, storm or rock, so as to be to it what the soul is believed to be to the body of a man." Nor could he find any failure to "distinguish between animate and inanimate things": "when an owl in a story talks and cooks food, both actions are on a level not of supposed fact but of fancy."[64]

Codrington felt much the same way about "totemism," which, in its religious aspect, was regarded by evolutionists as a particular form of animistic belief. Responding to the questionnaire sent out by James G. Frazer in 1888, Codrington said that he did not believe "any real *totem,* as I understand *totem,*" was to be found in Melanesia; where something resembling a totem was to be found, he considered that it had "to do with the fancy of individuals" to be "remembered by certain things"—and added a parenthesis: "Do people know how exceedingly modern family crests are in Europe?" He did not believe "that any people there" actually thought themselves "descended from birds or fish"—though he did not doubt that "it might be got out of them by questioning that they do": "a man given to totems would find them in Melanesia," but "I never did."[65]

What Codrington did find throughout Melanesia, and indeed, throughout "the whole Pacific," was in important respects quite different from Tylor's "animism." Codrington described it in a letter to Max Müller in 1878, and Müller used it in his Hibbert Lectures to attack evolutionary interpretations of religion: "the religion of the Melanesians consists, as far as belief goes, in the persuasion that there is a supernatural power belonging to the region of the unseen; and, as far as practice goes, in the use of means of getting this power turned to their own benefit." Throughout the Pacific, this power was called mana: "it is a power or influence, not physical, and in a way supernatural" which showed itself "in physical force, or in any kind of power or excellence which a man possesses." "All Melanesian religion consists, in fact, in getting this Mana for one's self, or getting it used for one's benefit" through "prayers and sacrifices." Fifteen years later, after attending Tylor's lectures, Codrington reprinted that letter as a footnote in his general Melanesian ethnography, where the discussion was cast in much the same terms. While there were analogies here to Tylor's animism, insofar as all spirits had mana, which one might seek to appropriate by prayer and sacrifice, the essential basis of religion was quite different: far from being a kind of ill-founded attempt to explain the natural world, a kind of science gone astray, religion was based on an irrational feeling of awe in the face of extraordinary power.[66]

Missionary Ethnography and Paradigm Change

Fison and Codrington had much in common, including a sense of the great difficulty involved in collecting reliable ethnographic information, a mistrust of most previous ethnography, a considerable respect for each other as ethnographic observers, a disdain for much armchair anthropology, and, notwithstanding, an active epistolary relationship to major figures in the metropole. But from the very beginning of their own epistolary relationship, there is evidence of a marked difference in their anthropological perspectives, and in their relationship to contemporary and subsequent anthropological paradigms.

Returning to Fison a kinship schedule filled out with the Mota data, Codrington suggested that "there appears to be a fallacy in the use of the English terms 'son,' 'daughter' etc. as translations of the native terms"; "by saying that a Mota man calls his brother's son his own *son,* you introduce the English notion of sonship, and tend to impute a promiscuous relationship which is far from being in accordance with their own ideas and feelings." In a subsequent letter he elaborated: "Of course these terms don't now—if ever they did—mean father and son with the sense of generation"; "the word used for child is used for all small objects in the comparative sense and I imagine that to be the original meaning of the word."[67]

Codrington was quite willing to collect kinship data for Fison, and included an extended discussion of kinship in his Melanesian ethnography. He noted there some recent changes that marked an "advance towards the patriarchal system," and certain linguistic "traces of a communal system of marriage." But he posed against the latter the fact that the people had "no memory of a time when all the women of one side were in fact common wives to the men of the other side," and he was in general little interested in issues of evolutionary sequence. His purpose was "the exhibition of the Melanesian people as they now appear"—and it was not the failure of evolutionary hypotheses or a growing sense of their empirical inadequacy, but rather his initial and continuing modesty and scepticism, that led Codrington to feel—as Fison eventually did—that that was "quite enough."[68]

Although he was in direct contact with both Tylor and Frazer, Codrington's relationship to the development of anthropological theory was perhaps better exemplified by his earlier epistolary link to Max Müller. Like Müller's, his underlying anthropological orientation was that of the pre-evolutionary ethnological paradigm embodied in the work of James Cowles Prichard—a transformation, under the aegis of comparative philology, of the migrational paradigm implicit in the early books of the Bible. Like Müller, Codrington made a certain surface accommodation to evolutionism, but remained critical of some of its fundamental assumptions. By denying that his Melanesians exemplified it, he called into question the very category of "savagery" upon which so much of evolutionary reconstruction was founded. Although Codrington lacked Müller's direct ties to the German philosophical tradition, and was not given to arguing general epistemological issues, at a pragmatic ethnographic level his concern with category definitions and problems of translation may also be considered part of an "anti-positivist" counter current that bubbled up here and there during the era of classical evolutionism.[69]

That same concern is resonant of issues Franz Boas was beginning to raise at about the same time, although the critique of classical evolutionism came later in Britain than in the United States and took a somewhat different course. But as we shall see, the earlier phases of the reaction against the "intellectualist" tradition in British anthropology were influenced by Codrington's ethnographic account of mana; and when a more general reaction took place after 1910, there were quite a few links to the tradition Codrington represented. W. H. R. Rivers, whose "genealogical method" seems perhaps foreshadowed in Codrington's chart of "A Mota Pedigree," did his fieldwork from the deck of a later *Southern Cross;* his primary Melanesian informant, John Patteson Pantutun, was the son of one of Patteson's native teachers, and Codrington's own fictive "grandson." When Rivers abandoned evolutionism in 1911, it was not simply to embrace a reemergent version of the pre-evolutionary "ethnological" paradigm; *The History of Melanesian Society* in fact argued a migration sequence recalling that proposed by Codrington, with a similar distinction between kava and betel peoples.[70]

But while Rivers' "conversion" to the "ethnological analysis of culture" marked the continuity of Codrington's Melanesian ethnographic tradition, Rivers did not share the same degree of sensitivity to the problem of translating kinship terms, or the same reservations about the assumptions of the Morganian tradition. And although Rivers' own relation to that tradition did, as we shall see, have something of the character of "discovery," the Morganian current was already "available" within the broader tradition of British social anthropology. Through Tylor's paper, through Walter Baldwin Spencer—whose work with Frank Gillen in Central Australia was described by the latter as "a splendid verification" of the research done by Fison and Howitt two decades before—and on down to Frazer, Australian ethnography had a distinctively Morganian aura. During the same period, however, the evolutionary tradition in Great Britain was to undergo a considerable further development, modification, and questioning.[71]

TWO

Animism, Totemism, and Christianity

A Pair of Heterodox Scottish Evolutionists

Harking back a quarter of a century to "the pioneers of the investigation" and thence forward through "the later research of a generation of able investigators," Tylor conveyed, retrospectively, a strong impression of the paradigmatic character of "classical evolutionism"—in the loose sense of a focussed inquiry sustained for an extended period by a group of researchers sharing a common framework of theoretical assumptions which defined a body of relevant empirical data. That framework had emerged during the 1860s in the work of several innovative thinkers—most notably, Tylor and McLennan—who, in the context of an archeological revolution in human time, found the assumptions of Prichardian monogenist ethnology no longer adequate to answer traditional questions about the "early history of mankind." In the context of the Darwinian revolution, they were forced to ask very different questions about the origin of fundamental human institutions and the emergence and growth of human culture. By the end of that decade, sociocultural evolutionism, although still controversial elsewhere in intellectual life, was in anthropological circles well on its way to becoming a kind of theoretical orthodoxy.[1]

But as we have seen in reviewing the ethnographic careers of Fison and Codrington, the "paradigmatic" character of classical evolutionism was from the beginning somewhat problematic: theoretically, for those still influenced by pre-evolutionary Prichardian ethnology; philosophically, for those who did not find congenial the dominant positivism of the day; methodologically, for those who mistrusted "survival" as a method of historical reconstruction; empirically, for those who had trouble finding in the real world ethnographic data that were called for by evolutionary theory, or whose ethnographic data were otherwise recalcitrant to evolutionary interpretation; and existentially, for those who retained a commitment to traditional Christian religious belief. It was possible for the latter to accept evolutionism as a working framework while retaining an ultimate faith, as did Fison, or simply to pursue descriptive ethnography without systematically confronting evolutionary issues, as did Codrington; it was even possible, as we shall see, to enlist evolutionary argument in the service of Protestant Christianity. But in an era when the cultural centrality of religion was still widely assumed, and when the "conflict of science and religion" was often sharply felt, the evolutionary status of the dogmatic and ritual bases of the Christian religion was an issue that continued to be discussed after the pioneering figures of classical evolutionism had made their major statements on the evolution of religion.[2]

While Tylor's theory of animism was the most important such statement, there was another, less noticed at the time of its appearance, which in the last decade of the nineteenth century and the first of the twentieth was increasingly to become the focus of paradigmatic debate: McLennan's theory of totemism. In a footnote to "Kinship in Ancient Greece," which he published as a follow-up to *Primitive Marriage,* McLennan had suggested that the Greeks might once have had totems like those of the American Indians. In the context of Tylor's writings on animism in the later 1860s, McLennan devoted further attention to this question, culminating in a long essay on "The Worship of Plants and Animals." The matter was not a new one, but simply the age-old issue of the "origin of idolatry" in modern evolutionary dress. Traditionally, it had been particularly bothersome in relation to the Egyptians, a people who in many ways seemed to stand on a fairly high cultural plane, and in this respect it was analogous to the problem posed by the existence of numerous amoral divinities among the Greeks. Among Christian apologists, the phenomenon was likely to be explained, if not simply as the work of the devil, then in more generalized "degenerationist" terms: the original monotheistic revelation had been gradually lost or compromised by the materialistic propensities of fallen man, which demanded a physical embodiment of spiritual principle, sometimes with the connivance of a priestly class that retained some knowledge of the pure monotheistic truth.[3]

Following in the competing tradition of eighteenth-century rationalists such as Charles de Brosses, but writing now in the context of Darwinian evolution, McLennan wanted to show that "totemism" was a general stage in the evolution of man. In doing so, he was—as every major sociocultural evolutionary writer felt compelled to do—countering the theories of Friedrich Max Müller. According to Müller's "disease of language" theory (which resonated of traditional degenerationist argument), all of "Aryan" mythology was built on the "wonderment" felt by the "forefathers of the Aryan family" in the face of the "whole solar drama," and myth interpretation was largely a matter of making equations in linguistic roots (Greek Zeus = Sanskrit Dyaus, from the verb *dyu,* to shine), and following out solar mythic patterns—for example, the young hero (Baldr = Sifrit = Achilles) dying in the fullness of youth, as did the sun. Referring to Tylor's work, McLennan argued instead that the animism of primitive man led naturally to fetishism, or the idea that there was life in inanimate objects; in these terms, the sun was merely another kind of fetish. Pursuing his sociological bent, McLennan offered a definition of totemism as the linking of fetishism with three social phenomena: the idea that there was one fetish for each tribe; the hereditary transmission of the fetish through the mother; and the association of the fetish with marriage law through the principle of exogamy.[4]

For McLennan, whose ostensible purpose was to understand the plant and animal worship of the ancient Greeks and Romans, totemism itself was more an explanation than a thing to be explained (although there was a hint that primitive men might have retained a kind of memory knowledge of their own evolutionary origins). And in his later writings, McLennan was less concerned with the origin of totemism than with the question why the groups held together by religious regard for the totem should be exogamous. But although he had planned "to trace the progress of Totemism" upward "in connection with kinship and Exogamy," that task remained undone at his death in 1881.[5] Loosely conceived of as a principle of both religious belief and social organization, and never systematically investigated, totemism was thus bequeathed by McLennan to later generations of evolutionary anthropologists, not as a pioneering investigation ready for Tylor's retrospective paradigmatic summary in 1888, but rather as a problematic concept that was to trouble scholars throughout the two decades around the turn of the century.

For many of those scholars, sociocultural evolutionism itself did have a somewhat taken-for-granted paradigmatic character. It was not a body of assumption they themselves shaped in the fire of intellectual controversy, but rather a model of anthropological inquiry that was already "available" as they came of age, and in terms of which their own thinking was elaborated. Working within this already established framework, however, several of the second generation of sociocultural evolutionists were, in the 1880s and 1890s, to develop arguments which either called into question important paradigmatic assumptions or foreshadowed the direction that anthropological theory would take after the reformation predicted by Tylor in 1896.

Two evolutionary writers whose work was to figure in major ways in that reformation were Andrew Lang and William Robertson Smith.

Both came from Scotland, where cultural and political marginality and the survivals of the Celtic clan tradition had encouraged an anthropological attitude among some more adventurous intellects. Both were influential literary men who won their major contemporary reputations outside anthropology—Lang as "the divine amateur of letters"; Smith as one of the most highly respected academic scholars of his day. Both were direct disciples of the two major pioneers of British evolutionary anthropology: Lang, a follower of Tylor, and Smith, of McLennan—though both felt also the influence of the other founding figure. Both were concerned with understanding the evolution of religion, and both dealt with it in terms that reflected their personal religious experience—though Lang was more concerned with belief, while Smith (in his anthropological work) was more interested in ritual. Both were somewhat less than orthodox, from the perspective of sociocultural evolutionism as well as conventional religious belief: Lang described himself as deservedly "an outcast from the church anthropological"; Smith was in fact proclaimed heretical by the Free Church into which he had been born. Both figures help to illuminate the general movement of anthropological thought between 1870 and 1910: Lang, in ways that have been largely lost to historical view; Smith, in ways that have only recently begun to be adequately appreciated.[6]

Andrew Lang: From Tylorian Folklore to Primitive Monotheism

Although Robert Louis Stevenson later described him as a "La-dy, Da-dy Oxford kind of Scot," Andrew Lang was an authentic son of the Scottish Border, "that land of old discord and lingering romance." He was born in 1844 in the ancient town of Selkirk, near the confluence of the Yarrow and the Ettrick, the "many-fabled streams" of Scottish balladry, where his ancestors had lived for at least seven generations, and his great-grandfather was chief magistrate at the time when Sir Walter Scott first became Sheriff-Deputy. An unusually precocious eldest son, Lang at five foreshadowed the reading habits of his later years, by setting six books upon six chairs and reading from one to another as his interest waned and waxed—fairy tales, chapbook histories of Scottish heroes, Shakespeare's *Midsummer Night's Dream,* the Homeric stories, and anything he could get his hands on about "Red Indians." Unlike other "Scots of the pen," who "first absorbed, and later were compelled to get rid of" their early religion, he got "no harm" from the culturally prescribed exposure to the Shorter Catechism; according to his recollection, "Calvinism ran like water off a duck's back." On the other hand, the "half-world of legend, of kelpies in the loch and elves in the greenwood, and of miraculous happenings beyond mortal compass, was not too far off in time but that he could feel the waft of its flying wing." And having felt "the inebriation of romance" in his childhood, Lang never really lost his appreciation of the marvelous.[7]

At ten Lang spent two lonely years at the Edinburgh Academy, where his withdrawal into books helped preserve the childhood "touch of genius" that usually at that age, he believed, faded "into the light of common day"—and where he had his first introduction to Homer in Greek. In 1861, he matriculated at St. Andrews University, where he began more seriously to write poetry, to read in contemporary scholarship on mythology and folklore, and to learn about (and attempt to practice) necromancy and alchemy. After spending a year at Glasgow University in order to qualify for a Snell Exhibition to Balliol College, in the fall of 1864 he went to Oxford, where he was to become something of a blue-china aesthete, whose poetic paragon was Swinburne. But Lang also studied with the Greek scholar Benjamin Jowett, then Senior Tutor and soon Master, and with his own tutor, T. H. Green, a missionary of Hegelian idealism among the British empiricists. Lang, who at this time knew Darwin only in a "vague, popular way"—and Hegel through Green's lectures on Aristotle—concluded that Hegel had invented evolution before Darwin by showing the spirit at work within it.[8]

After taking first-class honors in "Greats" in 1868, Lang won a fellowship at Merton College, where for the next few years his aesthetic interests flowered. He devoted himself to poetry in a Pre-Raphaelite mode, to Renaissance and medieval French literature, to classical studies and to mythology, in a kind of backwards poetic evolution from recent French romanticism to paganism, which was to prove influential in the Renaissance studies of his close friend Walter Pater. Lang's intellect was too mobile, however, to suffer very long the constraints of any particular line of scholarship, and by 1875, when he settled in London after his marriage forced him to vacate his fellowship, he was already launched on a career as literary journalist. He wrote almost as fast as he read; writing "like a spiritualist automatist" while he was engaged in continuous animated conversation, he once composed a lengthy review during a short trip by rail, depositing the finished product in the post upon detraining. From the time he published *Ballads and Lyrics of Old France* in 1872, until his death in 1912 stopped his pen in the midst of *Highways and Byways on the Border,* Lang kept producing books—alone, in collaboration, or by translation: biography, children's books, criticism, essays, fairy tales, fiction, folklore, histories, parodies, poetry, renditions of and commentaries on Greek classics—until the total in the British Museum catalogue came to over 350, not counting uncollected reviews and essays published in almost every major magazine of his day.[9]

Lang was, literally, a cultural phenomenon: the apotheosis of "the man of letters"—Oxford and Cambridge men who met the demand for a kind of middle-brow version of Arnoldian "culture" for a large middle-class readership—in the period when that social category was beginning to be eclipsed by an emergent category of "intellectuals." As "the droopy aristocrat of letters," it is said that he ridiculed or disparaged "practically every important novel that came his way," including those of Conrad, Dostoevski, Hardy, James, Tolstoy, and Zola. Praising Barrie, Doyle, Kipling, and his close friends Stevenson and Rider Haggard (with whom he co-authored the *The World's Desire,* and whose *She* he gently parodied with *He*), Lang was more than any other critic responsible for the great surge of interest in romance in the 1880s and 1890s. Romance may have served Lang as a kind of sublimated anthropology; be that as it may, there were moments when Lang felt that he had missed his calling. Walking late in life with a friend on Merton Street in Oxford, he remarked nostalgically "if I had stayed on here when I was a young Fellow, and stuck to one thing . . . I should have been a really big swell at anthropology." From the 1880s on, his contributions to that field were almost as numerous as his multicolored sequence of children's "fairy books"; if little known to anthropologists today, they were not without considerable influence in their own time.[10]

Lang came at anthropology from the study of folklore and mythology, which in the later nineteenth century were closely allied studies. In Tylorian terms, the "doctrine of survivals" was the basis for a kind of evolutionary sequence of genres—all of which Lang practiced—from mythology (the efforts of primitive men to explain the natural phenomena of the world around them) to the folklore of the modern European peasantry, on up to the nursery tales of civilized children (whose mental development was widely assumed to recapitulate a similar phylogenetic sequence). And in the imaginary other-world of the Victorian psyche, fairies and savages were antithetic projective images of middle-class respectability—the former, diaphanously veiled, always singing, always dancing; the latter, butt-bare and brutal, but just as careless of the morrow.[11]

By the time he arrived at St. Andrews, Lang had already read George Dasent's influential *Popular Tales from the Norse* and other diffusionist folklore studies written under the influence of Max Müller's essay on "Comparative Mythology"—which was said to have swept all the materials of British folklore "into its orbit" for almost two decades. But although he himself may have felt the direct influence of Müller at Oxford, Lang's characteristic viewpoint was defined by the two pioneer figures of British classical evolutionism. He later recalled that he had first been attracted to "savages" by McLennan's essays on totemism; products of the "most acute and ingenious" of all the minds he had known, the essays were "revelations which led on to others." Lang concluded that "the usual ideas" about mythology and folklore were "the reverse of the truth, that the common theory had to be inverted"—a notion which was already "in the air," but which, "like the White Knight in Alice," Lang "claimed for [his] own invention." The issue that was to preoccupy him was one of the paradigm issues of evolutionism, cast into the classical world in which his Oxford studies had made him at home: whether the myths of the Greeks were, as Müller maintained, degenerative products of a disease of language, or whether the "cruel, puerile, obscene" elements in them were signs of an earlier savagery. And by the time Lang came to argue the matter systematically, his airborne notion was rooted not only in McLennan's totemism but also in Tylor's theories in *Primitive Culture,* which he read in 1872, shortly after Tylor had been introduced to him in an Oxford salon as author of "a large book, all about savages."[12]

Over the next fifteen years, Lang authored what has been called his "exegesis" of the "new gospel of Tylor," bringing an end to Müller's domination of British folklore studies. The assault began in May of 1873, in an essay on "Mythology and Fairy Tales"—the "opening salvo in a withering attack" on Müller's mythological system, and the first systematic attempt to apply anthropological method to the comparative study of myths. Lang soon found himself in correspondence with several other Tylorian folklorists: Edward Clodd, who like Lang had stepped over the "threshold of full manhood" during the "*Sturm und Drang* period" of the 1860s, and who continued to publish Tylorian accounts of animism and magic well into the twentieth century; Edward Sydney Hartland, who moved from *The Science of Fairy Tales* to *Primitive Paternity,* and was still writing books on *Primitive Society* and *Primitive Law* in the 1920s; and George Lawrence Gomme, the author of several guides to the study of folklore, in which the "science" was defined in Tylorian terms as "the comparison and identification of the survivals of archaic beliefs, customs and traditions in modern ages." In 1878, the four men joined with others in founding the Folk-Lore Society; together, they have been called "the Great Team" of late-nineteenth-century British folklore.[13]

It was Lang's critique of Müller, however, that led the way; and the essays he collected in 1884 as *Custom and Myth* (and dedicated to Tylor) lay bare in a very clear form the basic assumptions of the "anthropological" as opposed to the "philological" approach to the study of mythology and folklore. For Lang (who proclaimed himself "a revolutionary mythologist") "the method of folklore" was structured by a series of analogies: between the relics of the material and the immaterial world, between the sciences that studied those relics, and between the peoples that produced or employed them in the past and in the present. It proceeded by comparison: "when an apparently irrational and anomalous custom is

"The droopy aristocrat of letters": Portrait of Andrew Lang, painted in 1885 by his friend Sir William Blake Richmond, R.A. (Courtesy of the Scottish National Portrait Gallery)

found in any country," it looked "for a country where a similar practice is found, and where the practice is no longer irrational and anomalous." In contrast to the "scholarly method" of the comparative mythologist—who would compare only "the myths of races which speak languages of the same family" and of races "which have, in historic times, been actually in proved contact with each other"—the folklorist, like the "unscholarly anthropologist," would compare the myths of races "widely severed" in space and time and would "not be surprised if Greeks and Australian blacks" told the same tale about the Pleiades. The "object of both myths" was "to account for the grouping . . . of the constellations"; like flint arrowheads from widely separated sites, the myths resembled each other "because they were originally framed to meet the same needs out of the same material." And if the ground of that similarity in "the common simple ideas of human nature" was not immediately evident, then the folklore of the peasants or "non-progressive classes" among civilized races provided "a mean term" in the process of understanding: "the conclusion will usually be that the fact which puzzles us by its presence in civilisation is a relic surviving from the time when the ancestors of a civilised race were in a state of savagery." On this basis, the essays that followed were a series of confrontations with Max Müller, designed to show that the myth of Cronus eating his children was a "product of the period of savage fancy," that there was "no end to Aryan parallels" of savage beliefs and practices, and that "myth was a disease of thought, far more than a disease of language"—produced by "men in similar mental conditions of ignorance, curiosity, and credulous fancy."[14]

From the perspective of Lang's later writings, the most interesting essay was the long one "Fetichism and the Infinite," which was a rebuttal of Max Müller's Hibbert Lectures on *The Origin and Growth of Religion*. Although Lang made a point of not committing himself to fetishism as "the first moment in the development of worship," he argued against Müller's degenerationist insistence that it was a "parasitical growth" or a "corruption" of religion, suggesting instead that it was "one of the earliest traceable steps by which men climbed to higher conceptions of the supernatural." Lang's insistence that religion was not "an extension of the idea of Vastness" grounded in "the emotion of awe," but rather "a development of ideas of Force" expressing itself in an "interested search" for "something practically *strong* for good and evil," has a certain resonance of Codrington's idea of mana; and Lang was more inclined than Tylor to emphasize the role of religion "in the growth of society." But the argument was essentially Tylorian: man did not have an innate "faculty of apprehending the Infinite"; on the contrary, "savage religion, like savage science [was] merely a fanciful explanation of what lies beyond the horizon of experience."[15]

Four years later, Lang authored a more systematic two-volume presentation of Tylorian thought in *Myth, Ritual, and Religion*, which according to Hartland gave the *coup de grâce* to the Müllerian school. Paradoxically, however, during the 1890s Lang became a vocal critic of Tylor's theory of animism, adopting positions on the evolution of religion that were in some respects quite consonant not only with traditional Protestant orthodoxy, but also with the anthropological assumptions of his intellectual antagonist Max Müller. It was a shift that required quite significant revisions when the second edition of *Myth, Ritual, and Religion* was produced in 1901.[16]

What may have occasioned this move must remain somewhat speculative, given a certain reticence Lang displayed about the evolution of his own religious beliefs. There is at least a suggestion, however, of a pattern that was by no means unusual among Victorian intellectuals at the end of the nineteenth century: an exposure to conventional religion during a pre-Darwinian childhood, a period of rationalistic doubt in the early heyday of evolutionary naturalism, and then a movement back toward supernaturalism, either of the conventional religious or the spiritualist variety—in a context of impending personal mortality, unease about the progress of European civilization, a reaction against "positivism" and "materialism," and a heightened intellectual interest in irrational psychological phenomena.[17]

After first reading Tylor, Lang spoke of himself as holding an orthodox "Darwinian" view of religious evolution. In the early 1880s, he co-authored with Tylor a "Double Ballade of Primitive Man" which contained the lines (drafted by Tylor, but strengthened by Lang in the published version): "Theologians all to expose,— / 'Tis the *mission* of Primitive Man." In *Custom and Myth,* he wrote of "the periodical resurrection of superstitions"—including the Cock Lane Ghost, spiritualism, and the divining rod—which might even "win the belief of the credulous among the educated classes." But with the death of friends of his youth, and of close relatives, Lang wanted very much to believe that "dear friends shall meet once more / Beyond the sphere of Time." Sometime after he met Rider Haggard in the late 1880s, he was urging the necessity of "letting civilisation die decently, as it must, and as we have no fight in us"; in a letter to Edward Clodd (who remained an ardent unbeliever) he commented: "you believe in Progress, do you? I'd rather believe in wraiths." And so Lang did.[18]

A person of "vivid imagination" given to very clear "waking dreams," Lang, by his own account, had seen two wraiths and a possible ghost by 1894—the latter back in 1869, when, while walking on Oriel Lane, he saw an Oxford professor who was at that moment actually some distance away and "either dead or dying." Lang had been among the founding members of the Society for Psychical Research in 1882, and by 1890 was avowing his own paranormal experiences in print. In 1894, he published a book called *Cock Lane and Common Sense,* in which he called into question the Tylorian view of animism, on what he insisted were strictly empirical grounds. Confronted with evidences of paranormal phenomena in civilized society, anthropologists—who wanted *not* to believe—were "wont to ejaculate that blessed word 'survival' " rather than studying the live manifestations of persons in the same mental condition as the Maori. Granting that much of modern spiritualism was fraudulent, Lang felt that it was stretching probability too far to regard the vast number of reports of such phenomena from Australia and ancient Alexandria to modern London as simply imposture. The only certain thing about such apparitions was that "they really are perceived"; and whether they were "actual objective facts of unknown origin" (and frequently counterfeited) or "identical and collective hallucinations," they were worthy of serious investigation.[19]

After three hundred pages of somewhat random documentation—interspersed with discussions of contemporary psychological theories of hypnosis, hallucination, and unconscious cerebration—Lang offered more general comments on what he called "The Ghost Theory of Religion." Although we were told of tribes without religion, closer study indicated that they believed in spirits, and better information often showed they also had theistic concepts of a Maker or a Judge. The fact that monotheistic civilized nations retained the belief in spirits suggested that all the elements of religion were distributed universally in all degrees of culture. In contrast, anthropological theory had argued a kind of devolution, which gradually deprived all nature save mankind of soul and left only one God. "The last scientific step, it may be inferred, is to deprive the universe of a God, and mankind of souls," and this would naturally be taken by those who see the process of ghost- and god-making as a "mere set of natural and inevitable fallacies." But if savages reasoned not only incorrectly from the "normal" facts of dreams and death, but correctly from the "abnormal" facts that science was wont to dismiss as imposture or hallucination, then their conclusions might not have been totally wrong: "man may have faculties which savages recognize, and which physical science does not." Purely materialistic theories of the world must be reconsidered; and the doctrines of theism and of the soul might not after all be false.[20]

Four years after this still somewhat tentative sally, Lang mounted a two-pronged assault on the "modern Science of the History of Religion," which had taken for granted as proven the assumption that the ideas of God and the soul were based on "early fallacious reasonings about misunderstood experiences." The first half of his argument was an attempt to find out "what, if anything, can be ascertained as to the nature of the 'visions' and hallucinations which, according to Mr. Tylor . . . lent their aid to the idea of 'spirit.' " The second was an attempt to "collect and compare" accounts of "High Gods and creative beings worshipped or believed in, by the most backward races" in order to determine whether these "relatively Supreme Beings" were "mere developments from the belief in ghosts of the dead."[21]

In pursuing the first task, Lang insisted that he was engaged in a "legitimate anthropological proceeding": following "Mr. Tylor's example" by collecting "savage *beliefs*," he took the further step of posing these against "attested records of similar *experiences* among living and educated men." Lang proposed to carry anthropology into "the X region of our nature," where in fact savages had anticipated some of the latest developments of contemporary Western psychology—hypnotism, "alternating personalities," and the remarkable cures that "the school of the Salpêtrière" would ascribe to "suggestion."[22]

Lang began by reviewing the history of the "scientific attitude towards X phenomena," which was encapsulated in Hume's rejection of miracles, and the more recent development of anthropological thinking on the origin of religion, as exemplified by Thomas Huxley, Herbert Spencer, and (in greater detail), Tylor. Noting a paradox that may in fact be seen in other aspects of social evolutionary thought, Lang suggested that the weakness of the anthropological argument was that it was not *au fond* evolutionary. Because Tylor had written before recent developments in psychology, he took it for granted "that the earliest, remote, unknown thinkers on life and the soul were existing on the same psychical plane as we ourselves." But a real Darwinian must acknowledge that "we know little more about the mental condition and experiences of the earlier thinkers who developed the doctrine of Souls than we know about the mental condition and experiences of the lower animals." Quoting Dessoir and citing Taine, Lang suggested that recent developments in "modern psychology and physiology" showed that the "'fully conscious life of the spirit' in which we moderns now live 'seems to rest on a substratum of reflex action of a hallucinatory type.'" And if "early men were ever in a condition in which telepathy and clairvoyance" were prevalent, "one might expect that faculties so useful would be developed in the struggle for existence" and that "they may still exist in savage as in civilised races."[23]

Lang went on to review a number of categories of paranormal experience (clairvoyance, divination, hallucination, demonic possession), juxtaposing the evidence of Tylorian ethnology with that of modern spiritualism, the studies of the Society for Psychical Research, and the work of contemporary psychologists (most notably, Charcot, Janet, and especially William James). Much of the evidence came from Tylor's sources, but "the question, however, on which Mr. Tylor does not touch, is, *Are any of the stories true?*" If, as Lang's evidence was designed to show, there were good grounds for believing that they were, then "the belief in human souls may be, in part, at least, based on supernormal phenomena which Materialism disregards." And if this was true of animism, then it was also true of fetishism, or "the belief in the souls tenanting inanimate objects."[24]

Having discussed the "supernormal aspects of the origins of religion," Lang devoted the second half of his book to whether, "when once the doctrine of souls was conceived by early men, it took precisely the course of development usually indicated by anthropological science"—according to which the "Idea of God" evolved gradually out of the idea of spirit or soul. Against this, Lang argued that the idea of God (in the sense of "a primal eternal Being, author of all things, the father and friend of man, the invisible omniscient guardian of morality") occurred "rudely, but recognisably, in the lowest-known grades of savagery," and therefore could not have arisen from "the later speculation of men, comparatively civilised and advanced, on the datum of ghosts." The ensuing chapters examined "the high gods of low races," in order to show that "certain low savages are as monotheistic as some Christians" and that these "supreme gods [were] not necessarily developed out of 'spirits,'" but belonged "to another branch of faith than ghosts, or ghost-gods, or Totems." Ranging over the world for ethnographic evidence, Lang relied rather heavily on Codrington's suggestion that the Banks Islanders distinguished between *tamate,* or ghosts of the dead, and *vui* ("beings who were not, and never had been, human")—which Lang insisted was "the usual savage doctrine." He relied even more heavily on accounts by Howitt of Darumulun, the "Supreme Spirit" of the Kurnai, who punished transgression of five ethical precepts, including both the fifth and the seventh of the Ten Commandments. There were, in short, not one, but "two streams of religious thought, one rising in the conception of an undifferentiated Being, eternal, moral, and creative, the other rising in the ghost-doctrine."[25]

If the former was less in evidence ethnographically than one might expect, it was because the ghost-doctrine was "best adapted to everyday needs and experiences" and often contaminated the primitive monotheism, introducing "sacrifice and food-propitiation" into its ritual. Similarly, the "conception of 'spirit,' once attained, would inevitably come to be attached to the idea of the Supreme Being," because it was difficult to think of "an eternal, powerful, and immortal being" merely "as *being*." Granting that all this smacked of "the old degeneration theory," Lang insisted that "in this particular respect" the degeneration theory was "as undeniable as any fact in human history." It was simply a result of "the attractions which animism, when once developed, possessed for the naughty natural man, 'the old Adam,'" who would not rest satisfied with "a moral creator" who would "not favour one man above his neighbour, or one tribe above its rivals, as a reward for sacrifice which he does not accept, or as constrained by charms which do not touch his omnipotence." Man would "'go a-whoring' after practically useful ghosts, ghost-gods and fetishes which he could keep in his wallet or medicine bag." And as "culture kept advancing" on "the material plane," the crafts and arts arose, "each needing a god," and these would proliferate, until "thought became clearer," and the conception of a single "Unknown God, Cause of Causes" would reemerge. However, it was only within the tradition of the religion of Jehovah that the original moral element of monotheism had been preserved or revived, and even here it had suffered degradation; furthermore, Judaism had been "strangely indifferent to the animistic element in religion." Only Christianity, at last, combined "what was good in Animism, the care for the individual soul as an immortal spirit under eternal responsibilities, with the One righteous Eternal of prophetic Israel, and so ended the long, intricate, and mysterious theological education of humanity."[26]

Setting himself against the whole tendency of Tylorian anthropology, and against the materialism of nineteenth-century science (which he saw as itself based upon an act of faith) Lang had ended in a position very near the degenerationism of Max Müller, whose work he had made his anthropological reputation attacking—although he insisted that, in contrast to Müller, *he* had shown how degeneration really worked. A man given to contrariety and paradox, Lang savored the idea ("highly paradoxical to our generation") that "what the Bible tells us" about the development of Hebrew religion was "precisely" what had occurred. But one suspects that other needs were being served than those of paradox. In the phrase of William James, which at one point he cited, Lang had by this time a strong "Will to Believe" in something approximating traditional Christianity. In contrast to Tylor's "minimal" definition of religion, Lang's required "the belief in the existence of an Intelligence or Intelligences not human, and not dependent on a material mechanism of brain and nerves, which may, or may not, powerfully control men's fortunes and the nature of things." It also required the belief that there was in man "an element so far kindred to these Intelligences that it can transcend the knowledge obtained through the known bodily senses, and may possibly survive the death of the body." In their present form they were "the faith in God and in the Immortality of the Soul." Although it came as a great surprise to Edward Clodd, Lang had for some time been in the habit of saying his prayers twice daily; shortly after his death, he was memorialized as "in the deepest sense, a Defender of the Faith."[27]

From the perspective of the evolutionary faithful, however, Lang was an apostate; during the decade before his death, he played the role of critical gadfly to the heir of Tylorian evolutionary rationalism, James G. Frazer. And for some time before that, Lang had caused the aging Tylor himself no small theoretical discomfort. *The Making of Religion* was offered to the public as "representing" the Gifford Lectures Lang had given in 1888 at the University of St. Andrews, although the original text had been lost in the interim (perhaps conveniently, in view of striking changes in his thought), and the published version therefore contained "very little that was spoken from Lord Gifford's chair." In 1890 and 1891, Tylor had also given two series of Gifford Lectures on "Natural Religion" at the University of Aberdeen. For the next fifteen years, British anthropologists awaited the publication of what Lang, in Tylor's festschrift, called "the great work with which he has long been occupied." But although four chapters of Tylor's anticipated magnum opus were actually set in type by 1904, the work never appeared.[28]

As preserved in Tylor's published bibliography, the analytic contents of his Gifford Lectures suggest that they stayed close to arguments he had by that time been making for a quarter of a century. With the addition of some material on the evolution of marriage institutions, and an attempt to place Tylor's own thesis in relation to the seventeenth- and eighteenth-century debates on natural religion, the Gifford Lectures seem to have been virtually a rehash of the major arguments of *Primitive Culture*. A generation further on, it was still the polemical context of the Darwinian decade that governed Tylor's argument, which was devoted to showing that religious ideas were not God-given, but had developed gradually over an immense span of time out of the primitive germs of animism. By 1891, when the battle for an evolutionary view of human development had long been won (and the third edition of *Primitive Culture* had just appeared), it may have seemed just a bit tedious to rewrite this argument for yet another publication. This sense of a repetitively elaborated and exhausted theoretical viewpoint is evident also in the surviving galleys and page proofs of a decade later. There again it was animism one more time, now in the more systematically classifactory mode of Tylor's later anthropology, presented in a series of schematic charts, each representing a different stage of technological and civilizational development: Tasmanian animism for the Lower Paleolithic, Algonquian and Melanesian animism for the "higher Stone Age," Mexican animism for the Age of Bronze, Graeco-Roman animism for the "great religions of the Iron Age," ending with a chart schematizing the animistic elements in Christianity itself.[29]

However, the last two of the chapters in galleys dealt with more specific issues that for Tylor raised once again the spectre of Revealed Religion. The third was devoted to rebutting Lang's views on the "high gods of low races"; the fourth, to the problem of "Deluge Legends," which seemed to confirm the historicity of the Bible. In both cases, Tylor's basic strategy was to argue that such ideas were not aboriginal, but had been introduced by Christian missionaries since the first European contact. What is most interesting about Tylor's defense is the fact that, in reasserting the evolutionary position, he drew heavily on diffusionary arguments similar to those of Franz Boas. Thus if one plotted the geographical distribution of the "Great Spirit" idea on a map of North America, it fitted "not with a theory of reinvention in several districts, but with a geographical transmission from a single point of origin, historically connected with the religion which had but lately passed into America from Europe." Tylor, of course, had never abandoned entirely the early interest in diffusionism which was his own inheritance from pre-evolutionary Prichardian "ethnology." Nevertheless, in terms of the logic of evolutionary argument as it had developed in the 1860s, diffusion had had a distinctly subordinate place. But now that the evolutionary paradigm itself was coming under attack, diffusion could play a role in buttressing it, by helping to explain away what might otherwise be major empirical anomalies for a developmental view of religious ideas.[30]

Even with this diffusionary buttress, Tylor's late evolutionary edifice was never to be completed. In 1896, Tylor suffered a serious illness, and although he published several important articles after that time, it seems to have marked the beginning of a general mental decline, which by 1904 had become quite severe. When Tylor was knighted in 1912, Clodd wondered in his diary if he was even aware of it, since "he has been long mentally dead."[31] But one wonders today whether a sound mind would have made the difference.

There is evidence to suggest that just as Prichardian ethnology in the 1850s had found it increasingly difficult to cope with the growing body of ethnographic data amassed by early-nineteenth-century explorers, travellers, and missionaries, so did some evolutionary anthropologists after 1890 find it difficult, in the context of resistance like that of Codrington, and criticism like that of Lang, to cope with a growing body of ethnographic data of a somewhat more sophisticated sort. Despite the promise of his "method of adhesions," Tylor in 1896 complained to Clodd that "nowadays the new anthropological material has become so enormous that before one thing has been got up to date another falls behind." Even had senility not fogged his faculties, it seems unlikely that an aging Tylor could ever really have come to terms with what Lang described as "the enormous quantity of fresh information as to the customs, institutions, and beliefs of backward races" that had "come to our knowledge" since 1891—which Lang felt had established the "*fact* of *non*-animistic religion." But "new hypotheses" were "not less common than new facts," and Lang had on several previous occasions reminded readers that *his* new hypothesis had not yet been rebutted. When he suggested in his festschrift essay that the "anthropological world eagerly awaits Mr. Tylor's treatment of the evidence, and his criticism, if he chooses to offer it, of the new theories," the ironic barb of the disciple turned apostate was scarcely concealed, though Tylor's mind could perhaps no longer feel the prick.[32]

William Robertson Smith and the Merry Sacrificial Feast of Totemism

Never having been a full convert to the evolutionary faith, William Robertson Smith never became its apostate. But the qualified evolutionism he did embrace was quite enough to make him heterodox to the elders of the church in which he had been reared, and they had him tried for heresy. Though he remained, in his own terms, a staunch defender of his parental faith, he was dismissed from his professorship at the University of Aberdeen. Forced further up scholarly paths along which he otherwise might not have fared so far, Smith went on to write works which, while not apostate, were to contribute substantially to the reformation of the doctrine of "classical evolutionism."

Smith was born in the immediate aftermath of his father's participation in the formation of a new religious community, and his childhood in that paternal community was to be a paradigm for his later thought, in which the "continued existence of a religion" depended on "the maintenance of a religious community" united by "handing down the knowledge of God from father to son by inculcation not only of religious doctrine but of religious praxis." His father had been born in the days when rationalist "Moderates" dominated the Presbyterian church; "by nature a scholar," he had taken all the first prizes at the University of Aberdeen, and gone on to become headmaster of a school in that town. At the time of the "Disruption" of the Church of Scotland in 1843, however, the elder Smith embraced the evangelical side with "whole-hearted enthusiasm." Joining in the formation of the Free Protesting Church, he was ordained minister of a country parish in November 1845, a year before William Robertson's birth. It was apparently simply by the coincidence of his father's given and his mother's maiden name that the younger Smith was named after the famous principal of the University of Edinburgh, William Robertson, who had been a leading architect of the Moderatism which the elder Smith rejected. But it was a portent nonetheless, for although the son never abandoned the experiential evangelical faith of his father, there were nevertheless to be resonances in Robertson Smith's mature religious thought of the developmental historicism and liberal religiosity of his accidental eponym.[33]

The dominant influence in Smith's early life was his father, a loving patriarch who in the education of his own children combined "strict orthodoxy" with "the practice of complete intellectual freedom and honesty." A sickly but precocious child, Smith was "prematurely awakened" to "the most serious and speculative subjects"; asked where he got the proof of the Trinity he had given to his younger brother (because "incomprehensible," it must be true, since "man could not have invented it") he replied, with unconscious irony, "that he had invented it for himself." After the departure of a visiting (and boringly loquacious) cleric, he is said to have drawn up his stool before his father's knee and pleaded: "And now, Papa, let us have some *rational* conversation." That same rational conversation about matters ultimately incomprehensible by reason alone, which Smith learned at his father's knee, was in fact to continue throughout his adult life.[34]

At fifteen Smith left his father's house to undertake a more formal education. Accompanied by the oldest of his younger brothers, and by his elder sister—all three of them tubercular—he was sent off to the University of Aberdeen, where his sister took over their mother's role as uncomplaining manager of domesticity. At Aberdeen, Smith studied rhetoric, logic, and psychology with the utilitarian empiricist Alexander Bain, who (despite their philosophical antagonism) regarded Smith as his most brilliant student; the young scholar was equally impressive to his instructors in science, mathematics, languages, and classics. The Shorter Catechism, however, had not run quickly off Smith's back as it had from Lang's; during his second year at Aberdeen, he dedicated himself to the ministry, and his resolve was strengthened when the ardors of a frugal academic life in a difficult climate claimed first his sister and then his brother, who died just three weeks after his graduation.

After a year recovering his own health, Smith (accompanied this time by a younger sister as housekeeper) began formal studies for the ministry at New College, Edinburgh, which had been founded by the Free Church in the year after the Disruption. There he continued his work in physical science, wrote an essay attacking Herbert Spencer's theory of "the materiality of the soul," and became the favorite of the more liberal of the two professors of Old Testament Exegesis—as against the one who argued that the Bible was "not a congeries of books, but a unit." Smith had more direct contact with the "higher criticism" during two summer trips to Germany, where he was much influenced by the Göttingen scholar Albrecht Ritschl, who after training in the Tübingen school had gone on to become the leading Protestant systematic theologian of his time. Although Smith found it "quite an anomaly to use the word *Sabbath*" to designate a day the Germans spent in a very lax fashion, he decided that it was "quite absurd to regard the heterodox Germans as infidels." And although he had begun New College embracing "the extreme positions of the Presbyterian orthodoxy," by the time he gave his inaugural address as president of the Theological Society in November 1869, he had arrived at a "dialectical" theology which provided an "organic" framework for the evolution of all his later religious speculations.[35]

The "only way to escape the wave of violent unbelief which has already swept over the German Churches" was "frankly to recognize the need of progress in our theological conceptions, not to suppress the new currents of thought as wholly dangerous, but to urge the positive side of a movement which if discouraged by the Church can express itself only in doubt and negation." Insisting that "principles which are to form the basis for the activity of a whole life cannot be given from without," but must "grow up within us and gradually unfold themselves before us as the explicit development of what is already a necessary part of our life," Smith argued that the doctrines of theology had to be "evolved by dialectical necessity from the assurance of the primitive act [of faith] itself." Granting that "a religious consciousness must always find its canon in Scripture," he nonetheless maintained that theology "had a life and growth of its own" which was "specifically determined, now in this direction, now in that, by historical circumstances and individual or national character." Theological progress was impossible so long as "the absolute truth" of the existing "confessional dogmatic" was maintained; and all theology must advance, because "the Christ of the Gospels so far transcends the theology of any age that to cling to an unchangeable dogma is really to cease to look to Him."[36]

Such a degree of theological liberalism did not forestall Smith's election by the General Assembly of the Free Church of Scotland to the chair of Hebrew and Old Testament Exegesis in the Free Church College of Aberdeen the following May. But even before then Smith's intellectual career was turning down a path that would eventually lead to his removal. Late in 1869 Smith joined with a number of other "literary and scientific men in or near Edinburgh" in the formation of "The Edinburgh Evening Club"—"the object being to have one man at least well up in every conceivable subject." Among these was "M'Lennan, an advocate," whose *Primitive Marriage* had of course put him "well up" in what would now be called social anthropology. McLennan was at that time involved in his researches on totemism, and over the next several years Smith discussed with him "the traces of nature religion" in the Bible. Smith insisted that the religion of the Old Testament did not "grow out of, but [rather] confronted and destroyed" these earlier totemistic tendencies, and he remained, in his own terms, a believer in the divine inspiration of the Old Testament until his death. But in the decade after he met McLennan his religious views developed along lines that brought him into protracted conflict with his church; and in the final crisis, McLennan's totemism was to play an important role.[37]

The early years of Smith's professorship were marked by a string of ministerial, pedagogical, and scholarly successes, including a series of articles presenting the results of recent Continental biblical scholarship to the readers of the *British and Foreign Evangelical Review*. In 1874, he was chosen by the editor of the ninth edition of the *Encyclopaedia Britannica* to write a number of articles on religious topics; the following year he was invited to join the Committee for the Revision of the Authorised Version of the Bible, on which he served until the work was completed in 1884. The "little party of enlightenment in the Free Church" were delighted; still nodding in dogmatic slumber, "the party of ignorance" did not immediately realize "the gravity of the situation." But when the second volume of the *Britannica* was reviewed by a conservative churchman, they awoke.[38]

The opening line of Smith's article on the Bible insisted on its literal etymological plurality (Biblia = books), which "correctly" expressed "the fact that the sacred writings of Christendom are made up of a number of independent records," the origin of each of which formed "a distinct critical problem." Although the argument that followed was by contemporary German critical standards rather tame stuff, it seemed to Smith's aroused antagonists that he had challenged the Bible's "authenticity, its veracity, its morality, its integrity, [and] its authority." Smith was charged with asserting that "the Pentateuch was only finished 800 years after Moses"; that "Prophecy never extends beyond the prophet's own time"; that various biblical books contained "poetical inventions," or were "mixed with other unknown authors," or had been "systematically altered"; that "Canticles is a political satire against Solomon"; that the "three synoptical gospels are non-apostolic digests of tradition." From Smith's perspective the fact that "the religion of revelation" was a "gradual development" did not in the least compromise its divine authority; but from a literalist point of view there was ample evidence in his article to document most of the charges, and on June 4, 1877, by a vote of 491 to 113 in the General Assembly of the Free Church, he was suspended from his chair at Aberdeen.[39]

The next four years of Smith's life were taken up largely with defending himself from further charges—a first "libel" or indictment; an "amended libel"; and finally, a "short libel"—that he had published opinions "of a dangerous and unsettling tendency in their bearing on the doctrine of the immediate inspiration, infallible truth, and divine authority of the Holy Scriptures." Smith was not without "enthusiastic sympathizers," especially among his students, who upon occasion greeted his entry to the crowded General Assembly with "wild cheering"; and he was a brilliant controversialist, whose lengthy speeches, delivered in a "thin, sharp" voice, were impressive even to his antagonists, whom in each of these stages he was able to forestall. But they remained persistent, and his continued scholarly development gave them new ammunition.[40]

A month after the short libel had been dismissed in May 1880, with the expectation that "the defects referred to will be guarded against and avoided in time to come," Smith published two articles that reopened the whole matter: one on "Hebrew Language and Literature" in the eleventh volume of the *Britannica,* the other on "Animal Worship and Animal Tribes among the Arabs and in the Old Testament" in the *Journal of Philology.* The former covered some of the same ground as the earlier article on the Bible, but after five further years of development in Smith's thought, it was now more unapologetically grounded in ethnological and comparative philological argument. The latter was explicitly an extension of McLennan's earlier essays to the field of Semitic religion, to the end of showing that the Semites were not "constitutionally monotheistic," and that the "superstitions with which the spiritual religion had to contend were not one whit less degrading than those of the most savage nations." Although Smith made this argument to show that Israel could not have risen above heathenism "by its own wisdom," his references to female kinship, polyandry, and infanticide were quite enough to elicit a charge from the General Assembly that his views "concerning marriage and the marriage laws in Israel" were "so gross and so fitted to pollute the moral sentiments of the community that they cannot be considered except within the closed doors of any court of this Church." Almost immediately a further charge of heresy was instituted, leading a year later to Smith's dismissal from his professorship at Aberdeen.[41]

Within a few days of that event, Smith's liberal friends had arranged for him to participate in the editorship of the ninth edition of the *Britannica,* first as joint and then as sole editor. He was later accustomed to explain his fabled erudition by saying that he had read every word of the *Britannica,* and he did in fact himself write over two hundred of its articles. But if in some respects his departure from Aberdeen was a kind of intellectual liberation, Smith's agonizingly protracted trial was the central and determinative episode of his life. To have been denounced as heretical by the religious community his loving "Papa" had joined in founding shortly before his own birth posed in the most painful personal terms the problem of the nature of religious community itself; and there is a sense in which all of Smith's later intellectual career was devoted to this issue. From this point of view, one may interpret his four book-length works as a series of commentaries on the Old Testament, each of them probing deeper beneath the literal text he had been accused of blaspheming, to get at the fundamental grounds of religion—in which had been planted the "living seed of the Divine word," preserved until "the fulness of the time when He was manifested who transformed the religion of Israel into a religion for all mankind."[42]

Conceived as part of Smith's defense against the "second case," *The Old Testament in the Jewish Church* was both an explication of the method of biblical criticism and a response to those charges having to do with the historicity of the Pentateuch. The "three great strata of laws embodied in the so-called books of Moses" were not all of one age but corresponded to "three stages in the development of Israel's institutions." The fully developed "Levitical system," which allowed "access to God" only "through the mediation of the Aaronic priests at the central sanctuary of the ark," had developed on a base of "popular religion," in which every worshipper might approach the deity through the central religious act of sacrifice, carried out in a local sanctuary which was, "as it were, the meeting-place of heaven and earth." Presented first as a series of public lectures in Glasgow and Edinburgh early in 1881, to audiences averaging "not less than eighteen hundred," the book appeared in print just as the second case against Smith was coming to a climax—to the further consternation of more conservative churchmen, one of whom insisted that Smith's doctrine of sacrifice "cut away the basis on which the whole doctrine of salvation rests." When the church courts "abruptly terminated" the second case against him by what he called "an act of violence," Smith gave a second and less popular series of lectures, *The Prophets of Israel and Their Place in History,* in which the characteristically historical (and anthropological) style of his thinking was very clearly displayed.[43]

Because "the records of our religion are historical documents," Smith insisted that they should be treated by the methods of "historical science," which had made "vast strides" in recent years. The essential point was an elaboration of an argument he had made a decade before in terms of contemporary psychological theory: that prophecy was a development "of the ordinary processes of the intellect." The prophets "apprehended the laws of Jehovah's dealings with men, not in their universal form, but in the particular shape applicable to [the] present circumstances" of their day. Rather than being a literal prefiguring of the events of the New Testament, the prophecies of the Old could be interpreted only in terms of the "actual condition of the people to whom the prophets spoke." Although Smith, like Tylor and the rest of his British contemporaries, still spoke of "culture" in a hierarchical and humanistic sense, his approach was nevertheless quite "anthropological" in the modern sense. To get behind the "literalistic view of prophecy," one had to "learn to enter with simplicity into [the] point of view" of the prophets and their audience, and this involved, among other things, a careful attention to the differing meanings of words and concepts which modern literalists took for granted, such as "sin" or "holiness." And what lay furthest behind the modern literalist meaning was a materialistic heathenism, "embodied in sexual analogies of a crass and physical kind," into which the people of Israel had been in constant danger of falling back, and out of which the prophets gradually led them to a "spiritualization of all the service of God." It was to the study of that underlying stratum of Semitic social organization and preprophetic religion that Smith's last two major works were devoted.[44]

His study was informed by a direct familiarity with the cultures and languages of the area. During the libel fight, Smith had taken two extended trips to the Middle East. Late in 1878 he travelled to Cairo, up the Nile, and then back to Palestine and Syria; the following year, he returned for six months to western Arabia. His diary of the first trip suggests that it was more a holiday than a research expedition. Travelling with a large entourage, Smith spent much of his time hunting antelope, comporting himself like a British sahib of the most traditional sort. When one of the Arabs in his retinue beat a slave girl who had run away, Smith made "a running kick at the beast," bowling him "clear over, howling," and then administered three lashes with his hippopotamous-hide whip for each mark he counted on the girl's naked body. He did, however, also undertake the study of Arabic, and do a bit of amateur archeology; on his return, he wrote the article on animal totems that provoked his dismissal. By the second trip, his purposes seem to have been more systematically scholarly, even anthropological. Garbed in Arab costume and accompanied by five servants who spoke only Arabic, Smith penetrated into areas of Arabia where few Europeans had been. And he did so with a clearly ethnographic goal, defined in terms of McLennan's theories. His efforts were rewarded with a wealth of "totem facts," which crowded upon him at every turn, "crying aloud to be registered."[45]

In part on the basis of his direct knowledge of the Middle East, and his by now fluent Arabic, Smith was chosen in 1883 as Lord Almoner's Reader in Arabic at Cambridge—the chair having become vacant when its previous occupant, not so lucky as Smith, had been killed by Arabs while on a political mission in the Sinai Peninsula. For the next eleven years, until his death from tuberculosis in 1894, Smith remained at Cambridge—as Reader, as Fellow of Christ's College, as University Librarian, and finally as Professor of Arabic. He continued to be preoccupied by the *Britannica* until the completion of the ninth edition in 1888, when his scholarly activity began to be restricted by the breakdown of his health. During this period Smith was nonetheless able to produce two further works of a more traditionally "anthropological" character, which form the basis of his subsequent reputation.

The first of these, *Kinship and Marriage in Early Arabia,* like McLen-

William Robertson Smith, in the guise of "Abdullah Effendi," 1880. (Courtesy of Robert A. Jones)

nan's *Primitive Marriage,* can be read as an essay on "the position of women," full of ulterior sexual assumption deriving either from prevailing cultural ideology or from personal psychological patrimony. But the relationship between the two books is more direct: Smith's preface made it clear that his study was a work of intellectual discipleship. The problem he set himself was "the genesis of the system of male kinship . . . which prevailed in Arabia at the time of Mohammed," a problem of origins suggested by the earlier debate between McLennan and Henry Maine over the priority of the "patriarchal" and the "matriarchal" families. In *Ancient Law*—and the fact that it was "ancient" and not "primitive" is diagnostic of Maine's pre-evolutionary provenience—Maine had argued that the original basis of society was the *patria potestas* (the absolute dominion of the father over the person and property of his children), and that the elementary social form was the family based on kinship through males. As Tylor recalled in 1888, it was against Maine that McLennan had pioneered the alternative view of "the antiquity of the maternal system" in *Primitive Marriage,* and the better part of McLennan's scholarly energies after 1865 had been spent in controverting Maine. In this polemical context, the genesis of the system of male kinship prevailing among a Semitic people was a critically important test case for the social evolutionary paradigm, since Maine's hypothesis had in fact been based in part on the social order of the ancient Semites as recorded in Genesis. What Smith did was to go behind the apparent patriarchalism of a more recent Semitic population to reveal its underlying matrifocal base. Furthermore, in his last chapter, he extended the argument from the "southern" to the "northern" Semites—that is, to the people of the Bible themselves.[46]

However, as a serious biblical and Semitic scholar, Smith was tied to traditions of research much different from McLennan's social evolutionism, traditions in which the canons of historical method had been enriched by the "comparative method," but not abandoned to it. Indeed, although his research was intended to support his late "lamented friend" against Maine, Smith was by methodological and conceptual predisposition in some respects quite close to Maine (whom he had certainly read), as well as to Fustel de Coulanges, whose work on *The Ancient City* foreshadowed some of Smith's views on the relations of religion and social organization. These ties to a more traditionally historical comparativist scholarship, oriented toward the study of documentary sources within a single cultural tradition rather than to "the comparative study of early institutions" throughout the world, are evident in Smith's preface. While his evidence "might easily have been disposed under heads borrowed from [McLennan's] exposition," he wished to speak "not only to general students of early society, but to all who are interested in old Arabia." He therefore "thought it best to attempt to build a self-contained argument on the Arabian facts alone, following a retrogressive order from the known to the unknown past, and not calling in the aid of hypotheses derived from the comparative method until, in working backwards on the Arabian evidence, I came to a point where the facts could not be interpreted without the aid of analogies drawn from other rude societies." It was only after he worked along Mainian lines back within the surviving documentary materials of a single ethnic and historical tradition to a point where he could go no further that Smith called upon the assumptions of the evolutionary comparative method of which McLennan had been the most self-conscious exponent.[47]

The effect of this structure, however, was to make McLennan's hypothesis the book's dramatic climax as well as its theoretical underpinning. Smith started from the formal models of Arab social organization held by the genealogists of Mohammed's time: models that were very Mainian, in some respects anticipating the "lineage theory" of later British social anthropology. According to "the theory of the Arab genealogists," the ultimate groups, out of which all larger unions were built up

> were all patriarchal tribes, formed, by subdivision of an original stock, on the system of kinship through male descents. A tribe was but a larger family; the tribal name was the name or nickname of the common ancestor. In process of time it broke up into two or more tribes, each embracing the descendants of one of the great ancestor's sons and taking its name from him. These tribes were again divided and subdivided on the same principle, and so at length that extreme state of division was reached which we find in the peninsula at the time of the prophet. Between a nation, a tribe, a sept or sub-tribe, and a family there is no difference, on this theory, except in size and distance from the common ancestor. As time rolls on the sons of a household grow into septs, and finally the septs become great tribes or even nations embracing several tribes.

From this starting point, however, Smith went on to find a number of contradictions and anomalies within the Arab patriarchal system that seemed to lead back to a social condition of a very different sort.[48]

The fact that some tribes still traced their origin to a female eponym, along with the prevalent "grammatical personification of a tribe as feminine," suggested that "all over Arabia the rule of female kinship must gradually have given way to a rule of male kinship," with the earlier pattern "so deeply rooted in language that it survived as a law of grammar in spite of the universal adoption of patronymic theory." The ritual "commingling of blood by which two men became brothers" suggested a time when the "social bond was not necesarily dependent on fatherhood," when kinship was not a matter of individual relationship in family lines, but rather a matter of "the blood of the tribe as a whole." The fact of adoption and fictive kinship suggested a time when the tribe was heterogeneous rather than homogeneous, when "local groups" ordinarily consisted of "unstable aggregates of fractions of different stock-groups." The continued existence of *mot'a* or temporary marriage, in which "the woman did not leave her home, her people gave up no rights which they had over her, and the children did not belong to the husband," suggested a stratification of three distinct marriage forms. Various bits of linguistic evidence showing that in Arabia paternity had originally to do with nurture rather than with procreation suggested a time when "physical fatherhood was not the basis of any important social relation." Along such lines of evidence Smith was led from the official patriarchalism back to a form of polyandry "so rude" as to be "to our view indeed no better than prostitution": indeed, "no other condition of things can be supposed as the antecedent alike of *beena* and *mot'a* marriage, of *ba'al* polyandry, and of the continued licence of the poorer classes."[49]

It was at this point—where Smith felt that "we are far beyond the range of authentic tradition"—that it became necessary to extend the frame of evidence and method beyond the geographically narrow one of Semitic historical scholarship to McLennan's wide world of evolutionary comparison. Because "the origin of an institution so fundamental as the system of kinship must lie in a stage of the evolution of society so remote that the special characteristics of individual races, like the Semites, cannot be thought to have been developed," it was "hardly probable that we can get beyond these results by observations or arguments drawn from the Semitic races alone, without comparison of the course of social development in savage races generally." Smith was less interested in the general argument of McLennan's *Primitive Marriage,* however, than in what it suggested about the homogeneity or heterogeneity of social groups. For him, the significance of "marriage by capture" was that "if captive women were brought into a kin in any considerable numbers, the local group in the second generation would contain representatives not only of the original stock but of all the stocks from which captives had been made"—and this initial heterogeneity would be intensified by the "law of exogamy," which made it incest for a man to marry in his own kin group. It was in this context that "totemism" took on great social significance: "in such societies a man's stock is not determined by counting degrees, but each kin has its stock-name and its stock-emblem or totem, which in tribes of female kinship descends from mother to child." Those emblems enabled a man to "know what persons are united to him by blood-ties and what persons he may not marry." Though it had "religious as well as social aspects," the "primary importance" of totemism was that "it supplied the necessary machinery for working a law of exogamy and enabling a man to fulfill the obligations of kindred" in a complicated social state—one in which blood-feud might at any time break up the local groups of a district, with "the several stocks rallying together in forgetfulness of all those home-ties which to our ideas are much more sacred than the blood, or totem, bond."[50]

Having established his comparative sociological reference point, Smith returned to his Arab texts to argue that "the Arabs were once divided into totem-stocks," in which "the belief that all members of the tribe are of one blood is associated with a conviction, more or less religious in character, that the life of the tribe is in some mysterious way derived from an animal, a plant, or more rarely some other natural object." The "relics of the system" were of three types: "the existence of stocks named after plants and animals; the prevalence of the conception that the members of the stock are of the blood of the eponym animal, or are sprung from a plant of the species chosen as totem; [and] the ascription to the totem of a sacred character, which may result in its being regarded as the god of the stock, but at any rate makes it to be regarded with veneration, so that, for example, a totem animal is not used as ordinary food."[51]

With the case made for the Semites of Arabia, three final tasks remained. First, it was necessary to generalize the argument to the northern Semites—where the "primitive organisation" of the Hebrews was "profoundly modified, at an early date, by the Conquest of Canaan, the transition to agricultural life, and the absorption of a considerable part of the aboriginal population." Having found there even more fragmentary survivals of a totemistic phase earlier "in date to the Semitic dispersion," it became necessary to offer a "summary sketch of a possible line of progress" that would lead from this stage to the system that "prevailed among the Arabs before Mohammed"—which Smith did by drawing heavily on the eighth chapter of McLennan's *Primitive Marriage*. Finally, it was necessary "to say something, at least by way of conjecture," as to the "very different" history of the northern Semites, which reflected the need of invading tribes to restrain "mutual feuds" among themselves as they attempted to subjugate the former inhabitants of the northern areas.[52]

Smith thought that it was the great advantage of McLennan's totem hypothesis over "all previous theories of primitive heathenism" that it did justice "to the intimate relation between religion and the fundamental structure of society which is so characteristic of the ancient world." Focussing "on the social side of totemism," *Kinship and Marriage* had defined "the fundamental institutions" of Semitic social life; on this basis, Smith's last major work was a study of "the fundamental institutions" of "the religion of the Semites." But one cannot understand this study of the evolution of religious ritual save in the context of his own religious evolution.[53]

For Smith, the "intelligent moral relationship" of man to his "heavenly father" was modeled on "the relation of affection and reverence" between a "loving father and a son," which was "not of mere physical origin, but grows up with the growth and training of the child." In his own case, the religious commitment nurtured by his father's training was strong enough to survive unscathed the long ordeal of his heresy trial. His mentor McLennan could never understand Smith's holding on so tightly to what he himself had easily shed. A year after the attack began, McLennan hoped that Smith would "shake himself free of his enemies"; in 1879, he could not see "what the fight is now for"; in 1880, he felt that Smith and those who defended him should "all leave, like men, a church whose standards they no longer agree with." But Smith would not leave voluntarily, and when in April 1887 he received from the trustees of the Burnett Fund an invitation to return to Aberdeen to lecture on "the primitive religions of the Semitic peoples, viewed in relation to other ancient religions, and to the spiritual religion of the Old Testament and of Christianity," it was a kind of vindication—since, broadly stated, this was in fact the issue that had led to his dismissal.[54]

Smith originally planned to give three series of lectures over a three-year period, the first on ritual institutions, the second on "creed and dogma," and the third on the influence of early Semitic religion "on the formulas and structure of the great monotheistic faiths." The invitation, however, coincided with a series of traumatic events in his personal life, and the full agenda was never realized. By this time his parents, along with a sister and a younger brother, had retired to a house Smith bought for them in Aberdeen—only to have his father suffer a paralytic stroke and his brother die of tuberculosis. It was in this stressful context that Smith himself began to suffer the extremely painful eczema and sciatica that marked the beginning of his own decline. The second series of lectures, given in the immediate aftermath of his father's death in February 1890, was limited to three, spoken from fragmentary notes; the third topic was never to be treated as such, although Smith did give three further lectures on Semitic beliefs in 1891. Even so, it was fairly evident that the first series of nine lectures, given in October 1888 and March 1889 and supplemented by two more in the published book, was, like so much of Smith's work, in fact an indirect treatment of the third topic. Addressing once again an audience of his "fellow-townsmen," who, like all good Scots, took for granted that "a right understanding of the religion of the Old Testament was the only way to a right understanding of the Christian faith," the returning heretic ventured to tell them what their religion had once been all about.[55]

As Smith suggested in the concluding paragraph of the published version, "redemption, substitution, purification, atoning blood, [and] the garment of righteousness, are all terms which in some sense go back to antique ritual." The central antique ritual was sacrifice, and the "fundamental idea of ancient sacrifice [was] sacramental communion"—the "merry sacrificial feast" when men met their god, who was "part and parcel of the same natural community," and "the whole community was stirred by a common emotion": "universal hilarity prevailed, men ate drank and were merry together, rejoicing before their God [*sic*]." Or so it was once, "in the old joyous type of worship," before "the development of a gloomier type of worship under the pressure of accumulated political disasters." In a religion of this kind, there was no room for an "abiding sense of sin and unworthiness," and the "habitual temper of the worshippers" was "one of joyous confidence in their god, untroubled by any habitual sense of human guilt, and resting on the conviction that they and the deity they adore are good friends." In this older religious community, "a man did not choose his religion or frame it for himself; it came to him as part of the general scheme of social obligations and ordinances laid upon him as a matter of course, by his position in the family and in the nation." But at the same time, there was no such thing as "intolerance" in the modern sense of the word; the religious community "never persecuted a man into particular beliefs for the good of his own soul." It was enough that he carry out "the correct performance" of "the series of acts and observances" that constituted the true basis of religion.[56]

If such a religious community seems a far cry from the Free Church, it was not unrelated to Smith's own religious experience. Smith saw his religious commitment not as an individual choice of belief, but as an inherited membership in a religious community; he clung to it almost instinctively—McLennan would surely have said irrationally—even as some of its leaders sought to expel him on the grounds that his beliefs now excluded him from membership. This experience provided Smith with a model of religion in general. It was social not individual in its essential character; it was emotional rather than rational in its psychological basis; it was embodied in ritual act rather than in dogmatic belief; and it was ultimately epitomized in the act of sacrifice, in which one member of the community gave up his individual life to reaffirm the living bonds of the social whole. Viewed from this perspective, Smith's lectures to his "fellow-townsmen" were thus both the explication of an idealized basis of religious community that existed only in a past golden age, and an *apologia pro vita sua*. If the Free Church had in fact been constituted according to this model, Smith's trial for heresy might never have taken place, and the spiritual community he had inherited from his father might never have been ruptured.

But the Free Church was not so constituted, and for reasons more deeply rooted in developmental process than in the Disruption or the Protestant Reformation. Like Rousseau's *Discourse on the Origin and Foundations of Inequality*, Smith's *Lectures* may be read as an allegory of failed primitivism: a story at once evolutionary and devolutionary. Explicitly, it is an account of the formation of the religious community of the "merry sacrificial feast," which grew up "under the action of unconscious forces operating silently from age to age." Implicitly, it is an account of the transformation of that "traditional" community in the later historical phases of religious development in the ancient world, in the very processes that were to lead eventually to the "positive" religions of Judaism, Christianity, and Islam.[57]

Although Smith took for granted the prior existence of maternal kinship, his concern now was the "fixed relations" of men and gods (usually conceived of as male) in a society in which "the members of one kindred looked on themselves as . . . a single animated mass of blood, flesh, and bones, of which no member could be touched without all the members suffering," in which "there were no binding precepts of conduct except those that rest on the principle of kinship," in which "no sharp line of distinction was drawn between the nature of gods, of men, and of beasts," or between "the gods proper" and "the lower orders of demoniac beings," in which "the god and his own proper worshippers make up a single community and the place of the god in the community is interpreted on the analogy of human relationships," and in which the world was "parcelled out between demons and wild beasts on the one hand, and gods and men on the other." In such a society—which must have evolved out of an earlier stage of totemism—religion was as much a matter of place as it was of kinship: through "fixed relations" to a local god who was "the parent of their race," and who himself had "fixed relations" to "a definite sphere of nature," human groups were brought into "permanent alliance" with parts of nature beyond their "will and control." Religion thus set men free, "within a certain range, from the crushing sense of constant insecurity and vague dread of the unknown powers" that surrounded them, and thereby facilitated "the gradual subjugation of nature by man." Each god had its local sanctuary, or holy place—"holiness" being, in origin, not an ethical matter or an attribute of persons, but rather the character of a place that was withdrawn from ordinary use. Because such a place was "charged with divine energy," energy that was infectious upon contact and ready at any moment to be discharged "to the destruction of the man who presumes to approach it unduly," the sanctuary and the natural things associated with the local god were *taboo* (a Polynesian category which Smith's friend James G. Frazer, under his guidance, had just treated comparatively for the *Britannica*). And because "holiness admits of degrees," it was "natural to mark off an inner circle of intense holiness," which became the "fixed-meeting place between the worshippers and their god," and the locus of the act of sacrifice, "the typical form of all complete acts of worship in the antique religions."[58]

In the act of sacrifice (the subject of the last five of Smith's *Lectures*) kinship resumed priority over place. The whole community, "conceived as a circle of brethren, [were] united with one another and with their god by participation in one life or life-blood." Because that blood flowed also "in the veins of the victim," its death was "at once a shedding of the tribal blood and a violation of the sanctity of the divine life." But this violation was permitted, even required, on solemn occasions, because only by "participation in the flesh of a sacrosanct victim" could "the sacred cement be procured" that created or kept alive "a living bond of union between the worshippers and their god"—which, if impaired or attenuated, might lead to the withdrawal of divine assistance, and to "famine, plague, or other disaster." In a passage deleted from the second edition of the book, Smith made explicit the link between ancient sacrifice and Christian doctrine: "that the God-man dies for His people, and that his Death is their life" was foreshadowed in "germ" in a "very crude and materialistic form" by "the oldest mystical sacrifices."[59]

Between those two moments stood a developmental history, in which there had been not only prophets, but also losses. The ancient religion of the Semites against which the prophets had struggled was not so much that of the primitive sacramental communion as of the forms that had evolved from it, along two lines. On the one hand, there was the "gradual degradation of ordinary sacrifice," as men "above the state of savagery" found it impossible to "retain a literal faith in the consanguinity of animal kinds with gods and men" and (responding to "the pressure of hunger") developed "the taste for animal food." Along another line, Smith traced the development of piacular or expiatory sacrifices by a complex process involving the rejection of "the disgusting idea of cannibalism" with "growing civilisation." With the emergence of "the idea of property, a "new view of holiness" began to "swallow up all earlier formulas for the relations of persons and things," and sacrifice began to be conceived of as a gift or tribute to a god whose relations to men came to be conceived of more in terms of divine kingship than in terms of the fatherhood of the clan.[60]

Here, again, one notes Smith's somewhat ambivalent feelings about the course of religious evolution. Although "the introduction of ideas of property into the relations between men and their gods seems to have been one of the most fatal aberrations in the development of ancient religion," it was necessary to human material progress that the ideas underlying the "merry sacrificial feast" of totemic origin be superseded, "since the vague dread of the unknown supernatural" turned man aside from "his legitimate task of subduing nature to his use." It was only by referring all supernatural processes to the will and powers of known deities, "whose converse with man is guided by fixed laws," that progress could resume. From the perspective of spiritual progress, it was unfortunate that these laws should have been "largely based on the principle of property," which "materializes everything that it touches"; indeed, this made it "impossible to rise to spiritual conceptions of the deity and his relations to man on the basis of traditional religion." From the same perspective, it was only by building on the "element of permanent truth" contained in the earlier idea of a "living communion between the god and his worshippers" that ancient heathenism was able to lay the basis for the *ethical* conception of holiness that ultimately replaced the primitive *physical* conception. But if the ethical conception was built on the idea of primitive communion, it eventually transcended it. In the end, the primitive conception of holiness, like the primitive conception of kinship, was of a lower order than our conception of holiness—just as "traditional" religion was of a lower order than "positive" religion. In the last lines of his book, Smith abandoned all traces of religious primitivism: ritual might be historically prior to belief, but it was by its very nature materialistic, and none of the ritual systems of antiquity, whether based on ideas of communion or of property, "was able by mere natural development to shake itself free from the congenital defect inherent in every attempt to embody spiritual truth in material forms." That, as he had suggested in the opening paragraph of his first lecture, was the task of the "great religious innovators, who spoke as the organs of a divine revelation, and deliberately departed from the traditions of the past."[61]

Although Tylor wrote a number of articles for the *Britannica,* and cited Smith's work on Arabian kinship in 1888, the two men did not confront each other directly on issues relating to the evolution of religion. The contrast between them, however, was both striking and portentous. As a leading representative of what was later to be called the "English intellectualist" (or "utilitarian-positivist") tradition, Tylor conceived of religion primarily in terms of the rational thought processes of individual men. Its essential function was explanatory, and it had no constitutively social character. For Tylor, religion was preeminently a matter of belief; insofar as he dealt with ritual, it was as a secondary phenomenon—on the one hand, as "expressive and symbolic performance, the dramatic utterance of religious thought, the gesture-language of theology"; on the other, as a practical "means of intercourse with and influence on spiritual beings." In contrast to Smith, Tylor saw the gift theory of sacrifice not as a secondary development, but as its original basis: conceptualized in individualistic utilitarian terms, sacrifice was the attempt of a weak being to propitiate a more powerful one, often with the specific expectation of receiving something in exchange.[62]

Smith did not reject Tylorian assumptions entirely. Some of his reasoning on the relations of men and gods to physical nature and material objects was (although not by explicit citation) based on Tylor's concept of animism, and his account of the gradual subjugation of nature by man was conventionally utilitarian. He was also quite willing to call on the "comparative method" or a generalized sequence of evolutionary stages, or to appeal to "primitive habits of thought," in order to augment the evidence of the Semitic field. But for Smith, man was not entirely or simply a rational animal; reason was characteristically constrained or compartmentalized, or was a secondary manifestation. Whereas Tylor saw magic and religion as essentially similar expressions of animistic belief, for Smith the two stood in stark opposition, and it was only magic—fear-based, antisocial, and utilitarian—which might perhaps be thought of as the product of misguided individual reason. And while Smith, like Tylor, relied on the notion of "survivals," there was a subtle difference. For Tylor, the emphasis was on the survival of old ideas as artifacts of earlier practices, and the function of reason was to recreate the past context in which what was now irrational superstition had once been rational belief. For Smith, the emphasis was on the survival of old practices into the present, outliving their associated belief, so that the function of reason was to rationalize, to recreate in the present a context in which the apparently irrational practice would seem rational. Thus for Smith, rituals did not consist of "forms invented, once for all, to express a definite system of ideas," but were rather "natural growths, which were slowly developed through many centuries, and in their final form bore the imprint of a variety of influences, to which they had been subject under the changing conditions of human life and social order." Under such circumstances, one could not "fix a definite interpretation on any of the developments of ancient ritual." Rather, one could "trace in the ceremonial the influence of successive phases of thought, the presence of which is attested to us by other movements in the structure of ancient society," or alternatively, "show how features in the ritual, of which the historical origin had been forgotten, were accounted for on more modern principles, and used to give support to new ideas that were struggling for practical recognition." For Tylorians like the early Lang, the comparative method and the psychic unity of man made possible a quick transformation of the apparently unintelligible survival into the easily intelligible belief; for Smith, it was "precisely the things that seem obvious which in a subject like ours require the most careful scrutiny." [63]

Unlike the Tylorians, for whom it was a point of methodological principle (though not necessarily of ideological conviction) to sharply delimit the significance of race, Smith was quite capable of appealing "to the sensuality so strongly developed in the Semitic race." But he also insisted that the differences that developed between Semitic and Aryan religion were "not altogether an affair of race and innate tendency, but depended in a great measure on the operation of special local and historical causes": in the West, where kingship fell before the aristocracy, the tendency was "toward a divine aristocracy of many gods"; in the East, under the influence of "Oriental despotism," the "national god tended to acquire a really monarchic sway." As these examples suggest, "race" for Smith was less a matter of physical type than of historically conditioned traditional habits of thought. His primary concern was the "old unconscious religious tradition" which could not "be traced to the influence of individual minds," but "formed part of that inheritance from the past into which successive generations of the Semitic race grew up as it were instinctively." Positive religion could not "start with a *tabula rasa*," but must appeal to "religious instincts and susceptibilities that already exist in the audience." And it could only do this by "taking account of the traditional forms in which all religious feeling is embodied," "by speaking a language men accustomed to these old forms can understand." Furthermore, these ancient faiths had a systematic character—using the word "system" in "a practical sense, as when we speak of a political system, and not in the sense of an organized body of ideas or theological opinions." At that point, Smith was perhaps closer, in practical conceptual terms, to the later anthropological ideas of "culture" and "social system" than Tylor had been in the often-cited opening lines of *Primitive Culture*.[64]

The Revolt against Positivism and the Revolution in Anthropology

For intellectuals reconsidering the cultural grounding of religion in an age of science, the Greeks and the gods were topics of great fascination. In this context, the anthropological writings of both Lang and Smith had a general intellectual resonance in the 1880s and 1890s; each of them was an influence, for instance, on the "Cambridge Ritualists," whose thinking was molded in this period. Neither of them, however, was closely tied to anthropology as an emerging academic or professional specialty. Lang, self-proclaimed anthropologist manqué, became instead a professional gadfly, buzzing at its margins; Smith, quite content to be a Semitic scholar who read anthropology, died before the reformation in anthropology anticipated by Tylor in 1896. Both men, however, played an important role in the debates that swirled around the figure of James G. Frazer after 1900: Lang, as Frazer's most acerbic critic; Smith as a formative influence both on Frazer's thought and on the anthropological orientation that was to succeed it.[65]

The intellectual positions of Lang and Smith were, of course, in some important respects strikingly different. Lang wrote on ritual, and was to have some interesting things to say from a sociological perspective on the problems of Australian totemism; but he remained very largely within the Tylorian tradition even as he attacked its single most important substantive concept, animism. As he insisted on many occasions, Lang was only using the evolutionary anthropologist's comparative method in a more systematic way, applying it to data which, if it did not come from Tylor himself, was of the same sort. Comparing similar phenomena, without regard to racial origin, Lang sought to get at underlying psychic processes universal to mankind. Although he attacked rationalist assumptions at various points, insisting on the empirical reality of "irrational" phenomena and making them the focus of his study, his savages were still very like Tylorian savage philosophers, who reasoned soundly about phenomena which were nonetheless empirical for being abnormal. Lang was still, in short, very much within the British tradition in conceiving of religion in essentially individual terms; it had an ethical function, and was social in the sense of making individual men behave in a moral way, but it was not fundamentally social in origin. Although he helped to direct attention to "non-animistic" religion, the most substantial direct influence Lang had on subsequent anthropological thinking about religion was on the Central European Catholic school of Father Wilhelm Schmidt, who took inspiration from his advocacy of primitive monotheism. There was, in short, still some distance between Lang and Durkheim.[66]

In contrast to Lang, whose relation to modern social theory was as tangential as his relation to modern literature, William Robertson Smith was a major influence on several of the writers who revolutionized thinking about "consciousness and society" in the years around 1900—most strikingly, perhaps, in the case of Freud's *Totem and Taboo.* Although he drew on the whole literature of totemism from McLennan on, and most heavily on Frazer, Freud's most famous "just-so story" (the slaying and eating of the patriarchal father by a band of brothers) was derived from Smith's conception of the totem meal, which, in Freud's words, was "the beginning of so many things—of social organization, of moral restrictions, and of religion." It was this bit of highly conjectural history which, perhaps more than anything else in Freud, contributed to the alienation of a later generation of anthropologists from psychoanalytic theory.[67] In the case of Durkheim, however, Smith's influence was to be more systematically constitutive, both on Durkheim himself, and through him, on later British anthropology.

According to Durkheim's own testimony, the course he gave on the sociology of religion in 1895 "marked a dividing line" in the development of his thought on "the essential role played by religion in social life"—to such an extent that all of his previous researches "had to be taken up afresh in order to harmonize with these new insights." And the key factor in that reorientation was "the reading of the works of Robertson Smith and his school." Although Durkheim did not go into detail, we may assume that he had in mind such characteristic Smithian ideas as the notion that religion is basic to social order, the definition of religion in social rather than individual terms, the idea that the core of religion is to be found in the unity of the social group, the emphasis on ritual as opposed to belief, the priority of the emotional to the intellectual, the conception of the sacred, as well as the substantive focus on totemism and the rite of sacrifice. The relationship was complexly dialectical, and when the Durkheimians covered the same ground in detail (as Hubert and Mauss did in *Sacrifice: Its Nature and Function*), they had serious criticisms of Smith along lines that emphasized his ties to the British evolutionary tradition. But if Smith remained in some respects within the older British tradition, and was subject to criticism by later British social anthropologists, there can be no doubt that he contributed substantially to the definition of the mature Durkheimian sociology, which, in the context of further debate on the problem of totemism, was to be a major influence in the definition of the functionalist social anthropology of Malinowski and Radcliffe-Brown.[68] But as Lang's barbed tribute to Tylor suggested, all of this was to take place after a two-decade accumulation of "new facts"—many of them collected by men quite different from the ethnographers of the period before 1888.

THREE

From the Armchair to the Field

The Darwinian Zoologist as Ethnographer

Despite its self-consciously innovative statistical method, Tylor's paper of 1888 was a quintessential product of "armchair anthropology"—though perhaps not in a literal sense, since the tabulation of all that data, as well as the correspondence by which a good deal of it was collected, could only have been done at a desk. But the paper still took for granted the division of labor previously assumed by *Notes and Queries,* between the "travellers and residents in uncivilised lands," who were "not anthropologists themselves"—and whose observations it sought to improve—and those who would carry on "the scientific study of anthropology at home." Tylor remarked on Lewis Henry Morgan's having lived "among the Iroquois as an adopted son," and on John Wesley Powell as an observer who "had both the opportunity to see and the skill to see what he was seeing." Having been to Washington, D.C., four years earlier, at the time of the first overseas meeting of the British Association for the Advancement of Science in Montreal, Tylor had first-hand familiarity with the United States government's Bureau of Ethnology, which under Powell's direction had since 1879 been sending investigators to collect information among the Indian tribes of the United States. He knew of the work of Frank Hamilton Cushing at the Zuni pueblo in the early 1880s, which was one of the more richly presaging premonitions of the ethnographic style of twentieth-century anthropology. Tylor in fact ended his talk with a call for an international effort to carry on "a prompt and minute investigation" among the "hundred or more peoples in the world" on the verge of extinction, in order to save "some fast vanishing memory of their social laws and customs." But there was no explicit indication that this effort was to be carried out by investigators different from those for whom *Notes and Queries* had been intended.[1]

By 1888, however, Tylor was in fact already himself involved in ethnographic enterprises foreshadowing a more modern model. At the Montreal meetings of the British Association, where he had served as first president of the newly formed anthropological section, Tylor played a leading role in the establishment of a committee "for the purpose of investigating and publishing reports on the physical characters, languages, and industrial and social condition of the North-western Tribes of the Dominion of Canada." The committee was founded with an eye to Powell's bureau, which was already "sending out qualified agents to reside among the western tribes for purposes of philological and anthropological study." However, it began in the mode of *Notes and Queries* (which had recently gone out of print), by preparing a "Circular of Inquiry" (of which Tylor was apparently the principal author) for the use of government officers, missionaries, travellers, and others likely to "possess or obtain trustworthy information." This information was to be edited and synthesized by Horatio Hale, who had accompanied the United States Exploring Expedition to the islands of the Pacific five decades before, and who was then living in retirement in Canada. But while thus taking for granted a mediated relationship between the subjects of ethnography and the anthropologists at home, the new questionnaire also reflected the ethnographic sensitivity of Tylor's more sophisticated epistolary ethnographers (including, one assumes, Codrington, who must have interacted with Tylor while attending his lectures in 1883). It was largely stripped of the orienting theoretical remarks with which Tylor, especially, had embellished his sections of *Notes and Queries*. Indeed, there was no explicit reference to "animism," although inquirers were still directed toward many of its presumed empirical manifestations. More strikingly, in trying to reach "the theological stratum in the savage mind," they were cautioned against asking "un-called for questions," and urged to watch "religious rites actually performed, and then to ascertain what they mean." Similarly, the collection of myth-texts "written down in the native languages" and "translated by a skilled interpreter" was "the most natural way" to get at "ideas and beliefs which no inquisitorial cross-questioning" would induce the Indian story-teller to disclose—an approach Codrington would surely have counselled.[2]

Furthermore, Tylor was no longer willing to rest satisfied with research by questionnaire. From the beginning of the Northwest Coast project, it was assumed that, on the basis of the results of such an initial inquiry, some of the "more promising districts" would be the subjects of "personal survey" by Hale or (when it became evident that his age would make this impossible) by an agent who "would act under his directions." The first such agent was in fact a missionary, the Reverend E. F. Wilson, who had worked for nineteen years among the Ojibwa, travelling in summers farther west to recruit Indian children for his mission school. But he was soon to be replaced by an investigator of a very different sort: the German-born physicist-turned-ethnologist Franz Boas. After receiving his doctorate at the University of Kiel in 1881 for a dissertation on the color of seawater, Boas had undertaken experimental psychophysical studies of perception before going off to Baffinland to investigate the Eskimo knowledge of local physical geography. Led thence to historical ethnology and the traditional problem of the peopling of the North American continent, Boas in 1886 had carried on research among the Indians of Vancouver Island which brought him to the attention of Hale and the British Association committee; for the next ten years, Boas' ethnographic work was carried on in part under its auspices. While the history of ethnographic method, like that of anthropological theory, was to follow a somewhat different course under Boas in the United States than it did after Tylor in Great Britain, it was in the longer run a convergent evolution, marked by many similar phases. By the time Tylor published his 1888 paper, one of these was just beginning: the collection of anthropological data by academically trained natural scientists who came to define themselves as "anthropologists," who were directly involved in the evaluation if not the formulation of anthropological theory, and who were to train other "anthropologists" to carry on such work in an even more focussed manner.[3]

These developments depended of course on changes in the institutional situation of anthropology, which was still by and large an avocational activity of scholars either of independent means or of other professions. In London, the Anthropological Institute of Great Britain and Ireland had only a limited capacity to initiate research; it was in any case more concerned with prehistoric archeology and physical anthropology. The activities associated with the peripatetic yearly meetings of the British Association were intermittent and diverse; the most ambitious (aside from Tylor's committee) was an ethnographic survey of the British Isles. Other than this, the barely emergent institutionalization of anthropology was a by-product of the curatorial requirements of certain museum collections—most notably, those that had developed since the later eighteenth century at the British Museum. The early 1880s, however, were to see the establishment of anthropological collections at both traditional universities. At Cambridge, the archeological collections of the Cambridge Antiquarian Society were turned over to the university in 1883, and under the curatorship of Anatole von Hügel were to form the basis for the later Museum of Archaeology and Ethnology. During the same year, negotiations were completed at Oxford for the establishment of a museum to house the archeological and ethnological collections of General Augustus Henry Lane Fox Pitt Rivers, with the additional stipulation that a lecturer be appointed to give regular instruction in anthropology. However, the readership thereby given to Tylor was in fact a personal status, adjunct to the position he assumed as Keeper of the University Museum. His lectures were not part of a formal academic training program, and were given to rather heterogeneous audiences—which over the years became ever smaller (and increasingly female) until, according to anecdote, they were on one occasion addressed only to his wife: "and so, my dear Anna, we observe . . ."[4]

Anthropology did, however, benefit in a marginal way from the university reforms of the 1870s, insofar as they helped make it possible for several Darwinian biologists (notably the physiologist Michael Foster at Cambridge and the comparative anatomist Henry Moseley at Oxford) to initiate serious research in the biological sciences, which in this period were often seen as subsuming "anthropology."[5] These figures in turn trained the first college men in Britain who could realistically expect to make their living as university scientists. It was an economically marginal career decision, but a possible one—especially if one were willing to emigrate to universities at the imperial periphery, where the traditional subject matter of anthropology, more immediately in view, became an attractive focus for research. Two who followed this trajectory, the one from Oxford to Australia, the other from Cambridge to Ireland and Melanesia, were Baldwin Spencer and Alfred Haddon. Because their natural science training prepared them to unite systematic observation with the consideration of theoretical problems, they were to have a significant impact on an inquiry in which theory and observation had been kept sharply distinct, and lawyers and literary men had for several decades played leading roles.

Baldwin Spencer and Frank Gillen: Getting down to Bedrock in Central Australia

Among those who attended Tylor's early lectures at Oxford, watching with fascination as he actually made stone tools in a practical demonstration of the comparative method and the psychic unity of man, was young Walter Baldwin Spencer. Born in 1860, Spencer was the second son of a staunchly Nonconformist entrepreneur who ended his life as chairman of the Manchester textile firm of John Rylands and Sons, leaving an estate of over £200,000. After an early education at a school near his family's suburban estate, and a year studying art in Manchester, in 1879 young Spencer entered Owens College (later the University of Manchester) to study medicine. There he came under the influence of the zoologist Alfred Milnes Marshall, a "fiery apostle" of Darwinism, who put Spencer's artistic skill to service rendering specimens in the Zoological Practical Laboratory, and claimed him for the "new faith of biology." Two years later, Spencer won a four-year scholarship to study natural sciences at Oxford, where he became a member of Exeter College, the first in a line of anthropologists identified with that foundation. During this period Spencer shed his family's Methodism for a Huxleyan agnosticism, willingly entertaining the proposition that life originated in a "lucky thunderstorm." Along with other Oxford biologists, he was worried by the debate then taking place about the use of university facilities for vivisection. And he was stirred also by the "University Settlements" idea, which he saw as "a modified form of Socialism" through which " 'varsity' men" might bring to "the lower classes" a bit of "what Matthew Arnold would call 'sweetness & light.' "[6]

But the greatest influence on Spencer was Henry Moseley, who, after having sailed around the world in the early 1870s as naturalist of the *Challenger* expedition, had subsequently been appointed Linacre Professor of Anatomy. Spencer's methodical assiduity so impressed Moseley that instead of "plying questions" at the viva following his written exams in 1884, Moseley simply congratulated Spencer on the excellence of his work. The following year Moseley chose him as his full-time demonstrator, charged with supervising laboratory work and giving a course of lectures, as well as assisting Moseley and Tylor in the transfer of the Pitt Rivers ethnographic collection to its new museum adjunct to the University Museum. With Moseley's encouragement, Spencer in 1886 applied for (and was elected to) the newly established professorship of biology at the University of Melbourne. He was not eager to emigrate, but after an engagement of three years he was anxious to marry; and however brilliant his prospects, an overseas university was the only place a twenty-six-year-old scientist could expect to find a £750 salary and a social ranking as high as his merchant father's back in Manchester.[7]

During his first several years in Melbourne, Spencer was kept busy teaching zoology and botany, politicking successfully for the construction of a new laboratory building, and making occasional short excursions as a field naturalist during university vacations. In 1889 he met Lorimer Fison, who was then editing a Methodist newspaper in Melbourne, and tried unsuccessfully to get a lectureship established for him at a Methodist denominational college attached to the University of Melbourne (there being no chance, as Spencer reported to Tylor, for a regular professorship when the university had as yet no chair in modern languages). Spencer's own introduction to ethnographic work took place five years later, when the governments of three Australian colonies organized a scientific expedition, financed by a businessman named William Horn, to go 2000 miles by camelback into the central Australian desert.

Spencer's official role was as expedition zoologist; the anthropological work was allocated to E. C. Stirling, director of the South Australian Museum and lecturer in physiology at the University of Adelaide. Stirling found evidence of Fison and Howitt's marriage classes among the Arunta, though he doubted the hypothesis that they resulted from a conscious reformatory movement to prevent consanguine marriage. He was more interested, however, in technology and physical anthropology. According to Horn—who himself described the Aborigines as "absolutely untameable" and totally lacking in either "religious belief" or "traditions"—Stirling had not gained "much insight into [their] manners and customs." In contrast, Spencer's enthusiasm for observation in the field was as expansive as his personality; he quickly began to venture beyond zoology, and unlike Stirling was prepared to take advantage of a unique ethnographic opportunity which presented itself at Alice Springs.[8]

It was there, in the very middle of the continent, that the expedition encountered Frank Gillen, who for twenty years had served as station manager of the transcontinental telegraph station, dreaming of escape by gambling in gold mine shares. An Australian-born Irish republican bearing "all the marks of his race," Gillen was boisterous, impetuous, generous, and witty, and he had a way with the Arunta who hung around the station and its outbuildings. Although he characteristically referred to them as "my niggers" or "nigs," he was a relatively activist Sub-Protector of Aborigines, in the face of pastoralists who took up the best lands for their stock and "relegate the Nigger to the barren wastes which are often destitute alike of game and tradition." Gillen made it a point not to trespass on the camping spots of the Arunta, and when they stole insulators off the telegraph line to use the glass for making tools, he got them to desist by supplying them instead with broken bottles. Over the years, he had collected a certain amount of miscellaneous ethnographic data, and in the report of the Horn Expedition he included twenty-five pages of notes on Arunta manners and customs. Gillen did not hit it off with Stirling, and at a certain point refused entirely to send him further ethnographic information. But he took immediately to Spencer, whom his Arunta domestic described as "very good Whitefellow, no mindey yab longa me." "Yarning" over whiskey late at night, the two men began a friendship that lasted until Gillen's death in 1912—despite his dismay at Spencer's growing Toryism, and his occasional outbursts against Spencer's "arrogant assumption of superiority so characteristic of your Nigger assimilating race."[9]

After the Horn Expedition's departure, Gillen visited Melbourne, where Spencer introduced him to Fison and Howitt, and Gillen agreed to cooperate with Spencer in a joint publication, which Spencer was to write on the basis of reports Gillen sent every six weeks when the mail left

Alice Springs. Although Gillen was reluctant to pursue issues without "the guidance of [Spencer's] scientifically trained mind," he followed up every lead Spencer suggested, including the collection of anthropological "types" *au naturel*—to the considerable consternation of his domestic, who objected vehemently to "potografum lubra cock." Spencer, however, was most interested in social organization, on which he accepted the guidance of Fison and Howitt. Gillen quickly fell into the spirit of social evolutionary speculation in the Morganian mode, suggesting that Howitt's pirrauru system of temporary wives had in fact been instituted to modify an earlier promiscuous intercourse. Repeating a description of the Lurilcha of Tempe as "all same wild dog, him catchum him sister, jump up longa one fellow mother," he asked whether Fison and Howitt had known of any tribe totally lacking a system of marriage classes. Reporting to Spencer that the eight-class system of the ChiKinca (described to him as "that one very good, him make um walk straight") was rapidly being adopted by all of the tribes of the Macdonnell Ranges, Gillen suggested that "the fact of these niggers being in the very act of changing their system" from four to eight classes was "a most interesting discovery, which showed that "they were struggling upwards towards the light." At Spencer's suggestion, Gillen considered marriage classes and totem groups in a presumed sequence of four stages: tribes with no classes, but totems; tribes with classes to which certain totems were restricted; tribes in which all the totems were confined to certain classes; and tribes in which there was no "vestige" of a relation between class and totem—although Gillen suspected that there must once have been a time when the totems influenced the marriage laws. Like Fison he worried that they might "never discover genuine promiscuity amongst any of these tribes" and wondered if such a thing still existed "amongst any savage people." And he found it "just a trifle depressing" that their work might be only "a 'splendid verification' of that done by Howitt and Fison."[10]

In the same letter to Spencer, Gillen complained about the utter hopelessness of "getting at the 'why' of things," because, "when driven into a corner," informants always took "refuge" in what they called the "alcheringa." As it happened, however, Gillen was by then on the verge of gaining access to "the elusive alcheringa." For a long time he had been on the track of "a big ceremony called Engwiera," which was held at long intervals and attracted Aborigines from hundreds of miles away. Further inquiry indicated that the engwura was an initiation ceremony linked to food production, and that each totem had its own ritual. After much "palaver with the old men," Gillen was able to arrange to have the ceremony held at Alice Springs in November 1896, during Spencer's summer vacation, by agreeing to provide the rations for all who came.

Gillen had long been spoken of by Alice Springs Arunta as a member of the witchetty grub totem, and he arranged for Spencer to attend as his *wetecja*, or younger brother ("blood *and* tribal"). The ceremonies "would last at least a week," and in order to "see everything" it would be necessary for them both "to live at the camp." Gillen also told the Arunta that he would describe the ceremonies to two great *oknirabata* (men of influence) of southeastern Australian tribes, who could themselves send out churinga and make boys into men, and who would know whether the Arunta accounts were "crooked" or "straight." On the basis of pictures drawn upon the ground, the Arunta concluded that Howitt's totem was the lizard and Fison's the wildcat; dubbing Howitt "Echumpa" and Fison "Okurabala," they were later eager to find out what the two had "thought of their Corroborrees."[11]

The ceremonies, which in fact lasted for almost three months, were a "real red letter period in tribal history"—never again would "'bacca be so plentiful or flour so liberally dealt out." They were also a red letter moment in the lives of Spencer and Gillen, who later wished "we could live our Engwura life over again"—though he confessed that "it was an anxious time," in which there was "always a danger of the thing bursting up." Gillen's prodigality with provisions had in fact created a somewhat artificial situation, in which adaptations and compromises were introduced to facilitate the participation of a large and diverse gathering. But in the process, a window was opened to a sacred traditional world whose very existence Horn had denied—although his expedition had unknowingly desecrated it, by uncovering a secret Aboriginal cache of sixty carved wooden boards and fifteen incised stones, which, in a spirit of ethnocentric uplift, they had replaced with the steel axes and knives of technological civilization. Gillen himself had previously amassed a collection of over one hundred "Chooringa" by means more unabashedly plunderous. But during the engwura, he and Spencer began to appreciate that these caches were depositories of the "special men of the Alcheringa," or "far distant past," who had "wandered about and descended at those spots into the earth where their Churinga, the very ones which are now within the storehouse, remain associated with their spirit part." When Gillen later discovered that an old man had been killed for divulging the locality of churinga to a policeman who was assisting their inquiries, he bitterly regretted "ever having countenanced" churinga robberies, and resolved that there must be no more. But he could only fully realize "what they meant to the natives" when he watched them "reverently handling their treasures" at the engwura.[12]

Camping in a wurley of gum boughs opening upon the ceremonial area, with the temperature as high as 110° in the shade, Spencer and Gillen were given an unprecedented ethnographic opportunity to

Baldwin Spencer (left) and Frank Gillen, with Arunta (Aranda) tribesmen, under a wurley at the engwura ceremonies, Alice Springs, 1896. (Courtesy of the Museum of Victoria Council, W. B. Spencer Collection)

observe, to photograph, and to interrogate—for the most part, in pidgin English, since Gillen's knowledge of Arunta (and several other Aboriginal languages) was in fact rather less fluent than Spencer had assumed. Their shelter became a social center for off-duty elders, who came to squat and gab between the dances, which continued around the clock. Like Howitt in Gippsland, Spencer had with him a supply of wax matches for informants to arrange upon the ground to display kinship or totemic relationships. But thanks in part to the sacred alcheringa status which, unknowingly, they had given to Howitt in the process of describing "Echumpa," Spencer and Gillen were able to move beyond the social organizational issues they had inherited from Howitt and Fison into an unexplored world of ceremony and traditional belief. Gillen's influence with the Aborigines had been greatly heightened, and, after Spencer's departure, they now invited him to their ceremonies "as a matter of course." When at Spencer's suggestion Gillen undertook to follow up the traditions of the totem wanderings in the alcheringa, old men came from all over to talk to him, delighting now "in raking up their traditions" because they really believed, he reported, that "I look upon them with sympathetic credulity."[13]

Despite the fact that he continued to refer to fieldwork as "nigger-ing," Gillen was, after his fashion, capable of a considerable empathy. Although the extinction of the Aborigines was "inevitable & rapidly approaching," it should, he thought, be made "as pleasant as possible." He was profoundly disturbed by what he called the "true degeneration*" (explicated in a footnote as "*from our, which is the proper, point of view") which followed when they dropped their "old habits and customs." And he had no use for mission stations, where the extirpation of tradition was not an accident of contact but a deliberate policy: "if ever niggers in this world were being systematically degraded, . . . I should say debauched, these people are." Gillen wished that he could still believe as his "poor dead brother" had, and often used his lost Roman Catholicism as a reference point in interpreting the "quaintly pathetic old superstitions" of the alcheringa. Comparing "Churinga" (which he insisted should be capitalized) to the sacramental wafer, he suggested that it conveyed the same meaning as the English word "sacred": men sprang from churinga "just as the Virgin Mary appears at Lourdes." It was a trope his colleague (whom Gillen described as possessing a "generous and ready sympathy") seems to have found congenial, if we may judge from Gillen's self-deprecating remark that "the blackfellow eating the flesh and blood of his totem in the same spirit that the Christian takes the sacrament is a thing that would never have dawned upon my muddy mind."[14]

After their engwura experience, the two ethnographers felt more confident of getting at "the 'why' of things," which they thought of in purposive terms, as a matter of trying to get at the "essential" or "fundamental idea" behind a customary or ceremonial act. At least once, they appealed to what "the natives themselves say," when informants spoke of the engwura as making the initiates "*ertwa murra oknirra,* words which respectively mean 'man, good, [and] great or very.'" But they immediately provided their own gloss: "Evidently, the main objects [are] . . . to bring the young men under the control of the old men . . . , to teach them habits of self-restraint and hardihood . . . [and to show them] the sacred secrets of the tribe. . . ." More often, however, it was difficult to get at "the idea which [was] present in the native mind," because the natives could "offer no explanation"; and in these instances the ethnographers had to offer their own. Sometimes these were in terms of self-interest: thus, food restrictions were associated with the idea of "reserving the best things" for the elders or for the men as against the women. Sometimes "purpose" was simply equated with "result," conceived of in more sociological terms: the engwura's "main result is undoubtedly to preserve unchanged certain customs." Sometimes the explanation was straightforwardly utilitarian: although the intichiuma ceremonies of different totems were "no two of them alike," they all had "for their sole object the purpose of increasing the number of the animal or plant after which the totem is named" and thus the "total food supply" of the tribe. Sometimes, explanation was symbolic: the presentation of the knocked-out teeth of initiates to female relatives was an "indication" that they had "passed from the control of the mother into the ranks of the men or women." Or the appeal might simply be to the commonplaces of evolutionary assumption, as when (without explicit reference to Tylor or Frazer) the churinga belief was interpreted as a "modification" of the idea of an external soul, which found expression "in the folklore of so many peoples": "primitive man, regarding his soul as a concrete object, imagines that he can place it in some secure spot" outside his body.[15]

Just as there was an ultimate limit on relativizing empathy (*our = proper), so was there an ultimate ground of ethnological interpretation. Gillen was quite capable of resisting Spencer's evolutionary leads, insisting, for instance, that one tribe was not in the paleolithic stage, because he had observed them grinding (rather than chipping) their stone axes. But although he always measured evolutionary speculation against his reading of the ethnographic data, Gillen operated for the most part quite comfortably within a theoretical agenda which, transmitted by Spencer, was defined by major figures of social evolutionism: Tylor, Morgan, McLennan, and (as we shall see) Frazer. The geological metaphor ("getting down to bedrock") Gillen occasionally used to describe his fieldwork was in this sense quite appropriate—for *The Native Tribes of Central Australia* remained, *au fond*, an evolutionary ethnography. When, after "endeavouring as best we could to enter into their feelings, to think as they did, and to become for the time being one of themselves," Spencer and Gillen concluded that "one or two of the most powerful" Aborigines might introduce a "fundamental change of custom," it was only a slight qualification of their immediately preceding comment that "as amongst all savage tribes, the Australian native is bound hand and foot by custom"—and in fact fitted quite well with Morgan's notion that progress in the evolution of social organization was the result of "reformatory movements." And in writing for a more general audience, the two men were quite capable of offering an image of "naked, howling savages" whose ceremonies were "crude in the extreme" and whose nature was never more vividly expressed than when they smeared each other with blood—although here, as in all their published work, the rhetoric was surely Spencer's.[16]

Despite its evolutionary grounding, *The Native Tribes of Central Australia* represented a substantial departure from nineteenth-century ethnographic norms. In contrast with *Kamilaroi and Kurnai* or *The Melanesians*, it was governed by a particular context of observation and inquiry. Going beyond the elicitation of customary rules as general statements illustrated by a few particular instances, it presented an extended account of observed ceremonial behavior, supplemented by information gained from informants in the immediate context of ceremonial performance: "it was while watching and questioning closely the natives during the performance of the Engwura ceremony—a description of which will be found in a later chapter—that we were able to find out the way in which the totem names of the individuals originate and to gain an insight into the true nature of their totemic system." As that reference to "a later chapter" suggests, the transition between the two modes is in fact quite marked, one third of the way into the book, where the text begins to be thickened with photographs of the actual ceremonies. Before that, the ethnography was still recognizably in the mode of Fison and Howitt, to whom the book was in fact dedicated; after that, one feels that one has stepped into the ethnographic world of the next century.[17]

It was, however, a world that Spencer and Gillen did more to foreshadow than to create. One can find in their correspondence material for Malinowskian mottoes, as when, regarding a proposal of Stirling's for work at Tempe Downs, Gillen agreed with Spencer that "without living amongst them and possessing their entire confidence it will be valueless." But despite their continuing personal dedication to the ethnographic enterprise, the two men seem not to have played a major role in establishing a new methodological model. In 1901, when they both managed a year's leave, they used money from Spencer's father to underwrite an expedition across Australia from south to north, which produced a second joint ethnography. Ten years later, when Gillen was near death, Spencer was still at it in the northern territories, where he was able to get himself appointed Chief Protector of Aborigines and did a considerable amount of fieldwork around Port Darwin. Even after his retirement in 1919, Spencer kept going, returning to the Macdonnell Ranges in 1923 and to Alice Springs in 1926. And when he died three years later, it was in a hut on a storm-wracked island off Cape Horn, where, accompanied by a much younger woman, he had come to do fieldwork among the Fuegians. Faithful to Tylor to the end, he sought to disprove the existence of monotheism among a group which, from the time of Darwin's encounter in the 1830s, had vied with the Australians for the status of most primitive living humans. Spencer died, however, without leaving academic ethnographic progeny; despite his efforts upon several occasions, the University of Melbourne did not establish instruction in anthropology before his retirement, which was occasioned in part by its most recent refusal to do so. There were, as a result, no "Spencerian" ethnographers.[18]

In contrast, *The Native Tribes of Central Australia* had a powerful influence on anthropological theory. According to the later recollection of

Tylor's successor at Oxford, Robert Marett, the book "took the scientific world by storm." Writing in 1913, Bronislaw Malinowski estimated that half the theoretical work in the years since its publication had been based on Spencer and Gillen's book, and that nine-tenths had been "affected or modified by it." Although he was by that time himself critical of some of the book's most important conclusions, Malinowski's continuing concern with the presumed ignorance of savages about the sexual facts of human reproduction was sustained by Spencer and Gillen's observations among the Arunta: "time after time we have questioned them on this point, and always received the reply that the child was not the direct result of intercourse," which "merely prepares the mother for the reception and birth also of an already-formed spirit child who inhabits one of the local totem centres."[19] A more systematic line of influence, however—one which Malinowski was to reject—was the reinforcement of the Morganian tradition within British anthropology, as previously naturalized in the work of Fison and Howitt.

Although they did not mention Morgan by name, Spencer and Gillen made a point of disputing "Mr. McLennan" on the terms of relationship being "merely for the purpose of addressing each other." Without exception in all the tribes they had studied, the terms coincided with "the recognition of relationships, all of which are dependent on the existence of a classificatory system, the fundamental idea of which is that the women of certain groups marry the men of others." Without any "prejudice in favour of one theory or another," their studies had convinced them that the observed facts of social organization could not "receive any satisfactory explanation except on the theory of the former existence of group marriage, and further, that this has of necessity given rise to the terms of relationship used by the Australian natives."[20] Although there was to be considerable further debate about primitive promiscuity and group marriage, the Morganian position on the significance of kinship terms was henceforth to be a powerful force in British social anthropology.

The Native Tribes of Central Australia also had a major impact on another area of theoretical concern to which McLennan's name was linked: the discussion of totemism. Not only did it provide the first evidence from a living people for Robertson Smith's theory of the primitive totemic sacramental meal; it also had a somewhat disruptive effect on thinking about the role of totemism in the regulation of marriage. Spencer and Gillen still found this association among the Urabunna, where each tribal moeity was divided into a number of exogamous totems, inherited in the female line. But in the eight-class system of the Arunta, the totems had nothing whatsoever to do with marriage and descent. They were strictly local, and the totem of a child might or might not be the same as that of either the father or the mother, since the child "belongs to the totem of the spot at which the mother believes that it was conceived," by the entry into her body of a particular spirit from the Alcheringa time. Commentators in England saw all of this as quite revolutionary—an "overthrow" of all "recognized principles" of the totemic regulation of marriage. Picked up especially by James Frazer, who was to become their armchair mentor, Spencer and Gillen's Arunta ethnography was to be at the center of the debate that swirled around totemism throughout the prewar period.[21*]

Retrospectively, the most important product of this discussion was perhaps Durkheim's *Elementary Forms of the Religious Life*. Previously influenced by Robertson Smith's interpretation of totemic religion among the ancient Semites, Durkheim later found in Spencer and Gillen's work a body of detailed ethnographic data on a functioning totemic system that seemed to provide the "crucial experiment" by which he could lay bare the fundamental principles of religion. Already interested in the problem of Australian social organization, Durkheim devoted much of his attention to the reinterpretation of the Arunta materials in terms of his own developing theoretical viewpoint. In contrast to other writers, for whom the Arunta data contributed to the separation of the social organizational and the religious aspects of totemism, Durkheim saw totemism as essentially constitutive of Aboriginal social organization, and found in the Arunta ceremonials evidence for the function of religion in "upholding and reaffirming at regular intervals the collective sentiments and the collective ideas which make the unity and the personality of a society."[22]

But if they provided ethnographic grist for the mills of theoretical debate, Spencer and Gillen were not themselves active participants in it. Their ethnographic agenda was theoretically constrained, but their

*Although it retains today a place in the Australian ethnographic canon, the ethnography of Spencer and Gillen has been subject to serious criticism, most decisively by T. G. H. Strehlow, the son of a Lutheran missionary ethnographer who lived among the Western Aranda and spoke their language. Although the elder Strehlow attained an excellent knowledge of myth and social organization, his knowledge of ceremonials was only second hand, because, from missionary principle, he never attended "pagan rites." Dismissing his work as a product "entirely [of] the study," Spencer contributed to its marginalization from Australian anthropological discourse. The younger Strehlow, who himself was fluent in the Western Aranda language from childhood, later drew on his own research and on his father's manuscripts to make a careful analysis of the ethnographies of Spencer and Gillen. Granting their competence as visual observers, Strehlow concluded that their work was "defaced" by "many serious inaccuracies." Because they were forced to rely on younger Aranda intermediaries who were able to speak pidgin, they had in fact been misled on many points, including the issue of nescience of physiological paternity (Strehlow 1971:xxii, xxvi, xxviii, xxix, 596–97). For a systematic discussion of the problem of Australian Aboriginal nescience, which offers a provocatively different interpretation of a number of the themes of this book, consult Wolfe (1994).

ethnographic noses were never too tightly pressed against any theoretical grindstone. Theoreticians like Durkheim could give their Arunta materials a kind of archetypal evolutionary status; but they themselves insisted on the "very considerable diversity" of custom among Australian tribes, some of whom were "in a less highly developed state than the Arunta."[23] Despite their evolutionary predilections, they were both firmly committed to ethnographic observation: Gillen, by virtue of twenty years of residence on the ground; Spencer, by virtue of an academic training still much in the tradition of the field naturalist. During the same period in which Spencer and Gillen were carrying on their Arunta ethnography, however, that tradition was also undergoing transformation in the work of Alfred Cort Haddon, which had less impact on the development of anthropological theory, but much more on the development of institutionalized ethnographic practice.

Alfred Cort Haddon and the Cambridge University Anthropological Expedition to Torres Straits

With Haddon, as perhaps with Spencer, one has a sense of what Tylor's anthropological career might have been had he come along a second time in his own wake, a generation later, when the universities were open to dissenters, evolutionism was a scientific orthodoxy, and careers in scientific fields neighboring to anthropology were a serious possibility—and as the ebbing tide of mid-Victorian liberal optimism was overtaken by the cresting wave of empire. Like Spencer, and Tylor earlier, Haddon came from a dissenting entrepreneurial family. His grandfather had been the founder of a London printing firm specializing in missionary tracts; his father became the sole proprietor of it in 1855, the year of Haddon's birth. His father was apparently more interested in Baptist religion, philanthropy, and a leisured middle-class existence enriched by gardening and music than he was in the family business, which suffered as a result. But until 1870, Haddon was able to enjoy a life in country houses outside London, where he obtained a "scrappy and precarious" education first at home and then at a series of schools. His mother, who wrote children's books on religious and natural history topics, encouraged his scientific interests, which even in his childhood included a collection of skulls. Although a participant in Dwight Moody revivals, and still deeply religious, he had by 1871 felt the influence of Darwinism, and dreamed of a career in zoology. Acceding to his father's wish that he enter the family business, he tried to relieve the drudgery of the office by taking evening classes in anatomy and geology, and by giving lectures himself at the

YMCA and at the girls' school his Aunt Caroline ran at Dover. Eventually, it became evident even to his father that he was not earmarked for the business world, and with the help of his aunt, who knew Michael Foster, he was sent off to Christ's College, Cambridge—despite Foster's warning that "the life of a scientific man is a very hard and unremunerative one" and that he would perhaps be better off to stay in publishing, and use his leisure time for scientific activity.[24]

A protégé of Darwin's "bulldog" Thomas Huxley, Foster had come to Cambridge in 1870, where he began to develop practical laboratory instruction in physiology and other biological specialties. Haddon was powerfully influenced by Foster's undogmatic experimental approach, and even more by the almost religious scientific dedication of his brilliant student F. M. Balfour, with whom Foster had co-authored a textbook in embryology in 1874, and for whom Haddon served as demonstrator. Exchanging his childhood belief for Huxley's agnosticism and Balfour's religion of science, Haddon pursued a compensating interest in the origin of the lowest life forms. Although he performed well in the recently established Natural Science Tripos, he failed to win an assistantship in zoology at the British Museum. He went instead for six months to study marine biology at the zoological station at Naples, serving upon his return as curator and demonstrator in Cambridge. But with Huxley's support, he won appointment in 1881 to the chair in zoology at the Royal College of Science in Dublin, and felt financially secure enough to marry.[25]

Living for the next thirteen years in a kind of cultural exile among a quasi-colonial population, Haddon's participation in the lively if somewhat parochial life of the Dublin scientific community was complicated by the anti-British feeling aroused by the Home Rule question. He was shocked to hear his students cheer the news of Gordon's defeat at Khartoum, and he later lost an attractive fellowship when the "patriotic [i.e., Irish] element" combined against the "very few scientific men" on the selecting council. A gentle and empathic person by nature, and later a socialist, Haddon had a good deal of sympathy for the Irish people; but there was no doubt about his basic cultural identity. When Prince Edward came to Dublin for a state visit in 1885, Haddon and his wife Fanny, along with the rest of the English elite, were part of the crush at the soirées; and though he could not afford the dress required for a royal presentation, he did take the viceroy for a Sunday visit to the zoo. Haddon also developed a heightened sense of the cultural—or, as he would have put it, the "racial"—identity of the Irish. When one of his several dredging expeditions for marine specimens took him to an Irish fishing village, this "peep into another world" with different "ways of thought" convinced him that the "ordinary Saxon" was incapable of either understanding or governing the "typical Irish": "theory is all very fine, [but] the facts of Irish idiosyncracies refuse to be treated in a logical manner."[26]

After failing in the competition for the chair in zoology which Spencer won in Melbourne, Haddon began to make plans for a major research expedition that might get him out of the dead end of a provincial professorship. Sustained by his regular participation in the meetings of the British Association, his ties to the metropolitan scientific world remained strong enough to win him both counsel and support. Moseley suggested that he do research on Ascension Island; Alfred Russel Wallace urged him to go to the West Indies. But Haddon chose instead the islands of the Torres Straits, between New Guinea and Australia, which Huxley had visited on the H.M.S. *Rattlesnake* four decades previously. With a £300 grant won with Huxley's help, Haddon in 1888 sailed off on a solo expedition to study a problem that would have interested Darwin himself: "the fauna, structure and mode of formation of the coral reefs in Torres Straits."[27]

Although Haddon's background in anthropology at this point was virtually nil, he realized that there might be opportunities in Torres Straits for ethnographic work. However, after consulting with Sir William Flower, the director of the natural history collections of the British Museum and a recent past president of the Anthropological Institute, "about taking measurements of natives," he decided not to bother because "a good deal was known already about them." But he did nevertheless take along a copy of *Notes and Queries*, and, at James Frazer's request, a copy of Frazer's privately printed *Questions on the Manners, Customs, Religion, Superstitions, etc., of Uncivilized or Semi-Civilized Peoples*—as well as a letter certifying Haddon's membership in the Dublin lodge of the Free Masons. Although Haddon did in fact complete the researches for which he went to the islands, his interests quickly began to shift from marine biology to anthropology.[28]

After landing on Thursday Island, the administrative center of the area, Haddon accompanied the Acting Government Resident on his island rounds, bartering calico, "jewsharps," and hatchets for native "curios" to sell to museums to recoup some of his expenses. At each stop he "dived" into native houses "to see what was going on and to look out for spoil," and at several places he got the natives to put on a *koppa-koppa* or ceremonial dance. Sketching and photographing the islanders, he cajoled the women into abandoning the missionary calicoes which, forewarned by a local headman, they had "donned in our honour" to replace their usual grass skirts. Later on he settled for a while on Mabuiag Island, where for some weeks he was "the chief of the island and the only white man there." His days were occupied with dredging reefs and examining specimens in an empty fishing station that served as laboratory. But in the evening he joined the natives round the campfire for their evening prayers, and when groups of them came later to his home (the deserted mission house that was kept for him by the wife of the Polynesian mission teacher), they talked on into the night in pidgin about what life had been like "before white man he come—no missionary—no nothing." As one old man would tell a traditional legend, the others jogged his memory and corrected his mistakes, nodding with approval when the informant was "telling the story properly." Similarly, Haddon would submit for their correction the sketches of ceremonies he composed on the basis of their descriptions.[29]

The rather random ethnographic observations Haddon was able to collect have a definite ring of anthropological naivete—as when, after noting that the sons and daughters of the same man by two wives were not regarded as brothers and sisters, he observed somewhat heavy-handedly, "hence there is a matriarchal and not a patriarchal system here." Perhaps not surprisingly, the "Ethnography of the Western Tribe of Torres Straits" which he published in the *Journal of the Anthropological Institute* upon his return was in fact cast in the categories of *Notes and Queries*. What is surprising about Haddon's early ethnographic experience is his unusual sensitivity, for an anthropologist of his day, to certain aspects of what today would be called the "colonial situation" of his ethnography. Undated manuscript materials and short published pieces from the period after his return from Torres Straits reveal a humanely relativizing (although still ethnocentric and even racialist) ethical sensibility. Squirming uncomfortably under the weight of the "white man's burden," Haddon tried to find a standpoint from which he could both study and defend natives whose traditional customs and beliefs were being radically transformed, if not effaced, by the encroachments of a civilization and an empire of which, albeit ambivalently, he was himself a part. While still in the field, he was pleased that the Resident's "willingness to assist" was "backed up by the power and the authority of the official": at every island he visited, the local native police were put under Haddon's orders, and their boat made available to him for dredging. Working under the umbrella of British colonial authority, he had been lucky enough "to arrive at a time when the old order is changing, giving place rather to a negation than to a 'new' ": "They know, poor souls, that they now have no need for these things and they have a need for 'baccy." Although not twenty years ago the islanders had shown "a fierce determination to slay the encroaching white man," they would now walk thirteen miles to dance the same day "for the delectation of an Englishman they have never seen."[30]

But upon his return to England he expressed dismay that the

"Anglo-Indian and the Colonial" so often referred to natives as "niggers," which he described—in a passage stained by unconscious ethnic assumption—as "a term of reproach which implies a hatred and superciliousness similar to that with which the Jews regard the Gentiles, the Greeks the Barbarians, and which the Chinese still hold for 'foreign devils.'" Similarly, his own vindication of the natives was often cast in ethnocentric terms: "there are few Irish cottages which would compare favorably [for cleanliness] with this heathen woman's home." At other times he was more relativistic, as when he attacked those who "confuse clothing with morality." He clearly felt the pathos as well as the methodological inconvenience when, "from their connection with white men," natives got the "idea that their customs are wrong or foolish," and therefore could "hardly be induced to talk about them." But the elegaic tone sometimes resonated with patronization: "although the results are usually incongruous and often comic, yet there is always something pathetic in an isolated race at a low level of development semi-consciously striving to be in touch with the result of centuries of civilization and culture." At one point, he explained the presumed collapse of the old island culture by the fact that "the new civilization" was so "incomparably superior" that the natives lost faith "in all the past" and accepted "the new *en masse*." But he also insisted that "civilization did not consist of railways, telegraphs, representative government, nor even of those characteristic British exports—beer and Bible," but rather of "right living and the cultivation of morality." "We" had a right to protect life and property in "all the countries that come under our sway," but if "the native political or social organization" were able to do this and "keep the native population in order," there was no reason to try to "change their religious forms or their moral codes."[31]

Furthermore, Haddon was not unaware of how "our sway" had been established. While it was not easy "in every case of conflict between the white man and the native" to tell "who was the aggressor," it was usually the former who was "the wilful or ignorant disturber of the peace": "the ordinary white man is not only ignorant of the meaning of native intimations and careless of the sanctity of tabu and sacred ceremonies, but he cannot imagine that he has not the right to go where he likes and do what he pleases." So it was that the map of the world was splotched with "the red paint of British aggression."[32]

Although he thought the sufferings of the natives were "heartrending," and that "they would be less than men if they did not rebel," Haddon did not suppose the red paint would be soon erased. He did feel, however, that Britain should be concerned with the "responsibilities" as well as the "emoluments" of imperialism, and one of those responsibilities was anthropology. Fearful that the recently founded Imperial

Institute was to be simply "a temple to the gospel of ten per cent," he proposed that it should include a bureau of ethnology, which would collect and disseminate information on all the native groups of the empire. Unlike its American model, however, such a bureau would also provide for training in anthropology; and because experience at Oxford had shown that instruction by itself was not enough, Haddon urged that the subject should be included in the examinations for the Indian and Colonial Services, and special credit be offered to already-appointed officials who studied it. Given its "inevitable tendency to develop a more sympathetic and cordial attitude towards our dependencies and to modify our precipitate attempts to uproot institutions which are due to profound ethnic differences," such training would "unquestionably reduce the cost of maintaining our ascendancy." Anthropology, in short, should be part of the white man's burden: by enlightening imperial self-interest, it would reduce its weight, not only for the English, but for the savage—whom Haddon had seen bear the brunt of it.[33]

It was a theme to which Haddon recurred many times throughout his life; but at the time his proposal was stillborn. Huxley, to whom he had sent an early draft, felt that "a project for the 'conversion' of the heathen" was more plausible than an attempt to convert the Imperial Institute. He even doubted that anthropological knowledge would in fact "improve the relations of Englishmen with other races," since our "too frequent brutality has a moral rather than an intellectual source." Rather than try to publish the article, Haddon, he suggested, should work through existing agencies to collect more anthropological data.[34]

By this time, Haddon was no longer an outsider to those agencies. During the months he spent in England after his return in the late spring of 1889, he was urged by several leading scientists he met at meetings of the British Association and the Anthropological Institute to give up zoology for anthropology. Although Huxley concurred, he doubted that "a devotee of anthropology" could find the "irreducible minimum of bread and butter the need of which is patent to a physiologist if not a morphologist."[35] Rather than burn his bridges, Haddon returned to his chair in Dublin, and continued to publish in zoology for some years to come. But his commitment to anthropology had been made. Zoology would be possible for a long time to come, but the ethnic variety of mankind was rapidly disappearing from the face of the earth.

At a time when an academic man with ethnographic experience overseas was a rarity in British anthropology, Haddon quickly moved to the front ranks of the discipline. In the early 1890s he became involved in the kinds of empirical research that were most characteristic of British anthropology at this time: notably, physical anthropology and folklore. Within an evolutionary context, these two inquiries each bore on a problem of practical political and ideological as well as theoretical significance: the origin of the differentiating features of contemporary European populations, as viewed in the somewhat confused racial-cum-cultural terms characteristic of the period. Physical anthropology presumed to offer methods by which underlying racial "types" could be specified; folklore collected the surviving evidence of their cultural characteristics—and their presumed mutual relevance was in fact reflected in the organizational history of British anthropology. When the Anthropological Institute entered the doldrums at the end of its first decade (when prehistoric archeologists had played the leading role), it was the physical anthropologists—with an eye to the flourishing state of physical anthropology in France and Germany—who led in its reinvigoration in the 1880s, when William Flower, Francis Galton, and John Beddoe served as presidents. And by the time Haddon came upon the scene, ties with folklore had become so close that the Anthropological Institute seriously considered a proposal from the Folk-Lore Society that the two groups amalgamate. Although Haddon himself seconded the motion, the proposal ran aground on financial issues. It is in the context of this near conjunction of folklore and anthropology (in which physical anthropology was dominant) that Haddon's early anthropology was formed.[36]

Coming from zoology, Haddon naturally found physical anthropology congenial; in 1891, he joined with D. J. Cunningham, Professor of Anatomy at Trinity College, in establishing an anthropometric laboratory in Dublin modelled on Galton's in London. Living at the center of the arc of the "Celtic fringe," and sharing the prevailing belief that the folk bore "the same relation to educated people that savages bear to civilized communities," Haddon clearly felt that research among local populations could be a functional equivalent of ethnographic fieldwork in Torres Straits—and a lot easier to manage. In 1892, he suggested the possibility of a general ethnographic survey of the British Isles to the Anthropological Institute, the Folk-Lore Society, and the Society of Antiquaries. Edward Brabrook, a lawyer-scholar who played a leading role in all three groups, took the lead in gaining the sponsorship of the British Association for the Advancement of Science, which set up a committee to organize a large-scale "Ethnographic Survey of the United Kingdom" with a view to determining "as far as possible the racial elements of which it is composed." Although migration, industrialization, and urbanization had destroyed the "ethnic quality" of much of the kingdom, there were still scattered places where "families have dwelt in the same village from father to son as far back as their ancestry can be traced," where "custom and prejudice and superstition have held men bound in chains which all the restlessness of the nineteenth century has not yet completely severed," and where the Ethnographic Survey hoped "still to find sure traces of the past." Haddon's own major contribution to the project was a study of the ethnography of the Aran Islands in Galway Bay, an isolated and uncontaminated region where he found the inhabitants singularly free of lying, drinking, and the other commonly assumed vices of the Irish character.[37]

On the basis of his Torres Straits and Irish researches, Haddon by 1898 felt confident enough of his identification as an anthropologist and his mastery of its methods to become a spokesman of the discipline—although in his characteristically modest and eclectic style. *The Study of Man* was not a "treatise on Anthropology," but "merely a collection of samples of the way in which parts of the subject are studied."[38] Its emphasis was on methodology in the study of physical anthropology and folklore; the last chapter was largely a collection of the circulars of the Ethnographic Survey of the United Kingdom. Haddon's anthropology, however, also had a more systematic aspect; and while his folklore studies were very much in the Tylorian tradition, when it came to interpreting his Melanesian materials, his approach differed from that of Tylor and other earlier sociocultural evolutionists in ways that reflect the general changes then under way in British anthropology.

Unlike Spencer, whose early Australian fieldwork linked him directly to an already-established line of social evolutionary ethnography, Haddon had first worked in an area where there was as yet no strong ethnographic tradition. Drawing on his background in biology, he constructed an evolutionary approach that differed significantly from classical sociocultural evolutionism of the Morganian or Tylorian sort. What concerned Haddon in the first instance was not so much the documentation of a universal sequence of development, but—like Darwin in the Galapagos—the distribution of forms within a single geographical area. Specifically, he was interested in the forms of material culture, which he insisted need not be treated as "the mere collecting of curios." Thus he was pleased when he found on Prince of Wales Island the missing link in "a series of stages in the evolution of houses" from the Australian wind screen to the Papuan pile house, precisely on the very island which "from its geographical position might reasonably be expected" to supply it; similarly, he hoped to use his sketches to trace the variation of artifacts (and customs) from one island to the next.[39]

Shortly after his return from Torres Straits, Haddon had written to Havelock Ellis, the English sexual psychologist and scientific popularizer (and a friend of his avant-garde Aunt Caroline), proposing a "general work on Anthropology written from a biological point of view," which he justified on the ground that "savages" were " 'arrested' " or " 'generalized types' " like the mud-fishes, persisting "in the fag ends of continents."

The book subsequently included in Ellis' Contemporary Science series, *Evolution in Art,* was Haddon's attempt to bring to bear on that subject the methods of the zoologist, who he suggested engaged in three distinct sorts of activities. The "analytical zoologist" recorded and classified the fauna of a district; the "more synthetically-minded" student mapped the distribution of a particular species, seeking to account for its variations, to "ascertain the place of its evolution," and to trace its subsequent migrations; the "philosophical student" studied the general development of animals so as to shed light on their "genealogies and relationships." Much of Haddon's book was in fact cast in the "philosophical" mode, attempting to work out certain general principles of the development of artistic design in terms of "skeuomorphs" and "biomorphs"—the "objective originals," either artificial or natural forms—which were "gradually transformed into aesthetic conceptions." And in the spirit of his proposal to Ellis, the text was replete with the evolutionary metaphors, the racial "tendencies" and cultural "stages," and the conventional ethnocentric wisdom about the minds of savages that were commonly characteristic of late-nineteenth-century anthropology—rather more so, in fact, than in Tylor's work, since Haddon was intent on casting his argument in "biological" terms.[40]

At one point, however, Haddon acknowledged his own preference for zoological work at a more empirical level: "no part of the study of Biology is more fascinating than that which deals with the geographical distribution of organisms." In this mode, Haddon was interested in establishing "artistic provinces," in the value of characteristic art forms as criteria for the definition of ethnic or racial relationships, and in tracing the migrations of people and the diffusion of culture through borrowing. And while his concern with these problems was rooted in zoology, it also linked him to an earlier diffusionist/migrationist "ethnological" tradition. Pushed from the center stage of anthropological speculation with the emergence of the classical evolutionary paradigm in the 1860s, diffusionism was still a part of the chorus of anthropological voices throughout the later nineteenth century; shortly, with Haddon's help, it was again to take a leading role.[41]

Although its intellectual provenance was quite different, Haddon's approach in fact displayed significant analogies to that which Franz Boas had adopted in the study of the distribution of the adhesions of folklore elements on the Northwest Coast of Canada—although Boas was somewhat critical of Haddon's general statements on the evolution of art and had no sympathy for his social Darwinism. Haddon did not formulate a general critique like "The Limitations of the Comparative Method of Anthropology" that Boas offered in 1896, but he was nevertheless well aware of some of the limitations. Unconsciously echoing Henry Maine, he suggested that "it is only when the indigenous material is insufficient, or fails in its results, that the comparative method should be employed, and then only when history, tradition, or other lines of evidence warrant its use." And just as Boas wanted to limit comparison to phenomena that were actually historically related, so also Haddon insisted that "one great advantage in the method of confining attention to a limited area is that similar designs very probably have a genetic connection, whereas this is by no means the case if objects from different regions are compared together." Another way of avoiding the confusion of "analogy" and "homology" was to make "careful inquiries" of "the natives themselves" in order to elucidate "the meaning of the devices of savages." From this perspective, the "most important and pressing work in this subject"—and Haddon would surely have extended this from art to anthropology—was the collection of "oral information" in the field. Within several years, he was himself to organize a major expedition to that end.[42]

Balancing his socialist disapproval of the private ownership of property in land against the hope that propinquity might lead to an academic position in a place where his anthropological ambitions would be more easily realizable, Haddon in 1893 settled his family in a house in Cambridge. By this time, an annual term of lectures in physical anthropology had been included by Professor Alexander Macalister as part of the training offered in human anatomy, and in 1894, when the incumbent lecturer left to accept a post at Manchester, Haddon was hired to take his place at a salary of £50 a year. Although he continued to hold his Dublin chair, Haddon tried in every way he could to expand his Cambridge beachhead. For those who cared to attend, he offered lectures in ethnology and sociology—an interest inspired by Patrick Geddes, a botanist turned Le Playian sociologist and advocate of city planning, in whose Edinburgh summer extension schools Haddon had participated. Early in 1897, Haddon confided to Geddes a plan to return to Torres Straits, because he felt that the material he had previously collected was inadequate for an ethnographic monograph the Cambridge University Press had agreed to publish. By this time, however, Haddon's already embracive conception of anthropology had broadened to include the "psychology and sociology of savage peoples," which were "really of more importance" than their "physical characteristics." In order to accomplish the range of investigations he now considered necessary, Haddon proposed to take with him "a linguistic expert, a trained experimental psychologist and one or two young men to train as field anthropologists"—apparently assuming physical anthropology and sociology as his own areas of expertise. Haddon's motives were institutional as well as intellectual: "I am certain that the best way to start a School of Anthropology at Cambridge is to boldly go in for research work of this kind," which, in contrast to "stay at home work," could only be "satisfactorily done in the present and immediate future."[43]

The linguist had already been chosen. After his first expedition, Haddon had followed the advice of James Frazer to ask Codrington for help in working up the linguistic materials. Because he was busy writing *The Melanesians,* Codrington had suggested Sidney Ray, a teacher of arithmetic in London elementary schools, who had for several years filled his leisure time analyzing the native gospels printed by the British and Foreign Bible Society, and who in 1893 co-authored with Haddon a study of the languages of the Torres Straits. With a little pressure on the London school board to arrange a leave, all that remained was to provide the £48 subsidy that would keep Ray's family from starving during the year he was away.[44]

The selection of the psychologist was more complicated. In an era when anthropological speculation was rife with unexamined assumptions about racial mental differences and the "concrete" mental processes of childlike savages, as well as of the "psychic unity of mankind" and "independent invention," it was a very significant step to take a practitioner of the new "experimental psychology" into the field to study basic perceptual processes. Haddon may have been led to it by his interest in the "psychology of symbolism" in primitive art, on which his reading had been guided by Ellis. Be that as it may, he found at Cambridge a specialist in the physiology of the sense organs, with a particular interest in vision: W. H. R. Rivers. After training in medicine at the University of London and St. Bartholomew's Hospital, Rivers had accepted an appointment at the National Hospital for the Paralysed and Epileptic in 1891. There he assisted at the operations of the leading brain surgeon, Victor Horsley, and, in addition, came under the influence of Hughlings Jackson, whose studies of the evolution of the nervous system were landmarks in the emergence of modern neurology. He also met young Henry Head, already on his way to becoming England's leading neurophysiologist, who had worked on vision with the German physiologist Ewald Hering. Inspired by Head, Rivers made several trips to Germany, where he studied psychopathology and experimental psychology. In 1893 Rivers was invited by Sir Michael Foster to teach the physiology of the sense organs at Cambridge, where he established the first systematic practical courses in experimental psychology in Britain; in 1897 he was elected to a newly established lectureship in physiological and experimental psychology.[45]

Rivers, however, at first declined Haddon's invitation, suggesting instead his student Charles Myers, who had previously attended Haddon's lectures on physical anthropology. Upon hearing from Myers of the venture, William McDougall, another of Rivers' most promising students, proposed that he also go along. When Haddon accepted them both, Rivers, feeling "rather run down" and "much in need of a holiday," decided after all to join the group if Haddon would have him; as a result, the expedition included not one but three psychologists. The trainee in field anthropology was Anthony Wilkin, who as an undergraduate at King's College had heard Haddon lecture on sociology. Finally, there was another volunteering friend of Myers and McDougall, a young medical pathologist named Charles Seligman, whose persistence in the face of doubts about his health and personality was at the last minute rewarded.[46]

Haddon was not able to find the private benefactor from whom he had hoped to get £2000, and six of the anthropologists had to pay their own way. Cambridge University contributed £475, along with its name, and the promise of a publication subvention from its press. Donations from the British and Queensland governments and several scientific societies raised the total to £1275, which covered the substantial cost of phonographic, photographic, cinematic, and psychological-testing equipment, as well as such items as camp furniture and "articles for native trade." As a result of advance publicity in various scientific journals, the venture came to the attention of Charles Hose, a Cambridge graduate serving as district magistrate in the government of Charles Brooke, the Rajah of Sarawak, who at Hose's instigation invited the group to come there with all expenses paid. Although Haddon emphasized that the major purpose of the expedition was to study the islanders of Torres Straits in relation to "their neighbours in New Guinea and Australia," arrangements were made to allow several months' work on Borneo.[47]

After a six-week trip by boat, on April 22, 1898, six of the expedition members arrived at Thursday Island, where they were met by Seligman, who had gone on ahead. From there they sailed east in two groups, one of which endured a week-long trip in a crowded, storm-tossed ketch. At Murray (Mer) Island, they were welcomed by the long-resident schoolmaster and magistrate, Jack Bruce, and by the natives, to whom Haddon showed photographs from his first visit: "it was a steamy and smelly performance, but it was jolly to be again among my old friends." For the next four months, Rivers, Myers, and McDougall remained on Mer, carrying out the first extended series of psychological and physiological tests ever performed on native populations. After three weeks of collecting medical, linguistic, physical anthropological, and general ethnographic data, the other four left on the London Missionary Society's schooner *Olive Branch* for Port Moresby, and thence for a tour of mission station villages down the southeastern coast of New Guinea; on July 20 three of them returned to Mer, leaving Seligman to work in the Rigo district. After another month on Mer, Myers and McDougall went off as an advance

The members of the Torres Straits Expedition, with unidentified assistants. Alfred Haddon (looking down) and Anthony Wilkin in the front row; William Rivers and Sydney Ray in the second; Charles Myers, William McDougall, and Charles Seligman in the rear. (Courtesy of the Cambridge University Museum of Archaeology and Anthropology)

guard of the expedition to Sarawak, and two weeks later, on September 8, Haddon, Rivers, Wilkin, and Ray joined Seligman for a tour along the western shore and among the islands of the Gulf of Papua. They all spent a fortnight on Kiwai in the Fly River delta, where they enjoyed the hospitality of the Reverend James ("Tamate") Chalmers; Ray stayed there to work on linguistics, while the others went for a month to Mabuiag Island, where Haddon had worked a decade previously.[48]

Toward the end of October, Rivers and Wilkin sailed for England, while Haddon, Ray, and Seligman went for three weeks to Saibai, southwest of the Fly delta, before sailing (via Hongkong and Singapore) for Sarawak. Three weeks after arriving in Kuching on December 12, they sailed northeast along the coast to join McDougall and Hose at Limbang. Although Myers had by this time left for England, the others travelled with Hose by dugout up the Limbang and Madalam Rivers, across the watershed, and back down the Baram River to Marudi, through jungles where three years earlier a punitive expedition had been sent to punish "rebel" headhunters. (Haddon, although favorably impressed with the "mild despotism" of the "white Rajah," considered it illogical to allow the Iban Dyak members of punitive expeditions against "a recalcitrant headhunting chief" to keep any heads they managed to procure along the way.) From Marudi, the four remaining anthropologists made several journeys up river into the interior with Hose, into areas where "only three or four white men had previously been," before departing finally for England late in April 1899.[49]

The Cambridge Anthropological Expedition to Torres Straits was described by later social anthropologists as a "turning point" and the "beginning of a new phase" in the history of British social anthropology. And indeed it was. Not, however, in terms of the impact of its ethnographic data on anthropological theory, nor (with one major exception) in terms of its contribution to ethnographic method.* Certainly, it did not mark the beginning of fieldwork in the modern anthropological sense—which was better exemplified in the work of Spencer and Gillen. Myers spoke of his Borneo venture as "a delightful way to spend a holiday and to acquire a general knowledge of the customs and character of the people," but believed that "more than this is difficult owing to the reserve and suspicious bearing of the natives towards strangers and to the difficulties of language." Most of the expedition's work before the Borneo tour consisted of brief stays among missionized natives; none of the investigators learned a native language, and much of the ethno-

*In addition to psychological testing, the Torres Straits Expedition experimented with several other innovative modes of data gathering, including wax cylinder sound-recording and ethnographic cinematography, of which several minutes survive in the Cambridge Museum of Ethnology and Archaeology. With Haddon's encouragement, Spencer also filmed Aborigines in 1901 and 1912 (De Brigard 1975:36).

graphic data they collected had a somewhat random character. Despite Haddon's scientific dedication and transcultural geniality, the surviving documentary evidence suggests that he was not an impressive fieldworker. Although he collected a great many skulls and artifacts, actual fieldnotes form a minuscule part of his extensive papers, and are far outweighed by his reading notes on the writings of others and by letters sent to him by missionaries, traders, and others with whom he remained in correspondence (in contrast, the proportion of such material in the papers of Malinowski is insignificant).[50]

There was, however, one major methodological innovation associated with the Torres Straits Expedition that was to have far-reaching significance: Rivers' "genealogical method." Although he was not the first ethnographer to collect genealogies or to suggest their more general usefulness to anthropology, Rivers came to genealogies independently through Francis Galton, whom he had consulted before leaving England. His original goal was similar to that which had motivated Galton's own earlier *Inquiries into Human Faculty:* "to discover whether those who were closely related resembled one another in their reactions to the various psychological and physiological tests." But when he realized that the genealogical memories of the islanders went back as far as three or even five generations, Rivers began, with "Dr. Haddon's encouragement," to collect the data for its potential sociological value as well. Using only a few basic English categories ("father," "mother," "child," "husband," "wife"), Rivers tried in pidgin English, sometimes clarified (or further complicated) by native interpreters, to get from each informant (usually male, and in general statements referred to as such) the personal names and marital connections of his parents, siblings, children, and grandrelatives: "what name wife belong him?" "what piccaninny he got?" He also tried to ensure that the terms were used in their "real" or "proper English" (i.e., biological) sense, and did not elicit some classificatory or adoptive relative: "he proper father?" "he proper mother?" Viewed with retrospective sophistication as to the ambiguities of social and biological kinship, this image of Rivers' ethnography-in-process may elicit a condescending smile. But to Rivers the method seemed self-correcting against error or deception, because the same sets of relationships could be elicited on separate occasions or by different observers from different informants (since the genealogies overlapped). Thus even after Rivers had returned to England, the "chief" of Mabuiag, anxious to draw up his own record "for the use and guidance of his descendants," created another version (recorded and sent along by the local trader) which, save for "minor discrepancies," confirmed information previously collected by Rivers.[51]

As we shall see, Rivers' genealogical method led him back to the

Morganian tradition of social evolutionism, and thence to theoretical issues of great significance for the future of British anthropology. But his work was equally influential from the perspective of ethnographic method. It seemed to offer a methodological shortcut, by which scientifically trained observers, "with no knowledge of the language and very inferior interpreters," could in a "comparatively short time" collect information that had remained hidden from the most observant long-term European residents, even to the point of laying bare the basic structure of the indigenous society. It provided a framework in which all members of a local group could be located, and to which could be attached a broad range of ethnographic information on "the social condition of each person included in the pedigrees": data on residence, totems, clan membership, miscellaneous behavioral and biographical information. Beyond such sociological matters, it could in fact be used to study demography, physical anthropology, migrations, linguistics, even magic and religion. Most important, it enabled the observer "to study abstract problems, on which the savage's ideas are vague, by means of concrete facts, of which he is a master"—thereby making it possible "to formulate laws regulating the lives of the people which they have probably never formulated themselves, certainly not with the clearness and definiteness which they have to the mind trained by a more complex civilisation." Not only could the observing scientist delineate the actual social laws of a particular group, he could detect also how far its laws, whether explicit or implicit, "were being actually followed in practice."[52]

It was in this context of evolutionary and methodological hubris that Rivers' "genealogical" method was to be elaborated, in the fourth edition of *Notes and Queries*, as the "concrete" method. Its power was attested not only by students but by independent observers who might have been biassed against academic presumption—"men on the spot" such as G. Orde Brown, who, after telling Rivers that kinship data were unobtainable among a particular group in Kenya, had been urged to try Rivers' method: "and now I find that he was right, and that I was completely wrong, in spite of my then three years experience of these people."[53]

But if Rivers' work was a landmark in the development of ethnographic method, the ethnographic results of the expedition as a whole had nothing like the impact of the monograph that Spencer and Gillen had published the very year that it returned. Two years afterward, Haddon published for a popular audience a plodding narrative account of the expedition, *Head-hunters, Black, White, and Brown*, in which the uncertain relativizing of his ethnocentric assumption is suggested by his comment that when it came to "dealing with primitive peoples," he preferred "humanising" as opposed to "civilising" or "Europeanising." The impact within anthropology of the expedition's seven large volumes of *Reports* was diminished somewhat by their rather slow appearance in print. Appropriately, in view of the personnel and the originating goals of the expedition, the two large parts of the volume on *Physiology and Psychology* were the first out, in 1901 and 1903. The two volumes on the *Sociology, Magic, and Religion* of the western and eastern islanders appeared in 1904 and 1908; Ray's on *Linguistics* in 1907, and Haddon's on *Arts and Crafts* in 1912. Haddon's *General Ethnography* (which was originally listed as a volume on *Physical Anthropology*) did not in fact see print until 1935. By that time the embracive evolutionary conception of anthropology that justified such a diffuse and multidisciplinary enterprise had been called seriously into question. Far from being accepted as a general methodological paradigm, the Cambridge Expedition became something of a methodological albatross for several early academic anthropologists who, alone in the field, attempted to carry on a similar range of inquiries.[54]

The difficulties of such a general anthropological enterprise had been evident to Haddon from the beginning. As early as the end of his first stay in the Torres Straits he had concluded that to be a "proper anthropologist" required "wider knowledge and more versatile talents" than any one person could claim. Such a paragon should be "a linguist, artist, musician and have an extensive knowledge of natural and mechanical science, etc."—and by 1898, Haddon had in fact upped the disciplinary ante with the addition of psychology, physiology, and sociology. Perhaps with the larger nineteenth-century maritime expeditions in mind, he had adopted the idea of a multidisciplinary team of investigators. A man who called his secretary "comrade" and liked to think of scientific work as a cooperative enterprise to which "we all contribute our mites," Haddon continued for a while to plan in large-scale terms. In 1906, he presented to the Royal Geographical Society a scheme for an expedition that would operate throughout Melanesia from a large ocean steamer which would have a permanent staff, consisting of director, doctor, photographers, and typists, and would drop off field investigators at suitable spots, returning at intervals to collect their information and provide them access to its facilities. But in his numerous pleas on behalf of what he began to call "field work" (a term he seems to have introduced into anthropology) there is in fact a shift toward an ethnographic model quite different from that of the Torres Straits Expedition.[55]

In speaking of "field work" (sometimes with a unifying hyphen) Haddon probably had in mind the activity of the field naturalist. Certainly, his thinking on the matter was cast very much in biological terms, even as he moved toward a model much closer to that of the classic period of modern ethnography. He thought of the Melanesian islands as "a fairly well-marked biological province," whose anthropology had only begun to be studied, and would soon no longer be possible, because of the "dying out or modification" of culture and the "shifting and mixing of populations." In order to elucidate "the nature, origin and distribution of the races and peoples of the West Pacific," what was required was a series of "intensive studies of restricted areas." Although "intensive study" was a logical follow-up to the "survey work" of the Torres Straits Expedition, it would not, in Haddon's view, entirely replace it. Since "all cultures were mixed," "surveys" should be taken of the neighboring cultures that might have influenced the one being studied intensively. "More extensive surveys" would also serve to "elucidate the broader aspects of [the] distributions" of physical types, material objects, and "customs or cults" as well as to suggest "promising sites for more intensive investigation." It was, however, the "intensive study of a limited area" which became the emblematic slogan for the brave band of academically trained "field-anthropologists" Haddon hoped to create.[56]

In the early stages of his campaign, Haddon still tended to accept a division between "synthetic students" who were a sort of "intelligence department" directing "the workers in the field" and even to think of fieldwork itself as a kind of interim salvage project that would "save for posterity that information which we alone can collect," thereby creating a "mine of information for present and future generations of students of man." But he also insisted on the need for "trained observers"—"scientific men trained in anthropological methods"; and if in 1910 he still accepted a division between "field-workers" and "arm-chair" workers, he now argued that "the most valuable generalisations are made, however, when the observer is at the same time a generaliser."[57]

Although his more ambitious schemes were never realized, Haddon's efforts largely succeeded in redefining the image of what it was to be an ethnographer. Not himself a brilliant fieldworker, nor the articulator of the model which gradually emerged, he did nevertheless have a strong sense of "field-work," and of the training of academic fieldworkers, as a missionary project. When Seligman later said that "field research in anthropology is what the blood of martyrs is to the Church," he was speaking as a representative of the "Cambridge School" which Haddon had done more than any other man to establish.[58]

The "Cambridge School" and the Redefinition of "Intensive Study"

Haddon's hope that the Torres Straits Expedition would lead to the founding of a "School of Anthropology at Cambridge" soon began to be realized. While he was overseas, the work of lecturing on physical anthropology to students of anatomy had been taken over by a medical man, W. H. L. Duckworth; when Haddon returned he had nothing but the Dublin post which since 1893 had been the means to "earn the bread" that let him "work at anthropology in Cambridge for nothing." However, James G. Frazer (long at Cambridge, though he taught no anthropology) and William Ridgeway, the Disney Professor of Archaeology, joined in organizing support for Haddon among other faculty members, and in May of 1900, he was appointed University Lecturer in Ethnology. The salary was only a quarter of the £200 a year he had hoped to receive, and for a time Haddon thought of abandoning anthropology entirely. But his situation began to improve in 1901, when he was made a Fellow of Christ's College and felt secure enough to resign his Dublin post; a year after that, he was also appointed the first Lecturer in Ethnology under the newly organized program in sociology at the London School of Economics. By that time, the support for anthropology that for more than a decade had been slowly growing in various sectors of the Cambridge faculty coalesced in a Memorial on the Study of Anthropology signed by thirty-one members of the senate—including Frazer, Haddon, Rivers, Ridgeway, the historians Bury and Ward, the zoologist Sedgwick, and Baron von Hügel, the curator of the Museum of Archaeology and Ethnology. Within a year, a Board of Anthropological Studies was established to provide instruction in "Prehistoric and Historic Anthropology and Ethnology (including Sociology and Comparative Religion), Physical Anthropology, and Psychological Anthropology." In 1908, the board was empowered to grant a diploma upon completion of a thesis; the year after that, Haddon was finally appointed as Reader in Ethnology, with the salary he had hoped for ten years previously—which enabled him belatedly to enjoy the relatively comfortable life of an Edwardian academic gentleman.[59]

Haddon himself did no further ethnographic fieldwork after 1914; but he was recognized as leader of the "Cambridge School." In the first instance, it consisted of the personnel of the Torres Straits Expedition itself. Not all were to continue in anthropology. Although Anthony Wilkin accompanied two archeological expeditions to Upper Egypt, and did research among the Berbers of Algeria, he died prematurely from dysentery in Cairo in 1901—the promise he showed being remembered only in the popular account of his Berber work and the research fellowship that his parents established in his name at Cambridge. Sydney Ray's fate was perhaps symbolic of the marginal status of linguistic inquiry in the emergent tradition of British social anthropology: although he continued to publish on linguistic matters, and was widely acknowledged as a brilliant student of Oceanic languages, he lived out his life as an elementary schoolmaster, despite various efforts Haddon made to secure something better for him. Both Myers and McDougall were in the long run to remain in psychology, where each was very influential. Myers in 1909 published what was long the standard text in experimental psychology, and was for many years the leading figure in the British Psychological Society. McDougall wrote influential textbooks on physiological psychology and social psychology, before turning to racially oriented speculations about the "group mind"; he subsequently emigrated to the United States, where he instituted parapsychological research at Duke University and published a critique of American democracy. But in the early days of his career, each man made an anthropological contribution—Myers, in the form of an extensive anthropometric study of soldiers in the Egyptian and Sudanese armies in 1901; McDougall, as co-author (or "midwife") of a two-volume ethnographic survey, *The Pagan Tribes of Borneo,* based on Charles Hose's twenty-four years of experience as ambulatory administrator.[60]

Of the alumni of the Torres Straits Expedition, it was Seligman and Rivers who, both as fieldworkers and exemplars, were to provide the active ethnographic core of the Cambridge School. Seligman, the only child of a well-to-do Jewish wine merchant, had trained as a pathologist, and in fact for a decade returned to that career. In 1904, however, with support from a wealthy American he met on a fishing holiday, he went back to Melanesia for a further coastal survey which led to a volume that was to serve as the basepoint for later studies in the region. The following year he married Brenda Z. Salaman, who gave up her own premedical training to become his ethnographic partner. She became a specialist in kinship and social organization, while Seligman collected data for a more traditional ethnological classification (physical types, material culture, customs, etc.). In 1906, at the suggestion of Haddon, who was anxious to have studies of "the most backward peoples," the couple worked among the Veddahs of Ceylon. In 1909 they were off on the first of three survey expeditions into the Anglo-Egyptian Sudan, where Brenda remarked how "queer" it was to see the otherwise quite "primitive" Nuba men, "absolutely nude," carrying rifles. Typically, she would "plug away" at genealogies, "mostly in Arabic," while "Sligs" would take head measurements. The eventual result was another benchmark survey, *The Pagan Tribes of the Nilotic Sudan.*[61]

During the same period, Rivers (whose career we will consider in much greater detail) went on to do research among the Todas in India, before returning twice to Melanesia.[62] Both Seligman and Rivers were to play important roles in training the rising generation of fieldworkers who worked increasingly in the "intensive" mode: Rivers at Cambridge in cooperation with Haddon; Seligman at the London School of Eco-

C. G. Seligman, interviewing informants on the verandah of the mission house at Hula on the Hood Peninsula on the southeastern coast of New Guinea, 1904. (Courtesy of the Cambridge University Museum of Archaeology and Anthropology)

nomics, where in 1910 he joined the Anglo-Finnish sociologist Edward Westermarck, who himself had done extensive fieldwork in Morocco. At Oxford, both Rivers and Seligman, along with Haddon, served occasionally as informal extramural ethnographic mentors to the fieldworkers who began to be trained there after 1905.

The first of the new generation of academically trained anthropologists to go into the field was Radcliffe-Brown, who went to the Andamans in 1905. But there were at least nine others who undertook the "intensive study of a limited area" before the Great War. Gerald C. Wheeler of the London School of Economics and Arthur M. Hocart of Oxford accompanied Rivers on the Percy Sladen Trust Expedition in 1908; Wheeler spent ten months among the Mono-Alu in the Western Solomons; Hocart stayed on in Fiji for four years, where as schoolmaster he collected a rich body of ethnographic data. Diamond Jenness, an Oxonian from New Zealand whose sister had married a missionary in the D'Entrecasteaux, spent nine months on Goodenough Island in 1910, and then went off for several years of intensive work among the Eskimo. Two young Finns followed Westermarck to England to work under Haddon's tutelage: Gunnar Landtman left in 1910 for two years on Kiwai Island; Rafael Karsten worked among three tribes in the Bolivian Chaco in 1911 and 1912. And despite Haddon's gendered image of the "trained scientific man," there were in fact two Oxford-trained women: Barbara Freire-Marecco, who worked among the Pueblo Indians of the American Southwest, and Marie Czaplička (like Bronislaw Malinowski, a Polish émigré), who spent a strenuous year on the Arctic Circle among the Tungus in 1914. And when Malinowski in the fall of that year set off for the southeastern coast of Papua to follow up another Torres Straits survey with more intensive study, yet another offspring of the Cambridge School, John Layard, was settling in for two years' work on Atchin off the coast of Malekula.[63]

That the contribution of these ten inheritors of Haddon's initiative should have been obscured in the disciplinary memory by Malinowski's tithe is in part a reflection of biographical accident (emigration, military service, mental breakdown, early death) and institutional marginality (careers outside of England or outside of anthropology). Some of the other nine seem clearly to have been, by present standards, quite competent ethnographers; Hocart's fieldnotes reveal him as an unusually sensitive fieldworker. But their monographs were slow in appearing and conventional in style, and they seem not to have thought of or represented themselves as ethnographic innovators.[64] Landtman, who like Malinowski was sent out to follow up a Torres Straits survey with a more "intensive study," may perhaps stand for the rest.

Insofar as one can infer from photographs and from Landtman's long letters to Haddon from the field, his ethnographic situation was somewhere between that of Malinowski in Mailu and in the Trobriands: the Kiwai natives were less acculturated than the former but more missionized than the latter. Although Landtman preferred to live at the mission station, there were times when he lived "among the natives"—who, after he joined them on dugong hunts, described him, he said, as "this white man he another kind, all same me fellow." Landtman recorded observational data, but he seems to have conceived of his method primarily in terms of working closely with individual (and paid) informants (or, as he put it more aptly in one letter to Haddon, "teachers"). Although he did learn some Kiwai, and wrote a perceptive little essay on the nature of pidgin as a language in its own right, the many passages of quoted material in his ethnography make it clear that he worked primarily in the latter tongue. Even so, his monograph received Malinowski's imprimatur as that of "a master of the modern sociological method in fieldwork."[65]

Malinowski could afford to be generous after the fact, for although Landtman had gone into the field before Malinowski came to England to enter the service of the Cambridge School, his book did not appear until four years after Malinowski's epoch-marking monograph. Landtman's fieldnotes had been lost in a shipwreck on his return to Europe, and he had to hire a diver to recover the trunk that contained them. By the time his ethnography appeared in 1927, he had already returned to Finland, where he became Westermarck's successor as Professor of Sociology. The book he left behind was cumbrously entitled *The Kiwai Papuans of British New Guinea: A Nature-born Instance of Rousseau's Ideal Community*. A rather prosaic descriptive ethnography, it had none of the mythopoeic resonances of Malinowski's *Argonauts*, nor anything approximating the self-proclaiming methodological charter of Malinowski's opening chapter.[66]

And yet, as Malinowski's review suggested, both he and Landtman were products of the "school" that had grown out of the Torres Straits Expedition. Of that school's leading figures, it was Rivers who articulated most clearly just how "intensive study" should be carried on. Reflecting on his own further ethnographic efforts and those of others (notably Hocart, with whom he worked for three months on Eddystone Island), Rivers by 1912 had moved far beyond the insouciant scientism of some of his discussions of the "genealogical method."

Five years previously, the British Association for the Advancement of Science had established a committee to prepare a fourth edition of *Notes and Queries*. Tylor, who had chaired the committees that produced the editions of 1892 and 1899 (the latter little more than a reprinting), was by now superannuated, and the new committee was chaired by Charles Hercules Read, who had long been associated with the Department of British and Mediaeval Antiquities and Ethnography of the British Museum. Read had in fact written a preface for the section on ethnography in the two 1890s editions which gave a clear premonition of an impending paradigm change in ethnographic method. Read was by then aware that the volume's numbered queries were not so easily answered as the armchair founders had assumed. Even to get "superficial answers" to many of them "would necessitate a long-continued residence among a native race." The "timid answers of natives" to questions transmitted by a "native interpreter" were unreliable, and more apt to produce "confusion" than "benefit to comparative anthropology." Read gave the matter an evolutionary explanation: the limits of "vocabulary or of ideas" in a "savage in the lower stages of culture" often made it extremely difficult to phrase a question "in such a way that he can comprehend it." The result was that "from timidity, or the desire to please, or from weariness of the questioning, he will give an answer that he thinks will satisfy the inquirer." "If time serve," these difficulties might be overcome in "friendly intercourse," facilitated by equality of physical status ("if they sit upon the ground, he should do the same") and by "checking of answers through different individuals." But for the most part, Read thought it doubtful that the amateur traveller could accomplish very much in "a short stay among a savage people," and he retreated into a kind of indexical positivism: "the best plan seems to be to devote as much time as possible to the photographic camera or to make careful drawings, for by these means the traveller is dealing with facts about which there can be no question, and the record thus obtained may be elucidated by subsequent inquirers on the same spot."[67]

If in 1899 Read could only hint at an ethnographic alternative to the numbered questionnaire, by 1912, when the fourth edition of *Notes and Queries* was published, that alternative had begun to be realized in the practice of the Cambridge School. With Read on the committee of revision were four Torres Straits alumni: Haddon, Rivers, Myers, and, later, Seligman. The publication that finally appeared, after some conflict between the old guard and the young turks, was in many respects a new departure. It was still ostensibly directed to "travellers" and others who were not anthropologists but who might "supply the information which is wanted for the scientific study of anthropology at home." And despite the urging of "friendly critics" that a "narrative form" be adopted, many sections still reflected the "old lists of 'leading questions' " of the three Tylorian editions. But the "friendly critics" had clearly had a great impact. John Linton Myres, the Oxford archeologist who was the only contributor to write more pages than Rivers, described Rivers' contribution as "a revelation" that set a new "standard for worksmanship in the field." It was quite evident that the "workers in the field" for whom Rivers wrote were not casual travellers but people in a position to undertake "intensive study."[68]

The centerpiece of the whole volume, Rivers' "General Account of Method," was in effect a programmatic systematization of the ethnographic experience of the Cambridge School. Here, the distinction between "survey" work and "intensive study" was recast in linguistic terms: because (as was suggested elsewhere in the volume) "language is our only key to the correct and complete understanding of the life and thought of a people," Rivers insisted that the investigator's "first duty" was "to acquire as completely as possible" a knowledge of their language—although he still felt that it was better to rely on an interpreter than on "an inadequate knowledge of the language." Although Rivers still gave special prominence to the genealogical method, it was now valued as a means of enabling the inquirer "to use the very instrument which the people themselves use in dealing with their social problems," so that in studying "the formation and nature of their social classifications," the "influence of civilised categories" might be entirely excluded.[69]

Although Rivers still appealed to the nature of "the thought of people of the lower cultures" to justify his first rule of method ("the abstract should always be approached through the concrete"), he now placed great emphasis on the problem of category differences: "the greatest caution must be used in obtaining information by means of direct questions, since it is probable that such questions will inevitably suggest some civilised category." Indeed, special attention should be paid to volunteered information, even if it interrupted one's train of thought: instead of complaining of the difficulty of keeping an informant to the point, the investigator should recognize that "the native also has a point, probably of far more interest than his own."[70]

Rivers' "investigator" was still more an "inquirer" than an "observer"; he was strongly encouraged, however, to get the corroboration of "two or more independent witnesses" and was cautioned that disagreements among them were "one of the most fruitful sources of knowledge": "a man who will tell you nothing spontaneously often cannot refrain from correcting false information." Wherever possible, the investigator was to supplement verbal accounts with the actual witnessing of ceremonies, and was told to "take advantage of any events of social importance which occur during your stay," since "the thorough study of a concrete case in which social regulations have been broken may give more insight into the moral ideas of the people than a month of questioning about what they think right or wrong." Last but not least, the inquirer was to develop "sympathy and tact," without which "it is certain that the best kind of work will never be done." Although Rivers urged this on grounds of expedience ("people of rude culture are so unaccustomed to any such evidence of sympathy with their ways of thinking and acting" that it would "go far to break down their reticence"), he cautioned that natives would be "quick to recognize whether this sympathy is real or feigned."[71]

As a kind of footnote to the new edition of *Notes and Queries,* Rivers the following year published a statement on the needs of anthropological research in which he narrowed and refined the conception of "intensive study" that had emerged in the work of the Cambridge School. Indeed, this essay may be taken as marking, at the programmatic level, the transition in British anthropology from the ethnographic model of the Torres Straits Expedition (in which a team of investigators divided the labor of a multifocal general anthropological survey) to the usual modern model of more narrowly focussed sociological inquiry by a single "participant observer." On the one hand, Rivers explicitly subordinated certain traditional concerns of a general anthropology, either because their data were less immediately endangered (as in the case of archeology) or because pursuing them risked destroying the rapport necessary for intensive "sociological" study (as in the case of material culture and physical anthropology). Similarly, because of the "disturbance and excitement produced among natives by the various activities of the different members of an expedition," Rivers now urged that ethnographic work should be carried on instead by a single investigator "working alone." As further justification, he argued that the labor of ethnography should not be divided, because the subject matter was indivisible. In a "rude" culture, the domains civilized men designated as politics, religion, education, art, and technology were interdependent and inseparable, and it followed that "specialism in the collection of ethnographic details must be avoided at all costs." Rivers did insist, however, on the specialization of the ethnographer's role itself. Government officials and missionaries could not do the job because their regular duties left them little time, because they lacked the appropriate training, and because their occupations brought them into conflict with native ideas and customs—even, in the case of missionaries, to the point of embracing the "duty to destroy them." Rivers therefore felt that ethnography was best carried on by "private workers," preferably with special training or experience "in exact methods in other sciences."[72]

Such were the conditions of "intensive work," which Rivers defined as that "in which the worker lives for a year or more among a community of perhaps four or five hundred people and studies every detail of their life and culture; in which he comes to know every member of the community personally; in which he is not content with generalized information, but studies every feature of life and custom in concrete detail and in the vernacular language." That, of course, was exactly what Malinowski did in the Trobriands, and later retrospectively archetypified in what was to become the better-known public charter of modern ethnographic method. But as Rivers' argument in fact implies, and as was evident elsewhere in the 1912 *Notes and Queries*, the practice of "intensive" ethnographic study by the "concrete" method had correlates in the realm of anthropological theory. As long as "the aim of anthropology" was "to teach us the history of mankind"—as Rivers still felt it to be—the bustle of village activity could have only mediate rather than intrinsic interest. It is not accidental that the period in which the "intensive study of limited areas" became "participant observation" was also a period of considerable theoretical ferment as well.[73]

FOUR

The Frazerian Moment

Evolutionary Anthropology in Disarray

When Bronislaw Malinowski was asked to write the article on "Anthropology" for the thirteenth edition of the *Encyclopaedia Britannica* in 1926, he did so by recounting developments since "the events of 1910"—which, although he did not mention it, had been the year of his own arrival in England. The publication of James G. Frazer's four-volume evolutionary study of totemism in that year, followed by William Rivers' move from "evolutionism" to "diffusionism" in 1911, had marked the beginning of a fifteen-year period of theoretical contention ending in the triumph of the "functionalist" anthropology of which Malinowski's article was a major manifesto. And indeed he had more than personalistic justification for regarding the end of the first twentieth-century decade as a significant marker in the history of British anthropology. But the theoretical and methodological issues Malinowski encountered when he got to England had in fact been developing over a somewhat longer period—a process roughly paralleling (and interacting with) the emergence of the fieldwork tradition whose paradigmatic exemplar Malinowski was to become.[1]

In contrast to the situation in the United States, where the reaction against evolutionism in anthropology may be clearly marked in retrospect by the publication of Boas' essay on "The Limitations of the Comparative Method of Anthropology" in 1896, the movement away from evolutionism in the British anthropological tradition was a relatively gradual process, focussing on a somewhat different set of anthropological issues. In the Boasian tradition, the anti-evolutionary impulse was expressed in a general reconsideration of the biological and cultural differences between "primitive" and "civilized" "races"—on the one hand through a fairly systematic critique of static typological notions of race, and on the other through a more implicit pluralization and relativization of the hierarchical evolutionary conception of culture. In Britain, there was nothing approximating the Boasian critique of race until the 1930s, and the reconsideration of the idea of culture took a different course to a different outcome.[2]

To cast a complex matter in simplifying biographical terms, in 1896 there was no British Boas. The period of Boas' anthropological ascent in the United States was the period of Tylor's anthropological decline in Great Britain—but there was no single figure who emerged from Tylor's shadow to play an institutional and intellectual role analogous to that of Boas in the United States. In general anthropological outlook, Haddon was closest; but his intellect lacked the critical cutting edge of Boas', and his academic persona was of a less dynamic sort. Haddon's most serious theoretical effort took the form of a somewhat pedestrian attempt to apply biological methods to the study of cultural forms; for the most part, his generalizing writings were popularizations of a rather traditional ethnological sort (the races of man, the migrations of peoples). His institutionalizing endeavors took place within a much more constraining academic tradition, and after the establishment of the Cambridge School, had only modest success. Coming slightly later on the scene than Haddon, William Rivers was to cut a very large swath in the fifteen years after 1910, but his energies were never permanently focussed entirely on anthropology, and his theoretical and methodological concerns pulled in several different directions. Rather than sweeping the field, his "conversion" to diffusionist ethnology in 1911 simply opened it further to theoretical competition, in which evolutionary anthropologists were active participants long after some of their underlying assumptions had been called into question.[3]

Retreating gradually into senescence after 1896, Tylor was not himself a likely candidate to lead a "reformation in anthropology" or to tighten its "logical screw." But with the British anthropological world awaiting the appearance of his magnum opus, Tylor nevertheless continued for a time to be an evolutionary presence, despite the apostate goadings of Andrew Lang. It was in this extended moment of slowly waning paradigmatic potency that James G. Frazer, whom some more recent social anthropologists have had difficulty taking seriously, even in retrospect, was to be a major figure on the anthropological scene—if only by serving as the focal point of conceptual debate.*

*An extreme manifestation of the long-dominant British social anthropological attitude toward Frazer was expressed in several articles by Edmund Leach. One of these, written in 1966, was a response to the attempt by Ian Jarvie to reorient British social anthropology on rationalistic, comparativist lines, and in the process to renarrativize its history (1964). (See also Leach 1961.) More recently, there have been evidences of a reappreciation. Kuper (1988:211–16) has credited Frazer's treatment of cross-cousin marriage in *Folklore in the Old Testament* (1918:II, 97) as the ultimate source of the "alliance theory" of Claude Lévi-Strauss. In the aftermath of the reaction against structural-functionalism, anthropologists

Though his "intellectualism" was a focus of discussion, Frazer was not himself a direct participant in this debate; holding his theoretical opinions loosely, he had little taste for controversy, the more so as it might distract him from the pursuit of his own literary agenda. There were, however, other "third generation" evolutionists, also influenced by Tylor, but more évolué than Frazer, who came upon the scene in the 1890s and were more active contributors to disciplinary discourse and who helped to define the later direction of British anthropology: notably, Edward Westermarck and Robert Ranulph Marett.

Significantly, the anthropological careers of all three men were at one point oriented to traditional philosophical issues—epistemological, psychological, or ethical—that were in some sense problematic for the evolutionary tradition. Although Frazer was an academic protégé of William Robertson Smith and was for a time at personal odds with Tylor, his anthropology remained the most traditionally Tylorian—until long after Tylor was dead and evolutionism had been pushed from the center of anthropological speculation by tendencies that Westermarck and Marett helped to form. Beginning their careers under Tylor's aegis, both men took up lines of speculation that were to call evolutionism into question; both, however, remained in a broad sense evolutionary anthropologists throughout their careers. Although one of the three (Westermarck) had in fact substantial fieldwork experience, and the other two were strongly supportive of field ethnographers either in the older epistolary or the newer academic mode, all three of them remained very much in the earlier tradition of "armchair anthropology." But in rather different ways, each of them contributed substantially both to the disarray of evolutionary anthropology in the period before World War I and to the formation of the issues out of which the major postwar tendencies were to emerge.

James Frazer and *The Golden Bough*: From Magic to Religion to Science

When William James was in Rome in December 1900, he chanced to stay in the same *pensione* as James and Lilly Frazer: "he of the 'Golden Bough,' 'Pausanias,' and other three- and six-volume works of anthropological

associated with the "literary turn" in anthropology, struck by the fact that "functionalists write, too," have developed a certain sympathy for Frazer (Boon 1982:9–21, 1983; Strathern 1987:80, whose essay is presented as "a confession of someone brought up to view Sir James Frazer in a particular way who has discovered that the context for that view has shifted"). There has also been interest in such Frazerian problems as divine kingship (Vaughn 1980).

erudition, Fellow of Trinity College, Cambridge, and a sucking babe of humility, unworldliness and molelike sightlessness to everything but *print;* she a deaf and lebenslustig cosmopolitan Frenchwoman, clever in all sorts of directions, a widow with a motherly heart, who has adopted him and nurses him." William James was no stranger to the intellectual life of the nation in which his brother Henry had settled. As early as the 1870s he had been a frequent contributor to the psychological/philosophical journal *Mind;* during a lengthy visit in 1882 he became part of a circle of defenders of empiricism against the invasion of Hegelian influences, as well as a critic of traditional associationist psychology—and an active participant in the Society for Psychical Research. His *Principles of Psychology* was a major influence on the development of the field in Britain after 1890; a few years later, *The Will to Believe* announced the radical and voluntaristic empiricism of his mature philosophy. Before a breakdown of his health forced a change in plans, his trip to Europe in 1900 had originally been occasioned by an invitation to give the Gifford Lectures in Edinburgh, which were published in 1903 as *The Varieties of Religious Experience.* It was in this context that James found it "amusing" that the man who "after Tylor" was "the greatest authority now in England on the religious ideas and superstitions of primitive peoples" knew nothing of psychical research, and thought that "trances, etc., of savage soothsayers and the like are all *feigned!*" Fortunately, however, Frazer was also "conscience incarnate," and James was confident that after his "stirring him up," Frazer would "now proceed to put in big loads of work in the morbid psychology direction." James overestimated the power of human reason to convert to the cause of human irrationality a latter-day Tylorian child of the Enlightenment. Despite the moments of sociological pessimism that occasionally marked his anthropology, Frazer never showed any interest in "morbid psychology"; his life was instead, in the words of his biographer, "a monument to sublimation."[4]

First of four children to survive from birth, Frazer was born in 1854 to the wife of a respectable and God-fearing Glasgow chemist, a Gladstonian Liberal and Free Churchman who "accepted the Bible in its literal sense as the inspired and infallible word of God." Withdrawing inward in reaction to the "passionately activist character" of his father, Frazer enjoyed an unusually protected and idyllic childhood lived largely in the world of books that filled his father's substantial library. According to the amanuensis of his later years, Frazer's only actual encounter with "a member of a primitive tribe" took place when a nursemaid took him into a fairground tent to see "The Wild Man of Borneo," and young Frazer retreated "howling with terror"—preferring to satisfy his taste for exoticism by reading Scott, Cervantes, and *The Arabian Nights.* For Frazer, exoticism of whatever sort was always contained within strict limits of propriety: although he was eventually to write a good deal about human marital practices, his amanuensis later joked that he "did not even know the four-letter words, but was limited to the three-letter abstractions of sin and sex." Far from chafing at the restrictions of the strict Presbyterian Sabbath, Frazer found a quiet pleasure in filling the intervals between divine services with edifying books, and "attended church and took part in acts of worship for most of his life." But if there seems to have been no crisis of disbelief, Frazer clearly shed his parents' creed at an early point; later in life, he declared to a friend, with the force of long conviction: "I am not a Christian, on the contrary I reject the Christian religion as utterly false." What he did retain was the lifelong habit of reading about religious belief and the persistent desire to explain why mankind should ever have believed in the first place.[5]

After getting the rudiments of Latin and Greek, and a taste for classical studies, at a suburban academy, Frazer matriculated at the University of Glasgow in 1869. There he felt the influence of three professors: George Ramsey, whose "powerful impulse" directed "the main current" of Frazer's studies "for many years to the classics of antiquity"; John Veitch, the "last representative of the line of purely Scottish philosophers" extending from Hume to Hamilton, "direct heirs and disciples" of Locke and Berkeley—men who wrote "like gentlemen in the language of polished society, and not like pedants in the uncouth jargon of the schools"; and William Thomson (later Lord Kelvin), who gave him "a conception of the physical universe as regulated by exact and absolutely unvarying laws of nature expressible in mathematical formulas." Frazer graduated in 1874, harvesting honors along the way; like Andrew Lang a decade previously, he looked south to Balliol College, Oxford, for further education. But like McLennan a generation before, he was sent instead to Cambridge by parents who feared the "contagion" of Romanizing tendencies in what was still thought of as Cardinal Newman's alma mater.[6]

After four years at Trinity College, where he continued to read classics and reap honors, Frazer yielded to his father's urging and studied law at the Inns of Court. But although he was admitted to the bar in 1882, he never practiced. In 1879 he had competed successfully for a fellowship at Trinity, submitting a dissertation on "The Growth of Plato's Ideal Theory." The subject was inspired by the lectures of Henry Jackson, co-editor of the *Journal of Philology,* who later published a series of articles in which he attempted to assimilate Plato's "Ideas" to the "natural kinds" of John Stuart Mill. Frazer, however, attacked Plato from an empiricist standpoint: citing Mill's *Logic* at several points, he argued that Plato had been guilty of a "gigantic and yet splendid error, which converted [Socrates'] true theory of knowledge into a false theory of being." In a passage foreshadowing much of his future work, he suggested that

Fellowship photograph of James G. Frazer, 1879 (Courtesy of the Master and Fellows of Trinity College Cambridge)

Plato had committed "the same mistake into which savages fall when, from the analogy of their own acts, they ascribe the action of inanimate objects to a principle of life, thought, and feeling inherent in these objects." Renewed at five-year intervals, Frazer's fellowship became tenable for life in 1895; although he ceased actually to live in college several years after his marriage in 1896, he continued for another dozen years to work there, with his wife in attendance, "usually being there from 8 A.M. to midnight!"—a schedule he was to maintain for the rest of his life.[7]

Although his later epistemological position was apparent early on, it took Frazer some time to find his characteristic subject matter. For a brief period in the early 1880s, he fancied himself a philosopher-psychologist. At Trinity, his first two mentors had been Jackson and James Ward, a student of the German idealist Lotze. After abandoning a career as a Congregationalist minister, Ward had come to Trinity as Fellow just before Frazer's matriculation, and was beginning to formulate the critique of associationist psychology he published in the *Encyclopaedia Britannica* in 1886. Frazer, however, seems to have been touched by his mentors' idealism only to a limited extent, and by the critique of associationism not at all. His more important philosophical and psychological models were John Stuart Mill and Herbert Spencer, whom he read in large doses as a Trinity undergraduate. His own psychological aspirations are evident in a notebook on "Philosophy" he began in 1880, in which he proposed to treat "scientific results from a psychological point of view." Arguing that "the only objects of knowledge possible to man are the operations of his own mind," he began by insisting that "the science of Nature is therefore the science of Mind," and went on to maintain that "the increasing differentiation of the brain" was dependent on a prior "increase in thinking"—by means of a Lamarckian evolutionary associationism clearly derived from Herbert Spencer. From there, Frazer went on in a series of fragmentary notes to embrace a Benthamite ethics and a Comtean hierarchy of science, to argue that from "false beliefs (exhibited in systems of philosophy, religions, superstitions, etc.) general truths may be extracted," to suggest (apparently against himself) that "in order to understand Man we must first understand Nature," to discuss the problems of measuring sensations, to reconcile Idealism and Materialism as two complementary views of "the same reality," to propose a means by which Darwinism might overthrow Teleology, and to contrast Talent (Aristotle and Gladstone) and Genius (Plato and Disraeli). As a philosopher Frazer could not claim either—but the notes did carry many of the characteristic markings of his later anthropological writings.[8]

Before he came to anthropology, however, Frazer established what was to be a parallel (and intertwining) strand of his scholarly life: the edition of classical texts. His very first publication was an edition of the Roman historian Sallust, commissioned by a London publishing firm for their Grammar School Classics series. Shortly after its appearance in 1884, he arranged with the publishing house of George Macmillan (who was to become a close friend and the publisher of all his major writings) to prepare an edition of Pausanias, a Greek antiquary and geographer of the second century A.D. Pausanias' *Description of Greece* was full of richly ethnographic accounts of religious practices, myths, and folklore extinct in Athens by the time he wrote but still alive in the Greek countryside. When Frazer's edition finally appeared in 1898, the one volume originally proposed by Macmillan had grown to six volumes, and Frazer's interests had shifted toward anthropology. But after World War I Frazer returned to editing classical texts, and all of his anthropological work was in a sense a commentary upon the sort of cultural disjunctions that Pausanias had observed. Recast in a larger historical and ideological framework, these were the same problems that had motivated Lang's anthropology: the survivals of underlying savagery within the Graeco-Roman and Christian tradition.[9]

The explanation of survivals was, of course, a quintessentially Tylorian project. Frazer had been introduced to Tylor's *Primitive Culture* by James Ward, with whom he took a walking tour in Spain in the spring of 1883, and by early 1885 he had begun to envision his own classical interests in Tylorian terms. Writing for classicists in Jackson's *Journal of Philology,* Frazer tried to explain the obligation of Vestal virgins to tend perpetual temple fires, by venturing a "little way from the weary high-road of Greece and Rome into the virgin forest of comparative custom and religion." What followed was one of those anthropological Cook's tours which filled so many pages of Tylor's *Primitive Culture,* and which were to fill so many more in Frazer's later work. Setting sail from South Africa, Frazer touched at the Andaman Islands (where the natives had not yet learned to start fires, but could keep alive the ones set by lightning); he then hopped off via Tasmania to the New World (where, "to the anthropologist," Louisiana was "a mere step" from New Mexico) before returning to the customs of European peasants. When at the end of his ethnographic odyssey he finally unravelled the mystery that had led him back from ancient Rome "to the embryo state of human civilization," it was not by "any profound [i.e., Müllerian] theory of the relation of the life of man to the courses of the heavens," but in practical utilitarian terms. The fire-tending role of the Vestals could be explained by the "elementary difficulty of rubbing sticks together"; its status as a "survival" was evidenced by the fact that this was the way the Vestals rekindled the perpetual fire on occasions when it accidentally went out. Here, in comparative methodological embryo, was most of Frazer's later anthropology.[10]

There was, however, an important methodological footnote, which was offered in the even more explicitly Tylorian talk Frazer gave to the Anthropological Institute in March 1885—with Galton in the chair, and Herbert Spencer and Tylor in the audience:

> It is to be observed that the explanations which I give of many of the following customs are not the explanations offered by the people who practice these customs. Sometimes people give no explanation of their customs, sometimes (much oftener than not) a wrong one.

Still a novice in evolutionary anthropology, Frazer quite casually, as an aside, proclaimed its authoritative interpretive power—and, by an extension he could not foresee, that of the functionalist fieldworkers who followed after.[11]

The paper itself was important in establishing, at the very beginning of Frazer's anthropological career, his conceptual as well as methodological relationship to Tylor. Entitled "On Certain Burial Customs as Illustrative of the Primitive Theory of the Soul," it clearly foreshadows the basic plot structure of *The Golden Bough*. Frazer started from a single "curious custom" recorded by Plutarch: any man who, "falsely reported to have died abroad, returns home alive," was required to reenter his house by the roof rather than the door. After another extended ethnographic tour in search of ghost beliefs, Frazer concluded that because the man had been defined as dead, and the door of the house was ghost-proof, he was only able to reenter "down the chimney"—after which he was reborn and went through "all the stages of a second childhood."[12]

In the discussion that followed, Galton, who had a penchant for finding problems in other people's evolutionary arguments, raised a fundamental (and, indeed, characteristically Boasian) methodological issue: confronted by a widespread and enduring custom, should one assume its derivation from a single motivational root, or could its manifestation in a variety of conditions rather be the result of diversity of origin and "a concurrence of [different] motives" in sustaining it? Galton himself avoided mentioning the names of the recently dead before their relatives, but for "totally different reasons to that by which the savage was principally governed." Tylor, apparently no more troubled then by such issues than he was to be in 1888, congratulated Frazer on treating classical authors not as "mere ancient texts," but as "repositories of real facts full of anthropological value." Subsuming Frazer's paper within his own conceptual framework, he called it an "ingenious" and "original" contribution to the study of "animistic" funeral customs, although Frazer, while citing Tylor frequently, had not in fact referred explicitly to "animism." Acknowledging Galton's objection only to dismiss it, Frazer expressed his "deep gratitude" to Tylor—whose writings "had first interested him in anthropology," and thereby "marked an epoch" in his life.[13]

But if Tylor led Frazer to anthropology, it was Robertson Smith who guided him toward the topic of his monumental anthropological project. The two Scotsmen met in January 1884, after dinner in the combination room of Trinity College—of which Smith had been a member for two years before migrating to Christ's. When their conversation turned to Arabs in Spain, Frazer ventured to disagree with Smith, despite knowing "next to nothing on the subject." Beaten down "in the kindest and gentlest way" by Smith's erudition, Frazer "yielded [him]self captive at once," and "never afterwards attempted to dispute the mastership which he thenceforward exercised over me by his extraordinary union of genius and learning." Frazer's captivation in fact obscured fundamental differences, both religious and anthropological; but these seem not to have troubled an emotional/intellectual relationship which Frazer's biographer has characterized as one of "courtship" and "love." Then at work on the "P" volume of the *Britannica*, Smith invited Frazer to contribute a number of short articles (Penates, Priapus, Proserpine), and a longer one about Pericles. Frazer recalled that when he had run into difficulties while working on the last, Smith "actually came to my rooms and began writing with his own hand at my dictation or from my notes to oblige me to make a start with it." Jump-started by Smith, Frazer's writing engine never again slowed down (except, briefly, at the onset of a period of depression after Lang started hacking away at *The Golden Bough* in 1901).[14]

With Pericles out of the way, Smith in 1886 asked Frazer to write two nonclassical essays for the "T" volume: one on "Taboo," another on "Totem." Given the direction Smith's own anthropological work had taken in the 1880s, it is not surprising that he took "much personal pains" with the latter, "guiding Frazer carefully in his treatment." The essay in fact took seven months to write, and could be included in the "T" volume only in abridged form; the full version became Frazer's first anthropological book. Together, the two topics were to provide the thematic core of almost all of his subsequent anthropology.[15]

The short article on taboo was essentially descriptive and classificatory, with only the briefest attempt at evolutionary explanation: taboos were "not the creation of a legislator but the gradual outgrowth of animistic beliefs, to which the ambition and avarice of chiefs and priests afterwards gave an artificial extension." And despite Smith's supervising hand, the essay on totemism was also, by Frazer's own later account, "little more than a classified collection of facts" drawn from perhaps five hundred different ethnographic sources; he had as yet "formed no theory either of totemism or exogamy." It does, however, serve to define the status of knowledge at the point when discussion of the two phenomena McLennan had paired twenty years earlier was about to take off into a twenty-year period of constantly intensifying debate—and to suggest something of the orientation of one of its central participants.[16]

In contrast to a "fetich," which was an isolated individual object, Frazer defined a totem as "a class of material objects which a savage regards with superstitious respect, believing that there exists between him and every member of the class an intimate and altogether special relation" which was "mutually beneficent." Of the three major kinds of totems (individual, sex-group, and clan), "by far the most important" was the last, which Frazer defined as "a body of men and women who call themselves by the name of the totem, believe themselves to be of one blood, descendants of a common ancestor [the totem creature], and are bound together by common obligations to each other and by a common faith in the totem." Thus, totemism was "both a religious and a social system"—although in its later history these two aspects tended "to part company," and Frazer treated them separately in his essay.[17]

Under the heading "Totemism as a Religion," Frazer discussed beliefs and myths about totems, "totem taboos" and the penalties for their violation, the benefits conferred by the totem, inanimate totems, totem markings, and a variety of "totemic ceremonies," ending with a consideration of "individual" and "sex totems." Infrequently, Frazer offered explanatory asides. Some of these were straightforwardly utilitarian, as when he discussed the marking of tents: "the same desire for protection against supernatural danger may be the motive of similar totemic customs, if not of totemism in general." Others were more sociological, as when he discussed "ceremonies at puberty": "when we remember that the fundamental rules of totem society are rules regulating marriage, or rather sexual intercourse, . . . persons of the same totem being forbidden, under pain of death, to have connection with each other, the propriety of imprinting these marks on the persons of the clansmen and inculcating these rules on their minds at the very moment when transgression of these all-important rules first becomes possible, is immediately apparent." But even when the goal was social order rather than individual protection, the sense of rational invention, if not by an individual legislator, then by a generalized savage philosopher, was very strong: "the rules which it is the object of these ceremonies to inculcate are probably deductions from that fundamental and as yet unexplained connection between a man and his totem, which constitutes the religion of totemism."[18]

In the "Social Aspect of Totemism," Frazer treated three topics: rather briefly, the clan obligation of blood feud, and at much greater length, the rules of exogamy and descent—drawing heavily on the Australian data of Fison and Howitt. His more general theoretical sources were suggested in a comment on tribes like the Dieri, in which the line of descent was neither female nor male, but "half-way between the two": "after the researches of Bachofen, McLennan, and Morgan, we may be sure that such a wavering marks a transition from female to male descent, and not conversely." And as this remark suggests, there were several passages foreshadowing Tylor's "adhesions" paper of the following year. There was also a hint of anticipation of Emile Durkheim in the suggestion that the piling up of totems (individual, sex, clan, subphratry, phratry) was perhaps "a rudimentary classification of natural objects under heads which bear a certain resemblance to genera, species, etc." and in the case of some Australian tribes was "extended so as to include the whole of nature."[19]

In the end, however, Frazer's understanding of the "social aspect of totemism" returned to the mind of the savage philosopher—not as an embodiment of a *conscience collective,* but as an archetypal individual refining his ideas about the world (or perhaps as an imagined collectivity of such speculators). Offering a brief "view of the growth, maturity, and decay of totems," Frazer placed his major categories in a recurring cyclic sequence: subtotems as growing, clan totems as grown, subphratric and phratric totems as "successive stages of decay." Eventually, however, "the change of female to male kinship and the settlement of a tribe in fixed abodes" disrupted this "constantly shifting kaleidoscope of clans," and society was "shaken down into a certain stability and permanence of form." With "the longer memory which accompanies an advance in culture," those totems that had been "generalised into the divinities of larger groups" would no longer "pass into oblivion," but would "retain an elevated rank in the religious hierarchy, with the totems of the subordinate tribal divisions grouped under them." Thus over time "the tribal totem tends to pass into an anthropomorphic god": "As the attribution of human qualities to the totem is of the essence of totemism, it is plain that a deity generalised from or including under him a number of distinct animals and plants must, as his animal and vegetable attributes contradict and cancel each other, tend more and more to throw them off and to retain only those human qualities which to the savage apprehension are the common element of the totems whereof he is the composite product." With the rise of one such totem "more and more into human form," the others would correspondingly fall, until, at a later age, the links "which bound them to the god having wholly faded from memory, a generation of mythologists arises who seek to patch up the broken chain by the cheap method of symbolism." As to the origin of totemism itself, Frazer had little to say. Rejecting Herbert Spencer's theory of the "misinterpretation of nicknames" by associating it with "so-called comparative [i.e. Müllerian] mythology," Frazer concluded that "no satisfactory explanation of the origin of totemism has yet been given."[20]

In all of this characteristically Frazerian explanatory ad-hockery (the memory of longer memory fading within a single paragraph), the resonances of Tylor ring much louder than any of Robertson Smith. Whatever guidance Smith may have given Frazer in composing the essay on totemism, it clearly did not include effective indoctrination in the sociology of religious ritual and belief—matters on which their personal beliefs and practices were of course at sharp odds, though they had both grown up in the Free Church. Careful comparison has documented the differences between the two men on a whole series of fundamental methodological and conceptual issues: the aims and uses of the comparative method, the relative priority of myth and ritual, the relationship of magic and religion, the significance of taboo, the origin and function of totemism, the nature of sacrifice, and the relationship of evolution and social progress. Like Tylor, Frazer thought of religion as essentially a philosophical system, and a mistaken one at that; his writings tended—with varying degrees of animus and ambivalence—to undermine the grounds of individual religious belief. In contrast, Smith remained always a believing Christian; his writings sought to understand the sociological bases of religious community, a community that in his own life had been disrupted by the rational analysis of the authoritative texts of religious belief.[21]

While evident retrospectively in a comparison of their major published works, these differences had begun to show themselves at an early point in the relationship of the two men—in a context that helps to clarify Frazer's general view of "the mind of primitive man." Arguing with Henry Jackson in 1888, Frazer disputed the notion that men "start institutions on a strictly utilitarian basis but afterwards invent absurd (superstitious) reasons to account for a sensible practice"—suggesting that it was in fact a variant of the Müllerian "disease of language" schema. Against the view that "superstition is invented to account for an institution," Frazer argued "conversely that the superstition gives rise to the institution": it was not that "superstitions are similar all over the world because institutions are similar," but rather that "institutions are similar because superstitions are so." Jackson's problem was that he assumed that savages initially saw the world "exactly in the way in which it appears to us in the year 1888," and that only later did they fall into irrational error. But as Frazer suggested to another correspondent the following year, in fact "primitive man looks at the world from such a totally different point of view from us, that what seems simple and obvious to us almost certainly did not appear so to him; and, *vice versa*, what seems simple and obvious to him is almost always so entirely remote from our ways of thought that we should never have dreamed of it." But despite his apparent departure here from the doctrine of psychic unity, and despite the fact that he defended his position in relativist terms ("there is no *absolute* way of looking at the world," but only "a perpetual approximation ever nearer and nearer to what we call the facts"), Frazer's underlying commitment to a version of Tylor's evolutionary rationalism was clearly evident in his exchange with Jackson.[22]

Like Tylor, Frazer believed that the external world "suggested certain ideas to the primitive man" on which "he acted and could not help acting." His actions were different from ours not because his mental processes were different, but "because the ideas which he received from the world were different from those which we receive." Although Frazer did not refer to Tylor, his argument closely paralleled Tylor's theory of animism, in which, after an initial mistaken conclusion based on sound empirical perception (the leap from the real experience of dreams to the false doctrine of the soul), humanity gradually over time corrected the early evolutionary error. As Frazer put it to Jackson: "the first incorrect ideas suggested by the world and the institutions based on them have been gradually corrected by the rise of truer ideas and hence of better institutions." What was at issue was the traditional one of progress versus degeneration. Whereas Frazer believed that "progress or development has been steady and continuous," Jackson believed that "man began with reason, lapsed into unreason, and then struggled out of the quagmire back into reason." Since this was, in fact, "the Fall of Man," Jackson might as well "throw Adam and the apples into the bargain, and swallow the whole."[23]

That all of this bore on Frazer's differences with Smith was evident in his request that Jackson "keep this letter and show it to R. Smith": "I am always having little tiffs with him on these same lines but have never had a pitched battle." That Frazer never fully appreciated the grounds of his difference with Smith is suggested by his subsequent complaint to Jackson that he had no one to talk to about "these subjects": "even R. Smith is so stern a utilitarian that to talk to him of ghosts and spirits is to venture on delicate ground." Smith was no stern utilitarian, nor was he, as Frazer came close to suggesting after reading *The Religion of the Semites,* guilty of "making the early Semites reason like nineteenth-century people." Frazer was closer to the mark when, years later, he suggested to Smith's biographer that Smith, "influenced probably by his deeply religious nature, under-estimated the influence of fear, and over-estimated the influence of benevolent emotions (love, confidence, and gratitude) in moulding early religion." Frazer felt that on this basis Smith conceived of sacrifice "as mainly a form of communion with the deity instead of a mode of propitiating him and averting his anger." Granting that sacrifice might sometimes "involve" such communion, Frazer insisted that "the old gift theory"—which was of course Tylor's theory—was "substantially correct." But even here, Frazer portrayed Smith in his own individualistic psychological terms, reducing Smith's sociological interpretations to a difference of motivating individual emotion, and portraying communion as a relationship between the individual and his deity.[24]

Having been led from Pausanias to the cross-cultural study of totem and taboo, Frazer set about collecting further ethnographic data, and looking for a frame in which to present it. In 1887 he prepared the

Questions on the Manners, Customs, Religion, Superstitions, etc., of Uncivilized or Semi-Civilized Peoples which he asked Haddon to take to Torres Straits. That same year, he seems to have been preoccupied with the topic of taboo: for several weeks in the fall, he engaged Henry Jackson in an intense discussion of taboos relating to sexual intercourse, especially those surrounding menstruation—when among the "lower races" women were "regarded as most dangerous." He in fact suggested to Jackson that he was "inclined to put aside all other work," including Pausanias, to write a volume that he might "have out in a year." Although he later spoke of having been at work in this period on "a general work on primitive superstition and religion," this could well have referred to an extension of his essay on taboo. In the event, however, Frazer found his focus in a particular cultural practice at the temple of Aricia, in the Alban hills southeast of Rome, in which, according to the Greek geographer Strabo, "the people set up as a priest a runaway slave who has slain with his own hand the man previously consecrated to his office." Pausanias had commented on it, and corrobative evidence uncovered in 1885 by British archeological excavations at Nemi was reported in several journals that Frazer would have read. In 1885 the practice was also treated in a philosophical drama, *Le prêtre de Némi,* by the French Orientalist Ernest Renan, whose extensive positivistic writings on the history of religion, though anathema to Smith, were an important influence on Frazer. A possible explanation for the custom followed at Nemi occurred to Frazer in the spring of 1889, when he read a late-seventeenth-century travel account of a similar periodic ritual-killing of the king on the Malabar Coast in India. In this context, he was able within a few months to employ on a much more ambitious scale the same plot device he had tried out in his two early essays on temple fires and burial customs: the use of the "comparative method" to explicate an apparently mysterious custom in classical antiquity—in this case, the rule by which the priest of the sacred grove of Diana could assume his office only by first plucking the "golden bough" and then killing his predecessor, thenceforth to live in constant fear "as the priest who slew the slayer, and shall himself be slain."[25]

Although in the third edition it was expanded to twelve volumes, the solution to the mystery of the "Golden Bough" was offered in a letter Frazer wrote to George Macmillan early in November 1889, announcing the impending completion of a "study in the history of primitive religions," written as "an explanation of the legend of the Golden Bough:"

> By an application of the Comparative Method I believe I can make it probable that the priest represented the god of the grove—Virbius—and that his slaughter was regarded as the death of the god. This raises the question

of a wide-spread custom of killing men and animals regarded as divine. I have collected many examples of this custom and proposed a new explanation of it. The Golden Bough, I believe I can show, was the mistletoe, and the whole legend can, I think be brought into connexion, on the one hand, with the Druidical reverence for the mistletoe, and on the other with the Norse legend of the death of Balder. Of the exact way in which I connect the Golden Bough with the Priest of Aricia I shall only say that in explaining it I am led to propose a new explanation of the meaning of totemism. This is the bare outline of the book which, whatever may be thought of its theories, will be found to contain a large store of very curious customs, many of which may be new even to professed anthropologists. The resemblance of the savage customs and ideas to the fundamental doctrines of Christianity is striking. But I make no reference to this parallelism, leaving my readers to draw their own conclusions, one way or the other.[26]

There was little in *The Golden Bough* that was by itself strikingly original. The fundamental conceptual and methodological debts were to Tylor. The project of explicating minor mysteries in classical scholarship by comparison to savage custom and belief had been anticipated by Andrew Lang, whose critique of Max Müller's solar Aryan theories provided the immediate background of Frazer's own "inquiry into the primitive religion of the Aryans." The reliance on "the popular superstitions and customs of the peasantry" in modern Europe as "the fullest and most trustworthy evidence we possess as to the primitive religion of the Aryans" was simply an extension of an approach being pursued in the work of the Tylorian folklorists who had come together in the Folk-Lore Society: Edward Clodd, G. L. Gomme, E. S. Hartland, and Alfred Nutt. Much of the specific substance of the comparison was, as Frazer acknowledged, taken from the work of the German scholar Wilhelm Mannhardt, who "by oral inquiry, and by printed questions scattered broadcast over Europe, as well as by ransacking the literature of folklore," had collected a mass of evidence regarding "the superstitious beliefs and rites connected with trees and cultivated plants." And Frazer's central idea, "the conception of the slain god," was by his own admission "derived directly" from Robertson Smith—to whom *The Golden Bough* was dedicated.[27]

What was distinctive of Frazer may be seen as a concomitant of his adoption of a plot-type echoing a genre very much in fashion at the *fin-de-siècle:* that of the mystery story. In contrast to Tylor, for whom savage animism was a relatively straightforward affair, once its underlying principle was articulated, Frazer revelled in the uncovering of obscure motives. Why would presumably rational human creatures do this bizarre customary thing? At the very beginning of his odyssey of explanation, in one of the most richly rhetorical (and reiteratively hypothetical) renderings of the "comparative method" ever ventured, the chord of "motive" rings four times within a single periodic sentence: "If we can show that a barbarous custom, like that of the priesthood of Nemi, has existed elsewhere; if we can detect the motives which led to its institution; if we can prove that these motives have operated widely, perhaps universally, in human society, producing in varied circumstances a variety of institutions specifically different but generically alike; if we can show, lastly, that these very motives, with some of their derivative institutions, were actually at work in classical antiquity; then we may fairly infer that at a remoter age the same motives gave birth to the priesthood of Nemi." Although it is not a contrast Frazer or his contemporaries would have drawn, one may perhaps distinguish between an anthropology of "motive" and an anthropology of "meaning." Both are mentalistic terms, and both have to do with human intention; but the one is prior and the other is consequent. Motive, both etymologically and in the range of its historical meanings, is directly linked with purposive individual action; meaning is more open to interactional or contextual complexities of signification. Whereas "meaning" encourages a move toward culture in a modern anthropological sense, "motive" seems almost inherently psychologistic. Certainly in Frazer's case, the search for motive was characteristically conceived of in individualistic, intellectualistic, and utilitarian terms, and the idea of culture was kept within the bounds of its older humanistic cum evolutionary meaning.[28]

In the first edition of *The Golden Bough,* which was subtitled *A Study in Comparative Religion,* the key to "motive" was simply the inability of the savage to conceive of "the distinction commonly drawn by more advanced peoples between the natural and the supernatural." Imagining the world to be "worked by supernatural agents" acting "on impulses and motives like his own," he saw "no limit to his power of influencing the course of nature to his own advantage" by "prayers, promises, or threats" to "secure him fine weather and an abundant crop from the gods"—or from the god that had become "incarnate in his own person." This rather simple utilitarian anthropomorphism was complemented by another view of the world, "in which we may detect the modern notion of natural law as a series of events occurring in an invariable order without the intervention of personal agency," which Frazer called "sympathetic magic," and which he discussed at much greater length in the second edition.[29]

Subtitled *A Study in Magic and Religion,* the second edition was reworked in the period when resurgent irrationalism—marked by Lang's apostasy—had begun to threaten the Tylorian edifice, and a "sharp distinction" was now drawn between the two modes of thought. Religion receded into the background of primitive belief, and—inverting Lang's perspective on the Australians—the previously mentioned resemblance of "savage ideas and customs to the fundamental doctrines of Christianity" was more strongly suggested. In this context, Frazer's treatment of savage theories of magic was greatly elaborated. Like Tylor's animism, sympathetic magic was a "crude philosophy" based upon two principles: "first, that like produces like, or that an effect resembles its cause; and second, that things which have once been in contact, but have ceased to be so, continue to act on each other as if the contact still persisted." The former was the basis of what Frazer called "mimetic" or "imitative" (or later, "homeopathic") magic, in which, for example, an "Ojebway Indian" desiring to work evil on an enemy shoots an arrow into his effigy. The latter, or "sympathetic magic in the strict sense" (later, "contagious magic") was apparently derived from another Tylorian folklorist, Sydney Hartland; its "most familiar example" was the use of a person's hair or nail cuttings to work one's will, "at any distance, upon the person from whom they were cut." Citing Tylor's *Primitive Culture*—and by indirection, the whole tradition of British empiricist psychology back to Locke—Frazer suggested that they were each "mistaken applications" of either one of two "great fundamental laws of thought": the "association of ideas by similarity and . . . by contiguity in space or time." The very literal-mindedness and concreteness of the savage mind, the constant confusion of word and thing, of simile and metaphor (the constitutional incapacity, even, for metaphor), paradoxically gave rise to a mental world of make-believe and even madness. But with the savage's "train of reasoning" clearly in mind, it was possible to explain the motives of the apparently bizarre, and to understand how rationality, misapplied, might lead to a world of irrationality—as well as how, in the slow course of evolutionary time, some men had got their train of reasoning back on the right track.[30]

Frazer's thinking on these matters may be illuminated by considering his successive theories of the origin of totemism. Although he had offered none in 1887, Frazer did attempt one in the first edition of *The Golden Bough*. Drawing on the work of two Tylorians, the folklorist Edward Clodd and the Dutch ethnologist G. A. Wilken, he suggested that totemism had originated in the belief in an "external soul." Unable to conceive of life abstractly, savages thought of it as a concrete material thing, which, for safekeeping, could be deposited in an external object; the generalized relation of reverence in which savages held totem species was simply a consequence of their inability to distinguish the particular plant or animal in which an individual's soul was deposited: "as he does not know which the dear one is, he is obliged to spare them all from fear of injuring the one." Although Frazer later concluded that this was "at most only a partial solution of the problem," he left it deposited for safekeeping in his subsequent writings on totemism.[31]

Frazer's second theory of totemism was stimulated by Spencer and Gillen's Arunta ethnography, which came to his attention when Lorimer Fison forwarded to him a letter Spencer had written Fison just after the start of the engwura ceremonies of 1896. Frazer was struck by Spencer's observation that in five of the ceremonies totem members ate their own totem. Recalling Robertson Smith's concept of the totem sacrament, Frazer wrote immediately to Spencer, who was somewhat doubtful of the notion, and instead discussed churinga beliefs which seemed to support Frazer's earlier theory of the external soul. Spencer did, however, offer further information on the rules governing the eating of the grub totem ("to which Mr. Gillen and myself belong") during and after the intichiuma ceremonies held for their increase, along with similar practices among several other totem groups. Frazer, who soon took over from Tylor the task of seeing the Arunta book into print, was struck by its extended description of ceremonies which were not previously reported "from any other part of the world." On the basis of Spencer's further description, Frazer concluded that "among these tribes totemism was a system expressly devised for the purpose of procuring a plentiful supply" of "all the desirable things in nature" by dividing them up among totem groups, each of which would have responsibility for the flourishing of its own totem species for the benefit of the tribe as a whole. Originally, the groups would have eaten their own totems; but gradually a taboo against eating them might have arisen by the following train of thought:

> I am, e.g., a Kangaroo man, and I want to make as many kangaroos come and be eaten as I can. Now if I kill and eat them myself, the kangaroos will regard me with fear and distrust as a dangerous creature, not as a genuine kangaroo at all. I must therefore be very kind and gentle to my brothers and sisters the kangaroos. I must never injure them myself, and then I shall be able to induce them to come quietly and confidingly to be injured (in fact to be killed and eaten) by my fellow tribesmen. [But] if I occasionally take a bite or two at a joint of kangaroo when no kangaroo is looking, no great harm will be done, especially if I take care not to eat the best of the flesh, but only the inferior parts. Indeed, in order to be (as I am) a real Kangaroo, it is necessary that I should occasionally eat kangaroo; for unless I have real kangaroo flesh and blood in me, . . . I should only be a sham kangaroo, and . . . the other kangaroos would know at once that I was an imposter, and not one of them would come near me when I wanted to catch them.[32]

Having thus extended the principle of psychic unity from mankind to the animal world (in a style of thought which Radcliffe-Brown was said to have ridiculed as the "If I were a cow" mode), Frazer drew further necessary consequences from his "new theory of totemism." On the hypothesis that "totemism exists for the multiplication of the totem plants and animals," one might have expected a rule of endogamy rather than exogamy, since a union of a Kangaroo man and a Kangaroo woman should, "by sympathetic magic," increase the number of real kangaroos; but this seemed not to be the case. In part to obviate this empirical difficulty, Frazer suggested that the religious side of totemism ("the superstitious relation of the man to his totem animal") was the "original element of totemism," and that the social element ("the prohibition to marry a woman of the same totem") had been "tacked on to it subsequently, and not in all cases."[33]

On the whole Spencer was quite enthusiastic about Frazer's theory, but he suggested several modifications—including a proposal as to how Kangaroo endogamy "might possibly" have preceded the present exogamous rule, on the Morganian assumption that "the division into what we call classes and sub-classes" was "deliberately introduced" into "a well-developed totemic system" in order to regulate marriage. On one issue, however, he remained adamant: there was "no evidence of any feeling of conciliation" in the attitude of a savage toward his totem; it was simply a matter of having "a special power" over it. Picking up on the former point, Frazer suggested a sequence of bisections within a totemic community, arguing that there was an essential distinction between totemism and exogamy. Picking up on the latter, he concluded that "sympathetic magic is a more primitive method of securing a food supply than propitiation," suggesting an essential distinction between magic and religion:

> In fact, I am coming more and more to the conclusion that if we define religion as the propitiation of natural and supernatural powers, and magic as the coercion of them, magic has everywhere preceded religion. It is only when men find by experience that they cannot *compel* the higher powers to comply with their wishes, that they condescend to *entreat* them. In time, after long ages, they begin to realize that entreaty is also vain, and then they try compulsion again; but this time the compulsion is applied within narrower limits and in a different way from the old magical method. In short, religion is replaced by science. The order of evolution, then, of human thought and practice is, magic—religion—science.

In this context—further elaborated in a two-part article in the *Fortnightly Review*—totemism was neither a form of social organization nor a form of religion, but was purely magical in origin and essentially economic in purpose.[34]

By 1905, after widespread discussion among anthropological writers, much of it critical, Frazer, "on mature reflection," rejected his second theory because it was "too rational," and because it implied a social organization "too complex to be primitive." Returning to the Arunta data, he realized that "the clue had been staring us in the face for years": the Arunta notion that a person's totem was defined not by inheritance from the mother or father but from the totem center (where the souls of the dead resided, awaiting reincarnation) nearest the spot where the mother first felt the stirring of the "spirit child" that had made its way into her womb. According to this third or "conceptional theory," the "ultimate source of totemism" was the "savage ignorance of the physical process by which men and animals reproduce their kinds." This granted, everything else about totemism followed "in a simple and natural manner"—for example, hereditary totems by the tendency of mothers to return to the same spots or of fathers to insist that they do so.[35]

Frazer suggested that his new theory could be generalized to explain totemism over the whole world. If humans evolved from animals, "there must have been a period" when "mankind would have been ignorant of paternity," which was "a matter of inference only, not of perception": "how could the infantine intelligence of the primitive savage"—exemplified still among the Australians—"perceive that the child which comes forth from the womb is the fruit of the seed which was sowed there nine long months before?" But "so soon as he began to think at all," man inevitably turned his thought to this "most mysterious event" which was "so essential to the continuance of the species." In this case, however, the savage philosopher suddenly underwent a sex change: "what more natural than to identify [the quickening] with something that simultaneously struck her fancy"—a kangaroo that "disappeared into a thicket," a "gay butterfly that flickered past," even "the moonbeams sparkling and dancing on the water," or "the sighing of the wind in the trees." Although thus based ultimately on "the sick fancies of pregnant women," totemism might even have an actual "physical basis" if we were to accept the still-prevailing notion that the "impressions made on a mother's mind" during pregnancy were "really imprinted" on her unborn offspring—as the "figure of a lizard" might be on the mother who was "visited by a lizard while she had a child in the womb." In these terms, even the preservation of a clan physical type under "a rigorous rule of clan exogamy" could be explained: where residence was patrilocal, the wives would bear the impressions of their husbands' families; where matrilocal, the impressions of their own.[36] One is tempted to suggest that out of the sick fancies of repressed men, theories of totemism arise—each the expression of a basic cultural preoccupation of Victorian respectability: religious belief (the preservation of the soul); economic enterprise (the division of labor); and the control of sexuality (or how to have babies without enjoying sex).

Frazer's first theory of totemism had been the occasion of a break with Tylor in 1898. Although Tylor had in the past refrained from writing about totemism because of "its really bewildering complexity," he was quite critical of the way in which ethnographic evidence had been used originally by McLennan and more recently by Frazer. By implication, he defended the priority of his own theory of animism, protesting "the manner in which totems have been placed almost at the foundation of religion," and suggesting that Wilken—whom he accused Frazer of inadequately acknowledging—had been on the right track in seeing the transmigration of souls as the link between totemism and a prior stage of ancestor worship. Tylor insisted that there had been as yet no real proof of Robertson Smith's totem sacrament, and looked forward to the "remarkable new information" that would soon be forthcoming in Spencer and Gillen's monograph. When Frazer had Macmillan send Tylor proofs, Tylor suggested that he compress passages in which "there is diffuseness and the matter is sometimes repulsive"—the very passages which to Frazer furnished "the first well-attested case of what appears to be a real totem-sacrament," and which he defended as readable even by "a girl at boarding school," since they contained no reference to sexual matters. Although the dispute was patched over in correspondence, Tylor's (perhaps self-interested) plea for theoretical caution was lost on Frazer, and relations between the two men were for some time very cool.[37]

Despite his tiff with Tylor, and his increasingly close ties to the Morganian tradition in Australian ethnography, Frazer remained to the end essentially Tylorian. There was, however, a difference of emphasis—a drawing-out of one potential of the Tylorian view of the mind of savage man. Like Locke's madmen, Tylor's savages reasoned soundly from false premises or inadequate experience; accepting that view, one could emphasize the psychic unity of the process or the radical disjunction of the product—a disjunction made more radical by the opposition between human reason itself and the animal instincts of sexuality. Methodologically, Frazer still accepted psychic unity, which was necessary in order to reconstruct the savage's "train of reasoning"; but attitudinally, he was often more inclined than Tylor to insist on disjunction, and to view it in a somewhat different psychological and ideological perspective. Taboo, he had suggested in 1888, "subserved the progress of civilization, by fostering conceptions of the rights of property and the sanctity of the marriage tie" until they were "strong enough to stand by themselves and to fling away the crutch of superstition which in earlier days had been their sole support." To which he added a characteristic rhetorical flourish: "thus on the taboo were grafted the golden fruits of law and morality, while the parent stem dwindled slowly into the sour crabs and empty husks of popular superstition on which the swine of modern society are still content to feed."[38]

Tylor's anthropology was that of an optimistic mid-Victorian liberal. Product of "the age of equipoise," Tylor could still think of anthropology as "a reformer's science" rooting out "the remains of crude old culture which have passed into harmful superstition." In contrast, Frazer's anthropology was that of a disenchanted later Victorian liberal, responding in the 1880s to a decade of economic depression, land war in Ireland, and the stirrings of socialism at home. By 1909, when apprehensive rumblings of gender, class, racial, and international conflict could be heard beneath the conversation of the Edwardian garden party, Frazer began to see superstition as more than simply a crutch. Speaking now as its "advocate" not as its "executioner," he argued in *Psyche's Task* that for long periods of human history superstition had been the primary support of "the pillars on which rests the whole fabric of civil society"—government, private property, marriage, and respect for human life. But if in the now safely evolutionary past superstition buttressed social order, in the potentially revolutionary present it threatened social chaos. In a lecture given in 1908, Frazer heaped up metaphors of impending doom, all in a single paragraph: the "smooth surface of cultured society" was "sapped and mined by superstition"; "the ground beneath our feet" was "honeycombed by unseen forces"; we were "standing on a volcano which may at any moment break out in smoke and fire to spread ruin and devastation among the gardens and palaces of ancient culture wrought so laboriously by the hands of many generations." He could still believe in progress, but only as "the avowed creed of the enlightened minority"; in contrast, "the real, though unavowed creed of the mass of mankind appears to be almost stationary [because] in the majority of men, whether they are savages or outwardly civilized beings, intellectual progress is so slow as to be hardly perceptible."[39]

Just as Tylor wrote to as well as from and of his times, so was this even more true of Frazer. More than any other anthropologist of his day, he spoke, "in the first place," as Robert Marett later suggested, to "the public" at large. If Andrew Lang was an anthropologist forced to be a man of letters, Frazer was a man of letters posing as an anthropologist. The record of his correspondence with his publisher gives ample evidence of the great importance of commercial literary considerations in his career, the management of which was eventually taken over by his wife Lilly, who saw to it that every scrap he wrote was published and republished—including, toward the end of his long life, extensive selections compiled by his amanuensis from the manuscript notebooks in which he had recorded passages from his ethnographic sources. And after a slow beginning, Frazer was both financially successful and intellectually influential.[40]

Frazer's intellectual influence was certainly not due to his power as a theoretician; he himself provided testimony to the ad-hockery of his hypotheses. At the beginning of the third edition of *The Golden Bough,* he acknowledged that he was quite capable of "stretching an hypothesis too far, of crowding a multitude of incongruous particulars under one narrow formula." And toward the end—after recapitulating a series of "principal points on which I have altered my opinion"—he dismissed all his theories as simply "convenient pegs on which to hang my collections of facts." But Frazer's theoretical modesty may have helped to preserve the pose of science—the more so since he presented his compilations of ethnographic data in a Gibbonesque style unmatched by anthropologists of greater scientific pretensions. Discarding the "austere form," but not—he hoped—"the solid substance of a scientific treatise," Frazer offered to his readers "in simple and sensuous language" an erudite mass of often titillating exotic detail, cast into travelogue, detective story, even epic drama of evolutionary scope.[41]

Instead of editing one, like his friend Robertson Smith, Frazer "actually composed an encyclopaedia"—"a corpus of assorted evidence" offering a "panorama of the primitive life and mind." Joining him on an odyssey of exploration among the peoples "of rudimentary culture" at the farther reaches of the British empire, whose fate was now "in the hands" of "our imperial race," the reading public could vicariously brave the perils of the primitive unknown, assured of a quick and safe return to the accustomed comforts—and the equally vicarious colonial responsibilities—of modern civilization. Not, however, without feeling a disconcerting rumbling of its underpinnings. Interspersed by the comparative method among the accounts of savagery, tales of the surviving customs of European peasant folk brought the primitive close to home. Although Frazer had no use for "that creature Freud," he, too, had written a story of irrational savagery beneath the civilized veneer of prewar Europe—in which sex was never far beneath the surface. For many intellectuals—especially after the Great War—this was the bitter fruit of *The Golden Bough*. But like the horrors of traditional nursery tales, *The Golden Bough* could in fact be read quite innocently: all those savage scandals were merely the "childish doings" of "very naughty" children—and "was it not human to derive satisfaction from the story of one's infant peccadillos?" For many, Frazer's "golden treasury of stories for grown-up children" was ultimately a message of reassurance, in which rational understanding (both in the author and the race) struggled to overcome the primitive irrationalities of myth, magic, superstition, and taboo.[42]

Frazer's ambivalence and self-contradiction may even have broadened his appeal. He had written (especially in the second edition) "the most devasting attack anyone had made on Christianity since William Godwin"; but in reducing the drama of the Saviour's death and resurrection to yet another variant of the divine god slain to guarantee the corn, he could also be read as universalizing Christianity—a view which the more moderate tone of his later work helped to sustain. Tasting Frazer's cake of relativism, one could still hold on to the hope of truth: if "the moral world [was] as little exempt as the physical world from the law of ceaseless change," the study of "the amazing diversities of ethical theory and practice" would nonetheless help us replace "what is false by what is true."[43]

Thus it was that amid the now sometimes endless-seeming longueurs of the now no longer quite so alien-seeming customs of the tribes of the "Amongsthas" ("Amongst the M'Bengas . . . , Amongst the Aht . . . , Amongst the Koraks . . ."), there could once be found "objective correlatives" both to evoke and to provoke the states of mind of several generations of readers. In the decade after 1911, as many as 36,000 copies of the twelve volumes of the third edition of *The Golden Bough* were published, and it continued in print during the decade to follow, when over 33,000 copies of the one-volume abridgment were also sold. By this time, its "leading ideas" were "so widely diffused through academic, literary, and journalistic channels" that they were known to many who had never read the book. Sir James, who was knighted on the eve of the First World War, was still a frequent figure in the popular press on the eve of the Second.[44]

The reaction of his scholarly confreres was at the time and has since been somewhat problematic. Among a later generation of British social anthropologists, it was a disciplinary scandal that Frazer, the very model of an "armchair anthropologist" (who is said to have responded "but heaven forbid!" to William James's query, had he ever met a savage?), should ever have represented anthropology to the intellectual world at large. Reflecting this widespread attitude, Frazer's biographer opened his study with a stark disclaimer: "Frazer is an embarrassment." But in an era when the fieldwork model was only beginning to be established and the relationship among anthropology, European folklore, and early classical texts of Western civilization was closer than before or since, there was a well-established role open for Frazer—the more so as it became evident that Tylor could no longer fill it.[45]

The most striking comment by a contemporary on Frazer's reception was a subsequent recollection of Jane Harrison, a leading figure among the group of Cambridge Ritualists who between 1900 and 1915 reinterpreted the origins of Greek drama and religion in anthropological terms: "Tylor had written and spoken; Robertson Smith, exiled for

Sir James Frazer, with Rudyard Kipling (right), and Paul-Emile Appell, Rector of the Sorbonne, on the occasion of receiving an honorary degree in 1921. (Courtesy of Robert Ackerman)

heresy, had seen the Star in the East; in vain; we classical deaf adders stopped our ears and closed our eyes; but at the mere sound of the magical words 'Golden Bough,' the scales fell—we heard and understood." Although recent scholarship has suggested that Harrison's reminiscence overstated an influence that was in reality more Smithian than Frazerian, it is nonetheless the case that the Ritualists' interpretations were all built upon the central image of Frazer's dying, fertilizing god.[46]

As the history of the Cambridge Ritualists suggests, Frazer's real impact came with the second edition of his book, which the *Quarterly Review* compared in "pre-eminence" to Tylor's *Primitive Culture:* "till Mr. Tylor gives us the new book on which he is understood to be engaged, Mr. Frazer need fear no rival." Even then, however, the scholarly reaction was mixed: with the exception of the folklorist Alfred Nutt, who embraced what he called the "Mannhardt-Frazer" hypothesis, the eight reviews in *Folk-Lore* ranged from Haddon's "mild demurrer" to the "ferocious onslaught" that inaugurated Andrew Lang's continuing intellectual vendetta. A decade later, the folklorist Edward Clodd confided to his diary that Haddon regarded Frazer as a "literary man, not a man of science," who did not "know human nature and allows his theories to obsess him."[47*]

But there is also evidence that Frazer's work was taken very seriously by his fellow anthropologists. Reviewing the third edition of *The Golden Bough,* Robert Marett suggested that although "official anthropology was at first inclined to stand aloof," regarding it as a "literary rather than truly scientific work," the second edition was "backed by anthropologists almost to a man"—"it might have been a fairy-tale once: but now it was science." There was a tone of gentlemanly irony in Marett's review, which went on to raise fundamental questions about Frazer's theories of magic and religion. But that is in fact the historical point: in the two decades after 1900, one had to take Frazer's theories seriously, even if one disagreed with them; if he did not set the agenda for anthropological research, his works were nonetheless a constant reference point.[48]

Nor was this merely a matter of armchair debate; Frazer was taken seriously also by members of the emergent group of field anthropologists. When Seligman went down the Nile in 1910 after reading Frazer's *Early History of the Kingship,* he found that the Shilluks had a divine king, who "until the last few years was ceremonially killed when he began to get old or invalidish." Fifteen years later, when Isaac Schapera arrived at the London School of Economics to pursue graduate work in anthropology, he proposed to Seligman a doctoral dissertation on divine kingship. Although Frazer himself insisted on a sharp separation of ethnography and theory (which "should regularly and rightly be left to the comparative ethnologist"), he was quite active in encouraging ethnographic fieldwork, both by missionaries, like John Roscoe in Africa, and by academic anthropologists, like Radcliffe-Brown in Western Australia. On a number of occasions he modestly suggested that their ethnographic data would outlast his own theoretical speculations.[49]

As late as 1928, in the seventh of the lectures established in Frazer's name, Edward Westermarck could still describe Frazer as "the supreme

*There is further evidence of such private chafing among folklorists of Frazer's era, who, working in the same genre, may well have felt unjustly overshadowed. Mrs. Clodd, writing to Haddon, referred to Lilly Frazer as "a pusher," and her husband as "the best advertised man in England"; Mrs. Hartland, quoted in the same letter, was shocked by a form letter Frazer had sent regretting that "lack of space" had prevented him from inviting the Hartlands (and others) to the festivities surrounding the Frazer Lecture (ACHP:3/10/27; see also Filby 1958).

commander" of social anthropology, "who *should* not expose himself to the dangers attending action on the field." To be sure, this might be dismissed as ceremonial froth, appropriate to a moment when Frazer's public reputation—and growing theoretical irrelevance—had reduced him to an anthropological icon. But there was a time earlier in both men's lives when it was much closer to the truth. For as Tylor retired from the anthropological scene, Frazer was able to pick up his mantle, sustaining the evolutionary paradigm in a period when it was beginning to be seriously questioned. Despite his waverings and shiftings on a series of specific issues, Frazer remained tenaciously committed to all the basic principles of evolutionary anthropology: the comparative method, the psychic unity of man, independent invention, the stages of cultural development, the doctrine of survivals. As the most publicly visible defender of the evolutionary faith in a period of incipient scepticism, he was for a decade at the epicenter of anthropological debate.[50]

Edward Westermarck: Marriage and Morals in Human Evolution and in Morocco

On February 15, 1889, Edward Westermarck gave a lecture to the Philosophical Society of the University of Helsingfors "On the Method for an Ethnographically-Based Sociology, Illustrated by an Investigation of the Earliest History of Marriage and the Family." From the similarity of title, and from Westermarck's later reference to Tylor's method, it would seem that this lecture was stimulated in part by Tylor's paper on adhesions, a version of which had in fact been given at Oxford in June 1888, when Westermarck was still in England on the first of many visits there. Accounts of the contents of Westermarck's lecture suggest, however, that Westermarck himself had already arrived at a critical position on two central assumptions of social evolutionary theory: primitive promiscuity and the priority of matriarchal marriage forms.[51]

Born to a well-to-do academic family in Helsingfors in 1862, a half-century after Sweden had ceded the Grand Duchy of Finland to the Russian Empire, Westermarck had an early experience of linguistic and cultural diversity—and the advantage of being a native speaker of Swedish when it was still the official language of university education and government administration. A sickly child, he was extremely close to the mother without whose "unceasing care" he would "scarcely have survived." After an unhappy (but academically successful) secondary schooling, he entered the university which his father served as bursar, and where his mother's father had taught the history of ideas. Moving from aesthetics and literature to philosophy, he was quickly alienated by the German metaphysics then in vogue, and was soon attracted to the

British empirical tradition. After reading, in Swedish translation, Herbert Spencer's *First Principles* and Mill's essays on religion, he gave up Christianity for agnosticism—but without abandoning an optimistic view of human life on earth. His honors thesis asked the question, "Does Civilization Increase the Happiness of Mankind?"; employing the "hedonic calculus," he answered with a definite "yes."[52]

Westermarck spent his summers on walking tours, two of which were particularly significant. Wishing to improve his Finnish and learn more of the life of the peasantry, he spent the summer of 1883 in a country village, where at a wedding feast "the veil of modesty was discarded and the wedding company literally wallowed in sensual enjoyment." When the attentions of the host extended beyond "offers of meat and drink" to those that "could not be accepted," his "earlier friendliness changed into a rage"—and Westermarck "just escaped being struck in the face by a discarded boot." Two years later, on a mountain jaunt, he met the English psychologist James Sully, who had written a book on pessimism. They talked (in German) about Westermarck's honors research, beginning a friendship that, despite the twenty-year difference in their ages, "grew in intimacy with the passage of the years."[53]

Pursuing his doctoral studies, Westermarck began to read evolutionary theory: Ernst Haeckel's *Natural History of Creation,* more of Herbert Spencer (in German translation), and a recent Swedish rendition of Darwin's *Descent of Man.* After his earlier experience of peasant sensuality, reading Darwin made him wonder, "how are we to explain the veil of modesty and discretion that is drawn over the sexual life, in contrast to other manifestations of human nature?" In following up this question, Westermarck was led to a "much more comprehensive problem": the historical development of "the relations between the sexes in general." Despite Darwin's counterargument from primate sexual jealousy, Westermarck at first accepted the view that "primitive man lived in a state of promiscuity"; and in order to consult the social evolutionists Darwin cited, he learned English. Westermarck soon decided, however, that "marriage must be studied in its connection with biological conditions, and that the tendency to interpret all sorts of customs as social survivals, without a careful investigation into their existing environment, [was] apt to lead to the most arbitrary conclusions"—an approach which became for him "the first principle" of sociological method, although he never entirely abandoned an interest in the study of survivals.[54]

In September 1887, Westermarck went to England to pursue his researches in the British Museum, staying in London with a family to whom Sully introduced him. He was a "constant guest" in Sully's home, where he "came into personal contact with the intellectual movements in England at that period"—including neo-Darwinian biologists who, under the influence of August Weismann, were calling into question the inheritance of acquired characters. A reading of Darwin's *Life and Letters* gave him a further lesson "in strict scientific method"; although he objected to the doctrine of sexual selection, he became in other respects a staunch Darwinian. By Christmas, he had a sketch of his book, but he continued to collect material, including twenty-five responses to 125 written inquiries he had sent to people "living among savages." Although Westermarck considered writing the book in German, he decided before he returned to Finland in July of 1888 that his English was sufficiently idiomatic to allow him to go ahead in that language. Over the next year he composed a doctoral dissertation which was subsequently to form the first six chapters of *The History of Human Marriage*.[55]

Westermarck sent copies of the dissertation to various English scholars, including Tylor and Alfred Russel Wallace. While Tylor worried that "some of the data in it are too sexual for even a special public," he was flattered by Westermarck's reference to his paper on the development of institutions, and helped to arrange publication by Macmillan. But Tylor left it to Wallace to write a highly laudatory introductory note praising "the new comer who has so boldly challenged the conclusions of some of our most esteemed writers"—among whom Wallace included Tylor, along with Darwin, Lubbock, Morgan, Spencer, and "many others." Tylor was chagrined to find himself "bracketed with Mr. Herbert Spencer, whom both personally and in his works I dislike." And he asked Westermarck to see to it that in the introduction to the second edition, he would be "put right," as "an unbeliever in primitive 'communal marriage.'"[56]

On that issue Tylor found Westermarck's extended critique of the evidence at least "partially convincing," although he was critical of the argument in terms of natural selection, and worried about Westermarck's "extreme patriarchalism." But five years later he acknowledged (with specific reference to Westermarck's work, along with that of Starcke and Letourneau) that a reaction had set in against the "theory of primitive matrimonial anarchy" which in the last thirty years had come to be considered "almost as a fact established by anthropology," and that it was likely "to be transformed, or to pass away altogether." By then he felt that the upholders of the priority of Maine's "patriarchal system" had "the weight of the evidence on their side," provided they did not insist on "its fully developed form." In this context, Tylor went on to rework the argument of his 1888 paper on the political advantages of exogamy to account for its widespread coexistence with the maternal system at an intermediate point in human social evolution.[57]

In doing so, Tylor sought to counter Westermarck's use of data from the 1888 paper to support what was to be his most controversial thesis:

that exogamy originated in an "instinctive horror of incest" that made "sexual love between the nearest kin a psychical impossibility," not because of the physical relationship itself, but because "there is an innate aversion to marriage between persons living very closely together from early youth." Having already argued that Morgan's classificatory system was not a system of blood ties, but (as McLennan had suggested) rather a system of "terms of address" springing largely from "the close living together of considerable numbers of kinfolk," Westermarck had used Tylor's data on the adhesions of exogamy and classificatory relationship to document an argument that exogamy was the end-product of this instinctive aversion. Tylor, in contrast, insisted that "the reason of exogamy is not moral but political."[58]

Tylor had felt that the "distinguishing feature of Dr. Westermarck's whole treatise" was "his vigorous effort to work the biology-side and the culture-side of anthropology into one connected system." That three decades after Darwin this could be seen as an innovative approach is confirmation of the fact that sociocultural evolutionism, although a response to problems presented by the Darwinian revolution, had not been elaborated in Darwinian terms. Westermarck differed from Darwin on a number of points. Against Darwin's suggestion that "racial differences are due to different standards of beauty," he insisted that "the different standards of beauty are due to racial differences." And in order to defend his position that the family, not the tribe or horde, was "the primary social unit of the human race," he argued, against Darwin, that the manlike apes led a solitary rather than a gregarious life. But in defining marriage in relativistic terms as "nothing else than a more or less durable connection between male and female, lasting beyond the mere act of propagation until after the birth of the offspring," he was not so much rejecting a Eurocentric viewpoint as adopting a trans-species natural historical one, which he defended in terms of "the survival of the fittest." Darwin had been the most important single influence on Westermarck's work, and at critical points he appealed to natural selection as the basis of the instincts—notably, in the case of the aversion to incest, which, although peculiar to humans, also led to "the survival of the fittest" by "preventing injurious unions." If Westermarck placed "particular stress" on "psychological causes," it was because "the mere instincts have played a very important part in the origin of social institutions and rules."[59]

Westermarck was, in short, a neo-Darwinian social evolutionist; rather than misguided human reason, it was naturally selected instinct which explained the behavior of savage man. Believing in the survival of the fittest, he was critical of the Tylorian notion of survivals, which implied the survival of the unfit: "nothing has been more fatal to the Science of Society than the habit of inferring, without sufficient reasons, from the prevalence of a custom or institution among some savage peoples, that this custom or institution is a relic of a stage of development that the whole human race once went through." However, Westermarck's arguments were in many respects still cast in the classical social evolutionary mode. Using a comparative method to criticize conclusions of the comparative method, he filled page after page with one-sentence characterizations of customs culled from travellers' accounts of the evolutionists' universal tribe, which, for one less inclined than Frazer to literary archaism, were simply the "Amongthas." While Westermarck was critical of traditional sequences of stages in the evolution of marriage, he was in no doubt about its direction. Passion had become more "refined" and marriage more durable "in proportion as the human race has advanced"; the dominant tendency had been "the extension of the wife's rights," until she was "no longer the husband's property," and "according to modern ideas, marriage is, or should be, a contract on the footing of perfect equality between the sexes." Seeking a "well-rounded period" to finish off the book, his editor composed a sentence that was to make Westermarck a minor hero of the feminist movement: "The history of human marriage is the history of a relation in which women have been gradually triumphing over the passions, the prejudices, and the selfish interests of men." But when "further research" convinced him that the improving status of women had not "kept pace with the advance of civilization," Westermarck deleted this sentence from later editions. And though his book on marriage was "the most momentous happening" in Westermarck's life, his own sexual inclinations were such as to sustain a lifelong bachelordom.[60]

While he was working on his history of marriage, Westermarck "conceived the idea of writing another work dealing with the origin and development of the moral consciousness." Again, his starting point was Darwin's *Descent of Man,* which he discussed at a meeting of the Philosophical Society in 1890, arguing that "social instincts have been acquired through natural selection and from these instincts arise many of the actions we call moral." But another influence seems to have been the theory of emotions that William James had enunciated in 1884 (widely known as the James-Lange theory), which Westermarck accepted in qualified form: "the emotions are feelings which attach to perceptions of certain conditions in our bodies." That influence was surely reinforced in 1897, when he went to England for the third time (having met Tylor and Marett at Oxford in 1893) and, at the meetings of the Aristotelian Society, met Alexander Shand, of whom he was to become an intimate friend.[61]

Although Shand was a rather leisurely gentleman-scholar whose only book, *The Foundations of Character,* did not appear until he was over fifty, he had already formed its principle hypothesis by the middle 1890s. His project was the realization of the "science of character" that John Stuart Mill had envisioned as "ethology" in 1843, but which had been aborted by "the dominance of the Laws of Association as explanatory principles." In contrast, Shand used the James-Lange theory of the emotions to argue that characterological types were determined by "systems of sentiments," which were derived from instinctually based emotions and expressed in different "relative ethics." Shand spoke of Westermarck (along with William McDougall) as one of those who had accepted his hypothesis, and Westermarck in turn acknowledged Shand's influence—although he was also subject to other more specifically philosophical influences in the early 1890s. Along the way, Westermarck became convinced that "moral judgments are ultimately based, not on the intellect, but on emotions," and that there could be "no moral truths because the contents of an emotion fall entirely outside the category of truth." Ethics as a science could have no other task than to "investigate moral consciousness as a fact" by studying the variety of moral ideas among peoples, which were "most plainly expressed in their customs and laws.[62]

Westermarck began in the characteristic comparativist manner, by excerpting books on slips of paper and categorizing them by subject matter. And when he decided that he should study the problem "not only from books but from life," it was still in comparativist terms: he had in mind an ambitious itinerary that would have carried him to the Amazon, Tierra del Fuego, Polynesia, Australia, Malaya, and India. When he actually departed from England, via Spain, in 1898, Morocco was to have been the first stage of a venture he hoped would take him eventually to "Ceylon, the South Sea Islands, and Heaven knows where." By the end of a three months' stay, when the portmanteau containing all of his scientific notes was stolen in the night from his tent in Marrakesh, Westermarck had concluded that "a journey for ethnological research is a serious undertaking, needing much time and patience." During twenty-one such journeys to Morocco over the next several decades, he was in fact to spend a total of seven years in the field, including over two years without a break between 1900 and 1902.[63]

In an era when there was "not a single road made in the whole of Morocco," and the heads of rebel tribesmen were upon occasion still put on pikes around the walls of Mequinez, fieldwork there was at least as demanding as at Alice Springs or Murray Island. However, disregarding the Sultan's requirement that foreigners must be accompanied by a military escort, Westermarck relied instead on the baraka of Sîdi Abdsslam, a shereef of the Baqqâli family, whose "holiness" was so strong that people were "even afraid of their goatherds." Sîdi Abdsslam later went to Finland with Westermarck to help him learn Arabic, and thereafter accompanied him on all his field excursions—eventually being knighted by the president of Finland for his services.[64]

Characteristically accompanied by a retinue of eight, Westermarck moved around Morocco, "living like a nomad in my tent, travelling from tribe to tribe and settling down for weeks or months, now in one, now in another country village where I found useful work could be done." Although he usually pitched his tent no more than two nights in the same place, since the traditional duty of hospitality was "limited to three days," he also spent lengthy periods in a number of places, including half a year in Fez, six months in a village in the mountains of Andjra, three months among the Shlöh of the Great Atlas range (whom he regarded as "a superior race to the Arabic-speaking Bedouins of the plains") as well as frequent summers in villas on the Mediterranean coast. Occasionally, Westermarck doffed his European suit to attend ceremonies "disguised as a Moor," and he once took advantage of a hole in the floor of a second-story room to gain "an insight into the more intimate family life of the Berbers." But his more usual fieldwork mode was to select a "teacher" to come "every day and instruct me in the tribe's manners and customs." In Dukkala, it was literally "the village schoolmaster"; in Marrakesh it was a "scribe from Glawi" who taught him Berber to complement the Arabic he already had mastered; in Fez, he had a whole "staff of new teachers," including a divorced woman from an Arabic-speaking mountain tribe, who made him promise not to disclose the "magic arts by which married women can get their husbands under their thumbs." If it was perhaps not yet fieldwork in the full Malinowskian mode, Malinowski himself later said that "no better field-work exists than that of Westermarck in Morocco"; since then, "several generations of Moroccanists" have consulted Westermarck's lengthy indices to discover what he "did happen to know about almost any matter that one wants to pursue concerning things Moroccan."[65]

The matters that Westermarck himself particularly wanted to pursue were those aspects of the "folk-lore" of the Moroccans that would illustrate the "close connection between moral opinions and magic and religious beliefs." Much of *The Origin and Development of Moral Ideas* was in fact written during the four years he spent in Morocco before 1906, and Westermarck began the book by noting the frequent references made "on my authority, to customs and ideas prevalent among the natives of Morocco." But in fact these references were rather infrequent, and clustered in the chapters on religious beliefs, and in the discussion of "homosexual love"—which Westermarck assured his publisher contained no details that "may be regarded as 'scandalous,' even by a judge," and which was on several occasions reprinted in German and French translations. The vast body of Westermarck's ethnographic data was separately published, at first in occasional articles, and later in a series of major monographs.[66]

What Westermarck called "my Moorish investigations" have been more recently described as reading "like a territorially restricted Frazer" (the "Amongthas" now regional rather than global and described on the basis of fieldwork instead of reading). Westermarck himself recalled that when he first went to Morocco he carried with him the two volumes of *The Golden Bough*, along with "tents and rifles and other necessary things." In treating the general evolution of morals, Westermarck's intellectual reference points were the major figures of the British and Scottish philosophical traditions from Hume and Bentham to Bain and Spencer. But in treating Moroccan customs and beliefs, the reference point was often Frazer. Sometimes Westermarck was critical, and on substantial issues—using his Moroccan evidence to argue against Frazer's hypothesis that "the human victim who is killed for the purpose of ensuring good crops is regarded as a representative of the corn-spirit and is slain as such." At others, he was simply emendatory—suggesting that the new king was supposed to inherit, "not the predecessor's soul, but his divinity or holiness," or baraka. He defended himself at length against Frazer's critique of his theory of the origin of exogamy (which Frazer explained instead as an "accidental result" of savage superstition, an "unconscious mimicry" of the scientific fact that infertility was "an inevitable consequence of inbreeding through many generations"). Nevertheless, Westermarck took Frazer's discussion of magic and religion as the "starting point" for his own work on *Ritual and Belief in Morocco*—although its fundamental concept, baraka, tended to blur the distinction between the two.[67]

The thrust of Westermarck's work, however, was much more relativistic than Frazer's. Instinctualist rather than intellectualist, he denied any "absolute standard of morality," on the grounds that "moral concepts are ultimately based on emotions either of indignation or approval." Westermarck did, however, seek to establish moral universals comparatively. On the one hand, he found that "among mankind at large there is a moral rule which forbids people to kill members of their own society." On the other, he found in the maternal and paternal instincts a universal human basis for an extensionist theory of altruism, with marriage, local proximity, common descent, and common worship uniting ever larger units within the bonds of sympathetic obligation. Reversing this universalizing tactic, Westermarck argued, in contrast to Frazer's pervasively negative view of savagery, that certain characteristics commonly attributed to savages were not in fact universal. Thus, while "nowhere in the savage world is truth held in less estimation than among many of the African races," even there many peoples had been described as "hostile to falsehood."[68]

But despite these important differences, Westermarck's view of the development of moral ideas remained within the evolutionary tradition and was roughly consistent with the stages Frazer had outlined in the second edition of *The Golden Bough.* He spoke of the "higher stages of moral development," in which ("among peoples of culture") the "doctrine of resentment" was complemented by the "doctrine of forgiveness." And just as "the extension of duties towards neighbours" had embraced "wider and wider circles of men" as they moved "on the upward path from savagery to barbarism to civilisation," so, over time, had the constitutive role of "sentiment" itself been superseded by that of "reflection." Like Tylor, whom he defended against Lang on the issue of Australian monotheism, Westermarck rejected any necessary linkage between morality and religion. The moral ideas of uncivilized men were "more affected by magic than by religion"; religious influence was most powerful in intermediate "stages of culture"; "increasing knowledge" lessened "the sphere of the supernatural," which in the future would be even more constricted. Despite Westermarck's pruning of *The Golden Bough,* Frazer would surely have recognized here the sequence of magic, religion, and science. It was not by accident that Westermarck spoke of the outdoor study at his English country home as "the sacred grove"—or that he dedicated the third of his trilogy of Moroccan ethnographic studies to Frazer.[69]

In sharp contrast to Frazer, however, Westermarck was also very active in the groves of academe. Frazer's only pedagogic venture was an ill-starred stint in 1908 as Professor of Social Anthropology at the University of Liverpool, undertaken on condition that he be required neither to teach nor to examine—and even so abandoned after five months. Westermarck, on the other hand, was for much of his life simultaneously professor at universities in two different countries: the University of Helsingfors, where he was first docent, then Professor of Practical Philosophy, and the Åbo Academy in Finland, where he was founding Rector; and the University of London, in the London School of Economics and Political Science.[70]

Hybrid offspring of Fabian socialism and late Victorian university reform, the London School of Economics was founded in 1895 as the brainchild of Sydney Webb. In 1900 it became a school within the newly reorganized University of London, and in 1903 its curriculum was extended to include the study of sociology. The same year had seen the founding in London of the Sociological Society, an unstable and temporary coalition of "racial sociologists," town-planning or "civics sociologists," and "ethical or social work sociologists," brought together by a common concern with the quality of life and of human populations in the deteriorating urban environment of modern civilization and by a belief in the possibility of a "science of society" which might improve them.

The leading eugenicist in the group was of course Francis Galton, whose occasional interest in the methodology of cultural comparison was distinctly secondary to his systematic interest in the presumed hereditary differences among races, classes, and individuals and in the possibility of improving the "average civic worth" of the British population by active social intervention. The leading civics sociologist was Haddon's friend Patrick Geddes, who preferred to think of "Place, Work, and People" (Le Play's Lieu, Travail, Famille) in terms of a dynamic interaction between organism and environment. Although a less well defined group, the ethical sociologists may be exemplified by Leonard Hobhouse, who had been influenced by the Hegelian T. H. Green at Oxford, and who insisted in his inaugural editorial for the *Sociological Review* in 1908 that "any deep-reaching definitions, classifications, any conception of growth, development or decay in human society will consciously or unconsciously be framed in terms of our conception of the common good." However, the society's organizing spirit, the banker Victor Branford, and its chief financial angel, the wealthy businessman Martin White, were both Scottish disciples of Geddes; it was White whose support made possible the development of sociology at the London School of Economics.[71]

Before Westermarck returned to London in 1903 to arrange for the publication of the first part of his study of moral ideas, Branford wrote inviting him to participate in the Sociological Society and upon his arrival introduced him to White, who subsequently became a close personal friend. Within weeks, Westermarck was asked to give seven lectures at the London School of Economics on "Early Customs and Morals," and in the following year White funded three-year lectureships there for Westermarck, Hobhouse, and Alfred Haddon. In 1907, when a Department of Sociology was formed, White endowed a permanent professorship for Hobhouse and a five-year personal chair for Westermarck. From then on until his retirement in 1930, Westermarck spent at least one term a year teaching at the London School of Economics—where the student body was, by his account, "the most international" and "the most varied in colour of any university in the world" and where the seminars had just as wide a range.[72]

Like Westermarck, Hobhouse had been strongly influenced by Tylor, whose lectures he attended at Oxford; and like Westermarck (although in anti-biologistic intellectualist terms), he published a comparativist study of the evolution of morals. In 1915, Hobhouse and two students produced a comparative study of the "material culture and social institutions of the simpler peoples," subtitled "an essay in correlation," which used a variant of Tylor's method of adhesions in order to establish a general "orthogenic" trend of social and mental development. Given the evolutionary orientation of the two major figures, it

Edward Westermarck (center), on the verandah of his house outside Tangier, lunching with his friend Martin White (right), benefactor of the London School of Economics, 1907. (Courtesy of the Collection Åbo Akademis bildsamlingar)

is thus not surprising that the first syllabus of the London School of Economics Department of Sociology was structured by the categories of social evolutionary comparativism: among its topics were "the principle of evolution applied to social phenomena"; "maternal and paternal descent"; "the clan and the tribe"; "the development of social control"; and "animism, ancestor-worship, polytheism."[73]

Although Branford had hoped that "the academic Department of Sociology might grow up in active cooperation with the Society," there were in fact tensions from the very beginning—within the Sociological Society, between the society and the Department of Sociology, and apparently also within the department itself. Hobhouse, who opposed both biological and environmental determinism, was hostile to both the eugenics and the civics sociologists. By 1907, the former had gone their own way with the formation of the Eugenics Education Society. Among the civics sociologists who remained, there was dissatisfaction with Hobhouse's rather abstractly academic sociology; Branford had in fact refused to include Tylor's works in the society's bibliographies on the grounds that anthropology "had no practical focus." By 1911, dissension had reached a point of crisis, and Hobhouse was forced to resign as editor of the *Sociological Review*. Although until his death in 1929 he remained the only professor of sociology with a regular appointment in Britain, his interests turned increasingly to philosophy. Morris Ginsberg as his successor remained devoted to him, but there was no Hobhousian school. Whether Hobhouse's anti-Spencerian liberal sociology represented a viable theoretical tradition has been disputed; however, his most sophisticated explicator has described Hobhouse's work as "remote" from the "characteristic concerns of modern sociology," and it is generally agreed that there was a hiatus in the development of sociology in Britain after its brief Edwardian efflorescence.[74]

In the meantime, however, the encompassment of anthropology by sociology at the London School of Economics had long since begun to break down. An internal administrative memoir on the teaching of anthropology and ethnology suggested an incipient differentiation from sociology: ethnology was "that part of anthropology which investigated the characteristics of different races, their geographical distribution and migrations, and their affinities"; in contrast, "anthropology" was the study of "those characteristics which are common to civilised and uncivilised races"—the rest of civilization being left to "sociology's other branches." The appointment of Charles Seligman in 1910 to the ethnology lectureship originally held by Haddon and then in 1913 to a permanent position as part-time Professor of Anthropology gave a further impetus to the development of a separate ethnographically oriented anthropology. And in the work of other anthropologists than Seligman, this empirical tradition developed along theoretical lines quite different from that represented by Hobhouse's evolutionary sociology, with its purposive ethical focus and its strongly intellectualistic and individualistic tendency.[75]

For somewhat different reasons, neither did it develop along the theoretical line represented by Westermarck. Although there is much in Malinowski that can be traced to Westermarck's biologically grounded sociology, the major theoretical influences on later British social anthropology came from people inclined to draw a sharper line between biology and sociology. At the time of the Sociological Society's founding in 1903, Emile Durkheim was one of several Continental sociologists whose advice was sought on the constitution of a science of society. But the methodological and conceptual opposition between the emerging British and French sociological traditions was clearly evident in the two papers by Durkheim included in the first volume of the society's *Sociological Papers*. Durkheim was sharply critical of those who interpreted religious beliefs and practices as "the outcome of feelings which are born and nurtured in the individual conscience," and who had no adequate understanding of society as "the determining cause of the action of which it is the scene." And in reviewing Westermarck's *History of Human Marriage* a decade earlier, he had criticized the attempt to "rest sociology on Darwinism" as "contrary to proper method" in sociology.[76]

A similar issue had previously been raised from within the British tradition by the man whose study of ritual had played a formative role in the development of Durkheim's sociological thought: William Robertson Smith. Shortly after Westermarck's *History of Human Marriage* appeared, Smith charged that despite its title, it was really a work in "natural history" rather than "history." It was based on the "tacit assumption" that "the laws of society are at bottom mere formulated instincts," and Westermarck had offered "no evidence to satisfy anyone that is not prepared to share the assumption with him." The "crucial test" was his explanation of the origin of exogamy, which actually took for granted "the very custom that it professes to explain," insofar as the postulated instinctive aversion to inbreeding was explained as the product of the natural selection of groups that "through many generations" had avoided "wiving within the group"—that is, that already practiced as a custom the exogamy Westermarck wished to ground in instinct. In seeking a "sounder method of handling the evidence drawn from the usages of rude societies," Smith looked backward toward his own mentor McLennan. But his suggestion that Westermarck's definition of marriage as "the habit of pairing" was "totally inapplicable" within "the sphere of law and custom" looked forward to the later Durkheimian tradition in British social anthropology.[77]

Robert Marett and the Magico-Religious: The "Laws of Association" and the "Will to Believe"

Although the anglicization of Durkheim is appropriately associated with the name of Radcliffe-Brown, there was before him another important mediator: Robert Ranulph Marett. Durkheim's nephew Marcel Mauss, who inherited the ethnological portion of his uncle's sociological estate, once suggested that "an early exposure to customary law in the Channel Islands" was an important asset for a number of British anthropologists—among them A. M. Hocart, Robert S. Rattray, and Marett. Marett's birth in 1866 on the island of Jersey, within a few miles of the coast of Normandy, symbolized a greater receptivity to the French sociological tradition than many of his British anthropological confreres were to exhibit. Marett's maternal and paternal families were both deeply and endogamously rooted in the island gentry; his father, a scholar of insular law and custom and founder of the local antiquarian Société Jersiase, had studied at the Sorbonne before serving in a series of important local administrative posts. But as the title of Marett's autobiography suggests, his cultural life was oriented from the Norman periphery toward the English center. From the time that he came up to Jowett's Balliol in 1884, he was "a Jerseyman at Oxford"—a gentleman academic, for whom anthropology, whether of the sociological or intellectualist mode, was always somewhat avocational to his collegiate life.[78]

Coming to Balliol as "an old-world Tory" and a "Church-and-State man," Marett soon became a member of the Russell Club, "a hot-bed of radicalism," and a participant in the social work of Toynbee Hall—although in retrospect he was inclined to accept as "near the mark" a later student's denunciation of him as "a palaeolithic Conservative disguised under a thin coating of Victorian Liberalism." As one of "Jowett's men," Marett considered himself a Platonist in respect to "divine philosophy"; but while he resisted religious scepticism, he handed "the whole department of [worldly] domestic affairs" over to that "most efficient handmaid," natural science. He was distrustful of Balliol Hegelianism and the "haughty Oxford logicians who had no practical acquaintance with scientific method"; his own philosophical leanings were "secretly on the side of J. S. Mill." And when a tutor advised him to consult Lang's *Custom and Myth* about certain Roman gentile names "that suggested a connection with animals and plants," Marett became "an enthusiastic, if extremely ignorant, disciple of the school of Tylor" against the linguistic Aryanism of Max Müller.[79]

After an undergraduate career interrupted by meningitis and a recuperative year of travel on the Continent, Marett chose the life of an Oxford don. In 1891 he competed successfully for a fellowship at Exeter College, to which he remained attached for the rest of his career, serving after 1929 as Rector. Before he arrived at Exeter, his "nascent appetite for anthropology" had been tickled by the topic announced for the triennial T. H. Green Moral Philosophy Prize: "The Ethics of Savage Races." For the next three years he "read up the manners and customs of savage folk"—doing his best "not to allow either the old light of Tylor or the new light of Frazer to dazzle my half-awakened eyes"—with the thought that lectures on "ethics in its evolutionary aspect" might become part of the "Greats" curriculum. Marett soon discovered that "savage life, being relatively undifferentiated in contrast to civilisation with its diversity of special functions, must be studied as if all of one piece, so that ethics merged into morals, and morals covered also religion, law, government, and, in short, the social custom as a whole." Although never published, his essay won the prize, bringing Marett into direct contact with Tylor, who was one of the examiners, and whose successor and biographer he eventually became. In the shorter run, Marett helped Tylor, whose memory was already failing, with revisions for the fourth edition of *Primitive Culture,* and (less successfully), with the reworking of the Gifford Lectures.[80]

During the seven-year bachelorhood still required of newly elected fellows, Marett seems to have been preoccupied with teaching and with college responsibilities—as well as holidays abroad and golf at home. Although he continued to use a "slip-system" to cull abstracts from ethnographic sources, he wrote little in this period. In the early 1890s he contributed to the *Economic Review* a number of reviews of books on economic and social topics, as well as an essay sharply critical of Herbert Spencer's "Ethics of Industrialism," which he glossed as grossly Darwinistic, without any appreciation of "the power of Ideas" as a "factor in Progress." After 1897, he reviewed a number of sociological and psychological works for the *Oxford Magazine*.[81]

At the same time, Marett was coming directly under the influence of a psychology quite different from Tylorian and Frazerian associationism: the voluntaristic empiricism of William James. Aside from its general vogue in British psychology in this period, James's thought was specifically available to Marett through his undergraduate acquaintance F. C. S. Schiller, who had gone to teach in the United States, where he was James's friend and philosophical disciple. Upon his return to Oxford in 1897 Schiller became the leading British exponent of Jamesian pragmatism, and later secretary of the Oxford Philosophical Society, which Marett served as president. It was to this group that Marett presented the only published version of his ethical studies: an essay on "Origin and Validity in Ethics" in which he attempted a synthesis of the "rational utilitarianism" of the evolutionary school and the voluntaristic intuitionalism of an empirical introspectionist psychology. Although Marett did not cite James either here or in his early anthropological essays, it is clear that he felt the influence of a man whom he had come "to know very intimately" during one of his visits to England. James's approval of his ethics essay was was "reward enough" to have justified Marett's effort; similarly, it was a letter from James that convinced Marett of "the soundness of the position" he later developed in *The Threshold of Religion*.[82]

Marett's return to anthropology came in 1899, in the aftermath of his marriage (to Nora Kirk, the daughter of a Scottish colonial administrator), which he seems to have experienced as a liberation of creative force. On the eve of the British Association meetings that fall, his Oxford colleague John Myres, a classical archeologist, asked him if he could enliven the anthropological section with something "really startling." Writing on Jersey, with only a "small bundle of extracts" his wife had culled for him on the history of religion, Marett produced a paper attacking the hypothesis that "had commanded the allegiance of all men for some thirty years": Tylor's animism. But rather than arguing for the existence of savage beliefs in a supreme being, as Lang did, Marett suggested that primitive religion was at once a "wider" and a "vaguer" phenomenon than Tylor's "belief in spiritual beings." His interest was in "residual phenomena which a strictly animistic interpretation of rudimentary religion would be likely to ignore." Groping about "amongst the roots of those beliefs and practices that at a certain stage of their development have usually been treated as forming a single growth which is labelled animism," Marett found evidence for a "pre-animistic religion." Although he was reluctant to "crib, cabin, and confine" research by creating a new definitional "pigeon-hole," he proposed to call it "animatism": the "basic feeling of awe, which drives a man, ere he can think or theorize upon it, into personal relations with the supernatural." The essence of religion was not to be found in the "shifting variety" of beliefs, but in "that steadfast groundwork of specific emotion whereby man is able to feel the supernatural precisely at the point at which his thought breaks down." As Marett later put it, savage religion developed under conditions that favored "emotional and motor processes" rather than "ideational" ones; it was "something not so much thought out as danced out."[83]

Marett's paper caused a sensation in the small world of British anthropology and folklore, in which he now began to participate actively. Having attacked the aging father of evolutionary intellectualism, Marett next turned his critical attention to the work of the latter-day scion. In 1904, he published a long essay in *Folk-Lore* criticizing the three-stage theory of intellectual evolution Frazer had advanced in the second edition of *The Golden Bough.* Marett's paper addressed Frazer's argument that religion had arisen when a "primitive philosopher," slowly realizing that "time and trial" had shown that magic lacked the causal efficacy claimed for it, concluded that other unseen beings, "like himself but far stronger," directed the course of the world, and that they must be propiatiated in order to accomplish what "he had hitherto believed to be dependent on his own magic." In a passage with far-reaching critical implications for evolutionary method, Marett suggested that "one's first impression is that a purely analytical method has escaped its own notice in putting on a pseudo-genetic guise, that mere heads of classification have first been invested with an impermeable essence, and then identified with the phases of a historical development which is thereby robbed of all intrinsic continuity." Frazer had suggested that magic could be "deduced immediately from elementary processes of reasoning"—the "laws of association by similarity and by contiguity in space or time." Granting that this might have "passed muster" thirty years ago, when Tylor "first formulated the same theory," Marett insisted that since then "an all-sufficient associationalism" had "for sound reason been banished from psychology."[84]

Frazer's rationalistic interpretation was another instance of the "psychologist's fallacy," in which "the standpoint of the observer" was confused with "the standpoint of the mind under observation." Although

Marett conceded that a "considerable amount of real inference may be operative at certain stages in the development of magic," he nevertheless took as his "working principle" the assumption that theory grew out of practice, "rather than the other way about." His paradigm case of "rudimentary magic" was the act of a rejected suitor angrily throwing a "faithless maiden's portrait into the fire." Although the man knew he was only pretending to harm the woman, the "will to believe" built a bridge between the symbol and the ulterior cathartic reality (the quotes around the title of James's highly influential essay were Marett's). Similarly, primitive man knew he was pretending, but he was "loth to abandon a practice rooted in impulse and capable of affording relief to surcharged emotion." And as the shaman might believe in the efficacy of his catharsis, so might the victim of a spell: "just as the savage is a good actor, throwing himself like a child into his mime, so he is a good spectator, entering into the spirit of another's acting, herein again resembling the child, who can be frightened into fits by the roar of what he knows to be but a 'pretended' lion." Make-believe could be efficacious, "stirring all manner of deep-lying impulses and automatisms."[85]

Magic was not, as Frazer thought, a misguided "savage equivalent of our natural science" based on the assumption of a mechanical regularity in nature. It was rather an act of "imperative willing" whose ideal mechanism was the spell, since "nothing initiates an imperative more cleanly, cutting it away from the formative matrix of thought and launching it on its free career, than the spoken word"—the "very type of a spiritual projectile." And inasmuch as magic was based on a generalized notion of "quasi-personal agency," it was never clearly distinguishable from religion. It was, however, finally "swallowed up in unmistakable religion" by a "gradually-intensifying personification," which followed naturally from the fact that the magical act was "an inter-personal, intersubjective transaction, an affair between wills."[86]

Although referring to savages in condescending, evolutionary, and ethnocentric terms, Marett showed great sensitivity to problems of definition—and to what Franz Boas, at about the same time, would have called "premature classification." If Marett's critical stance was perhaps more explicitly philosophically based, it, too, was strongly affected by ethnographic considerations. He seems to have been particularly influenced by Codrington's representation of the Melanesian idea of mana, which he cited in his discussion of "pre-animistic religion" and treated at greater length in several essays a decade later. In 1907, Marett played the primary role in organizing a festschrift in honor of Tylor's seventy-fifth birthday. Directing his own contribution again to Frazer, who had "universalized Dr. Tylor's partial correlation" of taboo and magic, Marett called into question a number of evolutionary assumptions, including the idea that human history could be shown "to be subject to hard-and-fast laws." Taboo was in the first instance a social rather than a psychological phenomenon: "a portion of the unwritten law of society." And when considered psychologically, it was better seen as a "mystic affair" than as "a misapplication of the laws of association of ideas." Frazer had a right to his own definition of magic, since it was "not a savage concept," but "merely a counter for the use of the psychology that seeks to explain the primitive mind not from within but from without." But taboo was in fact a native concept, which should be understood in native terms; instead, "we are merely bidden to despise it." Looking for "genuine primitive notions" that "may with relative appropriateness be deemed equivalent to the idea of magic, as that idea is to be understood . . . by a psychology that tries to establish a community between savage and civilized peoples," Marett was led to the idea that taboo was a kind of "negative *mana*"—"an awe as towards mystic powers recognized by society and as such tending to be reputable."[87]

Doubtful of the category pretensions of the intellectualizing armchair anthropologist-philosopher, Marett was nevertheless willing to attribute a kind of empirical speculation to protophilosophers of a Jamesian bent. Speaking to the Oxford meeting of the International Congress on the History of Religions in 1908, he argued that although it might not have "acquired in the aboriginal mind the full status of an abstract idea," the idea that "religion consists in getting *mana* for oneself" had "long been more or less articulately felt by the Melanesian mind." The task of the science of comparative religion was to explicate the notion "in just those terms that would naturally suggest themselves" if the native mind were "somehow quickened into self-consciousness and self-expression." On this basis, Marett proposed to generalize the "*tabu-mana* formula" to characterize the negative and positive aspects of supernatural power, suggesting that for analytic purposes both should be subsumed within a single undifferentiated sphere of the "magico-religious."[88]

At several places in these two discussions of mana, Marett referred to the work of the Durkheimians, which he had first become aware of in 1905—at a point when there was no copy of the *Année sociologique* in the Oxford library. Marett was put off a bit by their "socialistic" tendency, and he did not think it "feasible to deal in their concrete way with an abstraction, such as social man must be if you leave out his individual aspect." But as a counter to "the opposite tendency running through so much of British work," the Durkheimian emphasis on "the purely social element" was "very enlightening," and in the first volume of the new *Sociological Review*, Marett published an essay elaborating his own "sociological view of Comparative Religion."[89]

Recasting the "British school" somewhat in his own anti-Frazerian image, Marett suggested that it used a "psychological method" to understand religious consciousness "from the inside," penetrating behind ritual, language, organization, and other "outward signs" to "those subjective factors of which the objective manifestations formed the more or less loose-fitting garment." In contrast, "the rest of the world" sought explanations of a more "objectivist" sort; Marett instanced the biological school of Novicow and Espinas, the racialism of Lapouge and Ammon, economic interpretations deriving from Marx, and the anthropogeography of Ratzel—all of which he rejected as apriorist or reductionist. What was left was the sociological school of Emile Durkheim, whose "objectivism" was "psychological" rather than "materialist," and whose determinism still left room for "the phenomenal existence of the contingent in the shape of human purpose." From the Durkheimians, the British could learn the necessity of "a Social, not an Individual, Psychology." British students of religion had fallen victim to the "fallacy of Psammetichus"—the Egyptian king who isolated infants to see what language they would instinctively speak; reversing this "incubator" approach, Marett suggested that transplanting a savage child to civilized surroundings would make clear "that the supreme determining influence must rest with the social factor."[90]

Marett was not ready to abandon individual psychology entirely, or to subordinate social psychology to social morphology, but he insisted that "Social Psychology must work with Social Morphology ever at its elbow." Although he would not go so far as to "say that a religion is identical with a particular organization of society," he did argue that the "meaning and purpose" of religion existed "not for the individual tribesman taken at random," but "for the society as a whole"—and that "social meanings and purposes exist mainly as embodied in social institutions." In the study of primitive society, where "self-caused ideas as moving forces are but rarely to be met with," this meant taking ritual rather than belief as the starting point of analysis: "out of it proceed the random whys; back to it go the indecisive therefores; and at this the common centre the meanings coalesce and grow ever more consistent, so that at last, perhaps, they react as one systematic idea on the supporting custom, and may henceforth rank as an originating psychical force of the higher order."[91]

Marett's commitment to social psychology reflected certain ulterior ideological motives. Although these were manifested in a critique of Frazerian assumption, they were not dissimilar to those that in the same years were impelling Frazer toward a reconsideration of *Psyche's Task.* Ever the academic gentleman, Marett began corresponding with Frazer before his initial critique in 1904, and in 1911 the two men quarelled politely by mail as to who was the true theoretical heir of William Robertson Smith. Frazer rejected Marett's assertion that Smith, too, had believed in the historical priority of ritual to dogma; Marett insisted that Smith had attributed to savages only the "unconscious" principles embodied in religious practice rather than any "reasoned" religious belief. After apologizing for the "over-vigorous" response necessary "when one is up against a giant like you," Marett retreated to the underlying ideological point: "All that some of us—McDougall, for instance, and Lévy-Bruhl, etc. in France—have been trying to do is to emphasize the *mobbish* character of primitive religion and primitive life." Like Frazer—and many of the social scientists of his day—Marett was fearful of the irrational forces stirring beneath the surface of Edwardian society. And in a broad sense he, too, remained an evolutionist, editing the works of Baldwin Spencer and publishing books on evolutionary topics on into the 1930s. But along lines that now seem much more forward-looking than the anxious protofunctionalist resonances of *Psyche's Task,* Marett's work contributed to the reformation of British social anthropology; much of what we associate with Malinowski and Radcliffe-Brown is in fact foreshadowed in Marett—whom around 1910 both of them read.[92]

Marett was almost as much an "armchair anthropologist" as Frazer; aside from several archeological digs on Jersey, his fieldwork was limited to five hours with some pygmies in London (to whom he referred in discussing the magico-religious), and an afternoon watching Aboriginal dances when the British Association met in Australia in 1914. But his sense of the difficulties of ethnographic translation was manifest in an essay entitled "The Study of Magico-Religious Facts" he contributed to the 1912 edition of *Notes and Queries.* The hyphenation was both a reflection of the fact that "framers of general theory" were "in dispute," and an exhortation to the ethnographer to collect data from the "point of view" of primitive folk, "uncoloured by his own." Eschewing questionnaires, Marett argued that "the real scheme of topics" must be framed "by the observer himself to suit the social conditions of a given tribe." The ethnographer must not ask "why" but "what," focussing on the rite in all its complex concrete detail, "keeping at arm's length our own theological concepts, as well as our anthropological concepts, which are just as bad, since they have been framed by us to make us understand savagery, not by savagery to enable it to understand itself."[93]

Although anthropology was always for Marett an "overtime employment," his influence was enhanced by his institutional activities at Oxford. It was he who made Exeter College a "nursery of anthropologists": Rattray, Hocart, and Evans-Pritchard were all his pupils. But it was also Marett who, after Tylor, became the focal figure of anthropology at the university level in Oxford. Although Tylor's readership had been augmented by a titular professorship in 1895, his attempt that year to

Faculty and students of the Committee for Anthropology, Oxford, c. 1910. Left to right (seated): Henry Balfour, Arthur Thomson, R. R. Marett; (standing): Wilson D. Wallis, Diamond Jenness, and Marius Barbeau. (Courtesy of the Pitt Rivers Museum, University of Oxford)

establish anthropology as a regular academic subject had been defeated by the combined forces of the "clerical" and the "classical" parties in the university electorate. Associated at this point primarily with the School of Natural Science, anthropology was still tarred with the *odium scientificum* that had been directed against Darwinism and vivisection. But as British anthropology moved toward the European classical world, it gained support in the arts faculty. In 1902, the debate was reopened by John Myres, who had attended Tylor's lectures before going on to do archeological research on Cyprus; and by 1904, Marett had joined in the campaign. The following year saw the establishment of a Committee for Anthropology, which "kept steadily in view the need of inducing classical scholars to study the lower culture as it bears upon the higher," and two years later, under Marett's leadership, organized a series of lectures on "Anthropology and the Classics." But it was also made clear that anthropology would not encroach too much on established scholarly fields: early on, Marett suggested that "the Anthropological Course would concern itself exclusively with past and present *savagery*." On this basis, a broad coalition was created, with members of the arts faculty outnumbering the natural scientists on the Committee for Anthropology by eleven to five, and a diploma course was established.[94]

Initially, the syllabus required candidates to pass examinations in both "Physical Anthropology" and "Cultural Anthropology," with the "comparative study of social phenomena" included in the latter under the heading "Sociological." But when Marett was appointed Tylor's successor two years after his retirement in 1908, his title was listed as Reader in Social Anthropology. By 1914 the "increase in the number of students of Social Anthropology," who were previously "dependent on the hospitality of Exeter College," was such that separate accommodation was sought for this "department" within the "School of Anthropology." Although the first use of "social anthropology" is commonly associated with the title of Frazer's ill-fated professorship at Liverpool, the rubric proved as inappropriate for Frazer as the professorship. By 1921, with a better view of how "social anthropology" might develop under the Durkheimian influences Marett had helped to mediate, Frazer decided that a better alternative to "physical anthropology" was after all "mental anthropology." By that time, however, "mental anthropology" in the Frazerian mode seemed to many itself out of date, and Marett's contribution to its passing was by no means insignificant. Although he never again wrote anything so seminal as those early critical articles, it was Marett who, from within, first clearly formulated the critique of what his student Evans-Pritchard later spoke of as the "Intellectualist (English) Interpretation of Magic."[95]

The Early Critique of Frazerian Assumption

Westermarck and Marett may be taken as representing two distinct lines of internal critique of the intellectualist tradition: one of them biologically oriented (and leading toward Malinowskian functionalism); the other, sociologically oriented (and leading toward Radcliffe-Brownian structural-functionalism). Both men began their anthropological careers under Tylor's aegis, and as successive Frazer Lecturers in the 1920s were still defending "the scientific tradition [Frazer] so stoutly championed" against the attacks of diffusionary anthropologists.[96] But if they refused to join a frontal assault on the evolutionary school, they had themselves already raised substantial, even transformative, issues for the intellectualist tradition. Nor were they the only British anthropologists to do so in the years around 1900. There were others—gentlemen scholars without university connections, whose contributions lie below the horizon of an emerging academic anthropology: some of them, critics from within; one of them, frankly apostate.

Perhaps the most outstanding among the former was Ernest Crawley, a schoolmaster whose obituarist described him as a "famous player and teacher of ball games, especially lawn tennis, [who] was also known as an anthropologist." Crawley, who had been a student of classics at Cambridge in the late 1880s, described himself as a follower of both Tylor and Frazer. His reading of their work had convinced him that "prevalent theories of marriage origins were based on an imperfect understanding of primitive custom and thought," and Westermarck's subsequent critique of "the old theory of primitive communism and the matriarchate" had confirmed his rejection of these "pseudo-syntheses." Crawley regarded Tylor's adhesions paper as "an important departure," but argued that before attempting comparisons, it was necessary first to analyze "every custom and its adhesions in the light not only of the whole culture of the given peoples, but of all primitive and elemental psychology." Taking from Tylor the notion of avoidance and from Frazer the idea of taboo, Crawley in 1902 published a work that brought into focus the repressed sexual themes running beneath the surface of intellectualist anthropology.[97]

In dedicating *The Mystic Rose* to Frazer, Crawley praised him for showing "that the origin of the marriage system was to be found in some primitive conception of danger attaching to the sexual act." Indeed, Crawley's peroration, in which he equated the "Mystical Rose" [sic] with the "Maiden-Mother" as a member of the "Holy Family" of Christian Europe, suggests an obvious parallel to Frazer's project, which had sought the savage prototype of another member of that "divine trinity." However, Crawley's account of the evolution of the religiously sanctioned taboos surrounding the "sexual crises" of the human life cycle followed Westermarck in assuming their basis in human physiology and instinct. While his psychology remained staunchly individualistic, it was equally staunchly anti-intellectualist: "all primitive psychological attitudes" arose from "what may be called physiological thought," which was "more or less reflex and subconscious" and became "practically inherent in the human mind." Furthermore, the primitive taboos surrounding the relations of the sexes were "repeated in the average civilized man, not as mere survivals, though their religious content has been narrowed, but springing from functional causes constant in the human organism." The Freudian resonances were later obvious to Crawley's editor, whose numerous additions to the posthumous second edition also included a number of references to the work of Malinowski.[98]

Not all of the British critics of Frazerian assumption in the decade after 1900, however, dedicated books to Tylor's heir. Andrew Lang, respectfully apostate to the master, was scathingly critical of the disciple. Having found "high gods" in Australia, Lang was not receptive to Frazer's suggestion that magic had preceded the development of religion. He described *The Golden Bough* to a friend as "the most inconceivably silly book of recent times": "One laughs out loud in bed at the absurdity of it." And Lang did his best to make the world laugh with him, dubbing Frazer's the "Covent Garden" or "vegetable school" of mythology, and devoting nearly a whole book to a case-by-case criticism of its classical and ethnographic evidence.[99]

Lang, however, was as much concerned with totemism and exogamy as with vegetative gods; and given his commitment to primitive monotheism, he had a strong motive for rejecting Frazer's conclusion that totemism was religious or magical in origin and that its social aspect was a secondary manifestation. Lang insisted that totemism must be viewed primarily as a social phenomenon which was only "later invaded by religion." In sharp contrast to Frazer, whose notions of social organization led back through Spencer and Fison to Morgan, Lang was more sympathetic to McLennan, despite disagreeing with him on several fundamental issues. Although Lang rejected Westermarck's instinctual explanation of the origin of exogamy, he accepted his critique of primitive promiscuity. Just as he insisted that the primitive religion of mankind was monotheistic, so did he insist that "the Family is the most ancient and the most sacred of human institutions." But in the process of defending what were, in terms of the larger culture, quite traditional beliefs, Lang developed what, in the culture of anthropology, has been viewed as a very forward-looking critique.[100]

While he proclaimed himself unpersuaded that mankind shared ancestry with "the great extant anthropoid apes," Lang started from the Darwinian view of primitive society developed by J. J. Atkinson, a cousin of his who had lived for years in New Caledonia, and whose manuscript on *Primal Law* Lang published as a complement to his own work on *Social Origins*. Following Darwin's reasoning from primate behavior, Atkinson assumed that man "aboriginally lived in small communities, each with a single wife, or, if powerful, with several, whom he jealously guarded against all other Men." In this primal patriarchal context, the only way young males could stay in the group was by capturing wives from the outside—a practice which (here influenced by Crawley) Lang suggested was the unconscious basis for a strict mystical taboo against incest. Totem names were simply "unfriendly *sobriquets*" applied by one group to another, who came in time to adopt the "nickname" applied to them and to give it a religious aspect. As such internally heterogeneous groups grew in size, and as the fact of internal heterogeneity was formally recognized, the totemic system within a given locality might began to approximate the McLennian form: exogamous clans with female descent.[101]

Against Frazer and the Morganian tradition, Lang saw the development of a "dual organization" not in terms of bisection, but rather in terms of "the amalgamation of two separate and independent local totem groups." Instead of being a conscious reformatory attempt to limit certain kinds of incestuous relations, "the growth of exogamy [was] non-moral, gradual, and almost unconscious, till it is clinched and stereotyped by the totem tabu." The class divisions within phratries were part of yet another "set of savage rules, which, whatever their origin, prohibit marriage *within the generation*"—and which were quite distinct from the prohibitions against marrying within the phratry or the totem group.[102]

In this context, Lang called into question the use of classificatory kinship terminology to reason backward about the development of social organization. Spencer and Gillen had insisted that in studying classificatory systems it was necessary to "lay aside all [our] preconceived ideas of relationship"; one could not assume that "father" meant "biological father." But in fact, Lang argued, the whole force of their reasoning backward depended on the terms having just that meaning—if one called a whole group of men "father," this implied a period when no man knew his true biological father. But insofar as we had knowledge of the actual meaning of such terms in each native language, it tended to show that classificatory terms defined "customary legal status" (age, sex, generation, etc.) rather than biological relationship. If "an Urabunna calls a crowd of men of his father's status by the same term as he calls his father," this might mean simply that he "styles his father by the name denoting a status which his father shares with many other men." If this were the case, then classifactory terms, rather than being survivals of different kinship practices in the past, were simply reflections of present customary social relationships. Rather than assume their origin in communal marriage, Lang preferred to assume that the terms had originated in small primeval totem kin-groups to describe relations of biological kinship or close continguity, and "in the evolution of tribal customary law" had been "extended out of their *family*, or fire-circle, into their *tribal* significance"—into terms "including all who have the same status, rights, and duties."[103]

Just as he questioned that particular customs were survivals of the primitive social state, so did Lang question the portrayal of that state by any particular presently existing tribe. Far from representing the primitive state of humanity, the Arunta were a sport, degenerate in some respects, highly or anomalously evolved in others. Accepting the Arunta as primitive, Frazer had taken various Arunta myths as describing earlier historical realities; in contrast, Lang, insisting on the priority of ritual to belief, argued that their myths were what Boas would have called "secondary rationalizations" to explain their anomalous practices. And in contrast to Lubbock, Spencer, Frazer, and others, Lang based his theory on "the group, not the individual," as the "social unit."[104]

Lang was by no means a consistently systematic critic of ethnocentric evolutionary assumptions—which manifested themselves rhetorically even in the critical process: thus, the Arunta "theory of things" was so complex that "one would scarcely believe it possible for naked savages." And while he maintained that "no Australians are now in or near 'the chrysalis' state of humanity," he had not by any means abandoned the search for origins. But in advancing his own theory of the "origin of totems," Lang knew that he was "guessing"; and in criticizing the evolutionary assumptions of others, he willy-nilly called into question the assumptions of British evolutionism in general—along lines analogous to those Marett was also pursuing.[105]

In 1903, Lang was conscious that he was going against the mass of learned anthropological opinion (though interestingly enough, he counted Emile Durkheim as an ally on some issues). But he had his followers, including notably Northcote W. Thomas, a fellow member of the Society for Psychical Research (and later government anthropologist in Nigeria), who with Lang's guidance carried on in 1906 a library study of "kinship organisations and group marriage in Australia." Although Thomas disagreed with Lang on certain points, he supported the "unconscious evolution theory of Mr. Lang" against the "conscious reformation theory." And with regard to the argument for group marriage from classificatory terminology, he concluded that "so far as Australia is concerned, [it] falls to the ground."[106]

Commenting in 1905 on an ethnographic account which he felt sustained his viewpoint, Lang suggested that there were "two chief points in dispute" in Australian ethnography: "the nature and origin of the marriage laws" and "the nature and origin of such among their ideas and practices as may be styled 'religious'"—or, in other terms, the problems of exogamy and totemism. Nor did these problems seem near solution: discussing "Australian Problems" in the Tylor festschrift of 1907, Lang concluded that "we seem lost in a wilderness of difficulties."[107]

That loss of direction must be seen in the context of developments in ethnographic practice. In 1898, Lang had criticized Tylorian comparativism as being based on the testimony of "observers ignorant of the language" and "prejudiced by one or other theory or bias": "How can one pretend to raise a science on such foundations?" But the development of a fieldwork tradition in fact exacerbated the problem, by uncovering ethnographic evidence that did not easily fit with evolutionary assumptions. The concern with the quality of ethnographic data manifest in the 1912 edition of *Notes and Queries* may be seen as an attempt to find a route out of Lang's "wilderness of difficulties." Another route was a more systematic regional comparativism, analogous to that proposed by Boas. Following the pattern of Northcote Thomas's study of Australian kinship, Westermarck commissioned two comparative studies of the same area, one in 1910 by Gerald Wheeler, another in 1913 by Bronislaw Malinowski. In each case, however, the result (if not the motive) was to expose further problems in evolutionary argument.[108]

Although the problems of totemism and exogamy were perhaps the most frequent and most controversial topics in *Man*, the "Monthly Record of Anthropological Science" initiated by the Anthropological Institute in 1900, at the end of the decade they seemed further from solution than they had in the beginning. By this time (according to one later summary) there had been over twenty different theories of totemism, which since Spencer and Gillen had been among the primary focussing issues of ethnographic fieldwork. In 1910, Frazer made his own attempt at synthesis: a four-volume compendium of world ethnographic data (and of his own earlier writings) on "totemism and exogamy." But far from ending the discussion, Frazer's work simply confirmed the inability of evolutionary theory to resolve, in the continent where primitive social organization and culture presumably still survived, its central theoretical problems.[109]

A more appropriately symbolic—although much less noticed—evidence of the disarray into which classical evolutionism had fallen appeared the following year, in the last book by the last active member of the original triumvirate of classical British evolutionists: Lord Avebury's *Marriage, Totemism, and Religion*. Returning to anthropological topics after a long absence, Avebury (John Lubbock) rallied to the defense of primitive promiscuity and totemism; but in the very process, he was forced to call attention to the way in which different evolutionary writers contradicted each other. By this time McLennan's original linkage of religious belief and matrilineal social organization had been pulled apart, as theorists tried to cope conceptually with contradictory ethnographic data. Among Boasian anthropologists, a more systematic ethnographic critique of evolutionary categories carried this centrifugal fragmentation even further. By an inversion of Tylor's "method of adhesions," Alexander Goldenweiser argued that the presumed distinguishing features of totemism (exogamous clans, totemic clan names, religious regard, totem taboos, and belief in hereditary descent) were actually to be found together in the world ethnographic record only in a small minority of cases. The question could well have been asked—as it later was by Lévi-Strauss—to what extent totemism was a "real" phenomenon in the primitive world, and to what extent a creation of the Victorian evolutionary imagination. Noting that the vogue of totemism coincided with that of "hysteria," Lévi-Strauss suggested that "once we are persuaded to doubt that it is possible arbitrarily to isolate certain phenomena and to group them together as diagnostic signs of an illness, or of an objective institution, the symptoms themselves vanish or appear refractory to any unifying interpretation."[110]

Neither totemism, nor Frazer, nor evolutionism passed from the scene in 1910. The next several years saw the publication of what in the general world of social science were surely the two most influential books on the problem of totemism: Freud's *Totem and Taboo* and Durkheim's *Elementary Forms of the Religious Life*, both of which were stimulated at least in part by Frazer's work, and both of which stimulated discussion of totemism on into the interwar period. Frazer, of course, continued to be published, and honored; and there were others of the same cohort of folklore-anthropologists (notably Hartland and Clodd) who continued to defend fundamental evolutionary assumptions into the 1920s. As late as 1929, Marett could still remark, with just a touch of irony, that "the majestic windmill is in working order." He did so, however, in defending Frazer and Tylor against the resurgent diffusionism which Malinowski had noted as one of "the events of 1910."[111]

FIVE

The Revival of Diffusionist Ethnology

Rivers and the Heliolithic School

At the Portsmouth meetings of the British Association for the Advancement of Science in September 1911, the disarray of evolutionary anthropology was displayed in a small international symposium on the problem of totemism. There was a paper by Haddon on "the present position" of the topic. There were two by Americans: the sociologist Hutton Webster, who spoke on the relation of clans and secret societies, and Alexander Goldenweiser, who presented a version of his critique of totemism as a cross-cultural category. And there were also two by Continental scholars: the German diffusionist Fritz Graebner, who, like Goldenweiser, called into question the existence of totemism as a cultural entity; and the Belgian sociologist Emile Waxweiler, who, along Durkheimian lines, argued the need for a functional interpretation. But the symposium was somewhat overshadowed by William Rivers' presidential address to the anthropological section, in which he announced his "conversion" from evolutionism to the "ethnological analysis of culture."[1]

Acknowledging that "the last few years" had seen "great additions" to the "facts of anthropology" and "decided advance" in its methods, Rivers was nevertheless concerned that "the theoretical side" had lagged: "the main problems of the history of human society are little if at all nearer their solution, and there are even matters which a few years ago were regarded as settled which to-day are as uncertain as ever." In contrast to zoologists or botanists, who everywhere shared the same set of "guiding principles," the anthropologists of different nations belonged to "different schools of thought." British anthropologists, inspired "primarily by the idea of evolution founded on a psychology common to mankind as a whole," interpreted cultural "similarities in different parts of the world" as the product of "independent origin and development." French anthropologists, too, were evolutionists, but insisted that "the psychology of the individual cannot be used as a guide to the collective actions of men in early stages of social evolution," and that "the study of sociology requires the application of principles and methods of investigation peculiar to itself." The Americans, preoccupied with ethnographic documentation, devoted little attention to "theoretical problems," although there was a movement there to put "the evolutionary point of view on one side" and study social problems from a "purely psychological" standpoint closer to the British than the French. It was in German anthropology, however, that there was "the most fundamental difference in standpoint and method."[2]

Although Adolf Bastian's *Elementargedanken* (elementary thought forms) had been "a most convenient expression for the psychological means whereby evolution is supposed to have proceeded," there had been a "general revolt" in Germany "not merely against Darwinism," but "even against the whole idea of evolution." Friedrich Ratzel's "geographical movement," as developed by Graebner and Wilhelm Schmidt, had insisted (against Bastian) that similarities of culture "could only be explained by direct transmission from one people to another"—in some cases, even arguing the influence of "one and the same culture" over "widely separated regions." Whereas the British were inclined to see "transitional forms" as evidence of "independent processes of evolution based on psychological tendencies common to mankind," the Germans saw only "the evidence of mixture of cultures, either with or without an accompanying mixture of races to which these cultures belonged."[3]

Although Rivers' historical perspective extended no further back than "recent years," his comment that the German movement would be "more fitly styled 'ethnological'" in fact suggests a somewhat greater depth in time, and the religious resonance of his "conversion" suggests roots even deeper yet. Diffusionary ethnology was not a new thing in Britain in 1910, or in Germany in 1883, when Ratzel had published his *Anthropogeographie.* It is in fact one of the ur-forms of anthropological speculation in the Western European intellectual tradition. If "evolutionism" can be traced to early Greek speculations, "diffusionism" is as old as the Old Testament; until the dehistoricization of anthropology after World War I, these two were the major traditional paradigmatic alternatives structuring speculation about human differences, which were characteristically seen as products of change in time. In the first half of the nineteenth century, the biblical diffusionism that traced all human groups back to Shem, Ham, and Japheth had been transformed into "ethnology," or "the science of races"—a development which in Britain can be followed in the work of James Cowles Prichard. In contrast to increasingly outspoken polygenists, who viewed races in static physicalist terms as aboriginally adapted to distinct climatic regions, monogenist ethnologists saw existing races as the historical products of movement through differing environments; by establishing physical, cultural, and linguistic connections, they sought to trace the relationships of present human groups back through time and space to a single original source.[4]

In the 1860s, Prichardian ethnology was pushed from the center stage of anthropological speculation: on the one hand, by the polygenist physical anthropologists associated with James Hunt's Anthropological Society of London; on the other hand, by the monogenist evolutionists, biological and cultural, who revitalized the dormant Ethnological Society of London, and who, at the end of the decade, dominated the Anthropological Institute that was formed in the amalgamation of the two competing groups. It was in this historical moment that what has been called "classical evolutionism" was established as an anthropological paradigm. Paradoxically, however, the anthropology that emerged from this period of paradigm reorientation was not systematically Darwinian in character. Later-nineteenth-century physical anthropology tended to see human differences in static typological terms reminiscent of pre-Darwinian polygenism. And insofar as post-Darwinian sociocultural anthropology used the comparative method to fill the evolutionary space between the ape and European man with a series of "stages" of cultural or social development, it may be said to have substituted a series of typological ladders for the branching Darwinian tree. Franz Boas noted this paradox in a letter he drafted in response to Tylor's 1888 paper, in which he suggested that it was "a most characteristic sign of the diversity of our present methods of thinking in physiological and psychological science that in the former we are inclined to derive genetically similar forms from *one* source; while in psychological science we are inclined to believe that an idea can develop independently in different communities or individuals." In effect, Boas was saying that while evolutionary anthropology emphasized independent invention, evolutionary biology (like traditional ethnology) was diffusionary.[5]

Since that passage was deleted from the version Boas actually sent, we can not be sure how Tylor would have responded to the suggestion that his anthropology was not consistent with biological evolutionism—although it is worth recalling that he was resistant to Westermarck's application of natural selection to the evolution of human marriage. But Tylor had long been aware of the explanatory alternatives Boas posed. When he responded to Galton's problem by suggesting that "transmission from a common source" was a "difficulty ever present in such investigations," he was in fact referring obliquely to an issue he had raised back in 1865, at a time when he was moving from diffusionary ethnology to evolutionism: whether a given instance of cultural similarity was to be explained by "the like working of men's minds under like conditions" (i.e., independent invention) or by "blood relationship" or "intercourse, direct or indirect, between the races among whom it is found." Although the classical evolutionary paradigm privileged independent invention, diffusion—either in the form of "intercourse" (i.e., "borrowing") or "blood relationship" (i.e., migration or race mixture)—remained an option in any given instance. Tylor himself never ceased to be interested in such questions, and continued to interpret the Aztec game of patolli in diffusionary terms on into the 1890s. However, what may be taken as his final statement on the topic—the concluding paragraph of the article on "Anthropology" in the eleventh edition of the *Encyclopaedia Britannica*—was in fact a strong reaffirmation of "independent invention":

> Anthropological researches undertaken all over the globe have shown the necessity of abandoning the old theory that a similarity of customs and superstitions, of arts and crafts, justifies the assumption of a remote relationship, if not an identity of origin between races. It is now certain that there has ever been an inherent tendency in man, allowing for differences in climate and material surroundings, to develop culture by the same stages and in the same way.[6]

But as Tylor's own case suggests (and as we have noted incidentally at several previous points) traditional "ethnological" issues did not disappear entirely from British anthropology during the later nineteenth century. Despite the rise of a typologically oriented physical "anthropology" in the 1860s, the problem of "racial" relationships continued to be discussed as an historical or "ethnological" problem. In 1895, Augustus Keane, Emeritus Professor of Hindustani at University College, London, published a widely read *Ethnology* which specifically acknowledged its debt to the Prichardian tradition—although in the characteristic fashion of post-Darwinian racialism, Keane attempted to reconcile it with polygenism. Thus it was only after a neo-polygenist account of the physical evolution of mankind, in which four primary branches of the "family tree of the Hominidae" separated sequentially from the main trunk, that Keane devoted the last half of his book to their further differentiation in the process of human migration into different regions of the earth.[7]

During the same period, the succession of population movements in Europe continued to command attention, as the subtitle of Isaac Taylor's *The Origin of the Aryans* attests: *An Account of the Prehistoric Ethnology and Civilisation of Europe.* While Max Müller had come to insist that "Aryan" was a linguistic rather than a "racial" category, his orientation to Aryan languages and mythologies remained broadly diffusionist. And despite the attacks of Lang and the other Tylorians, Müller continued to advance his own interpretations of religion and mythology, occasionally offering acute criticisms of fundamental assumptions of evolutionary comparativism—including, specifically, its image of the "savage." Even Tylorian folklorists pursued "ethnological" issues; thus Gomme in 1892 published a volume on *Ethnology in Folklore* in which he sought to remedy the failure of "the science of culture" to deal with "ethnological facts." Although Gomme's argument was developed in terms of intruding Aryans conquering indigenous savage groups, he, like Boas, justified his diffusionist approach with an appeal to Tylor's statistical method. And in the same year that Boas published his essay "On the Limitations of the Comparative Method of Anthropology," Gomme was also led to question many of the assumptions of evolutionary comparativism, which he suggested was pursued by the "exact opposite of Darwinian principles."[8]

At the level of day-to-day ethnographic practice, as opposed to comparativist theorizing, the ethnological approach never disappeared from late-nineteenth-century anthropology. Among the first questions one asked of any given group were "Who are they related to?" and "Where did they come from?" It was to investigate just such questions about the population of the British Isles that the "Ethnographic Survey of the United Kingdom" in which Alfred Haddon participated was undertaken in 1892. Similar issues motivated much of Haddonian ethnography overseas. The Torres Straits Expedition was of "some ethnological importance" because it focussed on the "frontier" between "large land areas inhabited respectively by Papuans and Australians," where there might be evidence of mixture or traces of "a migration of the Australian stock from North to South." Similarly, Seligman's work in Melanesia and later in the Sudan had to do with defining ethnic groups and tracing population movements. Issues of racial affinity were the starting point of any ethnographic survey, including the one carried on, under Haddon's influence, by Walter William Skeat during a Cambridge-sponsored expedition to the Malay Peninsula in 1899. Even at the basepoint of evolutionary comparativism, among the Australian Aborigines, there were those who found evidence of racial diversity, interpreting the fundamental division into two marriage classes as the result of the mixing of two racial groups, rather than being (as the Morganians would have it) "due to far-seeing deliberation on the part of savages."[9]

But if there were many precedents within the British anthropological tradition for the approach that Rivers (appropriately) styled "ethnological," it was his "conversion" in 1911 that initiated its resurgence as a distinct "school" in Great Britain. Although that episode has since been largely repressed in the disciplinary memory, it is impossible to understand the development of social anthropology in Britain without a further examination of the anthropological career of William Rivers and of the neo-diffusionist claimants of his tripartite anthropological inheritance.

W. H. R. Rivers: From the Evolution of Sensory Perception to the Diffusion of Primitive Social Organization

William Halse Rivers Rivers was in a sense baptized into the anthropological controversies of the 1860s. Three weeks after his birth in 1864, his maternal uncle, James Hunt, presented to him a copy of the translation of Theodor Waitz's *Anthropologie der Naturvölker* just published by the Anthropological Society of London, which Hunt had founded the year before. Given the fact that Hunt was a rather vitriolic polygenist racialist and Waitz a monogenist intellectual antecedent of Franz Boas, it was a somewhat paradoxical gift; in any case, the baptism did not take. When some years later Rivers was offered his uncle's valuable anthropological library, he declined on the grounds that "such books were of no use to him." But this was not all his uncle had to offer that Rivers was unable to accept. Hunt had come to anthropology through an interest in language, and practiced (by inheritance from his father) a system of speech therapy. By 1863, Hunt had established a center for the treatment of patients in Hastings, Sussex, where his sister also lived. Rivers' father, the son of a naval officer, was an Anglican clergyman who, after his education at Cambridge, had settled at nearby Chatham. Propinquity led to marriage, and temporarily to a new career. By the time Hunt died in 1869, Rivers' father had also become involved in Hunt's speech therapy practice, which he carried on until he returned to the active ministry in 1880. He was not, however, able successfully to apply Hunt's system to his son, who stammered badly. It was only in the years after his father's death in 1911 (the year of his own anthropological "conversion") that Rivers was able partly to overcome his speech impediment.[10]

That a man blocked in the expression of sensory stimuli should have turned to the study of sense perception (displacing sound to sight) seems perhaps worth remarking. But that turn was still some years in the future when Rivers received his Bachelor of Medicine degree in 1886—at twenty-two, the youngest medical graduate at St. Bartholomew's Hospital for decades to come. For the next two years, he served as ship's surgeon, travelling to Japan and North America, before winning his M.D. and election to a fellowship in the Royal College of Physicians in 1888. During his residencies at Chichester and St. Bartholomew's, Rivers became interested in neurological and psychiatric problems, publishing papers on delirium and hysteria, and in 1891 became house physician at the National Hospital for the Paralysed and Epileptic. Having read Herbert Spencer on his voyage to the Far East, Rivers was receptive to Hughlings Jackson's attempt to ground Spencer's mental evolutionism in empirical neurophysiological research—perhaps the more so because Jackson's research interests also included the linkage of speech defects and brain disorders. As we have already seen, this empirically oriented evolutionary viewpoint provided an essential underpinning for the research Rivers pursued when he settled at Cambridge after work in Germany with Ewald Hering (on color vision) and Emil Kraepelin (on psychiatric problems). When he finally turned to anthropology, thirty-five years after his uncle's attempt to baptize him into the profession, Rivers was already predisposed to accept the then still-prevailing social evolutionary paradigm.[11]

Rivers' shift to social anthropology did not take place immediately. For some years after his return from Torres Straits, his publications focussed primarily on the issues of visual perception that had motivated his "holiday" excursion. The attempt to transport the apparatus and the methodology of the academic psychological laboratory to the beaches of the Papuan Gulf had not produced such clearcut results as might have been expected on the basis of evolutionary racial assumption. The differences in sensory perception between Papuans and Englishmen (in some cases, the investigators themselves, in others, experimental subjects tested later on at home) were not clearcut. Although the investigators were inclined to explain some of them in terms of cultural experience, others they assumed to be innate. Thus McDougall concluded that the Papuan sense of touch was "twice as delicate as that of the Englishmen, while their sensitivity to pain is hardly half as great." Rivers himself seemed ambivalent; although it has been suggested that "the experiments disconfirmed conventional evolutionist wisdom about primitives' sensibilities," Rivers did in fact attempt to place the experimental results into a conventionally evolutionary framework.[12*]

Paradoxically, Rivers' initial conceptual reference point was the pre-evolutionary interpretation of Homeric color terms advanced by the British classicist (and Prime Minister) William Gladstone in 1858. On

*The results of the Torres Straits psychological testing were later to be interpreted as evidence against racial mental differences, most recently by Kuklick in the passage quoted above. Although the results certainly provoked scepticism, and in some cases may have sustained critique, the positions later taken by members of the expedition on such matters suggest that "disconfirming" is perhaps an overstatement. As the following paragraphs suggest, Rivers' subsequent writings on color perception and the epicritic/protopathic nerve distinction reflect a great deal of evolutionist assumption. Myers at the time suggested that reaction times might be the "expression of racial differences in temperament" (C. S. Myers 1903:223). McDougall later became a spokesman for the inequality of races, recalling his Torres Straits experience as evidence of the extroverted, sympathetic, and submissive racial temperament of the Negro (cf. Stocking 1968b:216–17, and above, 117). Some years later, the American psychologist E. B. Titchener wrote a critique of the tests, in which he was sharply critical of the work of both McDougall and Rivers, both from the point of view of their methodology and their ethnocentrism (Titchener 1916).

the basis of such phrases as "the wine-dark sea," Gladstone had argued that Homer "distinguished little beyond differences of lightness and darkness." Gladstone's suggestion had been picked up by several post-Darwinian writers who argued for "an evolution of the color sense in historical times," such that "the sense for blue had developed much later than that for the other colors," but it had not been widely accepted. However, on the basis of an analysis of color terms he collected among Australians of the Seven Rivers district, among Kiwai Papuans, and among eastern and western islanders of the Torres Straits, Rivers concluded that those four groups represented "progressive stages in the evolution of color language," with the "highest stage" having terms for both green and blue, but tending to confuse them. Despite the fact that his own tests showed that the islanders could recognize blue and distinguish "different shades or tints of blue," Rivers argued that it was "nevertheless possible that there may be some degree of insensitiveness to this colour" corresponding to the linguistic confusion; in the more popular account of his investigations, Rivers argued that such insensitiveness in fact existed. Pursuing his inquiries among the Singhalese and Tamils in Ceylon, among the natives of Upper Egypt, among eighteen Labrador Eskimos who were visiting London, and later among the Todas, he continued to argue in similar evolutionary terms—although to do so he had to exclude the Eskimos, whose "terminology for color appears to be extremely well developed," and to suggest that the apparent difficulty modern Egyptians had perceiving blue might actually result from sensory degeneration, in order to account for the fact that "the ancient language of Egypt" had a definite word for that color.[13]

It is worth noting the sharp contrast with Franz Boas, whose study of "alternating sounds" fifteen years earlier had dealt with a related problem of the categorization of sensory perceptions. Boas argued that the apparent inability of certain non-European groups to make the same phonetic distinctions as Europeans was "in no way a sign of primitiveness" but rather a reflection of the fact that the two groups distinguished sense perceptions in terms of a different set of linguistic categories. While Rivers granted that "the influence of language in testing" could not "be wholly excluded," he nevertheless spoke of his inquiry in terms of "the primitive confusion between blue and black," or "characteristic defects" of color language, rather than in terms of differences of classificatory categories. And although he was aware of a variety of methodological complications affecting his results, it is clear that he wanted very much to find an explanation in terms of "corresponding defect[s] in color sense" that would justify conventional evolutionary notions of the differences between civilized European and "races of low culture." His later-quoted suggestion that "pure sense-acuity is much the same in all races," was not in fact an affirmation of a generalized sensory egalitarianism, but an attempt to explain away the "frequent superiority of the savage over the civilised man in his recognition of what is going on around him in nature" as a result of training and habit. Wherever ambiguous results might be interpreted to justify traditional hierarchical views of capacity, Rivers was inclined to give "probability" the benefit of doubt:

> In these observations the Todas occupy an intermediate position between the two other races and probably but for certain adverse circumstances, this intermediate position would have been occupied still more frequently. The interest of this lies in the fact that in general intellectual and cultural development, the Todas undoubtedly occupy a position intermediate between the Papuans and the Englishmen, and the corresponding intermediate position found in the above observations suggests that there is a connexion between general intellectual development and such mental operations as are tested by the experiments recorded in this paper.[14]

As a neurologist in the tradition of Hughlings Jackson, Rivers took for granted that mental evolution was manifested at a level below linguistic concepts and sensory percepts. In collaboration with his friend Henry Head, Rivers in fact went on to perform a series of experiments which, although not specifically comparative, did in a general way reinforce assumptions about neurological evolution. Severing nerves in Head's left forearm, Rivers monitored experimentally its recovery of tactile sensitivity over a period of years—using Head's *glans penis* for "control tests." In their report of the experiments, Rivers and Head correlated two phases of Head's recovery of sensation with two types of response to tactile stimuli (the indiscriminate and the graduated) and two types of nerve fibres (the protopathic and the epicritic). It was only in the last paragraph that they hinted at a relation of their findings to "the developmental history of the nervous system," suggesting that "they reveal the means by which an imperfect organism has struggled towards improved functions and psychic unity." Elsewhere, Rivers clearly interpreted the dichotomy as one between the emotional/concrete and the rational/abstract aspects of the human psyche—a conventional evolutionary polarity long traditional in European speculation about "savage" or "primitive" mentality.[15]

By the time that the results of this experiment were published in 1908, Rivers' interests had turned definitively—although not permanently—to anthropology. Rivers came to anthropology with a number of orienting commitments from his previous scientific work. In addition to the obvious evolutionism (both at a theoretical and an ideological level), there was a strongly empiricist scientism, which combined an unusual degree of methodological self-consciousness with a certain conceptual

Henry Head (with eyes closed), as William Rivers (guided by a plaster cast) prepares to test the response of the regenerating severed nerve in Head's left arm, in Rivers' rooms in St. John's College, Cambridge, c. 1903. (Courtesy of Professor N. J. Mackintosh and the Department of Experimental Psychology, University of Cambridge)

flamboyance: when Rivers took the bit of an hypothesis in his teeth, he was sometimes willing to ride roughshod over empirical difficulties that got in the way, either by covering them with "probabilities," by excluding recalcitrant data (e.g., those eighteen color-conscious Eskimos), or by calling upon subsidiary hypotheses even if they ran counter to the main line of his interpretation (e.g., Egyptian degeneration).[16]

It took a while, however, for Rivers to redefine himself as an anthropologist. His early anthropological writings are those of an empirically oriented disciplinary outsider trying to find firm footing within the discursive traditions of an unfamiliar field. Initially, his interest in the "genealogical method" showed clear marks of its origin in Galtonian biological concerns: it was useful for the collection of both "vital" (i.e., demographic and biological) and "social" statistics. And although from the beginning he was quite ingenious in specifying the various "sociological" issues it could be applied to, his language sometimes betrayed his disciplinary marginality. Thus in 1900 he spoke of the kinship systems of Torres Straits as "of the kind known as 'classificatory.'" By 1904 Rivers had clearly consulted Morgan's *Systems of Consanguinity,* in which that "kind" of system had first been defined. In discussing the "system of kinship" of the Mabuiag people, he referred to "the ten characters which Morgan has called the indicative features of the classificatory system." It was not until 1907, however, that he made a systematic attempt to come to terms with Morganian theory.[17]

Before that time, Rivers had published what was to be his most extensive ethnographic study, on the basis of fieldwork carried on among the Todas of southern India during five months of the winter of 1901–1902. Having, as it were, accidentally discovered "the genealogical method" during his first ethnographic venture, he now returned to the field to apply it systematically in what he later presented as not simply "a record of the customs and beliefs of a people, but also a demonstration of anthropological method"—"the great need of anthropology at the present time" being "more exact method, not only in collecting material, but also in recording it."[18]

Because the Todas were "inveterate beggars," Rivers could not entirely avoid "the necessity of paying for information"; but until near the end of his stay, when he offered rewards for certain specific items of information, he made it a point simply to pay a stipulated sum "for the trouble taken in giving a day or half day to my service." He did not give much weight to the fact that his interpreter was "a catechist who had been endeavouring for ten years to convert the Todas to Christianity"; nor did he reveal that the man communicated with the Todas through Tamil, the third language of the Toda men, which was spoken by only a few women. He was confident that his interpreter had quickly overcome the initial resistance of some Todas to being questioned by one who had been assiduously missionizing them. Similarly, he felt that any linguistic difficulties had been largely surmounted by using Toda nouns and names wherever possible, so that both the Todas and Rivers got "the general drift" of questions and answers even before they were interpreted. Beyond that, precise information was a matter of cross-checking between as many independent accounts as possible, relying heavily on the genealogical method, and establishing a clear distinction between two types of inquiry: mornings devoted to psychological work and topics of a public character, and afternoons given to sacred topics that might be discussed with one or two informants privately.[19]

The mass of information collected by these means was embodied in a 700-page monograph that firmly established Rivers' reputation as a practitioner of "the new anthropology." Since then, *The Todas* has been hailed as the ethnographic exemplar that helped to convince later British social anthropologists they were "engaged in a science rather than a literary exercise"—a fulfilment of Rivers' hope that his tombstone might bear the inscription: "He made ethnology a science." There have, however, been slight reservations about Rivers' failure to note the existence of matrilineal units crosscutting the division into patrilineal clans, and about a general submergence of pattern in the masses of ethnographic detail. Rivers himself was aware that he might have "complicated, perhaps even obscured" his account by "the mass of detail with which it is accompanied," and he worried lest his desire to clearly indicate where his record was "of doubtful value" had led him to lay "undue stress on its uncertainties and deficiencies." But from an historical viewpoint, it is precisely some of Rivers' uncertainties that help to place *The Todas* in the movement of British anthropology away from evolutionism.[20]

Although Rivers did not make a point of it, in choosing to study the Todas he had selected an ethnographic case that, *prima facie*, implicated what had been central issues of evolutionary anthropology. Erstwhile practitioners of female infanticide, and still polyandrous, "the Tudas of the Nilgherry Hills" had been noted in McLennan's *Primitive Marriage* as part of the evidence that "the most ancient system" of blood relationship was "a system of kinship through females only." Furthermore, the major previous ethnographic account, Marshall's *A Phrenologist Amongst the Todas*, acknowledged a general debt to McLennan's book. In this context, Rivers had planned to investigate the "various social regulations" associated with "the custom of polyandry," and to see if there was a "system of exogamy." But when he arrived among the Todas, it was their religious and ceremonial life that preempted his attention, and rather than pursuing a comparative study among several tribes, as he had originally intended, he spent all of his time with the Todas, concentrating on their religion and sociology (as well as on their visual perception).[21]

In this context, Rivers' monograph can be read as documenting a failure of naively evolutionary expectations. His comment that a Toda custom "without any exact parallel in other parts of the world" must be an "independent invention" suggests that he was still not entirely accustomed to evolutionary usage, which in fact assumed that "independent inventions" would recur at widely dispersed points on the earth. Elsewhere, Rivers seems to have been checking the categories of Toda culture against certain traditional issues of evolutionary debate—often with negative results. Thus there was "little to indicate that ancestor-worship has played any part in the evolution of Toda religion" or to support "the idea that the gods are personifications of the forces of nature"; neither did the Todas provide "any definite evidence towards the solution of the vexed question of the relation between polyandry and infanticide."[22]

In other cases where the evidence was problematic, however, Rivers called upon the doctrine of survivals or the idea of transitional stages to sustain a generally evolutionary interpretation. Despite the Todas' polyandry and infanticide, Toda kinship was patrilineal; Rivers nevertheless found evidence of prior mother-right in the "social organisation" of the buffalo which were the focus of Toda economic and ritual life: "there is complete promiscuity, and the buffalo belongs to its mother's group because paternity is unknown or disregarded." Along similar lines, he suggested that the Todas had reached "a stage of mental development" in which "they are no longer satisfied with a purely classificatory system, and have begun to make distinctions in their terminology for near and distant relatives." They were now "in a state of social evolution in which the common bond constituted by membership of the clan has largely been replaced by the bond constituted by the family."[23]

At various points Rivers frankly acknowledged his difficulty in explaining a particular cultural practice. No doubt this was in part due to an unfortunate conjunction of events during the fourth month of his stay: three men who had given him information about sacred matters each suffered calamities, and Toda diviners decided that the gods were angry "because their secrets had been revealed to a stranger." As a result, his sources of information "ran dry to a large extent" just when he "had hoped to overcome the scruples of the people and to obtain information on many doubtful points." However, Rivers' difficulties may also have reflected a certain conception of explanation in terms of "origin," often construed as rationalistic or utilitarian "motive," either in the present or in the past. Thus Rivers argued that some features of Toda childbirth ceremonies "had their origin in the motive" of promoting lactation by imitating the flow of milk. To explain a custom in terms of motive, the field ethnographer began by asking people why they practiced it. But except in a very few cases, "the Todas were quite unable to give explanations of their customs," the answer to nearly every question being that the custom in question was "ordained by the goddess Teikirzi." As a result, Rivers had to make his own inferences about Toda motives, and in some cases he simply confessed his ignorance: "I could not satisfy myself as to what the people really had in their own minds when they were lamenting" a dying buffalo. Elsewhere, rationalistic psychological interpretation came up short against the veil of time: "possibly the Todas may have some clear ideas about the connexion between their bells, gods, and dairies, but I could not discover them, and am inclined to believe that the people are now very hazy about the exact place of the bell and the god in their theology."[24]

At a more general interpretive level, there was a recurrent problem of what might be called "evolutionary fit" which could not be easily resolved by the notions of survivals or transitional stages. Thus, the Todas combined the strictest regulation of marriage with what Rivers regarded as almost complete sexual promiscuity, both before and after marriage. Their religion, which Rivers considered to be of a higher order than might be expected "for a people living in such simple circumstances," was particularly recalcitrant to evolutionary interpretation. On the one hand, "the idea of 'god'" was "highly developed"; on the other, the Todas were completely indifferent to the desecration of the hilltop cairns associated with their gods. In a manner reminiscent of the way he dealt with those Egyptian color terms, Rivers resolved the dilemma by calling upon the notion of degeneration: the Todas had come to the Nilgiri Hills with "a religion of a higher order than they possess at present" and by a "long and slow process" their worship had been "transferred from gods, not to stocks and stones"—as one might expect, were the evolutionary order simply reversed—but "to bells and dairy vessels." Rather than casting light on the problem of totemism or "the evolution of religion from magic" they showed, "in little, the general traits characteristic of the degeneration of religion." Indeed, when all was said and done, the Todas really did not fit very well into an evolutionary framework. Thus Rivers asserted in the introduction that "one of the most striking aspects of the customs and ceremonies of the Todas is that these have in many cases no exact parallels in other places." Which was in fact to say that they ran counter to "perhaps the most definite result which modern research in anthropology has brought out": the "extraordinary similarity of custom" among "races so widely separated geographically and so diverse ethnologically that it seems certain that the customs must have developed in total independence of one another."[25]

Given this general failure of evolutionary categories and assumptions, it is perhaps not surprising that Rivers' specifically generalizing chapters in various ways disappoint or surprise our expectations. After devoting seventeen chapters to describing the various "religious institutions and ceremonies of the Todas," Rivers suggested that "there remains the general nexus which binds all these beliefs into a whole so that they constitute the Toda religion." In the context of the negative and degenerationist argument that followed, this phrasing belies the suggestion that Rivers' account was "among the most remarkable examples of internal cohesiveness in all ethnographic literature." For Rivers, the treatment of the totality of Toda religion was conceived of more in residual than in integrative terms. Similarly, the conclusion to the work as a whole, far from hinting at an integrative functionalist interpretation, foreshadows instead Rivers' later "conversion" to diffusionism. Turning away from evolutionary issues to quite traditional "ethnological" questions—"Who are the Todas? How do they come to be living on the Nilgiri Hills?"—Rivers advanced an hypothesis which he felt was "open to the charge of being highly conjectural." Largely on the basis of the religious data which had been so recalcitrant to evolutionary interpretation, Rivers suggested that the Todas had migrated a thousand years ago from the Malabar region, where they had been influenced by Christian and Jewish settlements, to the Nilgiri Hills, where under special environmental conditions their religion had undergone simultaneously a theological degeneration and an overelaboration of ritual.[26]

In an article written after the publication of his Toda ethnography, Rivers discussed the special relationship of a man to his mother's brother in terms that verged on, but then drew back from, a functional interpretation. Although this relationship was customarily explained as a "survival" of the "state of mother-right," Rivers argued it might instead have had a different origin, deriving "from the custom that a man should marry the daughter of his mother's brother, so that his maternal uncle is at the same time his father-in-law, either actual or prospective." Had he "been ignorant of the origin of the uncle-nephew relationship elsewhere," and sought explanation "in the character of the social organisation as it is at the present time," Rivers thought he would "naturally have found it" in this marriage rule. From a later perspective, we might rephrase this: had he not known the standard evolutionary explanation, he would naturally have offered a functionalist one. Rivers, however, introduced this functionalist possibility only to recast it in evolutionary terms, speaking of the rule as a "survival of the marriage regulation" rather than a present consequence of it. On the one hand, this led him to the conclusion that a "survival may have a twofold origin; that customs which seem to be identical may have arisen in different ways in different parts of the world." On this basis, Rivers (unconsciously echoing Boas' critique of 1896) suggested that "grave doubts must be cast on what may be called the current anthropological method of supporting hypotheses by the enumeration of examples from different parts of the world." On the other hand, Rivers still held tightly to the notion of "survivals," in terms that recall the difficulties of his Toda fieldwork: they were apparently "meaningless" customs "for which it would seem impossible to find any adequate direct psychological explanation in motives of any kind, whether religious, ethical, or magical"—but which became "at once intelligible and natural" when seen "as vestiges of an old social order." For Rivers the notion of survivals was thus a conceptual tool of great practical value, reempowering the authority of the psychologist/ethnographer encountering informants who either would not or could not tell him what their "motive" was when they engaged in what to the Western eye seemed an inexplicably curious custom.[27]

In Rivers' hands, however, the doctrine of survivals led away from a psychological to a sociological explanation—and back not to Tylor, but to Lewis Henry Morgan. If his reference to "the enumeration of examples" recalls Tylor's study of adhesions, Rivers' failure to use the term "cross-cousin marriage" in an essay dealing with that topic suggests that he was not directly familiar with Tylor's paper of 1888. And although he served as member of the three-man editorial committee for Tylor's festschrift in 1907, his own contribution made no reference to Tylor's work; instead he took the opportunity to write about Morgan, whose work he has been credited with "rediscovering" for British social anthropology.[28]

There was a kind of a priori "fit" between Rivers' "genealogical method" and Morgan's conception of a "system of consanguinity," which in 1871 had been defined in the following terms:

> Around every person there is a circle or group of kindred of which such person is the centre, the *Ego,* from whom the degree of relationship is reckoned, and to whom the relationship itself returns. Above him are his father and his mother and their ascendants, below him are his children and their descendants; while upon either side are his brothers and sisters and their descendants, and the brothers and sisters of his father and of his mother and their descendants, as well as a much greater number of collateral relatives descended from common ancestors still more remote.

A "system of consanguinity" was "but the formal expression and recognition of these relationships"—which were in fact exactly the relationships that Rivers had investigated among a number of specific egos on Murray Island.[29]

Rivers' references to Morgan, however, do not suggest a systematic reading of *Systems of Consanguinity.* Although he later occasionally cited the work correctly, his personal copy of the book remained in unannotated mint condition; and when in 1907 he turned to the problem he called "The Origin of the Classificatory System of Relationships," his references were to Morgan's *Ancient Society,* in which the "Barbarian" (second) stage of the evolution of the family had been renamed the "Punaluan." It was here, however, that Rivers began what he later referred to as "sifting out the chaff from the wheat" in Morgan's argument.[30]

Acknowledging that Morgan's overall scheme for the evolution of human marriage from "complete promiscuity" to monogamy had recently "encountered much opposition," Rivers suggested that critics (including Westermarck, Crawley, Lang, and Thomas) had failed to distinguish between two parts of Morgan's argument: that dealing with the existence of the "consanguine family and the evolution from this of the Punaluan family," and that dealing "with the existence of this latter form of the family itself." He proposed first to note a "radical defect" in the former, and then to restate the latter in the light of later evidence.[31]

Morgan's evidence for the consanguine family (Fison's "undivided commune") was based on the assumption that the Malayan (or, as Rivers preferred, the Polynesian) form of the classificatory system was the earliest. Comparing the kinship terminologies of the Australians, the more highly evolved Kurnai, the Mabuiag, the Murray Islanders, and the Hawaiians, Rivers noted a progressive elimination of the distinction between "cross" and "parallel" cousins (although he did not use those terms), which he felt correlated with the relative social advancement of those societies. On this basis, he maintained that the Malayan system of the Hawaiians was a *late* development of the classificatory system rather than its ur-form. Having thus shown that the classificatory system provided no evidence for the existence of the consanguine family, Rivers then proceeded to argue that it did support the existence of the Punaluan family or of "group marriage"—which he defined as "a marriage occuring in a community divided into definite groups, whether they be clans, classes [or] phratries, in which all the men of one group are the husbands of all the women of the other group," and vice versa. On this basis, it would be natural to distinguish within each of the two groups four categories of persons: childbearing women, sexually active men, children, and elders. The resulting categories in one's own moeity would naturally be designated by terms we would gloss as mother, mother's brother, brother/sister, and grandfather/grandmother; in the other moeity, by father, father's sister, father's sister's (or reversing the perspective, mother's brother's) daughter, and grandfather/grandmother—which, Rivers suggested, were "the chief terms we find in the classificatory system."[32]

Having inverted Morgan's sequence, Rivers then proceeded to invert his definitional assumption: rather than being in the first instance an expression of real or assumed biological relationships, the classificatory system was "in its origin expressive of status," to which "only the vaguest ideas of consanguinity need have been attached." But whereas earlier writers (presumably, McLennan) had argued that kinship terms were "merely" terms of address and had "nothing to do with status and duties so far as status implied any function in the social economy," Rivers had been impressed, from the time of his Torres Straits fieldwork, by the social "functions" attached to the status categories marked by kinship terminology, and he felt that "if Morgan were now alive" he would be, too. It was only his "unfortunate error" regarding the Malayan system that had prevented Morgan from seeing how the terms arose "out of purely status relationships." But Rivers' fieldwork had also convinced him beyond "the slightest doubt" that "at the present time the system is an expression of consanguinity and affinity to those who use it." And rather than pursuing his incipiently functionalist critique, he ended by appealing once again to evolution and the doctrine of survivals. Thus there were "definite indications" of an evolution by which the systems "are coming to express status less and ties of consanguinity and affinity more"; and the "special features" of the classificatory system among the American Indians made it "more probable that its general features are the survivals of some general form of marriage." Whatever his modifications of the specifics of Morgan's argument, Rivers did not question that prior marriage forms were determinative of present kinship relationships; in his view, it was this causal assumption that made it possible for them to be studied "scientifically."[33]

It was precisely that assumption that was attacked by Alfred Kroeber in a critique of Morgan's "Classificatory Systems of Relationship" published in the *Journal of the Royal Anthropological Institute* in 1909. Along lines resonant of Boas' essay "On Alternating Sounds," Kroeber (Boas' first doctoral student at Columbia) argued that the Morganian distinction between "descriptive" and "classificatory" was a "subjective" one. It originated in "the point of view of investigators" struck by the fact that other languages did not "discriminate certain relationships which the languages of civilized Europe distinguish"—and forgetful, as well, "that their own languages are filled with entirely analogous groupings or classifications which custom has made so familiar and natural that they are not felt as such." Generalizing, Kroeber suggested that the multiplicity of "slightly varying relationships" expressed in different languages could be reduced to eight "principles or categories": generation, age, sex of speaker, sex (and condition) of the connecting relative, lineality vs. collaterality, and blood vs. marriage. Although these principles facilitated the comparison of systems "along the basic lines of their structure," they did not justify a fundamental distinction of type: "judged from its own point of view, English is the less classificatory; looked at from the Indian point of view it is the more classificatory."[34]

Kroeber argued that the factors determining any given terminological lumping were "psychological," in the sense that they would reflect perceived similarities between two relationships. And they were "linguistic" insofar as these perceptions were expressed in terms of the resources of a particular language: "in view of the comparative paucity of terms as compared with possible relationships," it was "entirely natural that the same word or the same stem" should be used to denote relationships that shared a number of the eight distinguishing features. But because "terms of relationship reflect psychology, not sociology," they could "be utilized for sociological inferences only with extreme caution."[35]

From Rivers' perspective, however, "psychological" explanation had not served too well in the interpretation of ethnographic phenomena —as witnessed by the ambiguous results of his sensory investigations and by his subsequent difficulties with the "motives" of Toda customary behavior. Retreating (during this particular phase of his career) from psychology, Rivers had found in Morgan a sociological determinism that seemed a much stronger basis for a scientific ethnology. And in 1913 he defended that basis in a series of three lectures given at the London School of Economics (with Westermarck and Malinowski in attendance).[36]

To begin with, Rivers dealt again with McLennan's suggestion that "the nomenclature of the classificatory system" was simply "a body of mutual salutations" without sociological or biological significance. Drawing on Howitt, Spencer and Gillen, and his own Torres Straits fieldwork, he argued that ethnographic evidence showed that "one who applies a given term of relationship to another person has to behave towards that person in certain definite ways." Indeed, there was "a definite correlation between the presence of a term of relationship and special functions attached to the relationship." If McLennan "had known what we know today," he would never have attacked Morgan along this line.[37]

Rivers turned then to Kroeber, insisting that "many details of the classificatory systems have been directly determined by social factors." Using data from Fiji, the New Hebrides, and Guadalcanal, he suggested that various characteristics of those kinship terminologies followed logically from what he now called "cross-cousin marriage." And unless one was willing to accept what Rivers clearly regarded as the patently preposterous assumption that "the Fijians took to marrying their cross-cousins because such a marriage was suggested to them by their system of relationship" there was no real question which was "antecedent" and which "consequent."[38]

Having asserted the general principle, Rivers went on to propose that certain unusual forms of the classificatory system could be explained by "special forms" of marriage: specifically, that of the Banks Islanders, where Codrington had recorded some "very remarkable features," including the practice of cross-cousins referring to each other by the terms "otherwise used between parents and children." This could be explained, Rivers suggested, by a precontact social regulation which enjoined the marriage of a man to a "superfluous wife" of his mother's brother." Rivers then noted the more "bizarre" custom of the people of Pentecost Island, who applied the same kinship terms to relatives two generations apart. The clue to the explanation had been given him by John Pantutun (Codrington's "grandson"), who had served on Pentecost as a mission teacher, and who once rather dismissively remarked, "That is the place where they marry their granddaughters." To Rivers, this "fact"—later confirmed by talking to one "not very good informant"—accounted for the terminological lumping of alternate generations between which there was no conceivable "psychological resemblance."[39]

From there, Rivers broadened his argument to inquire more generally "how far we are justified in inferring the existence of a social institution of which we have no direct evidence when we find features of the nomenclature of relationship which would result from such an institution." The answer was, quite far indeed. Rivers was in fact willing to hypothesize "an extraordinary form of marriage" (the now-famous case of marriage to the widow of one's grandfather) even though "at the present moment any direct evidence for such a marriage is wholly lacking." Accusing doubters of ethnocentric blindness, he suggested that it was only those who were still "under the domination of ideas derived from [our] own social surroundings that [could not] believe in such a marriage." From there, Rivers went on to devote the bulk of his lecture to arguing (in anticipation of several later Americanists) that cross-cousin marriage had once been "a widespread practice in North America."[40]

Having justified the argument from survivals in specific instances, Rivers concluded by treating more general questions of historical change. On the basis of different forms of terminology in Oceania, he suggested that there had been an overall "progressive" and simplifying change in the classificatory system, from "the regulation of marriage by some kind of clan-exogamy" to "a mechanism based on relation as traced by means of [individual] pedigrees." Looking further backward in time and structure, he proposed that "the classificatory system as a whole" had its origin in the "dual organization"—"that special variety of the clan-organization in which a community consists of two exogamous moeities." Turning then forward (and westward) to *non*-classificatory kinship systems, Rivers replaced Morgan's single "descriptive" system by two "genera" (the "species and varieties" of which were dependent on particular "social conditions"): the "kindred" system of the Semites and the Sudanese, which arose out of the "patriarchal or extended family" and "our own" form, the "family system," which was based on the family "in the narrow sense" of "a man, his wife, and their children."[41]

There are many comments that might be made about the Kroeber-Rivers debate, which is one of the better known in the literature of kinship studies. To Raymond Firth it seemed that Rivers' somewhat "naive" and "limited" conception of marriage, which "focused almost entirely on its legalization of sex relations," may have been influenced by his "confirmed bachelorhood"—or, as others have suggested, by his "closeted" homosexuality. While some might hesitate to accept such motivational inferences, there would probably be general agreement today with Firth's opinion that much of Rivers' argument about kinship terms and abnormal marriage forms "cannot be sustained." Be that as it may, there can be little doubt that the British social anthropological tradition was long sustained by Rivers' commitment to the possibility of a scientific study of social organization. And while one must question Meyer Fortes' implied suggestion that Rivers' "rediscovery" of Morgan enabled the trans-Atlantic transposition of disciplinary founding fathers, the debate was a critical moment in the definition of the two traditions. Not all Boasians shared Kroeber's view of kinship terminology; even Kroeber himself later retreated on the issue of its sociological significance. But Kroeber's critique of Morgan's kinship categories was archetypically Boasian, and the general effect of the Boasian critique of evolutionism was to obscure if not efface Morgan's place in the history of American anthropology. And if Morgan never achieved an eponymic status in British social anthropology equal to that of Boas in the United States, his importance in the definition of that tradition—mediated in large part by Rivers—is undeniable.[42]

Although Morgan himself was less given than Tylor to positivistic proclamations, later writers have spoken of Morgan's "greatest discovery" as "the fact that customs of designating relatives have scientific significance." Reading Morgan through Radcliffe-Brown's monocle, Fortes suggested that his central concept was the notion of "system" as "a self-balancing, internally coherent, and harmonious arrangement of recognized relationships," the specific cases of which could each be allocated to their "proper class" by comparing them to the "paradigmatic case for each class of systems." Although the systemic emphasis is perhaps less strong in Rivers, his references to "genera" and "species" suggest a similar typological concern, in a somewhat different scientific idiom. And when it came to advocating the scientific status of the inquiry, Rivers' rhetoric was even more assertive than Tylor's had been. His three lectures on Morgan's "classificatory system" showed the operation "of the principle of determinism with a rigour and definiteness equal to that of any of the exact sciences," since "according to my scheme not only has the general character of systems of relationship been strictly determined by social conditions, but every detail of these systems has also been so determined." Rivers tended to be naively positivistic about the data from which "laws regulating the lives of the people" could be derived, assuming that "systems of relationship" were "bodies of dry fact the accuracy of which, especially when collected by the genealogical method, is about as incapable of being influenced by bias, conscious or unconscious, as any subject that can be imagined." But it was to an end quite characteristic of the classic phase of the later British social anthropological tradition: to make sociology "a science fit to rank with other sciences."[43]

Rivers and Morgan shared similarly disjunctive historical fates: in both cases, their own national anthropological traditions turned sharply away from the orientation to which their own personal intellectual evolution eventually led them, and they were, although in different ways, maltreated in the disciplinary memory—attacked, misappreciated, neglected, repressed. But there was a major difference. Morgan moved from diffusionary ethnology to social evolutionism, only to become a focal point of criticism when the dominant group in the discipline turned (for a time) back to history. In contrast, Rivers moved from evolutionism to diffusionism, falling into neglect when the dominant group in the discipline turned away from the study of temporal change.[44]

Although Rivers' shift was foreshadowed in his unsuccessful attempt to apply evolutionary categories to his Toda materials, he himself saw it as a later and sudden experience of "conversion" that occurred as he grappled with data collected when he returned to Melanesia in 1908. Having received a grant from the Percy Sladen Trust to "study mother-right communities in the Solomon Islands, and to trace the details of the transition from mother-right to father-right," Rivers set off via the United States, stopping off for a month in Hawaii and another in Fiji. In Melanesia, he was joined by Gerald Wheeler, a student of Westermarck's, and by Arthur M. Hocart, who had been an undergraduate at Marett's Oxford college. Rivers himself did "intensive work" for several months with Hocart on Eddystone Island in the Western Solomons, where they divided the ethnographic labor—Rivers studying kinship, social organization, ghosts and gods, while Hocart attended to fishing, warfare, and death. But the bulk of Rivers' time was spent following in Codrington's wake aboard the mission ship *Southern Cross*, as it sailed among the New Hebrides, the Banks, the Torres, the Santa Cruz, to the Solomon Islands, and back in reverse order six months later. Although this "survey work" was carried on through linguistic intermediaries during "hasty visits, sometimes of only a few hours' duration," Rivers was confident that the "genealogical method" had enabled him to uncover the systems of relationships, which "like fossils" gave "hidden indications of ancient social institutions."[45]

In writing up his material, Rivers first attempted a comparison of these kinship systems without regard to their linguistic forms. On this basis he was able to "demonstrate the existence either in the present or the past of a number of extraordinary and anomalous forms of marriage." These forms "became explicable," however, if the underlying form of social organization in Melanesia was the dual organization with matrilineal descent, "accompanied by a condition of dominance of the old men which enabled them to monopolize all the young women of the community." From there, Rivers had been able to "trace out" a "consistent and

Rivers with a group of Malekulans, 1914. (Courtesy of the Cambridge University Museum of Archaeology and Anthropology)

definite scheme" of the history of marriage in Melanesia, in terms of a sequence of stages "of a purely evolutionary character."[46]

When he then considered the kinship terminologies as linguistic phenomena, however, he discovered that the terms fell into "two main classes": one, widely diffused throughout Oceania, which his "comparative study of the forms of the systems had shown to have suffered change"; another, varying widely throughout the area, of terms (such as those for "mother" and "mother's brother") which "there was no reason to believe had suffered any great change of status." On this basis, Rivers hypothesized an initial linguistic diversity transformed into relative uniformity "by the incoming of a people from without." The combined "morphological and linguistic study" thus showed that the change he had traced "was not a spontaneous evolution, but one which had taken place under the influence of the blending of peoples."[47]

Rivers' conclusion had broader methodological implications. If

Melanesian society was "the resultant of the mixture of three or four main cultures," then one was no longer entitled to take out of the resulting complex "any institution or belief" and "regard it as primitive merely because Melanesian culture on the whole is more or less primitive." Although it was possible that mana might be fundamental to religion, there was no justification for regarding it as the basis of pre-animistic religion or as the common source of both religion and magic. The general methodological point was that "if cultures are complex, their analysis is a preliminary step which is necessary if speculations concerning the evolution of human society, its beliefs and practices, are to rest on a firm foundation."[48]

This position was of course close to that Boas had argued in 1896, and in both cases it implied a pluralization of the idea of culture—although Rivers continued to speak of "cultures" as "high" and "low." As in Boas' case, Rivers' pluralization of culture reflected an extended and methodologically self-conscious experience of fieldwork, a critical reconsideration of evolutionary assumptions, and (in a more superficial way) contact with the German anthropological tradition. But in Rivers' case, there was no systematic critique of evolutionary racialism, in which "culture" took over the determinative role previously given to "race." And while both Boasian and Riversian diffusionisms involved a fracturing of cultural phenomena into elements for the purposes of historical reconstruction, they did not take the same route back toward an integrative or systemic view.[49]

Although Kroeber himself was shortly to retreat from "psychological" explanations of "superorganic" (i.e., cultural) phenomena, the more characteristic Boasian approach to cultural integration was in fact psychological, with language providing the model. In a period in which, as Rivers put it, there was a general "revolt against the psychological assumptions current in the anthropology of the past," his own changing position on the role of psychological explanation is difficult to fix. In 1908 Rivers described his early psychological work in sensory perception, nerve regeneration, and the effects of alcohol on fatigue as in "that branch of psychology . . . to which the name of individual psychology is usually given." By "an extension," he had applied that approach "to the differences which characterise the members of different races," and had suggested implications for mental evolution. But Rivers seems to have been little aware of the various contemporary manifestations of supra-individual psychologizing among French and German writers (Le Bon's crowd psychology, Durkheim's *conscience collective*, Wundt's *Völkerpsychologie*). He was of course aware of his student McDougall's instinctualist *Introduction to Social Psychology*, but his early psychological interests were better represented by McDougall's textbook, *Physiological*

Psychology, and by the *Experimental Psychology* of another student and Torres Straits colleague, Charles Myers.[50]

When both his professional psychological armamentarium and the taken-for-granted psychological assumptions of social evolutionism proved inadequate for the penetration of Toda "motives," Rivers found refuge in his "sociological determinism," which he was to advocate even more strongly in the face of Kroeber's "psychological" critique. He continued to look forward to a future "social psychology" and to appeal to present social psychological knowledge to justify the occasional ad hoc psychologizing in his own ethnological analyses. But for a period after 1910 his more formal programmatic statements insisted on a differentiation between "sociological" and "psychological" explanation, and on the priority of the former. And when his psychiatric work during the Great War led him back toward psychological analysis, it was to be in terms of very different psychological assumptions.[51]

Thus in contrast to the Boasians, Rivers was not led by the Germanic notion of *Geist* toward an integrationist view of cultural patterning or the relationship of culture and personality. Although he made various statements arguing the interdependency of cultural features, his reconstructive methodology depended on "the analysis of rude cultures into their component elements," which were related to each other not in patterned synchronic terms but in stratified diachronic terms, as the layered residue of different episodes of cultural contact. Seeking a bedrock of coherence and duration in the life of any people, he found it in a particular privileged aspect of their culture: "social structure."[52]

Rivers insisted that "ethnological analysis" necessitated a distinction between "mere contact" and "intimate intermixture." Drawing an analogy to British colonial experience ("the spread of our own people over the earth's surface"), he arranged four primary "constituents of culture" in a hierarchical index of intermixture. While previous studies had taken "material objects" as their "starting-point," these were in fact the least trustworthy indices, since "a passing vessel which does not even anchor" might transmit the use of iron to otherwise untouched groups. Magico-religious beliefs were only slightly more resistant; and while native linguistic structures were not easily modifiable, it was not difficult to learn a new vocabulary or a lingua franca. But social structure, "the framework of society" was quite another matter:

> We find in Oceania islands where Europeans have been settled as missionaries or traders perhaps for fifty or a hundred years; we find the people wearing European clothes and European ornaments, using European utensils, and even European weapons when they fight; we find them holding the beliefs and practising the ritual of a European religion; we find them speaking a European language often even among themselves, and yet in-

> vestigation shows that much of their social structure remains thoroughly native and uninfluenced not only in its general form, but often even in its minutest details.

Modifiable only by "the actual blending of peoples" or "the most profound political changes," social structure was "the surest criterion of what is early and what is late in any given culture."[53]

That determination was possible, of course, only because the doctrine of survivals was part of the wheat Rivers sifted from the chaff of Morgan's theories. His new diffusionism, however, required Rivers also to assume in many cases the degeneration of certain aspects of culture in order to account for the presence of "advanced" cultural elements among people of "low culture." Thus it was that within a year or so of his "conversion" he published articles arguing both the "disappearance of useful arts" and the "persistence of the useless." If the latter assumption was necessary to the documentation of transitions in social organization, the former made it possible to account for the present low level of material culture among peoples, like the Australians, whose complex social organization Rivers attributed to the influence of small groups of immigrants with a superior material culture, the traces of which were now lost.[54]

It was from this standpoint that Rivers completed what was intended to be his ethnological masterwork, *The History of Melanesian Society*. No longer "under the sway of the crude evolutionary doctrine" that had compromised his earlier demonstration of method in "the collection and recording of ethnographic facts," Rivers now offered an exemplar of the method for the "theoretical treatment of these facts." The first volume was a "purely morphological study" of the social organization of different Melanesian groups. The opening (and most extended) account was devoted to the Banks Islands, which were exemplary of "the dual organisation" and "the seat of a highly developed secret organisation." These had been Codrington's primary ethnographic focus, and Rivers worked out from Codrington's account, using as his paradigm case a genealogy Codrington had collected; one of its members, Codrington's "grandson" Pantutun, was his primary informant, here and wherever else the Motu language served as lingua franca. Both in the Banks Islands account and in the single chapters devoted to other islands, Rivers also relied heavily on the assistance of the Reverend W. J. Durrad, who worked with him on the *Southern Cross* and later sent him extensive notes. As in his account of the Todas, Rivers made a point of describing how the data had been gathered. But although he frankly acknowledged the limitations of material characteristically collected from a single missionized informant through at least one intermediary language (outside of any observational or behavioral context), it usually came down to affirming its "probable" reliability.[55]

In the case of Tikopia, where Rivers himself spent only a single day, he was at pains to justify the credibility of John Maresere, who provided most of his information. A Roman Catholic native of Wallis Island, Maresere had lived on Tikopia for twenty years before he had been sent out to sea alone in a canoe—punishment for an offense Rivers did not specify, but which was in fact an adulterous relationship of the sort that Maresere was "most emphatic" in insisting *never* occurred in Tikopia. Returning to Tikopia on the *Southern Cross* after living for some time in the Banks Islands, Maresere provided a description of Tikopian culture in the Motu lingua franca to Durrad, who translated it into English for Rivers. Rivers was convinced that he and Durrad had been able to detect the "very few inconsistencies or contradictions" in Maresere's account, which was confirmed in its essentials by Durrad in a later visit of "several weeks." But given the complex series of linguistic and cultural barriers separating Rivers from his ethnographic data, it is not surprising that later extensive fieldwork should have shown that Maresere's account was "unreliable as Tikopia ethnography." It was, nevertheless, one of the linch-pins in Rivers' theoretical argument.[56]

That argument was based largely on the existence of several "anomalous forms of marriage," most of which had been "recorded for the first time and are unknown, or not yet discovered, in other parts of the world." Asking what social state could explain these marriages, Rivers hypothesized a gerontocratic dual organization with matrilineal descent, in which the old men monopolized the young women, and the younger men had to be satisfied with superannuated castoffs (with cross-cousin marriage a result of favored nephews being rewarded instead with daughters). From a state best exemplified on Pentecost Island, Rivers developed a sequence of four social organizational forms: dual organization with matrilineal descent, an organization in totemic clans, clan exogamy without totemism, and an organization without clans in which marriage was regulated simply by kinship. Although his linguistic comparison confirmed the priority of dual organization with matrilineal descent, it also led Rivers to conclude that later forms must have been the result of "an alien people, perhaps superior in culture, coming from a place with a very different social structure." Like John Pantutun, they would find marriage with persons classed as granddaughters or grandmothers "ridiculous"—and their attitude would "have a decided influence in breaking down such marriage regulations."[57]

Looking for "further evidence of this external influence," Rivers found it in the secret societies that had been described by "Dr. Codrington and others." These were most widespread and elaborate in the southern regions of Melanesia, which were "relatively backward in culture and possess the most archaic form of social organisation," but with "a certain degree of correlation" between the presence of secret societies and "general advance of culture." On this basis Rivers hypothesized a peaceable incursion of small (and predominantly male) groups who continued to practice in secret the religious ceremonies they had brought with them—although because present-day Melanesians were hostile to strangers, he had to assume as "motive" for their peaceful acceptance, that the aboriginal population believed them to be "the dead come back to earth."[58]

With an initial incursion thus established, Rivers found evidence of a series of population movements. The major intrusions upon the aboriginal "dual people" were by two related peoples who had come from Indonesia, whom Rivers labelled by their characteristic stimulants. The first to come were the kava drinkers (exemplified by Tikopia), who were widely diffused throughout Melanesia and who had peopled Polynesia as well. They were followed by the betel-chewers, whose influence was confined to the more northerly portions of Melanesia—and whom Rivers expected to be exemplified by the "intensive study" he and Hocart had done in the Western Solomons. However, the distribution of funerary practices suggested that the presumably aboriginal dual organization was itself the product of an even earlier fusion (rather than, as was commonly thought, the result of fission within a homogeneous grouping). And there were more recent complexities, including two distinct movements of a megalithic sun-worshipping people into Oceania—migrations which Rivers hoped might eventually be brought into "relation with other parts of the world, including our own islands." Moving out from Melanesia to Indonesia, and thence to India, China, and Japan, and even to America, "ethnological analysis" thus held forth the prospect that all of human cultural history might be encompassed within a single scheme.[59]

Rivers saw himself as standing midway between "the evolutionary school" and "the modern historical school" of Graebner in Germany, who did not appreciate "the evolutionary character of the blending of cultures." And *The History of Melanesian Society* was full of what might be called "survivals" of Rivers' earlier evolutionary orientation: many of the old elements (marital communism, the dual organization, totemism, the sequences from matriliny to patriliny and from magic to religion) were still there, mixed together in the new historical bag. He preferred a Frazerian to a Durkheimian definition of religion; and while he insisted that kinship terms were the reflection of prior marriage practices, in other cases he looked for the beliefs underlying current cultural practices. Rivers still thought of his stance as "essentially evolutionary" in spite of his method's "having become historical"; if he called his book the "history" rather than "The Evolution of Melanesian Society," it was because "it is the historical aspect of human progress, rather than the evolution which accompanies it, which should for the present be our main occupation."[60]

When Rivers wrote, there was as yet no "functional" school to which his work might have related; but his relationship to functionalist assumption is worth remarking. Although he most commonly used the term "function" in speaking of the rules governing the behavior of particular kinship categories, there are places where his analysis was functional in a more systematic sense. But when he affirmed that "social institutions only arise in response to definite social needs," he immediately went on to say that he did "not propose to consider such needs as may arise in a homogeneous community"—since he had already shown that the population of Melanesia was not homogeneous. And in his study of the social institutions of heterogenous communities, functional analysis was constantly "smothered in surmise."[61]

At many points, Rivers showed his bias toward ingenious complexity; he wanted explanations that would take care of every single detail. He frequently ran into apparent contradictions, discrepancies between theory and fact; sometimes he appealed for further fieldwork, but more often he tried to explain them away. Many of his positive arguments were linked sausages of supposition: "we have no evidence whatever that the Fijian secret cult was connected with the sun, but if the *nanga* of Fiji is the representative of the *marae* of Tahiti, and if the latter is connected with a cult of the sun, it will become probable that a cult of the sun formed at least one of the motives of the secret mysteries of the Fijian organisation." Once made, such amalgams of assumption were treated as established facts within larger structures of conjecture. Rivers was not unaware of "the logical method" he had been using: "the formulation of a working hypothetical scheme to form a framework into which the facts are fitted [in] a coherent whole, all parts of which are consistent with one another." Granting that some of his constituent arguments might appear circular, he argued that they were elements "in a complex structure no part of which in any way contradicts, or is inconsistent with" its component linkages. Rivers at one point distinguished between "less essential" features of his scheme, and others "so essential that if they are proved to be wrong the whole will have to go." But he professed a willingness for that to happen, so long as "its discussion has been the means of formulating any principles of ethnological inquiry which will be found to be of universal, or even of wide, application."[62]

The first of six such principles Rivers specified was "the fundamental and essential character of social structure"; the last, the role "of the contact of people in the history of human culture." In the longer run, the former principle was to become the most distinctive mark of British social anthropology. And as it did, *The History of Melanesian Society*—conceived as the exemplar of a new (or resurrected) anthropological paradigm—became instead a kind of anti-exemplar of the "conjectural history" in reaction to which social anthropology had emerged. Once a stimulus to research, Rivers' masterwork lapsed, unread, into semi-oblivion. But in the middle 1920s, when the older generation of evolutionists had not yet passed from the scene and the functionalists were just beginning to constitute a school, the "diffusion of culture" inspired both lively advocacy and sharp resistance.[63]

Elliot Smith, William Perry, and the Children of the Sun

In reaffirming the causal priority of "independent invention" in his *Encyclopaedia Britannica* article, Tylor chose "pyramid-building" as clinching example: "no ethnical relationship can ever have existed between the Aztecs and the Egyptians; yet each race developed the idea of the pyramid tomb through that psychological similarity which is as much a characteristic of the species man as his physique." It was not an accidental choice, for in the older tradition of diffusionist ethnology, Egypt had once had a special place. In order to maintain a biblical monogenism, it was necessary to show that the earliest Egyptian dynasty was in fact "far within the era" of the "second origin of mankind" after the Flood—and in 1819, James Cowles Prichard had devoted a major portion of his *Analysis of Egyptian Mythology* to that task. Postulating a divinely instituted theistic religion as the "original possession" of all mankind, Prichard suggested that there had been a "progress of superstition," from the doctrine of emanation through pantheism downward to Egyptian fetishism and "all the prodigious abominations in which a corrupt religion emulated and exceeded the actual depravity of man." Six years earlier, Prichard had noted the similarity between his own *Researches into the Physical History of Man* and "the system of Mr. [Jacob] Bryant, who had written" a widely read late-eighteenth-century attempt to rationalize the Mosaic account with the Egyptian and other mythological annals. Bryant had argued that the introduction of "the useful arts" was everywhere the work of a single "wonderful people"—the sun-worshipping, obelisk-building, sea-going Amonians (descendants of Ham), who despite their apostasy from the truth of primitive revealed religion, were great in "worldly wisdom." Through Bryant, Prichard thus linked his own inquiry to a tradition of historical speculation deeply rooted in European culture: the land of the pharaohs and the pyramids was seen as a center both of religious degeneration and of civilizational advance, of idolatry and of scientific knowledge.[64]

In the nineteenth century, the culture-bearing role of the Egyptians was increasingly compromised by racialism and by evolutionism, as the sequence of imperialist ventures from Napoleon's invasion of 1798 to the Suez crisis of 1882 reduced Egypt to colonial dependence. Anti-Prichardian polygenist writers cited Egyptian monuments depicting four distinguishable racial types as evidence of the stability of races over long periods of time. The focus of early historical inquiry shifted, as comparative philologists pursued linguistic relationships genealogically along a diagonal from India through Greece to the British Isles, leaving Egypt stranded among African peoples whose languages and body types were declared beyond the bounds of genealogical connection, and could only be treated typologically. When "prehistory" was incorporated into a vastly expanded temporal and evolutionary framework after 1858, the connections between early man and modern civilization were sought by other methods in other places. In Tylor's use of the comparative method, Egyptian hieroglyphics became simply one instance of the general process (evident also in Central America and in China) by which "picture-writing" evolved to "word-writing"; in McLennan's, Egyptian animal worship became part of the worldwide evidence for the evolution of totemism.[65]

Interest in ancient Egypt did not die out, however, after the "Egyptomania" of the earlier nineteenth century. In the later 1870s, when Britain became involved in the ownership of the Suez Canal and in international negotiations over the debts of Khedive Ismail's government, modern British Egyptology began to take off. By the time of the British military intervention in 1882, Flinders Petrie had already spent two six-month periods in Egypt, and the Egypt Exploration Fund had been established in London. Over the next several decades, Petrie's extensive excavations led to the reformation of Egyptian archeological method and to a new system of relative chronology. Inevitably, the extensive archeological excavations produced anthropological by-products—such as the studies Rivers conducted in 1900 of the color vision of peasants employed in the digging. But there were also to be more systematic anthropological consequences.[66]

By 1900, the administration of the British proconsul Lord Cromer had begun to offer career opportunities in Egypt for young men with British university credentials. Among them was a young Australian named Grafton Elliot Smith, one of the earliest of the colonial-born anthropologists who were to play an influential role in the history of the discipline. Elliot Smith developed an interest in physiology at the age of ten when his schoolmaster father brought home an elementary textbook; from the time he dissected a beached shark with his penknife, he was "specially intrigued by the brain." After medical studies at the University of Sydney he served for two years there as demonstrator of anatomy, publishing articles on the neurology of marsupials which quickly established him as a figure in Australian science. In 1896 he set off for England with a travelling scholarship, stopping on the way to spend a day with Baldwin Spencer in Melbourne. Settling in Cambridge, Smith worked under the tutelage of Alexander Macalister, the Professor of Anatomy, in the physiological laboratory, where he must have met Rivers. In 1899 (at a time when "University authorities did not always look kindly upon 'Colonials' ") he was elected to a fellowship in St. John's, which was Macalister's and Rivers' college. By 1900 he had won an international reputation for his studies of the cerebrum, and through Macalister's intermediacy was offered the first professorship of anatomy in the Government School of Medicine in Cairo.[67]

Over the next few years, Elliot Smith's continuing productivity in the areas of his primary research was to establish him as the world's leading comparative neurologist and authority on primate cerebral evolution. In 1909 he returned to England as Professor of Anatomy at the University of Manchester, and in 1912 he offered a synthetic view of human cerebral evolution as the presidential address to the anthropological section of the British Association. Later that year he was prominently involved in the analysis and interpretation of the remains "discovered" at Piltdown in Sussex—although not (as one writer later charged) in the perpetration of the fraud. During the 1920s several of his students were to make more substantial contributions to the study of fossil man—notably Raymond Dart's Australopithecines (which Smith interpreted as anthopoid apes) and Davidson Black's Peking Man (which Smith was disinclined to see as evidence for "the central Asiatic origin of the Hominidae"). Throughout this period, Elliot Smith remained a major participant in discussions of human evolution, in which he became a severe critic of the racial theories of the other leading British contributor, Arthur Keith—with whom he had first crossed swords over the interpretation of the Piltdown skull.[68]

Elliot Smith's turn to more strictly anthropological topics began in Egypt in 1900, when Rivers mentioned that the skulls uncovered at the excavation sites where he studied color vision had in some cases actually contained "dessicated brains." Over the next few years Smith himself became involved in the study of ancient Egyptian remains, both in the anatomical laboratory and at various archeological sites. In 1903, he undertook the first of a series of researches on the technique of mummification; in 1907, when the Aswan dam was raised by seven meters, he joined the salvage archeological project, supervising the study of six thousand skeletons and mummies in the first season alone. In 1911, two years after returning to England, Smith synthesized his Egyptological researches in a small volume entitled *The Ancient Egyptians and Their Influence upon the Civilization of Europe*.[69]

Like Rivers in Melanesia, Elliot Smith had begun his Egyptological studies within an evolutionary framework, but he "gradually came to realise that the facts of racial admixture and the blending of cultures were far more obtrusive and significant." While he remained staunchly evolutionary regarding the processes of mankind's emergence, he concluded that "evolution yields a surprisingly small contribution to the solutions of the difficulties which present themselves" in the study of "Man's history and achievements" over the "last sixty centuries." In approaching the latter problem, Smith took as his starting point three recent contributions to Egyptology: the evidence that "every stage in the history of the evolution of the working of copper" was represented in the predynastic graves of Upper Egypt; the advances in chronology that made it possible to "synchronize events" on the banks of the Nile and the Euphrates and to follow "the spread of the knowledge of copper" among the various peoples of antiquity; and the increased knowledge (largely through his own work) of the "physical characteristics of the Ancient Egyptians."[70]

Smith treated the latter issue in the style of nineteenth-century craniological raciology, notably Giuseppe Sergi's study, *The Mediterranean Race*. Sergi had argued, against the Aryanists of his day, that the primitive population of Europe derived from a dolichocephalic northern African "Hamitic" population. Smith's "Proto-Egyptians" were representative of this type, which he called the "Brown Race." The "nearest approximation to that anthropological abstraction, a pure race," they were distinguished sharply from "that most Ape-like race of mankind, the Negro," as well as from the broad-headed "alien" Armenoid type that he later discovered in Lower Egypt. Putting together the evidence of cultural advance and racial movement, Smith developed a complex series of hypotheses to explain Egypt's "three-fold influence upon the development of European civilization": in part by slow diffusion from tribe to tribe within Sergi's Mediterranean race; in part by the mediation of Asiatic groups who had learned the art of metal-working from the Egyptians; in part through direct Egyptian influence—including that of inferior migrant craftsmen, making "crude copies" of the monuments of the pyramid age, who had spread a "megalithic culture" along the Mediterranean and Atlantic littorals.[71]

After delivering his manuscript to his London publisher, Smith went up to Cambridge to serve as an external examiner. There his friend Rivers told him that this, his "first incursion into ethnology," was a "flagrant defiance" of prevailing evolutionary doctrines—which Rivers was even then in the process of recanting. Smith also found in the Cambridge museum a skull similar to his intrusive Armenoids, but which had in fact been collected in the South Pacific. Augmented by other cranial evidence, this discovery became the basis for a paper, given at the same meetings at which Rivers announced his conversion to ethnology, wherein Smith argued that the "peculiar distribution of megalithic monuments in India, Eastern Asia, Oceania and America," was due to "the influence, directly or indirectly, of Egyptian civilization."[72]

The next several meetings of the British Association were enlivened by "sometimes very heated" discussion of diffusionist papers given by both Elliot Smith and Rivers, who in 1915 "showed that the megalithic monuments of Oceania were probably the work of sun-worshipping immigrants." At the 1914 meetings in Australia, Smith discovered what was to be the "cornerstone" of a larger diffusionist edifice, when he happened to see two mummies from the Torres Straits in the museum at the University of Sydney. Upon closer examination, he determined that the technique of their mummification showed close similarities to that of the Egyptians twenty-five centuries before. Smith believed these to be too numerous to "have arisen by chance"—especially in view of the complexity of the mummification process and the fact that none of the conditions which had led to its development in Egypt existed in the Torres Straits. Convinced that he had uncovered evidence for the worldwide influence of the Egyptians, Smith excitedly reported his find to his colleagues at the British Association—only to have the Oxford evolutionary archeologist, John Myres, attempt to explain the phenomenon in terms of the psychic unity of mankind, and Alfred Haddon complain that there were "no links between Egypt and Papua to indicate that the custom had spread."[73]

Responding to the challenge, Elliot Smith published the next year a small volume, *The Migrations of Early Culture,* in which the basic position of what came to be known as the "heliolithic school" was set forth in greater detail. According to Smith, mummification was only "the most distinctive" element of an "intimately interwoven series" of "bizarre customs and beliefs" that together made up the " 'heliolithic' culture complex." These included megalithic monuments; sun and serpent worship; the swastika symbol; the practices of massage, circumcision, cranial deformation, and tattooing; stories of the creation, the deluge, the divine origin of kings, and the genesis of a chosen people from an incestuous union. These elements had no "genetic or inherent connection," but had become associated "purely by chance" over an extended period in ancient Egypt, and in the centuries after 900 B.C. had been carried westward and eastward in a series of maritime expeditions. Eventually reaching the American coast, the complex there "bore fruit in the development of the great civilizations on the Pacific littoral and isthmus, whence it gradually leavened the bulk of the vast aboriginal population of the Americas." Since many of these elements served "no useful purpose" and were "wholly misunderstood" by the populations among whom they were found, it was inconceivable that they had been inde-

Grafton Elliot Smith, in his laboratory at University College, c. 1925. (Courtesy of the Library, University College London)

pendently invented or that any "psychological explanation" or "theory of evolution" could account for them. Appealing to ethnologists to "recognize the error of their ways and to repent," Smith called on them to "admit that in former ages knowledge and culture spread in much the same way as they are known to be diffused to-day."[74]

Elliot Smith saw his hypothesis as "a further extension" of the argument of Rivers' "great monograph," *The History of Melanesian Society*. By showing how "small groups of wanderers" from a "higher culture" could exert profound influence on a "large uncultured population," Rivers had demonstrated "the means of transmission"; by showing how a people often "completely lost some useful art which it once had, and even more often clung to some useless practice," he helped to account for the frequent failure to preserve that influence entire. Although Rivers himself had little to contribute to the discussion of the heliolithic theory over the next few years, there was no question that he supported it. At a discussion of the issue at the British Association in 1915, Rivers indicated that although he had previously "hesitated to follow Elliot Smith" all the way back to Egypt, the evidence of the Torres Straits mummies had convinced him that "the complex most suitably known as megalithic developed in

Egypt and spread thence to the many parts of the world where we find evidence of its existence at the present time." Equally important, Rivers suggested, was the recent demonstration by W. J. Perry that the motive of migration was "the love of wealth": Perry's maps of distribution revealed "with a clearness which has few, if any, parallels in the history of ethnology, that the carriers of the Egyptian culture were impelled by the same motives as those which lead the people of our own time." Over the next few years, Perry was to play a major role in the further elaboration and propagation of the heliolithic theory.[75]

William James Perry was the son of an Anglican clergyman, headmaster of the school Perry attended until 1906, when he won a scholarship to study mathematics at Cambridge, where he attended the lectures of Haddon and Rivers. By 1910 he had become closely acquainted with Rivers, and remained in close correspondence with him after taking a post at a grammar school in Yorkshire in 1911. Although they were unrelated, by 1915 they were addressing each other as "My Dear Uncle" and "My Dear Nephew"—which in many Melanesian societies would have indicated the relationship of heir apparency (mother's brother/sister's son). In the autumn of 1913, Rivers suggested to Perry that he collect evidence for the existence of Megalithic monuments and a sun-cult in Indonesia—which in Rivers' scheme was the proximate source of the kava and the betel cultures, and, in Perry's words, "the sieve through which any extensive migration from the West to Oceania must pass." The results of his study convinced Perry that the stoneworks of Indonesia were the products of migrants who had entered the area in search of gold and other forms of wealth, and who had also introduced terraced irrigation, metal-working, and rice-growing, as well as a sun-cult and "a whole group of beliefs and tales concerning the sky-world and ideas about fertility and the use of phallic symbols." Although Perry's elements included some of Elliot Smith's, he did not insist so strongly on their accidental association; his training with Rivers was also reflected in an emphasis on social structural distinctions. Perry saw his project as the outcome of convergent inquiries: dedicated to Rivers, his book was published by the Manchester University Press at Smith's behest. Within a year, Smith had rescued Perry from the isolation of his Yorkshire schoolmastership by obtaining for him an appointment at Manchester.[76]

By that time Elliot Smith had provided another major link in the developing diffusionist argument, in a series of three lectures given over a two-year period and published in 1919 as *The Evolution of the Dragon*. While many of the programmatic statements of the neo-diffusionists attacking the idea of psychic unity and evolutionary parallelism had a strongly anti-psychologistic character, when it came to developing the positive argument for their position, they advanced psychological interpretations of their own. At critical points in their argument, it became necessary to provide "motives," both for the original elaboration of cultural practices and the migrations that led to their diffusion. And at these points, neo-diffusionism tended to become a sort of mirror-image of evolutionism, in which the philosophical basis for the development of civilization was sought in a different set of beliefs than those of animistic proto-science. For Smith, the dragon was "primarily a personification of the life-giving and life-destroying powers of water," and his first chapter was devoted to "the genesis of this biological theory of water and its relationship to the other germs of civilization." Taking as his unstated reference point Frazer's *Golden Bough,* Smith suggested that the water-king of the Egyptians, on whose vitality the fertility of the land was dependent, had refused to be slain at the height of his powers, but called instead "upon the Great Mother, as the giver of life, to rejuvenate him" through the elixir of human blood obtained by sacrifice—the "story of the slaying of the dragon" being "a much distorted rumour of this incident."[77]

In this context, Smith offered a theory counter to Frazer's on the relationship of religion and science: originally undifferentiated, both were attempts "to peer into the meaning of natural phenomena"—not, however, to explain them, but in response to "the instinct of self-preservation." The search for "the elixir of life" was "the great driving force that has compelled men to build up the material and the intellectual fabric of civilization." Religion was "archaic science enriched with the belief in supernatural control"; myth, in contrast, was "effete religion which has been superseded by the growth of a loftier ethical purpose." The "essential unity of the motives and incidents of the myths of all peoples" was not, however, a token of "independent origin" or "the similarity of the working of the human mind"; rather, it was evidence "of their derivation from the same ultimate source."[78]

As Reader in Comparative Religion at Manchester, Perry took on the task of elaborating more systematically Elliot Smith's somewhat disjointed notions on "the origin of magic and religion." Starting from the primitive Great Mother belief of the food-gathering peoples of the Paleolithic Age, Perry traced the emergence of irrigational god-kings among the food-producing Egyptians, whose practice of mummification had led to a more general belief in immortality. This in turn became a "powerful incentive" to "the search for the Earthly Paradise" and for various magical substances (polished stone celts, crystals, gold, pearl shells) that were regarded as "givers of life." Tracing the consequent "world-wide spread of culture" became the subject of the culminating work of British neo-diffusionism, Perry's *Children of the Sun.*[79]

There Perry began by studying the geographical distribution of certain key culture elements: irrigation, pottery-making, the working of metals, and the use of stone for polished implements, graven images, and construction. At the outer limits of each major cultural area lay the "food-gatherers" who were the earth's true primitives; they were of little concern to him. But among the "food-producers" in each area he was able to trace everywhere the same "culture-sequence," first in North America, then westward through Oceania, Indonesia, and India, in striking relation to the distribution of the sources of gold, copper, pearls, and other "givers of life." In each case, however, the sequence led back to the same "archaic civilization" that had been carried everywhere by "the children of the sun." Their culture-bearing role was in fact documented in stories of "culture-heroes" present in the mythology of peoples in every major area. Anthropologists, long obsessed with the idea of "continual upward cultural progress" and contemptuous of "native tradition," had refused to treat this evidence seriously. Echoing Lang's position on primitive monotheism, Perry proposed instead to "accept the tradition that culture was introduced, until it is disproved by irrefutable evidence."[80]

Lacking Smith's background in biological science, Perry was little interested in issues of "race." Although at several points he associated the "children of the sun" with the Phoenicians, it was the diffusion of Egyptian cultural elements rather than the ethnic identity of their carriers that concerned him. But as a student of Rivers, Perry was also interested in relationships that could be established "between the social, political and economic organizations, and the religious system of a people." His central chapters were devoted to a variety of such topics, in which the original inventory of the elements of archaic civilization was expanded to include human sacrifice, the great mother-goddess, mother-right, totemic clans, the dual organization, and exogamy—as well as "a ruling class in two divisions": the children of the sun, born of the sky-world and practicing incestuous unions; and war chiefs associated with the underworld. The "climax" of Perry's argument was an attempt to show "how and why these cultural elements originated, and to explain what caused Egyptian culture to begin its journey across the earth." Rejecting geographical determinism, Perry argued that it was not climate or any other "external determination" but "the mind of man" that was "of predominating importance, both in the production of the archaic civilization and in the determination of its distribution."[81]

That Perry should have supported this position by quoting a paragraph in which Frazer criticized Westermarck's dependence on "biological causes without taking into account the factors of intelligence, deliberation, and will" suggests again the paradoxical relationship between his own work and that of "the evolutionary school." Throughout *The Children of the Sun*, Frazer was a frequently cited source of evidence, both on matters relating to the fertility-enhancing role of god-kings and on the issues of social evolutionary theory Frazer had treated in *Totemism and Exogamy,* many of which were subsumed and reinterpreted in Perry's argument. Although Perry (perhaps symptomatically) was not given to the phrase "amongst the," his work had a similar world-geographical and world-historical scope, and it, too, was given unity of plot by the search for "motive." There was, however, a dramatic contrast in the general narrative structure of his book and Frazer's *Golden Bough,* a contrast more fundamental perhaps than that between independent invention and diffusion.[82]

Despite Frazer's fears of "the volcano underfoot," the progress of civilization was for him an upward one. But Perry's "culture-sequences" were all sequences of degeneration; once the archaic civilization left its Egyptian source, "the rule was that of the degradation of culture." How Western Europe had escaped this devolutionary fate Perry did not say: "the story of the coming of the modern world" was "a task for the future." But otherwise the pattern of history was everywhere the same: viewed from the periphery of migration rather than the Egyptian center, what Perry had written was a history not of the diffusion of culture but of its devolution, as elements were lost, or lost their meaning, as they were carried farther from their source.[83]

And there were in fact overtones of a more general Spenglerian pessimism throughout Perry's book. If the contemporary historical model for the genesis of neo-diffusionism had been the experience of British imperial expansion, the model for its culminating statement was the experience of World War I. The archaic civilization contained the seeds of its own catastrophic destruction in the hostility between the "two sides of the dual organization," which the children of the sun took with them and reproduced at every stage of their migrations. The rise of warrior classes (accompanied by "the subjection of women"), "the institution of the class system," and the competition for power among "ruling groups" had gradually "educated" mankind in the "violent and cruel modes of behavior" which ultimately "smashed" the archaic civilization, giving rise "to fresh communities of a warlike nature."[84]

Perry, however, apparently shared the mildly socialist politics of his mentor Rivers, and was not willing to assume that this cycle was everywhere irreversible. Warfare was not natural to mankind, which in the truly primitive food-gathering stage lived normally in "perfect peace" and "perfect equality." Warfare was a "deviation" produced in "the interaction between social institutions and human behaviour." Perry's study of that interaction (which was "one of the ultimate problems of social psychology") led him to the conclusion that warfare might disappear, if the "institution which gives rise to it"—the "class system"—could be "eliminated or modified." Fortunately, the "great democratic movement" of the modern era was "accompanied by the continual adoption of less violent modes of behavior." Social psychology—toward which Perry's study of history had in fact been pointed—thus suggested that it might yet "be possible to order society on the right lines."[85]

Perry's primary purpose, of course, was not the reordering of society but the reformation of anthropology. Following the publication of *The Children of the Sun*, Perry moved from Manchester to University College, London, as Reader in Cultural Anthropology in the Department of Anatomy Elliot Smith had come to head three years before. Perry's room in the new anatomy building, its walls decorated with charts of cultural element distributions and a worldwide migrational map, soon became an important center of anthropological discussion. Among the participants were the archeologist V. Gordon Childe and the social anthropologists Daryll Forde and A. P. Elkin, both of whom were to hold major anthropological professorships over the next few decades. But if neo-diffusionism remained a force throughout the 1920s, *The Children of the Sun* was more successful as a provocation to debate and criticism than as an alternative paradigm.[86]

Published in the year in which "the discovery of the tomb of Tutankhamen" had focussed "the attention of the whole world upon Egypt" as the home of "the highest expressions of material and social culture," Perry's account of how "so vast a civilisation utterly vanished from the earth" stirred the imagination of some popular reviewers. But the anthropological response was much less favorable, even among some who, like Alfred Haddon, were theoretically predisposed to migrational diffusionism. Having previously argued that the representations of elephants Elliot Smith had seen in Mayan stelae as proof of Egyptian influence were really only macaws, Haddon now launched an all-out attack on the evidence for the diffusion of "pearls as 'givers of life.'" Referring to documentary sources and the expertise of a number of fellow Cambridge scholars, he suggested that Smith and Perry had not faced up to the fundamental "racial and linguistic problems" of any diffusionist project. Although Haddon refrained from a "full discussion" of Perry's theories on the grounds that it would first "require a syndicate to check his references and statements," his final comment was quite scathing: "All writers are liable to slips, but careful students always bear in mind that the historical, as well as the scientific, method demands that . . . one should quote correctly, consult the original sources at first-hand, and that a clear distinction should be made between assumptions and definitely ascertained facts."[87]

While less predisposed than Haddon to diffusionism, Marett nonetheless accepted the "indisputable proof" of migration by a megalithic people into Oceania from the West. But he found "absurd" Perry's lumping together of so many different peoples "under the heading of food-gatherers." And although he had done no more fieldwork than Perry, he went on to contrast the fleeting fame of theory with the "immortality" of a "really sound piece of ethnographic research."[88]

It seems likely that the development of ethnographic fieldwork compromised the readiness of the emerging group of professional anthropologists to be receptive to worldwide comparativist enterprises, whether of the evolutionary or the diffusionary sort. The ethnographic material of Frazer's *Golden Bough* had been derived largely from travellers, missionaries, and other "amateurs" not likely to have a voice in scholarly anthropological discussion. By 1923, Perry relied more heavily on ethnographers with academic connections, some of them potential reviewers of his book. Unlike Frazer, he did not select data on a common theme from different tribes of the "Amongsthas"; rather, he professed to characterize the total culture of particular groups. But he was little concerned with the presently observed behavior of any group, privileging instead native tradition as a source of evidence about past history. Although he occasionally spoke of "cultures," the impact of his argument was radically to reduce the cultural diversity of the present ethnographic world: given his universal cultural key, "the form of culture possessed by any one community can be accounted for when its manner of derivation from the archaic civilization is known." To an emerging generation of younger academic anthropologists whose full certification was increasingly dependent on ethnographic research, the appropriation of their fieldwork in a comparativist enterprise widely regarded as extremely dubious must have seemed a somewhat disturbing prospect. As the twenties wore on, the discussion of heliolithic diffusion—which occupied a place in *Man* similar to that of totemism in the century's first decade—became increasingly critical.[89]

By the early 1930s, what might be called the Egyptian phase of modern British anthropology was clearly over. In 1913, when Seligman had attempted the first synthesis of the researches he and his wife Brenda conducted in the Anglo-Egyptian Sudan between 1909 and 1911, the influence of Elliot Smith was very much in evidence. It was Smith who had shown that "the predynastic Egyptians and earliest Nubians were not even Negroid." Seligman, who was the chief articulator of the now-discredited "Hamitic hypothesis," carried the argument a step further to show that the "features common to the social life and religion of ancient Egypt and tropical Negro-land" were due to "the infiltration of the latter with the ideas of that great White Race of which the predynastic Egyptians constitute the oldest known as well as one of the purest branches." Unlike Rivers, however, Seligman never accepted the worldwide cultural influence of the Egyptians. And after the dust had settled from "the diffusion controversy," he concluded (without once mentioning Elliot Smith) that the widespread belief in divine kingship in Negro Africa was not the result of "the transmission of a specifically Egyptian custom," but rather "an old and widespread Hamitic belief," to which a number of specifically Egyptian rites had "become attached."[90]

Perry's later years were marred by Parkinson's disease, first manifested following Rivers' sudden death in 1922. His last major work, although subtitled *An Introductory Contribution to Social Psychology,* was still very much in the style of *The Children of the Sun,* both thematically and methodologically. Elliot Smith's last contribution to "the diffusion controversy" was an attempt to reclaim Tylor for the diffusionist cause by postulating a split intellectual personality: Tylor's "reason" impelled him to accept the "reality of the widespread dispersal of civilisation in the world," but an "emotional intuition" stemming from his Quaker upbringing led him to postulate a universal animistic belief in "the continuance of the soul's existence after death." Holding these "diametrically opposite" beliefs simultaneously for most of his life, Tylor in his last published writing succumbed to the "popular fallacy" of independent invention, "which his own disciples seem to have imagined to be the essence of their master's teaching."[91]

By the time Smith wrote those words, however, Tylor's disciples had all but passed from the anthropological scene, and the protagonists of the new synchronic functionalism were not inclined to listen to advocates of what they had come to regard as "conjectural history." Meyer Fortes found Perry's book fundamentally flawed by his assumption of "the historicity of myth," and went on to suggest that "by pressing analogies in which any feature of one culture is considered to be homologous with any feature of any other culture, almost anything can be proved." And although Smith in 1922 was sufficiently representative of the discipline to take Tylor's place as the authority on "Anthropology" for the twelfth edition of the *Encyclopaedia Britannica,* his book on Tylor was not reviewed in the publications of the Royal Anthropological Institute.[92]

A. M. Hocart: The Boasian Ethnographer as Frazerian Diffusionist

The generation of academic anthropologists who entered the discipline during the interwar years later looked back upon the neo-Egyptian diffusionism of Smith and Perry as "uncritical to the point of extravagance" and "obviously fallacious"—"a bizarre ethnological theory" from which any serious anthropologist must be disassociated. Following a pattern already set by Rivers' Torres Straits colleagues, Haddon and

Seligman, they have tended to distinguish between an "early" Rivers and a "late" Rivers. The former contributed substantially to ethnographic method and the theory of social organization; the latter unfortunately got tangled up with Smith and Perry, who as Rivers' literary executors were even suspected of self-interested editing of his numerous posthumously published manuscripts. A similar dissociational tendency is manifest in the case of Arthur Maurice Hocart, who has recently been reappreciated as one of the most important members of the prewar cohort—but whose career was closely linked to all three of the neo-diffusionists.[93]

Like Marett, Hocart came from the Channel Islands, where his French forebears had acquired British nationality after settling on the island of Guernsey. His grandfather was a High Church clergyman who became a Wesleyan Methodist; his father, a Wesleyan minister who became a Unitarian and who wrote on a variety of religious topics—including the obstacles to the Protestant faith in Belgium, where Hocart was born in 1883. Hocart attended school in Brussels and at Elizabeth College on Guernsey, before matriculating at Oxford in 1902. There he lived in Marett's college, Exeter, until 1906, when he graduated with second-class honors in "Greats" (Greek, Latin, ancient history, and philosophy). During his first two years, his special subject was comparative philology, which he studied with "that remarkable man," Joseph Wright, a protégé of Max Müller's who had succeeded him to the professorship in 1901. During his last two years, Hocart studied psychology with one of the alumni of the Torres Straits Expedition, William McDougall. After graduation, he spent two years pursuing psychology and philosophy at the University of Berlin, where he must have studied the phenomenological psychology of Carl Stumpf.[94]

When Rivers chose two associates for the Percy Sladen Trust Expedition, he turned to London and Oxford to complement his own Cambridge affiliation; Hocart could have been suggested by either McDougall or Marett. On the basis of a passage in one of Hocart's letters to Rivers referring to the possible legal difficulties of having "flute duets" with a "precocious dandy" from Fiji, it has been intimated that the two men may have shared a homosexual inclination; be that as it may, there is no doubt that they hit it off emotionally and intellectually. If we may assume that Rivers taught Hocart the "genealogical method," it seems likely that the more empathic quality of Rivers' methodological prescriptions in the 1912 edition of *Notes and Queries* reflected his experience in the field with Hocart. Hocart's background in classical languages, comparative philology, and phenomenological psychology inclined him to a very different style of fieldwork from that typified by the "genealogical method"; as one obituarist put it, rather than asking detailed questions, he listened.[95]

Hocart's early fieldwork was probably the most extensive of any anthropologist of his generation. After working with Rivers for three months on Eddystone Island, he spent six weeks on Roviana before returning for further work on Eddystone. With Haddon's support, he then obtained the headmastership of a school for native boys in Fiji, where he served until 1912. For two years after that he investigated "race, crafts, and customs" in Fiji, Rotuma, Wallis Island, Samoa, and Tonga, working as a "graduate research scholar" first for Exeter and then for Jesus College, Oxford. The ethnographic notes preserved from this continuous six-year fieldwork stint suggest an unusual sensitivity to the difficulties of category definition and to the semantic nuances implicated in any attempt at intercultural translation—as well as to the problematic position of an imperial ethnographer in a colonized society.[96]

Trying to understand the native culture "from within," Hocart was also, in the language of a more recent anthropological sensibility, quite remarkably "reflexive." Among his earliest publications on Fiji was one in an English theological journal wherein he translated, "as closely as possible, attempting to render every word," the argument of a Christianized Fijian that the demographic decline of his race was due to the neglect of traditional native gods, to whom Jehovah, the God of the Spirit, had delegated responsibility for the "life of the flesh." Complementing this piece was a discussion of "the psychological interpretation of language," in which Hocart attacked the notion that savage languages were "poor in general concepts and rich in minute subdivisions of the species." Adopting what was to become a favorite trope—the Fijian ethnographer in England whose observations were then interpreted by a "Fijian philosopher" for a third Fijian back at home—Hocart argued that a language could only be evaluated in relation to the "uses it is put to and the thoughts that it is required to express."[97]

In 1914, Hocart returned to Oxford as a diploma student in anthropology. During the following year, he gave lectures on "Problems in Anthropology," served one term as Deputy Wilde Reader in Mental Philosophy for the absent McDougall, and wrote what may be regarded as his first theoretical statement: an attack on "the rationalistic utilitarian psychology" which, in the manner of Hobbes and Locke, first asked of any custom, "What can have been the intended use of it?" The curtain of social history "used to rise on highly intelligent White Men sealing a compact for the abolition of strife"; now, Frazer would have it rise "on a camp meeting of 'dull' Australian Blacks discussing how to prevent the injurious effects of incest." But since the dual organization did not in fact stop the incest between parent and child, the psychological anthropologist was forced toward the conclusion that "the savage does not think as we do," and to supplement rational utilitarianism with a "functional psychology" that explained savage customs by "association, emotion, confusion of thought, massive apprehension, analogical reasoning and so forth." To both of these, and to a third "biological psychology" that explained customs by "instincts, real or supposed, of the human mind," Hocart responded that one could not deduce "the ever-changing and endless variety of custom and belief throughout the world" either out of a uniform human mentality or from different mental constitutions. His own assumption was that the "congenital differences of character between races" were "negligible." But it was "precisely because savages think in the same manner as we do that they think different things; for the same processes working on different inherited material must lead to different results."[98]

The savage's mind worked on "inherited tradition and social organization"; and despite our confidence in "the absolute validity of our own systems," so did ours. A "curious savage," speculating on "the workings of the European mind" on the basis of accounts by "travelled friends" of European customs and beliefs about germs, might conclude—in the manner of Lévy-Bruhl—that "the White Man does not think logically as we do; he is post-logical." The "highly-strung natures" of white men saw everywhere "the workings of a mysterious power of Contagion, with which the whole world is loaded as with electricity"; the "theory of bacilli" was "merely the European way of justifying these feelings."[99]

Although it was clear enough that Hocart felt that ethnology could advance only by abandoning speculation about motive conceived of in individualistic, rationalistic, utilitarian terms, his positive programmatic alternatives were not well defined. "Having dispensed with Mind," Rivers had already "annexed" the province of kinship and social organization "to exact method." Anticipating the direction of his own work, Hocart suggested that religion might be the next region to be "threatened with subjugation." In the meantime, "the conflict between psychology and history for the possession of ethnology" had a "practical" as well as a "theoretic" importance. The "psychological point of view" led logically to two ways of dealing with natives: "the damn nigger" and the "little brown brother" attitudes—the former assuming the absolute psychological disparity of "the dark races"; the latter taking a patronizing posture toward the undeveloped intelligence and moral sense of the childlike natives.[100]

Hocart's anti-psychologism was at this point even more extreme than that of Rivers. Reviewing *The History of Melanesian Society,* he took his mentor to task for attributing differing "modes of thought" to "rude peoples" and Europeans, without actually studying their traditions or beliefs in detail. Rivers had been too fair to the "psychological school," producing a compromise between the methods of "the evolutionary school and that of the modern historical school of Germany"—rather than following "his own instinct" and becoming a "whole-hogger." Rejecting the English "psychological school," Hocart seems to have turned toward other anthropological traditions—not, however, that of his ancestral France, but to the German and the American. There were indeed striking similarities between Hocart's anti-ethnocentric and linguistically oriented approach and that of the Boasians, and during the war years he published articles in the *American Anthropologist*.[101]

After four years in the army, during which he served on the front lines in France and reached the rank of captain, Hocart resumed his anthropological career in 1919. Whether because of the scarcity of academic positions, or because of his own commitment to empirical research, he accepted an appointment as Archaeological Commissioner for Ceylon, devoting a preparatory year at Oxford to studying Sanskrit, Pali, Tamil, and Singhalese, and spending time in India as well, studying the conservation of Hindu and Buddhist monuments. Through most of the 1920s, Hocart was in Ceylon supervising excavations and attending to the preservation of monuments, many of them reachable only by difficult journeys through dangerous terrain. Severe dysentery forced him to take home leave in 1925; the years after his return to Ceylon were complicated by interdepartmental tensions and political squabbling involving the "official" and the "unofficial" (i.e., Singhalese) members of the legislature, and a succession of less-than-competent colonial governors. Failing in his attempt to procure the Disney Professorship of Archaeology at Cambridge in 1927 and suffering a near-fatal relapse of dysentery the following year, Hocart retired to England on a pension in 1929, where in 1930 he married the woman who had nursed him through his illness.[102]

By that time, Hocart had published two books that defined his characteristic anthropological style, which had both Boasian and Frazerian moments. Although rather drastically refashioned by the Bishop Museum's editors, the *Lau Islands, Fiji* was intended to be an ethnography of a sort Boas might have appreciated. In an unpublished methodological preface, Hocart described it as largely a "stringing together" of the verbatim statements of native informants. Trained in several specialist traditions of textual scholarship, Hocart sought to create a body of material that might play "the same part in the study of Fijian culture as the Brahmanas and Sutras do in India, Pausanias in Greece, [and the] Pyramid Texts in Egypt." As works of "supreme importance for the study of religion," these "original sources" would "remain while books written around them pass away." Similarly, his goal was to provide "a complete record of all the facts to which the theorist will always have to look for his material." Unlike Boas, however, Hocart did not exhibit a reluctance to theorize: "theory alone is worthy of our labour; the collection of facts is waste of time except to provide fuel for theory."[103]

That Hocart should have chosen "kingship," regarded as a religious phenomenon, as the focus for his theoretical constructions may reflect the fact that his time in Ceylon was largely spent in excavating temples associated with Buddhist kings; but there also were other predisposing factors. Borrowed from Frazer, "divine kingship" was a central topic of neo-diffusionist ethnology, with which, despite private reservations, Hocart nonetheless associated himself: "Mr. Perry's views may be modified . . . , but the broad fact remains of a culture involving megaliths and solar kings spreading from one end of the world to the other." And if neo-diffusionism may be interpreted in part as a rewriting of Frazer, this is even more the case with Hocart, who as a trained classicist would have known *The Golden Bough* from an early point in his career and whose scholarship (ranging across thirteen languages) rivalled that of Frazer. In announcing the completion of his book in 1925, he suggested that it dealt with a topic of which Frazer had just touched "the fringe." Rivers having seized the terrain of kinship and social organization, Hocart would now carry the flag of "precise method" toward the religious heartland of British evolutionary theorizing.[104]

Hocart opened his study of kingship by noting the "fierce battle" raging between "those who deny that the same thing is ever invented twice" and the "die-hards" who "automatically turn down every attempt at tracing common origins." Although he sought a moderate diffusionist middle ground, Hocart was little concerned with documenting the diffusion of customs or the migrations of peoples. Diffusion was for him rather a necessary methodological assumption, justifying the comparison of widely separated cultural phenomena as products of a single historically continuous process of differentiation. He wanted to discern "the main features of a religion" which "a long time ago attained to such a vogue that by degrees it overspread a considerable part of the world."[105]

In contrast to that of the evolutionists, Hocart's project was not a search for ultimate origins: there were "no first beginnings," but only "beliefs, older beliefs, and yet older beliefs," and "long and intimate intercourse with various peoples of the South Seas" had taught him "the consequent habit of taking all beliefs seriously." As the book's opening epigraph from Grimm suggested, the beliefs Hocart took especially seriously were those of "song and story." Although dismissed by rationalistically inclined historians of every age, myths when rightly read were "after all no more than sober history." They were not products of imagination (as those who argued the natural tendency of man to personify nature would have it); they were products of memory—not of events, but of rituals. Although an Oxonian, Hocart had obviously read the Cambridge Ritualists: creation myths were "memories, more or less accurate, of creation ceremonies."[106]

To study those ceremonies, Hocart relied on the methods "so successful in the study of language." Just as "the comparative philologist" analyzed language "into its smallest elements, which are sounds," Hocart broke coronation ceremonies into the "numerous rites and observances" of which they were composed. Labelling them alphabetically, Hocart noted their presence or absence in a series of cultures (Fijian, Indian, Cambodian, Egyptian, Hebrew, Roman, Byzantine, and English), concluding that these various "consecration rites" were all derived "from one common source": a "parent rite" that included "most if not all of the rites we have found, some here, some there."[107]

Although borrowed from comparative philology, Hocart's method of "dissection" was heavily laden also with the rhetoric of comparative anatomy. While the studies composing *Kingship* were "originally undertaken at random," they "invariably led us back to the institution of divine kings," gradually revealing this "earliest known religion" not "as an accidental conglomeration of ideas" but as an "organism." Altered "by the need of adaptation to new circumstances," its "mutually interdependent" parts might even "lose their old function, and with it their old form, in order to acquire a new one"; but "through all these changes" we might recognize the same "social structure." In short, all the rites he studied were "species" of a "genus."[108]

In retracing divergent developments back to "common origins," it was not enough to study "outward resemblances"; the anatomization of customs was a matter of discovering structural or formal identities. At various points, Hocart's argument in fact hinged on a series of equations: because "kings = gods," they could "perform wonders"; the king, being the sun, could "make the earth and men fruitful by imposing regularity on the universe and the tribe." Although at points Hocart was inclined to interpret beliefs in terms of an inadequate development of the "powers of abstraction," he cautioned against turning the "ritual conception of the universe into ridicule." Until we had "penetrated into the inner meaning of ancient dogmas" we had no right to "condemn them as preposterous." The equations of his analysis (like those of native thought) were not those of material identity: "it is through their forms . . . that things are brought into relation, identified, with one another and with man; it is through this conceptual identity that man can influence the world and mend it when it works badly." Regardless of their differing powers of abstraction, there was a psychic unity between the South Sea Islander and the European which (when utilitarian ethnocentrism was put aside) made anthropological understanding possible. And for Hocart (in contrast to Marett and others who reacted against Frazerian rationalism by

Arthur Maurice Hocart, late in life. (Courtesy of the Alexander Turnbull Library, Wellington, New Zealand; no. 94302.5)

stressing the emotional aspects of the human psyche) that unity (like the rituals in which it was manifest) was ultimately logical.[109]

Hocart's rejection of the rational utilitarian psychology of Frazerian evolutionism was, in the end, neither a rejection of psychology nor a dismissal of evolutionism per se. He repudiated the assumption that the Väddas (Seligman's Veddahs), or any other present people, were necessarily "as primitive in their customs as in their lack of clothes": "we cannot . . . base a whole science on an assumption which not only has never been proved, but is demonstrably false." On the other hand, he did believe that "there is more than an analogy between natural and human history, that the infinite variety of human customs is the outward manifestation of man's endless experiments in the acquisition of higher powers, his groping after new faculties that are raising him to an ever higher rank, that they are in short, nothing else than the evolutionary processes, viewed under a microscope." In this respect, as in a number of others, Hocart was close to Elliot Smith, who, beginning his career as a Darwinian comparative anatomist, remained *au fond* an evolutionist—diffusionism being, as we have noted several times, more compatible than independent invention with the branching pattern of Darwinian development. Hocart himself acknowledged his debt in 1929: "I think it will turn out that, as Professor Elliot Smith has suggested, the act of procreation gave rise to the idea of creation, and all sacrifice is an act of creation."[110]

It is not surprising, then, that despite reservations he had about the migrations of "the children of the sun," Hocart after his return to England joined the neo-diffusionists at University College, where he served as Honorary Lecturer in Ethnology from 1931 until 1934. Failing in his candidacy for the chair in social anthropology at Cambridge in 1932, he spent the five years before his death in 1939 as Professor of Sociology at the University of Cairo. During this period, he published a now-forgotten evolutionary textbook, *The Progress of Man,* and a recently remembered study, *Kings and Councillors*. There, and in several manuscripts published after his death by his literary executor Lord Raglan, Hocart pursued the ramifying theme of divine kingship toward a more general "comparative anatomy of human society." Some of Hocart's work—particularly the posthumous study *Caste*—was not without later influence and resonance, especially among French writers. But by the middle 1930s, other advocates of the scientific study of social and cultural phenomena—very nearly contemporary with Hocart, but untainted by neo-diffusionism and less marginal institutionally—had already redirected the British social anthropological tradition along quite different lines.[111]

Neo-Diffusionism and the Revolution in Anthropology

From the time of his "conversion" in 1911 until several years after his death in 1922, William Rivers was the single most influential figure in British anthropology—or, to be more precise, in those portions of it treating the temporal development and descriptive variety of human psychology, social organization, and culture (as opposed to the biological aspects of human variation). No account of that influence can be complete without reference to the force of Rivers' persona. Both contemporary observers and later commentators have noted a transformation of his personality, from a repressed, withdrawn, and somewhat conservative intellectualism to a more spontaneous and anti-establishmentarian conviviality, or, as one historian would have it, from a rather rigidly epicritic to a more flexibly protopathic personality. If it was this "later" Rivers that Arnold Bennett remembered as "the really great swell" to whom he had been introduced by Siegfried Sassoon, it is clear that the early Rivers, too, had a powerful personal influence on those with whom he worked closely. But whether narrowly focussed or widely diffused, Rivers' personal charisma could only facilitate an influence that depended primarily on his methodological and theoretical contributions to an anthropology which in the years after 1900 was in a state of considerable disarray.[112]

Initiated as the "genealogical method" on the Torres Straits Expedition, generalized as the "concrete method" in the 1912 revision of *Notes and Queries,* Rivers' ethnographic innovations provided a kind of methodological technology for a generation of younger academic fieldworkers in the new "intensive" mode. On the theoretical side, the sequence of his conceptual enthusiasms—the analysis of social organization, the ethnological analysis of cultural diffusion, and (still to be discussed) the anthropological implications of pathological psychology—represented three possible lines of development out of the crisis of late evolutionary anthropology. His sudden death in 1922 left heirs in each of these three areas to squabble over his anthropological estate—or better, to redefine anthropology along each of three different trajectories. At the time of Rivers' death, Malinowski had offered himself (in the first chapter of *Argonauts of the Western Pacific*) as exemplar of ethnographic method, and his early theoretical work may be read as an attempt to claim the psychological portion of Rivers' estate. By the end of the decade, Radcliffe-Brown had successfully claimed that of social structure, which over a slightly longer run was to subsume the whole. But for several years in the 1920s, the heirs of Rivers' neo-diffusionist portion were vocal claimants of anthropological primacy.[113]

Their claim was forestalled in part by certain limitations in the neo-diffusionist position, insofar as it emphasized the migration of a single culture-bearing group rather than a diffusion of culture traits or a "blending" of cultures. For a discipline that had long sought to define itself in strictly secular scientific terms, Rivers' suggestion to Hocart, recounted in the latter's review of Perry's *Children of the Sun,* that "we are coming back to the point of view of the 'Lost Tribeists' " must have rung a discordant note—especially since, by Hocart's account, the "astonishing similarities" spread by "the children of the sun" bore a striking relation to the traces left "in Mexico, in Peru, in Ireland and where not," by the "Ten Lost Tribes of Israel." And while the anthropological critique of racialism was not at that time so far advanced in Britain as in the United States, the over- and under-tones of racial superiority in the heliolithic tale of culture-bearing invaders seem, if only in retrospect, at odds with the movement of the modern discipline—although these tones were stronger in Smith than in Perry, and in the early 1930s both men were involved in or responsive to the critique of racism.[114]

Perhaps more to the point is the relationship of neo-diffusionism to the "culture" concept. As the evolutionary linkage of "race" and "culture" was broken by the pluralization of the culture concept in the early twentieth century, "culture" provided an increasingly compelling alternative to "race" as a mode of conceptualizing differences in human behavior. By the time Rivers moved from evolutionism to diffusionism, he had in fact begun to speak of "cultures" in the plural. But with the advent of a more extreme neo-diffusionism, this incipient pluralization of the culture concept was submerged in the single stream of culture emanating from Egypt. A similar comment might in fact be made regarding social organization: the dual organization, which in Rivers' thinking was linked to an analysis of classificatory kinship terminology in situations of cultural blending, was in Perry's simply "carried *bodily*" by the "children of the sun."[115]

From this point of view, neo-diffusionism may be seen as running counter to a more general "ethnographicization" of anthropological inquiry that was also strongly manifest in the other major center of the academic fieldwork tradition, the United States. In both countries, this ethnographicization was reflected in an increased attention to what it was that specifically characterized or unified the localized populations that were the focus of ethnographic inquiry. Although in Britain such integration came to be conceptualized in the idiom of "social structure" rather than of "culture," the tendency in both countries was to focus on processes or structures of integration as they were manifested in the present.[116]

In this respect, the movement in both countries toward a more ethnographically particular anthropology may be regarded as part of a general "dehistoricization" of sociocultural anthropological inquiry. For centuries the dominant axis of such inquiry had been the diachronic one. There were, of course, more synchronically oriented tendencies, such as the political sociology of Montesquieu in the eighteenth century. But more characteristically the empirical variety of human "others" distributed in contemporary space was interpreted in terms of change in time—as the reflection either of a general developmental process or of a gradual modification in the course of movement into different physical or cultural environments (often conceptualized in degenerative terms). Although opposed in many respects, the evolutionism of James Frazer and the "ethnological" analysis of William Rivers were both manifestations of this more general diachronic tradition. Given the limitations of archeological knowledge and the absence of documentary records, diachronic reconstructions of either sort were necessarily highly "conjectural"; and they seemed even more so with the development of more rigorous standards both in archeology and in other professionalizing fields of temporal inquiry. As the criteria of professional competence in sociocultural anthropology began to be redefined in terms of the empirical study of particular ethnographic entities existing in the present, and as the spokesmen for that inquiry sought to win support for it on the grounds of its practical social utility, "conjectural" history—whether of the evolutionary or the neo-diffusionist variety—became an obstacle to both the theoretical and the institutional development of anthropology.[117]

This dehistoricization (more pronounced, perhaps, in the British tradition than in the American) had consequences for the definition of "anthropology." In both traditions, the latter term encompassed several different inquiries—most notably, physical anthropology, prehistoric archeology, and linguistics—which had distinguishable historical roots, which on the European continent had not come together in the same way, and which in the twentieth century had somewhat divergent professionalizing trajectories. Even in the Anglo-American tradition, their integration within a single disciplinary framework was historically contingent and imperfectly realized. Insofar as this disciplinary integration had a meaningful justification in a paradigm of anthropological inquiry other than that of systematic racial determinism, it had found that justification in the two traditional forms of diachronic anthropology.[118]

Within Prichardian ethnology, the various manifestations of human diversity—linguistic, physical, cultural—were all the outcome of a single historical process; along with the evidence of archeology, the contemporary evidence from each of these three domains contributed to the goal of tracing contemporary human diversity back along the branches of a migrational tree toward a single root. And while Darwinism transformed the terms of ethnological inquiry, the problem still remained of reconstructing the physical, linguistic, and cultural modification of mankind in time. Although in practice its component inquiries developed along divergent and not always Darwinian lines, "anthropology" became the rubric which, in the Anglo-American tradition, encompassed a presumptively integrated discipline. The major institutional forms (the Royal Anthropological Institute, Section H of the British Association, and the early university departments) were at least juxtapositionally inclusive—as was the methodological manual, *Notes and Queries*. And with the emergence of neo-diffusionism, the basis for this integration may have been strengthened, insofar as the diffusionists' view of human development more closely approximated the divergent branching model of Darwinian evolution, to which such major diffusionary figures as Rivers and Smith remained in principle strongly committed.[119]

Dehistoricization, ethnographicization, and professionalization, however, seriously weakened both the historically contingent and the paradigmatic bases for the tenuous integration of "anthropology." In contrast to the tendency to conceive of the entities of ethnographic inquiry in integrative terms, the discipline itself began to disintegrate. Although Rivers had encouraged a broad-ranging role for his "single investigator," there were limits to what a person "working alone" could accomplish, and these limits were more sharply felt as inquiries along different lines were measured by the increasingly professional standards of each particular line. Among those who came to anthropology in the evolutionary and neo-diffusionist phases, there were several who cut a wide subdisciplinary path, but only a couple who could claim the authority to write an encompassing article on "Anthropology" for the *Encyclopaedia Britannica*. Tylor did it in 1910; Elliot Smith in 1922; Marett again in 1929, although not without a revision of the supplement on "Applied Anthropology" which Seligman had contributed in 1926. Hocart, who was the most complete anthropologist of his generation, might have accomplished three-quarters of the whole. All of these men, however, conceived of anthropology in fundamentally diachronic terms. But when Malinowski wrote the article on "Anthropology" for the thirteenth edition in 1926, his functionalist manifesto dealt only with "the science of culture" among "the modern living representatives of primitive mankind."[120]

SIX

From Fieldwork to Functionalism

Malinowski and the Emergence of British Social Anthropology

When James Frazer, soon to be Sir James, completed the third edition of *The Golden Bough* late in 1913, a group of friends and colleagues, led by the Cambridge Ritualist F. M. Cornford, initiated a subscription in his honor. The original idea was to establish a fund for the promotion of anthropological fieldwork, but the war intervened, and when the project was resumed in 1920, it took instead the form of an "annual lectureship in Social Anthropology"—although Frazer himself by this time was expressing a preference for the modifier "mental." The fourth lecturer in the series was Bronislaw Malinowski, for whose *Argonauts of the Western Pacific* Frazer had written a laudatory preface three years before.[1]

Living "as a native among the natives," and "conversing with them in their native tongue," Malinowski had derived "all his information from the surest sources—personal observation and statements made to him directly by the natives in their own language without the intervention of an interpreter." Like Cervantes and Shakespeare (and in contrast to Molière), Malinowski saw man "in the round and not in the flat," taking "full account of the complexity of human nature." Frazer considered it the special virtue of *Argonauts* that Malinowski rejected the idea that "pure sociology should confine itself to the description of acts and should leave the problems of motives and feelings to psychology." Seeking instead "to penetrate the motives" of the natives' behavior, Malinowski's work was evidence that "sociology cannot fulfil its task without calling in at every turn the aid of psychology."[2]

It was a theme which Malinowski himself had broached in a letter written from the Trobriands five years before in response to an inquiry from Frazer about his fieldwork:

> You are probably aware that there is now a tendency, supported among others by one or two leading field ethnographers [e.g., Rivers] and an eminent Egyptologist [Elliot Smith], to attack what they call the "psychological method." Personally, I think that we cannot study separately the institutions of a people and its mentality. Only by investigating them side by side, by seeing how certain ideas correspond to certain social arrangements, can both aspects become intelligible. . . . Living among them, learning their language; fitting into their customs and institutions and constantly examining the ideas, which refer to these customs and institutions; doing what they do (as far as this is possible) and trying to understand their instincts, their likes and dislikes—these are the two lines of inquiry which, I think, ought to run parallel in the study of a native race.

At that time, Malinowski announced his representational goals in terms of the "scene/act" ratio that has been seen as the "imaginative core" of Frazer's anthropology. Telling Frazer that it was "through the study of your works mainly I have come to realise the paramount importance of vividness and colour in descriptions of native life," he promised to "try to give the local colour" and describe "the *mise-en-scène* to the best of my ability."[3]

It is not surprising, then—the less so, given his tendency to politic flattery—that Malinowski, in reviewing the one-volume abridgment in 1923, described himself as "a faithful disciple of the *Golden Bough*." In the Frazer Lecture itself, he recalled how the three green volumes of the second edition were "the only solace of his troubles" when, as a university student back in Cracow, he was "ordered to abandon for a time my physical and chemical research because of ill-health, but was allowed to follow up a favourite side-line" and make a "first attempt to read an English masterpiece in the original"—or, as he had previously told Frazer, to have it "read to me aloud by my mother." From that moment on, Malinowski declared, he had been "bound to the service of Frazerian anthropology."[4]

It was in the same lecture, however, that Malinowski sounded the call for the anthropologist to "relinquish his comfortable position in the long chair on the veranda of the missionary compound, Government station, or planter's bungalow" and go out into the village and the garden, where information would flow "full-flavored from his own observations of native life, and not be squeezed out of reluctant informants as a trickle of talk." Malinowski's appeal for an "open-air anthropology" has been polemically glossed as the "manifesto" of an oedipal "revolution in social anthropology" directed at Frazer as the "chief-priest (or father)" of "armchair anthropology"—provoking a minor debate on the actual intellectual relationship of Malinowski and Frazer. That relationship was by no means aggressively oedipal, but it was historically complex. On the one hand, Malinowski did wrap himself in the mantle of leadership of what he himself referred to as a "revolution in social anthropology," and the call to come down from the veranda (or out of the armchair) into the open air may appropriately be heard as the battle cry of that revolution. On the other hand, it is also true that in both style and substance Malinowski's anthropology was in many ways Frazerian. Familiar with the foreshadowings of functionalism in *Psyche's Task*, he would surely have appreciated Durkheim's comment that Frazer's treatment of the "geographical and social conditions" in his descriptions of "the religious or domestic institutions" of particular tribes in *Totemism and Exogamy* implied "a rupture with the old methods of the anthropological school." If Malinowski's own *mise-en-scène* was to be the major island of a single archipelago, the topics that interested him—notably, "the importance of vegetable cults for primitive magic and religion"—were Frazerian topics. And beyond the Trobriands, the "big questions" to which its culture offered answers were defining issues of human nature of the sort implicit in Frazer's work. While Malinowski's approach to these was to be heavily influenced by the man whom Frazer had called "that creature Freud," there were nevertheless many Frazerian echoes in his psychobiological view of human nature.[5]

Frazer, however, was far from the only intellectual influence on Malinowski. Before he read Frazer, he had read Nietzsche and Mach. And because the "twelve volumes of the *Golden Bough* were too heavy and costly a burden to carry across sago swamps," the authors whose books he "re-read while in the field" or in "intervals between my expeditions" were "Westermarck, Karl Bücher, Ratzel, Marett, Hubert and Mauss, Crawley and Rivers." Of these Rivers, his "patron sain[t] in fieldwork," has a special place. To appreciate this, however, we must once again pick up the thread of Rivers' career in the years after he moved away from traditional British psychology, and consider how, during the Great War, he and several of his colleagues came under the influence of a psychology of a very different sort.[6]

Rivers and the Rapprochement of Anthropology and Psychology

Rivers began as a psychologist, and two of the three essays in press at the time of his death were on psychological topics. But between 1908 and 1917 he hardly published in this area, and after his "conversion" to ethnology in 1911, there were several major statements that tended to separate ethnological from psychological inquiry. The first of these was Rivers' response to the Durkheimians, or more specifically to Lucien

Lévy-Bruhl, who was then often seen as one of that group. "According to the French school," Rivers commented, "the work of practically the whole body of English anthropologists suffers from the radical defect that it supposes social institutions to have arisen in consequence of the realization of primitive ideas logically kin to our own"; against this the Durkheimians urged that "motive derived from the psychology of the individual state" had no place in the study of "social facts." In the absence of an attempt by other Durkheimians to "formulate the psychological character" of "collective representations," Rivers read Lévy-Bruhl's *Les Fonctions mentales dans les sociétés inférieures* as an attempt to do so—positively, in arguing that primitive thought was "under the dominance" of the "law of participation"; negatively, in suggesting that it was "not subject to the law of contradiction which dominates our own thought." Analyzing material he and Hocart had collected in 1908 on the Eddystone conception of death, Rivers rejected the notion that primitive thought was "pre-logical": "if it were once recognized that the natives have their own categories, which are different from those of the civilized, there is not only no contradiction, but their proceedings become strictly logical." Taking an implicit dig also at Frazerian psychology, Rivers suggested that it was "the anthropologists' fallacy" to suppose that "because a rite or institution fulfils a certain utilitarian purpose, it therefore came into being in order to fulfil that purpose." Anticipating Hocart, he remarked that a Melanesian returning to address the "native Philosophical Society" might treat the English mentality as "post-logical."[7]

In 1913, Rivers' dissatisfaction with both traditional English psychologizing and its collectivist French alternative led him to suggest that "in the present condition of the science of sociology we only confuse the issue by trying to explain social facts and social processes in psychological terms." While his language and his epistemological posture may have reflected a familiarity with Durkheim, Rivers' "sociology" was one of historical reconstruction, and as the first phrase suggests, what he proposed was a tactical separation, not a permanent divorce. Extending the argument the following year, he acknowledged that "the final aim of the study of society is the explanation of social behaviour in terms of psychology." In the meantime, however, it was possible to describe the actions of human beings in society "without reference to motives"—the discovery of which in his own ethnographic research had been a "more difficult task" than any other. It was not only possible, but necessary: "I suggest that it is the business of sociology to ascertain what happens and what has happened before it tries to explain why it happens and has happened."[8]

Even in justifying separation, however, Rivers suggested the basis of his later return. The "psychology" he referred to was now explicitly "social." Citing Graham Wallas' *Human Nature in Politics,* he acknowledged that "it has in recent years been gradually recognized that social conduct is not directed by intellectual motives, but predominantly, often it would seem exclusively, by sentiments or even instincts for which no intellectual ground can be assigned." And although he suggested that this justified his call for separation—on the ground that "no mental states are more difficult to analyse than emotions and sentiments, to say nothing of instincts"—he turned immediately to another "recent movement in psychology" which offered greater hope. On the one hand, it explained the failure of attempts to "learn the springs of social conduct" by "direct inquiry": "that which we are told, when we ask for an explanation of social conduct, is but a rationalistic interpretation" of conduct that "really depends" on "unconscious tendencies" and "deeply hidden motives." On the other, it suggested a variety of "indirect means" by which "the subconscious activity of the individual mind" could be studied, some of which "have possible analogues in the study of the social mind": "thus, the myth of the social group has been likened to the dream of the individual." Freud, in short, might offer a way of getting behind those Toda professions of ignorance. The very next item in Rivers' bibliography is a talk he gave in 1917 on "Freud's Psychology of the Unconscious."[9]

Rivers' return to psychology was a by-product of his service in World War I. In the summer of 1914, he had travelled with other anthropologists to Australia for one of the periodic overseas meetings of the British Association, where he gave a paper on the complexity of Australian culture. After the meetings, Rivers accompanied his student John Layard to the New Hebrides, pursuing the report of a living megalithic culture complex; after staying for ten days on the island of Atchin with Layard, he spent the next several months island-hopping on the *Southern Cross,* before returning to England early in 1915. Soon thereafter, Rivers received an "imperative telegram" from Elliot Smith, urging him to join Smith on the staff of a military mental hospital at Maghull, near Liverpool, where three others from the Torres Straits Expedition—Myers, McDougall, and Seligman—were also involved in the treatment of soldiers "shell shocked" by the horrors of trench warfare.[10]

Among the Maghull staff was T. H. Pear, a student of Myers who had become seriously interested in Freud. In the years before the war, Pear had taught at Manchester, where he "expounded Freud's views, new and very exciting then" to evening "prayer meetings" of a group of faculty that included the physicists Rutherford and Bohr as well as Elliot Smith; and later, in staff sessions at Maghull, the question was often asked of him "does Freud illuminate this or that problem?" Shortly after his arrival at Maghull, Rivers, who "wanted to catch up" on recent developments in psychology, asked Pear if he would "direct his

W. H. R. Rivers (seated) with his colleagues Dr. William Brown (left) and Grafton Elliot Smith at the Maghull Military Hospital, 1915. (Courtesy of Beth Dillingham)

reading" and discuss it "Cambridge fashion" on afternoon walks. He especially wanted to "grasp what Freud meant by the Unconscious," which he regarded as "the most important contribution to psychology for a long time." [11]

By 1916, Rivers had moved on to the Craiglockhart Hospital for

Officers in Edinburgh, where he hoped to discover if there were "consistent differences in the neurotic symptoms" of officers and "other ranks." His most notable patient was the poet Siegfried Sassoon, who after service in the trenches had turned pacifist, throwing his Military Cross into the Mersey River as a public protest. Wire-pulling by influential friends, and the testimony of his fellow officer (and poet) Robert Graves, saved Sassoon from serious punishment, and he was sent instead to Craiglockhart, shepherded by Graves, who, though apparently never a patient in the formal sense, was also strongly influenced by Rivers. Rivers diagnosed Sassoon as suffering from "a very strong anti-war complex," which he set about treating by therapeutic techniques that he formally described as "autognosis" (or discussion of traumatic experiences) and "re-education," which enabled the patient to turn "energy, morbidly directed, into more healthy channels." After four months of "lengthy conversations three times a week"—apparently as much about politics as about his experience in the trenches—Sassoon was overcome with guilt, accepted River's diagnosis, gave up his antiwar complex, and returned to the front.[12]

It has been suggested that the "covert intention of Rivers' therapeutic practice had been the reinscription of male gender anxieties in someone who had spoken out against the war," and by Rivers' own account, his relationship with Sassoon was less than straightforward. Analyzing later a "pacifist dream" he had after a conversation with a patient who "was not suffering from any form of psycho-neurosis, but was in the hospital on account of his adoption of a pacifist attitude," Rivers worried that his "official position" as an officer in uniform "might be influencing the genuineness of the views I was expressing in my conversations." Rivers was also aware that Sassoon might be influencing him, and speculated about "the situation that would arise if my task of converting a patient from his 'pacifist errors' should have as its result my own conversion to his point of view." Although at a critical point in his dream Rivers turned to the right when he was told to turn left (which contra the "psycho-analytic school," he glossed in conventional political terms), Rivers did in subsequent years move sharply to the left, and was standing as a Labour candidate for Parliament at the time of his death.[13]

Whatever its ulterior motives, the pragmatic "bucking up" style of Rivers' analysis of Sassoon was quite consistent with the rather British gloss Rivers gave to Freudian doctrine. The tone was set in the paper he read to the Edinburgh Pathological Club early in March 1917, in which he urged colleagues not to be put off by the Viennese origins of psychoanalysis: the preoccupation with "the cruder side of sexual life" (which might make it seem more a contribution to "pornography" than to medicine) was merely an "unfortunate excrescence." Rivers granted that "suppressed sexual complexes" played little part in war neuroses: the phobias and paralyses Rivers had treated occurred in rank-and-file soldiers "who seem to have been unusually free of those sexual repressions which are so frequent . . . among the more leisured classes of the community." However, the "denial of the validity of Freud's theory of the unconscious in the form currently held by its adherents" was different from its denial altogether. War experience confirmed abundantly Freud's "theory of forgetting," which was "the most striking and characteristic feature of his psychology." On this basis Rivers suggested that present treatment policies were the "direct opposite" of a proper therapy. "Instead of advising repression and assisting it by drugs, suggestion, or hypnotism, we should lead the patient resolutely to face the situation provided by his painful experience," emphasizing its good or even "noble side": "by such conversation an emotional experience, which is perhaps tending to become dissociated, may be intellectualised and brought into harmony with the rest of the mental life"—which was more or less the approach Rivers seems to have taken with Sassoon.[14]

It was also consistent with the approach Rivers adopted in his two more systematic ventures into Freudian theory: *Instinct and the Unconscious* and *Conflict and Dream*. Like others of "that brilliant band of workers who made Maghull a centre for the study of abnormal psychology," Rivers believed that the lessons learned from the treatment of "war-neuroses" could be applied more generally in the understanding of human behavior. To this end, *Instinct and the Unconscious* was an attempt "to put into a biological setting the system of psycho-therapy adopted in Great Britain in the treatment of the psycho-neuroses of war." More specifically, Rivers considered "the success and failure of suppression" (distinguished from repression as the involuntary rather than witting attempt "to banish experience from consciousness") as a means of "dealing with instinctive tendencies out of harmony with social life." He sought to place the major categories of Freudian discourse (as redefined by him) into a general evolutionary framework which was in the first instance biological and physiological and in which the protopathic/epicritic distinction of his prewar experiments with Henry Head was a constant reference point. In this context, instincts were suppressed forms of primitive behavior, and psychoneuroses were the result of a breakdown in the "state of equilibrium between instinctive tendencies and the forces by which they are normally controlled"—although ever the optimist, Rivers ended his book by suggesting that instability resulting from the failure of suppression and sublimation might be "the source of energy from which we may expect great accomplishments in art and science."[15]

Rivers' pragmatic, upbeat approach to psychotherapy is even more evident in the posthumously published *Conflict and Dream*, which attempted to bring dreams "within a formula closely comparable" to that of *Instinct and the Unconscious*—or, as it were, to anglicize Freudian dream theory. By his own account, when he first read *The Interpretation of Dreams* at Maghull, Freud's interpretations seemed "forced" and the method "so unscientific that it might be used to prove anything." It was only when reading it for a second time in mid-March of 1917 that Rivers had the dream which "went far to convince me of the truth of the main lines of the Freudian position." Interestingly, that dream had to do with his ambivalence about the presidency of the Royal Anthropological Institute—to which (as "S. Poole") he was attracted "for family reasons" (his uncle, James Hunt), but feared to accept because he still stammered on ceremonial occasions. However, it was not until several years later that he formulated the view that dreams were attempts "to solve conflicts which are disturbing the normal course of life." Insisting that the importance of universal sexual symbolism and early childhood experience had been "greatly exaggerated by Freud and his followers," Rivers argued that it was characteristically the conflicts of very recent life experience that appeared disguised in dreams, and that the "constructive function of the dream," like that of psychotherapy, was to solve "practical problems" or conflicts arising in daily life.[16]

Rivers illustrated that "constructive function" by another dream he had at the time of his second reading of Freud's dream theory, in which a Melanesian missionary's mention of "hidden sources" was interpreted by Rivers' dreaming self as referring to "survivals." Analyzing the dream immediately on awakening (as was his wont), Rivers was struck by the similarity between the anthropological notion of "survivals" and the Freudian idea of "unconscious experience." He glossed this as reflecting the "conflict" he was feeling in this period between his interests in ethnology and in psychology, and as pointing "the way to a means of reconciliation which had not occurred to me in the waking state"—although it was "only later" that he came to see that the conflict was unreal and that the two studies might be "mutually helpful." The product of that realization was a lecture he gave at Manchester on "dreams and primitive culture."[17]

By present standards, it is one of the most dated of Rivers' contributions—an expression, perhaps of the "desire for change and novelty" which he suggested elsewhere was "one of the strongest elements" in his "mental make-up." In this case, however, novelty took the form of a general regression to traditional evolutionary assumption, buttressed at points by diffusionary argument. Reglossing the essential features of Freud's "dream-work" as "dramatisation, symbolisation, condensation, displacement and secondary elaboration," Rivers argued that these were manifest both in the cultural productions of the Paleolithic period and in those of "existing savage peoples." While he granted that the latter were "not merely peoples who have been left behind in the stream of progress" and that each was the product of a "highly complex history" of borrowing and blending, Rivers suggested a distinction between "social" and "mental" development, arguing that we were "thus justified" in equating the dreams of the "civilised individual" and the customs and myths of existing savages as each representing "a similar infantile stage of mental development." Without specific reference to the Todas, Rivers once again appealed to the difficulty of eliciting "rational explanations" of "rude rites and customs," this time citing it as evidence of "their origin in the unconscious." He went on to suggest that "the myth reveals the unconscious history of the race just as the dream reveals the unconscious history of the individual." At a later point, Rivers was in fact willing to speculate also about social primitivity—notably, in arguing that Melanesians were instinctively "more gregarious than the average European," which he saw as support for Wilfred Trotter's notion of the "herd-instinct."[18]

In the years before his death, Rivers continued to write on problems in the "extensive border-region between psychology and ethnology." He published several pieces attributing the "dying out of native races" to a "psychological factor": the "loss of interest in life," which, "given the enormous influence of the mind upon the body" among "lowly peoples," could cause them actually "to sicken and die" when their traditional customs were destroyed. And in two presidential addresses to the Folk-Lore Society, Rivers commented on what psychology had to offer ethnology and vice versa—in both cases, from the perspective of a member of the "historical school" of Elliot Smith and William Perry.[19]

The first of these addresses, "Conservatism and Plasticity," offered a psychoanalytic solution to a basic problem facing the diffusionists: how small groups of migrating peoples could have such a far-reaching influence on those among whom they settled, given the "widely accepted" and indubitable fact that the savage "is far more a slave of custom than ourselves." Rivers suggested that among the Melanesians, where authority over the child was asserted by the mother's brother and (given the "communistic" nature of society) by the tribal elders as representatives of the ancestors, the "father ideal" of European society, generalized as the "group-ideal," was replaced by the "ancestor ideal," producing "a degree of conservatism greater than our own." In this context, innovation was possible only from the outside, and could be explained in terms of the psychoanalytic doctrine of "transference," reconceptualized in social terms. Confronted by strangers "with a culture, and especially a material culture, greatly superior to their own," savages transferred their "affective dispositions" to the invaders, adopting their customs as "compromise formations" in which the "demands of the old ideal" might still be met symbolically—a process Rivers illustrated by the influence of "representatives of our own civilisation who, during the last century, have settled among so many peoples of lowly culture."[20]

In his second presidential address, Rivers reversed the perspective, to see what ethnology could offer to psychology, specifically, the social psychology that had challenged the old psychology of individualistic introspection. Noting that "many different lines of research" had converged to show the "importance of symbols" in "collective behaviour," Rivers wanted to know whether there was "a universal system of symbolisation," and if so, whether it was due to "social heritage" or to "heredity"—as "Jung and Freud and their disciples seem to believe." Focussing on the symbol of rebirth, as discussed by Otto Rank, Rivers concluded, after a Frazerian tour of world ethnography, that it was not "part of the universal furniture of the human mind." Rather, it was found in "widely separated regions" in close connection with "the organisations known as secret societies"—which of course played a central role in the diffusionist argument.[21]

Throughout this period, Rivers continued to participate in the discussions of Freudian theory then going on in British psychological circles. In 1919, his paper on "Instinct and the Unconscious" was the centerpiece of a joint meeting of the British Psychological Society, the Aristotelian Society, and the *Mind* Association, to which Myers, McDougall, and Carl Jung also contributed papers. A month after his death an essay reinterpreting Alexander Shand's notion of "sentiment" as the epicritic evolutionary modification of the protopathic "complex" of Carl Jung was discussed at a symposium of the British Psychological Society in Manchester.[22]

It has since been suggested that had Myers, McDougall, Seligman, and Rivers remained in contact, a "culture-pattern theory" might have been developed, analogous, presumably, to that which emerged in this period among Boasian students of culture and personality. Although in broader historical retrospect that seems unlikely, it is clear nonetheless that the early 1920s were a distinct moment in the relations of English ethnologists and psychologists. As Rivers and others were so evidently aware, traditional British psychology had been called into question along a number of lines: the irrational, the instinctive, the abnormal, the pathological, the collective. Foreshadowed in the work of William James and in the psychic research movement, prefigured in the social psychologies of Graham Wallas and William McDougall (whose text went through twenty-one editions in twenty years), catalyzed by the experiences of World War I, which opened the way for a serious consideration of Freud, the reorientation of British psychology seemed to Rivers and others to provide the basis for a new relationship of anthropology and psychology.[23]

That relationship was the topic of Marett's lecture in a symposium entitled *Psychology and the Sciences* in 1924; in the same year it was the topic of Seligman's presidential address to the Royal Anthropological Institute, in which he used the "types" Jung had called "extravert" and "introvert" as the basis for an analysis of "the dreams of non-European races." And in March of that year there was apparently an agreement (never realized) that the Royal Anthropological Institute and the British Psychological Society would be housed "under one roof." It is in this context of a momentary rapprochement between British anthropology and the newer trends in psychology that one must understand the "functional" anthropology of Bronislaw Malinowski.[24]

From Cracow to the Trobriands: The Rider Haggard and the Joseph Conrad of Anthropology

Growing up in the southern portion of partitioned Poland that formed the Austrian province of Galicia, Malinowski would naturally have been oriented toward Vienna—metropolis of the Habsburg Empire, and more important for young Polish intellectuals, birthplace of cultural modernism. Malinowski's father was one of those scions of petty nobility who in this period were turning to urban intellectual occupations. After taking a doctorate at Leipzig, he went on to become the "founder of Polish dialectology" as Professor of Slavonic Philology at the University of Cracow, where a new modernizing Polish nationalism found an outlet in linguistic, historical, and scientific studies rather than in the revolutionary political activity of an earlier historical moment. As members of the "exclusive clan" of a great "university aristocracy," the Malinowskis lived in an apartment in the academic dormitory, which Malinowski's mother apparently continued to have charge of after his "stern" and "distant" father died when Malinowski was fourteen. Afflicted soon thereafter with an eye disease caused by a tubercular infection, Malinowski was forced to withdraw from gymnasium and spend months in a darkened room, where he was tutored by his mother, who taught herself Latin and mathematics in order to supervise his education. In 1899 she took him on the first of several recuperative trips to Northern Africa, Montenegro, and the Canary Islands. In 1902 he entered his late father's university, where he studied physics and philosophy.[25]

A quarter of a century later, Malinowski recalled that it was in that year, when he was eighteen, that he first heard of Freud—having been previously during adolescence distressed by dreams of incest and (before the fact) of his father's death. But at the time, the more powerful intellectual influence reaching him from Vienna was that of the physicist, psychologist, and philosopher of science Ernst Mach. Although Mach drew from Tylor's work, he was more consistently Darwinian in outlook: for him, the history of human mentality was characterized less by the lost rationality of the doctrine of survivals than by the positive rationality of the principle of "economy of thought." Mach saw the instinctive, organically adaptive behavior of savages as the ultimate basis of science, which was simply "the formulation, in clear, abstract and communicable terms, of what was instinctively known long before." In his epistemological magnum opus, *Knowledge and Error*, Mach elaborated his viewpoint at greater length, arguing that all the processes of the living individual were reactions in the interests of self-preservation: "ideas gradually adapt to facts by picturing them with sufficient accuracy to meet biological needs"; the formation of scientific hypotheses was merely a "further degree of development of instinctive and primitive thought."[26]

Malinowski's three major professors were all influenced by Mach; one had written the only Polish-language work treating the principle of economy of thought. That was also the topic of Malinowski's doctoral dissertation, a rather brief historical-critical essay in which he tried to come to terms with "the most outstanding representatives of the anti-metaphysical movement." Despite Malinowski's somewhat critical posture in the dissertation itself, it is impossible to read Mach's major epistemological works without sensing portents of Malinowski's later anthropological outlook. Like Malinowski, Mach was at bottom a methodological individualist; it was from the starting point of the famous drawing of the world as "presented to my left eye" that he developed his empirical view of science. Central to the endeavor was the concept of "function," which for Mach made superfluous the "ordinary concepts of cause and effect." While Malinowski's later use of function was broader than Mach's, this is consistent with his characteristic intellectual opportunism. Frankly willing to "accept all the risks which eclecticism carries," he remained open to a variety of influences, not in their full complexity, but as they seemed to offer standpoints from which to approach the large philosophical and anthropological questions that preoccupied him. For Malinowski, Mach was less a source of specific concepts than a font of general assumptions to which he often later returned, albeit in a detextualized and recontextualized fashion.[27]

Although a critically important one, Machian empiricism was not the only major influence on Malinowski in his intellectually formative years. Malinowski was a person of strongly dualistic temperament,

"Bronislaw Malinowski appears as Xerxes Yakshma in [Tadeusz] Micinski's [novel] *Nietota*" —Oil painting by Stanisław Witkiewicz, 1910. (From the collection of Eva Franczak and Stefan Okołowicz. Courtesy of Daniel Gerould)

pulled between intellect and passion, science and art. His vacations were spent in Zakopane in the Tatra Mountains, where a bohemian circle of intimate friends included several aspiring artists, novelists, and philosophers who looked for inspiration to the cultural modernism of turn-of-the-century Vienna and western Europe generally. Among them, Malinowski's closest friend was Stanisław (Staś) Witkiewicz, who was later to become a major Polish cultural figure as painter, dramatist, and author, whose early unpublished works included a fictionalized autobiography, *The 622 Downfalls of Bungo*—in which one episode (in real life an "isolated psychological experiment") was a homosexual encounter with the Malinowski character, the Duke of Nevermore. In the aftermath of his fiancée's suicide, Staś accompanied Malinowski to the southwestern Pacific in a Gauguinesque search for primitive regenerative experience; there, the friendship ended, for reasons that are unclear, though it is evident that the two men differed radically in metaphysical temperament. When Malinowski marked the rupture in his diary, it was by reference to two heroic icons of modernism: "Nietzsche breaking with Wagner." Malinowski, of course, was Nietzsche, and by his own later recollection, the preceding decade had been his "Nietzsche period." One of his early philosophical efforts had been an essay on *The Birth of Tragedy*, in which can be seen aspects of much of his later thinking on myth—although he read Nietzsche critically, casting the Apollonian/Dionysian opposition in physiological, even Darwinian, evolutionary terms.[28]

Malinowski was no systematic doubter of the values of science or civilization. Arguing in his dissertation for the "objective" validity of scientific laws, he had insisted that "even if only one normal man remained on the earth, and all others had lost the ability to make judgements which we would consider normal and logical, that one man would not need to doubt the value of the material and scientific conquests of mankind," since their "tremendous practical importance" would "enable him to completely annihilate his adversaries outright": "the relation of the white man to his less civilized colored brethren illustrates this sadly and emphatically." Knowledge and power—the laws of science and the Gatling gun—in the hands of a "normal" individual (male, white, European, and civilized) thus sustained each other, sadly but emphatically.[29]

As that sadness suggests, there was an elegiac undertone to Malinowski's attitude toward European civilization. Though he was more positivist than Staś, his several early experiences at the margins of Europe had inspired a romantic fascination with the culturally exotic. Given also his father's interest in Slavic linguistics and folklore (a scholarly tradition with which Malinowski was obviously familiar) and his own social position in a subjugated nation, which made him sharply aware of the variations of cultural belief and behavior in different social strata, it is not surprising that he should have turned from physics to anthropology—or that he should have done so in a cultural evolutionary context.

Upon completing his university studies, Malinowski, still seeking a healthier climate, travelled with his mother to the Canary Islands, where he stayed for two years in an environment he found "extremely primitive and Spanish"—"a hundred years behind in respect of culture." When he returned, his doctoral degree, upon appeal to Emperor Franz Josef, was granted with the special imperial accolade *sub auspiciis Imperatoris* and bestowed "with great pomp" to the accompaniment of "a flourish of trumpets." Malinowski then followed in his father's footsteps to Leipzig, where he spent a year studying *Völkerpsychologie* with Wilhelm Wundt, reading Simmel on the state of German sociological thought and attending the lectures of Karl Bücher, an economic historian who had written on the nature of work among savage and civilized peoples. While in Leipzig, Malinowski also began an affair with a pianist from South Africa, whom in 1910 he followed to London. There it was his intention to study anthropology in the country where that discipline was most advanced—and where "culture has reached its highest standard."[30]

Given his earlier interest in sociology, as well as the greater cosmopolitanism of the London School of Economics—and the fact that Frazer did no teaching—it is not surprising that Malinowski (apparently at Haddon's suggestion) became a student of Charles Seligman and Edward Westermarck rather than of Haddon and Rivers. At the School of Economics he served an armchair apprenticeship in Westermarck's seminar, reading Crawley, Lang, Robertson Smith, and Durkheim, as well as Rivers on the Todas; it is clear also that he found an important theoretical resource in Westermarck's revisionist evolutionary sociology. In this context, he began to consider more critically the work of Frazer, composing an unpublished Marettian critique of *The Golden Bough,* and an extended and devastatingly critical review of *Totemism and Exogamy*—published, however, back in Poland in a language Frazer probably did not read. Malinowski's first substantial anthropological publication in English, in Westermarck's festschrift in 1912, was also a contribution to the ongoing discussion of totemism. Taking off from Frazer's suggestion that the division of labor embodied in the Australian intichiuma ceremony was a good principle misapplied, which under totemism led to no positive results, Malinowski argued that the ceremonies were in fact a "collective and regular system of labor" involving a higher and more "economic" type of work than savages were normally capable of. It had, in Bücher's terms, the essential characteristics of "civilized" labor, insofar as it was organized, collective, continuous, regular, periodical, and involved systematic planning and definite goals. Echoing the abortive functionalism of Frazer's *Psyche's Task,* Malinowski suggested that strong stimuli were necessary to force savage man to work in a style repugnant to him and that magic and religion had supplied the necessary "coercive forces," although he rejected "any universal scheme of evolution . . . among all the races of mankind."[31]

The structuring role of evolutionary assumption was manifest also in the monograph Malinowski published the following year, *The Family among the Australian Aborigines.* Substantively, the book was an attempt, following the line pioneered twenty years before by Westermarck, to attack such evolutionary war-horses as "primitive promiscuity" and "marriage by capture," as well as the whole Morganian notion of the "classificatory system of kinship." Its argument was based on a systematic analysis of all the available literature from the ethnographic realm that provided evolutionists with their type-case of truly "primitive man." At the same time, the work may be regarded also as a methodological exercise—another attempt to tighten Tylor's "logical screw." Malinowski was much concerned with defining analytic categories that were not "directly borrowed from our own society," and even more with developing rigorous method in the evaluation of ethnographic evidence. To the latter end, he turned to history in a quite technical and professional sense: using Langlois and Seignobos' textbook in historical method as a model for treating the Australian ethnographic literature by "the strict rules of historical criticism," he analyzed conflicting testimony so that future fieldwork might be focussed on key issues of fact.[32]

Constructively, the book was Malinowski's most Durkheimian work: his primary concern was to demonstrate the interrelation of the ideas of kinship and of the family with the "general structure of society." A Durkheimian chord was struck in the very first pages, when Malinowski declared that "each social institution must be studied in all its complex social functions as well as in its reflexion in the collective psychology." A key footnote made clear that the idiom of "social facts," "social morphology," and "collective ideas" was borrowed from the "French school of Prof. Durkheim and his associates"—to which Malinowski, like Rivers and others, assimilated Lévy-Bruhl's notions of savage "prelogical mentality." The book's central argument clearly derived from a reading of the Durkheimian literature: social (as distinguished from physiological) consanguinity was defined relativistically as "the set of relations involved by the collective ideas under which the facts of procreation are viewed in a given society."[33]

Even here, however, Malinowski's use of the term "social function" was by no means consistently Durkheimian, and his future disagreements were anticipated in a note insisting that in referring to "collective mind," he did not "postulate the existence of any metaphysical entity." In general, Malinowski felt that his interpretation was constrained by the "complete absence in our ethnographic information of any attempt to connect the data of folk-lore and the facts of sociology," or as he was sometimes inclined to pose the issue, "social belief" and "social function"—a term which in Malinowski's often rather *un*Durkheimian usage tended to mean "actual behavior." From this point of view, the Australian monograph was not so much an armchair exercise as the prolegomenon to his future fieldwork.[34]

Malinowski's subsequent response to Durkheim's *Elementary Forms of the Religious Life* pursued further the issue of methodological individualism. Quoting liberally to establish his grammatical-cum-methodological point, Malinowski argued that society was "the *logical* subject" of many of Durkheim's arguments, rather than merely "the atmosphere in which *individuals* create religious ideas." Malinowski formulated his own approach to "the genesis of religion" in a monograph published in Poland on "primitive beliefs and forms of social organization." Despite his earlier refusal to "find the origins of religion in crowd phenomena," he still drew heavily on Durkheim in his discussion of the "sociological side of religion." Reflecting the British reaction against the intellectualism of Tylor and Frazer, Malinowski insisted that religion, like all other cultural phenomena, must ultimately derive from individual psychic processes. As he had put it in notes for Westermarck's seminar, it was "the crystallization of ideas from emotional states"—fear, love, anxiety, hope, expectation—"which compels us to grasp strongly a certain idea and desperately cling to it"; ideas "born in this way radically differ from ideas born by simple contemplation, observation and other everyday experiences." Although the notes make it clear that he was influenced here by Marett, Malinowski's viewpoint was quite explicitly an extension of Westermarck's neo-Darwinian interpretation of the evolution of moral ideas into the "magico-religious" realm.[35]

Malinowski had early lost his inherited Roman Catholicism, and like Mach sought to purge himself of all metaphysical residues; but his anthropological readings (enlivened, perhaps, by all those conversations with Staś about matters of ultimate belief) had led him toward a view of human religiosity that rooted it firmly in the primitive nature of man. Although his last pre-fieldwork publication was in fact to call into question, on empirical ethnographic grounds, Durkheim's distinction between the sacred and the profane, the general import of his armchair speculation was to mark off, still in evolutionary terms, a realm in which instinctual irrational emotional impulses held sway, impulses which were subsequently rationalized and socialized in the form of religion: "Man, especially primitive man who lives in a constant struggle for survival, . . . is mainly emotional and active, . . . and it is easy to show that these very elements lead him to the performance of such acts and activities which constitute the germ of religion."[36]

From the beginning of his stay in England, it was assumed that Malinowski would do "an intensive study of a restricted area." With the help of Seligman, as well as Haddon and Rivers (from both of whom Malinowski received guidance), Malinowski pursued various possibilities for fieldwork sites, including the Sudan—or if no funding could be found, back in Poland "among our peasants." It was not until 1914, however, when the British Association met in Australia, that Seligman got Malinowski a travelling fellowship, and he received free passage to the antipodes as secretary to Marett, the recorder for the anthropological section. Rather than a study of Australian Aborigines, for which his armchair anthropology had prepared him—and which would have embedded his enterprise in a well-defined theoretical and ethnographic tradition—Malinowski's project was clearly designed by Seligman as a further follow-up to the Torres Straits Expedition: specifically, to focus more intensively on the boundary region between two major groups that earlier survey work had distinguished.[37]

"Taking leave of civilization" after the British Association meetings,

Malinowski arrived in Port Moresby on September 12, 1914. The next day he made the obligatory visit to Government House, where "the crew of fuzzy-headed savages in government uniforms" gave him "very much the 'sahib' feeling." There he paid the requisite courtesy call on Hubert Murray, who was the very archetype of a paternalist proconsul—and who had read Tylor and Maine, and was a friend of Seligman. Although Murray considered Malinowski a German, and took a personal dislike to him, he respected his ability, and did not at this point stand in his way. Afterwards, Malinowski met Ahuia Ova, an ardent Christian convert who had served so well as village constable that Murray had made him Central Court Interpreter—and who a decade previously had been Seligman's primary informant. Save for a few days of enforced idleness when Ahuia was busy at the trial of a European who had "hung up a native for five hours," Malinowski spent a month doing a kind of linguistic and ethnographic cramming "on the verandah of the house where [Ahuia] lived with his uncle," the old village chief.[38]

Malinowski quickly became dissatisfied, however, with these "ethnographic explorations," because he had "rather little to do with the savages on the spot" and did not speak their language. These "defects" were to be largely rectified during "intensive" work on the island of Mailu, two hundred miles southeast in Seligman's boundary zone, where the London Missionary Society had maintained a station since 1894. Malinowski's "travelling companions" on the trip down the coast in the steam launch *Wakefield* were a sampling of the stereotypic figures of the Melanesian colonial situation: a "brutal" German captain, who was "continually abusing and bullying the Papuans"; an English Quaker planter, from whom Malinowski got quite useful ethnographic information; and Mailu's resident aristocratic vagabond, who though "cultured" lived a "completely uncivilized" life in a "house without walls," where Malinowski was to enjoy occasional "lubrication." Also on the *Wakefield,* though unmentioned as a travelling companion, was Igua Pipi, fluent in the lingua franca Motu, who was to serve as chief factotum in Malinowski's retinue of several native "boys."[39]

Once on Mailu, Malinowski became the paying guest of the Reverend W. J. Saville, the author of "A Grammar of the Mailu Language," from whose mission house Malinowski "went to the village" each day during the next few weeks. Saville was to become the negative archetypal focal point of Malinowski's ambivalent feelings about the "civilizing" mission of colonialism. Although dependent on him, Malinowski was repelled by Saville's "persecution of people unfriendly to the mission." In the beginning, he made a slight allowance for the fact that Saville played cricket with the natives and treated them with "a fair amount of decency and liberality"—"were he a German, he would doubtless be downright loathsome." But over the first few weeks Malinowski's "hatred for missionaries" increased, and he began to ponder an "anti-mission campaign": struggling "consistently and ruthlessly against everything old," missionaries destroyed "the natives' joy in life," their "psychological *raison d'être*," while the "new needs, both material and moral," which they created were "completely beyond the savages."[40]

More immediately, Malinowski began to see Saville as a serious impediment to effective fieldwork—and as a kind of anti-model to the archetype he would later construct of "the Ethnographer." Still at this point an ethnographic novice, Malinowski carried into the field the fourth edition of *Notes and Queries,* and his published report on Mailu reflected quite clearly its topically interrogative categories. But the British Association manual also contained Rivers' "General Account of Method," in which a more participatory fieldwork style was clearly enunciated, and there are various passages both in Malinowski's diary and in his Mailu ethnography which suggest that his own ethnographic experience was leading him along the same path. He quickly became quite fluent in Motu, an accomplishment sufficiently remarkable that, lest it be discredited, he felt it necessary in his published account "to explicitly boast of my facility for acquiring a conversational command of foreign languages." And before the end of his stay, he was able to employ this fluency in a more directly interactive way.[41]

On a trip he made in early December surveying groups along the far southeastern New Guinea coast, in several villages Malinowski stayed in the *dubu* or men's house—on one occasion for three successive nights during a native feast. Although "the stench, smoke, noise of people, dogs and pigs" left him exhausted, he sensed the ethnographic potential of more direct involvement, and returned to Mailu resolved to "begin a new existence." During the next few weeks, when Saville chanced to be away, Malinowski took up residence in a previously abandoned mission house, where Igua Pipi and several Mailu men were wont to gather in the evening. Despite moments of frustration—including a week in January when he was left with "*absolutely* nobody" to work with, because he foolishly refused to pay the £2 the Mailu demanded to allow him to go with them on a trading expedition—Malinowski later described this as his most productive period. Recalling his difficulties in getting at "magico-religious" beliefs, he told how at a certain point the Mailu became convinced his deserted mission house was ghost-ridden and stopped sleeping there. When one evening the conversation turned to ghosts, Malinowski, professing ignorance, asked their advice about how to protect himself and got a great deal of information about topics previously closed to him. Generalizing in the published account, he suggested that work done "while living quite alone among the natives" was "incomparably more intensive than work done from white men's settlements, or even in any white man's company": "my experience is that direct questioning of the natives about a custom or belief never discloses their attitude of mind as thoroughly as the discussion of facts connected with the direct observation of a custom or a concrete occurrence, in which both parties are materially concerned."[42]

Implicit in that last phrase is a participatory mode of fieldwork that went well beyond that of Rivers' "general account of method." It was, however, a mode that in practice was characterized by asymmetries of involvement and ambivalences of attitude. Malinowski was quite willing to try (unsuccessfully) to "exert a certain pressure through the village constable" when six sticks of tobacco to each of the actors failed to get them to perform a ceremony a second time in full daylight so that he could photograph it. He enjoyed "the pleasure of having a crowd of boys to serve you"—which in Igua Pipi's case involved massaging him while telling stories about "murders of white men, as well as his fears about what he would do if I died in that way!" Echoing Conrad's Mistah Kurtz, Malinowski at one point suggested that his "feelings toward the natives" were "decidedly tending to '*Exterminate the brutes*' "; but in the next moment he worried about the "many instances in which I acted unfairly and stupidly." While he could be disingenuous in eliciting esoteric information, he deliberately refrained from publishing certain passages of a magical incantation, lest it fall into the hands of some white man "eager to put down superstitions" and "unscrupulous enough to divulge the charm among the natives."[43]

Insofar as Malinowski's Mailu ethnography departed from the sequence of categories in *Notes and Queries,* it was largely in the total omission of physical anthropological data and the relegation of technology to incidental treatment—and in the extensive consideration of "Economics." Although an interest in economic problems was quite consistent with Malinowski's prior intellectual concerns, it also reflected the importance of native labor and land tenure in the colonial context. Early on, he discussed "native labor" with a government official in Port Moresby, and later described himself as "obsessed by the thought of some ethnological government post in N.G." When he returned from the field to Australia to write up his results, he made a brief report on his fieldwork to Atlee Hunt, the Secretary of the Australian Department of External Affairs, who, often at odds with Murray, was a consistent supporter of the economic interests of white settlers in New Guinea. Malinowski emphasized that he had "paid special attention to the economic and sociological aspects of native life" and (though the ethnography did not in fact reflect it) the "process of adaptation to their new conditions." Convinced that Malinowski's emphasis on "the mental attitudes and peculiar customs of the people" rather than "measurements of bodies, etc." was "one likely to be of much use to the Government in our dealing with the natives," Hunt became his sponsor, obtaining funds to further his research and overcoming Murray's resistance to his return to New Guinea.[44]

While in Australia, Malinowski also made important connections in the scientific establishment, including Baldwin Spencer, E. C. Stirling of the Horn Expedition, and David Orme Masson, who had come from Scotland in 1886 to take the chair of chemistry at Melbourne (and who, like the other two, later received a British knighthood). Malinowski spent a month in Stirling's home in Adelaide, working on the Mailu manuscript—and, somewhat to the consternation of her parents, falling in love with Stirling's daughter Nina. When Malinowski failed to inform the military authorities prior to one of his trips to Adelaide (a technical violation of his status as enemy alien), it was Stirling's intervention that saved him from reporting to a "Concentration Camp"; it was Stirling also who offered stylistic corrections to the Mailu manuscript and facilitated its publication.[45]

With his Mailu ethnography off to the press, Malinowski began a second round of fieldwork. Although Seligman wanted him to go southeast to Rossel Island to examine another ethnic boundary region, Malinowski preferred the Mambare district on the northern coast of Papua, where a series of prophetic cults were causing the government concern. On the way, however, he stopped off in the Trobriands, "the leaders of the whole material and artistic culture" of eastern New Guinea, in order "to get an idea of what is going on among them" and to seek the help of the Resident Magistrate, R. L. Bellamy, in securing some museum specimens before Bellamy left to serve in the European war. Bellamy was an enthusiastically paternalistic administrator; after ten years he had finally got the Trobrianders to line the paths of Kiriwina with 120,000 coconut trees—by imposing stiff penalties for failure to do so. With a jail, a hospital, twelve white residents, and a thriving pearl industry in its lagoon, Kiriwina (the largest Trobriand island) was one of the "best governed and most 'civilized' places" in the region. It was also, however, a lushly idyllic tropical isle, little touched by the labor trade, whose chiefly aristocracies and erotic dances had already begun to sustain a popular image, "part noble savage, part licentious sybarite."[46]

Several years before, Rivers, generalizing from his own Melanesian experience, had suggested that "the most favorable moment for ethnographical work" was from ten to thirty years after a people had been brought under "the mollifying influences of the official and the missionary." That was long enough to ensure "the friendly reception and peaceful surroundings" that were essential to such work, but "not long enough to have allowed any serious impairment of the native culture" or "to have witnessed the passing of a generation who had participated in any "rites and practices" that might "have disappeared or suffered change." Long enough, that is, to enable the anthropologist to work under an umbrella of colonial power, but not so long that its shadow would have entirely withered the practice of the precontact culture, or darkened the memory of the way things used to be before the intrusion of the white man. In many respects a mythical time, it had nonetheless a powerful reality, if only in the minds of anthropologists in transit from the surviving evolutionary past to the evanescing ethnographic present.[47]

Malinowski's epoch-marking fieldwork in the Trobriand Islands came within the optimal period Rivers had defined: a decade after a permanent government station, a decade and a half after the last internal fighting and an abortive attempt at violent resistance to colonial power, two decades after the Methodist Overseas Mission headquarters had been established at Losuia. He arrived during the *milamala* festival, the ceremonial high point of the annual cycle, when "dancing and feasting and sexual license" went on "with great intensity." His attention was immediately engaged by the "ceremonial gardening"; the "beliefs and ceremonies about the spirits [called] Balom," and the "peculiar and interesting" trading ring "called Kula"—which, with the significant addition of Trobriand sex life, were to be the topics of his later monographs. On Kiriwina, these cultural phenomena did not have to be *recaptured* from the memories of elders, or *reconstructed* from fragmentary data surviving in the present, or *recreated* by people cajoled into performing defunct ceremonies; they could be directly observed. Malinowski was clearly captivated, and when he heard of the unexpected departure from Mambare of the missionary from whom he had hoped to get an ethnographic orientation, he decided instead to extend his Trobriand stay, apologizing to Seligman for remaining in an area he had already covered. After two months, Malinowski had enough Kiriwinian so that he only used pidgin English "a sentence or so per diem" and was able to dispense with his interpreter. Having moved in from the government station to the village of Omarakana, he was now "absolutely alone amongst niggers"; denying himself the "white man's solace" of whiskey and sex, he was getting "such damned good stuff" that he decided to abandon the Mambare project. Save for "Capuan days" he enjoyed every fortnight with the pearl-traders Billy Hancock and Rafael Brudo back on the coast in Gusaweta, he remained in Omarakana continuously for almost six months.[48]

According to one mythistorical account, it was Malinowski's Trobriand fieldwork that revolutionized ethnographic practice in British anthropology. Before then, the "standard methods of ethnographic research"—in which the native was a specimen to be measured, photographed, and interviewed—"were such that the social superiority of the investigator was constantly emphasized." But by pitching his tent in the middle of the village, learning the language in its colloquial form, and observing native life directly "through the 24 hours of an ordinary working day"—something "no European had ever done"—Malinowski "changed all this." While not every social anthropologist would have portrayed Malinowski in such heroic terms, it was not until 1967 that his role (and image) as ethnographic innovator was seriously called into question.[49]

In that year Malinowski's ethnographic heirs were shaken by the striking contrast between the methodological injunctions of the first chapter of *Argonauts of the Western Pacific* and the intimate revelations of his newly published field diaries. While there is no denying the contrast, if one makes a certain allowance for the hortatory and prescriptive character of the *Argonauts* chapter as mythic charter, it does not seem that Malinowski grossly misrepresented his ethnographic practice. His "aloneness" among the Trobrianders was by no means "absolute"; but if his "Capuan days" in Gusaweta and his bouts of novel-reading inside his tent were more frequent than methodological prescription implied, there is little doubt that his fieldwork was in general consistent with that which Rivers had called for in 1912, and which Malinowski himself had begun to implement (and further develop) in Mailu.[50]

Without a surviving diary for his first Trobriand sojourn, Malinowski's ethnographic practice at this point must be gleaned from other sources. Later reflections indicate that despite having dispensed with an interpreter, he was not yet able to "follow easily conversations among the natives themselves." And by his own account, he was still very much under Rivers' influence: "it was my ambition to develop the principle of the 'genealogical method' into a wider and more ambitious scheme to be entitled the 'method of objective documentation.'" But for contemporary evidence, the best source is "Baloma: The spirits of the dead in the Trobriands," which he wrote during the interval between his first and second Trobriand trips.[51]

The *baloma* was "the main form of the spirit" in Kiriwinian belief, in contrast to the *mulukuasi,* the "ghoulish" and "dangerous" female sorcerer who attacked the living and fed on the bodies of the dead, and the *kosi,* the meek and frivolous ghost of the deceased who "vanishes after a few days of irrelevant existence." Immediately after death, a baloma left its body and travelled westward to the island of Tuma, where it might be visited by and whence it might return to visit privileged living Kiriwinians; once a year the baloma returned as a group to receive gifts at *milamala*. Baloma played only a vague role in Kiriwinian magic, which depended primarily on the power inhering in the actual words of magical spells. But they played an absolutely critical role in reproduction, which could take place only when an aged baloma, having sloughed its skin and become a spirit child, returned from Tuma and entered a Kiriwinian woman of the same subclan whose vagina had been previously "opened" by sexual intercourse—which otherwise had nothing whatsoever to do with reproduction. Malinowski's discussion of garden magic ran by implication counter to Frazerian assumption, inasmuch as he made no mention of sympathetic magic and attributed to the Kiriwinians a practical knowledge of agricultural cause and effect. But the essay's climactic discussion of reproduction was presented, in clearly evolutionary terms, as a vindication of the primitive ignorance of paternity first suggested by Hartland, "brilliantly confirmed" by Spencer and Gillen, and supported by Frazer's "illustrious opinion."[52]

While the notion of the Trobrianders' ignorance of the physical processes of reproduction was long to be a matter of anthropological dispute, Malinowski's own interest in the issue was as much methodological as substantive. Despite the suggestion of one critic that Malinowski's (actually, Marett's) slogan was "study the ritual and not the belief," and despite the characterization of Malinowski as an "obsessional empiricist," what is striking in "Baloma" is precisely the attempt to penetrate native belief, and Malinowski's insistence on the inadequacy of uninterpreted "pure facts"—and by implication, of Rivers' "concrete method"—to that task. "Baloma" reveals Malinowski as an aggressively interactive fieldworker, by temperament disinclined to rest satisfied with professions of ignorance or appeals to *bogwa bubunesmasi* ("our old custom"). In contrast to *Notes and Queries,* he defended the use of leading questions under certain circumstances; he posed hypothetical cases and devised behavioral tests of the strength of belief; he challenged beliefs the natives took for granted, pointing out contradictions and suggesting alternatives; he pushed them, as he said, "to the metaphysical wall"—and was upon occasion pushed himself, as when asked why, if pregnancy was the result of sexual intercourse, the cause, "which was repeated daily," so rarely produced the effect. Rejecting the notion that it was "possible to wrap up in a blanket a certain number of 'facts as you find them' and bring them all back for the home student to generalize upon," he insisted that "field work consists only and exclusively in the interpretation of the chaotic social reality, in subordinating it to general rules."[53]

Malinowski's fieldwork style may well have led him astray on certain issues—including, it would seem, one implicated in the question of Trobriand paternity. In 1918, his trader friend Billy Hancock wrote to report the "rude shock" he got when several native women insisted that once the baloma arrived in Tuma, they did not ever return. Reminded that "you told the Doctor that it was so," they replied that "the Doctor told us it was like that & we were afraid to contradict him." Against this and other errors, confessed by him or imputed by others, must be posed not only Malinowski's richly anecdotal discussion of his fieldwork methods—which suggests other modes of interaction—but the large and variegated body of information he was able to collect. In marked contrast to the ethnographic notes of Haddon, which contain a disproportionate amount of second-hand material, derived from printed sources or correspondence with "men on the spot," and with those of Rivers, which have the schematic character one might expect of the "concrete method," Malinowski's fieldnotes are rich in the records of his own participant observation, recorded to a very considerable extent in the native language.[54]

From a substantive point of view, "Baloma" was a treatise on the "sociology of belief." Though he acknowledged a debt to Durkheim, Malinowski made a point of speaking of "social ideas" rather than "collective ideas," rejecting "the postulate of a collective consciousness" as "barren and absolutely useless for an ethnographical observer." In contrast, he was much concerned with the problems posed by informant variation: how was one to synthesize as one "belief" the "always fragmentary" and "at times hopelessly inadequate and contradictory" answers to the question "How do the natives imagine the return of the *baloma?*" Malinowski's solution—arrived at afterwards in the analysis of his field data—was to distinguish between "social ideas or dogmas" (beliefs embodied in institutions, customs, rites, and myths, which, "believed and acted upon by all," were absolutely standardized), "the general behavior of the natives toward the object of a belief," and opinions or interpretations (occasionally even sceptical) that might be offered by individuals, groups of specialists, or even the majority of the members of a community. Some such distinction between cultural idea and individual opinion, often overlaid with another distinction between rules and regularities of actual behavior, was to be characteristic of all of Malinowski's later methodological prescriptions, as well as his more theoretically oriented ethnographic writings. Often seen as anti-Durkheimian, it was anti-Riversian as well. Though it assumed a customary or institutional realm where native belief was homogeneous, it gave tremendous weight to the conflict of cultural rule and individual impulse which, as Malinowski later suggested, made savage society "not a consistent logical scheme, but rather a seething mixture of conflicting principles."[55]

"Baloma" was written in Melbourne, where Malinowski settled for eighteen months after his return from the Trobriands in March 1916, and where he enjoyed the patronage of Baldwin Spencer. He also resumed his earlier acquaintance with the Massons, whose youngest daughter, Elsie, deeply affected by the death of her fiancé at Gallipoli, had begun training as a nurse at the Melbourne hospital. She had recently published a book based on her experiences among Aborigines in the Northern Territory, and Malinowski, favorably impressed, asked her to help with his Trobriand materials. The two became the center of a circle of young intellectuals who called themselves "The Clan" and who discussed the latest trends in European thought—on which Malinowski was a kind of privileged native informant. Gradually, his relationship with Elsie became more intimate, and they began to talk of marriage. Unfortunately, however, Malinowski was still involved with Nina Stirling; having broken off direct "personal association" at her parents' insistence, he and Nina had continued an intimately supportive correspondence during periods when each, successively, was seriously ill, and Malinowski could not bring himself to break the relationship completely by announcing his new attachment.[56]

It was from this complicated romantic situation that Malinowski finally returned to the Trobriands in October 1917. During the early part of his Australian interval, he had still planned to pursue Seligman's Rossel Island project once he had "worked out his Trobriand material." An abortive attempt to write a Kiriwinian grammar led him to "a good deal of linguistic reading and reflection," and it is clear that his understanding of "intensive study" evolved *pari passu*. Writing to Frazer, he noted that "whilst in the field, . . . the more elementary aspects" of many subjects "become soon so familiar they escape notice"; however, "once away from the natives," memory could not take the place of "direct observation." He had therefore spent much of the Australian interim going through all his material to create a "condensed outline," which had opened "a whole series of new questions." Fortuitously, he was denied official permission to go to Rossel and was left free to return to Kiriwina.[57]

Although Malinowski did not settle this time in Omarakana, his return to the same vicinity, after having left it for an extended period, seems likely (as the experience of other anthropologists suggests) to have enhanced the intensity of his study, by implying that his involvement had not been simply a sojourn, but might be more enduring. His relations with the Trobrianders, however, were by no means those of "social parity" which have been suggested as a precondition of successful participant observation. His retinue of several New Guinea "boys" may call up images of colonial "petty lordship." So also, the image of him conducting a census: "I sit on a chair, which the *gwadi* carry around the village"—though some might find this less (or more?) "colonialist" if told that *gwadi* was the Trobriand term for "children." But in a stratified society like the Trobriands (where the chief sat upon a platform so that commoners need not crawl on the ground in passing), "social parity"—which bears a problematic relationship to ethnographic understanding—is itself a rather problematic notion. That Malinowski, in return for half a tobacco stick a day, had been allowed to pitch his tent in the restricted central area of Omarakana, that he was apparently addressed by terms connoting high rank and doubtless did not walk bent-backed in front of his next-door neighbor, may have opened up more areas of Trobriand life to him than any other readily available status—even as it may also in some respects have constrained his perspective.[58]

Again, a critical issue would seem to be the mode of interaction and the quality of relationships he was able to establish. The diary (which, as we shall see, was not really "about" his ethnographic work per se) offers a limited and somewhat distorted picture. The spare phrase "*buritila'ulo* in Wakayse-Kabwaku" is the sole reference to a major event in his fieldwork, a competitive food display recounted in some detail in *Coral Gardens and Their Magic*. Insofar as the activity of a fieldworker may be divided into different modes (participation, observation, interrogation—or perhaps more neutrally, doing, seeing, talking) it is no doubt true that Malinowski (like most fieldworkers since?) gathered more information by the last two than the first. But while the diary does indicate that a good bit of Malinowski's "talking" was in one-on-one sessions with informants compensated by tobacco, it was often done in a context of activity: "I went to a garden and talked with the Teyava people of gardening and garden magic." There were many situations where his participation was indeed severely limited. His diary indicates that he was always left behind when the natives left on a kula expedition; and *Argonauts* suggests why: when a voyage he had been allowed to join late in 1915 was forced back by adverse winds, this bad luck was attributed to his presence. But if he was often forced to rely on simple question and answer, and if he felt that the collection of texts was an essential component of a correct style, his methodological ideal—which his ethnographies make clear was frequently realized in practice—remained that established in Mailu: discussion with one or more informants of a mutually (if differently) experienced activity or event. Only thus could one "integrate native behavior into native significance."[59]

At the level of methodological principle, Malinowski insisted on the critical importance of "personal friendships [to] encourage confidences and the repetition of intimate gossip." How "real" these friendships were is a moot point; one may perhaps assume that taking place, as it were, out of ordinary time and space and across barriers of power and culture, they were, like virtually all ethnographic relationships before or since, inherently ambiguous and asymmetrical. At one point, Malinowski complained of living "always in a world of lies here"—and there must have been times when he was rebuffed, either because he sought privileged information or because the Trobrianders were wearied by his questions or hurt by his occasional angry outbursts. But any number of details in both the diary and the ethnographies—particularly *The Sexual*

Life of Savages, which is the most revealing of the imponderabilia of his daily ethnographic behavior—testify that he was usually on fairly good terms with the Trobrianders. Clearly, it would be a mistake to take at face value the ironic passage in *Argonauts* suggesting that he was accepted as a "necessary evil or nuisance, mitigated by donations of tobacco." The number of his informants (who frequently appear as identifiable individuals in the ethnographies), the *kayaku* or congregations in his tent, the magic offered for him when he was ill, the numerous sexual confidences, suggest something more than this. No doubt in Trobriand minds he remained a European, set apart by many things—some of them rather paradoxical, like his encyclopedic collection of private magic, of which no Trobriander commanded more than a small fragment. But he was clearly a European of a special sort—as evidenced by their surprise that he, so unmissionary in other respects, should have argued the "missionary view" of physiological paternity. It was evidenced also in the complaint of magistrate Bellamy that during his absence at the front Malinowski had "undone" much of the work of ten years—which may perhaps be glossed as referring to the subversion of "progressive" cultural innovations and the violation of the still fairly recently established etiquette of race relations. And many years later, after Malinowski's death, it was evidenced by the memory of him as "the man of songs"—perhaps from the times when, walking at night with several Trobriand companions, he sang "kiss my ass" to melodies from Wagner in order to frighten away *mulukuasi*.[60]

Even so, there is a striking attitudinal contrast between Malinowski's public ethnographical reflections and the more Kurtzian moments of his diary. Clearly, he took for granted many of the perquisites of colonial power, and enjoyed the occasional exultations of petty lordship: "delightful feeling that now I alone am the master of this village with my 'boys' "—foreshadowing, in one instance, his later claim to ethnographic authority: "feeling of ownership: it is I who will describe them or create them." At times, he felt the impulse to exercise the ultimate colonial prerogative of physical aggression: "the natives still irritate me, particularly Ginger, whom I could willingly beat to death." In such a mood he even empathized with the worst of colonial aggressors: "I understand all the *German and Belgian colonial atrocities*." On one occasion one of his "boys" so "enraged" him that he "punched him in the jaw once or twice"—at the same time worrying that "this might degenerate into a brawl."[61]

And there are those often angry references to the Trobrianders as "niggers" that so greatly disturbed a later generation of anthropologists—suggesting as it did to some that the putative founder of modern ethnographic method, with its presumed basis in empathic identification, might in fact have been "an anthropologist who hates the natives."

Trobriand participants observing ethnographic authority: "The Ethnographer" at work, Omarakana. (Courtesy of Helena Wayne Malinowska and the London School of Economics)

In Malinowski's defense it has been suggested that the epithet did not then have its later racially pejorative meaning, or that it was a mistranslation from the Polish. But as we have already seen, the word had long been in use on the colonial periphery as what Haddon called "a term of reproach"; and Malinowski used it also in letters written in English. Its absence from the Mailu diary suggests that its later use may have reflected his acculturation to the informal discourse of race relations in the Melanesian colonial situation.[62]

However, unlike Gillen, whose references to "nigs" have sometimes a patriarchally affectionate ring, Malinowski's use of the term usually had an aggressive edge, sometimes explicitly expressed as "hatred." Context, of course, is relevant: many instances occur in moments of ethnographic frustration ("I was fed up with the *niggers* and with my work"). In general, it seems likely that the diary functioned as a safety valve for feelings Malinowski was unable or unwilling to express in his daily relations. Perhaps as often, however, the context of frustration was apparently sexual; and to understand that, we must consider what the diary of his second Trobriand stay was really "about." In contrast to the Mailu diary—which was an account of "a new epoch in my life: an expedition all on my own to the tropics"—the second diary was "a diary in the strict sense of the term": not simply a "mirror of the events, [but] a moral evaluation, [a] location of the mainsprings of my life." A Joycean (better, Witkacian) stream of consciousness without an index, it is only incidentally "about" his fieldwork. It is better understood as an account of the central psychological drama of his life: an extended crisis of identity in which certain Freudian undertones were obvious even to Malinowski himself.[63]*

Save Malinowski, the major characters in the drama were all female. Back in Poland, threatened by the flow of battle on the eastern front, was his mother, to whom, by his own acknowledgment, he had a very strong oedipal tie. His Viennese friend Paul Khuner suggested that the reason he had difficulty making emotional attachments to women was that all his emotions were centered on his mother. His relations with women clearly evinced a characteristic oedipal tension between the spiritual and the erotic—evident in the Mailu diary in the contrast between Zenia and Toska, the "incomparable mistress" with whom he had broken at the time of his mother's last prewar visit to London. In Australia, there were Elsie Masson and Nina Stirling. Toward Elsie—who had "the miraculous power to absolve sins"—he felt an "intellectual and personal attraction without much lust"; at many points in the diary he imagines himself in intellectual conversation with her. In contrast, Nina fitted his "sensual apperceptions" and "emotional longings better than E.R.M."—but without a sense of intellectual communion: "we would have talked to each other as though shouting from different rooms." Although he left Australia thinking of Elsie as his fiancée, he continued to feel the pull of a "simpler" romantic love for Nina. In January, shortly after having formally proposed to Elsie by letter, he watched a dying Trobriand woman hemorrhage, and was struck with remorse about his "betrayal" of Nina,

*Extracting an autobiographical plot from a diary that reads as free-associational pastiche is a problematic task, both practically and theoretically. In the diary's published form, the phrase quoted above, "a moral evaluation," is part of an opening epigraph and is matched, at the end of the diary, by the concluding phrase, "truly, I lack real character." To what extent this freighted framing is an artifact of editing is not indicated in the prefatory material, which refers instead to "illegible passages" and "editorial omissions" of "a few extremely intimate observations" (1967:vi, xxi). It is my understanding—based on informal anecdotal evidence, rather than consultation of the original manuscript texts—that a number of the elisions refer obliquely to instances of autoeroticism, and might thus conform to the interpretive line suggested here. In general, however, my reading of Malinowski must be regarded as tentative, pending the completion of the biography now in process by Michael Young. Interested readers may also wish to consult *The Story of a Marriage,* a two-volume collection of the letters of Malinowski and Elsie Masson, edited by their daughter Helena Wayne, which appeared as *After Tylor* was in press.

who apparently had a serious heart condition; momentarily, he decided that he wanted to be with her "at any cost, to allay her sufferings." The psychological complexities of the situation are suggested by the fact that although Elsie was later explicitly equated with his mother—with a parenthetical reference to "Freud's theory"—Malinowski at this time dreamed that his mother reproached him for not marrying Nina.[64]

Closely bound up with this unresolved erotic attachment was the problem of Malinowski's national identity. An enemy alien taken by some to be German, he had been greeted upon his first return from the Trobriands by an army corporal assigned to prevent him from travelling to Brisbane. Others knew him as Slavic: Elton Mayo, a fellow member of "The Clan" who later became an influential industrial psychologist in the United States, spoke of Malinowski as living in "Slavonic squalor" and "the depths of Sociologico-Slavic gloom." However brilliant, he was not the sort of man Australian British fathers wanted for a son-in-law. And despite Malinowski's own deeply ingrained Anglophilia, he was at times moved by "a strong hatred for England and the English." He feared that if he married Elsie, he "would be estranged from Polishness"; as late as mid-April 1918, he vowed that "I shall go back to Poland and my children will be Poles."[65]

The last half of the second Trobriand diary recounts the resolution of this extended crisis. Despite moments of "strong emotional longing" for Nina, Malinowski's commitment to Elsie became ever stronger, and on April 30 he decided to write Nina "an absolutely irrevocable letter," but could not manage to finish it. Two weeks later Malinowski had brought himself "round to the knowledge" that "physical contact, frenzied self-surrender is valuable only against [a] background of true spiritual communion"—and that Elsie was "the only woman for whom I have this feeling." Although she was not "the fulfilment of all the potentialities of woman," she was "the ideal wife" for him, and on June 4 he decided that "de facto" they were married. Even then, the relationship with Nina was not finally broken off (by her) until after Baldwin Spencer made known to her parents (and the Massons) letters he discovered in private papers Malinowski had left for safekeeping in a room in the Melbourne museum—ironically, to save them from his prying landlady while he was in the Trobriands.[66]

On June 11, 1918, Malinowski received the news of his mother's death, and the diary (as published) rushed to a conclusion. The "shadow of death," which in January had threatened to separate him from Elsie, now drew them closer together. Life had been "pierced with the arrow of grief, guilt feelings, irretrievable things," and Poland now stood in the past, on the other side of a "black abyss, a void" in his soul. But even as "the tears flow[ed] constantly" in his grief, "external ambitions" helped to "tie [him] to life"; crawling over him "like lice," they were at this point clearly linked to England: F.R.S. (Fellow of the Royal Society), C.S.I. (Companion of the Order of the Star of India)—perhaps even "*Sir*" Bronislaw Malinowski.* Although thoughts about Elsie were "painful," she was now the anchor of his future and the redeemer of his past. In the diary's last paragraph, Malinowski recalled how his last evening with his mother in London had been "spoiled by that whore" (Toska), and suggested that "if I had been married to E.R.M. I would have behaved very differently."[67]

Although necessarily schematized, this biographical detail may tell us something about how the experiential dynamics of Malinowski's fieldwork may have conditioned his emerging theoretical orientation. Malinowski was a highly erotic individual, who at times suffered from "the metaphysical regret" of "you'll never fuck them all." His ethnographic style placed him in close physical proximity to grass-skirted native women whose bodies excited him and whose relatively uninhibited sex lives were a primary subject of his study. However, he had deliberately chosen to restrain his erotic energy throughout this period of his fieldwork, having resolved to remain faithful to Elsie in both deed and thought. Although on at least one occasion he "pawed" a Trobriand woman, he seems to have managed the former. His impulses, however, were quite another matter. The attempt to cope with them is in fact a primary psychological theme of the diary, whose function was the "taming of my lusts [and] the elimination of lecherousness."[68]

Malinowski's erotic impulses both drew him toward and separated him from the Trobrianders. Watching a group of native woman draw water at a spring, he thought "how easily" he "could have a *connection*" with one whom he found "very attractive." Immediately, he regretted "that this incompatibility can exist: physical attraction and personal aver-

*Who among the British anthropologists got knighted is perhaps a matter worthy of brief note, although it goes unmentioned in Leach's otherwise provocative perspective on "insiders" and "outsiders," in terms of a "spectrum" of "Englishness." In the pre-functionalist period the list includes major evolutionists (Lubbock, Tylor, and Frazer), officials of the British Museum (Flower, Franks, Read), a folklorist (Gomme), two colonial officers (Im Thurn, Temple), two Oxbridge archeologists (Ridgeway and Myres), and a colonial professor (Spencer). Malinowski did not make it, though four other of the nine "White" (counter-revolutionary) intellectuals whom Perry Anderson (1969:230) held in part responsible for the lack of a totalizing view of English society did (Berlin, Gombrich, Namier, Popper). Neither, of course, did Radcliffe-Brown, whose background was distinctly lower middle class. The social anthropologists knighted in the next generation were Evans-Pritchard ("a very English Englishman despite his Welsh name"), Richards ("true English"), Firth ("near English" despite his colonial background), and of course Leach himself—who, despite "becoming a rude mechanical," did "not cease to be a snob" (Leach 1984:16, 10). For the backgrounds of some other social anthropologists, see below, 407–9.

sion. Personal attraction without strong physical magnetism." Following her back to the village, he "admired the beauty of the human body," as "the poetry of the evening and the sunset permeated everything"; thinking about "how marvelously E.R.M. would have reacted to this," he "realized the gulf between me and the human beings around me."[69]

But it was not that gulf which was the ultimate meaning Malinowski drew from his field experience; rather it was an appreciation of shared humanity. When he formulated the "deepest essence" of his ethnographic work in November 1917, he echoed the goal he had set for his own diary:

> to discover what are his [the native's] main passions, the motives for his conduct, his aims . . . . His essential deepest way of thinking. At this point we are confronted with our own problems: What is essential in ourselves?

In seeking the mainsprings of his own life, Malinowski resolved to watch himself "right down to the deepest instincts." Alone in "the heart of darkness," he tried to penetrate the darkness of his own heart, and was confronted there by instinctual forces common to all men: "Now I often have the feeling of being 'at the bottom of consciousness'—the feeling of the physical foundation of mental life, the latter's dependence on the body, so that every thought that flows effortlessly in some psychic medium has been laboriously formed inside the organism." There, at "the bottom of consciousness," behind what he later called the "ever-imperfect wall of culture," all men, savage or civilized, were motivated by the same biologically based drives he had felt so acutely in the course of his own psychological drama in the Trobriands.[70]

At this point, however, it is clear that Malinowski still thought of this shared mental makeup in rather traditional evolutionary terms. In the elision between "aims" and "deepest ways of thinking" in the diary passage just quoted, there was in fact a starkly disjunctive parenthesis: "(Why does a *boy 'sign on'?* Is every *boy,* after some time, ready to *'sign off'*?)." Recalling Malinowski's neo-Frazerian contribution to Westermarck's festschrift, and looking forward to the argument of *Sex and Repression in Savage Society,* it is possible to integrate the elided passage into the broader themes of Malinowski's anthropology, and of his ethnographic experience. Like this disjunctive parenthesis (which referred to "signing on" for plantation labor), his early essay on the "economic functions" of the intichiuma ceremonies had to do with the transition from "savage" to "civilized" labor; in contrast, *Sex and Repression* makes it clear that the passage from savagery to civilization was also a passage away from a relatively easy and harmonious genital sexuality. For mankind as a whole, the long-run evolutionary consequence of "signing on" might be seen as loss as well as gain—and the loss more sharply felt by a European living on a tropical island, who had vowed to deny himself the sensual pleasures associated with such exotic realms. Denied the compensating gains of civilization, why, indeed, would the native "boy"—or anyone else—"sign on"?[71]

It was in the Trobriands, in April 1918, that Malinowski conceived the notion of a "New Humanism" centered on "living man, living language, and living full-blooded facts," for which he planned to organize "a kind of humanistic R[oyal] S[ociety]" when he returned to England. Although the "Society of Modern Humanism" did not materialize, the New Humanism was explicitly discussed in an article published after his return, in which (echoing Rivers) he explained the currently debated "depopulation of Melanesia" in psychobiological terms. In their "fanatical zeal to prune and uproot," convention-bound "morality mongers" and parochial middle-class "petty inquisitors of primitive life" had choked off the natives' "joy of living" by suppressing the institutions that gave "zest and meaning to life"—the flute playing of the Dobu, the drums around Port Moresby, the dancing of the Trobrianders. Malinowski was particularly incensed by attempts to tamper with "the most powerful human instinct"—the sexual instinct—and with the system of regulations and liberties which "a natural biological and social development has built around it" in a particular culture. In this context he offered one of his earliest published statements of the functional integration of culture, expressed in essentially psychobiological instrumental terms:

> every item of culture . . . represents a value, fulfils a social function, has a positive, biological significance. For tradition is a fabric in which all the strands are so closely woven that the destruction of one unmakes the whole. And tradition is, biologically speaking, a form of collective adaptation of a community to its surroundings. Destroy tradition, and you will deprive the collective organism of its protective shell, and give it over to the slow but inevitable process of dying out.[72]

Malinowski's gradual perception, while in the field, of an "undercurrent of desire" must thus be understood not simply as a matter of the opposition of individual impulse to societal "convention, law, and morals," but also as a deepened appreciation of the grounding of such cultural rules in the regulation of instinct by tradition. If Westermarck—and in a somewhat different fashion Mach and Nietzsche—had prepared Malinowski to see cultural life as founded on human instinct, it was his field experience of human sexuality (his own as well as that of the Trobrianders) that prepared him later to consider this relationship in a specifically Freudian context.[73]

In the spring of 1918, however, the focus of his theoretical concerns was still William Rivers, in the latter's pre-Freudian, anti-psychological, diffusionist mode; despite frequent disagreements with his views, reading Rivers made Malinowski "simply *bubble up with theoretical ideas.*" He did not reject history entirely—"a being endowed with memory must be understood though its history"; indeed, as late as 1922, he spoke of doing a migration study in the Riversian mode. But he was very doubtful about the "projection of space onto time," and in the course of his engagement with Riversian historicism, "social psychology" emerged as the privileged inquiry. Responding to some (unspecified) "criticisms *ad hominem*" Rivers had made of Seligman, Malinowski thought of formulating his "theoretical ideas" ("for E.R.M.") and of writing an "Int[roduction] to the Study of Comparative Sociology": "*'Socio-psychological correspondences' = The main study is to understand how ideas (social) & social institutions react on each other. The study of the mental (which is always individual, differential) becomes objective, consolidated into an institution, & this again reacts on the individual.*"[74]

In all of this, Malinowski thought of himself as probing more deeply than Rivers had into the cultural dynamics of the human psyche. The contrast was suggested in notes for the preface to his planned ethnography: "[Jan] Kubary as a concrete [i.e., Riversian] methodologist; Mikluho-Maclay as a new type. Marett's comparison: *early ethnographers as prospectors.*" It is in the context of this implied contrast between the surveying of an ethnographic surface and the mining of its deeper psychological meaning—as well as in the context of transforming national identity—that one must gloss Malinowski's reported proclamation of his ultimate anthropological ambition: "Rivers is the Rider Haggard of anthropology; I shall be the Conrad."[75]

Functionalist Forays toward a Scientific Theory of Culture

In March 1919 the "penniless Pole" and "the English miss" were married in a Melbourne registry office, with her parents in attendance despite their fear that he would bring a "wild influence into family life." When Poland became independent, they both became Polish citizens; as late as 1922, Malinowski seriously considered accepting the offer of the new chair of ethnology at Cracow. In the meantime, however, his intellectual and career orientation continued to point him toward Britain; it was there that the goal (already articulated in the Trobriands) of a "revolution in social anthropology" would have to be pursued. After some months in Australia, where he worked on his Trobriand materials (and suffered from the Spanish flu), he and Elsie sailed for England, and then stayed for a time with her relatives in Edinburgh. Soon, however, Malinowski's ill-health (subsequently diagnosed as tuberculosis) forced them to retreat to the Canary Islands, the central site of those early ventures with his mother into extra-European otherness. It was during this idyllic year with his new wife, far from "the trouble and irritation of Europe," that he crafted the manuscript most strongly expressive of the romantic literary impulse in his divided intellectual persona—the opening chapter of which defined the ethnographic mode thenceforth associated with his name.[76]

Malinowski was acutely aware of the chasm between "the brute material of information . . . and the final authoritative presentation of results," or, as he elsewhere revealingly phrased it, between "the slight dust of little bits of information—here and there, chaotic, unequal even in their credibility" and the "final ideals of knowledge": "the essential nigger as an illustration and document to our Conception of Man." The problem was how "to convince my readers" that the ethnographic information offered them was "objectively acquired knowledge" and not simply "a subjectively formed notion." It was, in short, the problem of establishing his "ethnographic authority"—which may be regarded as the prototype for the authority of all modern ethnography.[77]

At the level of explicit formulation, Malinowski tended to speak in terms congenial to a physicist-turned-ethnographer under the methodological shadow of Rivers. The critical thing, as in physics or chemistry, was to be "absolutely candid" about one's method, which Malinowski discussed under three headings: "proper conditions for ethnographic work"; knowledge of the "principles," "aims," and "results" of modern "scientific study"; and the application of "special methods" of "collecting, manipulating, and fixing" evidence. The latter, too, could be grouped under three rubrics: "statistic documentation by concrete evidence" of the "rules and regularities of tribal life"; collecting "the imponderabilia of actual life and typical behavior" in order to put "flesh and blood" on the "skeleton" of the tribal constitution; and the creation of a *corpus inscriptionum* of native opinion and utterance to illustrate "typical ways of thinking and feeling." Beyond these general prescriptions, Malinowski's more specific methodological injunctions—the keeping of an "ethnographic diary," the making of "synoptic charts," and the preliminary sketching of results—all emphasize the constructive, problem-generating role of the ethnographer. But what was absolutely critical was to place this "active huntsman" in a certain situation. Cut off from "the company of white men," he would "naturally" seek the society of natives not his "natural companions," engaging in "natural intercourse" with them rather than relying on "paid, and often bored, informants." Waking up "every morning to a day presenting itself more or less as it does to the native," he would find his life soon took "quite a natural course very much in harmony with his surroundings." Corrected for repeated "breaches of etiquette," he would "learn how to behave"; taking part ("in a way") in village life, he would cease "to be a disturbing element." Such were the means by which the ethnographer might observe a culture from the inside, and thereby "grasp the native's point of view, his relation to life, and realize *his* vision of *his* world."[78*]

Although Malinowski tried to formulate the "ethnographer's magic" as a practical "application of a number of rules of common sense and well-known scientific principles," his real problem was not so much to tell his readers how to accomplish the ultimate divinatory task as to convince them that it could be done, and that he had done it. If "empty programme" were to be translated into "the result of personal experience," then his own experience of the native's experience must become the reader's experience as well. And that was a task that scientific analysis yielded up to literary art.[79]

To this end, Malinowski's reading of Frazer served his ethnography very well indeed. Throughout, Frazer's "scene/act" ratio was employed to place the reader imaginatively within the actual physical setting of the events Malinowski reconstructed: "When, on a hot day, we enter the deep shadow of fruit trees and palms, and find ourselves in the midst of the wonderfully designed and ornamented houses hiding here and there in irregular groups among the green . . . ." More important was a device one might call the "author/reader equation": "Imagine yourself suddenly set down surrounded by all your gear, alone on a tropical beach close to a native village . . . ." As its original title ("Kula: A Tale of Native Enterprise and Adventure in Eastern New Guinea") suggested, this ethnography (in contrast to most "scientific" ethnographies, including his own later ones) had a narrative structure. Beginning with the construction of a *waga* or canoe, through its launching and departure, readers were taken on an ambitious expedition across the sea arm of Pilolu (with a pause for the account of a mythical shipwreck), on to the Amphletts, Tewara, and Sanaroa, stopping for magical ceremonies on the beach of Sarubwoyna,

*Malinowski, aided by Billy Hancock, also took a great many ethnographic photographs in the Trobriand Islands, the most symbolically resonant of which languished unpublished in the Malinowski collection at the London School of Economics until the 1970s (see 262, above). Frequently reprinted in recent years, it displays an obviously self-conscious construction (Trobrianders watching the ethnographer at work writing in his tent) which marks it even more clearly as a visual representation of his auctorial authority—too strong, perhaps (or too laden with ironies), for use in the ethnographic charter of that authority (see Stocking 1993d). Although Malinowski later reproached himself for not taking photography more seriously as an ethnographic tool (1935a:I, 461; cf. T. Wright 1991), his work has been linked to a "major change of direction in anthropology" in which visual representation became "just another ancillary tool in the fieldworker's arsenal . . . , a technique perceived as recording surface rather than depth" (Edwards 1992:4).

to the climactic kula exchanges in Dobu, and then the journey home—there to witness a return visit from the Dobuans, and tie up the loose ends of the "inland Kula" and its "remaining branches and offshoots." With Malinowski along to intervene when necessary to explain particular ethnographic details or to provide more extended disquisitions on the sociology, mythology, magic, and language of the kula, his readers could follow the Trobrianders through the epic event that periodically focussed all the energies of their existence. At the end, Malinowski's readers were prepared to believe that they had glimpsed the "inner meaning and the psychological reality" of a life that was "outwardly strange" and at "first sight incomprehensible."[80]

This narrative technology of "I-witnessing" was enhanced in numerous ways. Characteristically, chapters opened with references to a present action or situation: "the canoe, painted and decorated, stands now ready to be launched." There were occasional contrasts between "nowadays" and "olden days," and several chapters in fact ended with historical diffusionist speculations; more characteristically, however, Malinowski wrote in the active voice and the present tense. By bringing the reader along as eyewitness to the ongoing kula events, he established the conviction that they exemplified life in the Trobriands to that very day. Previous ethnographies had described reconstructed behavior as if it were present practice, but it was Malinowski's *Argonauts* that, more than any other, validated the temporal context in which modern ethnography was customarily to be situated: the vague and essentially atemporal moment that later came to be called "the ethnographic present."[81]

As the Homeric (and Frazerian) echoes of its actually published title suggest, something was going on in this primal ethnographic scene besides the narrative re-creation of actual experience. In discussing the Trobriand shipwreck myth, Malinowski suggested that it was not always easy to distinguish "mere mytho-poetic fiction" from "actual experience"; despite his professed methodological candor, a similar problem exists in his own work. A reader must pay close attention to realize from the printed narrative that Malinowski never actually sailed with a kula expedition after that ill-fated venture toward Kitava in 1915. At one point he did note that most of his narrative was "reconstructed," arguing that for one who had seen the "native's tribal life" and had "a good grip over intelligent informants," such reconstruction was neither "fanciful" nor "very difficult." But along the way, ambiguous phrases ("I have seen, indeed followed") encourage the reader to believe that he had done something more than catch up in a cutter. Similarly, while attentive readers may have realized that Malinowski did sometimes pay informants, it is only his diary that reveals just how often (roughly, once a fortnight) he retreated to Billy Hancock's compound at Gusaweta for refuge from a "surfeit of native." The diary also suggests that his time-reckoning was not entirely reliable—in general, he was not in the field for quite so long as *Argonauts* suggests.[82]

A certain vagueness as to the situation of events in time is one aspect of the myth-making process. Another is the peopling of the mythopoeic moment with characters of archetypal stature. It is worth considering in this context the cast of characters in *Argonauts*. Most numerous were the "natives": distinguished often by tribal group or status, frequently named, they were occasionally subsumed within the category "savage" (and in the privacy of his diary, by the epithet "nigger"); they were, however, most explicitly denied the archetypifying capitalization of Primitive Economic Man—a rubric Malinowski was at some pains to critique. Brushed at times with the exotic colors of noble savagery, the Trobrianders were more often painted in rather ordinary tones; though once referred to as "Homeric heroes," they were not in fact the heroes of Malinowski's romance. His attitude toward them was often that of "gentle irony"—a literary mode characteristic of much of modern ethnography. As "the Ethnographer," Malinowski was not only capable of sharing their vision of their world, but knew things about it that they would never know, bringing to light "phenomena of human nature" which "had remained hidden even from those in whom they happened."[83]

Such phenomena were hidden also from a second group of characters: "the minor cast of cramped minds" who had "gotten the natives all wrong" in the past: administrators, missionaries, traders, all "full of the biassed and pre-judged opinions inevitable in the average practical man" who had "lived for years in the place . . . and yet hardly knew one thing about them really well." Sometimes archetypical representations of painful experiences Malinowski had had with very real people (e.g., the Mailu missionary Saville), they appear briefly in the methodological introduction as a "stock of strawmen" who by stark contrast highlight the virtues of Malinowski's method.[84]

Posed against these two sets of characters is a third, who stands apart, capitalized, in heroic singularity: the Ethnographer. Appositional equation to the first person singular leaves no doubt as to his actual identity, and the equation is confirmed iconographically by photographs of "the Ethnographer's tent" placed strategically at the beginning and the end of the book, before and after the expedition it recounts. Marking him off from all other Europeans, the methodological introduction has affirmed his divinatory powers. By the book's end we know that only he, who ventured there alone and made his loneliness the instrument of divining knowledge, could have guided us also into and out of the heart of darkness. Considered in this light, *Argonauts* may be regarded as a kind of euhemerist myth—divinizing, however, not its ostensible Trobriand heroes, but the European Jason who brought back the Golden Fleece of ethnographic knowledge. Long before Susan Sontag used Lévi-Strauss as the model of the "Anthropologist as Hero," Malinowski had created the role for himself.[85]

Malinowski did so, however, not simply to make his book more saleable or to advance his own career, but to launch the "revolution in social anthropology" he had imagined in the Trobriands. This required him to convince not only readers, but also apprentice ethnographers, who would begin their fieldwork "paralyzed with fear of all sorts of traps and barriers," that his methods were adequate to the ethnographic task. From this point of view, one might suggest that the introduction to *Argonauts* was never intended as a "true description" of Malinowski's own fieldwork experience; description was simply the device by which he made prescription compelling. It would not have served either his career-advancing or his confidence-inspiring purposes to include there the (relatively innocuous) "confessions of ignorance and failure" which, from a position of established eminence, he was to offer a dozen years later. Rather, he wanted to make the apprentice ethnographer "aware beforehand that we had a way of attacking" all those "initial difficulties which are so very hard to surmount." More than that, he wanted to legitimate the style of fieldwork on which that novice was to embark. In writing for novice ethnographers as well as general readers, Malinowski's problem was not so much to enumerate principles of method (though he did this); it was to demonstrate to them that the task could be done. In this context, every aspect of *Argonauts*—structure as well as argument, style as well as content, anecdote as well as precept, implication as well as statement, omission as well as inclusion—all contributed to the euhemerist validating myth.[86]

The fieldwork style that Malinowski sought to establish as the basis for his "revolution in social anthropology" depended ultimately on placing oneself in a situation where one might have a certain kind of experience. Like the situations that elicited Trobriand magic, it was initially threatening and potentially dangerous, one in which "elements of chance and accident" often determined success and failure. As Malinowski was several years later to suggest in his Frazer Lecture, "Myth in Primitive Psychology," the function of magic was to bridge over "the gaps and inadequacies in highly important activities not yet completely mastered by man." The gap between the specific methodological prescriptions of fieldwork and the vaguely defined goals of ethnographic knowledge had thus to be filled by what Malinowski himself called "the ethnographer's magic." And just as in primitive psychology myth functioned "especially where there is a sociological strain," so in anthropological psychology it functioned especially where there was an epistemological strain. Myth was not "an explanation in satisfaction of a scientific interest, but a narrative resurrection of a primeval reality, told in satisfaction of deep religious wants, moral cravings, social submissions, assertions, even practical requirements." Malinowski emphasized the intermingling of its pragmatic and legitimating functions: myth was at once "a warrant, a charter, and often even a practical guide to the activities with which it is connected." Expressing, enhancing, and codifying belief, vouching for "the efficiency of ritual," it came "into play when rite, ceremony, or a social or moral rule demands justification, warrant of antiquity, reality and sanctity." While the central rite (and moral rule) of the new social anthropology professed to be innovative rather than antique, it did demand the justification of presumed reality, and it was this mythic charter that *Argonauts* sought to provide. Effectively appropriating to himself experience that in fact had been shared by others (including "The Ethnographer's Tent," which Westermarck had taken to Morocco), at once archetypifying it and rendering it in concrete narrative form, Malinowski validated not only his own fieldwork but that of "modern anthropology."[87*]

With Rivers recently dead, it was Haddon ("the Leader and Dean of British Field Anthropology") who spoke in public for the Cambridge School, lauding the book as "the high-water mark of ethnological investigation and interpretation," which would "prove of great value for the guidance of future fieldworkers." Despite the fact that *Argonauts* was dedicated to him, Seligman—whose ethnographic taste was as prosaic as his fieldwork style—continued to regard "Baloma" as Malinowski's best effort, and thought that much of his work of the 1920s was compromised by proselytizing purpose. But it was Seligman, part-time Professor of Ethnology at the London School of Economics since 1912, who used his

*On several occasions my reading of Malinowski's methodological prescriptions has been assimilated to the work of those who treat (or are presumed to treat) the "ethnographic authority" of modern anthropology as merely a matter of literary artifice, or as the product of the colonial situation, or as an instrument of colonial power. Acknowledging that my work may be vulnerable to such assimilation—and granting (indeed, insisting) that such interpretations may enrich our historical as well as our critical understanding—I want to insist also that, from my point of view, this does not imply a devaluing deconstructivism. Edmund Leach, for whom Malinowski was "a great hero," once associated me with those for whom he was "a fraud, a man who preached the gospel of 'participant observation' but did not practice it" (1990:56). Against this, I would appeal to Malinowski's own notion of the empowering charter function of myth, which makes it possible to "get on with the work" of that highly problematic process of participant observation, and to produce ethnographies, which although of varying quality, are many of them at least as valuable and permanent contributions to our understanding of the variety of humankind as the efforts of those who would deconstruct them. Of these, surely among the most valuable and permanently interesting were those of Malinowski (see also Dauber 1995; Stocking 1995).

independent means privately to support Malinowski's career, and who shepherded him to the academic position from which a "revolution in social anthropology" might be successfully waged.[88]

Before the war, Malinowski had lectured briefly at the School of Economics on primitive religion; in 1920 he gave a series of lectures on primitive economics. When he was considering a Polish chair in 1921, Seligman reported to him that Rivers felt his future was in England—though not at Cambridge, where two of Rivers' own students (both, one notes, of British ancestry) had priority. Seligman promised to do something himself at the School of Economics, and the opportunity came the following year, after the British Association for the Advancement of Science had set up a committee on the teaching of anthropology. In this context, a competition developed between the School of Economics and University College, where Elliot Smith (beneficiary of a large grant from the Rockefeller Foundation) was trying to establish a base in the Department of Anatomy for his diffusionist anthropology. After extensive negotiations, an agreement was reached whereby there would be two readerships, one at University College for William Perry in cultural anthropology, one at the School of Economics for Malinowski—at his suggestion, in "social anthropology," since the School of Economics was "the centre for sociology and all that pertains to it," and Frazer had legitimized that usage in his Liverpool lectures.[89]

The treatment of a "relatively benign" tubercular condition prevented Malinowski from assuming his position until the fall of 1924, and he spent the interval in Oberbozen (Soprabolzano), a village in the Italian Dolomites where he had bought an Alpine house that was to be his home away from London for the next few years. Responding to Frazer's thanks for his very laudatory review of the abridged *Golden Bough,* Malinowski portrayed himself and Perry as started "on a sort of race" in which Perry had a year's head start, but in which he himself was the beneficiary of "a strong movement" to provide an "antidote against Elliot Smithism." Under the misapprehension that Frazer actually taught anthropology, Malinowski expressed a hope that he might help him to "secure a foothold" as his assistant in Cambridge, where there would surely be an attempt also to "establish a culture-contact monopoly and to try and gag all those heretics who do not believe that Kultur is One, that She was born in Egypt and that E.S. is Her Prophet and Perry his barber."[90]

Malinowski was inclined to treat "Smith, Perry & Co. like a basketfull of rotten eggs: with the greatest care and consideration, not to say respect"—and refrain from attacking them directly. But there is no doubt that in the aftermath of Rivers' death he saw them as the chief rival claimants to leadership in British anthropology and that his own problem was to define a theoretical position from which to counter their claim. *Argonauts* had established him as the exemplar of a new ethnographic mode. But though the descriptive analysis of the ritual exchange of *vaygu'a* (red shell necklaces and white shell bracelets) between trading partners, clockwise and counterclockwise around the kula ring, had a certain power at the level of what has been called "clinical theory" (and was to stimulate Marcel Mauss's classic discourse on the principle of reciprocity) *Argonauts* was not itself a work that made ambitious theoretical claims. It was only in the last pages that Malinowski discussed "the meaning of the Kula," largely in psychological terms: the "complex emotional and intellectual attitude at the bottom of it." "Functionalism" was barely hinted at in a brief reference to the possibility of a "new type of theory"—an alternative to "evolution," the "contact of cultures," and environmental determinism—which would study "the influence on one another of the various aspects of an institution" and "the social and psychological mechanism on which the institution is based."[91]

Given Malinowski's commitment to an ethnographically grounded anthropology and his evident appreciation of cultural specificity, as well as his pervasive interest in psychological processes, one might have expected that his anthropology would develop along Boasian lines, as a pluralistic study of the variability of culture and personality. His ethnographic goal, like that of many of his anthropological contemporaries, was to get behind the experience of recent contact, to reveal the essential ethnic characteristics of the group he had studied—what in his later magnum ethnographic opus he called "the essential Trobriander," "tenacious of [his] own culture," flourishing as it had "for ages, unknown and untouched by Europeans."* But even there, the Trobrianders were quickly linked to "Oceanic civilisations" and "human nature in general." Characteristically, Malinowski's interest in cultural psychology had a universalistic thrust, in which the Trobrianders, as full-blooded exemplars of human nature in its "savage"—that is, "essentially human"—state, were posed against what appears in retrospect as an evolutionary strawman, or used to explicate more general human cultural and psychological processes. And while the latter were increasingly to be formulated in "functionalist" terms, there was often a residue or underpinning of evolutionary assumption. When Malinowski, reviewing *Children of the*

*In 1935, after his turn to the study of "culture contact," Malinowski acknowledged as "the most serious shortcoming of my whole anthropological research in Melanesia" his failure to treat adequately the "decay of custom under European influence." He had in fact noted many facts "registering the influence of European culture," including the eclipse of the power of the chief by that of the resident magistrate, as well as the influence of missionaries and traders. "Brought up," however, in an anthropology "still mainly interested in the 'real savage' as representative of the stone age," in which human history was revealed in surviving custom, he had not given them serious consideration (1935a:I, 479–81).

Sun, spoke of an "acute crisis" in anthropology, it was Perry's that was the "new anthropology." In contrast, he himself retained "a firm belief in the uniformity of human nature, and all his theoretical bias [made] him remain faithful to the old school." If, as he later suggested, evolutionism was "nowadays generally discredited and discarded," it was nonetheless "fundamentally sound when correctly set forth."[92]

If functionalism thus emerged in the shadow of Frazer, the shade of Rivers was lurking close in the background; and while Malinowski was critical of Rivers' diffusionist turn, it was his psychological views that were especially pertinent. In 1913, when Rivers read his paper on "Survivals in Sociology," to the Sociological Society, Malinowski prepared critical notes as a basis for comments at the meeting. Rejecting Rivers' definition, he argued that all customs were in one sense survivals insofar as one aspect or another had lost its utility, but that no custom, "however out of fashion," did not perform *some* social function. The problem lay precisely in Rivers' rejection of "the validity of psychol[ogical] explanations in sociology." If one shut one's mind to the psychological meaning of social institutions and customs, it was impossible "to see how far they are survivals and how far they are not." Frazer and Robertson Smith had clearly demonstrated that communion was a survival when viewed in "crude materialistic" terms—but any believing Christian would find it "simply absurd" so to regard his religion's single "most vital function." It was impossible to take a step in sociology "without using psychological terms," because one could understand the "social function of institutions" only in terms of the "ideas and emotions" associated with them.[93]

During Malinowski's years in the South Pacific, Rivers' evolving position was a constant point of reference for him as he sought a standpoint from which to interpret his ethnographic experience. Early in 1918 he became aware of Rivers' return to psychology, when Seligman sent him "a short account of dreams" and a book "on insanity from the modern point of view" and encouraged him to collect dreams from his Trobriand informants. Malinowski responded that he already had a "fair idea" of Freud's theory, having read several ethnological articles in *Imago* and a part (as was often his wont) of the *Traumdeuting*. He later recalled that Seligman's letter had stimulated reflections on how the Oedipus complex might manifest itself in a matrilineal community, but when he assured Seligman early in 1919 that he had finished Rivers' "Dreams and Primitive Culture," he added that he was not "very up yet" on the subject.[94]

Malinowski was, however, continuing to search for his own social psychological alternative to the rationalistic psychology Rivers had rejected. After returning to Australia, Malinowski attended a philosophical seminar early in 1919, in which he read William James and reread

Mach, and attempted to redefine the basis of his own scientific point of view. Dividing experience into the "objective" and the "subjective," and ranging the sciences in a hierarchy (Physics, Biology, Evolution, Psychology, Sociology, Humanistic), he suggested that psychology—conceived of as an awareness or mastery "of our own body from within" by "the coordination of our brain & other nervous systems"—was "the basis of all other disciplines" of the subjective realm.[95]

Central among these other disciplines was "social psychology," which was the focus of much of Malinowski's reading after he completed *Argonauts* in April 1921. Anticipating a job at the London School of Economics, he immersed himself in current British sociological and social psychological literature, including works by Moncure Conway, Morris Ginsberg, Leonard Hobhouse, William McDougall, Wilfred Trotter, and Graham Wallas—as well as Walter Bagehot on "the cake of custom," and Gabriel Tarde on imitation, which he saw as the "starting point of the most important investigations in Social Psychology." Although he was interested in the biological and instinctual bases of human behavior, Malinowski dismissed as "survivals of Hegelian thinking" all notions like the "herd," the "crowd," or the "group mind," which seemed to postulate the existence of supra-individual entities. He insisted that the basis of all social organization was "a common stock of ideas," which he spoke of in terms of the *Kultur* of each group. Defining *Kultur* in functional terms as "the means of satisfying human needs through general social cooperation," he argued that "the real problem of Social Psychology" was how "the Group through its social organisation achieves unity of Action, which implies a definite coordination of ideas, as well as of functions." As he suggested in some undated early notes toward a book on kinship, his goal was to solve "the fundamental Mystery of the Social": "When we understand how this system [kinship] comes into being, how it imposes the prototype values of future social morals: respect for authority, personal loyalty, subordination of impulses to feelings—when we discover that, we have really answered (in a concrete instance, but one which allows of a simple generalization by extension) the main question: how does society impress its norms on the individual." It was in this context that Malinowski approached the writings of Sigmund Freud, who, by providing "the first concrete theory about the relation between instinctive life and social institution," offered an inspiration for the "exploration of the difficult borderland between social tradition and social organisation."[96]

In turning to Freud, Malinowski was catching the crest of the postwar interest in psychoanalysis both within and outside anthropology. In the newly founded journal *Psyche*—a forum in which the broad realm once called the "spiritual" could be explored by intellectuals whom the Great War had disillusioned—the psychoanalytic fad was described as "almost without parallel in the history of scientific progress." With Rivers, the leader of the psychoanalytic movement in anthropology, now deceased, it must have seemed a likely move, for an aging young man anxious to establish himself, to take up the problem of the cultural variability of the Oedipus complex, a problem which Rivers in fact had recently broached.[97]

A month after Rivers' death, Malinowski's publisher expressed satisfaction that he was turning to "Studies in Erotica and Psychoanalysis among Savages"; six months later, Malinowski was getting bibliographical advice from Seligman, and he seems also to have had conversations with at least one member of the Freudian inner circle on one of the trips he took to Vienna from Oberbozen. Malinowski approached Freud through three major works: *Three Contributions to the Theory of Sex,* the *Introductory Lectures on Psychoanalysis,* and *Totem and Taboo.* Although Seligman had encouraged him to study dreams, it was primarily the libido theory that engaged Malinowski, and like Rivers, he was critical of Freud's narrowly sexual focus: "a theory of sexuality must be based on [a] sound view of instinct," which must also include other biologically based needs besides sex—notably the nutritional. Even so, Malinowski felt that Freud "embraced an enormous field" and that his contribution was "most valuable." His early reading of *Totem and Taboo* evoked little of the criticism he was later to develop—leading him merely to suggest that Freud's argument did not necessarily entail his assumption of a "mass psyche," and that he did not "sufficiently lay stress on the dynamic value of social atmosphere in belief."[98]

Late in 1923, Malinowski stepped forward as a prospective Freudian revisionist, seeking both to apply psychoanalytic concepts to anthropology and to modify them in the light of ethnographic evidence. His first substantive contribution was a straightforward ethnographic account of beliefs about procreation and parenthood in the matrilineal Trobriands; broader thoretical implications were only hinted in the opening and closing paragraphs, in which he affirmed his conviction that "ignorance of paternity" was "an original feature of primitive psychology," which must be kept in mind "in all speculations about the Origins of Marriage and the Evolution of Sexual Customs."[99]

The significance of this data for Freudian theory was suggested in a letter on "Psycho-Analysis and Anthropology" the following month in *Nature:* when "the original constitution of the human family" was examined, "not in any hypothetical primitive form, but as we find it in actual observation among present day savages," we find not the "tyrannical and ferocious father" of *Totem and Taboo,* but a situation in which "the two elements decisive for psycho-analysis, the repressive authority and the severing taboo, are 'displaced,' distributed in a manner different from that in the patriarchal family." This being so, and assuming that "Freud's general theory" was correct, "the repressed wish formation" ought to and did "receive a shape different from the Oedipus complex."[100]

That possibility was pursued more systematically in a second article in *Psyche,* published in April 1924, at a point when the relations of psychoanalysis and anthropology had become a matter for discussion before the Royal Anthropological Institute—to the considerable irritation of the aging evolutionary folklorist, Edward Clodd. Clearly writing as an outsider, Malinowski glossed the notion of "complex"—as Rivers had done—in the idiom of Alexander Shand's "sentiment." But his essay was intended to contribute to psychoanalytic theory, which, by emphasizing the "libidinous nature" of primitive man, had "given the right foundation to primitive psychology." Distinguishing between the psychological, biological, and sociological aspects of Freudian thought, Malinowski largely accepted the first, was somewhat critical of the second, and offered his own contribution to the last, which he felt had only begun to be touched in J. C. Flugel's *Psycho-Analytic Study of the Family*. Malinowski's goal was no less than to confront "the main task of psycho-analytic theory," by showing how the formation of the "nuclear complex" would vary with the varying "constitution of the family" in different forms of society and in the social strata of our own. Along the way, he would offer a more precise scheme of ontogenetic stages, to augment Freud's theory of "the stratification of the human mind, and its rough correspondence to the stages in the child's development."[101]

Malinowski went on to trace the formation of the nuclear complex in "the two most radically different types of family known to empirical observation"—the "matrilineal family" of the Trobriands and the "patriarchal family of modern civilisation" (with occasional asides on the peasantry and working classes)—through the stages of infancy, babyhood, childhood, and adolescence. Accepting in general the psychoanalytic view of the development of the Oedipus complex in European society—where "the institution of father-right crosses and represses a number of natural impulses"—he drew a contrast with "the social arrangements of Trobriand matriliny," which were "in almost complete harmony with the biological course of development." The Trobrianders, however, paid a cultural evolutionary price: whereas the latency period of the European upper classes represented "the triumph of other cultural and social interests over sexuality," the harmonious continuity of sexual development among "savages" was "destructive culturally," since genital sexuality, early and easily established, was "never to be dislodged again." But if there was no friction between the father and the son, and the child's "infantile craving" for the mother gradually spent itself "in a natural spontaneous manner," the Trobriander nevertheless eventually "submitted to a system of repressions and taboos" in the form of the matriarchal authority of his mother's brother and the strongly asserted prohibition of all contact with his sister—the persons who became, respectively, the objects of a young man's homicidal and incestuous wishes. Describing his hitherto unsuspected alternative "type of nuclear complex" as "a notable confirmation of the main tenet of Freudian psychology," Malinowski proposed a study of "every type of civilization, to establish the special complex which pertains to it." Having argued "the sociological nature of family influences," Malinowski turned six months later to the social consequences of variability in the nuclear complex. After briefly contrasting the "hearty" Trobrianders with the "community of neurasthenics" he had found in the sexually repressive culture of the Amphletts, he examined Trobriand dreams, folklore, and mythology to show that all these cultural phenomena reflected the matriarchal complex.[102]

As it happened, Malinowski's Freudian revisionism was proposed at the moment when a major rift was developing in the psychoanalytic movement. In *The Trauma of Birth* (a book which Malinowski cited), his Vienna psychoanalytic contact Otto Rank had recently suggested that mental conflicts had more to do with the mother than the father—an argument for which Malinowski could be seen as providing ethnographic validation. It was in this context that Freud's lord lieutenant in England, Ernest Jones, took up the problem of "mother-right and the sexual ignorance of savages." Acknowledging Malinowski as a fieldworker of "remarkable acumen," he suggested that the Trobriand denial of paternal procreation was in fact "tendentious," arguing that the matrilineal system with its avunculate complex arose "as a mode of defense against the primordial Oedipus tendencies." Far from forcing a revision in Freudian theory, Malinowski's apparent ethnographic exception merely proved the universal oedipal rule.[103]

With his revisionism unrequited, Malinowski became more critical of Freud. Although he had planned an ambitious volume evaluating Freudian theory from an anthropological perspective, when he got around to publishing *Sex and Repression in Savage Society* in 1927, it consisted only of two of the earlier articles, followed by two new ones responding to Jones, in which he now offered a critique of *Totem and Taboo*. The first carried somewhat further a range of issues A. L. Kroeber (whom Malinowski had met in the United States in 1926) had first raised in 1920. Arguing that Freud's origination of culture in the aftermath of primal parricide in fact assumed the prior existence of culture—since the guilt feelings that led to the imposition of totemic sacrifice must themselves have been "imposed upon man by culture"—Malinowski insisted that the transition from the state of nature to culture was not accomplished in a leap, but was the product of "many infinitely small steps integrated over enormous stretches of time." In contrast to Freud, Malinowski found his beginning not in the deed, but in the need, insisting that an understanding of culture must be founded on an understanding of the role of instinct in man.[104]

Malinowski's readings in the early 1920s had included much on the problem of instinct, and in a review of a work by August Forel on the social world of ants and men, he had argued the "plasticity" of human instincts in the "secondary milieu" of culture. His developmental approach to the problem, however, was in a broad sense Freudian; if he owed the primacy of the nuclear family to Westermarck, it was his reading of Freud that made critically problematic what Westermarck took for granted: the repression of incestuous impulses. That problem was central to the genesis of culture, in its socially constraining, as opposed to its individually creative, aspect. Drawing evidence from Havelock Ellis on sexual periodicity in animals and humans, Malinowski now saw sexuality as "the original sin of man." The "most difficult to control" of all human instincts, its channelling was essential to "the establishment of the first foundations of culture"—since without the incest taboo, "at maturity we would witness the breaking up of the family, hence complete social chaos and an impossibility of continuing cultural tradition."[105]

The repression of incestuous sexuality, however, was only one of two problems of cultural continuity; the other "main peril of humanity," the "revolt against authority," had also to be dealt with if the "new type of human bond" for which there was "no prototype in the animal kingdom" was to be maintained. Although Malinowski insisted on the instinctual basis of paternal love (just as he insisted on the cultural conditioning of maternal love), he saw its transformation into a "principle of force, of distance, of pursuit of ambition and authority" as culturally essential. Despite his insistence that "male authority is not necessarily that of the father," he tended to see the supersession of male tenderness by male coercion in phylogenetic evolutionary as well as ontogenetic familial terms. Mother-right, which embodied the two principles in two different men, was more useful "at a level of human organization where kinship plays a paramount sociological part"; but as "culture advances" father-right "naturally becomes dominant."[106]

Rebuffed by the most loyal guardian of Freudian orthodoxy, Malinowski had drawn away from psychoanalysis; he expended considerable effort in *Sex and Repression* on a more systematic recasting of the ideas of complex and repression into the conceptual idiom of Shandian sentiment. Malinowski's book was more often to be remembered as the book which "disproved" the universality of the Oedipus complex than as a contribution to a "neo-Freudian" psychoanalytical anthropology. But if the psychoanalytic moment in British anthropology was rather brief, and Freudianism faded quickly from the forefront of functionalist theory, themes developed in *Sex and Repression* were still to be manifest in the posthumous systematization of Malinowski's viewpoint in *A Scientific Theory of Culture*—although reproduction was there only one of eight "basic needs," and the psychological assumptions had been recast in terms of the stimulus/response psychology of the behavioralists at Yale, where Malinowski spent the last months of his life.[107*]

To speak of "functionalist theory" in the middle 1920s verges, however, on anachronistic misnomer. Although there are among Malinowski's manuscripts various short experiments in theory which anticipate later formulations, his published writings in this period are better regarded as a series of opportunistic theoretical forays, in which he brought to bear his Trobriand ethnographic material on issues currently mooted within or outside of anthropology. And while the shibboleths against which he deployed these materials usually had an evolutionary character, his own arguments were grounded also in evolutionary assumptions from which "functionalism" only gradually separated itself. These early functionalist forays may be divided into two (overlapping) groups: one having to do with human knowledge, broadly conceived, in which the major intellectual reference points were Frazer, Lévy-Bruhl, and, more distantly, Mach; the other, with human sociality, in which the main antagonists were Rivers and Durkheim. Despite Malinowski's theoretical opportunism, there were common themes—emanations of his pragmatic philosophic predisposition, his evolutionary heritage, his fieldwork experience, and his readings in the early 1920s—which pointed toward a more systematic "functionalist" formulation.[108]

The first of these forays appeared as an appendix to one of the most influential books of the decade, C. K. Ogden and I. A. Richards' *The Meaning of Meaning*—an early publication in Ogden's *International Library of Psychology, Philosophy, and Scientific Method*, which, like *Psyche*, was one of the spaces in which intellectuals could seek new meanings amidst the wreckage of Victorian verities. Malinowski's involvement may have been mediated by Alan Gardiner, the prominent Egyptologist, who had corresponded with him in the field, encouraging him to collect and pub-

*It is worth noting, however, that Seligman continued to be interested in psychological issues and psychoanalytic theory. His manuscripts in the archives of the Royal Anthropological Institute include boxes of letters and questionnaires describing the dreams of individual Britons, submitted in response to a BBC lecture he gave in 1931 (CSAI); his Huxley Lecture of 1932, in which he referred to the work of Evans-Pritchard, Meyer Fortes, Reo Fortune, Audrey Richards, and others of the rising generation, suggests that, at least as far as Seligman was concerned, the psychoanalytic option was still a live one in the early 1930s.

Bronislaw Malinowski and his wife Elsie Masson Malinowska with their daughters (left to right: Józefa, Wanda, and Helena) near their villa in Oberbozen in the Dolomite Alps, c. 1926. (Photograph by Raymond Firth; courtesy of Helena Wayne Malinowska)

lish "the actual native texts" of his informants and not to present them only in translation, and whom Malinowski had hoped to involve in his humanistic Royal Society. Malinowski now thought it remarkable that Gardiner, Henry Head (in his work on aphasia), Ogden and Richards, and he himself, from different starting points, had since then arrived at "similar Semantic theories based on psychological considerations"—attributing this in his own case to "fundamental difficulties" he had faced in translating Trobriand texts. Offering the notion of "context of situation" as an equivalent to the "sign-situation" of Ogden and Richards, Malinowski suggested that the "Ethnographic view of language proves the principle of Symbolic Relativity": "since the whole world of 'things-to-be-expressed' changes with the level of culture," the meaning of a word "must always be gathered from an analysis of its functions, with reference to the given culture." This ambiguous usage of "culture," in which evolutionary "level" coexisted with an idea of the particularity of a "given culture," is worth noting. When Malinowski spoke of "phatic communion" and the "magical attitude towards words," insisting that language "in primitive communities is primarily a mode of social action rather than a mere reflection of thought," he was echoing not only Marett but the Rivers-Head distinction of the protopathic and the epicritic. Appealing to "modern" (i.e., Freudian) psychology, Darwin on the expression of the emotions, and his recent experience with two children of his own, Malinowski pursued the parallels of child and savage, ontogeny and phylogeny, in order to develop an adaptive evolutionary (and Machian) view of language, in which "the grammatical categories with all their peculiarities, exceptions and refractory insubordination to rule, are the reflection of the makeshift, unsystematic, practical outlook imposed by man's struggle for existence in the widest sense of this word."[109]

When Malinowski a decade later returned more systematically to linguistic issues in the second volume of his long-delayed ethnographic magnum opus, with its "ethnographic theory of language" and its *corpus inscriptionum agriculturae quiriviniensis,* he explicitly rejected, as a "serious error," his earlier opposition of "civilized and scientific to primitive speech." But in the 1920s, he pursued his evolving functionalist agenda into areas of human knowledge and belief that had been Frazer's special evolutionary preserve. This move began with his appreciative review of the abridgment of *The Golden Bough,* which Malinowski glossed in un-Frazerian pragmatic terms as both a manual for fieldwork and a presentation of "primitive man as he really is, not an idle onlooker on the vast and varied spectacle of Nature, evolving by reflection a sort of speculative philosophy as to its meaning and origins, but an eager actor, playing his part for his own benefit, trying to use all the means in his power towards the attainment of his various needs and desires: supply of food, shelter and covering; satisfaction of social ambitions and sexual passions; satisfaction of some aesthetic impulses and of sportive and playful necessities."[110]

Malinowski's full-blown treatment of "Magic, Science, and Religion" appeared in 1925 in a volume originally conceived as "Cambridge Essays on Science and Religion" and sponsored by the Society for the Propagation of the Gospel. Edited by the biochemist Joseph Needham, with contributions by such luminaries as the astronomer Arthur S. Eddington, the book's tone was set by the Vice-Chancellor of Cambridge University, who cited Malinowski's contribution as ethnographic evidence that there need be no "conflict between religion and science," that "their relations were not so much competitive as complementary."[111]

Departing from the more euphonious sequence of his own title, as well as that of Frazer's evolutionary triad (magic, religion, science), Malinowski began by universalizing science. Just as there were "no peoples however primitive" without religion or magic, there were "no savage races lacking either in the scientific attitude or in science, though this lack has frequently been attributed to them." Every primitive community made a distinction between two domains, "the Sacred and the Profane; in other words the domain of Magic and Religion and that of Science." Combatting the notion that primitives were "pre-logical" and "hopelessly immersed in a mystical frame of mind"—a view articulated by Lévy-Bruhl, but shared by unnamed other "anthropologists and philosophers of renown"—Malinowski argued that in relation to certain practical activities (arts, crafts, economic pursuits) every community had "a body of rules and conceptions" derived from experience by "logical inference" and "open to control by experiment and critique by reason." He had found evidence even of a certain "thirst for knowledge" among native antiquarians interested in the details of myth and tradition, native naturalists observing the marine world, and even among native sociologists—"the ideal informant, capable with marvelous accuracy and insight to give the *raison d'être,* the function, and the organization of many a simpler institution in his tribe."[112]

Turning then to the domain of the sacred, Malinowski distinguished between the magical act carried out "as means to an end"—which could "easily be elicited from any native informant"—and the religious ceremony, which was not "a means to an end but an end in itself"—and for which it was "only possible for the sociologist to establish the function." His discussion of religious ceremonial was a recasting of Frazer and Durkheim in the terms of an emerging biopsychological and instrumental functionalism that had been foreshadowed in the "New Humanism" essay he conceived toward the end of his Trobriand fieldwork. The "sociological function" of initiation ceremonies was argued in terms of the "survival value" of a sanctified tradition as a mechanism of social cohesion in primitive societies, where "the complex apparatus of modern science" did not exist "to fix the results of experience in imperishable molds." As a "ritual and dramatic expression of the supreme power and value of tradition" initiation ceremonies served to ensure "continuity in tradition" and the maintenance of "tribal cohesion." Malinowski discussed totemism in terms resonant of Frazer's second theory: the "biological importance of primitive religion in the sacralization of food" and the "desire to control" useful animal and plant species. Mortuary rituals he treated as expressions of the instinct of "self-preservation" channelized to maintain social cohesion: "in short, religion here assures the victory of tradition and culture over the mere negative response of thwarted instinct." Granting that "Robertson Smith, Durkheim, and their school" had made an important contribution even in their "very exaggeration of the sociological aspect of primitive faith," Malinowski insisted on its basis in individual instinctive and emotional need; the role of social cooperation was facilitative, and although "indispensible for its enactment," was essentially "a matter of technique."[113]

In treating magic "among the stone age savages of today," Malinowski was back on the ground of "purely practical acts" for the satisfaction of individual human biopsychological needs. Implicitly rejecting Marett's undifferentiated "magico-religious" realm, he distinguished three types of magic: a "dramatic expression of emotion" (much in the Marettian mode); a Frazerian rite that "imitates its end"; and the direct invocation of the power contained in the spell itself. Although none of them implied "an abstract conception of universal power" such as "mana," they all were based on a "universal psycho-physiological mechanism." Magic was "revealed to man in those passionate experiences which assail him in the impasses of his instinctive life and of his practical pursuits, in those gaps and breaches left in the ever-imperfect wall of culture which he erects between himself and the besetting temptations and dangers of his destiny." Its "fallacious claims" were sustained by the memory of positive cases and the strength of the magician's "outstanding personality." They were also upheld by the power of myth, which was not the product of speculation about origins or contemplation of nature, but a "warrant" for the truth of magic, a "pedigree" of its filiation, a "charter of its claims to validity." Magic was, as Frazer had suggested, a kind of "pseudo-science," governed not by logic but (as Marett might have had it) by desire; its "function" was to "ritualize man's optimism," without which he could not have "advanced to the higher stages of culture." Although Malinowski did not include *Psyche's Task* among the several references to Frazer in his bibliographical note, the resonances nonetheless ring clear.[114]

But if Malinowski thus justified magic in Marettian and Frazerian terms, his final comment on the "cultural function" of science and religion was cast in terms of their "biological value." Influenced as well by Mach, Westermarck, Freud, and Shand, he had done a fair amount of reading in biology in the early 1920s, when biological issues (instinct, sexuality, marriage, reproductivity, depopulation) were at the forefront of his (and general cultural) concern. In contrast to Frazer, what was universal in mankind for Malinowski was not a psychic unity conceived of as a principle of rationality (leading, among savages, paradoxically to unreason); it was rather a biopsychic unity, based in instinct and passion, but expressed in pragmatic, instrumental behavior directed toward adaptive ends.[115]

On the other hand, as the central section of his Cambridge essay suggests, Malinowski was also vitally interested in the forces of social cohesion, seeking a solution to the problem of social order in individually based terms that would avoid the mystical supra-individual entities he saw in Durkheim and theorists of the "group mind" or the "herd." This more sociological line toward functionalism was developed in reviews and lectures, culminating in 1926 in a brief volume, *Crime and Custom in Savage Society*, published in Ogden's *International Library of Psychology*. Aside from Durkheim, Malinowski's theoretical antagonists here included the aging evolutionary folklorist and lawyer Sydney Hartland, whose recent *Primitive Law* marked the culmination of a long career in the shadow of James Frazer. Even more important was Rivers, whose diffusionist literary executors had reconstructed from his surviving lecture notes a book that was to be his last word on *Social Organization*.[116]

Rivers and Hartland were taken by Malinowski as representing the widespread notion that "in primitive societies the individual is completely dominated by the group"—that "automatic acquiescence," "instinctive submission," or a mystical "group sentiment" accounted for "the harmonious working of communal ownership" and ensured "the peaceful character of a communistic system of sexual relations" without any "definite social machinery for the exertion of authority." Questioning this vision of a "Bolshevik paradise," Malinowski used the ownership of a Trobriand canoe as the starting point for what was in effect an extensionist theory of social order, in which individual actors were bound together in chains of reciprocity that were "part and parcel of a whole system of mutualities." The "dual organization" of "Dr. Rivers and his school" resulted neither from "fusion" nor "splitting," but was simply "the integral result of the inner symmetry of all social transactions, of the reciprocity of services, without which no primitive community could exist." Reinforced by "social ambition" and "enlightened self-interest," reciprocity was "the basis of social structure" and of law as "a body of binding obligations"—the "fundamental function" of which was to "hem in and control human instincts and to impose a non-spontaneous compulsory behavior."[117]

Rather than being, however, a single system "in equilibrium," native law was in fact a "composite body of systems" subject to the constant "strain of circumstances." Analyzing the suicide of a boy guilty of a "breach of totemic clan exogamy," Malinowski suggested that there was in fact "a well-established system of evasion"; offering a glancing attack on the "classificatory system of kinship," he suggested that as "kinship recedes," the "stringency" of incest rules was lessened. Similarly, a chief required by the rules of "mother-right" to make his nephew "the legal heir to all his dignities and offices" might be led by an instinctive paternal feeling to favor his sons—which in Omarakana had led to a serious feud and the imprisonment of the nephew of the principal chief. Though "ideas" might emphasize the dogma of "the unity of the clan," "sentiments" did not always follow their lead: "human cultural reality [was] not a consistent logical scheme, but rather a seething mixture of conflicting principles"—a "constant struggle of human passions against the law" and of "legal principles with one another," which could be sorted out only by the careful analysis of material collected by "direct observation" in the field.[118]

Despite its title, and its frequent references to the "primitive," *Crime and Custom in Savage Society* was the least evolutionary of Malinowski's functionalist forays. At the end, he noted that it had "not once been necessary" to resort to "any evolutionary or historical reconstructions." He had simply analyzed certain facts "into simpler elements" and traced "the relations between these elements," correlating "one aspect of culture with another" to "show which is the function fulfilled by either within the scheme of culture." Without excluding "a further investigation" of the "evolutionary level" or "historical antecedents" of such customs, Malinowski claimed a place for a type of investigation in which "the student of Man" could proclaim *"hypotheses non fingo."*[119]

That same year, following in the footsteps of Tylor and Elliot Smith, Malinowski contributed the article on "Anthropology" to the latest edition of the *Encyclopaedia Britannica*. Explicitly limiting himself to the "science of culture," he offered a kind of autobiographical intellectual history of "progress" since "the events of 1910," categorizing briefly a "number of one-sided and incompatible tendencies": the psychological interpretation of culture, diffusionism, sociological theories, theories of primitive mentality. Elliot Smith and Perry were dismissed in a short aside, on the grounds that their use of data was "unsatisfactory" and their argument really belonged to archeology, where it had met with "adverse criticism." In contrast, "the functional analysis of culture" aimed at "understanding the nature of culture rather than at conjectural reconstructions of its evolution or of past historical events." Functionalism was the result of modern fieldwork, which—ruthlessly banishing conjecture, but not theory—demonstrated that "every custom, material object, idea and belief fulfils some vital function" and "represents an indispensible part within a working whole." But it was also the inevitable outcome of evolutionism properly considered—not as a "sequence of forms," but as "the gradual cystallisation of well-defined institutions" and the "better adaptation of [each] institution to its function." Implied in the "best achievements of modern fieldwork (notably of the American anthropologists)," "active in the work of the French school," "predominant among the soundest theories of the comparative school," functionalism was, however, to be found systematically only in the fieldwork and theory of four anthropologists, listed modestly in alphabetical order: W. Hoernlé, B. Malinowski, A. Radcliffe-Brown, and R. Thurnwald. The bulk of the article, drawn from his own writings, was an "analysis of concrete problems"—marriage and the family, economic organization, the supernatural, and primitive knowledge—from a "functional point of view." Finally, there was a brief summary, in which he suggested that "to explain any item of culture" meant "to indicate its functional place within an institution" which in turn had "to be placed within the system of culture"—and in which he looked forward to resituating culture in the broader scheme of "organic evolution."[120]

If his sociological analysis was still grounded in a biopsychological and individualistic instrumentalism, it is clear in retrospect that at this point Malinowski's "functionalism" had broken out of the framework of diachronic assumption. In 1932 he explicitly offered "an evolutionist's recantation," insisting that (though he did "still believe in evolution") any attempt to reconstruct the past would be possible only on the basis of a systematic knowledge of the "laws and regularities" of process in the present.[121]

The previous year, in the article on "Culture" in the American *Encyclopaedia of the Social Sciences,* Malinowski offered a lengthier and more systematic statement of the functionalist viewpoint. Here the concept of "institutions" was elaborated in a somewhat materialist mode. Arguing that culture was "a reality *sui generis,*" and insisting that evolutionary inquiry "must be preceded by a functional analysis of culture," Malinowski divided its "well organized unity" into two "fundamental aspects": a "body of artifacts and a system of customs." Artifacts (of which he himself had collected more than two thousand) were "integral parts" of "organized systems of human activities called institutions" (e.g., gardening), each "built up around the satisfaction of a deep human need." But although constructed on a "material substratum," the "cultural mode of satisfaction of the biological needs of the human organism created new conditions" by imposing "derived" or "instrumental imperatives." These "cultural needs"—which must be "fulfilled if the community is to survive and its culture to continue"—were independent of the "conscious motivation" of individuals (but not beyond the ken of the functionalist anthropologist). They were satisfied by custom, "a standardized mode of behavior traditionally enjoined on the members of a community"; in every human culture, it was tradition itself which somehow "chose" from a "number of possible ways of behavior," fixing "a special type" and endowing it "with a hallmark of social value." In this context, the bulk of the essay (drawing somewhat redundantly on his functionalist forays of the 1920s) was devoted to the specific instrumental imperatives that were "part of the universal scheme which underlies all concrete cultures": procreation, economic organization, law and education, magic and religion, knowledge and art. At the end—after at least a dozen quotable definitions—culture was once more defined as "an intrumental reality," the "cumulative creation of man," which "deeply" modified "human innate endowment," making man "into something essentially different from a mere animal organism." From this point there was a direct rhetorical/ theoretical line to the charts, tables, and terminology of the posthumous *Scientific Theory of Culture*.[122]

The Emergence of the Functional School of Anthropology

Working in the shadow of Frazer and Rivers, affiliating himself with the "old" anthropology in the race against the school of Perry and Elliot Smith, Malinowski by the later 1920s had claimed for himself the laurels of the "new." In 1932, in a characteristic moment of self-mockery, he marked his *Britannica* article of 1926 as the moment when "the magnificent title of the Functional School of Anthropology" was "bestowed by myself, in a way on myself, and to a large extent out of my own sense of irresponsibility." "Fully aware" that he "was speaking of a New Movement, which hardly existed," he had made himself "into the captain, the general staff, and the body of privates of an army that was not yet there." He was, however, constantly seeking recruits and allies, both within and outside anthropology. Writing to Brenda Seligman the same year, he asked if, when he issued "some new Functional Manifesto," he might include her name among "the active and ruthless adherents of the Functional Method"—which he thought of not as a "rigid school" but a "live movement."[123]

From the time he had conceived of his "revolution in social anthropology" and the Society of Modern Humanism in the Trobriands, Malinowski obviously felt that the field on which his campaign must be waged was wider than that encompassed by the still marginally institutionalized discipline of anthropology—and that the forces of the discipline must not themselves be dispersed over too wide a realm. Anthropology must appeal to a broader public, both intellectually and in terms of its practical social or administrative relevance; by the same token, it should itself be intellectually focussed on themes and problems that could demonstrate such relevance, and gradually discard "the purely Antiquarian associations with Archaeology and even pre-history."[124]

It was a campaign which, for a time, was extremely successful. Today, after decades of criticism of functionialism as either platitude or tautology, obvious or dubious, one hesitates to attribute this success to the power of Malinowski's often rhetorically overinflated theoretical writings—which in 1957 his last protégé pronounced "not merely dated, but dead." But it might be argued that Malinowski, who himself often spoke of functionalism as "common sense," was not in any systematic way a theorist. Theory was what made fieldwork function; fieldwork was what made theory functional. Occasionally, although in a different register, he seemed to echo Frazer's self-deprecating thought that it was the fieldwork that really mattered. But whether proclaimed in theoretical manifesto or proffered at a level that would later be called "clinical" theory, "functionalism" had a resonantly innovative, clarifying quality, at once liberating and reassuring, in the intellectual and ideological context of the 1920s—not only for aspiring anthropologists, but for others beyond the discipline who hoped that the problems of the postwar, post-Victorian, world might somehow be amenable to a new type of human scientific understanding.[125]

Like Tylor and Frazer, although within a more restricted temporal and geographical range, Malinowski still sought answers to the "brave, 'big' questions." Concerned with generically human problems (work, reproduction, marriage, belief) and generically human motives (hunger, passion, vanity, fear), he offered a vision of the other and the self in terms of the "essentially human." If Tylor, in the period of high Victorian optimism, had placed savagery and civilization on a single upward ladder of progress, the intervening years had destabilized that gradual evolutionary sequence, giving new meaning to the psychic unity of mankind. If for Frazer the ladder still stood, there were moments when it seemed very shaky indeed—moments when, fearful of "the volcano underfoot," he conveyed a sense that savagery lay very close beneath the surface of modern civilization. Writing after the volcano had exploded, Malinowski pushed the ladder aside, virtually collapsing the distance between the two states. Reducing "the exotic to the familiar" (while continuing to rely on the appeal of its exoticism), he found the "universally human" among Trobriand savages, not as rationality gone astray, but in minds that were on the whole as pragmatically rational as those of civilized men. And he found it in a culture whose center had not ceased to hold. To study such a group by methods that proclaimed themselves empirical and practical and "functional," in an era when that term had a cultural resonance far outside of anthropology, from biology and psychology to architecture and furniture design; to do so by a method and a theory which professed to cast light on every aspect of human cultural activity, in a potentially integrative way; to do so within a restricted temporal range, at a moment when the past had discredited itself; to do so in a way that shook up traditional assumptions, but left foundations largely intact, which had an edge of radicalism but was in many ways profoundly conservative—professing, among other things, to offer a more humane and economic basis for an empire that had just attained its apogee—all of this must have made functionalism very attractive indeed.[126]

Once he had established a position at the School of Economics, Malinowski moved more and more into the public realm, debating diffusionists in a more pointed way than his cautious early comments, urging the value of a "practical anthropology" in colonial administration, speaking as an authority on problems of marriage and the family, working closely with the British Social Hygiene Council—always proclaiming the virtues of the "functional" approach. His extradisciplinary ties were in fact international: in 1926 he made a whirlwind tour of American universities, including a "star" performance before an elite group of American academics at the Hanover Conference of the Social Science Research Council; in 1928, he was invited by an American editor to join with such other English luminaries as Havelock Ellis and Bertrand Russell in "spreading light and learning in the field of sex and morals among our educated but uncivilized Americans."[127]

Closer to home, and within anthropology, Malinowski's "functionalism" had begun to attract students to his seminars at the School of Economics. The alternatives in academic anthropology were at this point quite limited. Prewar initiatives had given anthropology a makeshift and underfunded foothold at Oxford and Cambridge, but there was little dynamism to be found at either place in the postwar decade. In a conservative and "socially arrogant" institutional culture "quite unaffected at heart" by the reforms of the Universities Act of 1923, anthropology managed only a precariously marginal existence. Patchwork staffs of three or four persons, most with multiple responsibilites, had somehow to cover all its fields (physical, prehistoric, technological, social, ethnological), while simultaneously curating museums, or demonstrating anatomy, or giving cohorts of colonial probationers a smattering of general anthropological and regional ethnographic knowledge. At Cambridge, Rivers' student William Armstrong, who shared his mentor's diffusionist inclinations, was chosen in 1922 (unanimously, from a field of five that included Malinowski) to carry on instruction in "social anthropology." But when it came to replacing Haddon in 1926, the readership in ethnology went to T. C. Hodson, an anthropological mediocrity whose years in the Indian Civil Service made him a likely mentor for colonial probationers, but whose selection seems to have been motivated by Haddon's desire (over some opposition) to keep the position out of the hands of the extreme diffusionists. When the chair in archeology was filled the following year, Haddon failed in an attempt to push a much more promising (and more acceptably diffusionist) candidate, A. M. Hocart. At Oxford, there were Henry Balfour, who had been curating the Pitt Rivers Museum for decades, and Leonard Buxton, Lecturer in Physical Anthropology after 1922, whose *Primitive Labour* was one of the few books in which Malinowski—who was politic even with Perry—could find nothing to praise. Marett was by his own account preoccupied with Exeter

College, of which he became Rector in 1928, and the promise of his early essays was dissipated in volumes harking back to evolutionism. While he continued to attract students to social anthropology, the best of them, Evans-Pritchard, went off to London, as did the best at Cambridge—including Gregory Bateson, Reo Fortune, Audrey Richards, and Camilla Wedgwood—if not as regular students, then as visitors to Malinowski's seminar.[128]

Viewed as paradigmatic alternatives, the options were equally uncompelling. Sociocultural evolutionism had by this time been around for sixty years in much the same by now rather tired form, and was largely in the hands of an older generation, many of them outside the academy—and quite a few literally the "grey-beards" against whom postwar youth were rebelling. Diffusionism, despite a certain vogue, seems to have been less attractive to younger scholars. Although the seminar at University College for a time rivalled Malinowski's, the average age in 1930 of interwar Ph.D.s at University College was fifteen years more than at the School of Economics. While the overshadowing of University College was due in part to the fact that Malinowski became the favorite of the Rockefeller Foundation and was able to dispense substantial fellowship support for field research, the attraction of his program embodied *in propria persona* was surely a major factor. A man of great intellectual dynamism and personal charisma, he made himself the exemplar of a new paradigm which, in rejecting the study of the past, broke radically with the past of anthropology. Confronted now directly in the present, rather than through the medium of the printed page, the still-exotic variety of humankind offered the prospect of a new knowledge with practical implications for its future.[129]

The excitement of that early Malinowskian moment is clearly evident in the recollections of his students. Widely read, in a sometimes casual but confidently knowledgeable fashion, Malinowski could draw on a broad range of social theory, in several different languages, outside the conventional anthropological literature—and unlike the theorists whom he sometimes used as "strawmen," he had molded theory in the "living reality of native life." Given to calling up his own Roman Catholic Polish past, among nearly "savage" peasants, as a comparative cultural reference point, he seemed not only international, but even himself somewhat exotically "other." His functionalist explications of "the usefulness of the apparently senseless antics" of "savages" seemed "brilliantly new," offering the "fascination of a game for which the *chose donnée* was the necessity of the custom or institution under discussion to the individual, the group, or the society": "we began actually to visualize ourselves in the field." His seminars were legendary: "with a suave question, a caustic word, or a flash of wit, he would expose a fallacy, probe for further explanation . . . and after inviting opinion from all sides, he would draw together the threads in a masterly way, lifting the whole discussion to a higher theoretical level." Emotionally sensitive, unafraid of self-revelation, willing to resolve fierce arguments in mutual self-analysis, he drew students into the orbit of his work, enveloping them in the aura of his personality. Sometimes active research assistants on his books (which they took down in dictation), they were occasionally invited to Oberbozen, where they talked intensely about Trobriand mythology, or the latest thesis chapter, or some general problem of social theory, on walks through Alpine meadows, or over the supper table, or on the balcony, where Malinowski reclined, "often nude in the sun, with a green eyeshade, scrubbing himself with a solution of iodized salt." Back in London, there was an apartment in Bloomsbury that circulated among his students, to which Malinowski would lead his troop for evenings of wine and intellectual conviviality. For they were, after all, a troop: part of the excitement was the continuing controversy, in refectories and pubs as well as journals and on public platforms, with the members of that other, diffusionist, seminar, at University College.[130]

Not all who came in contact were (or remained) enthralled by all this intellectual excitement and disciplinary controversy. One with whom it did not sit so well was the man who had guided Malinowski's entry into British anthropology—but who was not about to be recruited into Malinowski's army. Although in 1927 Malinowski had been made Professor of Anthropology to work in consultation with Seligman as Professor of Ethnology, when Seligman went on leave in 1930 he managed the appointment of the historian of medicine Charles Singer rather than Malinowski as interim chairman of the Board of Studies in Anthropology of London University. When the following year Seligman without consultation appointed a sabbatical replacement for Malinowski, his protégé let him know that he felt deprived of the right to have lectures given "in the spirit" of his own approach. In response, Seligman avowed his own adherence to the anthropology Malinowski was attacking as "antiquarian"—as well as to "Victorian manners"—saying that he was "appalled" by the tone of "semi-popular propaganda work" Malinowski had written "in the manner of the more strident kind of journalist." To Malinowski, however, it seemed that Seligman was confusing "decided criticisms of theories and sarcasms directed against erroneous points of view with personal attacks"—apparently regarding him as he, Malinowski, saw Elliot Smith: "a perambulating compound of megalomania, monomania and self-seeking"—when in fact the functional method was really only a theoretical justification of "the purely objective analytical interests" that had guided both Seligman's fieldwork and his own.[131]

At the time, the matter was smoothed over by a "gentleman's agree-

E. E. Evans-Pritchard with a group of young Azande, c. 1928. (Courtesy of the Royal Anthropological Institute)

ment" regarding the advising of students. If they were interested in social anthropology they should work with Malinowski; if they were interested in fieldwork method or regional anthropology or prehistory or physical anthropology they should work with Seligman—a triage Malinowski documented with the case of Evans-Pritchard, whom he had sent to

Seligman because Evans-Pritchard preferred to go directly into the field without (like Audrey Richards) writing a theoretical thesis beforehand. Within a year, however, the gentleman's agreement had broken down, over whether Malinowski's students must attend lectures on technology, prehistory, and the races of man. Seligman felt that a good student should spend two or three hours a week on parts of anthropology other than social anthropology, and that a doctorate in anthropology should not be given if in fact a person was "only studying one branch." Although Seligman took the matter to the Board of Studies in Anthropology for the University of London, in the end the dispute seems to have been resolved by his own poor health, which led to his retirement in 1934.[132]

By that time, however, fissures had also begun to develop in the "functionalist movement" itself. As this happened, some of the limitations—and the overreachings—of Malinowskian functionalism were brought to the forefront of intradisciplinary debate, and an increasingly professionalized cadre of academic anthropologists, including some of Malinowski's own students, began to turn toward a social anthropology more narrowly defined.

SEVEN

From Cultural Psychology to Social Structure

Radcliffe-Brown and the Delimitation of Social Anthropology

To carry on fieldwork in the Malinowskian mode is one thing; fully to actualize the ethnographic authority it validates is quite another. Between the lived fullness of ethnographic experience and the fieldnotes in which it is embodied lies a process of selection and compression that leaves few traces, save in the gradually fading memory of the ethnographer. Between a body of fieldnotes and the ethnography eventually produced from it lie processes of interpretation and representation whose principles may be reduced by theory but nevertheless remain unsystematically various. And between an ethnographer's total corpus of fieldnotes and his or her total published ethnographic ouevre, there is often the relation of iceberg to tip. Malinowski was acutely conscious of such disjunctions. Justifying to Seligman in 1919 his need for further write-up time, he pointed out that Rivers had taken four years to produce *The History of Melanesian Society;* his own material was much bulkier and his "theoretical ambitions quite as far reaching." Although the 1920s saw the publication of his monographs on Trobriand exchange and sexuality, in 1931 Malinowski remarked that "large portions" of his data were "still in my notes as raw material"; a full descriptive account would take four or five substantial books. In the event, only the two-volume work *Coral Gardens and Their Magic* was to be realized.[1]

Nor were these unrealized ethnographic volumes the only books left unwritten in Malinowski's anthropological career. There was also a publicly promised but never completed work on the psychology of kinship. First thought of as part of *The Sexual Life of Savages,* it survives only as a series of outlines, notes, and chapter drafts in his manuscripts. The earliest outline of "the theoretical part of [the] sex book as conceived in 1922–23 in Oberbozen" clearly reflects Malinowski's psychoanalytic preoccupation at the time; in later outlines, he seems concerned rather with "the puzzles of the classificatory system." But whereas he had seen himself as contributing constructively to a psychoanalytically oriented theory of kinship, his attitude to the systematic study of kinship terminology in the tradition of Morgan had been unsympathetic since the period of his Australian family research.[2]

For Malinowski, Morgan's work was vitiated by the assumption that kinship terms expressed an assumed relationship of biological consanguinity based on sexual intercourse. Following Westermarck on the universality of the nuclear family, Malinowski saw kinship as based ultimately on the relationship of parent and child, whether or not that relationship was conceived of in biological terms. Seeking its definition in the "central collective ideas" of different groups, Malinowski had insisted that the "essence of kinship" was that "in one way or another" it affirmed "a very close, intimate tie between offspring and parents." What varied, given an ignorance of physiological paternity, was whether the relationship of father and child was to be understood in biological or social psychological terms. In this context, Malinowski had been also somewhat critical of Rivers' genealogical method, insofar as it "defined the unknown by what is still more indeterminate."[3]

When he returned to the problem of kinship in the 1920s, in the aftermath of Rivers' death, Malinowski clearly thought that psychoanalysis, grounded as it was in the nuclear family, would provide a more adequate basis for a generalized anthropological approach to kinship. When he then moved away from psychoanalysis, he tried to deal with "the puzzles of the classificatory system"—largely, however, by way of critique. His notes, like his published writings, are full of derogatory references to "kinship algebra," the "pseudo-mathematics of kinship" and the "classificatory obsession." But as the latter phrase suggests, this was the direction kinship studies were going in the 1920s. Far from controlling the course of the kinship discussion, Malinowski became increasingly isolated from it, as it moved along lines he found fundamentally uncongenial. Whether or not one accepts the view that he could not complete his kinship book because "his theoretical premises ran counter to those on which any analytical study of a kinship system or kinship in general must be based," the fact that it remained unwritten is historically significant. Kinship had been from the beginning a major preoccupation of his scholarship, and his public reputation was largely based on his role as anthropological spokesman on matters of sex, marriage, and kinship. And yet what should have been his summa on this subject lay incomplete throughout the last decade of his life.[4]

Malinowski's was not, however, the only book in the history of British anthropology that was, significantly, left unfinished. Aside from what was to have been Tylor's magnum opus, there was also one by the man who from Malinowski's point of view had helped to lead the study of kinship astray. Among William Rivers' manuscripts is a book that his literary executors left to gather dust—though they managed the posthumous publication of four others. Its subject matter was the social organization of the people of Ambrym, an island in the New Hebrides which, according to Rivers' historical reconstructions, illustrated the very earliest stage of kinship in Melanesia, and whose culture approximated that of the original population of the region, before the arrival of the kava people. Later study by several of his students was to suggest the presence there of dual matrilineal moeities and a marriage class system of a new type, with six sections rather than the two-, four-, and eight-section systems found on the Australian continent. To have discovered this would have been a critical piece of "puzzle solving" within the kinship paradigm Rivers had developed, and yet he remained unaware of its existence: preoccupied by patrilineal local clans, he treated evidences of matrilineal kinship as "survivals," and failed to see the matrilineal dual division, despite the fact that he had originally anticipated finding one.[5]

Close analysis of his surviving text has suggested two reasons for this failure: the inadequacy of Rivers' field data, and his preoccupation with anomalous marriage forms in a diffusionist historical context. His key data had been collected, using the genealogical method, from a single native of Ambrym, William Temar, whom Rivers encountered briefly on the island of Tangoa in 1914; as it later turned out, other Ambrym people did not agree with Temar's version of things. But when Rivers was later informed of this fact by one of his correspondents in Melanesia, he did not reject Temar's account, apparently because it fitted quite well with his gerontocratic theory of anomalous marriage forms. And although he eventually did abandon this particular marriage anomaly as far as Ambrym was concerned, he was never able to cope adequately with the Ambrym system and in the unpublished manuscript retreated to a "dull particularism."[6]

The solution to the Ambrym puzzle was to emerge in the work of a series of young Cambridge anthropologists, heirs of Rivers, whose claims to his social anthropological estate were in one way or another forestalled by circumstance. First in the sequence was John Layard, who like Malinowski took advantage of the British Association meetings in Australia to travel to the antipodes for fieldwork in 1914, and who went with Rivers to Atchin, an island which (like Ambrym) lay off the coast of Malekula in the New Hebrides. Abandoned there by Rivers, who sailed off on the tour in which he met William Temar, Layard did fieldwork on Atchin for a year, entering into native life in an even more participatory way than Malinowski—on one occasion joining in a dance clad only in a penis sheath. Returning from "my paradise" to the war-torn "civilization" of Europe, Layard experienced extreme culture shock, and for a brief period was in therapy with Rivers, until the "transference" failed because Rivers could not accept "the homosexual content of our relationship." It was more than twenty years before Layard, by then a Jungian outsider from the mainstream of British anthropology, was able to complete his work on *The Stone Men of Malekula*.[7]

After Layard came William Armstrong, who in 1919 did the fieldwork Malinowski had been urged to do on Rossel Island, and who for four years took Rivers' place as lecturer on social organization at Cambridge, before his career as academic anthropologist was subverted by the appointment of Hodson to Haddon's readership in ethnology. As an appendix to his *Rossel Island* ethnography, Armstrong published a three-stage evolutionary theory of the classificatory system, in which "open-class systems" could develop into either "closed class systems" or "classificatory systems" without classes—on the basis of which he postulated "the former existence of a class system in Melanesia."[8]

Next on the road to the solution of the Ambrym puzzle was T. T. Barnard, an Oxford graduate in zoology who was recruited into anthropology by Rivers and, after a year's training, was sent off to the New Hebrides in 1922 to fill gaps left by Rivers in his 1914 tour. Upon his return, Barnard was given access by Elliot Smith to Rivers' unpublished fieldnotes, which he used for a thesis on "The Regulation of Marriage in the New Hebrides." In it was a chapter on Ambrym, where Barnard himself had collected genealogies from five informants. While in the field, Barnard had hypothesized the prior existence of an eight-class system of the Arunta type; but after obtaining access to Rivers' material—which he described as "a classic example of an interrogator with firm preconceived ideas asking the wrong questions and misinterpreting the right answers when he got them"—he concluded, somewhat tentatively, that there might have been a six-class system. Barnard's thesis, however, was never published, and after eight years as Radcliffe-Brown's successor at Cape Town, he dropped out of anthropology.[9]

The full solution to the Ambrym puzzle was the contribution of the most brilliant of Rivers' aborted heirs, Bernard Deacon—one of that small group of ethnographers who by their actual martyrdom affirm the romantic image of the anthropologist as hero. Born and reared in prerevolutionary Russia, where his father worked for a shipping firm, Deacon was sidetracked from a career in the foreign service by Haddon, who persuaded him to read for the Anthropology Tripos. Deacon read Rivers, was taught by Armstrong, and had access to Barnard's thesis; he also wrote a paper offering three hypotheses for the evolution of Australian class systems, one of which proposed an intermediate step of "partial fissure" by which a four-class system might have developed into one of eight. Late in 1925, he was off to Malekula—by his own later account, in order to "have a go at Ambrym, as a test-case" or "crucial experiment."[10]

While the degree of his foreknowledge has been disputed, there is no question that Deacon, a "disciple" of the "earlier" Rivers, saw himself in a somewhat critical relationship to the "later." Six months into his field-work, he complained to Margaret Gardiner (the daughter of the Egyptologist), with whom he had fallen in love at Cambridge, that though he had been "brought up" there on "Rivers' theory," he now found it "a hindrance": "it clogs me." While he did not "share Malinowski's scorn for the historical people," he was interested in creating a "cyclopaedia of distributions" as a "check" on "theories like Perry & Smith's, which slur over gaps & by selecting here and there, distort the actual complexity." In December of 1926, Deacon reported that he had found in Ambrym "a class system of marriage of the type of those among Central Australian aborigines." It was in fact the six-class bilateral system that had eluded Rivers and which Barnard had only hypothesized.[11]

Deacon sent an account of his discovery off to Radcliffe-Brown, who had just taken up the newly established chair of anthropology in Sydney, and to Armstrong and Haddon in Cambridge; Haddon, in consultation with Radcliffe-Brown, arranged its publication in the *Journal of the Royal Anthropological Institute.* Rivers, Deacon argued, had been misled by his misunderstanding of John Pantutun's remark that the men of Pentecost "marry their granddaughters," which had been the stimulus to his interpretation of anomalous marriages in the region. Rivers had been the victim of an artifact of the classificatory system: the fact that mother's brother's children's children were classed as own grandchildren, so that the actual marriage being referred to was only one generation apart, not two. This suggested to Deacon the possibility "of derivation from some system of matrimonial classes within the moieties," which he found in the "remarkably lucid exposition of the [six] class system by the natives themselves," using stones and sticks arranged upon the ground. Descent was "really both patrilineal and matrilineal equally," a fact which Deacon was still inclined to interpret in diffusionist terms as the result of immigration by a patrilineal group. But he insisted nonetheless that Rivers' theory of Melanesian gerontocracy would "have to be modified"—specifically insofar as Rivers had stated that it was "'impossible to derive the peculiar Melanesian marriages directly from the matrimonial classes of Australia.'"[12]

By the time his paper was published, Deacon was dead of black-water fever contracted while he was waiting for the steamer that would have taken him back to Sydney. The six-class system was received in the anthropological community as a discovery of great importance, and with the demise of the discoverer, anthropologists of various persuasions sought to control its interpretation. John Layard stepped forward as prospective editor of Deacon's manuscript materials, but he was by this time thought to be "working in conjunction with Elliot Smith and Perry"; at the suggestion of Radcliffe-Brown, Haddon gave the job instead to his own student, Camilla Wedgwood. Brenda Seligman—a moderate diffusionist who in the years immediately after Rivers' death was the leading authority on classificatory kinship—complemented Deacon's published essay with a lengthy paper in which she argued that "those social groups known as 'marriage classes' have come about by the decidedly inconvenient method of tracing descent on the bilateral principle." Although she still believed that the Ambrym system itself was the "result of outside influence," she thought that Malinowski's work had shown that matrilineal and patrilineal influences deriving from the nuclear family could "be found in any culture" without calling upon foreign influences to account for ties between father and son.[13]

Malinowski himself, however, contributed nothing to the discussion of Deacon's discovery. As far as he was concerned, Deacon was simply one more participant in the "recent kinship enthusiasm" which, manifesting itself in a "spuriously scientific and stilted mathematization," had led to "the impasse on kinship." That impasse would be broken only when other anthropologists joined him in putting aside "kinship algebra" for "full-blooded sociological research" based on an "extensionist" study working out from the "initial situation" of the nuclear family.[14]

Had Deacon lived to take the boat to Sydney, he would have assumed a position as lecturer under Radcliffe-Brown, to whom he had sent copies of his notes from the field, and who greeted the six-section system as "one of the most important discoveries that has been made in Melanesia"—confirming, he believed, the position he had taken in a private debate with Rivers. In its published version, Deacon's essay was followed by another of the same title, contributed by Radcliffe-Brown, linking Deacon's Ambrym kinship system to the systems of Australia. The Australian and Ambrym systems had developed, "not one out of the other, but both from the same or a similar original system which existed in parts of Melanesia and in India," and the development of the two systems, although divergent, showed "a striking similarity due presumably to the action of the same or similar sociological principles." Radcliffe-Brown—who like Deacon regarded himself as a disciple of the "early" Rivers (before "Elliot Smith got hold of him")—was not inclined to pursue the "early history of Melanesia"; his primary interest was in the "capital importance" of the Ambrym system for "sociological theory." Despite his disagreement with Rivers, it was Radcliffe-Brown who emerged from the lively discussions of social organization in the 1920s to claim Rivers' position as the arbiter of that field in British social anthropology.[15]

"Anarchy Brown" in the Andamans and Australia: The Evolution of Totemism and the Function of Survivals

Raymond Firth, who knew them each well, and remained friendly with both, contrasted Malinowski and Radcliffe-Brown in aesthetic terms as representing the "romantic" and the "classical" modes. For Malinowski, "imaginative insight" had priority over scientific generalization, if the "formal expression of observed regularity meant forcing "the diversities of the human creature into an artificial mold." For Radcliffe-Brown, who valued precision, proportion, and restraint, the notion of "system" had priority, sometimes "to the neglect of the full content of phenomenal reality." [16] That same predisposition of Radcliffe-Brown's intellectual character was manifest in a tendency toward retrospective systematization of his own viewpoint, which tends somewhat to obscure his intellectual development. The matter is further complicated by the fact that he travelled very light throughout a peripatetic career. According to some invidious anecdotes (of which there are a number, as there also are of Malinowski) he carried with him only his volumes of *L'Année sociologique*. Unlike Malinowski, who preserved a large body of manuscripts from the various loci of his own activity, Radcliffe-Brown left manuscript traces that are relatively few and widely scattered, and for his early history we must rely largely on his own later reminiscences.

Christened Alfred Reginald, he came into the world unhyphenated, at Sparkbrook, Birmingham, in 1881. Of undistinguished Warwickshire stock, he explained his much later adoption of his mother's maiden (and elder brother's middle) name by the fact that there were "so many Browns in the world." The family were left penniless by his father's death in 1886, and the three young children were taken in by their maternal grandmother while their mother went to work as a "companion." Suffering from tuberculosis throughout much of his youth, Brown was educated first at the Royal Commercial Travellers' School in Pinner, Middlesex. By his own later account, he early on developed a "structuralist" bias on the basis of studies in chemistry and human anatomy, even before he was admitted to the prestigious King Edward's School in Birmingham as a Foundation Scholar in 1896. After only two years there, he went to work in the Birmingham library, and later recalled being then "closely in touch" with Havelock Ellis—whose wife "used to accuse him of having swallowed an encyclopedia." He seems also to have known Prince Peter Kropotkin, the Russian anarchist:

> Like other young men with blood in their veins, I wanted to do something to reform the world—to get rid of poverty and war, and so on. So I read Godwin, Proudhon, Marx and innumerable others. Kropotkin, revolutionary, but still a scientist, pointed out how important for any attempt to improve society was a scientific understanding of it, and the importance in this respect of what our friend Elie Reclus called "Primitive Folk."

By Brown's account, by 1900 he was already "a sociologist" intent on devoting his life "to the scientific study of culture." At the urging of his brother, who began a career in South Africa as a mining engineer after being wounded in the Boer War, Brown read philosophy to prepare himself for the "little-go" examination at Cambridge in the spring of 1902. Awarded an exhibition to Trinity College (and assisted financially by his brother), he originally hoped to read for the Natural Science Tripos, but on the advice of his tutor chose Mental and Moral Science instead.[17]

At that time, the first part of the Moral Science Tripos—in which Brown placed in the first division of the Second Class—consisted of psychology (including psychophysics, with lectures by Rivers and Myers, and readings in Bain, Ebbinghaus, James, Külpe, Herbert Spencer, and Stout, among others); logic (lectures by Neville Keynes and readings in Mill and Jevons, as well as Whewell, Bacon, and Aristotle); political economy "with special reference to the condition of England at the present time" (lectures by Marshall and Pigou, and readings in Jevons, Keynes, Sidgwick, and Adam Smith); and ethics (lectures by Sorley and readings in Mill, Sidgwick, Green, and Herbert Spencer). Part II, in which Brown received a First, included work in metaphysical and moral philosophy, advanced psychology, and the history of modern (i.e., 17th–18th century) philosophy (taught by the Hegelian McTaggart), as well as politics and advanced political economy.[18]

There is little evidence to support the suggestion that Bertrand Russell (who was not in Cambridge) and A. N. Whitehead (who lectured in mathematics) were in this phase of Brown's career "neglected sources of structuralism." And although it is quite possible that Brown might have been reading social evolutionary and sociological writers of the Scottish and French Enlightenment whom he was much later to include in his own history of social anthropology, the tripos readings suggest rather the importance of the later British utilitarian and associationist traditions, German experimental psychology, and the Cambridge economists. Brown's much later memory that he had "all his life accepted the hypothesis of social evolution as formulated by [Herbert] Spencer as a useful working hypothesis" seems sustained—although Kropotkin, too, would have given him a great deal of nineteenth-century social evolutionism, along with a view of society as a harmonious system of interaction among individuals. But while it may indeed be true that Havelock Ellis called his attention to Durkheim "in 1899 when I was visiting him in Cornwall" there is, as we shall see, reason to doubt that the Durkheimian influence really took until five years after Brown himself had begun to study anthropology.[19]*

Brown's formal academic instruction in anthropology began during his last undergraduate year—the first year of the new Board of Anthropological Studies—when he studied physical anthropology with Duckworth, archeology with Ridgeway, ethnology with Haddon, and kinship with Rivers (at a time when he would have been working on *The Todas*). Retrospectively, Brown insisted that "from the outset" he and Rivers had "disagreed on the subject of method," and recalled having undertaken in 1905 a "long essay on the concept of function in science" as part of a general work on scientific method. Surviving evidence from a later period suggests, however, that his disagreements with his mentor emerged more gradually, and did not fully crystallize until 1913. After attending the British Association meetings in South Africa in 1905 as secretary of the anthropological section, Brown spent a further year preparing for fieldwork in the Andaman Islands. Although at one point he later said that he had deliberately gone there to study "a primitive people who had no totemism," contemporary evidence and subsequent retrospection both confirm that his goal (defined by Haddon and Sir Richard Temple, who had served as Chief Commissioner of the Andaman and Nicobar Islands) was to reconstruct the "primitive culture" of the Negrito race, which was presumed to have been the lowest of four population strata in Southeast Asia. Brown's fieldwork was modelled on that of the Torres Straits Expedition—but with all the functions of its divided scientific labor carried on by a single investigator: it encompassed every aspect of anthropological research, including material culture, physical anthropology, psychological testing—as well as the collection of string figures, which were one of Haddon's special preoccupations.[20]

Brown seems actually to have been in the field for only ten months of the two years normally listed for his Andaman expedition (1906–1908). His early fieldwork seems to have been carried on among "the hangers-on" at the settlement at Fort Blair, many of whom had "so far left their

*It seems likely that Radcliffe-Brown inherited more from Herbert Spencer—either directly, or through Durkheim—than "the hypothesis of social evolution." There are numerous points in Spencer's work, including the charts of the "structural" and "functional" aspects of society in his *Descriptive Sociology* (1874), which resonate of the "structural-functionalism" that is commonly associated with Radcliffe-Brown.

own mode of life" that "they do not remember 'the things of the old time.' " His attempt to work with a party of Önges from the Little Andaman Island—"the only ones who retain something of their old customs," and who "do not know a single word of any language but their own"—was hindered by his difficulties in communicating: "I ask for the word 'arm' and I get the Önge for 'you are pinching me.' " His actual time spent on that island seems to have been no more than only "several weeks"; he abandoned the venture when he realized that it would take "two or three years" to speak well enough to understand their answers to queries about customs and beliefs. Instead, he worked among North Andamanese, relying heavily on Hindustani, "which the younger men and women all speak more or less imperfectly"; he gradually gained "a knowledge" of several dialects, however, and toward the end of his stay found an interpreter "who spoke English well and was of considerable intelligence." Even so, his work in social anthropology was not so successful as he and Rivers would have hoped. Although he took a number of photographs, he had trouble collecting genealogies, and later admitted in print that "this branch of my investigation was a failure." Despite these difficulties, the thesis he presented in October 1908 won him a fellowship at Trinity.[21]

By the account of one who knew him well, Brown had "a peculiar reputation at Trinity." A strikingly handsome man who deliberately cultivated an unconventional style, he regarded the British as "barbarians and traders," and sought "to mould himself" in the pattern of the French—reading Gide, and dressing "like a Paris *savant*." Although he had by this time abandoned anarchism except "as an ideal," he was known at Trinity as "Anarchy Brown." Gossip had it, however, that he had lived in the Andamans "as a primitive autocrat, exercising a beneficent but completely authoritarian sway over the simple Andamanese." He could bring people "under his spell"—and in fact experimented with mesmerism. But if he was "gentle and very considerate to those who fell within the sphere of his concern," he "had no regard whatsoever for those who fell outside of it"—including, apparently, a number of women who "declared that he was 'no gentleman.' " "Unaffected by traditions," he allegedly declared that "everything should be judged and acted on from a self-made rational foundation." He was a "bit of a superman," who was "informed on *all* subjects," and was occasionally "led by his inventive genius to fabricate the stories he told." Despite his academic success and his obvious brilliance, the "erudite" and the "scholarly" at Trinity were "distrustful of him." He was, in short, "too dramatic a personality to fit easily into the conservative life of the college"—nor was he part of the set that was to become Bloomsbury.[22]

But if Brown had by 1908 developed a certain persona, he had not yet found his mature intellectual identity. Judging by the one long

A. R. Brown, in the period of his Trinity fellowship, 1909. (Courtesy of Cynthia Pike)

surviving published fragment (which may in fact *be* the Trinity fellowship thesis), the first version of Brown's Andaman ethnography was influenced more by Haddon than by Rivers, and showed not a trace of Durkheim. It seems to have been a quite traditional attempt at historical reconstruction on the basis of a comparative analysis of culture elements. Similarly, articles he published in 1909 and 1910 on the religion of the Andamanese reflect little of his later theoretical viewpoint; he was mostly concerned with disputing E. H. Man's notion that the mythical being Peluga was (like Lang's Baiame) analogous to the Christian God, though in defending himself against the criticisms of the German diffusionist Wilhelm Schmidt he did offer certain strictures against historical arguments based on the doctrine of survivals. It was apparently during the same academic year, when he lectured on Australian ethnology and the Kwakiutl potlatch at the London School of Economics, that Brown had his first systematic encounter with the Durkheimian literature—initially, one suspects, the material on Australian social organization, which had for several years been part of the discussion of totemism in British anthropological circles.[23]

Although the "beginning of British anthropology's long affair with Durkheimianism" has been associated with the Cambridge Ritualists, Jane Harrison's own account indicates her debt for the idea of pretotemistic societies "to views expressed by Mr. A. R. Brown in a course of lectures delivered in 1909 at Trinity College, Cambridge." Actually given in 1910, these lectures on "Comparative Sociology" were, Brown suggested in a letter to Marcel Mauss, the first attempt to expound in England "the view of sociology put forward in the *Année Sociologique*." The printed announcement indicates that there was a series of ten topics, moving from the aims and methods of sociology, to the classification of social types, the general laws of evolution, the evolution of social structure, and thence to a series of specific topics: religion, law and morals, economic institutions—all treated in evolutionary terms—the relation of society and the individual, the social origin of general ideas, and contemporary social problems. But as preserved in notes taken by or for Haddon, there is a somewhat different series of topics, and an obvious division between an initial set of six and a final two.[24]

The first six were of a general sociological nature, heavily derivative from materials in the Durkheimian literature, above all, *The Division of Labor*, specific pages of which are clearly reflected in certain passages of the lectures. The last two topics, which occupy almost half the notes, suggest the impact of this theoretical orientation on Brown's own ethnographic material. A series of reflections on "totemism and exogamy" must have been provoked by the appearance of Frazer's compendium while Brown's lectures were in progress. This was followed by a treatment of the evolution of religion, in which Brown drew on Robertson Smith and Hertz, as well as Durkheim. It was here that he made extensive use of his own Andaman material. It is as if suddenly, while he was explicating Durkheim, the results of his not too successful field trip took on a new significance. If he had found no classificatory system among the Andamanese, it was because they were the type case of the pre-exogamous society—indeed, the only one yet encountered. Drawing heavily on early Durkheim—the Durkheim of *The Division of Labor*—Brown offered a hypothesis as to how under the pressure of population such a society might divide and become exogamous, with the sharing of the animal world in the process—an early version of what Lévi-Strauss was to call Radcliffe-Brown's "first theory" of totemism.[25]

Brown later said that the last two chapters of *The Andaman Islanders* had been written in 1910 "as an attempt to develop a new method in the interpretation of the institutions of a primitive people," and some of the lecture material in fact roughly parallels certain portions of the book. But it seems clear that he had not yet fully developed his later analysis, if only because certain important theoretical catch-phrases (such as "social value") are absent from the notes. More important, considered from the perspective of his overall theoretical development, Brown had not yet made the crucial shift from a diachronic evolutionary viewpoint to that of synchronic analysis. That shift was to take place several years later, in the context of a disagreement with Rivers over the interpretation of data Brown collected during his second fieldwork expedition, to Western Australia.[26]

Initially suggested by James Frazer as an extension of the work Spencer and Gillen had done elsewhere on the continent, this project was developed at first within the Oxford Committee for Anthropology. Hearing of the venture, Brown, who was then lecturing on Australian social organization at the London School of Economics, proposed himself to Frazer, who was advising Marett. Frazer would have preferred Spencer, but he was unwilling to undertake the project without Gillen, who had just been stricken with an eventually fatal illness. When the expedition was finally realized, under the joint sponsorship of Oxford and Cambridge, its British personnel consisted of Brown and a young Trinity College zoologist named Grant Watson, several prospective Oxford participants having dropped out. Because Brown's departure was delayed for "private reasons" (presumably his marriage, which took place before he left) Watson went ahead to Australia, where he was later joined by Brown, a Swedish sailor named Olsen whom Brown had engaged as cook-handyman, and Mrs. Daisy Bates.[27]

Although their relationship started amicably enough, Daisy Bates was one of the women who concluded that Brown was "no gentleman." Born Daisy O'Dwyer in county Tipperary in 1863, she had emigrated to Australia in 1884, where she entered into a troubled marriage with a West Australia cattleman. In the 1890s, she retreated to England, where she worked as a journalist; in 1901, after returning to live with her husband at a cattle station near the northwestern Australian coast, she took up the study of Aborigines as a kind of hobby. Over time, her staunch identification with white pioneers—whom she defended against charges of exploitation—was gradually countered by a growing empathy for the people she came to think of as "my natives." In 1904 she was employed by the Registrar-General of Western Australia to collect material for a "Short Authentic Historical Record of the Habits, Customs, and Language of the Aboriginal Natives of this State." Dissatisfied with what her questionnaires elicited, she went to live among the Aborigines herself, compiling a manuscript which by 1907 she had begun to send to Andrew Lang, who in 1910 sent two chapters on to Brown.[28]

Before leaving for Australia, Brown wrote Bates offering comments on her work. Although he much later recalled having "persuaded" her to adopt the "genealogical method," at the time he in fact complimented her on being "the first student of Australian ethnology who has collected genealogies": Baldwin Spencer, although asked to do this on his last expedition, "apparently did not care to take the trouble." For the most part, however, Brown wrote in an instructive mode, sending along an article he had just published on Australian marriage and descent, with the suggestion that Bates adopt his method of representing marriage classes in order to facilitate comparative study. Commenting on the chapters Lang had sent to him, he criticized Bates for not having kept "facts" and "theories" separate and for failing to define her various totem categories. Because in "its present form" her manuscript did not do justice to her "magnificent material," he offered to advise her—with the warning that he would be "a merciless critic."[29]

Brown's relationship with Daisy Bates, and his own ethnographic goals in undertaking the expedition, have been the subject of considerable debate, much of it based on a footnote to *The Social Organization of Australian Tribes* in which (echoing Deacon) he retrospectively described his "discovery" of the Kariera class system as "the result of a definite search" based on an earlier "surmise," after a "careful study of Australian data," that "some such system might very well exist." An interview Brown gave in Perth upon his arrival suggests, however, that he actually had a more general evolutionary goal: to find evidence for the hypothesis he had advanced at Cambridge on the origin of totemism, on which his views were in critical aspects still rather traditional. Thus although Frazer had been forced to the conclusion that totemism and exogamy were institutions "fundamentally distinct in origin and nature," Brown still saw them as intimately related. He proposed nothing less than to "settle" the issues of the ongoing totemism debate. The Australian Aborigines "personified" a "stage" that "probably every race," including "our own ancestors," had passed through. By studying all the variations of Australian marriage regulations, his expedition would cast light on "the origin of the system," and on its "progressive development" from "two to four and from four to eight" exogamous classes. On the other hand, Brown's comment to Bates that the Northwest would "probably give the key to the change from 4 to 8 classes," and Watson's that the "main business" of the expedition was to "tabulate facts pertaining to the four-class marriage system," suggest that Brown hoped, by studying all the variants of the four-class system, to find one that would indicate the process of its evolutionary transformation.[30]

Ten days after Brown's interview, Daisy Bates was seconded by the government to join the expedition for six months, with the understanding that Brown would publish her previous work by "including it in the reports of the expedition" (to which Bates had convinced a friend to contribute £1000). Once in the field, however, relations between Brown and Bates began to deteriorate. Like Brown, she was "undoubtedly stubborn, arrogant, egotistical and authoritarian"—and a snobbish, old-fashioned Tory to boot. She had expected a Cambridge professor, and was confronted instead by a lower-middle-class young man twenty years her junior, who had abandoned anarchy only to believe in socialism (though he worried about the power of the state). Brown in turn concluded that her extensive ethnographic knowledge was "a most hopeless tangle," and that she was irredeemably amateur. And they both thought themselves rightfully the leader of the expedition.[31]

Trekking along with a wagon drawn by two horses, the group travelled three hundred miles into the "wild unexplored bush" in search of a "large corroborree" they had heard was about to take place. When they found it, Bates (who had previously been assigned to the Burung section) introduced Brown as her "son" (which according to the kinship system placed him in the Paljeri section), and they set to work. But one morning shortly thereafter, when they had returned to their tents at dawn from observing some initiation dances, a dozen white Australians came "riding through the camp, firing off their revolvers at the native dogs, shouting and swearing," and scattering the Aborigines "in all directions." It was a police posse looking for two men accused of murder—or, as Bates later reported to the Chief Protector of Aborigines, "spearings demanded by tribal law because of 'wrong' marriages." After the posse had left, dragging off one old man who protested his innocence, the two "murderers" emerged from Brown's tent, where he had given them refuge. Concluding that ethnographic work had been hopelessly disrupted, Brown decided to make the long trip northwest to Bernier Island, where syphilitic Aborigines from many tribes—victims of a disease introduced by whites—were brought in chains to be kept in isolation, and could easily be interrogated. Bates, however, insisted that the Aborigines who had fled from the posse would return to the camp, and refused to go—whereupon Brown left her alone in the bush.[32]

As it happened, the Aborigines did not come back, and Bates returned by train to Perth. After a difficult trip up the coast, she rejoined the expedition at Bernier, working with the women patients kept separately on an island nearby. Her relations with Brown continued to deteriorate, however, and when after five months he decided to go inland again along the Gascoyne River, Bates went back to Perth, her six months' leave by this time up. When Brown's group returned to Carnarvon after a few weeks, and he proposed a longer venture in the bush, Watson left the expedition on friendly terms. Accompanied by an Aboriginal interpreter, Brown himself worked in the region for another six months, among the Kariera, Ngaluma, and Mardudhunera, before returning to England—with Bates's manuscript still in his possession.[33]

Despite the agreement before the expedition, that manuscript was never to be published. In its original form, it was manifestly unpublishable. Macmillan, to whom Lang apparently sent all or part of it, rejected it, and a scholar who has studied a copy of the unmutilated version has commented that "after a good beginning" each chapter "deteriorates," until the "last pages are merely random notes from any one of her many field notebooks," full of "random observations and illogical arguments." In forwarding portions to Brown, Lang had suggested that "scissors are needed for that vast and wandering work"—and it is evident that Brown, in attempting to edit it, took his advice. Having already complained of her mixture of fact and theory, he also began to assume the role of theorizer, for whom her material was merely unsystematized data. When they had worked together on the manuscript during the expedition, she is reported to have defended herself against charges of "obvious inaccuracy or contradiction" by saying that she had recorded what the natives had said, and "therefore it must be correct." But for Brown, the presumption of system was overriding: "If you had been collecting the genealogies with any pretence at accuracy you would have gone over these again with the natives in the endeavour to discover the errors, understand how they came to be made, and then correct them."[34]

Six months after his return, Brown reported to Haddon that his editing was "too drastic for Mrs. Bates," and that she had asked permission to publish for herself the information she had collected before the expedition. Having by this time been relieved by the government of Western Australia of his own responsibility to publish the manuscript, Brown returned it to her, with the request that she send on information she had collected during the expedition, so that it might be incorporated into the reports. But although Brown had envisioned a multivolume report in the style of the Torres Straits Expedition (with one by Sydney Ray on linguistics), there were to be no reports of the expedition as such. Bates felt that the material Brown returned to her had been mutilated "beyond recovery," and several times accused him of plagiarizing it. When asked to comment on a paper on totemism he gave to the Sydney meeting of the British Association in 1914, she described it as "all an extract from my manuscript." And there were in fact some passages missing from the material Brown returned to her, including two and a half pages on the Kariera.[35]

It is evident, in this and other instances, that Brown had a somewhat cavalier attitude toward data collected by those he regarded as amateurs. However, a later scholar's comparison of the material Brown cut with his own published account has suggested that he collected his

Kariera material independently, and "kept her list so that he could compare it with his notes." Whether and in what sense Brown's Kariera system was a "discovery" has been debated. There is no doubt that knowledge of the Kariera and their four-section system had been in the published realm for a long time. What Brown did in his account of "Three Tribes of Western Australia" was not so much to discover the Kariera system as to define it, in two senses. On the one hand, he placed the four sections within a larger context: "the kinship system, the rules of marriage, the local groupings, the residence patterns, the division of labour, the totemic cults and the nature of tribal integration." On the other hand, he defined the Kariera system as the exemplary case of one of two basic types of Australian systems of relationships which (excluding the Kurnai) covered the whole continent: type I (the Kariera) in which a man married his real or classificatory mother's brother's daughter, and type II (typified by the Mardudhunera) in which he married his real or classificatory mother's mother's brother's daughter's daughter. According to Rivers, Brown's achievement was to show that Australian social organization was not unique, but was "nothing more than a systematization of the regulation of marriage by kinship which is generally associated with exogamous systems"—although Northcote Thomas quickly pointed out to Rivers that he had made that very point in his own synthesis of 1906, which Brown would certainly have read. Be that as it may, Brown's paper was the first formulation of a systematization of Australian social organization which was to become authoritative.[36]

At one point, Brown suggested that if the "complicated" relationship system of the four-class Mardudhunera were systematically applied, it would produce a division into eight subclasses, similar to that of the Arunta, who were in fact later to be substituted as the exemplars of type II. Although this might be interpreted as a conceptual "survival" of evolutionary assumption, it is striking that—in contrast to his pre-fieldwork hypothesis—Brown's post-field systematization was not cast in evolutionary terms. This quite fundamental shift in his anthropological orientation is reflected in a lengthy correspondence Brown carried on with his mentor Rivers while living in Birmingham after his return from Australia early in 1912.[37]

The first letter affirmed a not-yet-disrupted discipleship: Brown was pleased that a manuscript on childbirth customs fitted with Rivers' Melanesian work, and asked for a copy of the address Rivers had given to the British Association while he was in Australia, which he had previously "only glanced" at. Brown went on to suggest that he now had "a good working hypothesis of the origin of the Australian social organisation, and indeed of the origin of totemism in general." The key lay in the dual division, and he was "more wedded than ever" to his earlier theory that it was "essentially a mode of organising the 'oppositions' that arise in savage societies in connection with marriage, initiation, etc." For the present, however, he proposed to publish only factual data, leaving "questions of origin" until after further research. Although he expected the intermediate forms of the Lake Eyre tribes to provide the ultimate key, he hoped first to go to North Queensland to study "the local and relationship organisations in their relationship to the totemic clans" among a tribe whose "maternal descent of the totem" would contrast to the male descent he had found in Western Australia.[38]

Upon reading Rivers' surprising account of his conversion from evolutionism to diffusionism, Brown at first chose to define their differences in minimal terms. Accepting "fully" the proposition that "analysis of a mixed culture must precede sociological explanation," he simply insisted that Australian culture was in fact unmixed. Rivers' argument to the contrary depended on treating the system of marriage classes and the system of totem clans as separate institutions (à la Frazer), and associating each with a different population stratum. Against this, Brown insisted that both classes and clans were "inseparably bound up with the relationship system," and that the form totemism took in any group was a reflection of its particular social organization. It was "social structure" that was "fundamental"; "the specialisation of religious functions [was] the result of the specialisation of social functions." Although further correspondence was to reveal that basic matters of conceptualization and definition were at issue, Brown concluded by reiterating his "full agreement" with "the main point" of Rivers' Portsmouth address.

Rivers answer (no longer extant) apparently suggested that the two disagreed "quite fundamentally about Australia." In response, Brown further explicated his view of the "two essential features of the relationship system" on that continent: "the existence of clans due to the distinction of nearer and more distant relatives of the same kind," and "the classification of the world of natural objects" with religious or mythic significance into two divisions "according to the divisions of the human society." Although both together constituted "the totemic organisation of the Australians," the former was more fundamental, since "a society might possess the social organisation without the classification," but not "the classification without some sort of social divisions." However, until he carried out his proposed field study of the "connection of the local organisation, the relationship system and the totemic clans in tribes with female descent," he could not rebut Rivers' argument that the "intimate connection" of the latter two was "the result of blending."

In this context, Brown introduced new ethnographic data that were to bring matters more sharply into focus: the case of the Dieri of Central Australia, about whom Howitt had written extensively, and who (along with Spencer's Arunta) were one of the main subjects of controversy in the study of Australian social organization. Rejecting Howitt's work as "unreliable," Brown interpreted some recently published ethnographic evidence as showing that the Dieri had a double system of totems, one with male descent similar to those in Western Australia, and one with female descent similar to those of eastern tribes. In the next several letters he advanced a "working hypothesis" of the origin of the Dieri system: assuming a single developmental sequence of Australian totemism, the Dieri represented a special transitional state in which the new western paternal form had been superimposed by borrowing in a tribe that still retained the older eastern maternal totems. Although he was able to justify this "imitation" by a lengthy conjectural argument, Brown's resort to borrowing was in evolutionary terms somewhat incongruous, and left Rivers an obvious diffusionary alternative. In the meantime, however, Brown went on to react to Durkheim's recently published *Elementary Forms of the Religious Life*, in which the interpretation of the totemism of another Central Australian tribe had even further complicated "the whole question of the evolution of totemism in Australia."[39]

Brown had of course already accepted Durkheim's general thesis of "the sociological origin of religion," and he agreed with "almost everything" Durkheim said about the Arunta system per se. But he felt that Durkheim had not explained why totem objects were selected from "the practical economic life of everyday," and that he was wrong about the evolutionary position of Arunta totemism. Reaffirming the hypothesis of his Cambridge lectures, Brown argued that the Andamanese "pre-totemic" social organization had developed into the "classificatory system of Australia" with its "dual divisions" and its originally matrilineal clans. The Arunta, rather than being primitive, were a later stage. Beyond this, Brown disagreed with Durkheim's definition of totemism as "above all" a name or emblem; and this led him to pose explicitly certain definitional issues in an unpreserved note (or notes) on the concepts "totemism" and "clan." In regard to totemism he apparently emphasized the presence of "a specific magico-religious relation between the clan and some species . . . of natural object"; regarding clan he apparently emphasized, as he did in a subsequent letter, the distinction, within a system of kinship, between "near and distant kindred."

Rivers' only extant letter in this first series was brief, pointed, and a bit patronizing. He accused Brown of basing his definitions too narrowly on Australian materials, suggesting that this was justifiable only if one adopted the Frazerian view "that the Australians represent a stage in the evolution of human society in general." Arguing that Brown's definition of clan was too narrowly genealogical, Rivers offered his own somewhat overlapping definitions of the contested concepts: a clan was an exogamous group within a tribe, whose members were bound together *either* by "a belief in common descent" *or* by "the common possession of a totem"; totemism was simply the term he used for "a form of social organisation . . . in which the totemic link forms an essential element of social structure." Having chosen his definitional ground, Rivers had no objection to Brown's explanation of the Dieri case "except that it assumes at the outset" what had to be explained. If the Dieri already had two kinds of social grouping, he could see "how one of them may have taken on the magico-religious ideas and practices of western totemism." But it was the presence of two groupings in the first place that required an explanation, and by implication Rivers had one even if Brown did not: that they were a type-case of the blending that characterized all of Australian culture.[40]

Brown responded to the definitional issue by an appeal to his fieldwork. In Australia there were "two different sorts of social groups that may be totemic"; he used the term "clan" only for those based on the distinction between near and distant kin. Exogamy was not their defining characteristic, but simply a consequence of the fact that their members were closely related. These groups were sometimes totemic and sometimes not, sometimes constituted by male descent and sometimes by female, sometimes localized and sometimes not. Although he did not wish "to define terms in sociology on the basis of Australian facts only," these groups seemed to "correspond fairly closely" to what were elsewhere called clans—though what was important was "not the name but the facts." On the question of Dieri totemic groups, Brown felt that he could not deal with this adequately without offering "a theory of Australian social organisation in general," and in view of Rivers' criticisms, and many things in Durkheim's book, he was postponing the paper in which he would offer it. For the present it seemed best to "abandon" the correspondence.

Viewing the 1912 exchange as a whole, it seems clear that Brown had begun to move beyond the relationship of student to mentor. Despite the failure of his Andaman kinship work, he had by this time published papers on Australian kinship whose excellence Rivers was later to acknowledge. The exchange had also heightened Brown's sensitivity to certain definitional problems, which he insisted on treating in terms of his empirical data rather than in terms of traditional evolutionary categories. At the same time, his position was compromised by his continuing underlying commitment to a diachonic evolutionary viewpoint, and his simultaneous unwillingness to insist on that viewpoint when pushed on questions of "origin." When Rivers threatened to force him into a corner on an issue of conjectural history, Brown backed off from the battle.[41]

When the correspondence was resumed in the summer of 1913, it was clear that Brown had resolved some of the ambiguities of his viewpoint. It may simply have been that he realized that his position vis-à-vis Rivers would be much stronger if he put aside the diachronic framework entirely. However, one suspects that he did so in the context of a further immersion in the writings of the Durkheimians, with whom by this time he was in direct contact. The fifth chapter of *The Rules of Sociological Method*—which was not a source for his 1910 lectures, but to which he subsequently referred—would have given him the justification for an essentially synchronic approach to social facts.[42]

Be that as it may, the exchange opened on July 12, 1913, with Rivers commenting on the last chapters of *The Andaman Islanders,* which, although still incomplete, he had previously recommended for publication by the Cambridge University Press, where portions of it were already set in type. Brown's whole interpretation of Andamanese myth as an expression of their "system of social values" ran quite counter to a thesis Rivers had developed to the effect that myth usually dealt with the rare and exceptional in native life. Rivers nevertheless found Brown's argument compelling, and it was now he who minimized the differences between them. He did, however, call attention to the contrast between "psychological" and "what I should call sociological or historical interpretation," suggesting that the history of Andaman culture might not be "so hopeless" as Brown seemed to feel.[43]

In response to other no longer extant comments, Brown granted that he had not got "to the bottom" of Andaman kinship, and had decided therefore to back off from his argument that it was "really a preclassificatory system"—although he continued to believe that it was. Having thus withdrawn from the battlefield of conjectural history, Brown was now finally free to disentangle himself from issues of origin, which Rivers had apparently continued to press by pointing out that there were customs similar to those of the Andamanese elsewhere in the world. To this, Brown now responded, "I am afraid you will be sorry to hear that I feel quite comfortable with this." From his present point of view, it did not really matter whether the Andamanese customs were invented or borrowed, or simply adopted "from their own early ancestors," which "seems to me to be much the same thing." Whatever their origin, they must be "adapted to some need of the Andaman collective conscience (to speak teleologically, and not meaning a conscious need)." While historical questions were no doubt interesting and important, they did not "affect the questions of causal relations in the present." As Durkheim had argued, these had to do with how "the customs of a society" served "to maintain a certain system of ideas and emotions which in its turn is what maintains the society in existence with its given structure and its given degree of cohesion." Drawing analogies to the study of language and examples from Andaman technology, Brown distinguished between "dynamical" and "statical" problems. While the latter did not depend on the former, he was prepared to argue that "in many cases the dynamic (historical) problems must depend on the static (psychological) problems."

With this letter, the separation of two paradigms was in principle accomplished. The critical passages were those referring to "causal relations in the present" and "the needs of the Andaman collective conscience." The former rejected both the problem and the concept of diachronic causation; the latter redefined the framework of psychological interpretation from that of individual motivation to that of the functional needs of the whole culture—in the process, one notes, reinforcing the interpretive authority of the theoretical ethnographer, who by virtue of his external comparative perspective was able to perceive the coherence and define the needs of the culture as a whole. There were, however, still other issues to be dealt with, and it is significant that they came together in relation to the problem of "survivals," which was a critically important assumption to both the evolutionist and the Riversian historical approaches, and which Brown admitted would, if accepted, compromise his position.

Responding to the paper on "Survivals in Sociology" that Rivers had just published, Brown sent him on December 13, 1913, the draft of an essay elaborating his own view "of the methods to be adopted in the study of social institutions." He began by rejecting Rivers' antithesis of the "psychological" and the "historical" methods. Following McDougall, Brown defined "psychology" as "the science of human behavior," of which sociology was simply that branch dealing with "those modes of behaviour that are determined in the individual by the society." Sociology in turn encompassed both static and dynamic (or as Rivers would have it, "psychological" and "historical") problems. Assuming that there were "only a limited number of ways in which a human society can be constituted," social statics sought the laws governing "the causal relations subsisting between different elements of the same social organisation." Social dynamics dealt with "the causes that produce changes of social organisation, and therefore with the origins of social institutions." Where he and Rivers disagreed was on the order in which these two sets of problems should be approached.[44]

In this context, Brown turned to the problem of survival, which Rivers had defined as a custom "whose nature cannot be explained by its present utility but only . . . through its past history." Arguing that the notion of "utility" was "subjective," Brown suggested that calling the customs connected with the mother's brother in the Torres Straits "useless" depended on a prior conception of "the fundamental purpose or end of society." He proposed that society be regarded as "a condition of equilibrium or balance of forces of cohesion and disruption," suggesting that its purpose was "its own continued existence in a state of equilibrium," and that the "utility"—or better, the "social function"—of any social institution was the way it contributed to this end. Here, then, was an "objective" criterion of survival: "In any given instance the hypothesis that a custom or institution is a survival must depend on some hypothesis as to the function that such a custom fulfils (or on the nature of the necessary connections between such customs and the other institutions of the society)," which was in effect to say that "any argument about survivals must necessarily rest on hypothetical solutions of problems of social statics." Implicitly calling into question what had been an unexamined methodological assumption of anthropology for at least fifty years, Brown argued that it was not enough to appeal to "the mental disposition which we call conservatism." Conservativism itself needed explanation: "We must know what is the social function of conservatism in general and what is the cause of the variation of its intensity in different conditions."[45*]

Pushing his attack, Brown argued, on the basis of an analysis of the "logical" structure of arguments from survivals, that using them to reason from "the present condition of a society back to its past" depended on a general knowledge of the principles of social statics. Since in the present state of sociological knowledge, "almost nothing [was] known of the functions of social institutions and of the laws that regulate their relations one to another," arguments from survival were of value "only when we have independent historical evidence (not based on survival hypotheses) as to the process of historical change." In short, the idea of

*The "doctrine of survivals" was a critical component of social evolutionary reconstructivism, insofar as it enabled one to reason backward down the presumed scale of civilization (Hodgen 1936; Stocking 1987b:162–63; Wolfe 1994; above, xiv). From 1890 on there is evidence here and there of a growing discomfort with and occasional criticism of the notion, which may be taken as yet another sign of paradigmatic malaise (Westermarck 1891:549–50; Crawley 1902: II, 260; Lang 1903:104, 1907b:7, 10; Marett 1919; Malinowski, above, 277) Viewed from the perspective of paradigmatic change, the rejection of "survivals" was a precondition of the emergence of functionalism, insofar as it facilitated (and necessitated) the explanation of sociocultural phenomena without reference to diachronic assumption. Brown's private critique of survivals is analogous in this respect to A. L. Kroeber's published comments in 1915 rejecting the inheritance of acquired characteristics. Such an understanding was essential to the emergence of the culture concept in Boasian anthropology, insofar as Lamarckian assumption, by creating a circular relationship between race and culture, precluded the explanation of human difference in purely cultural terms (Stocking 1968b:258–60, 265–66). For a comment on the cultural context of the "social function of conservatism," see above, xiv.

survival had only limited utility for sociology; its main function was as a foil: "It is of extreme interest in social statics to determine which customs in a society are really survivals, if there be any such."[46]

In drawing his argument together, Brown returned to the general question of the psychological explanation of social phenomena, which (following Durkheim's *Rules*) he defined as "modes of thinking, feeling and acting common to all or to a great number of the members of a society and imposed upon them by the society itself." If Rivers would accept that definition, they might agree on the "proper task of the sociologist"; but Brown suspected that Rivers would exclude thinking and feeling, on the grounds that as "purely mental processes" they could not be "directly observed." Against this, Brown argued that since actions were determined by thoughts and feelings, any explanation would be incomplete that did not take these into consideration. But he felt that he could not proceed without having from Rivers an explicit definition of social phenomena—and awaiting that, he broke off the manuscript in mid-paragraph.[47]

Rivers' answer was brief. Without apparently considering its implications for his theoretical position, he "very largely" accepted Brown's comments on the issue of "utility." But he disagreed "absolutely" with his definitions of psychology and of social phenomena, and therefore felt that "as regards the main question," his own position was "wholly untouched." Refusing to go into the matter by letter, he said he planned to give a talk at Oxford the next summer on "the relations between sociology and psychology," and that meanwhile Brown might like to "defer rewriting" the paper until he had a chance to read Rivers' "little book on social organisation," which would appear shortly.[48]

Although Brown professed to find "hardly anything in it with which I do not agree," and to look forward "still more eagerly" to Rivers' forthcoming *History of Melanesian Society*, the appearance of Rivers' "little book," *Kinship and Social Organization*, did not so much resolve matters as make explicit the fact that the two men were talking past one another. While in 1912 Brown had taken the stance of an empiricist appealing to his data against a priori assumption, now that he had defined the basis for his own mature theoretical stance, he saw their roles reversed: whereas Rivers insisted that sociologists must confine themselves "to concrete or objective phenomena such as are capable of exact observation," Brown insisted that this could only produce "empirical generalisations," never "explanations," and that social institutions were dependent on fundamental laws of psychology. Brown felt that he got along "much better and ever so much more rapidly" when he had a "working hypothesis of the fundamental nature of human society, such as I have now." But this hypothesis "would be quite useless" unless he "worked out the psychological explanations" as he went along. The advantage of this "conscious psychological method" was that it protected one from unconsciously accepting the "unscientific" assumptions of "popular psychology" or "the associationist intellectualist psychology of thirty years ago." Rivers' empiricism in fact concealed such assumptions, and therefore they could neither reach agreement "nor even properly argue with one another" about specific issues.[49]

Early in 1914, Brown offered some final comments in the course of remarks on manuscripts each man had written for the journal *Anthropos* on the topic which more than any other had given focus to anthropological discussion since 1900: the definition of totemism. In opposition to Rivers' continuing insistence on defining totemism as a "form of social organisation," Brown now proposed to cut through the empirical and theoretical confusion surrounding the concept by using totemism to refer only to a "special magico-religious relation between each social division" and "some species of natural object." On this basis, he suggested that there were "five different types of totemism in Australia which *may* have originated independently of one another," but among which there was "a close relation of *psychological* dependence." Admitting that "his theoretical and methodological bias" had largely determined his choice of definition, Brown still insisted his definition was better, since it was more adaptable to historical problems than Rivers' was to psychological problems, and because Rivers' in fact presupposed a specific theory of "clan totemism." In the end, however, he appealed simply to his "prejudices": "What makes me cling so much to my own is that I do so strongly feel the necessity of dealing with many psychological problems before attempting to attack the historical problems."[50]

In view of the fact that Rivers was for most of his career well known as a psychologist, and Radcliffe-Brown was for much of his known to oppose psychological interpretations, it is more than a bit paradoxical that their parting of theoretical ways should have ended on this note. One way to resolve the paradox is to place both men once again in relation to nineteenth-century evolutionism—which, as Radcliffe-Brown later pointed out, had a dual character. On the one hand, the basic problem of evolution was one of historical reconstruction (broadly conceived of as change in time), and causation was conceived of in diachronic terms. On the other, this historical reconstruction was undertaken on the basis of assumptions about the fundamental laws of human psychology, conceived of in essentially individualistic, utilitarian, intellectualist terms; characteristically, it involved a determination of the "motives" lying behind present customs—motives which were thought to lie in the past. Up to a point, one can interpret the development of Rivers and that of Radcliffe-Brown as alternate responses to the crisis of evolutionism in the context of this basic duality. Rivers retained an historical orientation to the definition of problem and causation, but abandoned the psychological approach in terms of "motives." Responding in 1916 to "a private criticism of my earlier work by one whose opinion I value highly," he argued that it was possible to discuss "the actions of human beings as members of society without reference to motives." He even suggested that "it would be possible" to treat marriage as a problem in "pure sociology" without using "a single psychological term referring to instincts, emotions, sentiments, ideas or beliefs. . . ." In contrast, Radcliffe-Brown rejected the historical problem, but retained (for the moment) the psychological approach, on the basis of a redefinition of psychological assumption. "Motive," conceived of in individualistic, intellectualist terms, became "function," conceived of in unconscious collective terms.[51]

But however apt, this formulation of their opposition has nonetheless a somewhat fleeting situational character. As we have seen, Rivers was soon to return to psychology, albeit of a very different sort. And Brown did not in fact immediately abandon diachronic problems; nor did he ever abandon an underlying commitment to evolutionism. Furthermore, over the longer run he cast off the psychological idiom in which his own Durkheimian alternative was initially phrased. However, it was not until after Rivers' death that he offered in print a strong programmatic assertion of the differences between them. When he did in "The Methods of Ethnology and Social Anthropology" in 1923, it was in effect the completion of the essay he had broken off suddenly ten years before.[52]

A. Radcliffe Brown and the Emergence of Social Anthropology in South Africa

As he himself commented, Brown was a "very slow writer." This was due, he suggested, not to "any unwillingness to write," but "because I sometimes have to spend a week in research in order to permit me to make a definite statement." Whatever the cause, it is a fact that aside from *The Andaman Islanders,* he published no book-length work; his characteristic form was the lecture or the essay, the periodic distillate of a slowly evolving and constantly resystematized theoretical viewpoint. Formed in his early immersion in Durkheim and in his debates with Rivers, his anthropological orientation was gradually refined over the next twenty-five years. But if the essence remained the same, there were changes—augmentations, elaborations, erasures, and on some points even reversals—as he moved from one job to another around the British colonial periphery, until in 1938 he finally found a place in the English academic establishment.[53]

At every place along the way, there were lectures, ever more extended elaborations of themes first stated at Trinity College in 1910. The first such series, which survives only in a printed announcement and a few press clippings, was given at the University of Birmingham during the late autumn and early winter of 1913–1914—the university's response to a move in the British Association, led by Sir Richard Temple, that it should establish a "school of applied anthropology." Presented under the rubric "social anthropology" (rather than "comparative sociology"), the topics of the Trinity series were now bracketed by a somewhat qualified plea for the social utility of anthropology. Against "journalists and writers" who offered "Utopia at a few days notice," Brown insisted on the need for systematic knowledge of the "natural laws" governing human society. Social evolution was quite a different thing from social progress, which could not be defined scientifically, and "must be left to politicians and reformers." At home, the utility of social anthropology apparently lay in showing that "society was not a work of the hands" and could not be "changed by legislation"; overseas, it would provide "commercial benefits" and facilitate colonial administration by offering an understanding of "a different set of human beings, who acted and thought in a different way."[54]

The group he was most interested in were "the Aborigines of Australia," about whom he had just contributed a somewhat derivative account to a two-volume popular compendium, *The Customs of the World*. In April 1914 he outlined to Haddon plans for further research among the tribes of South Australia and Queensland. Because his work on sociology and religion "bid fair" to keep him occupied "for some time to come," he offered to send Haddon the considerable material he had collected on Australian technology, with the thought that it might provide the basis "for a complete study of the distribution of types and culture areas of Australia." But although he later recalled that he had intended to devote "the next eight or ten years" to the solution of "Australian problems" particularly important for "general theories of sociology," he managed only a few weeks of fieldwork in South Australia before his plans were disrupted by the outbreak of war. Left without adequate financial support—Baldwin Spencer being perhaps reluctant to assist someone who seemed a competitor on his home turf—he spent several years teaching geography in a Church of England grammar school in Sydney.[55]

In 1917, Brown was appointed Director of Education on the island of Tonga, where his responsibilities included supervising the sports (among them, wheelbarrow races) at the coronation of Queen Charlotte as Tui Kanokubolu. But he soon discovered, "as Hocart found before me, that it is exceedingly difficult to get anything out of the Tongans as to their former customs and beliefs": "those who would tell do not know, and those who know will not tell except to a man . . . who has spent years among them [and] who knows the language thoroughly." The most he could manage were a few notes, which he used to answer queries Haddon forwarded to him from a Manchester lawyer who had travelled in the Solomons and was now writing a book on *The Social and Political Systems of Central Polynesia.* The climate, furthermore, was not good for Brown's health; having been diagnosed as again tubercular, he decided late in 1919 to stay with his brother in South Africa until he was well enough to look "for some more congenial job." While there, he hoped to finish the first volume of a work on the sociology of Australian tribes—leaving "to the future" a second volume that would require a return to the field to "test some of my hypotheses."[56]

Some weeks after his arrival in South Africa, Brown wrote to Haddon suggesting that there was a "good chance of something being done for ethnology here in Africa," including the appointment of an ethnologist at the Transvaal Museum in Pretoria, and the chance that the new Unionist government of Jan Christian Smuts might be persuaded to establish an ethnographical bureau to conduct "an ethnographical survey of the Union." Haddon immediately sent off letters to both the museum and Smuts, a man of evolutionary philosophical interests whose daughter Cato was in fact to study anthropology at Cambridge with Haddon. Emphasizing Brown's earlier work on Andaman and Australian technology, the recommendation to the museum procured him a job cataloguing five thousand specimens, including a collection of native dolls. In the letter to Smuts, Haddon stressed the importance of the "modern methods of sociological research" pioneered by Rivers and the "very real practical value" of ethnology in avoiding the "friction and consequent expense" so often involved in the "government of native races," and commended Brown as "the most brilliant and experienced of the younger students turned out by the Cambridge School of Ethnology."[57]

Although the movement to establish anthropological studies at the University of Cape Town had begun several years before, Brown's appointment in 1921 should be seen in relation to social, economic, and political issues "bound up with the native question" which at that historical moment were running together "with a crash" that "shook the Union of South Africa to its foundations." Smuts had just set up a permanent Native Affairs Commission to cope with some of the consequences of the "increasing civilization" that accompanied his aggressive industrialization policy—including the breakdown of the old tribal system and the danger of the "half-educated agitator among a wholly uneducated constituency." Over the next several years, the commission had plenty of friction to deal with. In May 1921 scores of members of a black religious sect were shot down at Bulhoek when they charged eight hundred police mobilized at the urging of the commission. The following January there was a strike of white miners opposed to the substitution of cheap black labor, and by March 22 most of the Rand "was in the hands of revolutionaries one of whose first acts was to attack natives in some of the compounds"; the strike was ended only after Smuts himself led in troops, leaving 230 people dead. Two months later there was a rebellion of Hottentots in the newly mandated territory of Southwest Africa. Trying to cope with the stream of "detribalized" blacks coming into the towns, Parliament in 1923 passed the Urban Areas Act, closing the towns to Bantu "except on sufferance." By June of 1924, the Smuts government had fallen, leading to a realignment of politics along racial rather than economic lines. It was in this context that Brown assumed the chair in social anthropology that had been funded by the Union government for a five-year period in the School of African Life and Languages in the University of Cape Town. On the basis of the majority report of the advisory committee chaired by Haddon (and despite the reservations of Marett, who worried about his health, his "literary unproductiveness," and his "conceited and unsociable" personality) it was filled by "Mr. A. Radcliffe Brown"—the form which he had recently adopted.[58]

Brown felt it was "a detestable nuisance having one's work mixed up with politics, and particularly with the kind of politics that we have out here"—Smuts's followers having sought unsuccessfully to make membership in the Dutch Reformed Church a criterion of appointment to the chair he held. It is clear, however, that he felt public relations, if not politics per se, was a nuisance to which he must direct a considerable effort. A scrapbook that survives from this period is full of clippings from *The Cape Argus*, *The Cape Times*, the *Diamond Fields Advertiser*, the Johannesburg *Star*, and the *Rand Daily Mail*. There were accounts or reprints of Brown's lectures—"The Working of the Native Mind," "Back to the Primitive," "How to Understand the Bantu," "The White Man's Problem"—with comments on his presentation: "Young in years, spare and tall of stature, with the typical flowing hair of the care-free genius, he possesses a sense of humour and a *joie de vivre* in his subject, investing his discourse with reality and fascination." There were articles and book reviews by him: "Man and his Ancestor" (a discussion of the Broken Hill skull); "The Ascent of Man" (a summary of human physical evolution); "The Mind of the Savage" (a critique of Lévy-Bruhl). There was a reprinting of his introductory lecture at the second of two "vacation courses" offered for "missionaries and others whose work brings them into contact with the natives and who would gain from more thorough knowledge of native life and thought." There were editorials inspired by his work ("The Sociology of the Native") or, in the end, attributing his departure for Australia to the government's failure to offer enough support to "the Cinderella of South African sciences."[59]

A striking aspect of these public performances is their evolutionary cast; much of the rhetoric ("grades of civilization," "lower races," "laws of evolution") could easily have come from Tylor, and at one point Brown offered a definition of civilization that echoed Tylor's definition of culture. But for Brown, "evolution" was not to be equated with "progress" or with a fundamental difference in human capacity, and the idea of civilization—"what we acquired from the particular society in which we lived"—was essentially plural. Save for the Bushmen (the only local group who qualified as "true savages"), what was at issue was the relationship of "two civilisations." If in 1923 he posed the problem as "how to maintain in this country European civilisation," his parting discussion of "the white man's problem" in 1925 suggested that the result must "slowly" but "surely" be "a new product of civilisation" which would be "a combination of the two": "South African nationalism must be a nationalism composed of both black and white." What he offered to the public was a conservative critique of ethnocentric assumption, which was couched as an appeal to European self-interest, but held forth the possibility of a more liberal future social order—and which served, as well, as a defense of social anthropology as the means to ethnic understanding and social peace.[60*]

Brown's characteristic pronouncements on matters of native policy were posed in cautionary terms: missionaries must be taught to understand the function of witchcraft in providing "an outlet for the social passions," and to realize that *uku-lobola*—"payment of cattle by a bridegroom to the father of his bride"—was not wife-purchase, but a form of ritual compensation. As he suggested in an article on "Bantu Sociology" for the new journal *Bantu Studies*, it was by understanding the functional significance of native customs, their part in native economic, moral, and religious life, their relations to other institutions and to the needs of the "social organism," that conflicts such as Bulhoek might be avoided and "harmonious relations" established. The teaching and research of his new Department of Social Anthropology was organized with such practical problems "constantly in view." Their role, however, was sharply delimited. Practical considerations might influence the choice of research problems, but the goal of social anthropology was the discovery of laws; and lest the inquiry be contaminated by "pet political theories," immediate practical concerns must be excluded. By the same token, the practical

*Brown served in this period as vice-chairman of the Cape Peninsula Native Welfare Society, and his writings have been seen as an "immanent critique of apartheid," later carried forward by liberal social anthropologists trained by his protégé Winifred Hoernlé. Their work has been contrasted with that of *volkenkundige* Afrikaner "apartheid anthropologists" who were influenced by Malinowski—this perhaps without adequate appreciation of his changing views on such issues (R. Gordon 1990, 1988; Gluckman 1975; below, 414–15).

application of its results must be left to others: the administrators and missionaries for whom the vacation courses were intended.[61]

To claim practical relevance while keeping politics at arm's length was no doubt a policy well suited to the propagation of social anthropology in the charged and even convulsive South African milieu of the early 1920s. But the privileging of theory was less a matter of policy than a central feature of Brown's anthropological project. When *The Andaman Islanders: A Study in Social Anthropology* was finally published in 1922, it was greeted back in London as "a revolutionary theory of social anthropology." Sir Richard Temple, who had advised on Brown's project before its Durkheimian redefinition, complained that Brown had gone out of his way to denigrate "so meticulous and accurate a recorder" as Temple's friend E. H. Man, whose observations—in contrast to Brown's—had been "spread over a long series of years." Temple nevertheless thought that Brown's approach, "if it proves to be generally acceptable," would "revolutionise" the "method of studying primitive peoples," insofar as it called for " 'a series of investigations in which the observation and the analysis and interpretation of the institutions of some one primitive people are carried on together by the ethnologist working in the field' "—and because it insisted that the only " 'sound rule of method' [was] to formulate clearly and explicitly the working hypothesis on which the interpretation is based." On the one hand, there should be an end of armchair anthropology; on the other, fieldwork should be theory-driven.[62]

Brown's volume was in fact structured by a separation of ethnographic observations from their "interpretation," and, on the very page in which he spoke of the separation of hypothesis from observation as a "false division of labour," there was a footnote acknowledging that his interpretation of Andamanese customs "was not worked out until after I left the islands." His book was nonetheless quite explicitly offered as the basis for a different sort of anthropology, which at this point in Brown's theoretical development might appropriately be described as a "functional cultural psychology." As such, it was motivated by concerns similar to those that had impelled Malinowski's "Baloma" and his subsequent attempt to define a social psychology. Although only on the penultimate page did Brown reveal that what he had been discussing was "the nature and function of the Andamanese religion," he had already by implication addressed most of the issues in the British tradition of the anthropology of religion (animism, nature worship, ancestor worship, totemism). He did so in Durkheimian terms; but insofar as he dealt with a "pretotemic" society, he carried the argument beyond the *Elementary Forms of the Religious Life,* which regarded totemism as the "most primitive and simple religion which is actually known." And he did so in terms of a rather different psychology: the sentiment psychology of

William McDougall and Alexander Shand. Like much of Brown's early work, the book was implicitly directed to Rivers: the two interpretive chapters on ceremony and myth, which occupy nearly half the text, may be read as a commentary on the problem of informant nescience, which had so troubled Rivers among the Todas, and as an explanation of "the social function of conservatism."[63]

For Brown, "interpretation" was not an attempt to seek the origin of customs or beliefs, but to discover their "meaning," which he assumed was inaccessible to the Andaman Islanders, except as "vague feelings" or "vague notions" they were "quite incapable of expressing" in words, save perhaps as "rationalisations." It was up to the anthropologist to "formulate in words the beliefs that are revealed in [their] actions" and to explicate their "processes of symbolic thought"—being "careful not to fall into the error of attributing to [them] the conceptions by which we make clear to ourselves [their] indefinite sentiments and notions," and accepting as a "rule of method" that interpretation must explain "not only the custom but also the reasons the natives give for following it." Keeping in mind Frazer's preoccupation with the "motives" of "savages"—and Rivers' difficulties in determining them—one may read the shift to "meaning" (in this passage) and thence to "function" as a reassertion of the interpretive authority of the anthropologist in the face of difficulties that arose with the movement from the armchair to the field.[64]

Brown's own interpretations were based on a "general psychological hypothesis as to the real nature of the phenomena to be explained." In opposition to the "intellectualist hypothesis" of Tylor and Frazer, for whom "beliefs are primary," and to explanations in terms of "surprise and terror" (Max Müller) or "awe and wonder" (Marett), his hypothesis was Durkheimian, recast in the terms of sentiment psychology. Society depended on the existence "in the minds of its members of a certain system of sentiments" (defined as "an organised system of emotional tendencies centred about some object") by which the conduct of the individual was regulated in conformity with the needs of the society. Every feature of the social system and every event or object affecting "the well-being or cohesion of the society" was an object of this system of sentiments, which was "not innate but developed in the individual by the action of society upon him." And it was the "social function" of the ceremonial customs, as collective expressions of these sentiments, to maintain them "in the mind of the individual" and transmit them "from one generation to another."[65]

Analyzing various Andaman ceremonies in these terms, Brown appealed frequently to "psycho-physical theory," to the fundamental psychological laws "regulating the affective life of human beings," to the evidence of "recent psychology"—even to the "commonplace of psychology" that "esthetic emotions are largely dependent upon motor images." However, his key concept was that of "social value": the way any object or thing—notably, whatever was consumed as food—"affects or is capable of affecting the social life." "The social value of food" was powerfully impressed upon the members of society in initiation ceremonies, which were the means of "moral or social education." By "producing in the space of a few days a very intense emotional experience," these ceremonies taught boys and girls "self-control or self-restraint" in relation to "one of the two fundamental human instincts—hunger." Initiation also served to mold their "social personality," by "producing or reinforcing the feeling of elation accompanying the recognition by an individual of his own social value"—a value marked by customarily regulated methods of personal adornment. Taken together, the ceremonial customs of the Andamanese formed "a closely connected system" which was ultimately about power—"the moral power of the society acting upon the individual." As Durkheim, Hubert, and Mauss had maintained, this was experienced by the individual as "something outside his own self" and was "projected into the world of nature."[66]

Turning from custom to belief, Brown sought the meaning of myths and legends in terms of his previous analysis of ceremony. On the basis of a comparison of several versions of the same legend to determine their common "motives," he concluded that these had primarily to do with "social value," and that their collective "function" was "to express in general the system of social values that is characteristic of the Andaman social organisation." Projecting onto nature "the moral forces that he experiences in society," projecting onto the "ancestors" the sense of his own dependence on tradition, each Andaman Islander had nevertheless to adapt to his social order and through it to the order of nature which was "constantly acting upon the social order." Together, these made up an "order of the universe" which was "subject to law, [and] controlled by unseen forces" that were construed in moral rather than scientific terms. Witnessed in external events, this moral law and order was also "experienced in the man's own consciousness or conscience" (both words, one notes, being necessary to convey Durkheim's *conscience*). This "view of the world" was not "a philosophy" reached by the "painful intellectual effort" of "searching out of meanings and reasons and causes." It was rather "the immediate and inevitable result of the experience of man in society," and it was as "the expression or formulation of this view of the world that the legends have their meaning, fulfill their function."[67]

If meaning was thus in the end apparently equated with function, it was in part because the Andamanese, "like other savages"—whom at several points Brown compared to children—had not "acquired the power of thinking abstractly." Since their "thought necessarily deals with concrete things," and since in any case what was expressed was more a matter of feeling than of thought, stories became the means by which they "express and systematize their fundamental notions of life and nature and the sentiments attaching to those notions." If their legends did not always "apply the laws of logical consistency" (despite the fact that "in everyday practical life" they showed "as much sound common-sense as the inhabitants of a civilised country") it was because "their purpose" was "not to give rational explanations, but to express sentiments." Echoing perhaps the later psychoanalytic Rivers, Brown argued that the "mental processes" underlying their legends were those of "symbolic thought" which could "be found in dreams and in art." In this context, it fell to the anthropologist to restate "the content of the legends in abstract terms." The epistemological status of that extrapolation was somewhat doubtful: at one point Brown commented that "if my personal impressions are of any value, this is really the idea that does underlie the legend in the native mind"; but at another, he said that there were "many details of the Andaman mythology that I cannot explain, owing simply, I believe, to my lack of insight into the ways of thought of the natives." That lack of insight, however, did not forestall the analysis of meaning once it was reconstrued as function; at that point, the ways of thought of the Andamanese and the anthropologist were one.[68]

Although in undertaking his interpretation, Brown had explicitly forsworn "any comparison of Andamanese customs with similar customs of other races," in the end he insisted that his "methods and principles" ought to be applicable "to the interpretation of other cultures," and "with necessary modifications, must be true of all human society." "For a culture to exist at all, and to continue to exist, it must conform to certain conditions": it must provide a mode of subsistence adequate to the environment and the population density; it must provide for continuity by "the proper care of children"; and it must provide "cohesion"—all of which required the "regulation of individual conduct" by a "certain system of moral customs." While the "system of sentiments or motives will clearly be different in different cultures, just as the system of moral rules is different in societies of different types," there was a "general substratum that is the same in all human societies." There was, in short, the basis for a program of comparative studies, and the presumption of comparability.[69]

When *The Andaman Islanders* was about to be reprinted in 1932, Radcliffe-Brown suggested a small number of minor changes, most of them involving the deletion of the word "psychology" or the substitution for it of the word "sociology." Although none of these was adopted, they are nonetheless suggestive of the direction of his theoretical development—and the extent to which Rivers, while alive, constrained it. For in preempting sociology, defining it in historical terms, and embracing "the ethnological analysis of culture," what Rivers left for Brown to claim as his own was a cultural "psychology" defined in synchronic functional terms. But with Rivers' death in 1922, Brown was free to redefine his enterprise; and the first step in that process was the presidential address he delivered to the anthropological section of the South African Association for the Advancement of Science the following year. Entitled "The Methods of Ethnology and Social Anthropology," it was, in effect, a revision and elaboration of the paper that Rivers had suggested he put aside a decade previously. It was also a counter statement to Rivers' own methodological manifesto of 1911 and a continuation of the discussion of the relations of "sociology and psychology" which Rivers had offered in response to Brown's critique of the doctrine of survivals.[70]

As Rivers had done in "The Ethnological Analysis of Culture," Brown surveyed the recent history and various national manifestations of anthropology as "the study of culture or civilization." Starting from Tylor's definition ("that complex whole which includes knowledge, belief, art, morals, law, custom, and any other capabilities and habits acquired by man as a member of society"), he suggested that the field had been plagued by a confusion of method. On the one hand, there was the "historical method," which sought no general laws but the "actual temporal relations between particular institutions or events or states of civilization." Because there was "almost no historical data" for "uncivilized peoples," historical evidence could only be indirect, reconstructions were "hypothetical," and the history produced was "conjectural history." By drawing on a variety of data (linguistic, physical, cultural, archeological) it was possible in some instances (e.g., the peopling of Madagascar) to produce "a knowledge of events and of their order of succession" in which some things "will be quite certain," others "probable," and some will never "get beyond mere guessing." Although he did not mention it, Brown had in fact produced such an "hypothetical reconstruction" of Andamanese culture history on the basis of their "technical culture." But there was another form of inquiry, which Brown called "inductive," because "it is essentially similar to the natural or inductive sciences" insofar as it sought "to discover and prove certain general laws." Given the difference of aim and method, it was advisable to regard the two inquiries as "separate, though doubtless connected studies, and to give them different names." Making explicit "a distinction already implicit" in much general usage, Brown proposed to call them "ethnology" and "social anthropology"—a designation he preferred to "sociology" because in English-speaking countries that term was commonly used to refer to "a somewhat formless" and overly ambitious study.[71]

The failure to distinguish inductive and historical study had led to confusion also in the study of cultural evolution. Just as Darwinian biological evolution assumed "the continuous action of the principles of heredity, variation, and natural selection," so also the development of culture might be studied inductively as "a process of evolution" governed by "specific principles or laws." But in fact it had been studied from an historical point of view as "a series of successive stages of development" conceived in unilinear terms—a failure even Durkheim had been guilty of, and which was best exemplified by Lewis Henry Morgan—rather than in branching terms as "each society develops its own special type as the result of its history and environment."[72]

In recent years, the latter "so-called evolutionary school" had been subject to very extensive criticism in England, Germany, and America. In each of those countries an historically oriented "ethnology" had reemerged, coming out of the undifferentiated "ethnology-anthropology of the last century" as "a special science" limiting itself "more and more strictly to the historical point of view." Although each version was different in its specific methodological principles, all had in common the rejection of "all attempts to discover general laws" and, in the American version especially, the relegation of "such an inductive study of culture" to "psychology."[73]

Following Durkheim, Brown now wished "most emphatically to insist that social anthropology is a science just as independent of psychology as psychology itself is independent of physiology, or as chemistry is independent of physics. . . ." To illustrate this, he discussed the case of a man arrested for murder, differentiating its individual aspect from the social institutional aspect along lines which, paradoxically, echo the discussion of blood feud Rivers had used in 1916 to differentiate psychology from his own historical sociology. But with Rivers gone, Brown was now free to claim for himself a newly dehistoricized and rechristened sociology—the laws of which were "in no sense laws of psychology."[74]

Such an inquiry looked forward to the eventual discovery of evolutionary laws or principles analogous to those in biology, the continuous operation of which produced "the various past and present forms of society." But it rejected the search for "origins" as it had been conducted by the likes of Frazer, to whose conceptional theory of totemism Brown contrasted his own theory of the social value of food in undifferentiated and differentiated societies. His theory, which was "capable of verification" over time, "by the ordinary process of induction," was a theory of origin in a processual sense, analogous to Darwin's, rather than the unverifiable historical sense characteristic of "the older anthropology." Typified by "the theory of animism of Tylor and Frazer," the latter approach had impeded the development of social anthropology, which assumed that the development of custom was the result not of an intellectual search for understanding, but of the need for "collective action in certain definite circumstances affecting the society or group."[75]

Brown went on to discuss the relations of ethnology and social anthropology in terms echoing his earlier discussion of dynamic and static problems. Aside from a very few new facts, ethnology had nothing to offer social anthropology, which "must rely on [real] history, not conjectural history." But as Rivers' *History of Melanesian Society* in fact revealed, ethnology did depend on assumptions about general social processes ("what is likely to happen when two peoples of different cultures meet and settle in the same island"). The relation was thus one of "one sided dependence": social anthropology could do without ethnology, but not vice versa.[76*]

Nor could ethnology offer any results of practical value. As Kroeber himself had acknowledged in reviewing Lowie's *Primitive Society* (previously cited by Brown as the "conclusive criticism" of Morgan's theories), the products of historical ethnology seemed "rather sterile" and without applicability to the problems of the world. In contrast, social anthropology, by teaching us the laws of social change, might eventually help to build a more satisfactory society than "the civilization of to-day." In the meantime, it had much to offer (along lines sketched in "Bantu Sociology") to the "missionary or the public servant who is engaged in dealing with the practical problems of the adjustment of the native civilization to the new conditions that have resulted from our occupation of the country."[77]

And yet, except in France, social anthropology had suffered "undeserved neglect," while ethnology "in recent years" had had "more than its fair share of attention." This, at a moment in history that was "critical for the study of primitive culture." Just as social anthropology, after three-quarters of a century, was "finding its feet" in terms of method-

*There is evidence in what may be taken as Rivers' final general statement on social organization that he was in fact influenced by Brown's insistence on the priority of the study of static phenomena. A manuscript Rivers prepared in 1920 for lectures at Cambridge in 1921 and 1922, published after his death by his diffusionist disciple Perry, opens with the suggestion that social structure can be studied from two points of view, the "historical" and the "static." Studies in "recent years" (presumably Rivers' own and those of his followers) had emphasized the former, and in their "zeal towards this end," had "perhaps neglected the task, which must always come first, of understanding human societies as they are, before they can expect to understand how they have come to be what they are." Rivers' lectures, therefore, would "deal mainly with what may be called the static study of social organization, rather than with the dynamic," treating not only the "structure" of groups, but also "their functions" (Rivers 1924:3–5; cf. ACHP: Radcliffe-Brown to Haddon 5/9/27). Although the text that followed makes clear that Rivers had by no means abandoned diffusionism, it is worth noting the extent of his reliance on Brown's analysis of Australian social organization—to which an appendix was devoted (195–201), in addition to various references in the text itself (32, 75, 196ff.).

ological sophistication and the beginnings of institutional recognition, "its subject matter was disappearing with great rapidity." What was urgently necessary for South African science was to assist "in every way possible the science of social anthropology."[78]

As soon as he moved to Cape Town, Brown had begun "swatting up the Bantu." One of the first sources he would have encountered was Henri Junod's *Life of a South African Tribe.* A long-time Swiss Protestant missionary among the Ba Thonga of Portuguese East Africa, Junod had been inspired to take up ethnography in 1898 by the remark of a visiting English diplomat, Lord Bryce, about how thankful we would be today if "a Roman had taken the trouble to fully investigate the habits of our Celtic forefathers!" Like Fison, Junod later came under the influence of evolutionary anthropology, and in 1909 he began a more "systematic investigation" using Frazer's questionnaire. Although he had earlier been doubtful of evolutionary marriage sequences, under the influence of Sydney Hartland he came to the conclusion that "in former and very remote times, our tribe has passed through the matriarchal stage," interpreting the relations of the mother's brother to his sister's son as a confirming evidence (although without using the term "survival"). It was to this issue that Brown addressed the most important theoretical contribution of his South African period.[79]

There were tactical reasons for focussing on what was a rather short passage in an ethnography which Malinowski later described as "the only entirely satisfactory synthesis that embraces every aspect of tribal life," and which in other respects was surely grist for Brown's comparative mill. But despite Junod's great sympathy for the Ba Thonga, and his feeling that the "curses of civilization far exceed its blessings for the South African native," Junod had no doubt that lobola and polygamy must be eradicated, and his book was full of practical advice to the government and missionaries on how to manage this. For an anthropologist who had undertaken a similar advisory role from a more relativist perspective, a critique of Junod was a useful way to assert the power and the relevance of social anthropology—and, by implication, a further posthumous thrust at Rivers, whose *History of Melanesian Society* had depended on similar assumptions about the role of the mother's brother.[80]

For Brown, the theoretical challenge was to find an "alternative hypothesis" to that of matriarchal survival. The customs Junod described (the uncle's special care for his uterine nephew, and the liberties permitted the latter, who had claims on his uncle's estate and might even inherit one of his widows) were not unique to the Ba Thonga; similar customs were found among the Nama Hottentots, the Tongans, and the Fijians, all of whom were patrilineal. Calling attention to a "correlation" between these customs and the "particular respect and obedience" due the father's sister, Brown argued that these were not "independent institutions, but part of one system," and that the explanation of any part of the system must fit "with an analysis of the system as a whole."[81]

Since social relations in primitive societies were "very largely regulated on the basis of kinship," and since the number of "logically possible" kinship relations was very large, a "system of classification" was necessary, and the "principle of classification most commonly adopted" was that "of the equivalence of brothers." That principle, however, gave no immediate pattern for "either the mother's brother or the father's sister," and where "the classificatory system" was highly elaborated, that problem was solved by regarding the former as male mother and the latter as female father. Brown then sought to "deduce what ought to be the patterns of behaviour" toward these relatives in a patrilineal society by considering first those toward the father and mother. As evidenced by Junod, the former implied "respect and even fear"; the latter, "tenderness and indulgence," and it was these patterns that were extended to the father's sister and mother's brother, respectively—which was "exactly what we find" among the three groups discussed.[82]

But if it was "easy enough to invent hypotheses," the hard work began when "we set out to verify them"—an undertaking which, among other things, would involve research among matriarchal societies. This in turn required the elimination of certain "false ideas" about matriarchy and patriarchy. All kinship was ultimately bilateral, but because "society tends to divide into segments," a choice must be made. Breaking down matriarchy and patriarchy into attributes that echoed Tylor's (descent, residence, inheritance, succession, and authority), Brown argued that the distinction between the two forms was "not an absolute but a relative one." In Africa there were two regions of "strongly patriarchal" peoples separated by an east-west band in which "the tendency is towards matriarchal institutions." Among the only one of these that had been fairly well studied, the Ila of Northern Rhodesia, the mother's brother had greater power and was more honored than the father. Challenging Junod's theory to explain how this relationship could be changed to that which now existed among the Ba Thonga, Brown went on to point to patterns in other groups which Junod's theory would not explain.[83]

But on his own hypothesis, the matter was "fairly simple": because of the tendency in "primitive society" to "merge the individual in the group," there was a "tendency to extend to all members of a group a certain type of behaviour which has its origin in a relationship to one particular member of the group." Thus, "the pattern of behaviour towards the mother, which is developed in the family by reasons of the nature of the family group and its social life, is extended with suitable modifications to the mother's sister and the mother's brother, then to the group of maternal kindred as a whole, and finally to the maternal gods, the ancestors of the mother's group"—and likewise with the father. In conclusion, Brown argued that his analysis had "not only theoretical but practical interest," insofar as it helped clarify "the function of the lobola."[84]

Brown's paper has been subjected to a variety of criticism—including an ethnographic rebuttal by Junod. Even his disciples were retrospectively disturbed by its "dyadic paradigm" and "extensionist" analysis couched in the language of "sentiment." But even those who later came to regard its offspring as misconceived might grant that it had a "seminal influence" on the development of kinship theory over the next few decades.[85]

That influence was disseminated also through Brown's formal teaching. The reading lists for his courses were still full of evolutionary anthropology, including Morgan's *Ancient Society*, Tylor's *Primitive Culture*, and the two major works of Frazer. These, however, were primarily intellectual foils for his own lectures, into which he was "pouring out" the "accumulation of twelve years of thinking," giving his students "a theory of social structure, a theory of kinship, of law, of religion, and a theory of art"—notes from which were passed on by Isaac Schapera to Edward Evans-Pritchard in 1927.[86]

Over a longer run a key intermediary role was played by Winifred Tucker Hoernlé, who for many years taught anthropology in Johannesburg at the University of Witwatersrand. As a student at Newnham College before the war she had been "overawed" by Brown's renditions of Andaman lullabies, and had attended his Trinity College lectures of 1910, before going on to study psychology with Wundt and Külpe in Germany and sociology with Durkheim in Paris. It was Hoernlé's fieldwork among the Nama Hottentots of German Southwest Africa in 1912 and 1913, and again (with Brown's support) in 1922, that provided him with one of his comparative reference points in the critique of Junod. Although Hoernlé had planned to write a monograph under Brown's guidance, he involved her instead in a comparative study of African social institutions.[87]

As described to Rivers several months before his death, the project had an indirect connection to Tylor's adhesions paper: Brown offered as his model the "ethnographical catalogue" proposed by the Dutch anthropologist Steinmetz, whose work had in turn been stimulated by Tylor's paper. But the "correlations" Brown sought were quite different from Tylor's "adhesions"—or, as he suggested to Hoernlé, from the study of "complexes" by American ethnologists, to which "the method has a superficial resemblance." His plan was to pick a particular institution or "system of connected institutions" and to collect "all available information for Africa south of the Sahara," in order to "discover a type" and "study its variations." Starting with the attempt to "exhibit the majority

Winifred Tucker [Hoernlé], accompanied by a Mrs. Gilman and an unidentified wagon driver, crossing the Swakop River in German Southwest Africa in September 1913, during her second field trip into Namaqualand. (Courtesy of the University of Witwatersrand Archives)

of African systems" of kinship as "varieties of one type," the inquiry would proceed then to the cattle and agricultural "complexes," and then to marriage.[88]

The project, however, was sidetracked by Brown's decision to accept appointment to the newly created chair in anthropology at the University of Sydney. Already in 1923, when he first heard of the Sydney plan, he believed that he had "advertised and boomed anthropology" enough so that "neither Cape Town, Johannesburg or Pretoria will let the subject drop." It was left to Hoernlé to carry on what he had begun. Although she herself published relatively little, her 1937 article, "The Social Organization of the Bantu-speaking Peoples," was clearly in the spirit of Brown's project. Initiated into teaching at Witwatersrand in Johannesburg "with the most sympathetic and invaluable help from Professor Brown," she went on to recruit several students into anthropology, and was later "honoured with the unofficial title of the 'Mother of Social Anthropology in South Africa.'"[89]

A. R. Radcliffe-Brown and the Social Organization of Australian Tribes

The movement to create a chair in anthropology at Sydney had developed in part as response to the mandate system set up under the League of Nations, under which German New Guinea—which had been quickly taken over by Australian forces early in the Great War—and portions of Melanesia became "C" mandates (or virtual colonial possessions) of Australia. Among those involved was Hubert Murray, the paternalistic lieutenant governor of adjoining Papua, whose "Murray System" encouraged the protection of traditional village life within a policy of controlled economic development. Despite his ambivalence toward Malinowski, and his scepticism of both diffusionist and functionalist theory, Murray thought that anthropology might be of administrative use, and in 1921 he appointed two "Government Anthropologists." Three years later, a similar position was established in the mandated territory itself. The potential administrative relevance of anthropology was, in short, "in the air"—and there were men in Australian academic science who were anxious to precipitate it. Among them were Walter (now Sir) Baldwin Spencer, as well as Malinowski's father-in-law, Sir David Orme Masson, the president of the Australian National Research Council.[90]

The movement took shape in connection with the second Pan-Pacific Science Congress in 1923, at which Haddon chaired the anthropological section, and supportive programmatic statements were presented from Frazer, Seligman, and Malinowski. Putting aside his personal feelings, Murray noted the work his two government anthropologists were doing "on the intensive lines suggested by Dr. Malinowski." After it had been edited to remove its hyperdiffusionist specifics, a draft proposal prepared by Elliot Smith became the basis for the general resolution on anthropological research, to be divided along national lines, with Australia given a primary interest in Papua, the New Guinea mandate, and Melanesia. Two other resolutions were addressed to the commonwealth government on the teaching of anthropology and the study of Australian Aborigines.[91]

After a subsequent meeting with the Prime Minister, Masson wrote Haddon that a chair at Sydney was a certainty, indicating that although it would be in effect "a chair of Social Ethnology," the negotiators preferred to call it "a chair of Anthropology" so as not to preclude other studies or alienate physical anthropologists. They had not reckoned, however, on the influence of a British colonial officer, sent out to advise the Commonwealth on "the administration of native races," who was strongly urging that what was needed was "men of character" with a public school rather than university education, and that "an interest in Anthropology really interferes with the proper discharge of their duties." As a result, the government reneged on its commitment, and it was only when Elliot Smith offered the prospect of funding by the Rockefeller Foundation that the Sydney chair was actually established, to "provide anthropological training" for cadets and senior officers in New Guinea and Papua, to train research workers among Australian Aborigines, and to offer degree courses. Spencer had mixed feelings about Radcliffe Brown, whose work he respected, despite the fact that it was "rather written as if he were the great 'Pooh-Bah,'" without "sufficient regard" for the accomplishments of "men like Howitt." But with the continuing support of Haddon, it was a foregone conclusion that the committee of electors, meeting at his home in Cambridge, would choose Brown over the only other serious contender, A. M. Hocart, who had no teaching experience and had done no work in Australia.[92]

In June of 1926—having legally hyphenated his name several months before—Radcliffe-Brown landed in Sydney to begin another five-year period of booming and building "social anthropology." On the way out he had toured American universities at the invitation of the Rockefeller Foundation. In New York, where he stayed at the Yale Club with Malinowski (who was on a similar tour for the Laura Spelman Rockefeller Memorial), he "saw Boas and his supporters" at Columbia. Visiting also at Harvard, Chicago, and Berkeley, he felt that he had got in touch "with nearly all the anthropologists of note." At Berkeley, he discovered a "very promising young man, Lloyd Warner," who had "done four years anthropology," and whom he encouraged to do fieldwork in Northern Australia, after "further training in America" and "a month or so" in Sydney.[93]

It was a pattern that others were to follow in the next few years. As chairman of the Committee on Anthropological Research of the Australian National Research Council, the local dispensing agent of Rockefeller Foundation support, Radcliffe-Brown had a certain discretionary power, and until after 1930, there were no equivalent resources elsewhere within the British sphere. As a result, Sydney became a center from or through which field research was carried on, not only in Australia, but throughout the area. In addition to Radcliffe-Brown's own students, others from the United States (including Margaret Mead and Hortense Powdermaker), or from Cambridge (including Gregory Bateson and Reo Fortune), or from Malinowski's seminar (including Raymond Firth) would stop off before, during, or after their fieldwork. Although he had of course to deal with administrative "gatekeepers" like E. P. Chinnery, the government anthropologist in the mandated territory, Radcliffe-Brown had input into site selection even outside of Australia (where his students naturally went to areas he chose or approved). In consultation with Chinnery, he directed Bateson to the Baining; when Raymond Firth planned to work on Rennell Island, for which Radcliffe-Brown had already trained Ian Hogbin, he was sent instead to Tikopia—in place of Fortune, who had wanted to work there. Fortune's project was "psychological," and "as one who has tried psychological investigations amongst primitive peoples," Radcliffe-Brown was "very doubtful of the value of such work"—the more so, perhaps, because Tikopia had been a critical ethnographic instance in the argument of Rivers' *History of Melanesian Society*.[94]

Although Radcliffe-Brown had come to Australia with the tacit understanding that he was to build "social anthropology," his position required him also to deal with projects in other fields of anthropology: of the first four funded, three were in fact in physical anthropology. And insofar as he was still concerned with the issues of his debate with Rivers (the homogeneity of Australian culture and its relation to that of Melanesia), "ethnological" evidence—the "Australoid" features of skulls from Malekula or the relation of Papuan and Australian languages—remained highly salient. But "the real motive" impelling his return to Australia was the chance to pursue problems which "seemed to me of particular importance for the general theories of sociology," and it was toward that end that his research program was primarily directed.[95]

By 1929, there were a dozen men and women "working in the field within Radcliffe-Brown's general plan." In retrospect, it seems clear that this plan had both a narrow short-run and a broader long-run aspect. The first step was to create a comparative baseline such as Radcliffe-Brown had envisioned in South Africa, and soon after his arrival he began "the immense task of collating and indexing all the anthropological and ethnographical information about Australia, New Guinea and the Pacific." From there, the next step was the same one he had suggested to Hoernlé: to take, in order, a series of connected institutions, starting with kinship, and to show that Australian kinship systems were "varieties of one type." Since 1913, he had published two further "Notes on the Social Organization of Australian Tribes," and there was by this time a considerable body of ethnographic material, of varying quality, covering much of Australia. The problem was to fill in the blank spaces on his distribution maps; to this end he sent a half-dozen fieldworkers into areas across the northern reaches of the continent and conducted brief inquiries of his own near Sydney in 1929 and 1930. In 1930, he brought this material together in a three-part monograph, "The Social Organization of Australian Tribes."[96]

The first two parts were definitional and taxonomic. To begin with, Radcliffe-Brown distinguished two "basic elements of social structure" from which "the complex kinship organizations of Australia are built":

the family and the "horde" or local territorial group. Beyond these were "tribes" (defined in terms of linguistic unity), often divided into "sub-tribes," both of which were divided (by principles which transcended tribal boundaries) into two, four, or eight parts that were often unsuitably called "marriage classes." In the interest of "more systematic terminology," Radcliffe-Brown proposed to refer to these as "moieties," "sections," and "sub-sections," which were related as "couples" and "pairs" in "cycles"—without noting that he himself had once used the terms "phraties" and "classes" for the first two categories, or that the term "section" had been previously used by R. H. Mathews, a surveyor somewhat at odds with the British anthropological establishment, who had published several hundred articles in the turn-of-the-century period. By adding a further distinction in terms of matrilineal or patrilineal descent, Radcliffe-Brown was able to map the distribution throughout Australia of seven different groupings, all of them composed of people who regarded themselves as related—so that the named divisions were in each instance "part of a larger whole": "the *kinship system* of the tribe." In Australia, these systems were in every case "classificatory," which Radcliffe-Brown defined in terms of three "principles": the "equivalence of brothers" (or siblings); the grouping of affinal with consanguinal relatives; and the extension of the system without limit, so that everyone an Australian might have contact with was a relative "of one kind or another"—and subject to a certain expected "pattern of behavior" appropriate to his kind, including the regulation of marriage.[97]

To offer a "systematic description" of the "many variations" of Australian kinship systems, a classification in terms of a limited number of "norms" was necessary. For this purpose Radcliffe-Brown used the two "types" he had defined in 1913, one (the Kariera), based on matrilateral cross-cousin marriage, with two lines of descent; the other (now exemplified by the Aranda—Spencer's Arunta), based on marriage with the mother's mother's brother's daughter's daughter, with four lines of descent. Complicating the matter was the relationship of the kinship system to other social structural phenomena: a system of patrilineal local clans which Radcliffe-Brown felt was "normal, though not quite universal," a more infrequent but potentially coexisting system of matrilineal clans, and various forms of "totemism," to which he gave "brief reference" as part of a "larger structure in which the society and external nature are brought together."[98]

With the definitional framework established, Radcliffe-Brown went on to offer what was "really only a systematic catalogue" of fifty-one "types" known at that time. In addition to his own fieldwork and that of six students, he drew on previous Australian literature, with a caution that accounts like those of Howitt and Mathews should not be accepted "without careful criticism" (although both were frequently cited, along with Daisy Bates).* By the end of the catalogue, the concept of "type" was a bit ambiguous. Aside from the two main "types" and the entries that conformed to them, there were also a number of "variant," "anomalous," "intermediate," or "special" forms (among these several based on "the unpublished notes" of his own students, including Warner's Murngin, Elkin's Ungarinyin, and Piddington's Karadjeri, as well as his own Yaralde)—all of them also referred to as "types." He was nevertheless able to conclude that there was "an organization of a single specialised type over the whole continent."[99]

Without attempting "detailed sociological analysis," the final section consisted of a discussion of some "theoretical" issues. Siding with Rivers against Kroeber, Radcliffe-Brown insisted that there was "a close correlation between the kinship terminology of a people and their social institutions." But against "Morgan and those who follow him"—which on this issue would have included Rivers—he insisted that this "very thorough functional correlation" was not "a survival from some very different form of social organization in a purely hypothetical past," but an aspect of "the social organization of that tribe as it exists in the present." Formulating the "principles that are active in the Australian classification of kin," Radcliffe-Brown found four: the "equivalence of brothers," which, generalized, was the basis on which "the existing system is built"; "the distinction between the father and the mother" (and their respective relatives); the relations of "authority and subordination" between members of adjacent generations, and of "social equivalence" between those one generation apart; and reciprocity in marriage as an instance of a "wider principle of reciprocity." All of these principles were based on the recognition of "individual relationships" reflecting "actual genealogical connection" as it was socially construed, but with a distinction between "near and distant relatives" of the same category. Citing Malinowski, Radcliffe-Brown suggested that at the base of it all was "the recognition that the most significant and permanent social relations between individuals are those between parents and children and between children of the same parents."[100]

*Others besides Radcliffe-Brown had been critical of Mathews and his work. Australian ethnography has been described as "marred by quite exceptional ill will, bitterness, and personal vendettas"—including numerous charges of plagiarism. Mathews had been involved in debates with both Howitt and Spencer, as well as with Radcliffe-Brown, and his corresponding membership in the Anthropological Institute was in fact rescinded on a technicality in 1898, after a number of complaints against him (RAIA: Council minutes 3/8/98, 3/29/98). More recently, he has been reintegrated into the Australian ethnographic canon, as "winner" of his debate with Howitt, although faring less well with Spencer and Radcliffe-Brown (McKnight 1990:47–50; see also Elkin 1956, 1975; R. Needham 1974; Mathews 1905).

In a similarly presentist mode, Radcliffe-Brown treated the organization of the "horde" or "local group," the issue of exogamy, and the moiety, section, and clan structure. Here, individual kinship would not suffice; implicitly harking back to his 1910 lectures and to early Durkheim, but without at this point referring to it as a "principle of opposition," Radcliffe-Brown introduced "the growth of segmentary structures [as] a constant feature of social development." Although a classificatory system of terminology would serve to establish a kinship structure to regulate the social relations of individuals in a community of "limited size," it would be "unstable" until supplemented by a "segmentary organization" that would place "individuals into permanent and recognizable groups." Without using the term, Radcliffe-Brown was attempting to account for the "dual organization"; its "close correlation" with "the classificatory system" he saw (contra Rivers) as part of "a system behind which there are certain active principles, which not merely help to produce the institutions at their origin but serve to maintain them in existence as long as they continue."[101]

Rejecting "conjectural history," Radcliffe-Brown opted for what looks very much like a "conjectural functionalism"—at every point along the way offering comments on the "function" of this or that principle or feature. Some of them might be called Malinowskian: "the important function of the family is that it provides for the feeding and bringing up of the children." Some of them might be called Darwinian: the "function" of patrilineal descent within the horde was to preserve the detailed "local knowledge" necessary to survive in the "unfavourable environment" of Australia. But the most important were Durkheimian, insofar as they had to do with the maintenance of "social integration." Because "the family is a short-lived group," a more "stable structure"—based initially on the "principle of the solidarity of siblings"—had to be created: "every human society has to provide for itself a system of social integration whereby individuals are united into groups and collective action is provided for." Such "integrative systems" might differ in their numerical range or "level of integration"; and in any society there were factors tending to either expansion or contraction of "social solidarity." And behind Durkheim lurked Herbert Spencer. Looking again at the main varieties of Australian social organization, Radcliffe-Brown contrasted the Kariera as "one of the simplest integrative systems" and the Aranda as providing both a "wider" and a "closer" integration. Anticipating his posthumously published acknowledgment that "all his life he had accepted the hypothesis of social evolution as formulated by Spencer as a useful working hypothesis," he spoke of the Kariera and the Aranda as "two terms in an evolutionary process"—not in the sense that the Aranda system was "derived historically" from one identical with the

Kariera, but rather insofar as evolution was a process "by which stable integrations at a higher level are substituted for or replace integrations at a lower level."[102]

But if it seems thus to be embedded in assumptions and issues of the past, "The Social Organization of Australian Tribes" has also been viewed as a step toward a purely "jural" analysis. While Radcliffe-Brown did not yet speak in such terms, he was definitely looking to the future: his "chief purpose" had been to "remove certain misconceptions" that were "current in anthropological literature" and "clear the way for a sociological study of the Australian culture." His work was later to be criticized for privileging "ideal patterns" as opposed to actual behavior—to the extent of arguing that "'four or five sufficiently extensive genealogies' would suffice to reveal a tribe's kinship structure." Even its critics, however, granted that for a long time it did indeed provide the framework for the study of Australian social structure.[103]

But as his reference to "Australian culture" suggests, for Radcliffe-Brown "social structure" was in 1931 still part of a larger project. In the previous decade he had referred several times to writing an Australian book conceived of in terms resonant of *The Andaman Islanders;* at one point it was described as focussing on "social personality," linked to the concept of "value," and a "final and conclusive theory of the soul." Although that book was never to be completed, there were several publications on "totemism" which gestured toward a more inclusive project.[104]

Having come to anthropology when the discussion of totemism seemed to be leading either to a dead end or to interminable confusion, Radcliffe-Brown was slow to reopen it. *The Andaman Islanders,* largely written in that disillusionary moment, contained no reference to totemism, though much of its argument could be fitted into the four-part "theory of totemism" which (echoing his 1910 lecture) he sketched in print a year after the book appeared. Shortly before his departure from South Africa he published an account of the "practically universal" distribution of "the rainbow-serpent myth" in Australia—which, with Rivers again clearly in mind, he saw as evidence of the homogeneity of Australian culture. In the process, however, he offered comments on associated "totemic ceremonies" which in fact echoed Frazer's second theory: their "ostensible purpose" was to maintain the forces of nature at full power by "the cooperative efforts of the various totemic groups amongst whom the various realms of nature are distributed."[105]

Although worried that the concept of totemism might have "outlived its usefulness," Radcliffe-Brown returned to the matter in 1929. Drawing on his own recent and earlier fieldwork, as well as that of Ursula McConnell (sister-in-law of Malinowski's friend Elton Mayo), he suggested that this had demonstrated the wide distribution of a cult with three essential features: the association of local sites with particular natural species; a system of rites for their increase; and a system of myths. Whether to call this or the Aranda form (in which natural species were linked to the section system) "totemism" was not so important as to collect more information on the larger question of the relation of man and nature in ritual and myth as the basis for a "general theory of the social function of ritual and myth." The same year, at the fourth Pan-Pacific Science Congress, Radcliffe-Brown offered such a theory.[106]

With the early-twentieth-century discussion now two decades past, Radcliffe-Brown felt free to reassert a linkage of the magico-religious and the sociological along lines foreshadowed in 1910. Drawing heavily on his *Andaman Islanders,* and on a modification of the argument of Durkheim's *Elementary Forms,* he found the common element in the Australian social forms usually called totemistic in a "general tendency" to "characterise" the segments of society by associating each segment with "some natural species or some portion of nature" toward which a "ritual attitude" was adopted. It was possible, as in the Andamans, for a hunting and gathering society to have the ritual attitude without having totemism. But when in the course of "social development" such a society was "differentiated into segmentary groups such as clans," a "ritual specialisation" took place by which each segment acquired "a special and particular relation" to "one or more natural species." In contrast to Durkheim, who explained the tendency to see the universe as a moral or social order as "a projection of society into external nature," Radcliffe-Brown inverted the relationship, arguing that "the process was one by which, in the fashioning of culture, external nature, so called, comes to be incorporated into the social order as an essential part of it." And insofar as totemism characteristically arose in societies that were dependent "wholly or in part on natural productions for subsistence," there were echoes in Radcliffe-Brown of a utilitarian or materialist approach antithetical to the idealism of the later Durkheim.[107]

In Australia, as in South Africa, Radcliffe-Brown's generalized theoretical concerns were more systematically developed in his university lectures, and it is clear that much of his influence was a matter of immediate aural presence. Surviving notes from the South African and Chicago lectures suggest that these were built upon a base established in 1910, with modifications and elaborations appropriate to the development of his thought on particular issues. They were, however, received by many of his students as "a revelation." He "never used notes" and "always seemed to speak extempore," commanding "detail and principle with fluent ease" and to "telling" effect: "we all had the feeling of 'system' in all he said, a system that seemed to us clear, economical, and intellectually satisfying."[108]

Despite his verbal facility, Radcliffe-Brown regarded lecturing a burden—the more so in view of his various other activities "booming anthropology." In addition to the administration and supervision of field research, these included the inauguration of the journal *Oceania* as an organ for fieldworkers trained under his program, special courses for cadets in the administrative services in New Guinea, vacation courses for missionaries and others, and public lectures on a range of topics—including one on "racial problems in the British Empire," in which he called into question colonial rule "on the basis of domination," and looked forward to a future empire in which "the many different races" would become parts of a "Single System, so as to make them one people." To free more time for all this, he early on sought the appointment of a lecturer. When premature death forestalled his choice of Deacon, he rejected F. E. Williams, the government anthropologist in Papua, brought Camilla Wedgwood out from Cambridge for one year, and finally settled on Raymond Firth, Malinowski's first and favorite student.[109]

For fifteen months, Firth was part of an intimate social circle Radcliffe-Brown gathered round himself in Sydney (where he was again living without his daughter and his wife, from whom he was divorced in the early 1930s). Although he moved at times in the highest "white tie and tails" circles of Sydney society, Radcliffe-Brown preferred the small international group with whom he regularly dined at a little Swiss cafe, and whom he occasionally entertained with melodies from Rameau and Couperin on his upright piano. Among his intimates, he was then known as "Rex"—a name "suited to his bearing and his disposition," which Lloyd Warner nevertheless democratized as "Rexy." He held forth on "an amazing range of subjects," from Herbert Spencer and the theory of instincts, to the Earl of Oxford's authorship of Shakespeare's plays, to Javanese dance—which he demonstrated, clad in a sarong, at parties in his flat in the Oxford Hotel. He was also capable of lecturing people "upon their own subject," claiming as his own knowledge that was sometimes only second hand—an "intellectual deafness" which was "a reflex of his egocentrism": "all that he learnt became an integral part of himself and was fitted into his own personality."[110]

Among the "the clutch of aging knights" who dominated Australian science, there were some who were put off by Radcliffe-Brown's "elegant cultured life style," with its "whiff of British superiority," and after several years problems began to develop. In 1929, a dispute over the photographic expenses of a fieldworker from Melbourne University put Radcliffe-Brown at odds with Malinowski's father-in-law, Sir David Orme Masson. Sir Hubert Murray, hearing reports that Radcliffe-Brown's lectures to cadets and officers of the Papuan administrative service were too obscurely theoretical, became concerned that functionalism might

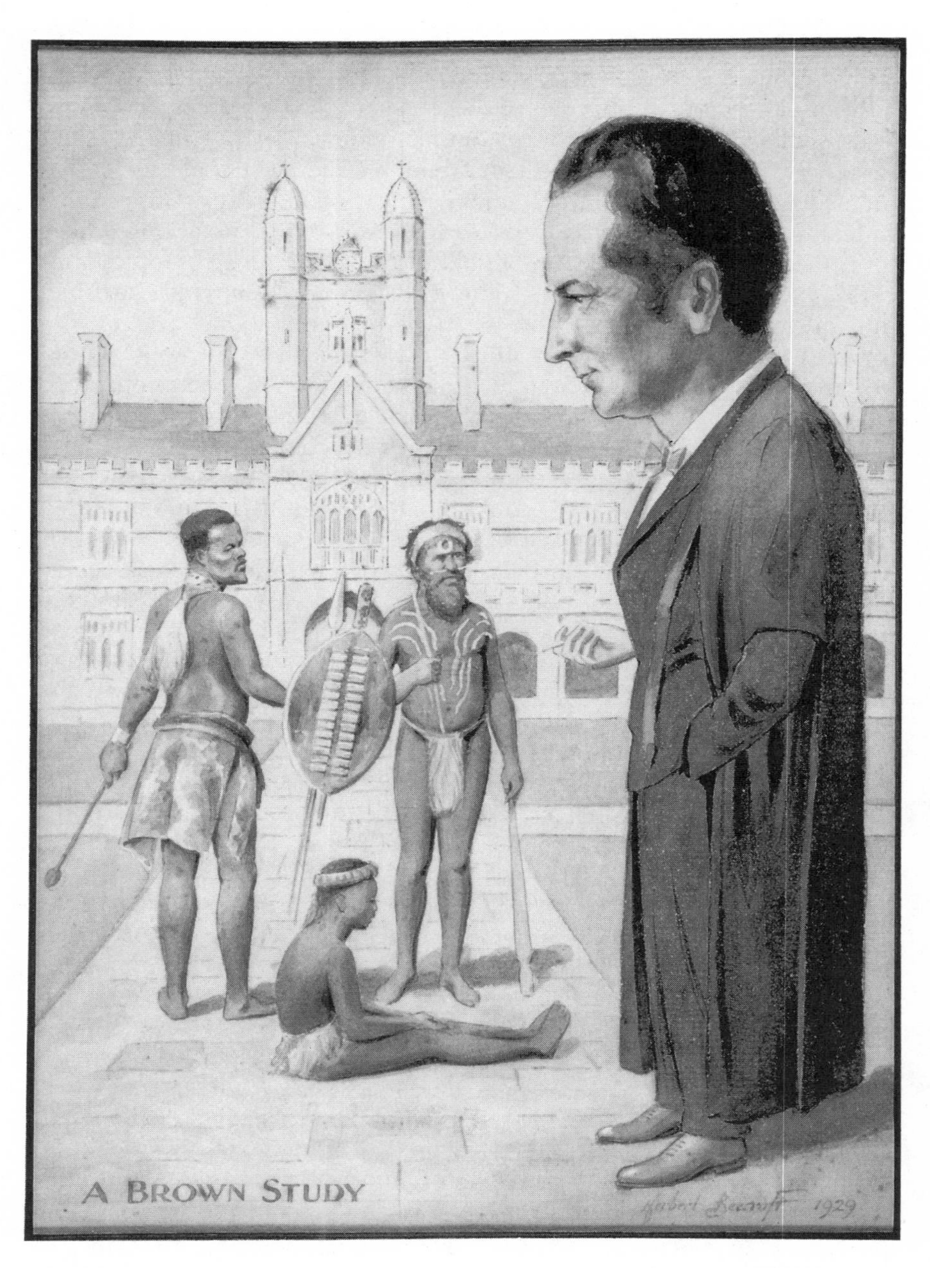

Radcliffe-Brown, in abstracted contemplation of the observing ethnographic subjects of his social anthropology: (left to right), a generic Bantu warrior, an Andamanese woman (cf. plate 14 in *The Andaman Islanders*), and a fig-leafed Australian Aboriginal—a wash drawing by Herbert Beecroft (b. 1865), who emigrated to Australia in 1905 and imagined this pre-postmodern pastiche in 1929. (Courtesy of the Institute of Social and Cultural Anthropology, Oxford)

justify noninterference with native practices he felt it necessary to stamp out. He took as deliberate provocation Camilla Wedgwood's article, in the opening number of *Oceania*, justifying native warfare as helping "to preserve a vigorous society." And he was more than a bit displeased when Radcliffe-Brown, at the meeting of Australian and New Zealand Association for the Advancement of Science in 1930, in the course of defending his theoretical and noninterventionist approach to "Applied Anthropology," not only reiterated the integrative function of native warfare, but questioned the right of the British empire to "exercise control over [the] destinies" of the peoples of India and Africa.[111]

Matters came to a head in 1930, when, after further disputes over administrative matters, Masson called for a review by the Australian National Research Council of "the conditions of award and the method of administration of grants in aid of anthropological field research." In an attempt to bypass the Research Council, Radcliffe-Brown appealed directly to the Rockefeller Foundation for money to set up an independent Institute of Anthropology. But when this circumventing initiative became known locally, it "caused an uproar" in Research Council circles, and was apparently a factor (along with the local reverberations of the world financial crisis) in the withdrawal of subsidies first by the government of Masson's home state, Victoria, and then by several other state governments. With the initial five-year Rockefeller grant coming to an end, the program he had worked hard to build seemed in jeopardy. Radcliffe-Brown, whose academic nomadism was as much personal style as product of circumstance, found reason enough to leave Australia. Although his time in Sydney had been "five of the best years" of his life, he had suffered there from "a chronic septic throat," and even before the blow-up was contemplating an appointment in the United States, on the grounds that his task in Sydney was accomplished: "the ideas in anthropology which I have maintained for twenty years are beginning to gain currency and acceptance amongst the younger people." In April of 1931, he accepted an offer to join the faculty of the University of Chicago, leaving Firth to carry on in Sydney for the next eighteen months. After that, the pieces were picked up by A. P. Elkin, an Australian-born Anglican "bush parson" who had taken a doctorate in anthropology at University College under Elliot Smith and Perry before joining Radcliffe-Brown's team of fieldworkers—and whose long-nurtured sense of betrayal and abandonment eventually produced a strikingly vitriolic obituary of his one-time mentor.[112]

In the summer before he arrived in Chicago, Radcliffe-Brown spent time in New York lecturing to Boasians at Columbia University, then returned briefly to London to give the presidential address to the anthropological section at the Centenary Meeting of the British Association for the Advancement of Science. To mark his ceremonial reentry upon the metropolitan scene after nearly two decades at the periphery, he offered an overview of "the present position of anthropological studies." Recapitulating and extending several of his earlier essays, he recast the historical development of British anthropology in the mold of his own career experience, so that his conception of social anthropology became at once the logical outcome of the past and the only appropriate program for the future. Later on, when, he was asked to state his interests for a directory of social anthropologists, he replied with a single word: "methodology"—one gloss of which might be "getting things in the right order." His primary task, he suggested in 1931, was "to indicate a new alignment of the studies which are grouped together under the name Anthropology": to place the "new" social anthropology (or "Comparative Sociology") in right relation to the rest of anthropology (physical anthropology, prehistoric archeology, and ethnology) and to adjacent sciences dealing with the human species (notably, psychology), as well as to the "old" social anthropology. Physical anthropology, where research effort in the past had been quite disproportionate to results, should in future become a part of human biology. While in principle he saw a point of contact in the investigation of what cultural differences, "if any," might be the result of racial differences, the difficulty of separating cultural from racial influences made it impossible at present to approach "comparative racial psychology" as a "scientific problem." Prehistoric archeology had by now established itself as a separate "specialized study"—to which he was now ready to relegate ethnology, insofar as it had legitimate historical purpose (as opposed to the "Egyptian theory" of Elliot Smith, the "culture-cycles" of Graebner, the equally "hypothetical" reconstructions of Father Schmidt and Leo Frobenius, or the attempt to derive culture from "a lost Atlantis").[113*]

This left social anthropology, from which Rivers had been converted in 1911, and to which Radcliffe-Brown thought he had been returning in the posthumously published *Social Organization*. The "new" social anthropology, however, differed from the "old" in important respects, which Radcliffe-Brown elaborated in relation to the study of totemism. Totemism was not an institution whose origin might be con-

*In the early 1920s, before the diffusion controversy heated up, Radcliffe-Brown and Malinowski both entertained the possibility that distribution studies might cast light on the history of culture. Brown had in mind a complete study of the distribution of Australian cultural elements, although he insisted that any historical hypothesis must be based also on a consideration of each element "in relation to the cultural system in which it occurs" (BMPY: Brown to Malinowski 11/6/22; see also Malinowski 1922a:232). While not uncritical of Frobenius, Brown had previously taken him (and the Boasians) much more seriously than he did Smith and Perry ([Radcliffe-]Brown 1925a, 1925c).

jectured in the absence of history. It was rather an "abstraction," "a particular form taken by what seems to be a universal element in culture": the tendency to establish relations between man and nature similar to those established among human beings in society. In this context, Radcliffe-Brown generalized the differences between the "old" and the "new" social anthropology. Rejecting hypothetical historical reconstruction and immediate psychological explanation in favor of "an ultimate psychological explanation of general sociological laws" that were to be "demonstrated by purely sociological inquiries," the new social anthropology attempted to give precise descriptions, in a suitably "exact terminology," in order to provide "a systematic classification." It was, in short, "functional, generalising, and sociological."[114]

Citing Haddon, Boas, Malinowski, and Margaret Mead (who had attended his Columbia lectures), Radcliffe-Brown suggested that the new social anthropology was based on a new type of fieldwork, which sought the "meaning of an element of culture" not in native explanations, but in its "interrelation with other elements" and its place "in the whole life of the people." If there was in this the danger of a "personal equation," this could be minimized by independent studies and by the development of sociological theory, which would relate the characteristics of any culture to "known sociological laws." These were to be discovered by "the comparative method" properly conceived of as a synchronic study of "many diverse types of culture" and of the "variations of a single culture type." Rejecting the polar division of the "peoples of the world" into Europeans and non-Europeans without "written history," cautioning against the use of the terms "primitive" or "savage" to characterize "the most diverse types of culture," Radcliffe-Brown insisted that comparative sociology would in principle study *all* cultural types, from the simplest to the most complex. But while he granted that every culture was "constantly undergoing change," it was the "less developed cultures" that were being "destroyed with appalling rapidity." In this context, he suggested that the comparative diachronic study of "processes of change" had best be left until some future moment when we had made "at least some progress in determining what culture is and how it works."[115]

Finally, Radcliffe-Brown commented on the relation of comparative sociology to yet another recently emergent branch of the discipline, one in which he had had experience over the last decade: Applied or Administrative Anthropology. In contrast to physical anthropology, prehistoric archeology, and ethnology, which offered nothing of practical value to colonial administration, social anthropology might provide "a scientific basis for the control and education of native peoples"—if only the empire, which had inflicted upon native peoples "irretrievable damage," "injustice," and "extermination" in the past, would make provision for "systematic study" rather than "go begging to America" and its philanthropical foundations for the support of ethnographic research.[116]

Whatever its retrospectively evident deficiencies, this was an ambitious program, offering a broad-ranging theoretical synthesis, an orientation toward fieldwork, and far-reaching practical application. It included an outline of a "scientific investigation" in which a series of studies on such problems as the "nature and function of the prohibition of incest"—the classic anthropological problem of the origin of exogamy, rephrased—might lead to "a theory of the nature and function of morality in general." In his peroration, Radcliffe-Brown looked forward to the "task of the twentieth and succeeding centuries" as "that of uniting all the peoples of the world in some sort of ordered community" including not only the great nations, but "the tribes of Africa, Asia and Oceania." Granted, the historical processes and cultural types that lay between those "tribes" and that "world community" were given very short shrift; it was nevertheless, in its intellectual and historical context, a program that could and did attract young anthropologists in both Britain and the United States—some of them of radical political inclination.[117]

Anticipating the next phase of his career, Radcliffe-Brown commented in passing on the varieties of sociology departments in the United States and on the fact that comparative sociology there as elsewhere (save in France) had tended to fall between disciplinary cracks—being "left by the anthropologists to sociology, and by the sociologists to anthropology." Fortunately, however, in the United States this unsatisfactory state of things was now beginning to be recognized, "partly as a result of the work of the Social Science Research Council." Although he did not mention it by name, one place where the new forces were manifest was the University of Chicago, an institution with a strong sociological tradition, oriented toward both urban fieldwork and social theory, with well-established connections to the Research Council and the Rockefeller philanthropies.[118]

"R-B" among the Boasians: From the Comparative Science of Culture to the Natural Science of Society

After languishing for several decades under an eccentric founding professor, within a combined Department of Sociology and Anthropology, anthropology at Chicago had in the middle 1920s experienced a renaissance under the leadership of Fay-Cooper Cole, who had received his doctorate from Boas at Columbia. With Rockefeller support, Cole had brought to Chicago Boas' most brilliant student, Edward Sapir, a linguistic and psychological anthropologist moving away from, but still within, the tradition of Boasian historical ethnology—whom Cole had known at Columbia as "the shark of the lot." Although by 1929 the anthropological section was strong enough to become a separate department, within a year Sapir decided to accept an appointment at Yale. In seeking a replacement, Cole was more interested in star status than in conceptual consistency; Radcliffe-Brown's "functionalism" was well known in Rockefeller social science circles, and his sociological orientation seemed likely to fit in well at Chicago. Oral tradition has it that a telegram to Australia forestalled a bid by Harvard, which communicated its invitation by mail.[119]

Although he originally thought he might be coming only for a year, Radcliffe-Brown stayed at Chicago until 1937—save for some months in the fall of 1935 when he was Visiting Professor at the University of Yenching in China (a venture he conceived of as opening yet another major global region to comparative sociological inquiry). Despite his Edwardian monocle and cape—which quite amazed his midwestern American students—he was able (now as "R-B") to adapt to a milieu in which the major newspaper had not yet forgotten the Revolutionary War. In a pluralistic department, his was not the only voice, but there was a compensating freedom from administrative responsibilities, from the necessity of training colonial cadets, and from the increasingly irksome burden of teaching physical anthropology. For students trained by Sapir—some of whom felt abandoned by him—Radcliffe-Brown's was a voice with a provocative message. Each year, he offered the entering cohort an introductory course on "The Comparative Science of Culture"; each year, there were five or more additional courses or seminars on law, religion, economy, art, and the family, as well as area courses on Africa, Polynesia, East Asia, Australia, and North America. Although the response was not so much discipleship as an attempt to combine the historical and the functionalist approaches, a number of students did become involved in his research project.[120]

As he had previously done both for South Africa and for Australia, Radcliffe-Brown quickly began an attempt to systematize North American kinship data. Apparently assuming that it would be a relatively easy matter to update Morgan's *Systems of Consanguinity and Affinity* and define a limited number of "types," he recruited Fred Eggan and then Sol Tax to survey and abstract the literature; in addition to this library research, a number of students were sent out for fieldwork among various groups. In the end, however, the project was frustrated by the great range of variation among North American tribes, and what was produced (as well as several doctoral dissertations) was not a synthesis but a series of festschrift essays on particular groups.[121]

Radcliffe-Brown's influence, however, extended well beyond his immediate circle of students. The Chicago Department of Anthropology was part of a powerful grouping of social science departments at the most influential academic institution of mid-America. Offshoot of the Boasian tradition but outside the Boasian institutional orbit, it was an ideal place from which to promulgate the functional program to yet another national anthropological constituency—the more so, since American anthropology was already undergoing an internal evolution. From about 1920, the trait-distribution diffusionary studies of the "American Historical School" had been giving way to studies of cultural integration in psychological terms, studies in which Margaret Mead, who had felt Radcliffe-Brown's influence during stopovers in Sydney on the way to the field, played a leading role. In the later 1920s the attenuated sociological impulse within Boasian anthropology had been reinforced by the work of Robert Redfield at Chicago, George Murdock at Yale, and Lloyd Warner at Harvard (who was inclined to think of his studies of Newburyport and other modern American sites as yet more social "types" for Radcliffe-Brown's comparative sociological project). On the other hand, the voices of traditional Boasianism were still strong. Radcliffe-Brown had occasion to realize this soon after his arrival, when, as part of a committee of the American Anthropological Association, he tried to promote a worldwide collaborative salvage anthropology project under Rockefeller Foundation auspices—only to see it at first imperilled by internecine bickering and finally defeated by the impact of the Depression on research priorities. For the first time, he had to operate in an anthropological milieu with a well-established prior tradition, which although evolving, was still quite distant in its outlook from the viewpoint he had spent the last twenty years elaborating.[122]

Well aware of the oppositional character of Radcliffe-Brown's message, his students encouraged confrontations across the paradigmatic divide. In 1933, Sol Tax, who as an undergraduate had studied with Ralph Linton at Wisconsin, arranged a debate—an oral form which Radcliffe-Brown obviously found congenial. After some trouble defining the proposition to be discussed, Linton and Radcliffe-Brown settled on a recent passage from Boas, which seems perhaps to have been written with Radcliffe-Brown in mind: "The material of anthropology is such that it needs must be a historical science, one of the sciences the interest of which centers in the attempt to understand the individual phenomenon rather than in the establishment of general laws which, on account of the complexity of the material, will almost necessarily be vague and, we might almost say, so self-evident that they are of little help to a real understanding." Although the debate apparently ended in a standoff, there was some communication of ideas through less public channels.

When Tax went back to Madison on weekends, Linton engaged him in long discussions about Radcliffe-Brown's lectures, some of the ideas in which were clearly manifest in Linton's sociologically oriented and widely used textbook, *The Study of Man*.[123]

The confrontation with American anthropology was evident also in two of Radcliffe-Brown's rather short list of publications in this period: the first, with a leading member of the historicist old guard intent on defending the priority of history over science; the second, with a representative of the younger generation seeking to define a "functional historicity." In the first case, Radcliffe-Brown assumed that a recent study by A. L. Kroeber of California kin terms was a veiled attempt to "controvert" the position he had held "for the past twenty-four years" that there was "a fairly close correlation" between the "terminological" and the "social" classification of kin. Kroeber had argued that California tribes with "almost identical institutions" had quite different kinship terminology, which he explained by an appeal to the linguistic history of the region. In fact, Kroeber's essay was part of the debate he had been carrying on since 1909, first with Morgan and then with Rivers; but on the question of correlation, Radcliffe-Brown was quite within that same tradition. Where he differed from it (and from Kroeber) was on the role of diachronic assumption in the study of kinship, and on this issue, he now argued along the lines of his own earlier debate with Rivers. Admitting the possibility that in any system there might be "functional inconsistencies" which would lead to "social change," he rejected all "hypothetical" (as opposed to "documented") history, insisting on the priority of a synchronic, scientific, sociological study, based on "working hypotheses" that might be tested by theoretically motivated fieldwork. Toward that end, he felt it would be better if ethnology and social anthropology were recognized as "two different disciplines having different aims, different methods, and different interests in field investigations."[124]

Kroeber, who was then carrying on his own debate with Boas on the separation of history and science in anthropology, might have been inclined to accept a distinction of aims and methods if not of disciplines. But Alexander Lesser, a recent student of both Boas and John Dewey, was trying to establish a bridge between the "historical school" and the "functional school." Accepting that "the primary subject of attention must be the present and contemporary functioning of things," Lesser insisted that some of the relations of present phenomena might be "merely coexistences" based on "prior events" which could only be understood historically. From Radcliffe-Brown's perspective, however, the most disturbing part of Lesser's argument was his undifferentiated conception of "functionalism." Among younger American anthropologists seeking to broaden the Boasian tradition by redefinition and rapprochement, there was a tendency at this time to regard their own emergent holistic approach to culture in psychological terms as a form of "functionalism"—in some cases, even to suggest that Boasian anthropology had always been, broadly, "functionalist." Thus Lesser spoke of "the stressing of psychological aspects of culture" as the "outstanding" aspect of functionalism, treating the emphasis on "sociological problems of aggregation" (by implication, Radcliffe-Brown) and "the detailed consideration of sexual life and education" (by implication, Malinowski) simply as further tendencies within a generalized (and Americanized) "functionalist" movement.[125]

Having spent twenty-five years honing a distinctive theoretical position, Radcliffe-Brown was not inclined to allow such a casual assimilation—the more so when it took the form of advocating a "functional historicity." Although he kept open a possibility of rapprochement, he was clearly intent on sharply differentiating his own position from those that, to less committed taxonomists, might appear to be varieties of the same species. Acknowledging that he had made "constant use of the concept of social function, in lecturing and in writing, since 1909," he nevertheless rejected Lesser's attempt to associate him with an ill-defined group "he regards as 'functionalists.'" Starting from Durkheim's *Rules of Sociological Method,* and proceeding by way of "the analogy between social life and organic life," he went on to offer as a "working hypothesis" the suggestion that social function could only be understood in social structural terms: "the *function* of any recurrent activity" was "the part it plays in the social life as a whole and therefore the contribution it makes to the maintenance of the structural continuity." He was still willing to accept a psychological conception of "function" insofar as the usages of a society "work or 'function' only through their effects . . . in the thoughts, sentiments and actions of individuals," and he continued to regard functional and historical explanations as, in principle, supplementary rather than conflicting. What *his* functionalism *did* conflict with was two views widely held, although often "without precise formulation": the trait-diffusionists' "'shreds and patches' theory of culture," and the belief "that there are no discoverable significant sociological laws."[126]

His own most important attempt to offer such laws during his Chicago period was an article, "Patrilineal and Matrilineal Succession," written in response to the assertion by a student of Kroeber's that unilateral kinship institutions were "anomalous and artificial." Radcliffe-Brown took this to imply that they must therefore "have had a single origin in some one aberrant people and to have spread from them, by a process of 'diffusion,' to vast numbers of peoples." Against this view, he argued that in order to exist every society had to solve the problem of determining "the status of an individual"—which he defined as "the totality of all his rights and duties as recognized in social usages," including not only the rights transmitted by the father or mother to the child, but also the rights of parents over children. Although in the great majority of societies the solution adopted was mixed, the tendency was for either patrilineal or matrilineal succession to "preponderate." In explaining this, Radcliffe-Brown appealed to three "sociological laws" (the second being a "special instance" of the first): the need for "a certain degree of functional consistency among the constituent parts of the social system"; the consequent need for the "establishment of a social structure" in which the "rights and duties" implicated in the relations of individuals and groups were defined in such a way as to resolve conflicts "without destroying the structure"; and the need not only for stability, but for continuity, which was the "function" of "corporations" exercising joint rights over persons and things. Noting, even granting, the charge of "American ethnologists" that such laws "must necessarily be truisms," Radcliffe-Brown insisted that, "even so, they would seem to need to be brought to the attention" of ethnologists who would explain social structure in terms of the diffusion of anomalies.[127]

Retrospectively, what is striking is not so much Radcliffe-Brown's repeated insistence on the requirement of functional consistency as a "sociological law," but the legalistic framework in which his argument was now cast. Meyer Fortes, Radcliffe-Brown's patrilineal successor in the study of unilineal descent groups, was later to see this essay as a critical moment in the emergence of a more systematically "social structural" analysis of kinship. Radcliffe-Brown had earlier been inclined to view kinship in "dyadic" terms, in a manner similar to Malinowski's psychological approach, as a bilateral network of relations "radiating outwards from the elementary family." Now he emphasized what he was later to call the "jural" aspect of kinship relations as systems of socially recognized rights and duties attributed to categories of persons and enforced by legal or moral "sanctions." From a broader historical perspective, this is also the moment when Sir Henry Maine, whose commitment to patriarchy had pushed him to the sidelines of British anthropology during its evolutionary and early post-evolutionary phases, reentered the emerging social anthropological mainstream, as the precursory theoretician of corporate groups. Although Maine was little if at all evident in Radcliffe-Brown's earlier writings or lectures—or even in the articles on "Primitive Law" and "Social Sanctions" he wrote for the *Encyclopaedia of the Social Sciences* shortly after his arrival—he was an available intellectual resource at Chicago, where his influence was clearly felt among the sociologists, and where the law school was part of a lively interdisciplinary scene. Radcliffe-Brown's succession article was full of the terminology of Roman law (rights *in personam* and *in rem*) and clearly drew on Maine at a number of points, specifically citing him on the decay of the Roman *gens*. From that point on, Maine was to be a potent influence on several generations of British social anthropologists.[128]

Radcliffe-Brown's characteristic mode of intellectual development —the gradual evolution, continual refinement, and periodic repackaging of an underlying Durkheimian functionalism—is further manifest in the culminating intellectual moment of his Chicago period: a series of presentations to the Dean's Seminar of the Social Science Division in the spring of 1937. Given orally, "without manuscript or even notes," they were transcribed by Lloyd Warner's secretary and, after an abortive attempt at reworking by Radcliffe-Brown, were much later published in their unedited form as *A Natural Science of Society*. Their original occasion had been provided by Mortimer Adler, an Aristotelian polymath brought to Chicago by President Hutchins and lodged in the law school when the philosophers refused to provide him a home. Adler had argued in a previous Dean's Seminar that "there was only one possible social science and its name was psychology." Against this, Radcliffe-Brown maintained that "a theoretical science of human society was possible"; that there could be "only one such science," which was "as distinct from psychology as physiology is from chemistry"; and that it would be achieved by "the gradual improvement of the comparative method" along three lines: observational method, definition of concepts, and "systematic classification of types of societies."[129]

In a context of epistemological confrontation, Radcliffe-Brown cast his by now nearly fully evolved position into a philosophical frame. Against Adler's Aristotelianism, he appealed to Heraclitus of Ephesus to justify the immanence of natural laws in the universe; at several points he referred to A. N. Whitehead and (in the aborted revision) to Bertrand Russell and A. J. Ayer, though he was critical of "positivism, logical positivism, and pragmatism" for leaving "the procedures of science and of common sense" without "philosophical justification." While it has been argued that there was a systematic philosophical position, derived from a presumed early contact with Russell and Whitehead, behind Radcliffe-Brown's emergent structuralism, his philosophy seems to have had a somewhat ad hoc character, as he drew upon more recent reading to re-present arguments that had developed from quite different sources. The transcript includes extensive discussion of "natural kinds," of the difference between a "class" and a "system," of the different types of "systems," of the role of "analogy" in science, and of the necessity of "expedient abstraction" as the basis of comparison and the formulation of "structural principles." But what is most striking is Radcliffe-Brown's recurrent insistence on the "phenomenal reality" of the central objects of *his* study, in contrast to the "abstraction" of the "culture" studied by American anthropologists.[130]

Some time during his Chicago stay, Fred Eggan had suggested to Radcliffe-Brown that by continuing to talk of a "comparative science of culture" he was simply obscuring the differences between himself and American cultural anthropologists; and in explicating his "natural science of society" Radcliffe-Brown had quite a bit to say about the idea of "culture." Revoking a "taboo" he had placed on it at an early point in the seminar, he defined culture in terms which are much more acceptable today than the omnibus definitions of the Tylorian tradition. Culture was a "certain standardization of behavior"—a "social coaptation"—which Radcliffe-Brown discussed in terms of three components: "a set of rules of behavior," certain "common symbols and common meanings attached to these symbols," and a "common set" of ways of feeling and thinking ("sentiments" and "beliefs")—which Durkheim had called *représentations collectives*. But while "such an analysis of culture" might "be used for scientific purposes," no "science of culture" as such was possible: "you can only study culture as a characteristic of a social system." Just as Durkheim had erred in reifying the "collective consciousness," so was the "reification of culture" a "fallacy": "culture patterns" could not act upon an individual because they were merely abstractions. Psychology, as the analysis of "a system we call mind," was possible as a science insofar as it dealt with phenomena that existed in the individual human mind—literally, "under the skin of one individual." Similarly, a natural science of society was possible because, although its subject matter was inter-individual (social relations, social usages), the interacting individuals were contained within bounded entities called societies that existed in the real world. Unlike culture, Tlingit society was "a perfectly concrete discrete thing," and although the "structural principles" of different "social structures" were only discoverable by abstraction, the social structures themselves had a "phenomenal reality" that was directly observable, insofar as it consisted of "the social behavior of actual individual human beings" who could be observed interacting in "territorially delimited" and linguistically homogeneous groups. Thus it was that social systems (unlike culture) were "never" abstract, but were "real, concrete phenomena."[131]

Much of the seminar, of course, was devoted to the method of studying social systems scientifically. Although a "relational mathematics" would ultimately be required, Radcliffe-Brown ruled out experiment and measurement as not essential to science. What was critical was the perception of analogy—which was "in essence, a comparison." The first step toward a science of society was therefore the creation of an adequate taxonomy, "and in the first instance, a classification of social systems themselves." These were to be studied by a "comparative method" that would differ fundamentally from Tylor's study of "adhesions" (or the trait-diffusion comparisons that had been derived from it), in seeking to obtain "natural laws": that is to say, generalizations with an ever-greater precision and probability. In front of a somewhat critical interdisciplinary audience, Radcliffe-Brown stated his aspirations in strikingly modest terms: although a "theoretical natural science of society" was possible, and although there was only one way to achieve it, it did not yet exist "except in its most elementary beginnings." Various obstacles stood in the way: the intrinsic difficulty of the subject, the "historical fallacy," the "psychological illusion," the greater appeal of practice rather than theory, and the "vested interests of the existing social sciences"—all of which left him "not particularly optimistic as to the prospects of its immediate realization."[132]

By the time Radcliffe-Brown began this series of seminar presentations, he had already decided to return to England to accept a chair at Oxford. At Cambridge, a chair had been created in 1932 with money from Trinity College and from a long-time friend of James Frazer's, William Wyse. Initially filled by the previous Reader, T. C. Hodson, the Wyse Professorship went in 1936 to another Indian civil servant/ethnographer, J. H. Hutton, much to the disappointment of several candidates from the "functionalist" movement. At Oxford, in the context of Marett's impending retirement as Reader, the creation of the Cambridge chair had encouraged a movement for a similar position, which was realized later in 1936 as a professorship in social anthropology—that having been for years Marett's rubric. Although there were several Oxford candidates (including Evans-Pritchard), the electors were inclined toward Malinowski, who excluded himself in favor of Radcliffe-Brown.[133]

As his Chicago colleague Robert Redfield suggested in the festschrift organized at the time of Radcliffe-Brown's departure in 1937, he had made an important contribution to the reorientation then in process in American anthropology. The distinction between history and science, which had never been sharply drawn in the Boasian tradition, was now clarified, and a "needed" emphasis given to the "scientific side," in "sociological" rather than "psychological" terms. If Radcliffe-Brown's "general laws" were better regarded as "general propositions," his clarification of concepts and his classification of problems were important as guides to research, and as counterweights to "the analytic and nonconceptualized procedure of Boas." Despite the resistance he had encountered, his influence could be "read between the lines of many American books already written or to be written" even by those who were unaware of it. At Oxford, he was to have an even greater impact.[134]

Bronio and Rex: From Pure to Hyphenated Functionalism

As Malinowski's support for Radcliffe-Brown's Oxford candidacy suggests, the two men had for a long time considered themselves colleagues in a single movement for the reformation of British anthropology. Although they rarely came into direct contact, they periodically exchanged letters; apologizing on one occasion for not answering, Malinowski felt that "we supermen need not stick to any conventions," since "my towering spirit and yours touch above the highest levels of microcosmic nebulas and there gaze in silence at one another." But in fact there were substantial underlying theoretical differences between them, which developed over time and eventually came to the surface. After Malinowski's death, Radcliffe-Brown traced their intellectual relationship through a series of moments: a meeting in Australia in 1914, when they "reached fairly complete agreement" on the aims and methods of anthropology; a conversation at the Yale Club in New York in 1926, when they had begun to differ over the use of the concept function; Malinowski's article on "Culture" for the *Encyclopaedia of the Social Sciences*, which marked the beginning of a new phase in which he developed a "biological theory of culture." In fact, however, Radcliffe-Brown had at the time greeted Malinowski's article as a "fine" piece, and regularly assigned it for his "Comparative Science of Culture" course. But if he was inclined to rationalize their differences in terms of Malinowski's theoretical devolution and his own theoretical constancy, they were nevertheless deeply rooted—not only in their initial intellectual starting points and trajectories, but in their differing predispositions of intellectual personality.[135]

After 1930, in a context of competition for influence over the disposition of funding at the Rockefeller Foundation, these tensions began to be more openly manifest. In 1934, it was Malinowski who first publicly threw down the theoretical gauntlet, in his introduction to Ian Hogbin's *Law and Order in Polynesia*, by insisting strenuously on a fundamental divergence in their points of view. Offering an extended critique of Radcliffe-Brown's article on "Primitive Law" in the *Encyclopedia of the Social Sciences*—which he took as an implied criticism of *Crime and Custom*—Malinowski appealed to his own article on "Culture" as the basis for a "functional theory of custom" that would start from the "living, palpitating flesh and blood organism of man which remains somewhere at the heart of every institution." Although he suggested that the "only point of theoretical dissension between Professor Radcliffe-Brown and myself, and the only respect in which the Durkheimian conception of primitive society has to be supplemented" was the "tendency to ignore completely the individual and eliminate the biological element from the functional analysis of culture," he nevertheless made his own position clear: this tendency "must in my opinion be overcome."[136]

Radcliffe-Brown's rather acerbic response disclaimed association with "the figment of an automatically law-abiding native," and suggested that the variegated nature of social sanctions was an "elementary truth" that required the creation of strawmen-opponents so that it could be "claimed as a discovery" made by Malinowski in the Trobriand Islands. Denying that he ignored the individual and eliminated the biological in the functional analysis of culture, Radcliffe-Brown maintained that the really important differences between himself and Malinowski were in "the uses of words." The "slow and laborious process of establishing a scientific terminology" in the social sciences required exact definitions that had the same sense in all societies and did not conflict with current usage. So far as he could tell "without the aid of a definition," it seemed that Malinowski meant by "law" any "socially sanctioned rule of behaviour." If he would only stick to that meaning in his writings, "he would find that not only do I not disagree with him, but neither does anyone else, since the greater part of his statements are commonplaces of social science, only made to appear novel and profound by a novel and obscure use of words."[137]

Obviously chagrined, Malinowski ironically pled guilty to creating a strawman by having described Radcliffe-Brown as one of social anthropology's "theoretically most acute thinkers." Defending himself against charges of truism, he insisted that he had advanced his "theory of primitive sanctions" *before* he went to the Trobriands, and that authorities such as Sydney Hartland had rejected it. But like Radcliffe-Brown, he still minimized their differences: it was only in regard to primitive law and economics that he had "ventured" disagreement on "certain specific points." That careful circumscription of differences was also manifest when Malinowski came to Chicago in April 1935, and students arranged a formal debate with Radcliffe-Brown. Although a "bloody confrontation" had been expected, the chairman, Harold Lasswell, described the encounter as "a love fest"—to which Malinowski is said to have responded: "The function of old age is tolerance." Privately, too, relations remained cordial. After receiving the offer at Oxford, Radcliffe-Brown wrote Malinowski a note (addressed "Dear Bronio" and signed "Rex"), thanking him for his efforts, looking forward to a continuing close association, and indicating that in formulating plans for Oxford anthropology, he would first seek Malinowski's advice.[138]

Although Radcliffe-Brown immediately faced at Oxford issues of subdisciplinary status similar to those that had troubled Malinowski's relation to Seligman, there is no evidence that he discussed them with Malinowski. His interest was rather in establishing an independent institutional base for his brand of "social anthropology"—which was not an easy thing to do at Oxford, where anthropology had long been closely linked to the Pitt Rivers Museum. Radcliffe-Brown offered formal proposals for redefining the relationship of social anthropology to general ethnology, archeology, technology, and physical anthropology, but the war intervened to delay any resolution of the problem. By 1940, however, he was able to report to Lloyd Warner back in Chicago that he had succeeded in his efforts to establish an Institute of Social Anthropology—apparently, according to oral testimony, simply by the printing of a letterhead.[139]

Two years previously, shortly after Radcliffe-Brown's return to England brought the two men together for the first time in direct competition for intellectual and institutional influence, his controversy with Malinowski had flared up again. In January 1938, Radcliffe-Brown attacked a book for which Malinowski had written a laudatory preface, calling it "another of those monuments of muddled thinking that are occasionally but still too frequently erected in the name of anthropology." In response, Malinowski indicated that he was drafting a reply "all in the same Blood and Thunder manner in which we conduct our printed correspondence." Instead, however, he proposed (through a third party, in the manner of a duel) that they hold a public discussion of the issues between them. As challenged party, Radcliffe-Brown chose the topic: "the use of the concept 'function' in sociology"; and at Malinowski's suggestion, he opened the discussion on June 17, 1938, at Le Play House with a formal statement of his position. Although its substance survives only in Radcliffe-Brown's typed summary of the thirteen propositions he would defend and in extensive notes Malinowski prepared for his rejoinder, it seems clear that this time the outcome was not a "love fest."[140]

Radcliffe-Brown opened by insisting that cooperative scientific work depended on the acceptance of a common terminology, which required "precise unambiguous definitions of all technical terms." In scientific usage, "function" had two precise but distinct meanings: physiological function referred to the contribution an organ made "by its activity to the persistence of the organic structure"; mathematical function, to expressions in which the substitution of a specific value for a variable would give a value for the expression as a whole. By a process of degradation, each scientific usage had in popular usage a corresponding "imprecise" meaning: one equivalent to "activity" or "effect"; the other, to "any relation of covariation." Radcliffe-Brown proposed to use the term "social function" in a sense analogous to the more precise notion of physiological function, as the contribution any usage or belief made "to the persistence of the total complex of social reactions [relations?] which constitute the social structure of that society." Appealing to Hsun

Tze, Montesquieu, Saint-Simon, and Durkheim, he made a point of "deprecating" the recent usage referring to "any and every relation of interdependence" or simply to the idea of "use" and "purpose."[141]

Responding in a "semi-serious, semi-jocular vein," Malinowski cast himself as the "humble craftsman" of functionalism, against Radcliffe-Brown's black-caped "High Priest" exorcising demons with black-magic formulae. In truth, both of them were functionalists with minor divergencies, sharing a belief in the "scientific analysis of actual reality" as opposed to speculation on origins or history; both of them were committed to the search for "general laws of cultural process"; both were convinced that "human society and culture [were] an integral subject of study." The trouble was that Radcliffe-Brown insisted on embellishing his fine empirical work with a "window dressing" of "verbal or scholastic" definitions. He spoke of science as if all science were one, whereas the essence of scientific definition was that concepts should be derived from the reality a particular science studies empirically.

Ridiculing the derivation of sociological concepts by analogy from physiology, Malinowski suggested that there was a sense in which the debate itself was an organism, with MG (Morris Ginsberg) its head, R-B its brain, he himself its liver, and the audience its bowels. But whatever their short-run utility, "no science can live permanently on analogies"; and the organic analogy (along with the "collective soul") had long since been found wanting in sociology. Deriding Radcliffe-Brown's "puritanism of prim precision," Malinowski insisted that true precision required not the polishing of definitions, but "turning to facts and developing your concepts always in touch with bedrock reality." For him, that reality was revealed in fieldwork, which had shown that culture was not a "scrap-heap," not an "evolving or still less a 'persisting' organism," but an active, integrative, adaptive, and instrumental process.

In this context, Malinowski defiantly embraced flexibility of usage, arguing that fieldwork in fact revealed four different levels of meaning for the concept function, correlating roughly with Radcliffe-Brown's four usages: use and utility, mutual dependence ("or, if you like, co-variation"), the satisfaction of "the biological needs of the human organism," and the satisfaction of "derived needs" or "cultural imperatives." All things considered, the difference between them was "not very much," if in Radcliffe-Brown's definition one glossed "contribution" as "use" or "purpose" and replaced "persistence" by "integral working" (on the grounds that "persistence" was "a moral issue"). All that Malinowski did was add "flesh and blood human beings to the shadow of a 'purely social system.'"

But this "small" difference was perhaps more consequential than Malinowski would allow. Indeed, the most revealing point in the notes

Malinowski on shipboard, on his way to the United States in 1938. (Courtesy of Helena Wayne Malinowska)

for the debate was a marginal annotation Malinowski appended to Radcliffe-Brown's suggestion that "the social function of a usage or belief is to be discovered by examining its effects." While these were in the first instance effects upon individuals, it was "only the effects upon the social relations of the individual with other individuals that constitute the social function." To which Malinowski commented in the margin: "to me the distinction is not relevant."

The relevance of the distinction was not, however, so easily denied. Each man returned to it in print during the following year. In an article entitled "The Group and the Individual in Functional Analysis" published while he was on sabbatical leave at Yale, Malinowski made a point of distinguishing "plain and pure" from "hyphenated" functionalism, insisting at some length on the priority of the biological individual "both in social theory and in the reality of cultural life." And in his Frazer Lecture on "Taboo," Radcliffe-Brown attacked Malinowski's derivation of magic from individual psychological need, arguing that ritual could as well cause as alleviate anxiety, and insisting at some length on the social function (as opposed to the psychological effects) of ritual activity. Although his argument was similar in its essentials to that advanced in *The Andaman Islanders*, there was no longer any reference to "sentiments." The following year, in discussing "joking relationships," Radcliffe-Brown carried the issue a step further, by insisting that what seemed manifestly to be individual "psychological phenomena" were in fact expressions of social structural relationships.[142]

Caught in the United States by the outbreak of World War II, Malinowski remained at Yale (save for an interval of fieldwork in Mexico) until his death in 1942, shortly after he had accepted a permanent appointment. Whatever the actual historical circumstances of his exile, or the decision, if any, on the day of the debate, its retrospective historical symbolism is clear enough. By 1938, the mantle of leadership in British social anthropology had passed from Malinowski to Radcliffe-Brown. While he, too, was to leave behind more than one unwritten book, Radcliffe-Brown's two lectures as president of the Royal Anthropological Institute in 1940 and 1941 were to give that inquiry its classic paradigmatic definition as "the study of kinship systems" and of "social structure."[143]

EIGHT

Anthropological Institutions, Colonial Interests, and the First Cohorts of Social Anthropologists

If one were to choose a single year to date the "revolution in anthropology," an obvious choice would be 1922, when Rivers died and Malinowski and Radcliffe-Brown published their first major monographs. However, periodization (including that marked by the title of the present volume) is very largely a matter of historiographical convenience; the actual historical process of intellectual change is rarely so disjunctive. New orientations are defined in interaction with previously dominant ones; in that process, allies and followers must be recruited, audiences and resources commanded, institutions taken over or created—lest the new paradigm fade from view, perhaps later to be rediscovered as a previously unappreciated precursor. The success of the functionalist "revolution in anthropology" must be understood in similar institutional terms.[1]

There are, of course, still broader frameworks in which the "revolution in anthropology" may be viewed. The year 1922 was also the one in which Frederick Lugard, retired elder statesman of British colonial proconsuls, published what was to be both the classic defense of British colonial rule and the justification for the new mandate system: *The Dual Mandate in Tropical Africa*. As "protectors and trustees of backward races," the "civilised nations," Lugard maintained, had a double responsibility. Carrying "the torch of culture and progress" to the "dark places of the earth" in order to develop the "abounding wealth" of the tropics for "the benefit of mankind," they must minister "to the material needs of our own civilisation" while simultaneously safeguarding "the material rights of the natives" and promoting "their moral and educational progress." This was to be accomplished by policies such as Lugard had previously implemented in Nigeria, policies later commonly spoken of as "indirect rule." Indirect rule in fact had its precedents elsewhere, and was variously manifest in different colonial situations; and Lugard's own role in Nigeria has been the subject of historical controversy. Nevertheless, the idea that colonial administration might be carried on more effectively, efficiently, and economically, as well as more humanely, by working through the medium of "traditional" native rulers (rather than by direct imposition) was to have a powerful influence on British colonial policy in the interwar period.[2]

In such a context, "functionalism" has been seen as the anthropology appropriate to a new phase of British colonialism. Whereas evolutionism had served primarily as the ideological legitimation of the initial conquest of "savage races" by "civilized" Europeans, the "function of functionalism" was to sustain an established and routinized colonial order by clarifying the principles of traditional native systems through which "indirect rule" could be carried on. Inverting the perspective, it has also been suggested that the ethnographic holism and cultural relativism of functionalism were as much "products of colonial practice" as they were "theoretical innovations of academic anthropology." During the late 1960s and early 1970s, anthropology was frequently metaphorically condemned as the "child," the "step-child," the "problem-child," or simply as the "tool" of imperialism; a generation of anthropologists felt themselves judged as morally and politically complicit in the maintenance of colonial exploitation.[3]

No doubt such interpretations have sometimes been argued by means of selective documentation based on theoretically motivated assumptions of "correspondence" between anthropological theory and colonial practice—sometimes in a polemically charged manner. In the interests of a more balanced historical understanding, one may eschew aprioristic correspondences, casual metaphorical characterization, and anachronistic moral judgment. There can be no doubt, however, that colonialism was a critically important context for the development of anthropology, and that the "colonial situations" of particular ethnographic episodes or ethnographic traditions are issues worthy of systematic historical investigation. This range of problems, however, lies outside the scope of the present narrative. So also, except incidentally, does the actual utilization of functionalist anthropology by colonial administrators, as opposed to its putative utility for the colonial system. What is very much to the present point, however, is the role of British colonialism in establishing a potential market for a new kind of anthropology—and in the process, facilitating the institutionalization of social anthropology in the interwar and immediate postwar years.[4]*

*Recalling my comment in the Preface about the bracketing of "contemporary British cultural ideology," and "social and political history" (above, xiv), I note here also the failure to treat (save incidentally) either domestic debate about colonial policy and practice or

That institutionalizing process had, inevitably, an oppositional or competitive aspect—at several different levels. Social anthropology emerged within a broader anthropological tradition which included physical anthropology and prehistoric archeology, and which had achieved a significant degree of cultural recognition and institutionalization in the later nineteenth century. In the 1920s social anthropology had also to compete for personnel, resources, jobs, and audience with another reorienting movement, diffusionary ethnology. In the early 1930s social anthropology was itself divided into two distinct and competing theoretical tendencies—Malinowski's "plain and pure" and "hyphenated" functionalisms. By the end of that decade, intellectual dominance was passing to what has since been called "structural-functionalism"—although not, however, to the exclusion of more Malinowskian orientations. It was only in the course of this last internal competition, in a quite different colonial situation from that of 1890 or 1920, that the institutional base of social anthropology was finally firmly established in the years after World War II.[5]

The Institutions of British Anthropology in the Era of the New Imperialism

Before Tylor presented his paper on adhesions to the Anthropological Institute in November 1888, he had also given it early in September at the Bath meetings of the British Association and before that in June as a public lecture in the University Museum at Oxford: a sequence of sites approximating the full range of late-nineteenth-century British anthropological institutions. In London, a group of leisured gentlemen, businessmen, and professionals with anthropological interests—including medical men, scholars and scientists in related fields, and several men employed full time as curators of museum collections—met together monthly at the Anthropological Institute. There they listened to papers (some later published in the institute's quarterly *Journal*) on the physical variety of humankind, the material remnants of its previous history, and

---

other domestic concerns that might have been reflected in anthropological discourse. On the former problem, P. B. Rich (1990) and A. P. Thornton (1959) are suggestive; on the latter, Perry Anderson, who glossed social anthropology as an export by "British imperial society" onto "its subject peoples" of a "totalizing" social analysis that was "proscribed at home" lest it call into question the hegemony of the dominant class (1969:264); Henrika Kuklick, who reads British anthropology in terms of (among other things) the "rise of the meritocratic ideal" and the "projection of British folkmodels of the state" (1991:21, 264); or Anna Grimshaw and Keith Hart, who argue that the anthropology of Malinowski and Radcliffe-Brown "was compatible in many important ways with a bureaucratic class on the rise" (1993:24).

the diverse customs of its many tribes and peoples. Although among the professional scientists there were some who included anthropology among their scientific interests, anthropology as a distinct professional livelihood could scarcely be said to exist. The museum men had more general curatorial responsibilities; the academics had appointments in other disciplines. Even Tylor, who at Oxford lectured to rather heterogeneous audiences as Reader in Anthropology, was also Keeper of the University Museum.[6]

Once a year, a number of the metropolitan group would travel to some provincial city for the meetings of the British Association, where anthropology was recognized as a science suitable for advancement in section sessions that might also be attended by local people with anthropological interests. Some "anthropologists" also published books or articles in journals of wider circulation. But if there was a certain cultural receptivity to anthropological topics, there was no effective external social demand for anthropologists as such, or for anthropological research.[7]

Although there were occasional references to the practical utility of anthropology in the annual presidential addresses of the Anthropological Institute, there was little sustained concern with that topic. Anthropology had long since severed its early connection (through the Aborigines Protection Society) with humanitarian colonial reform, and in the 1860s it had rejected a racialist political program. Despite Tylor's suggestion in the peroration of *Primitive Culture* that the critique of "survivals" made "ethnology" a "reformer's science," the political style of the discipline was better characterized by his later recommendation that it go "forward, like a horse in blinkers, neither looking to the right hand nor to the left"—which may be glossed as pursuing its purely scientific function, without becoming entangled in political matters at home or abroad. During the institute's first two decades, it was little involved in colonial affairs beyond the attempt to gather and purvey information: on the one hand, through the preparation of *Notes and Queries* as a guide to the more systematic collection of anthropological data by "travellers and residents in uncivilized lands"; on the other, by providing an audience for such information at meetings on their return to the metropolis, or in the institute's *Journal*. There were colonial administrators who read Maine and Tylor, but the Colonial Office had little interest in anthropology, nor the Anthropological Institute in the Colonial Office, beyond its facilitation of the distribution of *Notes and Queries*.[8]

While there was a conscious attempt to discipline anthropological observation at second hand, there was no systematic provision for the academic training of anthropologists as such. For the founding generation of the 1860s, whose own science was not grounded in such specifically disciplinary university training—and who until 1900 were still around as dominating elders—the issue did not perhaps seem so compelling as it does in retrospect. Insofar as anthropology achieved a foothold in the universities before 1900, it was either in connection with museum collections or as an aspect of some more established study such as anatomy or classical archeology. The resources for anthropological research were extremely limited, and largely generated within the anthropological or scientific community itself, in the form of membership subscriptions, small grants from the British Association, or the personal funds of well-to-do participants.[9]

Within this limited and inchoate institutional framework, precursory manifestations of "social anthropology" had a distinctly secondary place. For various reasons—including their role in the structure of evolutionary thought, the local accessibility of their subject matter, or their relatively greater technical elaboration—the dominant inquiries within the generalized anthropology of the Anthropological Institute were prehistoric archeology and physical anthropology. The *Journal* did of course publish ethnographic materials of a sociological character (among them, papers by Fison and Howitt) but the more generalized sociological concern reflected in Tylor's paper on adhesions was quite atypical. "Anthropologists" with sociological interests were more likely to be active within the Folk-Lore Society. And despite the institute's universalistic scope, and the central theoretical importance of "savage" races, in practical terms the anthropological research of its members was to a surprising extent Anglocentric, focussing on the physical types, the archeological remains, and the folklore of the British Isles.[10]

Such was the institutional context of anthropology in 1889, when Alfred Haddon returned from his first voyage to the Torres Straits. Centered in the Anthropological Institute, with its generalized agenda, anthropology was recognized as a science by the British Association, but had only a small niche in the museums and the barest foothold in the universities. It was carried on by men with no specifically anthropological training, with limited resources, and with no prospect of employment as anthropologists. Although it had a place, in a general way, in the culture of the time, it had no acknowledged practical role to play in the colonial empire. In the next decade or so, however, there were to be significant changes.

When Haddon composed his closet critique of colonialism in 1892, the juggernaut of imperialism was rushing into all the corners of the earth where "savages" and "backward races" still lurked. The British and the Germans had divided up eastern New Guinea in 1884; that same year the Berlin Conference precipitated the final scramble for Africa. From the four points of the compass—Rhodes in South Africa, Cromer in Egypt,

Goldie in Nigeria, Lugard in Uganda—British power, direct or mediated, was advancing toward the heart of the Dark Continent. By the time of Queen Victoria's jubilee in 1897, the red-stained sectors of the global map were to reach their widest spread before the Treaty of Versailles. Domestically, the imperialist movement was at its height; until the outbreak of the Boer War in 1899, the voices of critics of empire were all but drowned by the jingo roar. Sixty years before, the earliest institutionalization of British anthropology had taken place against a background of critique of "the injuries we have inflicted, the cruelties we have committed, the vices we have fostered, [and] the desolation and utter ruin we have caused" in colonial areas overseas. But as Huxley's response to Haddon implied, the early 1890s were not a moment when moral critique of colonial empire was a likely standpoint from which to launch a career in anthropology. What Haddon called the "red paint of British aggression" was for most Britons rather a symbol of their preeminent position among the carriers of European civilization, a marking of the realm in which the Pax Britannica should henceforth prevail.[11]

On the other hand, Huxley's doubts notwithstanding, the idea that anthropology might have some contribution to make to the more efficient and more humane governance of Britain's imperial realm seemed a timely one to others besides Haddon. So also, the further (or perhaps prior) thought that the institutional and intellectual development of the discipline might be linked to the needs and to the fact of empire. After several decades in which they had shown little interest in colonial issues, British anthropologists began in the early 1890s a series of appeals to various colonial authorities arguing the importance of anthropological knowledge for responsible colonial government, and the responsibility of colonial government for the advancement of anthropological knowledge.[12]

At the Ipswich meeting of the British Association in 1895, there was a discussion of "the contact of European and native civilizations," at which Haddon offered a shortened, expurgated version of his unpublished appeal. At Liverpool the following year, the anthropological section passed a resolution calling for the government to establish "a Bureau of Ethnology for Greater Britain, which, by collecting information with regard to the native races within and on the borders of the Empire, will prove of immense value to science and to the Government itself." As Hercules Read of the British Museum, the mover of the resolution, posed the issue: if the United States government, which had only one "race" to deal with, supported such a bureau, then "how much more is it the duty of Great Britain to attempt some record of the many vanishing or, at any rate, quickly changing races within her borders?" Pointing to several precedents in the British sphere—including notably the collection of ethnographic data in connection with Indian censuses, which had previously been encouraged by the association—Read called for the systematic collection of ethnographic information "by a uniform method," as part of the regular duties of colonial officers, who would transmit it to a "central office" in London. At the next several meetings of the association, the plan was further elaborated. The British Museum agreed to supply a room, and the Prime Minister, Lord Salisbury, directed that reports by officers in protectorates under the Foreign Office be forwarded to the proposed bureau in response to queries it might distribute. But an appeal to the Colonial Office for similar assistance went unacknowledged, and neither the government nor the museum provided funds; as a result, the plan lapsed.[13]

In the meantime, however, the Anthropological Institute itself had entered a period of reinvigorated activity, which its subsequent president and historian, Arthur Keith, attributed to a new willingness to "shoulder its burden and move forward to meet its Empire-wide responsibilities." After more than two decades of continuous decline, membership began to rise after 1895—with, by 1899, a doubling of the small number of women fellows. Among them was a Miss G. M. Godden, to whom was delegated in 1897 the preparation of a list of anthropological questions for members of the Indian Civil Service and officers of the Northeast Frontier. Better known today is Mary Kingsley, who had travelled in West Africa in the early 1890s and whose writings were influential in an emerging critique of colonial policy by advocates of "indirect rule." At once racialist and relativist, Kingsley sought to preserve African societies from the disintegrative impact of Western civilization, so that they might develop a civilization which, although inferior, would be an expression of the unique spirituality of the "African Mind." Kingsley's proto-functionalism resonates to that of other anthropologists in this period, and she in fact advocated giving anthropologists a voice in colonial affairs; but any role she might have had in organized anthropology was cut short by her death from enteric fever while she was serving as a nurse in the Boer War.[14]

By the century's end, there was also a new male cohort in the Anthropological Institute, including several academics with anthropological interests (notably the Oxford and Cambridge classical archeologists John Myres and William Ridgeway), a number of men with extensive colonial experience, and several returning members of the Torres Straits Expedition. Although amalgamation with the Folk-Lore Society continued to be discussed, negotiations seem to have bogged down in detail, as the face of the institute turned increasingly overseas. The year 1900 saw a general reorganization of the institute and the inauguration of a new monthly publication, *Man*, as a repository for the "Miscellanea"

A studio portrait of Mary Kingsley, who autographed one taken at the same session in 1897: "the melancholy picture of one who tried to be just to all parties" (Frank 1986:174–75). (By permission of the Syndics of the Cambridge University Library)

and "Reviews" of the existing *Journal*—with an emphasis on records relating to "the History of Non-European Cultures, which (in this country, at all events) have not hitherto had a periodical record of their own." Although there was a moment of crisis in 1903, when more conservative members of the institute felt that *Man* was costing too much, matters were patched over. And in 1907, after several failed initiatives during the preceding decade, the institute was "by His Majesty's gracious command" henceforth to be known as Royal—which the institute's secretary took as evidence that the "Imperial importance of anthropology," although it had "not yet obtained general recognition in England," might soon be more adequately acknowledged.[15]

In the interim, there had been further attempts to win support from various colonial authorities. In the second year of the Boer War, Haddon, on behalf of the institute, joined with Edward Brabrook of the Folk-Lore Society in preparing a memorial to Joseph Chamberlain, the Colonial Secretary, urging the "scientific study of the native laws and customs" of the black population of the regions "lately known as the Orange Free State and the South African Republic." These peoples were, "for savages, in a somewhat advanced social stage," with "a tribal organisation, religious institutions, and a morality of their own." But because these restraints tended to break down under "contact with civilisation," without being replaced by new ones, the natives were "difficult of management by a European Government"—and were made more so by the "oppression" to which the Boers had subjected them. Granted that some of their customs were such as "not to be tolerated by a civilised government," careful inquiry was necessary to determine their "precise meaning and consequences"—as instanced by the frequent misinterpretation of the practice of lobola. In this context, the memorial proposed the creation of a commission to collect a complete ethnographic record, so as to ascertain "what customs may be recognised, and what customs must be forbidden or modified" in order to facilitate the administration of justice, as well as the passage of legislation governing native labor in the mines and native relations with European settlers. By preserving "for all time an account of the culture of the natives at the moment when they came under British rule," such a venture would also have a "scientific value" that would be "difficult to over-estimate." Chamberlain, however, thought the moment inopportune, both at that time and two years later, when he expressed "regret" that he could not see a delegation of some forty leading members of both societies. Although Haddon broached the issue again when the British Association met in South Africa in 1905, it was more than a decade before a locally renewed initiative led to the formation of the School of African Life and Languages and the appointment of Radcliffe-Brown at the University of Cape Town.[16]

By the time the question of an imperial bureau was raised again in 1908, anthropology had gained formal institutional recognition at both Cambridge and Oxford. In each case, the board or committee included a number of scholars whose previous training and disciplinary identification were somewhat heterogeneous, but who were now strongly committed to the advancement of "anthropology" as an academic study. And in a field of limited resources, these men were slightly ambivalent about its development at the University of London, where, in addition to the work at the School of Economics, the movement had already begun which a decade later eventuated in the establishment of the School of Oriental [and African] Studies. When Ridgeway, as president of the Anthropological Institute, was asked in March of 1908 to cooperate in the formation of an "Institute of Oriental Research," he took the occasion instead to reopen discussion of an "Imperial Bureau of Ethnology." At about the same time, the question of anthropological training for colonial officers had been raised by Sir Reginald Wingate, Governor-General of the Sudan, who hoped that the two ancient universities might consider giving "instruction in Ethnology and Primitive Religion" to probationers in the Sudan civil service. While such arrangements were being made, anthropologists of the two ancient universities also cooperated in the preparation of memorials from each institution to the Colonial and India Offices, urging the establishment of similar programs for their recruits, as well as instruction for present officers home on furlough—cautioning that it would be a "grave misfortune" if any government aid were limited to the University of London. Simultaneously, the Anthropological Institute composed a memorial to the Prime Minister, Lord Asquith, and other relevant members of the government, extending the proposal beyond the training of probationers to suggest also the formation, within the Anthropological Institute, of an "Imperial Bureau of Anthropology." Sustained by an annual government grant of £500, such a bureau would collect and make available ethnographic information on all races—but "especially" those in the British Empire—as well as organize an anthropometric survey of the United Kingdom. Although it would not be a "teaching body," it could also confer diplomas on "officials, scientific travellers, and others who had submitted a proper test of their distinction in some branch of anthropology."[17]

Neither of these attempts seems, however, to have been very productive. After a deputation from Oxford and Cambridge was received at the India and Colonial Offices in August 1908 without apparent result, Ridgeway decided it would be best in approaching the Prime Minister "to keep the scientific side out of sight." An attempt to include several peers of the realm (including Lord Curzon, late Viceroy of India) having failed, the delegation of twelve was loaded with men active in administration and trade, including five M.P.'s and five knights, as well as

Ridgeway and his counterpart Myres from Oxford. But although Myres privately expressed the opinion that Asquith had given "unambiguous recognition of the practical value for administrative purposes of systematic anthropological training," the published account suggests no more than an expression of the government's "hearty sympathy." And as far as financial support for the Anthropological Institute was concerned, Asquith felt that it had no greater claim than fifty or a hundred other organizations carrying on "excellent work, all on a voluntary basis." A follow-up memorandum to the Treasury produced nothing, nor did anything come of a further memorial sent directly to the colonial premiers and others attending the coronation of George V in 1911.[18]

Along with these failed attempts to obtain government support for anthropology by negotiation at the center, there were also initiatives from the colonial periphery in the prewar period. In addition to Wingate's request for university courses, the Sudan government in 1909 had provided funds to the Seligmans for an ethnographic survey. And when the acting commissioner of Northern Nigeria was unable to make sense of responses to an ethnographic questionnaire previously circulated to political officers throughout West Africa, he appealed in 1908 to the Colonial Office for the services of an anthropologist. After consulting with Frazer, Tylor, and Read, the Colonial Office engaged Northcote Thomas, a Cambridge graduate who had recently published an armchair study of Australian kinship, and who was active in both the Anthropological Institute and the Society for Psychical Research. Later remembered in colonial circles as "a recognized maniac" who "lived on vegetables" and wore sandals even back in England, Thomas seems to have alienated local colonial officials from the moment he began work in Southern Nigeria. Discarding the existing questionnaire responses, he circulated his own questionnaire. The results were forwarded by the Colonial Office to the Anthropological Institute in 1910, with the request that they be evaluated by a committee of experts, in meetings where both Thomas and representatives of the Colonial Office would be present. On this basis, the committee was to advise whether or not to continue the work, and whether instruction in anthropology should be given to probationers in the tropical African colonies. In the spirit of the emerging fieldwork mode, the committee (which included Rivers and Haddon) noted with approval Thomas' use of the method "known as 'genealogical,'" but urged that in the future he should "fix his headquarters in some central place & should in the first instance devote himself to acquiring some knowledge of the local languages." They were, however, generally laudatory, and offered their "emphatic opinion" that, in the interests of "efficient administration," the work should be continued on a larger scale.[19]

Thomas returned to Southern Nigeria for two more years, and published extensive compilations of customary and linguistic materials on the Edo- and Ibo-speaking peoples. But he also continued to disturb his employers by spending too much time on "purely scientific research"—and by concluding that Africans' consumption of liquor had no deleterious effects. Among those he succeeded in alienating was Frederick Lugard, who upon becoming governor of a united Nigeria in 1912 managed to get Thomas transferred to Sierra Leone, where he again ran into difficulty. Having provided a report confirming the government's suspicion that the "Human Leopard Society" represented a regressive tendency among a group made more "savage" by the disorienting stresses of social change, Thomas refused, on the grounds of professional ethics, to divulge the identity of presumed murderers he had interviewed in preparing the report. After one tour of duty, he was sent home in 1915, ostensibly because retrenchment was necessitated by the European war.[20]

In the clubby atmosphere of colonial bureaucracy, the experience of Thomas as "government anthropologist" reverberated for the next decade, confirming a prevailing prejudice in favor of "practical" rather than "scientific" men: university men of the sort recruited into the colonial services, who might benefit from some anthropological training, but whose main qualifications were the moral attributes associated with a "gentlemanly" background. When the Cambridge anthropologists in 1914 urged the Rajah of Sarawak to employ a full-time ethnologist to study local tribes before their "primitive conditions" were "greatly modified by contact with western civilisation," they were informally told that the crucial factor was whether, "to put it bluntly, the man is a gentleman or not." Despite his Cambridge education, a man like Thomas—who had proposed to win native confidence by filing his false teeth in the African fashion—would never have satisfied.[21]

On the eve of World War I, there was a final organized push by anthropologists at the center, led by Sir Richard Temple—one of a small group of colonial officials who had developed "the anthropological habit of mind." After his undergraduate days at Henry Maine's Cambridge college, Trinity Hall, Temple put in twenty years of military service in India, Afghanistan, and Burma, ending his colonial career as Chief Commissioner of the Andaman and Nicobar Islands. Along the way, he pursued his developing anthropological interests first as founder-editor of *Punjab Notes and Queries*, and from 1884 on as editor-proprietor of *The Indian Antiquary*. When the Board of Anthropological Studies was established at Cambridge in 1904, Temple gave a welcoming speech on "The Practical Value of Anthropology," anticipating that the board might become a "School of Applied Anthropology"—a project Temple conceived of in mentalistic terms, as a matter of "tact" and "sympathy," a "habit of mind" that would enable administrators, missionaries, and traders to better "understand" the "thought" of "savages" (who "within their limitations [were] very far from being fools").[22]

Nine years later, Temple developed similar themes in his presidential address to the anthropological section of the British Association. The meetings were held in Birmingham, the adopted home of Joseph Chamberlain, the leading "new imperialist," who was also the first chancellor of the University of Birmingham. In what was clearly a coordinated move, a session was held on "The Practical Application of Anthropological Teaching in the Universities," at which several colonial administrators and university anthropologists spoke in favor of Temple's proposal that a "School of Applied Anthropology" be established at the university. One by-product of Temple's initiative was the course of lectures given at Birmingham that winter by Radcliffe-Brown, first scion of the Cambridge Board of Anthropology, whose Andaman research Temple had helped to plan and was later to review somewhat critically. Another by-product was a joint committee of the British Association and the Anthropological Institute, chaired by Temple, which sought to "encourage the systematic teaching of Anthropology to persons either about to proceed to or actually working in those parts of the British Empire which contain populations alien to the British people."[23]

In February of 1914, a conference was held at the hall of the Drapers' Company in London to consider the committee's recommendations. Chaired by the Earl of Selborne, who as High Commissioner for South Africa played a major role in the establishment of the Union of South Africa, the conference was attended by almost sixty academics, colonial officials, and dignitaries of various sorts, including an official representative of the Colonial Office. The main resolution was offered by Sir Henry Craik, long-time parliamentary representative of the universities of Glasgow and Aberdeen, both of which had sent out "more than their share" of men to "carry the 'white man's burden' " in distant parts of an empire that, as another speaker noted, covered "one-third of the world" and ruled "one fifth of its inhabitants." The resolution was seconded by Sir Everhard Im Thurn, who had attended Tylor's Oxford lectures before going on to a career as colonial museum curator and administrator in Guiana, Ceylon, and Fiji. It was, the resolution affirmed, in "the highest interests of the Empire" that university instruction in anthropology be extended, so that those "about to spend their lives" overseas might acquire an "accurate knowledge of the habits, customs, social and religious ideas and ideals of the Eastern and non-European races subject to His Majesty the King Emperor." Sir Harry Johnston (whose explorations and diplomatic activities had added to the empire some 400,000 square miles in East Africa) was concerned that a positive governmental interest was "sometimes baulked" by lower-level colonial officials who thought anthropology "a ridiculous new-fangled craze." But the conference nevertheless unanimously supported a second implementing resolution that yet another delegation be sent to Prime Minister Asquith, with the request that he appoint an interdepartmental committee to advise "as to the form in which the sympathy and support of His Majesty's Government can be best expressed." In the event, however, the outbreak of World War I forestalled further consideration of the matter.[24]

The quarter-century since Tylor's paper and Haddon's return from the Torres Straits had seen significant changes in the institutional structure and the colonial orientation of anthropology. By 1913 the discipline had a fairly firm foothold in the three major universities. At the British Association discussion that year, Marett was able to report that the number of students in the Oxford program had risen from one in 1906 to thirty-four in 1912. The total for those years was eleven men from the British Isles, eight from the colonies, seven from the United States, two from the Continent, "11 women of all nationalities," and twenty-one officers of the colonial services of various British colonies: "10 from West Africa, 9 from the Anglo-Egyptian Soudan and Egypt, 1 from British East Africa, and 1 from India." A dozen or so students from the three universities had by this time undertaken fieldwork overseas. There was, in short, an emerging cohort of academically trained anthropologists. While change was less dramatic at the traditional institutional center of the discipline, the Anthropological Institute was also now a more academically professional organization than it had been in 1888. Between 1893 and 1910 the proportion of scholars employed by universities and museums among the institute's officers and council had gone from less than half to over two-thirds.[25]

On the other hand, the institutional structure of British anthropology was still rather heterogeneously constituted, with no established professional career path for new recruits. Of the academic scholars among the leadership of the Anthropological Institute, more than half were natural scientists, academic physicians, and academics other than anthropologists. Excluding Herbert Risley, who superintended ethnological surveys in India, Haddon was the only "field" anthropologist among the ten men who served as president of the institute between 1900 and 1920; the others were museum scholars, physical anthropologists, archeologists, and a retired colonial official. The groups responsible for anthropological instruction at the universities were also rather diverse in disciplinary character, and there was as yet no significant social demand for the professional services of those they trained—although the emergence of a student cohort was still too recent for its professional employment to be a serious problem. The government had called upon several physical anthropologists in 1903 to help determine whether the low physical standard of recruits for the Boer War reflected a general racial deterioration of the British population. But otherwise all those memorials and delegations urging the utility of anthropology in the overseas empire had produced little more than expressions of sympathy.[26]

In the colonies themselves, there were more hopeful signs. While the experiment with a "government anthropologist" in West Africa was an ambiguous precedent, there was by now a well-established tradition of governmental ethnological work in India, and Wingate's appeal from the Sudan foreshadowed a more widespread demand for anthropological training for colonial probationers. But if the usefulness of a certain generalized ethnological knowledge for developing a sympathetic "habit of mind" among colonial officials was beginning to be recognized, it had yet to be accepted that such knowledge was best provided by academically trained anthropologists. Moreover, the knowledge anthropologists sought to gather abroad, or have transmitted to them at home, so that they could make it available for training purposes, was a knowledge oriented toward the past rather than the present or future. It was knowledge of the precontact cultural state that would enable anthropologists at home to solve the evolutionary or diffusional problems that were still the focus of general anthropological speculation; it was a sympathetic knowledge of the precontact native mentality (or "racial mind") that they in turn would offer to colonial officers and others to facilitate administration or missionary activity or profitable trade.[27]*

*As a footnote to the discussion of anthropology and colonial problems in the prewar period, and an indication of the way in which discourse about race developed in British anthropology, it is worth considering the participation of British anthropologists in the First Universal Races Congress, held in London during July 1911. Organized by Felix Adler and Gustav Spiller, the conference attracted twelve hundred "active" members and another thousand "passive" participants; although its dominant tone was defined by idealistic European "liberal internationalists," there were a substantial number of representatives of non-European peoples, among them some in the emerging Pan-African movement. There were also many of the world's leading anthropologists, including both Franz Boas and Alfred Haddon, whose respective contributions provide another point of comparison between the American and British traditions. Boas gave a paper on "the instability of human types" under environmental influences, which was central to his developing critique of racial assumption (Stocking 1968b:161–94). But despite a generally sympathetic (if occasionally somewhat patronizing) attitude toward non-European peoples, Haddon (who two years previously had published a book entitled *The Races of Man*) took issue with Boas' argument. Each race and nation had its own mentality, and although environmental change was possible, the "great race types" were permanent; while a mixture of closely related or "comparable" races could be favorable, one between widely divergent types was not; the fact that there were "no pure races now existing" was "no reason for jumping to the conclusion, as so many did, that there is no such subject as racial anthropology" (Haddon in Schirbel 1991:II, 665, 674; Haddon 1911a, 1911b, 1909c; Boas 1911; Rich 1984). Haddon's interest in racial differentiation—an aspect of his traditional "ethnological" orientation, as well as his background in zoology—continued in evidence throughout his career. This

By the beginning of the war, however, changes were already under way in the temporal orientation of anthropological knowledge. With the end of the war, there were also to be dramatic changes in its imperial context which, in a changing institutional framework, helped to provide the basis for the emergence of social anthropology as a clearly differentiated inquiry, whose practitioners were inclined to see themselves opposed to the grey-beard elders of the Royal Anthropological Institute.

The Dual Mandate and the Emergence of Government Anthropology

With the Versailles Treaty and the allocation of mandates by the new League of Nations, the British Empire approached its apogee. Although it did not reach an ultimate limit until the early 1930s, when its power was extended through the southern Arabian littoral, the peace settlement had meant the addition of almost a million square miles and thirteen million new subjects. But on the global map, many of those miles were now crosshatched rather than solidly red. The Class A mandates of the late Turkish Empire were "provisionally" independent, subject to "the rendering of administrative advice and assistance." And if the Class C mandates of Southwest Africa and the Pacific Islands were treated as "integral portions" of the territory of the Mandatory Power, that power was in fact wielded by white-settler colonies which were themselves independent members of the League of Nations. While these mandatories were also "dominions" within the "community of nations known as the British Empire," their status did not commit them to sending troops to defend Chanak, the empire's outpost on the Dardanelles, when it was threatened by the new Turkish state in 1922. Elsewhere, in response to nationalist movements in India, Ireland, and Egypt, the terms of imperial dominion were also being substantially attenuated. Even at home, imperial energy and enthusiasm had passed their peak, and critics of

---

was true, as well, of Seligman, whose festschrift (Evans-Pritchard et al., eds., 1934) included Alẽs Hrdlička's (somewhat qualified) defense of the study of skull form, as well as George Pitt-Rivers' "anthropological approach to ethnogenics," along with some rather atypical contributions by members of the emerging cohort of social anthropologists (Firth on dreams, Malinowski on stone implements). Although both Haddon and Seligman in the mid 1930s became involved in the developing critique of racism, it seems likely that their persisting interest in a racial ethnology was a factor in the belated development of that critique in Britain. There were, of course, other factors, including the general anthropological tradition and the social atmosphere of the Royal Anthropological Institute, in which racially oriented physical anthropologists, ethnologists, and former colonial residents continued to play an important role (cf. Barkan 1988, 1992; Stepan 1982).

empire were increasingly vocal. Four times as many people attended the British Empire Exhibition at Wembley in 1924 as had gone to the Crystal Palace in 1851; but the event was grist for the cartoon mill of *Punch,* and a number of anti-imperialist intellectuals spoke of themselves as WGTW—the Won't Go to Wembleys. Among those who in the aftermath of Armageddon reacted against all things Victorian, there was scepticism not only of empire, but of the very "civilisation" to which the "well being and development of peoples not yet able to stand by themselves" had been given in "sacred Trust."[28]

While the spirit of the "new imperialism" had waned, there were plenty of old "new imperialists" still around in positions of power and influence. And there were few, even among the critics of empire, who doubted that the empire which the "new imperialism" had created—recast in terms of the "commonwealth ideal"—would last for some time. True, India was launched on the road to eventual independence; but despite the stirrings of African nationalism in the Pan-African Congress of 1920, the future of empire in tropical Africa seemed to stretch out indefinitely. What was at issue was not the fact of empire, but the terms on which it was to be sustained. Having emerged from the war heavily in debt, the home government was anxious that this be done as cheaply as possible. And aside from the limitations imposed by fiscal policy, there were also ethico-political constraints. With a revolutionary party in power in Russia, and revolutionary movements threatening elsewhere, with nationalist movements aroused and erstwhile American allies advocating self-determination, with the ideal of responsible trusteeship reasserted against the image of an irresponsible German colonialism, the moral basis of colonial rule was itself at issue. As the later-to-be-governor of Kenya put the matter early in 1922, "if we do not proclaim our own moral belief and act up to it in every way there will be very serious trouble in store."[29]

Freshly retired from the governor-generalship of Nigeria and shortly to begin a decade of service as Britain's permanent member of the League of Nations Mandate Commission, Frederick Lugard was at that moment on the verge of publishing just that proclamation: *The Dual Mandate in British Tropical Africa*. Written as an answer to Leonard Woolf's Labour Party critique, *Empire and Commerce in Africa,* Lugard's book was to be the bible of "indirect rule" in the interwar period. But rather than foreshadowing functionalist anthropology, its rhetoric and its ideology seem redolent of the racialist evolutionism of the later nineteenth century. Lugard had no doubt that it was "the genius of our [English] race to colonise, to trade, and to govern" or that "the typical African of this race-type ["negro" as opposed to "Hamitic negroid"] is a happy, thriftless, excitable person, lacking in self-control, discipline, and foresight, naturally courageous and naturally courteous and polite, full of personal vanity, with little sense of veracity, [and] fond of music"—whose mind was "far nearer to the animal world than that of the European or Asiatic." From "the point of view of the administrator," the peoples of tropical Africa could be classified in social evolutionary terms. There were "primitive tribes," either settled or pastoral, ranging in "social status" from those who, recognizing no chief, were "still in the patriarchal stage," up to those with "well-defined tribal institutions"—which usually became "despotisms marked by a ruthless disregard for human life" and never evolved "any approach to culture." Where "more progressive" communities had emerged, it was because they adopted "an alien monotheistic religion [Islam], which brought with it a written language and a foreign culture." Finally, there were a small group of "Europeanized Africans," of whom Lugard took a rather sceptical view—which he documented by a comparative reference to the American racialist writer Lothrop Stoddard.[30]

"Indirect rule"—or, in Lugard's phrases, "dependent native rule" and "ruling through the native chiefs"—was his preferred mode of government for both primitive and more advanced groups. Its "essential feature" was that "native chiefs" were constituted "as an integral part of the machinery of the administration," although certain powers were to be permanently reserved to the "controlling Power as trustee for the welfare of the masses." Similarly, in cases where "the advent of Europeans" had "a disintegrating effect on tribal authority," or where it was necessary to "hasten the transition from the patriarchal to the tribal stage," a more direct rule might be necessary, until the people could be induced "to recognize a common chief." But the main point was gradually to "evolve from their own institutions, based on their own habits of thought, prejudices and customs, the form of rule best suited to them, and adapted to meet the new conditions." And because "European brains, capital and energy have not been, and never will be, expended in developing the resources of Africa from motives of pure philanthropy," it was also essential to involve Africans in the productive and profitable economic activity which was the other aspect of the dual mandate.[31]

Save for Henry Maine (on the evolution of land tenure), Everhard Im Thurn (on labor in Fiji), and Elliot Smith (on "lack of interests in life" as a cause of population decline), Lugard made no reference to recognizably "anthropological" writers in the British tradition. Neither were anthropological topics included among those treated in his discussion of "research" as "the second main line of development" in Africa. In regard to the selection and training of district officers, Lugard sought to attract "the right class from our public schools and universities, while excluding as far as possible the 'bounder,' the 'prig,' and the 'book-worm.'" He did, however (in a footnote), refer to the fact that "ethnology" was one of the topics on which candidates for the Dutch colonial service were examined. There was, in short, a rather small opening for anthropology.[32]

The first to enter it, however, were not functional anthropologists, but a cohort of government anthropologists. There were of course a number of colonial officers with little or no academic training in anthropology who before the war and on through the interwar period collected ethnographic information, some of it published, much of it contained in district officers' reports. But there were also some who did this on a regular basis after receiving diplomas or taking courses in anthropology with Rivers and Haddon at Cambridge or with Marett at Oxford. By the time Lugard's book appeared, several of them were already at work in colonies whose governors, responding to similar postwar concerns, had concluded that the collection of ethnographic information by officers with some anthropological training might facilitate an enlightened and cost-effective native administration—or were concerned that the knowledge of rapidly changing primitive peoples should not be "lost to mankind as was the South American language which was last spoken on earth by Humboldt's aged parrot."[33]

Among them was Papua's Hubert Murray, who acknowledged a debt to an essay Rivers had written in 1917 on "The Government of Subject Peoples." Anticipating the "new responsibilities" that would come with the incorporation of German colonies into the empire, and the "duty of meeting old responsibilities in new ways," Rivers had suggested "two chief lines of action": "the investigation of customs and beliefs by officers especially appointed for the task"; and training in anthropology for "those who are themselves to carry on the work of government." In 1920, at the end of a somewhat defensive review of his administration in Papua—in which he bemoaned the incapacity of colonial officers to "think black"—Murray announced plans to appoint a government anthropologist. Malinowski, who in 1914 had been "obsessed by the thought of some ethnological governmental post," had by this time higher aspirations, and was in any case not in Murray's good graces. Neither was Ernest Chinnery, an Australian who before the war had collected ethnographic data while serving under Murray as patrol officer, and who after a wartime stint in the flying corps had taken a diploma in anthropology under Haddon. Instead, Murray gave the position to William Strong, the territory's chief medical officer, who as government agent in the Mekeo district had participated in Seligman's expedition of 1904. Strong was assisted by Rivers' student William Armstrong, who was later offered Strong's post when he retired after two years. When Armstrong chose instead to return to Cambridge, in the unrequited hope of a permanent academic career as Rivers' successor, the position was given to Francis Williams, an Australian Rhodes Scholar who after service in France had returned to Oxford to study anthropology under Marett—and who had been the runner-up to Radcliffe-Brown for the chair at Cape Town. In the aftermath of the discussions at the Pan-Pacific Science Congress in 1923, Chinnery (who had been serving as Director of Native Labour with the New Guinea Copper Mines) was appointed government anthropologist for the Mandated Territory to the north. For the next decade or more he and Williams served as gatekeepers to the New Guinea field, Chinnery channelling academic fieldworkers out of Sydney into appropriate sites in the northern regions, Williams largely monopolizing the southern half for his own research.[34]

Although there were men in other areas (including Haddon's student L. F. Taylor in Burma), the second major focus of government anthropology was West Africa, where in the early 1920s district officers in Nigeria and the Gold Coast were seconded to anthropological work. Anxious to include ethnological information in the 1921 census report for the northern provinces of Nigeria, Lugard's successor Hugh Clifford entrusted the task to Charles Kingsley Meek, an Oxford man who had served as district officer since 1912. After returning to Oxford for anthropological courses with Marett, Meek began collecting ethnographic data, partly from the earlier reports of district officers, but mainly from his own fieldwork in the survey mode, and in 1925 published a two-volume ethnographic compendium, *The Northern Tribes of Nigeria*. In 1929, after "riots of an unprecedented kind"—in which mobs of Ibo women "armed themselves with cudgels, and marched up and down the country, howling down the Government, setting fire to the Native Court buildings, [and] assaulting their chiefs"—Meek was sent to work among the Ibo in the southeast. There he undertook a more intensive study, eventually producing a highly regarded monograph on Ibo social and political structure, as well as several further studies of northern Nigerian groups.[35]

On the Gold Coast, Robert Sutherland Rattray adopted from the beginning a more intensive fieldwork style. After service in the Boer War and several years as hunter for a trading company, Rattray entered the Gold Coast administrative service in 1907. He took advantage of his leaves to study anthropology with Marett at Exeter College and law at Gray's Inn, and he published works on the folklore of the Chinyanja, the Hausa, and the Ashanti. Although known as the "polyglot Mr. Rattray" for his facility in several native languages, he was not a success as an administrator, and in 1921 Gordon Guggisberg, one of several "forward-looking" colonial governors in the postwar period, found a more satisfactory role for him as head (and sole member) of a new Anthropological Department of Ashanti. Rather than establishing a clearing-house for the

Robert Sutherland Rattray, "with tracker of primitive forest type," in his pre-administrative role of elephant hunter, which he later continued to play at the call of farmers whose crops were being damaged. (From Rattray, *Religion and Art in Ashanti,* 1927, fig. 24; by permission of Oxford University Press)

results of investigations by others, which he believed would have yielded a mass of material "very difficult to classify, examine, and verify," Rattray chose instead to undertake himself "a detailed investigation into the beliefs and customs" of the Ashanti. By working with the elders, without an interpreter—gaining their confidence as one who could understand "their modes of thought and pride of race"—he hoped to get them to "pour out their store of ancient lore" as "a background for future research." Over the next few years, Rattray produced a series of volumes which to this day are an indispensable resource for students of Ashanti culture.[36]

The ethnography of government anthropologists has been characterized as "evolutionist," and there is no doubt that evolutionism, both as cultural ideology and anthropological theory, provided both a prior grounding and a continuing reference point for their ethnographic enterprise. But to suggest (as in the case of Rattray) that their anthropology was "closer to the nineteenth century than the twentieth" implies a somewhat greater intellectual backwardness than their work displays. Meek, Rattray, and Williams—who might almost be said to constitute an "Oxford School" of government anthropology—were followers rather than makers of anthropological fashion. But their work developed in relation to the anthropological movements of their own day, toward which they were not unwilling to adopt a critical attitude when their specific ethnographic materials seemed to warrant it.[37]

Meek, whose turn to anthropology came later in his career, began as the most obviously derivative and backward-looking of the three Oxonians. The discussion of social organization in his initial ethnographic synthesis, *The Northern Tribes of Nigeria,* was cast in terms of "survivals" of "totemism" and the change from "mother-right" to patrilineal institutions; his lengthy account of religion was presented as a progressive sequence of forms within a "common religion—that of Animism"—from "ancestor worship" to "fetishism" to "naturism" to "polytheism," with asides to Frazer and Seligman on the killing of divine kings. Meek, however, was also concerned with problems of migration and diffusion, and his later book on the Jukun-speaking peoples was clearly written with an eye to Perry and Elliot Smith's derivation of all human culture from Ancient Egypt. By the time Meek published his intensive study of the Ibo, "social structure" had become his organizing principle, and he prefaced the discussion with comments on the work of Malinowski and Radcliffe-Brown on "primitive law," taking a middle ground between the two.[38]

Starting from an earlier and more systematic training in anthropology, Rattray opened his ethnography of the Ashanti with an analysis of their "classificatory system," adopting the genealogical method "first successfully worked out by the late Dr. Rivers . . . and elaborated by Mrs. Seligman." Like Meek, he devoted the bulk of his volume to religion, but with constant reference to the experience of his own eyewitnessing at specific times and places. He was sharply critical of the prevailing tendency to reduce West African religion to "fetishism"—which he believed to be the result of misinformation communicated by educated Africans who despised "the unlettered past of [their] race," or by "bush" or "raw" natives through the distorting medium of an interpreter, as well as the adoption of "inappropriate European words" rather than the careful examination of "the distinction and nomenclature that the African himself observes." In contrast, Rattray approached the Ashanti "as a seeker after truths," which "not all the learning nor all the books of the white man could ever give to me." Although he had earlier referred to Marett's "school of working anthropologists" as built "upon the noble foundations laid by Sir E. B. Tylor and Dr. Frazer," Rattray insisted that the Ashanti belief in a supreme being who was the source of power of their numerous lesser gods was not the result of "contact with Christians or even, I believe, with Mohammedans," but rather the natural product "of the mind of a primitive people who live face to face with nature." Acknowledging his mentor Marett's critique of Arnold Van Gennep, Rattray nevertheless organized his later work on Ashanti religion in terms of a life-cycle sequence of *rites de passage*. Even in what was in some respects his most evolutionary work, *Ashanti Law and Constitution*, Rattray tested evolutionary hypotheses against the ethnographic data, upon occasion disconfirming them. In his final work as government anthropologist, *The Tribes of the Ashanti Hinterland*, he hypothesized an incursion of "small bands" of "soldiers of fortune" who were "familiar with the idea of kingship or chieftainship in our modern sense" and were "accustomed to a patrilineal manner of reckoning descent"—and who, as the ruling class over the more "primitive" autochthonous peoples, preempted an independent evolution from "Priest-King" to "Territorial ruler." Although Rattray spoke of his hypothesis as a late revelation of his own ethnographic research, and made no mention of Rivers, Perry, or Elliot Smith, the echoes of heliolithic diffusionism seem obvious.[39]

While both Meek and Rattray were later to express reservations about indirect rule, they both devoted themselves primarily to the documentation of precontact cultures, assuming that such information would provide a more adequate basis for the encouragement of development along native lines. Rattray's memorandum on the "Golden Stool" soon after his appointment in 1921, which enabled the government "to deal in a sympathetic spirit with the disturbing event of its desecration," in fact became a primary talking point for advocates of a native policy informed by anthropological understanding. While it has been suggested that Rattray had some influence in the implementation of indirect rule in the Gold Coast, his practical contributions seem to have been undervalued, and he was not replaced upon his retirement in 1930. Indeed, the considerable time lapse between ethnographic research and publication must generally have reduced somewhat the practical value of the work of government anthropologists. Provoked by riots in 1929, Meek's study of the Ibo did not appear until 1937, when its "practical conclusions" were contained in a single final chapter evaluating, not uncritically, "indirect rule" as it had developed in Nigeria, with suggestions for its future evolution.[40]

In contrast, Williams' New Guinea ethnography seems to have been initially driven more directly by concerns arising in the contact situation itself—notably, religious movements like the "Taro Cult" and the "Vailala Madness." And unlike the rather nostalgically romantic Rattray, who echoed Richard Temple's *tout savoir, tout pardonner*, Williams (as his mentor Marett observed), hit "a happy mean between too much and too little sympathy with the native point of view." In the mode of Rivers and Malinowski, Williams suggested that the Vailala madness was caused by the loss of *joie de vivre* after the suppression of just those activities "which our native followed with the greatest zeal." More characteristically, however, he evaluated the contact situation in pragmatic terms, judging what in each area of native culture was "good" (which should be encouraged), what was "indifferent" (which might be tolerated), and what was "bad" (which had to be forbidden). Committed in a general way to indirect rule, he offered quite a bit of direct practical advice: arguing for native "peasant proprietorship" against "capitalistic enterprise," he urged the substitution of "crop rotation" for the "rotation of areas" in Orokaiva horticulture, to facilitate intensive agriculture and closer settlement.[41]

The three may also be contrasted in their relation to anthropological theory. Accepting an older division of anthropological labor, Meek and Rattray responded to theoretical tendencies emanating from the center, but had no pretensions as theorists themselves; they might evaluate theory against their ethnographic cases, but it was the ethnographic material as such that was their primary contribution to anthropology. Rattray described himself as "a student of anthropology from its practical and applied rather than its academic standpoint," who had "little opportunity" to "elaborate theories." He in fact called upon academic anthropologists to deal with certain technical or general topics: Seligman on dreams, Buxton on the biology of cross-cousin marriage, Marett on "some general aspects of Ashanti religion." Perhaps because Williams received his anthropological training at a younger age, before he entered the colonial service, theory played a more direct role in some of his work.[42]

The theory that interested Williams was a kind of psychobiological evolutionism, grounded in Marett's work on magico-religious phenomena, but reflecting several other intellectual tendencies of the period. For Williams, the taro cult was a "cultural mutation" analogous to the mutations of biological evolution, and should be "added to our theories of the growth of civilization" as a supplement to "the theory of culture contact and transmission." He drew on McDougall's theories of crowd psychology and Seligman's theories of the "extravert" character of "primitive peoples" to explain the shaking fits associated with the cult. Although he thought the strength of these fits might vary by race, he suggested that they might be cured by "an unmistakable condemnation" in the form of temporary confinement to "the district jail," which "would serve well enough as hospital."[43]

Williams also offered his own theory of Orokaiva magic, which although ethnographically focussed, was, like Malinowski's extrapolations from the Trobriands, clearly generalizable to other "primitive" peoples. Although Marett chided Williams for speaking of the "symbolic" procedures of magic as "obviously futile," Williams' treatment, like Malinowski's, was based upon Marett's earlier discussion of magic as "imperative willing." Williams, however, went beyond Marett in a more systematic consideration of the manner in which an originally "spontaneous and unthinking" act "becomes customary and is believed to be effective," and in explicating the reasons for the belief "in its effectiveness." He had quite a bit to say about the "Similarity Symbols" and "Contact Symbols" which corresponded "with Frazer's laws of Homoeopathic Magic and Contagious Magic," about the "mystery of incomprehensibility," which underwrote the efficacy of magical substances or "specifics" (echoing Malinowski's "magical power of words"), about the "logic" (or "pseudo-logic") which gave the practitioner "unconstrained confidence in his own work" and about the ways in which men came to believe in and fear the efficacy of magic—all this along lines that call to mind Lévi-Strauss and Evans-Pritchard. His discussion was in fact rather more elaborate than Malinowski's in "Magic, Science and Religion."[44]

By the time Williams' reports were reprinted in England, however, Malinowski's essay was already in print, in a book addressed from Cambridge University to the world of British intellectuals at large; Williams' subsequent volume, *Orokaiva Society*, was straightforwardly descriptive. This exemplified the place of government anthropologists in the British anthropological tradition. If they responded, with varying temporal lag, to the theoretical concerns of the day, they were for the most part consumers rather than producers of anthropological theory; insofar as they attempted the latter role, they did so from geographically distant, institutionally precarious, and intellectually marginal positions outside the metropolitan mainstream. As producers of ethnographic grist for a general anthropological mill, they had a higher status within the discipline than travellers or missionaries; in several cases their ethnographies for a time preempted a particular field. But if government anthropologists continued to be appointed in various colonies after 1930, their role was never systematically institutionalized. They did not reproduce themselves, and over the longer run their ethnographic fields were subject to incursion by the students of those who did.[45]

Rockefeller Funding and Functionalist Social Anthropology

In the immediate postwar years, the shift toward academic anthropology was reflected in the fate of Sir Richard Temple's attempt at the meetings of the British Association in 1921 to revive interest in an "Imperial School of [Applied] Anthropology." At a conference on "anthropological research and teaching" convened by the association in May of the following year, the old idea of an imperial bureau of ethnology was resurrected in the form of a coordinating "Central Institute" in London, with the suggestion that the Anthropological Institute might take on this function.

The proposal met resistance, however, from Elliot Smith, who charged that the institute was under the "reactionary and paralysing influence" of the "British Museum Party." Claiming to speak for Rivers, who at the time of his death was president of the institute, Smith maintained that emphasis should be placed instead on the role of "the great teaching institutions." Although the institute's secretary insisted that it was not "reactionary" so much as "anemic," the dynamism of prewar years had by this time clearly dissipated, never really to be recaptured during the interwar period. Over the next few months, the idea of a central bureau was dropped; for the rest of the decade, the focus shifted instead to the promotion of anthropological teaching and research at existing academic institutions, which were represented on a "Joint Committee" established by the Anthropological Institute in 1923.[46]

Surviving records suggest that the Joint Committee's major (and largely unsuccessful) preoccupation was raising money for ethnographic research, either from government offices or through contributions to a "Research Endowment Fund." The hoped-for encouragement of anthropological teaching achieved only limited gains. Although there was some expansion of programs for the training for colonial probationers in 1924, the discipline continued to live a somewhat precarious existence at the two ancient universities throughout the 1920s. The somewhat greater institutional dynamism at the University of London was linked to the influx of money from abroad, specifically, from the Rockefeller philanthropies, which contributed substantially both to University College and to the School of Economics.[47]

Various ulterior goals—including the social control of the underclasses and the promotion of the American capitalist class as "new imperialists"—have been attributed to Rockefeller philanthropy in this period. In less radical terms, it seems clear that the Rockefeller trustees and the new cohort of academically trained and reform-minded bureaucrats who had the major input in the day-to-day management of Rockefeller funding shared a commitment to the preservation and advancement of capitalist democracy within a stable international system. But however one characterizes the motive, it is evident that the 1920s were a period of redefinition of philanthropic priorities as well as transition in administrative style at the Rockefeller philanthropies. Along with a broadening of Rockefeller activity overseas and a focus on the support of institutions of higher learning, there was a general shift toward the encouragement of research as the best means of promoting human welfare.[48]

After earlier Rockefeller initiatives in the social sciences had run aground on the conflict of corporate and philanthropic interest in the aftermath of the "Ludlow Massacre" of Colorado miners, the elder Rockefeller's creation of the Laura Spelman Rockefeller Memorial in 1918 to further his late wife's social reform concerns reopened the possibility of work in this area. The Spelman Memorial's director, Beardsley Ruml, was one of several academic social scientists who as Rockefeller bureaucrats emphasized the production of "a body of substantiated and widely accepted generalisations as to human capacities and motives, and as to the behavior of human beings as individuals and groups." Another was Edwin Embree, who as director of the Division of Studies established in the Rockefeller Foundation in 1924 played a key role in organizing a program of research in "Human Biology." Taken in conjunction with Ruml's inclusion of biology among the social sciences, Embree's program reflects a broadly "psychobiological" orientation that was influential in Rockefeller philanthropic circles in the early 1920s. Heavily conditioned by racialist and evolutionist assumptions, it implied a kind of theoretical unity underlying a number of social problems (immigration, crime, public health, mental hygiene, fertility, child development) and a generalized concern for the composition, quality, and control of populations in modern industrial society. To a considerable extent the story of Rockefeller anthropology in the interwar period is that of the redirection of this interest in human biology toward the study of human sociocultural differences, as foundation bureaucrats, committed to consultation with the relevant local academic communities and advised by a series of disciplinary experts, responded to developments within anthropology. In the British sphere, the major focus of Rockefeller philanthropy outside the United States, the result was a considerable reinforcement of the institutional and personnel base of social anthropology.[49]

In the immediate postwar period, however, it was not certain that this would be the case. The early 1920s were the heyday of heliolithic ultra-diffusionism, as well as the moment when a number of British anthropologists were taking a psychoanalytic turn. Race was still a major concern in anthropology, and there was as yet no British analogue of the critique of racism that Franz Boas had developed in the United States. Physical anthropologists played an important role in the institutions of the discipline, and at the margins there was a considerable overlap with the upsurgent eugenics movement. Subdisciplinary lines were not yet so sharp as they were later to become: Radcliffe-Brown devoted teaching time to physical anthropology and reviewed books about human evolution in the popular press. More generally, the influence of biological thinking in the social sciences was quite strong even among those relatively little affected by racialism and eugenicism—as witnessed by Malinowski's biological readings of the early 1920s.[50]

Many of these tendencies came together in the work of George Pitt-Rivers, grandson of the founder of the museum (and later a Mosleyite fascist), who studied with McDougall and Marett at Oxford before undertaking fieldwork in New Guinea. There Pitt-Rivers became intrigued by the "depopulation of Melanesia," an issue of broadly ramifying administrative and anthropological concern in the postwar period, and the topic of a volume Rivers edited in the year of his death. In 1927, Pitt-Rivers published a book, based in large part on his earlier Oxford thesis, whose content is suggested by its rather lengthy title: *The Clash of Cultures and the Contact of Races: An Anthropological and Psychological Study of the Laws of Racial Adaptability, with Special Reference to the Depopulation of the Pacific and the Government of Subject Races.* Replete with references to Nietzsche and Schopenhauer, it was a melange of the intellectual tendencies available to anthropology in the early 1920s, including Freudian and Jungian psychoanalysis, racial ethnology, and eugenicism, as well as functionalist anthropology—with which Pitt-Rivers identified himself. Pitt-Rivers found the key to the population problem in the cultural breakdown resulting from the confrontation of incompatible cultural forms (themselves based in part on inherent racial temperaments). Although Rivers had argued that the loss of "psychological well-being" was a key to the depopulation problem, Pitt-Rivers felt that he had, surprisingly, failed to appreciate the central importance of the "marriage system." Pitt-Rivers, in contrast, placed great emphasis on disruptions of the "vita sexualis," treating at great length such issues as the appropriate balance of miscegenation and inbreeding and the virtues of polygyny over polyandry (because an excess of semen presumably caused sterility in women). Although he dedicated the book to Malinowski (who enjoyed Pitt-Rivers' company despite his "Fascist Weltanschauung"), he was critical of Malinowski's emphasis on the native's vision of *his* world, since the native world was in so many ways being subtly modified: what was needed was the study of culture change.[51]

Over the next decade, the study of "culture change" or "culture contact" was to become a significant option for British social anthropology. But Pitt-Rivers' book, although perhaps more influential than has been appreciated, was more symptomatic of the theoretical turmoil of the early 1920s than of the future of the discipline. The pattern of its redirection may be traced in the fate of a series of initiatives presented to the Rockefeller philanthropies. The first of these developed in relation to the Rockefeller Foundation's activities in medical research and education, which in 1920 included a major benefaction to University College, London. A substantial part of the grant went to support work in human anatomy, the chair in which was held by Grafton Elliot Smith, whose interests ranged from neuroanatomy to fossil man to diffusionist ethnology. Smith found a place for "cultural anthropology" within the new Institute of Anatomy, and by 1923 had managed also the creation of a readership in cultural anthropology for William Perry. For the next several years, Smith was to serve as private anthropological advisor to the Rockefeller philanthropies.[52]

In this role—which although informal was intramurally acknowledged—Smith helped to mediate a second opening for British anthropology. In 1923 the American racialist Madison Grant, acting on behalf of the eugenicist Galton Society of New York, forwarded to the Rockefeller Foundation a proposal for a study of the effects of natural selection among Australian Aborigines (as a means of understanding "the artificial conditions of selection now operating in civilized communities"). The Galton Society proposal was referred to the newly organized Division of Studies, and in line with a general Rockefeller policy that its support should be linked to some local commitment of resources and personnel, Edwin Embree asked Smith to investigate the anthropological situation in Australia. At that point, the Australian anthropologists had already begun the push for a chair in anthropology at Sydney. Along with Perry, Smith had in fact been co-author of a "draft scheme" which became the basis for the proposal that emanated from the Pan-Pacific Science Congress. When that plan was obstructed by the advice of the Colonial Office representative, John Ainsworth, it was the prospect Smith brought of Rockefeller support that encouraged the Australian Prime Minister to reconsider the matter. The Australian National Research Council had from the beginning thought of the chair in social anthropological terms, and the death of the Professor of Anatomy at Sydney further undermined the biological aspect of the scheme. But when Embree came out in 1925 to investigate several proposals from institutions in the Pacific, he sent back a favorable report on the Australian scheme despite its turn away from biology. And when the three electors (one of them Smith) chose Radcliffe-Brown, who was still completely unknown to the Rockefeller people, he was invited to stop off in New York and to tour American anthropological institutions on his way to Sydney. By the time he arrived there, the Rockefeller Foundation had already voted a five-year grant for the support of Australian anthropology. Given Radcliffe-Brown's position as chair of the Research Council's supervising committee, it is not surprising that the bulk of the grant went to support social anthropological fieldwork in Australia and in the nearby southwestern Pacific.[53]

The third redirecting initiative was one in which Malinowski became centrally involved, and which in fact was to lead to a reorientation of his own anthropology along lines suggested by Pitt-Rivers. Malinowski's earliest foray into what might be called "applied anthropology" had come in 1916 when he testified on the problem of plantation labor before an Australian parliamentary commission concerned that the federation pick up its "due share of the trade formerly in German hands."

Malinowski provided advice—cast still in evolutionary terms—on how to handle native workers, especially in the management of their sexual behavior. But he also tried to present "the native's point of view" on work, which, while not "purely economic," nevertheless helped to make his "life worth living." Offering a glancing attack on German colonial regimes, which never considered "the welfare of the races they govern," Malinowski concluded with a preservationist appeal: if they could only be kept from "contact with the white man's civilization" and left alone "to their own conditions," there was "not much likelihood of the native Papuans dying out. . . ."[54]

The same preservationist impulse was apparent in the essay on the "New Humanism" that Malinowski had conceived in the Trobriands and eventually published in 1922 in the journal of the London School of Economics. In an evident attempt to define an anthropological standpoint that might win him a position there, he proclaimed modern anthropology to be the final step in the historical development of humanism, which since the Renaissance had gradually broadened to include "all civilization, including those [*sic*] of the savage races." The contribution that field ethnology offered to the scientific study of human nature depended on the fact that what "*time* has hidden from us forever, *space* keeps preserved for a while"—that is to say, on the preservation in the present of functionally integrated cultural forms from the human past. But beyond its role in anthropological theory, Malinowski's preservationism had implications also for applied anthropology: from the point of view of "the scientific management" of native populations, the goal must be to preserve "the integrity of tribal life as far as possible" in order to prevent their "complete extinction."[55]

There was, however, another more pragmatically developmentalist side of Malinowski's applied anthropology which resonated strongly to Lord Lugard's "dual mandate." It was not simply native lives that were at stake: so also were "millions" in European money. In the South Seas, where white labor was not viable and "Yellow and Hindu" labor involved a "serious political danger," native survival was essential to the solution of the labor problem. Despite his reservations about natives "signing on," Malinowski was quite willing to appeal directly to European economic interests to advance the cause of anthropology—including especially its establishment at the London School of Economics, the institutional locus of his own scholarly career.[56]

The Rockefeller connection at the School of Economics had developed in 1923, when Beardsley Ruml went to England looking for projects for the Spelman Memorial, and was favorably impressed by Director William Beveridge's interest in "social biology" as part of the "natural basis of the social sciences." Although the resulting grants for construction and research established a supportive climate (and provided Malinowski with research assistants), substantial Rockefeller contributions specifically for anthropology developed as a by-product of a quite different and originally nonacademic initiative, in which the major role was played by Joseph Oldham, a leading figure in the Protestant missionary movement. An Oxford graduate forced by ill-health to abandon his missionary work in India, Oldham had been secretary of the Edinburgh World Missionary Conference of 1910, a major turning point in the modern history of missions. As secretary of the conference's Continuation Committee, editor of the *International Review of Missions,* and secretary of the International Missionary Council formed in 1921, Oldham helped to give voice to a younger ecumenical generation critical of traditional missionary ethnocentrism. In a spirit echoing Robert Codrington—and reflecting postwar currents in anthropological and colonial discourse—Oldham thought of "the science of missions" less in terms of cultural conversion than of building on the best of indigenous religious tradition.[57]

One of the topics addressed at the Edinburgh Conference in 1910 had been native education, along the practical "industrial" lines advocated for Negroes in the American South by Booker T. Washington at the Tuskegee Institute. After World War I, Oldham joined with Thomas Jesse Jones of the Phelps Stokes Fund in New York and the South African educationalist C. T. Loram (a colleague of Radcliffe-Brown's at Cape Town), in a campaign to reorient native education throughout Africa, emphasizing the use of vernacular languages and the provision of practical agricultural training as more appropriate for economic development. During the same period, Oldham played a mediating role in the campaign against the forced labor program initiated in 1919 by the Chief Native Commissioner in the East African Protectorate (the same Ainsworth who later almost obstructed the establishment of the Sydney chair). In 1923, when the Colonial Office established a committee to advise on educational problems, Oldham was chosen to serve, quickly becoming the most active member. The following year, the secretary of the committee, Hanns Vischer, who had served as Minister of Education in Northern Nigeria under Lugard, joined with Edwin Smith, a missionary with anthropological interests, in organizing a small international conference of missionaries, administrators, and scholars to consider the problem of the "education of the peoples of Africa through the medium of their own forms of thought." At a follow-up conference in September 1925, the proposal was made to establish an "International Bureau" to promote "an understanding of African languages *and social institutions* with a view to their protection and use as instruments of education." In July 1926, the International Institute of African Languages and Cultures was established in London, with Lugard as chairman, Vischer as secretary-general, and an international group of scholars, missionaries, and administrators on the executive council. Among them were Seligman, soon to be joined by Malinowski, and of course Oldham, who had been the behind-the-scenes organizational entrepreneur and later became administrative director.[58]

Even before the 1925 conference, Oldham had gone to New York to seek Rockefeller support. On a follow-up visit he justified his appeal on the grounds that a nation with so many of the "African race" within its borders could not remain indifferent to the economic and social problems created by the rapid movement of capital into the African continent. Shortly thereafter, the Spelman Memorial voted "in principle" to support Oldham's proposals, at a meeting in which it also made a five-year grant of $17,500 to the Royal Anthropological Institute. A year later, however, it allocated $25,000 over a similar period to the by then established African Institute, which, through Lugard's intermediacy, was also receiving support from the governments of various British African colonies.[59]

By the time Oldham's request was being considered, the Rockefeller turn to functional anthropology had already begun. The invitation to Radcliffe-Brown to tour the United States was complemented by a similar "get acquainted" trip for Malinowski, whose promotion to professor a year later was underwritten by money the Spelman Memorial had given to the School of Economics. Malinowski's tour culminated at the annual Hanover Conference of the Rockefeller-funded Social Science Research Council in 1926, where the assembled elite of American academic social science heard the influential maverick Boasian, Clark Wissler, predict a "revolt" in the discipline in favor of "what my friend Malinowski calls functional anthropology." It was in this context that Oldham, who had previously shared the opinion, widely held in colonial circles, that "anthropologists were more interested in theoretic aspects of the subject than its practical application," was encouraged by Abraham Flexner of the Rockefeller Foundation to establish contact with the anthropologists at the School of Economics. Surprisingly, in view of Malinowski's general hostility to missionaries, the two men hit it off.[60]

Despite their favorable inclination toward Malinowski and Oldham, the Rockefeller philanthropies had briefly held back from further commitment to British anthropology, in part because of the "internecine strife" centering around Elliot Smith, whose loss of influence at the Rockefeller Foundation was marked by the rejection in 1927 of a proposal to support cultural anthropology at University College. But with the reorganization of the Rockefeller philanthropies in 1928, the director of the new Division of the Social Sciences, Edmund Day (who had been impressed by Malinowski at the Hanover Conference) moved to develop a more systematic program in cultural anthropology. Although Malinowski had by this time established a cooperative relationship with Radcliffe-Brown at Sydney, he was not inclined to rest satisfied with only indirect access to fieldwork support. With the Southwest Pacific in Radcliffe-Brown's hands, Malinowski moved toward Africa, and by the end of 1928 had joined forces with Oldham in a campaign to win major Rockefeller support.[61]

It was presumably at about this time that Malinowski briefed himself by reading Lugard's *Dual Mandate in Tropical Africa,* leaving a record of his reactions in some undated notes. Although he commented on Lugard's ignorance of "real Anthropology," and was at points sceptical of the disinterestedness of Lugard's motives, he lauded as "excellent" the attempt to "evolve" from native African institutions and "habits of thought" the "form best suited to them." Dismissing the earlier work of Thomas and Meek, Malinowski argued that functional theory made it possible "to collect in a few weeks all the facts necessary to answer the practical questions" regarding such matters as land tenure. Had Lugard "wanted to control scientific Anthropology to fit his imperial idea—he couldn't have done anything but to create [the] Functional School"; "Indirect Rule," indeed, was "a Complete Surrender to the Functional Point of View."[62]

Although Malinowski initially equated Lugard's approach to "the whole antiprogressive conception," it is clear that in seeking Rockefeller support for functional anthropology he was himself pushed toward problems of cultural change. The opening salvo of his campaign with Oldham, published in the newly founded organ of the African Institute after discussions at Lugard's country estate, was a plea for a "Practical Anthropology" that would study the pressing problems of land tenure and labor as they affected "the changing Native" and the colonial administrator fearful of "what might be called 'black bolshevism.' " When Day came to London in June 1929, Malinowski pursued similar themes: although functional anthropology offered "a special technique" of "rapid research" to solve such problems as how much labor must be kept in a tribe to maintain its economic base, the British universities (save the School of Economics) lacked an effective fieldwork orientation. The critical problem was to provide fieldwork money, and the most likely channel for it was the African Institute, which had already inspired favorable interest from the Colonial Office, where Sydney Webb, founder of the London School of Economics, was now (as Lord Passfield), the man in charge. At the same time, Malinowski forwarded to Oldham a confidential report on "Rockefeller Interests" by an unnamed "American Observer" suggesting that they would be receptive to a large-scale appeal stressing "the mutual unification of knowledge by practical interests and vice-versa"—

especially if it focussed on "problems of contact between black and white and the sociology of white settlement." Fearful that the Anthropological Institute and Elliot Smith at University College might be developing competing plans that would sacrifice "sound" anthropology for the study of fossil man and the diffusion of Egyptian cultural influences to Nigeria, Malinowski urged Oldham to "play any trumpcards" he held "with a clear conscience." Day, however, had already committed himself to Malinowskian functionalism as the coming thing, although he cautioned the Rockefeller representative in Europe not to let Malinowski know of "our favorable prejudice"—the first fruit of which was an arrangement that anthropological fieldwork might be supported under the existing Rockefeller scheme of postdoctoral fellowships.[63]

In the meantime, Malinowski and Oldham were working to develop a "million dollar interlocking scheme for African research"—interlocking, because a parallel initiative on behalf of the new Rhodes House at Oxford was supported by men so powerful politically that they felt forced to coordinate planning. In their private communications, however, Oldham and Malinowski made it clear that their own plans had priority. These were developed largely by Malinowski, who had begun to get an indirect, practical familiarity with the African scene through a series of informal "Group Meetings" in which missionaries, interested colonial officials, and anthropologists—sometimes confronting each other from separate sofas—discussed the problems created by culture contact. At the end of March 1930, a printed appeal was sent to the Rockefeller Foundation. In order to "achieve the task of Western Civilization" in Africa and to protect "the interests of the native population" in a period when world economic conditions foreshadowed "rapidly increasing exploitation," it was essential to carry on systematic field research along the lines of the study of the tribal context of native mining labor that was already being carried on in Rhodesia by Malinowski's student Audrey Richards. Toward this end, and toward the training of administrators and missionaries in a more enlightened understanding of African cultural values, the African Institute requested £100,000 over the next ten years.[64]

Despite opposition from the biological scientists in the Foundation and the threat of competing proposals in Britain, Malinowski and Oldham were successful in their campaign. After entertaining a Rockefeller representative at his Italian Alpine villa, Malinowski told Oldham that the key was to win over Selskar Gunn, a biologist in charge of all the Rockefeller activities in Europe. Warning Gunn of the "possibility of racial wars of considerable magnitude," Oldham described Malinowski's "enthusiastic" reception by a group of colonial governors at a meeting in London. With the biological opposition effectively neutralized, the Rockefeller Foundation voted in April 1931 to allocate $250,000 in matching funds to the African Institute over the next five years. Given the simultaneous rejection of the Rhodes House plan and the somewhat reluctant renewal of a small grant to the Royal Anthropological Institute, it was clear that Rockefeller philanthropy had made a major commitment to functionalist anthropology.[65]

What soon became problematic, however, was just what brand of functionalist anthropology it was committed to. When the impending termination of the original five-year grant to Australian anthropology and the rapidly deteriorating financial situation of Australian state and federal governments threatened the continuation of the Sydney program in 1930, Radcliffe-Brown had approached Rockefeller officials with an omnibus plan that would combine the extension of the Australian grant, a proposal of his own for South African research, and the Rhodes House and African Institute proposals then still under consideration. Suggesting that the time was ripe for more general appraisal of Rockefeller anthropological policy, Radcliffe-Brown argued that no other science was faced with so dire a threat as that posed by the rapid disappearance of "the lower forms of culture," which might well vanish entirely "within the next generation." Fortunately, in the few years left, the "newer anthropology" based on the "functional study" of cultures as "integrated systems" might still formulate "general laws of social life and social development." Focussing on the present and the future rather than the past, it might even approximate an "experimental science" that would be of "immediate service to those who are concerned with the administration and education of native peoples." What was needed was "the establishment of a number of research institutions around to the world" to undertake cooperative investigation of the surviving native peoples "area by area and tribe by tribe." Radcliffe-Brown, who was leaving Sydney on his way to Chicago, proposed to make his visit to London for the centenary meeting of the British Association in September 1931 the occasion for a concerted effort toward this goal.[66]

Although Radcliffe-Brown had asked for his help in promoting the "vanishing cultures" plan, Malinowski clearly viewed his fellow functionalist's return from the antipodes as a threat to his own plans for the study of culture contact. Vacationing in France, he received reports that Radcliffe-Brown was offering Oldham advice on how to implement the African Institute's "five-year plan," and that Oldham was taking seriously the suggestion that studies focussing on economic life in terms of "social cohesion" were preferable to more comprehensive ethnographic inquiries. Equally disturbing was Radcliffe-Brown's suggestion that the School of Oriental Studies, which at this point had also applied to the Rockefeller Foundation for massive aid, was a more logical institutional center than the School of Economics for anthropological re-

The twelfth meeting of the Executive Council of the International Institute of African Languages and Cultures at the Fondation Universitaire, Brussels, June 30–July 1, 1933. Left to right: Sir Denison Ross, Professor T. T. Barnard, Professor Dietrich Westermann (Director), Miss Brackett (Secretary), Major Hanns Vischer (Secretary-General), Lord Lugard (Chairman), Monsieur Tschoffen (Minister for Colonies, Belgium), Dr. J. H. Oldham (Administrative Director), Rev. Father Schmidt, Professor P. Ryckmans, Professor Conti Rossini, Rev. E. W. Smith, Rev. Father Dubois, Professor F. Krause, Professor De Jonghe, Professor C. G. Seligman (partially obscured) and Professor Malinowski. (Courtesy of the Bodleian Library, Oxford; MSS Lugard 160/1, no. 3)

search throughout the empire—a center that Radcliffe-Brown indicated his willingness to head.[67]

Malinowski was in fact influential in getting the School of Oriental Studies grant scaled down to $36,000 and redefined in complementary rather than competitive terms. However, when Radcliffe-Brown pursued the issue of cooperative research while he was in New York teaching at Columbia in the summer of 1931, Edmund Day concluded that there was "a strong presumptive case" for a more unified Rockefeller program in cultural anthropology, which might provide comparative data for a contemplated Division in Behavior and Personality. Formally recognizing cultural anthropology as "a special field of interest, the development of which presents an element of urgency," the Rockefeller Foundation's officers decided to undertake a full-scale survey of anthropological activities throughout the world.[68]

Although Day considered asking Radcliffe-Brown himself to take charge of the survey, it was carried out instead by Leonard Outhwaite, a former staff member of the Spelman Memorial who had studied anthropology with Alfred Kroeber at the University of California. Outhwaite's ties to the Boasian tradition inevitably affected the survey's outcome: he found Radcliffe-Brown "challenging" but "extreme," and although he thought Malinowski "reasonable," he was disturbed by his tendency to act as "Tsar" of anthropology; seeing no fundamental distinction between their viewpoints, he concluded that their differences were "not strictly scientific." The more clearly evident theoretical differences between British functionalists and American historicists he saw as reflections of the differing cultures they had studied. He opposed the functionalists' "narrowing" of anthropology, and while he accepted the systemic integrity of cultures, he insisted that this, too, must be seen as an historical phenomenon. In the end, Outhwaite associated himself with the "best and most conservative workers in each country"—among whom he included Haddon and Seligman.[69]

In the meantime, the American Anthropological Association, apparently at Day's urging, had established a research committee to develop its own plans for the study of vanishing cultures. With Radcliffe-Brown moderating his position to win the support of both Wissler and Boas, the committee forwarded to the Rockefeller Foundation an application for $5,000,000 to support a twelve-year program of fieldwork among three hundred groups throughout the world. But Outhwaite, who had himself formulated a proposal, on a slightly smaller scale, to be supervised by the Social Science Division of the foundation, recommended that the Anthropological Association's proposal be turned down in its initial form, and that its committee be urged instead to develop plans for work among American Indians that might be incorporated into subsequent foundation planning. In April 1933, however, the association was informed that the Rockefeller Foundation had decided not to pursue a major program in anthropology.[70]

One contemporary nonparticipant, Lloyd Warner, who knew them both, suggested that the decision had been influenced by a "series of undercover battles" between Malinowski and Radcliffe-Brown, and between each of them and the Americans. But there is also evidence to suggest that by the end of 1932, the two functionalists had joined forces in the attempt to win "the biggest anthropological pie ever concocted." The Rockefeller Foundation's decision, furthermore, seems to have been made on larger grounds than the internecine bickerings of anthropologists. With its income drastically reduced in the world economic crisis of the early 1930s, a reconsideration of the social science program was undertaken in the fall of 1932. Although Day was still inclined to give some support to cultural anthropology, it was he who now proposed a concentration on certain major practical problems of social engineering.

And as the United States plunged to the nadir of depression in the early months of 1933, a decision was made to shelve Outhwaite's report and declare a "moratorium in the field of cultural anthropology." A year later it was decided to terminate the anthropology program entirely, so far as the Social Science Division was concerned, and let the director of the Humanities Division "pick up any part he wants to salvage"—although certain institutions, including the African Institute, continued to receive support under various prior and "terminal" grants.[71]

By 1938, when these terminal grants had ended, the interwar phase of Rockefeller anthropology was over. Total support directly to anthropology was approximately two and a half million dollars—to which might be added an indeterminate amount of indirect aid through more general fellowship or institutional support programs. While this covered all anthropological subdisciplines, in all countries, British anthropology was a primary beneficiary. Within the British sphere, where alternative sources of support were very limited, the effect was to encourage a process of subdisciplinary differentiation, and within the general sphere of the sociocultural, to encourage some tendencies against others.[72]

Underlying the problematic unity of anthropology in the British (as in the American) tradition was the assumption that human variety was the result of changes that took place over extended periods of time, leaving their traces in the bodies, the languages, and the cultures of human groups, as well as in artifacts and bones that survived above or below the ground. The time span of these changes might be longer or shorter, and they might be discussed in terms of generalized stages or historically specific events—the former in the case of sociocultural evolutionism, the latter in the case of diffusionary ethnology. In either case, however, the varieties of human behavior in the present were relevant primarily as they revealed information about the past. The emphasis on the collection of physical objects made the museum the most likely institution from which anthropological activity might be carried on and the important extradisciplinary relations of anthropology were to the biological rather than the social sciences.[73]

While the move toward a fieldwork-based ethnography antedated the availability of Rockefeller funding, the impact of that funding was greatly to encourage this tendency. An early Rockefeller interest in paleoanthropology was not broken off completely; support for fossil-man studies in China continued into the 1930s. But by the end of the 1920s the Rockefeller interest in eugenically oriented anthropological research into the makeup and capacity of human populations had been largely transformed along lines which, while still sometimes cast in terms of "race," increasingly emphasized the cultural determination of human behavior in the present. Although a major component of the comprehensive program that began to emerge was justified in terms of a practical concern with the processes of racial and cultural contact and social change in colonies whose resources were being exploited by the major European powers, there was also a strong interest, both among academic philanthropoids and some of their anthropological petitioners, in a more theoretically oriented comparative inquiry into the "laws" of culture, as a necessary basis for practical social policy.[74]

The institutional allocation of Rockefeller funding reflected and encouraged these tendencies. The Royal Anthropological Institute—the traditional home of an inclusive anthropology, museum-oriented and grounded in evolutionary assumption—received small grants, and these somewhat reluctantly bestowed. In the academic sphere, major support went not to the ancient universities, but to the University of London; within that institution, University College, the stronghold of diffusionism, although it began the decade as a major recipient, was soon overtaken by the School of Economics. Within the School of Economics, it was Malinowskian functionalism rather than Seligman's more traditional ethnology that benefitted most from Rockefeller funding. Although Seligman, like Haddon at Cambridge, had been supportive of the newer sociological orientations, he still saw them as part of a larger inquiry conceived in broadly historical terms, one which required, among other things, a knowledge of technology and of racial types. While Malinowski had been less concerned than Radcliffe-Brown with drawing the line between ethnology and social anthropology, and had little use for "kinship algebra," his rejection of historical reconstructions and his later disputes with Seligman over the training of students clearly justify his association with "social anthropology"—which was the rubric he himself had chosen for his professorship.[75]

In 1927, when his own star was being eclipsed by Malinowski's, Elliot Smith could not understand why "the sole method of studying mankind is to sit on a Melanesian island for a couple of years and listen to the gossip of the villagers." Although the ethnographic locus shifted to another continent, it was the ethnographic style Smith parodied that was sustained by Rockefeller funding until near the end of the world depression. Early in 1931, Malinowski had noted privately that anthropology was the least able of all academic disciplines to support itself. Academic anthropologists spent their time breeding young anthropologists "for the sake of anthropology and so that they in turn may breed new anthropologists." Yet, he lamented, there was "no practical basis of our science and there are no funds forthcoming to remunerate it for what it produces."* The Rockefeller money of the last several years had

*Writing to Haddon from Sydney about a museum project he was pushing, Radcliffe-Brown had expressed a similar concern: "I want jobs for some of my students and there is no hope of getting any of them into any of the state museums. I can't go on training stu-

facilitated fieldwork; what must now be done was to capitalize on this "almost surreptitious deviation" and establish the discipline as a special branch of Rockefeller endowment. Similarly, the proposed research centers of Radcliffe-Brown's vanishing-cultures scheme were intended to provide "assurance that there will be openings" for the students who had been trained for fieldwork research. Neither scheme was realized. But in a period when alternative sources of fieldwork support were limited and academic jobs in short supply, Rockefeller funding helped significantly to sustain the field research and the professional aspirations of a rising cohort of students who came to identify themselves as "social anthropologists."[76]

The Implementation and the Fate of Practical Anthropology

Viewed somewhat stereotypically from a present perspective, nineteenth-century anthropology had a spatially divided demographic structure: ethnographic information was collected by "men on the spot" in the colonies; anthropological generalization was the work of men in armchairs or meeting rooms in the hub of the empire. After 1900, when ethnographic data began to be collected by academically trained anthropologists, and amateurs were gradually excluded from the enterprise, the discipline became at once more professionally unified and more imperially diverse. From the time that anthropology first began to be systematically studied at British universities, it seems to have attracted students from beyond the British Isles. Aside from Malinowski, the prewar cohort included Diamond Jenness from New Zealand, Gunnar Landtman and Rafael Karsten from Finland (courtesy of Edward Westermarck), Marie Czaplička from Poland, Marius Barbeau from Canada, and Wilson Wallis from the United States, as well as a number of colonial officials who took diploma courses. By the early 1920s, a complex "colonial exchange" had developed. People with ethnographic experience, government service, and/or undergraduate degrees from abroad came to English universities for anthropological training. Products of English university anthropology programs (recruited either from home or from abroad) went out for fieldwork in the colonies; fully trained anthropologist-ethnographers went abroad (or returned home) to take up academic positions more readily available than in England. A later stage in the process—prefigured by the careers of Westermarck and Malinowski himself—involved

dents and giving them experience in field-work if there are no permanent jobs for them" (ACHP: 1/13/30).

the settling of anthropologists from abroad in academic positions in British universities. Implicated in this imperial (later, commonwealth) diversity were also diversities of ethnicity, religion, gender, and class that were strikingly manifest in the interwar cohort of British social anthropologists.[77]

Although Haddon sent several men to teach in colonial universities, and several Australians followed Elliot Smith to University College, imperial (and international) diversity was most strikingly manifest at the London School of Economics, where Malinowski was the exemplar par excellence. A multilingual international European by birth and breeding, linked to Australia by residence and marriage, he aspired to the status and the honorifics of the British academic elite. From the beginning, the personnel of his seminar at the School of Economics reflected the diversity of the colonial (and international) exchange—as well as that of prior disciplinary background. Raymond Firth was a New Zealander whose interest in the "difficult social and economic problems" facing the Maori brought him to London in 1924 to read economics, but who stayed with anthropology after entering Malinowski's first seminar. Isaac Schapera was the son of a South African Jewish shopkeeper, whose early years were spent in a semi-desert village in Namaqualand, where he was "brought up upon the back of a Hottentot woman"; entering the University of Cape Town intending to study law, Schapera switched to anthropology under the influence of Radcliffe-Brown, and went on to London for postgraduate training. Jack Driberg, born in Assam to an Indian service family, had spent fifteen years in the Uganda and Sudanese colonial services before coming to the School of Economics to begin a new career as anthropologist. Gordon Brown was a Canadian war veteran with a doctorate in psychology from Toronto who came to the School of Economics as a Rockefeller Fellow. Audrey Richards, the daughter of a member of the Viceroy's Council in India, had studied biology at Cambridge, worked briefly as amanuensis to the Oxford classicist Gilbert Murray (brother of the New Guinea governor) and then for four years as a secretary to the League of Nations Labour Department. Lucy Mair's progress was similar; she went from Newnham College, Cambridge, where she read classics, via Gilbert Murray and the League of Nations, on to the School of Economics (where her Scottish mother was the school's secretary and confidante of the director, William Beveridge). Margaret Read was another (somewhat older) Cambridge woman who turned to anthropology. Although his background was in fact Welsh and Anglo-Irish, the most conventionally "British" of this early cohort was perhaps Edward Evan Evans-Pritchard, the son of an Anglican curate, who went on from the prestigious Winchester College public school to read history at Marett's Exeter College. But even Evans-Pritchard seems to have been prefigured for the colonial exchange; touched perhaps by the contemporary romantic aura of T. E. Lawrence, he went to Oxford parties wearing an Arab burnoose.[78]*

With the advent of Rockefeller funding at Sydney, the colonial exchange between London and the Southwest Pacific accelerated. Reo Fortune, Ian Hogbin, Ralph Piddington, William Stanner, and Phyllis Kaberry were Australian and New Zealand-born students who attended Malinowski's seminars, all but Fortune taking their first degrees at Sydney and their doctorates at the School of Economics during the 1930s. Among those who felt Malinowski's influence before venturing in the opposite direction were Gregory Bateson and Camilla Wedgwood, both Cambridge graduates from well-established families of the British "intellectual aristocracy."[79]

Once the Rockefeller Foundation made its commitment to Malinowski, and to the International African Institute, the currents of colonial exchange shifted course—drawing once again from Europe and flowing back and forth from southern Africa. Meyer Fortes, born of Russian Jewish parents in South Africa, became interested in the education of Cape Coloured adolescents as an undergraduate in Cape Town, and went on to University College for graduate study of psychology; after receiving his doctorate in 1930 for a dissertation on cross-cultural intelligence testing, he met Malinowski at the home of the psychoanalyst J. C. Flugel, joined his seminar, and was among the first cohort of African Institute fellows. Following in the footsteps of Schapera, Fortes was one of a number of South Africans who, after spending time in Malinowski's seminars, went on to do fieldwork in Africa, often with Rockefeller support. Among them were Monica Hunter (Wilson), whose undergraduate and graduate degrees were from Cambridge, Max Gluckman, who came from Witwatersrand to study under Marett at Oxford, as well as two other students of Hoernlé's—Hilda Beemer (Kuper) and Eileen Jensen (Krige).

*There were others, of course, who became well known outside British social anthropology. Hortense Powdermaker was an American of German-Jewish background who came to London seeking a change from her experiences as an organizer for the Amalgamated Clothing Workers (Powdermaker 1966:33–45). Montague Francis Ashley-Montagu, later a physical anthropologist and influential critic of racial theories, attended both Westermarck's and Malinowski's seminars (Montagu 1982:65); born Israel Ehrenburg in London's East End (Shipman 1994), he joked with Malinowski about his presumed aristocratic ancestors, signing one letter "Long Live the Judo-Slavs" (BMPL: Montagu to Malinowski 7/9/35, 3/2/36). Talcott Parsons was a graduate of Amherst College seeking to clarify the relations between economics and sociology; his experience in Malinowski's seminar was a formative influence in the development later on of his own sociological "structural functionalism" (Parsons 1970). Haddon's academic exports (or returnees) included T. F. McIlwraith (to Toronto), H. D. Skinner (to Otago), G. S. Ghurye (to Bombay) and A. J. Goodwin (to Cape Town)—along with T. T. Barnard and, of course, Radcliffe-Brown.

Another was Zachariah K. Matthews, a South African black who had followed Radcliffe-Brown's Cape Town colleague C. T. Loram to Yale, where he studied anthropology under Edward Sapir, before joining Malinowski's seminar. And given the international orientation of the institute, there were also a number of scholars from other countries, including Kalervo Oberg (a second-generation Finn from British Columbia who had completed a doctorate under Radcliffe-Brown at Chicago), Gunther Wagner (who had worked on Yuchi linguistics under Boas along the way to a doctorate at Hamburg), Sjoerd Hofstra (who had just completed a library dissertation at Amsterdam under the Tylorian comparativist S. R. Steinmetz), and Siegfried Nadel, a Viennese Jew with a doctorate in psychology and philosophy and training as musicologist.[80]

In addition to the African Institute fellows (for whom participation was required), there were others who added to the multi-ethnic character of Malinowski's seminars. In the 1930s these often attracted thirty or more "students" and "regular attenders"—among them American blacks: the actor and singer Paul Robeson and his wife Eslanda, and the political scientist Ralph Bunche, who was beginning a two-year research project funded by the American Social Science Research Council on the impact of colonial rule in southern Africa. Malinowski was quite conscious of the unusual diversity of his following, and in the earthy ethnic language he sometimes employed in private, yearned for someone, "not a Jew, Dago, Pole or any of these exotic products," who might become the "future mainstay of British anthropology." In the mid-1930s, his candidate was Godfrey Wilson, the Oxford-educated son of the Shakespearean scholar J. Dover Wilson; as "an Englishman," a "practicing" Christian, and "a gentleman"—"qualifications which none of our other Fellows satisfy"—Wilson seemed "specially precious."[81]

Although the African Institute fellows were all expected to do fieldwork, it had not yet become a predoctoral prerequisite in the training of anthropologists. Not only did a number of the fellows come equipped with doctorates in other fields (or from other anthropologists), but several of Malinowski's early students (including Firth and Richards) followed Malinowski's own pattern, in which fieldwork followed the completion of a library dissertation. For despite his frequently noted (and vaunted) empiricism, Malinowski constantly insisted on the importance of *Problemstellung* (the definition of research problems in relation to existing theoretical and ethnographic literature), and on the systematic collection and organization of ethnographic data in relation to universal functionalist categories. He brought the same approach to problems of "culture contact"—the practical study of which was of course the publicly proclaimed *raison d'être* of the African Institute's fellowship program.[82]

In implementing that program, the purposes, cross-purposes, and prejudices of various (not entirely homogeneous) groups had in varying degrees to be accommodated. There were the anthropologists themselves, many of them primitivist preservationists by inclination, who were consciously refashioning (or representing) themselves as practical students of culture change, with the hope of generating support for ethnographic fieldwork and jobs for academically trained ethnographers. There was the International African Institute, in which missionaries and retired (or practicing) colonial officials—as well as non-Malinowskian anthropologists—had an important voice. Across the Atlantic there was the Rockefeller Foundation, in which the commitment to Malinowskian functionalism faced competition both from other anthropological orientations and from a more pressing interest in research on large-scale social problems plaguing Euroamerican civilization in its own backyard. There were several tendencies within the Colonial Office, which had begun to experiment with more active developmental policies, but had not yet overcome its traditional distrust of anthropology and anthropologists—as well as the voices of politicians and public opinion in Britain. There were the local colonial administrations, upon whom anthropologists were dependent, but with whom they were often at odds, as well as the generally oppositional white-settler communities. And there were of course the changing African peoples who were being studied, to the varying ends—scientific and practical, preservationist and developmental, altruistic and self-interested—of the other groups. Active negotiators of ethnographic knowledge on the ground, sometimes resistant "tribal" subjects of colonial administration, they had also begun to produce voices of national and Pan-African consciousness, in Britain as well as in Africa.[83]

Although it is not possible here to treat systematically the variety of interests and issues involved in the implementation of the African Institute program, there are several moments in that process that cast light on the fate of Malinowskian functionalism in the interwar period. In the discussions leading to the establishment of the fellowship program, Audrey Richards' early fieldwork in Rhodesia was cited as an exemplar of the sort of practical anthropological research that fellows might carry on. Before going into the field, Richards had conducted a library study of "hunger and work in a savage tribe," in which the functional analysis of the cultural refashioning of basic biological needs, previously pursued by Malinowski in the realm of sex, was carried into that of nutrition. Although Richards later recalled the choice of her field site almost as a matter of "sticking a pin in a map," contemporary documentation suggests other factors may have been at work. When (through Gilbert Murray) she sought support from Lord Lugard for an application for funding from the Rhodes trustees, Lugard indicated (in what clearly seemed an implicit condition) that he would be willing to support a study of "the development of the mineral wealth of Northern Rhodesia," where native labor was employed at the Broken Hill copper mines. "To make my meaning clear," Lugard explained, there was a need for "data" to determine "the maximum length of contract which can be entered into without injuriously effecting [*sic*] village life," the maximum number of adult males that could be taken away, and the effect on social life of the absence and later return of contract labor. In response, Richards proposed to Malinowski that a meeting of the School of Economics anthropological society be devoted to the question—in order to show "that we were really buckling to on the lines of your article [on 'Practical Anthropology']"—and that he himself write a letter to Philip Kerr (Lord Lothian), of the Rhodes Trust, suggesting that "there is a lot of similar fieldwork to be done in Rhodesia with this discovery of minerals." Whether Richards' study (published ten years later as *Land, Labour and Diet in Northern Rhodesia*) served the purposes Lugard had in mind is a moot point; although its focus is overwhelmingly on traditional patterns of labor among the Bemba, there is a brief suggestion at the end that if a man spent two years at home making millet, he could "then spend two years at the mines, leaving his wife to plant the third year millet." What is clear, however, is that in the interests of obtaining support for field research, there was an attempt to accommodate the utilitarian concerns of practical-minded men interested in the effective and profitable exploitation of African wealth.[84]

There were also accommodations regarding the selection of personnel. In the fall of 1931, when the first cohort of African Institute fellows was being chosen, Oldham wrote to Malinowski proposing that Paul Kirchoff, a German scholar who had done research on kinship among South American Indian groups, might undertake fieldwork in Rhodesia—again, with a view to convincing the Colonial Office of the practical value of anthropology for the development of mining in Rhodesia. Shortly before Kirchoff's planned departure, the Colonial Office suddenly refused him entrance to any British colony, letting it be known that he was suspected of being a communist agitator. Although Malinowski momentarily contemplated resigning from the African Institute rather than accepting the Colonial Office's "bald veto," he was rather quickly swayed by Oldham's argument that "the large interests of anthropology and African research" should not be sacrificed in a "forlorn" crusade. Convinced that the whole matter was a misunderstanding, and that Kirchoff was guilty at most of youthful indiscretion, Malinowski tried to send him instead to New Guinea, where he felt that even "the most intensive communistic doctrines" would present "no great danger." But this plan, too, was forestalled at the last minute by the Australian National

Research Council, on the basis of confidential information from British governmental officials.[85]

While the Rockefeller Foundation, at Malinowski's urging, did give Kirchoff a small grant to write up his earlier Latin American research, the constraining influence of this incident should not be minimized. At the time, the major participants concluded that in the future there must be a "very careful scrutiny of the past records and personality" of all candidates. Malinowski seems to have retained a tolerant attitude toward youthful political radicalism: "If you are not a Communist before twenty-five you have no heart"; but only on the assumption that it was a passing phase: "If you are a Communist after that, you have no head." Many of his students leaned to the left, and on at least several occasions he warned individuals that they must choose between radical politics and scientific anthropology.[86*]

The question arose again in 1936, in the case of a student whose background was by Colonial Office standards very questionable: Jomo Kenyatta, one of a group of London-based Pan-African radicals, who had become interested in anthropology while supporting himself as a linguistic informant. In trying to persuade Lord Lugard that the African Institute should support him, Malinowski said that Kenyatta, upon his return to Kenya, hoped "to devote himself to anthropological field-work from the practical point of view." Acknowledging that Kenyatta "had a definite political bias" when he joined his seminar in 1934, Malinowski believed that this had been "almost completely eradicated by the constant impact of detached scientific method on his mental processes." The "highly depoliticising influence of scientific anthropology" had already worked "a remarkable change"; given another "two years of systematic study and the hall-mark" provided by a diploma in anthropology—as well as "the obligation" he would feel toward the institute—and Malinowski was certain the change would be completed. And "since Mr. Kenyatta has considerable influence on African students, also on the educated Africans in Kenya, the contribution will not only be towards the advancement of theoretical studies, but also towards the practical influence of anthropology."[87]

Apparently unconvinced of the brainwashing power of functional anthropology, Lugard was the lone dissenter when the matter came to a vote in the African Institute's governing bureau. Kenyatta, his mental processes still politicized, went on to become the leader of the indepen-

*Anecdotal evidence suggests that Radcliffe-Brown issued similar warnings—although he himself had suggested to a Rockefeller bureaucrat in 1931 that "our present capitalistic system bears within itself the germs of its own destruction" (RAC: J. Van Sickle "Conversations with A. R.-B 9/7–8/31").

dence movement and the first president of Kenya. But in 1938, when he published *Facing Mount Kenya*, Kenyatta was able to find in functionalism a justification for the value of traditional cultural practices that Europeans deemed "savage and barbaric, worthy only of heathens who live in perpetual sin": far from being "mere bodily mutilation," cliteroidectomy was "the *conditio sine qua non* of the whole teaching of tribal law, religion and morality." And although he had to keep "under very considerable restraint the sense of political grievances which no progressive African can fail to experience," Kenyatta nevertheless ended his book with a ringing call for "unceasing" struggle toward "complete emancipation."[88]

By 1938, Malinowski himself seems to have backed off a bit from the optimistic view of "practical anthropology" he had put forward in seeking funding for anthropological research. Although he had spent great effort since 1923 "courting administrators and missionaries," the "real point" was that anthropology "depends more on administration than vice versa." It had therefore become "the anthropologist's task" to "convince the government officials and capitalists that their long run interests are in harmony with the findings of anthropology." And the effort was not so successful as Malinowski had hoped: two years after the initiation of the fellowship program, he was still complaining to Godfrey Wilson:

> Anthropology for the present is not a recognized science. . . . If your good friends, the missionaries (God damn their eyes!) were not such bloody swine, and did not fight us on every point they can; if they recognized the necessity of Anthropological Knowledge, instead of messing about in a slough of ignorance; if further, the Colonial Governments, instead of treating us as a nuisance, would recognize our utility, we might be out of the soup. For the present, my dear boy, we are all fighting a battle, which may not be losing, but it is certainly not easy.[89]

Like most anthropologists of the interwar period, Malinowski had begun by accepting the post-Versailles colonial system as historically "given." The danger was that unenlightened exploitation, without regard to the welfare of native populations, might lead to "racial wars." In this context, he promoted anthropological research as a means of making the system "work" more effectively, from the point of view of capitalist development and administrative efficiency—as well as native welfare. But despite his aggressive promotion of "practical anthropology," Malinowski was at heart a somewhat "reluctant imperialist"—and there is evidence to suggest that he became increasingly reluctant after 1934, when during a two-month inspection tour of African Institute fieldworkers, he had first-hand experience in South Africa of the color bar, which he had previously defended as "at present a necessity."[90]

While he was in South Africa, Malinowski gave several lectures, two of them before audiences of white educators, and one on "African (Negro) Patriotism" to an audience of black South Africans. In talking to his white audiences, he attacked "schooling of unblushingly European type" which, depriving the native child of his "cultural birthright" to "his own tradition and his own place in his tribal life," did not offer in exchange "the charter of citizenship in our own civilization and society." Those who sought to "attach a positive meaning" to "segregation" must realize "that unless some political scope is given to the African he will not be satisfied with anything less than equal political rights with the white settlers." To avoid this, Malinowski proposed a vernacular education that would "not estrange the African from his tribal culture" or "develop in him claims and desires which his future salary and status will never satisfy"; and he offered "modern anthropological technique in fieldwork" to help in the project.[91]

But to the audience of blacks, Malinowski's message had a somewhat different twist. Setting himself off from "pseudo-friends" of "Sable-coloured brethren" who had in fact done little to prevent slavery, labor exploitation, and land-grabbing—and from the earlier tendency of anthropology to ignore or despise detribalized Africans—he insisted that anthropology was changing. Referring to his own work to document the shift, he argued that functional anthropology had offered, and still did, a "moderate but effective championship" for traditional African cultures, even to the point of defending witchcraft and cannibalism; resisting the taking of lands, the perversion of tribal laws, or the imposition of an alien Christian morality, it had favored political autonomy and economic development along "natural" lines. But it was now time for functional anthropology to face also the problems of the modern Negro—the need for equality of status, freedom to compete in the labor market, and the protection of racial self-esteem; it was time, in short, to "recognize the reality of the detribalized African and fight for his place in the world."[92]

Malinowski returned from his African trip "a wiser and a sadder man." Several years later, in a preface to a volume entitled *The Savage Hits Back,* he reflected on "how little the trained anthropologist" had "so far worked and fought side by side with those who are usually described as pro-native." Was it because "science makes people too cautious?" or because "the anthropologist, enamoured of the unspoiled primitive, lost interest in the native enslaved, oppressed, or detribalized?" In either case, Malinowski asserted his personal belief "in the anthropologist's being not only the interpreter of the native but also his champion." In the preface he wrote for Kenyatta's book, Malinowski found it "amazing" how Mussolini's Abyssinian venture had "organised public opinion" among "natives whom one would never have suspected of having any complicated views on the League of Nations, on the Dual Mandate, on the Dignity of Labour, and on the Brotherhood of Man," and how the "Chinese incident" was "uniting the world of coloured peoples against Western influence." Calling into question the historical realization of Lord Lugard's whole project, he commended Kenyatta for "help[ing] us to understand how Africans see through our pretences, and how they assess the realities of the Dual Mandate." The same year, in the introductory essay to the African Institute's memorandum, *Methods of Study of Culture Contact,* he noted the emergence of a "new African type of nationalism, of racial feeling, and of collective opposition to Western culture" which had been aroused by the systematic denial of certain essential "elements of our culture": the "instruments of physical power" and of "political mastery"; the "substance of economic wealth"; and the admission "as equals to Church Assembly, school, or drawing-room."[93]

Malinowski never ceased to trumpet the virtues of "scientific anthropology" and its applicability to the solution of practical problems. But though his rhetoric was often a reflection of mood and moment, it seems apparent that he became increasingly disillusioned in the inter-war period with the civilization that science had produced. Born "into a world of peace and order," to a generation that "cherished legitimate hopes of stability and gradual development," he had lived through a profound "historical demoralisation." By the middle 1930s, indeed, he spoke of "our ultra-efficient modern culture" as a "Frankenstein monster with which we are as yet unable to cope"—and in the preface to Kenyatta's book, quoting the words of William James, he referred to progress as "a terrible thing." Rather than extolling "the benefits of Western civilization as the ultimate goal of all humanity," we should be thinking of how "to prevent the spread of our own troubles and cultural diseases to those who are not yet affected by them."[94]

Enamored of the "unspoiled primitive" even before he came to anthropology, but taking for granted the overwhelming knowledge/power of European civilization, Malinowski had for much of his career been a spokesman for "the native point of view" of the precontact "savage." Seeking to propagate his science in the 1920s, he offered a "practical anthropology" as the means by which the interests of natives, colonizers, administrators, and anthropologists could be advanced. As he gained more systematic and direct experience with the processes of culture contact in the African colonial situation in the early 1930s, the "savage"—now often "so-called" or called into question by use of scare quotes—was pushed into the wings of practical anthropology. The "detribalized native" was given center stage, at first as the object of administrative policy, then with a greater appreciation of native "interests and grievances," and finally with an incipient awareness of the emergence of Africans as a political force in world history.[95]

It would be rash to assume that Malinowski's students—born a generation further on, of diverse backgrounds and predispositions, with differing ethnographic experiences—would all have followed a similar path. But at the very least, there are grounds for suggesting a fairly widespread ambivalence toward, or dissociation from, if not disillusion with, the program of practical anthropology. In some cases, this seems to have been there from the beginning, when Malinowski's appeal to the Rockefeller Foundation for the study of "culture contact" was countered by Radcliffe-Brown's for the study of "vanishing cultures." Although both approaches were justified in terms of the needs of colonial administration and development, the balance of the utilitarian and the scientific was quite different. When Radcliffe-Brown lectured on "Applied Anthropology" in 1930, he made a point of insisting on the priority of theory: while it was "not too early" to consider issues of "practical application," it was "the more rapid advance of pure science" which made it possible to "look forward to a time" when the government of native peoples "would make some approach to being an art based on the application of the discovered laws of anthropological science." And when he passed through London on his way to the United States, Audrey Richards interpreted his views as an implicit attack on practical anthropology. Reporting to Malinowski, then on sabbatical in the south of France, she suggested that Evans-Pritchard was adopting the same position: " 'We are a pure science, [and] we are degrading our work by listening to popular appeals and trying to help missionaries, etc., etc.' "[96]

The early record of attempts to turn functional anthropology to practical colonial purpose might well have raised doubts about the venture. Gordon Brown, who was involved in a government-sponsored project of native education in Tanganyika in 1928, ran into difficulties with "influential settlers" which led him, after two "wasted" years, to conclude that he must choose between being a government official and "nothing else" or "devoting himself to science." In the event, he reconsidered his resignation, and later embarked on a further experiment in the application of anthropology "to the problems surrounding the administration of an African tribe." But the account entitled *Anthropology in Action* that Brown co-authored with the local district officer in 1935 was a record more of problems encountered than of problems solved, offered with the pious hope that further experiments might be conducted in the future.[97]

The early history of a later venture in applied anthropology, the Rhodes-Livingstone Institute, was equally problematic and frustrating. The institute scheme was first broached in 1934 by Sir Hubert Young, Governor of Northern Rhodesia, apparently as a sop to local traders who were upset at the removal of government offices from Livingstone to the new capital of Lusaka. Proposing to the Colonial Secretary the establishment in Livingstone of a museum and research institute in "archaeology, geology and particularly anthropology," Young suggested that it might "assist toward the formulation of the correct administrative policy for the mixed African and non-African community." The initial resistance of the Colonial Office was not overcome until after a strike of African miners in May 1935; backed now by Lord Lugard and by Lord Hailey, whose monumental *African Survey* was then in process, the project won the approval of a new Colonial Secretary. With the somewhat reluctant financial support of the copper companies, in what has been described as a "form of hidden taxation" paid to keep in the good graces of the reformist colonial governor, the Rhodes-Livingstone Institute was formally established in 1937. After "considerable discussion," the directorship was awarded to Godfrey Wilson, who at that point was scrambling unsuccessfully for an academic job. His new position was seen by Malinowski as a steppingstone that might lead Wilson "out of the jungle into a comfortable Chair": "I hope that you will not remain for the rest of your life trying to help the Governor of Northern Rhodesia to prevent any serious anthropological work being done by puttering round his museum at Livingstone and listening to his idiotic views about anthropology."[98]

Although Wilson was committed to the study of "culture contact," he "chuckle[d] with mirth over the idea of my being an 'Applied Anthropologist.'" Anticipating "bland folly," he reassured himself that his employers, having little idea what he was hired to do, would be waiting for him to tell them—and he proceeded to immerse himself in Marx's *Capital*, with which he was much impressed: "it takes a very great man to be so convincingly wrong." But Wilson's research proposal, which called for work among urban miners after a preliminary study in a rural area, was given only very reluctant approval by the five trustees. Some months later, after strikes in which the military killed seventeen black miners, permission for him to do research at Broken Hill was withdrawn on the grounds that his "methods" (which included "fraternizing" with the miners) "might cause discontent and unrest." Although the trustees agreed to keep the Rhodes-Livingstone Institute going after war broke out in Europe, it was made clear to Wilson that his status as a conscientious objector (as well, perhaps, as his interest in Marx) "made it undesirable that he should be allowed access to large bodies of natives where an expression of his views might have a weakening influence on native morale and interfere with recruiting." Faced with this opposition, Wilson resigned as director in April 1941, and spent the next year working with his wife Monica (whom he had met in Malinowski's seminar) on their theoretical *Analysis of Social Change Based on Observations in Central Africa*, before entering war service in the South African Medical Corps.[99]

With Wilson gone, Max Gluckman, who had previously been hired as assistant anthropologist, took over as acting director, in anticipation that the directorship might be accepted by Audrey Richards. However, Richards, who had been passed over as founding director because she was "not only a woman but also a woman who was an anthropologist," preferred to pursue her war service back in London, working in the Colonial Office. Overcoming reservations about Gluckman's suspect loyalty (he was both a Jew and a communist sympathizer), the trustees in 1943 appointed him director retroactive to June 1942. With the Soviets now allies in the war against Nazism, Gluckman abandoned his earlier belief that "the scientist must be aloof and academic" and entered wholeheartedly into the preparation of a "Seven Year Research Plan." Quoting an unnamed colleague, he suggested that "our project" was "the biggest event in social anthropological history since Rivers' Torres Straits Expedition." The plan aimed to "deal with the most important social problems confronting the Government of the Territory," focussing especially on the study of labor migration. But the weight of the presentation (cast in Radcliffe-Brownian terms of "types" of social structure) was on the "widest possible range of comparative problems in both indigenous and modern social organization."[100]

Gluckman's seven-year plan was received by local administrators with "expressions of hostility and suspicion"—one of them complaining that anthropologists spoke a language "quite unintelligible to the ordinary human." Its implementation was at best a mixed success. In his own research among the Lozi, Gluckman was little interested in the mines themselves, but rather in their effect on the Lozi social system: "the two types of life are structurally distinct, and each as a social system can be studied directly." During the remainder of his tenure, Gluckman concentrated on the training of researchers; noting the difficulties of cooperation with government, he concluded "that we must aim chiefly at increasing general theoretical knowledge of African social systems, and at mapping the social systems of Central Africa." By 1947, he was off to a lectureship under Radcliffe-Brown at Oxford.[101]

The Rhodes-Livingstone Institute long survived Gluckman's departure, and was in fact a prototype for social research institutes established in Nigeria and Uganda after World War II. The point, however, is not to argue the total failure of applied anthropology initiatives in this period. It is rather to suggest that, within an evolving (and on the whole more supportive) climate of colonial administrative opinion, the cross-purposes of various actors and the conflicts arising in the practice of practical anthropology had a somewhat disillusioning effect on social anthropologists—most of whom were in any case predisposed to prefer the study of precontact natives, and the pursuit of academic careers when these become available. This is evident even in the case of Audrey Richards, who was (along with Raymond Firth) directly involved in the relations of anthropology and colonial administration at the center of empire.[102]

When Richards first came to Malinowski's seminar, she proposed to do a history of the "back to nature" idea from Rousseau on, hypothesizing that it sprang from unconscious reaction to the thwarting of basic instincts in modern economic society. Among the Bemba, she was still wondering whether they were happier than civilized man, and when copper miners whose wages had been cut were "for the first time saying 'why didn't you leave us as we were?' " she felt inclined to "compose a sort of 'Hymn to Retardation.' " Nevertheless, as Malinowski's lieutenant in the fall of 1931, she had fought hard for a contact-oriented practical anthropology against Radcliffe-Brown's typologizing of vanishing cultures. Two years later she was hoping she might get a position at the School of Oriental Studies, specializing in helping government officials, among whom, by birth and breeding, she was able to move with relative ease. She was not one of the several students of Malinowski (notably, Lucy Mair and Marjory Perham) who were directly involved in the preparation of Lord Hailey's *African Survey*—a volume as exemplary of the emergent policy of colonial development as the *Dual Mandate* had been of the earlier doctrine of indirect rule. But when Hailey headed the Colonial Research Committee established in 1942 to handle the substantial research funds provided by the Colonial Development and Welfare Act of 1940, Richards (whom he knew personally) was chosen as its only anthropological member—overcoming the previously expressed concern of Colonial Secretary Malcolm MacDonald that "anthropologists, as a class, are rather difficult folk to deal with." Richards worked closely with Hailey in planning the permanent colonial research organization, encouraging him to establish a unified social research council with disciplinary subcommittees rather than a series of separate committees for each discipline. When the Colonial Social Science Research Council was established in 1944, Richards was the representative of anthropology (though the discipline had a second voice in the council's secretary, Raymond Firth, whom Hailey had previously recommended to MacDonald as both "very suitable" and "acceptable to the younger school of anthropologists").[103]

By this time Richards was somewhat less enthusiastic about practical anthropology than she had been in the early 1930s. In evaluating the work of the African Institute in 1944, she suggested that despite hopeful beginnings, there had been only "moderate success" in accomplishing its goals: "it looks as though the Anthropologist [the archetypifying capitalization would suggest Malinowski] had been advertising his goods, often rather clamourously, in a market in which there was little demand for them." Focussing on the difficulties of the "practical anthropology" project, her review was in effect an appeal for a new start after the war, in which "applied anthropology" would be thought of in somewhat more limited and academic terms. The reports of the Colonial Research Committee and the Colonial Social Science Research Council in this period, as well as Richards' later reminiscences, make clear that while practical colonial concerns were still the ultimately driving force, emphasis was now to be placed on the "scientific" status of research. Colonial researchers were seen not as administrative personnel, but as members of a specific disciplinary community, who must be trained in its most up-to-date methods, kept in contact with its academic base, allowed to pursue research that reflected disciplinary theoretical and substantive priorities, and expected eventually to find permanent niches in academic life. They should not feel "in any danger of falling behind the progress of their sciences, or of losing their chances of advancement therein."[104]

Hailey himself, acknowledging changes in both anthropology and in "the objectives of Colonial administration," still thought in terms of a certain intimacy between the two. Insisting that "acquaintance with the practical problems of colonial development is an essential preparation for undertaking social or anthropological research in the colonial field," he encouraged anthropologists to present their results with "greater solicitude" for those who are "not equipped to deal with the more esoteric of their terminologies." And Firth, surveying research priorities in West Africa for the Colonial Social Science Research Council, gave great emphasis to contemporary social and economic issues. But retrospective evaluations suggest that the Colonial Office, the Research Council, and the colonial governments—in a spirit similar to that of Rockefeller philanthropy in the early 1920s—had accepted that "for the most part basic ethnographic field investigation and fundamental studies of social structure were indispensable to provide the anthropological knowledge required for tackling the manifold practical problems involved in the development plans formulated by the colonial governments after the war."[105]

The priority of the discipline's scientific needs had for some time been insisted on by social anthropologists. Although they appealed, with varying degrees of importunity, to practical colonial interests in seeking support for their "science," they were anxious lest its intellectual progress be impeded by utilitarian concerns—and they were often also ambivalent about the ethical and political implications of colonial involvement. The solution was to set themselves at a certain distance from the definition and implementation of policy and to assert the priority of academic anthropology, even as they offered the promise of utility. Emphasizing the tension between practical and scientific concerns, Evans-Pritchard argued that the anthropologist might best employ his knowledge and his time in the solution of scientific problems which had no practical value whatsoever. Acknowledging a limited role of the anthropologist as "advisor" to colonial governments, he nevertheless saw the future of anthropology primarily in terms of its academic development: what was needed was more and bigger university departments. Firth himself took a similar tack in discussing "anthropology and colonial affairs" at the Royal Anthropological Institute in 1949: "scientifically, colonial affairs can have only limited interest for anthropologists"—most of whom were interested "in understanding social process, not directing it."[106]

Fortunately, important groups within the world of colonial administration had shown themselves willing to accept the scientific status and the utilitarian promisory note of social anthropology. As Firth noted, social anthropology was "benefitting a great deal" from "its new relation to colonial affairs." New possibilities for fieldwork had opened up, and government money was now available to support it; anthropology would play a big role in the research institutes being set in West Africa, East Africa, and the West Indies. Fieldwork—which until the early 1930s was in many cases still postdoctoral—could now become the *sine qua non* of the doctoral degree. Glorified by Seligman a generation previously as the "blood of martyrs" to the church of anthropology, it could now be regularly demanded as a rite of initiation to the profession.[107]

Although Firth did not mention it, Evans-Pritchard's call for more and bigger departments was beginning to be answered. The report of the Scarborough Commission (the Interdepartmental Commission of Enquiry on Oriental, Slavic, East European and African Studies) in 1946 had recommended the training of students, the support of research, and the building of departments; within six years, the number of positions in anthropology in commonwealth universities had almost doubled. Although further, greater expansion of the academic base lay still in the future, the institutional framework for an ethnographically grounded social anthropology had been firmly established.[108]

From Culture Contact to Social Structure

Parallelling the disillusion with practical anthropology, there occurred a disillusion with the theoretical agenda of Malinowskian functionalism. The process was not simply intellectual, but reflected also the rather complex psychodynamics of Malinowski's relations with his students. If he did not demand discipleship, he did demand allegiance—and he could be demanding in other ways as well. As his research assistant, Isaac Schapera was not only briefed beforehand as to what questions to ask in Malinowski's apparently impromptu Socratic seminars, but was also expected to take Malinowski's shoes to be repaired—a demand

Meyer Fortes and Tallensi men assembled under the baobob tree shrine, during the prayer preceding the sacrifice to the clan founder, Mosuor, at Tongo in 1936. (Courtesy of Doris Fortes)

which precipitated a temporary break with Malinowski. When Schapera was later unable, after a fortnight reading Freud to find any passage documenting Malinowski's conviction that Freud had "suggested" to his patients "what they should say," Schapera "broke" from him for a second time. Freud, of course, would have appreciated the fact that the "break" with Malinowski was not an isolated phenomenon, but one experienced by a number of his male students—the women being, on the whole, more faithful to the Malinowskian program, both as functionalism and as practical anthropology.[109]

The most striking episode in this dynamic involved three members of the first cohort of African Institute fellows—Fortes, Hofstra, and Nadel—who sat together in the seminar, and whom Malinowski dubbed "the Mandarins." While he in fact expressed a high opinion of them in correspondence, Malinowski is said to have treated them "abominably," insulting and provoking them—by Fortes' own account, with a "catalytic virtuosity" that kept the seminar "at a high pitch." Trouble, however, developed after the three had gone into the field, when Malinowski received a copy of the memorandum they had sent to Oldham describing their plan of work. It was, he suggested to Oldham, "a partial plagiarism" of his own ideas, the use of which he had agreed to, but without any thought that the three might lay claim to originality. Although the matter apparently was not pursued at the time, Fortes later recalled that after their return from the field, he and Hofstra were invited to Malinowski's apartment and asked to sign a statement admitting Malinowski's priority—but which Fortes took with him and later returned unsigned. Contemporary documentation casts Fortes' "break" in a slightly different light. In March 1936 Malinowski wrote to Fortes suggesting that their original memorandum had in fact contained a "full acknowledgement" that had been omitted by some "clerical oversight" and asking him to sign an enclosed letter to that effect—so that Malinowski could proceed to publish the same ideas without fear of being accused of plagiarism himself. Although Fortes apparently did not sign that draft, he did send Malinowski a more detailed letter indicating that Malinowski had "very kindly consented to let us borrow freely from your seminar teaching, especially as to the use of the diagrammatic schemes, the terminology and the theoretical approach propounded by you," and that the original proposal (which was enclosed) had in fact contained such acknowledgment. Fortes went on to characterize his own proposed study of the African family as nothing but an application to a "special field" of "theoretical and methodological principles" he had become familiar with "both from the teaching I received from you and from my general reading in sociology and psychology." But whatever the contribution of "general reading," the proposal documents themselves were very much in the Malinowskian psychobiological mode, cast in terms of basic human needs, the functions and interrelations of institutions, and the study of life histories.[110]

In a period when his public disagreements with Radcliffe-Brown may have made him more anxious to claim authorship of his own "pure" version of functionalism, Malinowski thus demanded allegiance by acknowledgment. He was also willing to prod his troops into line by public criticism. When a series of papers on culture contact by African Institute fellows was reprinted in April 1938, Malinowski provided an introductory essay in which he noted that the seven authors did not present "a united front" on the fundamental issues involved. He managed to offer at least one criticism of every participant save Audrey Richards, a close family friend who in the period after his wife's death had become a surrogate mother to his children. Fortes, whose essay Malinowski had in fact praised on several points, spoke on behalf of the group in suggesting that none of them had "realized clearly that contact phenomena are in fact completely new cultural facts"—or, if they did, "felt unequal to the methodological task this poses and tried to evade it."[111]

A dawning (or in some cases gnawing) sense that Malinowskian functionalism itself might be "unequal to the task" was apparently a general problem among the rising cohort of social anthropologists. Several of them a generation later reflected on the impasse that functionalism seemed to have reached in the middle 1930s. With his diaries still unpublished, Malinowski's ethnographic practice was not then at issue, and there is in fact ample indication in his correspondence with students in the field that Malinowskian functionalism "worked," in the sense that it facilitated the collection and organization of large amounts of data. But in several cases problems seem to have arisen when it came to synthesizing the material. As Firth later posed the matter: "If everything is related to everything else, where does the description stop?" Richards, looking back on Malinowski's own grand synthetic effort, felt that *Coral Gardens and Their Magic*—which was discussed as work-in-progress in the seminars of the early thirties—had carried "institutional study" to the "furthest limit" by means of "correlating one set of activities" with "the whole": "it was a *tour de force,* but it was not practical politics to repeat such an experiment."[112]

A sharper sense of dissatisfaction was evident at the time in letters Gregory Bateson wrote to Malinowski after having read *Coral Gardens,* while he was completing his own *Naven.* "Where you emphasize the need for complete delineation of all the factors relevant to a total cultural situation, I emphasize the need to consider these factors one at a time, comparing the action of the same factor in a whole series of separate situations." Granting that the two approaches might each be valid "within their respective limitations," Bateson nevertheless considered Malinowski's "a hopeless muddle out of which simple scientific generalizations can never come." In reading *Coral Gardens,* Bateson had looked for the word "logic" as applied to Trobriand culture and found not a single instance. What he wanted was to dissect the monograph and rearrange its rich materials to show "not the whole of the mechanism but rather the working of each isolable sociological and psychological law."[113]

If Bateson's case suggests that it was not simply a matter of a previously viable functionalism running aground in Africa, this shift in ethnographic focus was perhaps a factor in the ongoing theoretical transition. If the issue of abstraction presented itself even to students of small and bounded Oceanic societies, it was likely to be more strongly felt by those dealing with the larger, more complex, and more loosely margined societies of Africa—particularly when the focus was on culture contact. Malinowski himself seems to have been aware of the problem. Commenting on the contact studies of his students, he suggested that the "main presuppositions of functionalism in its simple form"—the boundedness of single cultures "which through age-long historical development have reached a state of well-balanced equilibrium"—simply "break down" in the African setting.[114]

In the event—and for a time—a solution to the theoretical impasse was found in the greater degree of abstraction facilitated by Radcliffe-Brown's approach to social structure. Radcliffe-Brown's influence had of course been felt at Cape Town (directly in the case of Schapera, mediately in the case of Hoernlé's students) and at Sydney. But that influence began to have a different significance after 1930, when institutional competition, divergent research priorities, and sharpened theoretical disagreement were beginning to fracture the earlier functionalist united front. Radcliffe-Brown's stopover in London on his way to Chicago marked an early moment in the process. Evans-Pritchard, who in 1929 had written to Malinowski suggesting a correlation between his fieldwork experience and his theoretical orientation ("no fieldwork/Durkheim's views"; "limited fieldwork/Radcliffe-Brown's views"; "exhaustive fieldwork/Malinowski's views"), was apparently especially affected. Meyer Fortes later recalled his "particularly vivid recollection" of an evening in Evans-Pritchard's "sumptuous Bloomsbury flat" when Radcliffe-Brown, "with characteristic self-assurance," gave "a whole lecture on lineage systems," which nine years later were to be the focus of Evans-Pritchard's first monograph on the Nuer. If for Evans-Pritchard the "break" with Malinowski was by then complete, Fortes soon got over what Richards then called his attack of "A.R.Bitis." But when Radcliffe-Brown returned to England from Chicago in 1937, the intellectual, institutional, and interpersonal context was very different.[115]

Evans-Pritchard, who felt that Malinowski had done his best to keep him out of the London School of Economics, had by then returned from academic exile in Cairo to take up a lectureship at Oxford, which Marett had helped him get after he was an unsuccessful candidate for Radcliffe-Brown's chair. With the African Institute fellowships now terminated (and Malinowski departing for the United States), Fortes lectured for a year at the School of Economics before joining Radcliffe-Brown and Evans-Pritchard at Oxford. During the academic year 1938–1939, Radcliffe-Brown led a seminar every Friday in a local pub, where the three were joined by Max Gluckman and Brenda Seligman. Fortes later recalled that there was discussion "in great detail" of the field data of Evans-Pritchard, Gluckman, and himself on the Nuer, the Zulu, and the Tallensi. At his postdoctoral students' request "R-B" would also lecture to them on kinship, as well as on most of the topics he had been fine-tuning for the last twenty years. By Gluckman's later reminiscence, the fundamental idea was that of "system," along the lines of the recent seminar at Chicago. It was at the group's suggestion that Radcliffe-Brown presented the material on "social structure" and "the study of kinship relations" in his two lectures as president of the Royal Anthropological Institute.[116]

Another product of the group was of course the collective work,

African Political Systems, which appeared in 1940. Edited by Evans-Pritchard and Fortes (who drafted the introduction), the book reflected the comparative spirit of Radcliffe-Brown's Australian and North American kinship projects. Speaking for "the Editors and myself," Radcliffe-Brown's preface was "a brief statement" on the "comparative study of political institutions" as part of "a natural science of society." Half a century further on, the animating spirit was still recognizably that of Tylor's essay of 1888—with, of course, the fundamental qualification that what Radcliffe-Brown advocated was a synchronic typological comparison of social systems rather than a diachronic statistical comparison of social practices. Such a venture now presupposed, of course, detailed ethnographic studies in the Malinowskian mode. Every one of the eight contributors had been a member of Malinowski's seminar; four had contributed to *Methods of Study of Culture Contact in Africa;* six had been fellows of the African Institute, which joined with the Oxford University Press in publishing the volume. The book, however, was dedicated to C. G. Seligman, and the only reference to Malinowski was in a footnote to Gunther Wagner's essay on the Kavirondo (significantly, the one contribution singled out for criticism in Radcliffe-Brown's preface). Although Gluckman's and Richards' essays included brief sections on "The Period of European Rule" and "Post-European Changes," and an "Editors' note" looked forward to further research on this problem, the focus throughout was on the nature of precontact political systems. While it was hoped that the book would be "of interest and use to those who have the task of administering African peoples," it was "the anthropologist's duty" simply to present "the facts and theory of native social organization," leaving to "the decision of administrators themselves" whether these "could be utilized in the practical tasks of administration." Although the essays displayed a considerably greater conceptual diversity than the preface suggested, the book may nevertheless stand as the accomplishment of the transition in British social anthropology from "pure" Malinowskian functionalism to the "hybrid" structural-functionalism of Radcliffe-Brown.[117]

Epilogue
Moment and Tradition in the History of British Social Anthropology

Radcliffe-Brown's tenure at Oxford was almost as brief as the previous episodes of his academic nomadism. During the war, he went off to Brazil for two years on a cultural mission for the British Council, serving as Visiting Professor at the Escola Livre de Sociologia at São Paulo. After a statutory age limit forced his retirement from Oxford in 1946, he spent two years as Professor of Social Sciences at Farouk University in Alexandria, Egypt. In 1950 and 1951, he was Visiting Professor at Manchester; from 1951 to 1954, he was back in South Africa, teaching social anthropology at Rhodes University. The last sixteen months of his life were spent back in London, isolated and in ill-health—although he "rose from his sickbed in a London hospital" in 1955 to preside at the January meeting of the Association of Social Anthropologists.[1]

The Association of Social Anthropologists had been founded in July of 1946 when, at the initiative of Evans-Pritchard, the little group that had met with Radcliffe-Brown on Fridays before the war was joined at Oxford by another half-dozen younger anthropologists to organize "a professional association of teachers and research workers in Social Anthropology." It was to be an "independent body," with membership by invitation only, the "normal qualification" being "holding, or having held, a teaching or research appointment in Social Anthropology." The institutional reference point was of course the Royal Anthropological Institute. In fact, leadership at the institute by the late 1930s was for the most part in the hands of academics, and social anthropologists had begun to play a more substantial role. Even so, the institute continued to be perceived by many social anthropologists as an abode of amateurism, outmoded evolutionism, and an undifferentiated general anthropology, in which the interests of physical anthropologists, archeologists, and traditional ethnologists outweighed those of social anthropologists.

Professor A. R. Radcliffe-Brown, with research students and staff of the Institute of Social Anthropology, Oxford University, 1946. Left to right (front row): K. T. Hadjioannou, Phyllis Puckle (Secretary and Librarian), A. R. Radcliffe-Brown, Meyer Fortes (Reader, 1947–50), K. A. Busia; (back row): L. F. Henriques, W. Newell, W. Brailsford, A. A. Issa, M. N. Srinivas. (Courtesy of the Institute of Social and Cultural Anthropology, Oxford)

However, the complete separation advocated by Evans-Pritchard and several others at the Oxford meeting was forestalled by Brenda Seligman, a long-time member (and financial supporter) of the institute. Arrangements were made to have the new association's notices published in *Man*, with the prospect of closer collaboration once the association was "more firmly established." On the whole, however, the founding impulse behind the association was clearly an assertion of independent and rigorously guarded professional status.[2]

Although Evans-Pritchard was "Chairman," Radcliffe-Brown was given the title "Life President," and in fact chaired the early meetings. Along with Firth, Forde, and Fortes, they constituted an executive committee, which, until the next annual conference, was given the power to invite others (with "one blackball to exclude"). Although there were thirty-six members by 1949, the criteria for and selection of membership were a continuing preoccupation of the Association of Social Anthropologists. For many years—even after its membership was five times the 1949 figure—it retained its restrictive professional character. Despite internal tensions—notably, between Oxford and the London School of Economics—the association became a very effective professional group, part trade union, part debating society.[3]

In the early meetings, a primary concern was "the teaching of social anthropology in universities," and the early postwar years, when the Labour government was in power, saw a substantial increase in teaching positions. Having defined membership in those terms, the association was able in effect to coopt people of more diverse intellectual background and career experience. At University College, London, the postwar revival of anthropology was directed by Daryll Forde, who had trained there in geography and archeology in the days of Smith and Perry. Shifting to ethnography under Alfred Kroeber and Robert Lowie while on a fellowship at Berkeley, Forde undertook fieldwork in Africa during a fifteen-year tenure as the Gregynog Professor of Geography and Anthropology at Aberystwyth in Wales. During the war, he served as Deputy Professor of Social Anthropology at Oxford for one year during Radcliffe-Brown's absence; supported by Lord Hailey, he also became director of the International African Institute. When the war ended, and a separate Department of Anthropology was established at University College, Forde became professor, bringing in Malinowski's student Phyllis Kaberry as Reader (and for a time, Radcliffe-Brown as "special lecturer"). At the School of African and Oriental Studies, the chair established in the postwar expansion went to Christoph von Fürer-Haimendorf, a prewar product of Viennese diffusionist ethnology who, after two terms in Malinowski's seminar, had gone on to do fieldwork in India, where he spent the war years; although relatively little interested in theoretical issues, as professor he, too, became a member of the Association of Social Anthropologists.[4]

From the beginning, the association also included members from commonwealth universities, where a number of the prewar cohort returned to take up positions, and there were also émigrés like Nadel, who became the founding professor at the Australian National University. In Britain, several members of the association held new positions at institutions in the north, most notably, Gluckman's professorship at Manchester. But the most significant expansion took place at Oxford and the London School of Economics, the major producers of doctorates in the immediate postwar period. At the School of Economics, where the functionalist tradition was stronger, Firth assumed Malinowski's old chair in 1944, and by 1952 there were six positions. At Oxford, where structuralism found its home, Evans-Pritchard succeeded Radcliffe-Brown in 1946, and by 1952 there were a half-dozen social anthropologists.[5]

Significantly absent from the founding meeting of the association was John Henry Hutton, the Professor of Anthropology at Cambridge, which as academic home of Rivers and Haddon had played a major role in the earlier development of British social anthropology. After the election of T. C. Hodson to the readership in 1926, Cambridge anthropology had entered a long period of decline. Although Haddon was still influential into the 1930s, like Seligman he was not in tune with the developments of that decade, retaining his commitment to a more traditional generalist ethnology. When Gregory Bateson applied for the Cambridge chair in anticipation of Hodson's retirement in 1936, his correspondence with Haddon, who had been his first teacher in anthropology a decade before, showed just how wide the gap had become. Although he acknowledged a debt to Ruth Benedict's ideas about "the cultural standardization of personality," Bateson's application was heavily influenced by Radcliffe-Brown. It made a strong case for social anthropology as a "technical science," privileging professional research in vanishing cultures over the practical needs of colonial administration. Loosening its ties to physical anthropology, technology, and archeology, social anthropology would look instead to sociology, psychology, and economics, with the hope of "taking its place with the older sciences" within the next twenty years.[6]

Haddon's response, however, echoed instead themes of previous decades. He insisted that the professor of anthropology had an obligation to students who would "not take up anthropology as a career," most of them "Colonial Cadets" who required it primarily "to enable them to deal sympathetically and efficiently with the natives with whom they will be in contact." Given a good general knowledge of the field, they might also be able to "add items of information in various directions—distributional, archaeological and the like, and might do useful work in cultural anthropology and especially on the problems of the clash of cultures. . . ." Bateson's proposal might be appropriate for the needs of the very small number who sought a career in anthropology, but Haddon nevertheless worried that Bateson himself might "soar away from mundane anthropology, which would be left to prosaic, pedestrian teachers." In the event, that was precisely what happened: with nine applicants (including Firth, Forde, Fortune, Hocart, and Richards), the initial favorite, Jack Driberg, was edged aside for Hutton, whom Bateson accurately described as "an honest solid man though no high flyer as an anthropologist."[7]

During the war, Hutton was involved in planning for the postwar period—not in the promotion of anthropological research, but rather in preparing, for the Duke of Devonshire's Committee, a report on "Post-War Training for the Colonial Service," in which he urged the appointment of both "white and coloured" officers born in the colonies as "a great step in the direction of self-government." There was, however, the hint of a more research-oriented future in 1945, when Hutton was able to get Evans-Pritchard released from military service to accept what turned out to be a one-year appointment as Reader in Anthropology. Four years later, it was Evans-Pritchard, as one of the external electors for Hutton's successor, who played a key role in winning Cambridge for social anthropology. He and the other Oxford elector, T. K. Penniman, along with the Vice-Chancellor (who by tradition was expected to vote with the external electors), favored the candidacy of Meyer Fortes against Fürer-Haimendorf, who was Hutton's choice. Fortes, however, was opposed by three of the four internal electors, for what Evans-Pritchard recalled as anti-Semitic reasons, with the fourth, the psychologist F. C. Bartlett, remaining undecided. At one point Evans-Pritchard was asked to leave the room, and was told upon his return that the board was unanimous in proposing him. When he refused, they thought of Audrey Richards, but she had been previously discouraged from applying because the Disney Professor of Archaeology was a woman, and having two women in the same field was felt to be impossible. With Bartlett's support, Fortes was finally elected by one vote, and a generation after Hodson's choice had saved Cambridge from diffusionist extremists, it was finally won for social anthropology.[8]

Although numbering only several dozen, social anthropologists had thus by 1951 established a firm institutional base. Other components of a more generalized anthropological tradition still maintained their place at Oxford and at Cambridge—and within the Royal Anthropological Institute. But social anthropology was now established as the dominant mode for studying the present life-forms of non-European peoples. Nor was it limited to them; in the tradition of Radcliffe-Brown, complex societies were in principle included as other "types" in a comparative science of society. In the absence of a strong British sociological tradition, the influence of social anthropology soon spread to that discipline as well; several of the chairs later established in sociology were filled by people trained as social anthropologists. The impact of social anthropology was also felt abroad, especially in the United States. By 1950, British social anthropologists had been approached to accept appointments in several United States departments; students from the United States were spending academic years in Britain, and regularly undertaking fieldwork within the British sphere.[9]*

*It is worth noting, as a factor in the burgeoning influence of British social anthropology, that the "colonial [or commonwealth] exchange" continued into the postwar period. The three major British universities continued to train students from the periphery and to send back faculty, including, for instance, M. N. Srinivas, who, after undergraduate training with Haddon's student Ghurye at Bombay, studied under Radcliffe-Brown at Oxford and

During the 1930s, American anthropologists had begun to explore various more "scientific" and "sociological" alternatives to the long-dominant Boasian tradition of historical ethnology. With the death of Boas in 1942 as symbolic marker of transition, the postwar years witnessed a heightened receptivity to approaches to social phenomena in terms which professed to be scientific. One manifestation of this trend was the comparative cross-cultural study of social structure undertaken by George Murdock at Yale. Based on data collected from 250 societies for what was to become the Human Relations Area Files, Murdock's study was a direct methodological descendant of Tylor's essay of 1888—and included Morgan, Rivers, and Radcliffe-Brown among the ten predecessors to whom it was dedicated. Strikingly, however, "functional anthropology" was not among the "four systems of social science theory" that Murdock's study attempted to synthesize: Sumnerian evolutionary sociology, the Boasian critique of evolution, behavioristic psychology, and psychoanalysis. A decade previously, he thought it might have been, but contact with Malinowski at Yale, while intellectually stimulating, had provided "no fundamental point of view not previously acquired" from William Graham Sumner's disciple Alfred Keller. And although Radcliffe-Brown's work had in fact been the stimulus which first induced Murdock "to specialize in the field," its virtues had dimmed "on closer view"—fading "into insubstantiality with intensive study." Even so, Murdock spoke of the "revolution" functional anthropology had "wrought in the younger generation of American anthropologists" in whose hands lay "the future of anthropology, and perhaps even that of social science in general."[10]

It was in this context that Murdock in 1951 offered a general critique of British social anthropology in the *American Anthropologist*. By editorial prearrangement it was paired with a response from Raymond Firth, whom Murdock had entertained during a visit Firth made to New Haven in 1950. Taken together, the two documents provide an historiographic microcosm, in which a presumably unitary historical phenomenon is examined from two distinct standpoints—one external, one internal, but each marginal to its own tradition. As such, it may offer the basis for some concluding remarks on the subject of this volume.[11]

The immediate occasion for Murdock's critique was the appearance in 1950 of a third collaborative volume published by the International African Institute: *African Systems of Kinship and Marriage*, edited by Radcliffe-Brown and Daryll Forde. Harking back to Morgan and Rivers, Radcliffe-Brown's long introductory essay was his fullest and most systematic published statement of the approach to kinship he had

---

then returned to Baroda and to Delhi (Srinivas 1973; see also the successive Association of Social Anthropologists *Register[s] of Members*).

Raymond Firth, during the year (1958–1959) when he and Meyer Fortes, foreshadowing a later rapprochement of two traditions, joined George Murdock, Fred Eggan, and five other American cultural anthropologists at the Center for Advanced Study in the Behavioral Sciences in Palo Alto. (Courtesy of Sir Raymond Firth)

been developing over the preceding four decades; the volume itself was yet another instantiation of the comparative project he had previously pursued in South Africa, Australia, and North America. Although the nine authors of ethnographic case studies were (save Forde) graduates of Malinowski's seminars, his name went unmentioned in the volume. The contributors (six of them by now holders of professorial chairs) included most of the leading figures in the Association of Social Anthropologists. From the perspective of their transatlantic critic in 1951, they seemed to have all of "the characteristics of a 'school'"—which Murdock regarded as *prima facie* grounds for questioning their membership in an international scientific community of "anthropologists."[12]

Murdock granted the "school" an "average level of ethnographic competence and theoretical suggestiveness probably unequalled by any comparable group elsewhere in the world." But he felt that their work was characterized by "off-setting limitations" which justified their exclusion from the anthropological community: narrowness of substantive and ethnographic interests, theoretical parochialism, "disinterest" in general ethnography, "neglect" of history and the processes of cultural change in time, and a "widespread indifference to psychology." Not only did the narrow focus on kinship and social structure lead to a "fractionating tendency inconsistent with functional theory" and greatly increase "the dangers of reification"; it also implied the abandonment of "the special province of anthropology": "Alone among the anthropologists of the world the British make no use of the culture concept." They were, in fact, not anthropologists at all, but "professionals of another category," and, like "many other sociologists," they tried "to discover valid laws by the intensive study" of "a very small and non-random sample of all societies," without adequate "comparative or cross-cultural validation."[13]

As his limiting temporal modifier implies, Firth was inclined to view "contemporary British social anthropology" in somewhat less monolithic and more historical terms. Granting the strong influence of "their personal ethnographic experience," he suggested that the alleged narrowness of British social anthropologists was more apparent than real. More ethnography was "read than cited," and transatlantic movements of staff and students had "spread knowledge of the more important contributions to American social anthropology." However, it was by isolating a particular sphere of inquiry and developing a "more precise framework of ideas and substantial propositions" that British social anthropology had "got its character." But social anthropology was not peculiarly British, and was in fact oriented toward a broader scientific community.* That this community was not primarily composed of human biologists, students of primitive technology, or archeologists was of little importance. What was important was not to maintain "an old-fashioned—and spurious—unified science of man" but rather to strengthen meaningful interdisciplinary connections with other social sciences: "sociology in the narrow sense," psychology, economics, jurisprudence, and "such history as is problem oriented."[14]

But if Firth insisted that it was by "isolating its sphere of enquiry"

*There have, however, been various attempts to see something specifically (or generically) British in the social anthropological tradition: for example, Mary Douglas's speculations on what the Dogon and the Nuer might seem like if they had been studied respectively by the British and the French, rather than vice versa (1975); or more recently, Mary Bouquet's interpretation of the "British 'obsession' with kinship" by reading Rivers against Beatrix Potter (1993). The association of basic philosophical/scientific viewpoints with national traditions has itself a lineage extending back through Talcott Parsons (1937) at least to J. T. Merz's great chapters on "the scientific spirit" (1904). For other views of national traditions in anthropology, see Gerholm and Hannerz, eds. (1982) (including Stocking 1982a) and S. Diamond, ed. (1980). For the British and American contrast, see M. Harris (1980) and G. Watson (1984). See also Rivers and Marett, above, 168–69, 179–80.

that British social anthropology had achieved its "unequalled" ethnographic competence and theoretical coherence, he was nevertheless willing to concede that "much of what Murdock has said is just and calls more for reflection than reply." In general, his approach was, first, to insist on the legitimacy of a scientific strategy ("generalizations in the natural sciences are assumed to be valid for a wide field of phenomena without the need of testing every instance"); then, to grant in effect certain limitations in its actual implementation ("the unwillingness or inability of the theorist to state clearly how far he intended his analysis to describe the behavior of people in an actual named society at a given period of time"); and finally, to suggest either that not all British social anthropologists were guilty of such failings or that recent practice showed signs of taking them into consideration ("this view, however, is ceasing to be an effective British position"). After twenty-five years in which it had "done much to establish a more significant typology," British social anthropology now appeared to be "moving slowly and unevenly toward a more systematic study of variation, including variation over time."[15]

At the precise historical moment when its establishment had been secured, the very nature of British social anthropology as an historical and conceptual phenomenon was placed at issue in this debate. Murdock—marginal to the Boasian tradition, but still identifying himself as an American cultural anthropologist—reduced the variety of British anthropology to the uniformity of a single intellectual type. And by exempting almost every major British social anthropologist from some aspect of his criticism, he tended to collapse his "school" into a single individual: Radcliffe-Brown, who, unlike Malinowski, seemed never "to have modified his theoretical position in any significant way since its earliest formulation decades ago." Firth—an insider, but a non-Africanist, non-Oxonian who was "not afraid to be called eclectic"—attempted to reintroduce variety into British social anthropology by historicizing it. Paradoxically, however, his essay tended to reinforce the reduction to a single individual. In searching for "greater coherence" than Malinowski's theories seemed to offer, in rejecting culture for social structure, and in embracing Radcliffe-Brown's approach to the problem of abstraction, "some British social anthropologists," Firth thought, had "fallen into a trap." In contrast, his own insistence on the "varied interests" of British social anthropologists, and on the more recent changes in the field, was sustained by references to several general theoretical statements by leading social anthropologists, each of whom departed from Radcliffe-Brown in significant respects. Read against each other, Murdock's typologizing critique and Firth's historicizing defense would seem almost to collapse "British social anthropology" into the influence of a single individual during a rather brief historical moment: roughly, the period between *African Political Systems* and *African Systems of Kinship and Marriage*.[16]

At the end of that historical moment, three leading members of the Association of Social Anthropologists published books on the nature of social anthropology. It was a task their mentor had himself begun sometime in this period, but never completed; the five preliminary chapters published after his death were vintage Radcliffe-Brown. In contrast, all three of the mid-century overviews have since been described as presenting "challenges" to "the old Oxford orthodoxy." Firth's own *Elements of Social Organization* and Siegfried Nadel's *Foundations of Social Anthropology* did so along "neo-Malinowskian" lines consistent with their intellectual histories and institutional affiliations; each of them insisted on the inadequacy of a purely structural analysis, reintroducing a concern for the variability of human social behavior. But the challenge represented by Evans-Pritchard's *Social Anthropology* (and more dramatically by his Marett Lecture of July 1950) was more far-reaching; rejecting "the establishment of sociological laws" as the goal of social anthropology, Evans-Pritchard redefined it as "a kind of historiography," one of the humanities rather than the natural sciences. Coming from Radcliffe-Brown's successor, whose inaugural lecture two years before had been a very "orthodox" performance, the apostasy of Evans-Pritchard sent shock waves through the small world of British social anthropology.* Despite these challenges, "Oxford orthodoxy" continued to be manifest in the ethnographic monographs of the 1950s, and to be more systematically elaborated by Meyer Fortes (although he, too, never lost touch completely with his early psychological concerns). It was not until later

*Toward the end of his life, in a period when he offered a number of autobiographical reminiscences, Evans-Pritchard published a note on the circumstances of his inaugural lecture, which, although reflecting his break with Radcliffe-Brown, leaves somewhat in doubt the earlier history of their relationship. By this account, Radcliffe-Brown's own inaugural lecture had been "a disaster," because he was "used to talking to students in parts of the world where intellectual standards were not so high" and misjudged "the calibre of his audience." At the time Evans-Pritchard was preparing his inaugural lecture, Radcliffe-Brown brought to him his own still-unpublished manuscript and asked Evans-Pritchard to "emphasize" its "main points" in his lecture, and then to destroy it. Because he believed that he should "represent" the Institute of Social Anthropology and did not wish to "publicly dissociate" himself from Radcliffe-Brown (for whom he had "personal regard, though less intellectual sympathy or appreciation") or from his colleague Meyer Fortes, Evans-Pritchard agreed to do so. Even so, upon rereading it he felt that he "would not wish to speak very differently; for I was cautious." Less cautious, however, in later personal conversation, in which he denigrated Radcliffe-Brown as a lower-middle-class boy who did not really read French and alienated his colleagues at All Souls by his pretensions to authority—and spoke of Malinowski, from whom he had long been alienated, as "a cad, a swine, a shit—and a genius" (Evans-Pritchard 1970; interviews 5/30/69, 5/2/73).

in the decade that British anthropologists began to explore the alternative structuralism represented by Claude Lévi-Strauss. But already by 1951, the process had begun which twenty years later seemed to one observer to have produced an "epistemological break": "for practical purposes textbooks which looked useful, [in 1971] no longer are; monographs which used to appear exhaustive now appear selective; interpretations which once looked full of insight now seem mechanical and lifeless."[17]

The break between structural-functionalism and later British social anthropology (whether neo-Malinowskian, Anglo-French structural, poststructural, or postmodern) has more dimensions than the epistemological: most notably, of course, those implied in the end of the British Empire. Although this subsequent history lies beyond the confines of the present inquiry, it is worth noting that many later developments (as well as the retrospective criticisms that have since been made of "structural-functional" anthropology) were anticipated in the Murdock-Firth exchange. These include the questioning of African models, the turn to history, the interest in individual agency, even the recent return to an idiom of "culture"—symbolized most strikingly in the renaming of the Oxford Institute, which since 1991 has been "The Institute of Social and Cultural Anthropology." And just as Firth resisted Murdock's reduction of variety by typification, so do defenders and redefiners now appeal to variability within the classical moment or within the tradition out of which it emerged—historical interests that never died, submerged symbolic concerns, neglected figures rediscovered. Such alternatives can even be found in the archetypal master himself—as when Radcliffe-Brown made allowance for a "real" as opposed to "conjectural" history or suggested a more sophisticated view of culture in the very act of denying its scientific status.[18]

We are led, then, back to the question of the historical specificity of "British social anthropology." There is a certain sense in which Murdock's typological reduction echoes the narrative of this book. Although suggesting a more broadly and thickly contextualized complexity of origin and development, the story has nevertheless retained an essentially linear structure, culminating in an archetype. Some figures outside the canon have been reintroduced; others more briefly mentioned. There have been glances, even extended gazes, at the ethnographic process overseas, and glimpses of its colonial situation, as well as hints of its domestic political context. And there has been recurrent consideration of its academic and institutional development. But the movement from Tylor through Haddon, Seligman, Marett, and Rivers to Malinowski and Radcliffe-Brown, from the Anthropological Institute through the interknit confines of British academic life to the (then) small world of the Association of Social Anthropologists, has provided the backbone of the story. Along the way, there were fundamental, even paradigmatic, changes—methodological, theoretical, and institutional—marked herein by occasional polysyllabic "izations." But there was also continuity. When Evans-Pritchard spoke in conversation of the lineage of his own chair—from Tylor to Marett to Radcliffe-Brown to himself—that simplifying vision, while obscuring transformations, also bespoke a kind of historical (and sociological) reality. Though widely influential, the world of British social anthropology was a rather small one, and it was structured very much by lineage.[19]

There is also, however, a sense in which Firth's historicizing defense, while reinforcing the earlier narrative, at the same time places it in question. Scarcely had the archetype been realized historically than its typological unity began to fragment; British social anthropology was more diverse than Radcliffe-Brown, and it continued to thrive and to change long after he had passed from the scene. The story had always been more complex than teleological retrospect would suggest—more complex, by far, than even the present lengthy narrative has been able to indicate. And since 1951, the positions have proliferated from which meanings might be mustered.*

*For British social anthropology since 1951, the only general account is Adam Kuper (1983), the penultimate chapter of which is called "The Lean Years, 1972–1982." Writing a decade after Ardener's cautiously hopeful presentation (1971) of a "new anthropology" that he felt was emerging in the wake of the "epistemic break," Kuper was struck instead by the pervading "institutional stagnation, intellectual torpor and parochialism," which he attributed in part to the continued "intellectual dominance of the retired elders" (i.e., the founding and early members of the Association of Social Anthropologists). For developments since then, the reader had best consult *Man* (or, as it has recently been retro-titled, the *Journal of the Royal Anthropological Institute, incorporating Man*), which continues to represent, to some extent, the broader anthropology of the institute—as well as *Anthropology Today* (formerly *RAIN*), which since 1974 has been a lively forum for many of the newer tendencies (none of them yet convincingly paradigmatic) (Benthall 1990). Both journals evidence, in both authorship and subject matter, a continuing rapprochement with American cultural anthropology. So also, the decennial conference of the Association of Social Anthropologists at St. Catherine's College, Oxford, in July 1993, where over a fifth of the papers came from scholars at American institutions and kinship seemed to have "disappeared from the anthropological agenda," its place taken by the notion of "culture"—which "has indeed become ubiquitous in the West in recent years." In contrast to the 1983 decennial meetings, where there was "endless pessimistic introspection," the conference theme ("The Uses of Knowledge: Global and Local Relations") produced "lively and reflexive debate," despite the continuing "lack of a handy paradigm" (Stolcke 1993). Attendance had doubled since 1983, and there were complaints by some younger anthropologists about the number of papers and the lack of time for discussion—evidence, perhaps, of an emerging generation gap between the heirs of the elders and the current student population (Roberts 1993). But to one used to meetings larger by a factor of more than ten, it still seemed quite intimate, and there was a much greater feeling of continuity and coherence of discourse. Appropriately, the eldest surviving elder, Raymond Firth, offered after-dinner comments on recent

But if the story is far more complex and open-ended than this volume has suggested, there is a certain unity, which may be marked by a final microcosm: that of *Notes and Queries in Anthropology*, the ethnographic handbook periodically prepared and published under the auspices of the British Association and the Anthropological Institute—the final edition of which also appeared in 1951. Because the editions never began entirely afresh, but had something of the repetitively overwritten character of a palimpsest, there was a great deal of continuity built into them. But there were also major changes, which roughly mark the major phases of the history we have traced. The first edition, in 1874, was Tylor's, and provided, in principle if not in practice, the sort of ethnographic underpinning essential for his comparative "method of investigating the development of institutions." The second edition of 1892 and the third of 1899 (which was simply a reprinting) continued the comparative project, while reflecting a growing sense of the inadequacy of its ethnographic base. The fourth, of 1912, was that of Rivers and Marett, calling for a new kind of ethnography and questioning the categories of comparison. The fifth, of 1929, was Haddon's, routinizing the new ethnography, but steering clear of the still-unresolved theoretical disputes of the 1920s. The sixth, undertaken in 1936 and published in 1951, may be seen as Radcliffe-Brown's.[20]

By this time, the unity of anthropology which was the heritage of nineteenth-century evolutionism and general ethnology had clearly fragmented. When the status of the sixth edition was reviewed in 1947 after the war had interrupted its preparation, it was found that "the only subcommittee that functioned was that on Social Anthropology"—which included Evans-Pritchard, Firth, Forde, and Fortes and was chaired by Radcliffe-Brown. Although the published volume included a short section on physical anthropology and a more extended (and little revised) section on material culture, the bulk of the volume was devoted to social anthropology. Brenda Seligman was the general editor, and the authors of the specific chapters were not identified; but it is clear that the methodological section was Radcliffe-Brown's, with specific topics treated by members of the subcommittee (Firth, for instance, preparing the initial draft of the section on economics). Quite a few passages were taken verbatim from the previous edition, but the central theoretical rubric, "social structure," was one not present in 1929. Radcliffe-Brown and his colleagues had in fact accomplished a major reworking. The general movement was from a theoretical pragmatism to a more

trends, from the point of view of a friendly critic, for whom, behind the variety of local knowledges affirmed by many conference participants, there was still to be found a single universal standard of empirical knowledge.

self-conscious, somewhat formalistic, and implicitly comparative social scientism. Although the starting point of method was still "a sympathetic understanding," there was new emphasis on the maintenance of a certain distance. Method, in short, was governed by the goal of objectivity.[21]

But there was also a substantial underlying continuity which extended back beyond 1929. Despite successive purgations of evolutionary or ethnocentric assumption in the twentieth-century editions, their traces were still to be found in the sixth—often as older markings on the palimpsest, but sometimes inscribed anew. Although it was now urged that the terms "primitive," "savage," and "aboriginal" be avoided, there were constant references to "primitive peoples" and "primitive societies," without quotation marks or the modifier "so-called," in passages new to this edition. Indeed, the objects of study seem not to have changed too much over the years, despite changes in the world around them. There were occasional hints of a colonial situation, and a few references to historical process, social change, or the effects of European contact. But reading the volume as a whole, it seems clear that the focus of ethnographic inquiry was the "purely native society"—conceived of as a bounded entity to be accurately described and comparatively categorized so that it might contribute to the eventual formulations of "universally valid social laws." It was a goal that Tylor himself might have appreciated.[22]

It was also the end of an era. When an attempt was made in the early 1970s to prepare a seventh edition, planning got far enough to enlist editors for physical and social anthropology, as well as subeditors for a number of topic areas. By May of 1973, there was even a brief draft preface, in which it was acknowledged that "Colonial Empires are in the main defunct," that the "classical material of the Anthropologist is vanishing before our eyes," that many anthropologists "are now deploying their methods to the study of communities nearer home," and that in the future "Indigenous Anthropologists will no doubt play an increasing part" in anthropology overseas. The project, however, languished—another book unwritten, another turning point unmarked in the history of British social anthropology.[23]

Viewed from after the end of empire and on the other side of an epistemological break, *Notes and Queries* seemed an anachronism. Anthropologists who as graduate students carried the structural-functionalist sixth edition into the field retrospectively minimized its usefulness. Although a recent Association of Social Anthropologists manual on method—the first of a multivolume series—contained an historical essay in which *Notes and Queries* was given brief mention, elsewhere in the volume it was described in rather stereotypic and distanced terms (e.g., "the naive guidance for amateurs enshrined in *Notes and Queries*"). But despite a similar distancing from "positivism," the project sought to "standardize procedures" and "terminological usages" in order "to make comparison and evaluation easier and more productive"—evidence perhaps that the spirit of Radcliffe-Brown, and of Tylor before him, was still alive in British social anthropology.[24]

Notes
References Cited
Manuscript Sources
Oral Sources
Index

Notes

Sources of quotations are given first in each note, in order of their occurrence in the text. These are followed, after a dash, by additional primary sources drawn upon for specific factual material or otherwise relevant. Primary sources are cited by date of original publication; however, the pagination indicated will in some cases be that of a later edition, reprint, or collection—in which case the date of that source will be indicated in the list of References Cited. Manuscript sources are cited in the notes by acronyms, as indicated in the list of Manuscript Sources. For basic biographical information, I have occasionally relied, without citation, on the *Dictionary of National Biography*, the *International Encyclopedia of the Social Sciences*, and the *International Dictionary of Anthropologists* (ed. Christopher Winters).

Preface

1 For literature in the history of anthropology since 1973, see the twice-yearly *History of Anthropology Newsletter*. Recent monographic contributions to the history of British social anthropology include A. Kuper 1973, 1983, 1988; Langham 1981; Kuklick 1991; Urry 1993. On many issues and points of detail, readers might wish to consult these works, as well as other sources mentioned in the notes and References Cited. For previous work by GWS, see under Stocking.
2 Cf. Shapin 1992.
3 Kuklick 1991; Urry 1993; cf. Henson 1974.
4 Cf. Barkan 1992.
5 A. Kuper 1982, 1988:190–209.
6 See entries under Stocking in References Cited.
7 Stocking 1968b:1–12, 1993c:5, 9, 60–61, 215, 362.

Prologue: Tylor and the Reformation of Anthropology

1 Tylor 1865:281—1871, 1873, 1881a, 1881b, 1885b. See also Marett 1936; Leopold 1980; Stocking 1968c, 1987b.
2 Tylor 1888:245, 270—H. Spencer 1874. See also Koepping 1985; Stigler 1986:297; Cowan 1985; Forrest 1974.
3 Tylor 1888:245–46.

4 Ibid. 248.
5 Ibid. 249.
6 Ibid. 252.
7 Ibid. 253, 256—Bachofen 1861.
8 Tylor 1888:256. See also Hodgen 1936.
9 McLennan 1865, 1876b; L. H. Morgan 1871. See also Trautman 1987.
10 Tylor 1888:265.
11 Ibid. 266, 268—W. R. Smith 1885.
12 Tylor 1888:248, 269.
13 For comments on my use of the "paradigm" idea, see Stocking 1987b:xiv, 1992c:343–44.
14 Köbben 1952; Hammel 1980; Jarvie 1964.
15 Galton and Flower in Tylor 1888:270–72.
16 Strauss & Orans 1975; Dow 1984.
17 Tylor 1865:5. See also Stocking 1987b; this volume, passim.
18 Boas 1887, 1889a. See also Stocking 1974b.
19 Lowie 1947:305; Stocking, ed., 1974c:131–34, 1968b:133–60.
20 Boas 1889b, 1896. See also Stocking 1968b:207–11.
21 Tylor in Stocking 1968b:211—Tylor 1896b, 1892, 1893. See also Stocking 1989.
22 Fortes 1969:12–14; cf. Stocking 1968b:198–233.
23 Fortes 1969:1; cf. Langham 1981. See also Jarvie 1964; A. Kuper 1973, 1983 (cf., however, 1988); Kuklick 1991; Urry 1993.

1. Center and Periphery: Armchair Anthropology, Missionary Ethnography, and Evolutionary Theory

1 Tylor 1896b:88, 1861; Stocking 1971a. See also Stocking 1987b; Leopold 1980.
2 BAAS 1874: iv—Tylor 1871. See also Stocking 1983:71–73, 1993b; Urry 1972.
3 Man in Tomas 1991:81–82—Man 1885; H. Spencer 1874. See also Stocking 1987b:259.
4 Stipe 1980; Pels 1992.
5 Tylor 1888:262–63.
6 Frazer 1909a:211. See also Grattan 1963.
7 LFMM 3/16/64; LFPM 3/17/67, 9/27/70, 1/3/70—Williams & Calvert 1859. See also Blamires & Smith 1886:89–92; Findlay & Holdsworth 1921–24; Warren 1967:37–56; Stocking 1987b:87–92; Comaroff & Comaroff 1991.
8 Müller in LFPM: C. Smith to Fison 3/17/67; Fison in Resek 1960:128—L. H. Morgan 1871:568, 573. See also Stocking 1987b:56–62.
9 See Trautman 1987:84–114; Resek 1960; Stocking 1974a; Schrempp 1983.
10 L. H. Morgan 1871:480; LHMP: Morgan to Fison 10/31/71.
11 LFPC: Fison to Howitt 7/6/74.
12 LHMP: Morgan to Fison 8/19/70; L. H. Morgan 1877:53; LFPC: Fison to Howitt 9/17/74, Fison to Codrington 11/14/77, Fison to Howitt 8/17/76; LHMP: Fison to Morgan 8/1/79.
13 Frazer 1909a:230. See also M. H. Walker 1971.

14 Howitt in M. H. Walker 1971:210—Lubbock 1865. See also Mulvaney 1958, 1970, 1971.

15 LFPC: Fison to Howitt 2/19/80, Fison to Howitt 8/18/74; Howitt to Morgan 7/27/77 in Stern, ed., 1930:262; EBTP: Howitt to Tylor 11/21/81—Smyth 1878. See also M. H. Walker 1971:191, 226, 323–27.

16 Fison & Howitt 1880:180–86; EBTP: Fison to Tylor 11/7/81, Howitt to Tylor 6/4/83. See also Mulvaney 1970; Rowley 1970.

17 Howitt to Morgan 2/28/76 in Stern, ed., 1930:260–61.

18 McLennan 1876b:366, 372–73; Tylor 1878:67; Lubbock 1871. See also Resek 1960:136.

19 Fison to Morgan 7/15/80, 3/26/80, 1/27/79 in Stern, ed., 1930:431, 429, 275, 277.

20 Fison to Morgan 1/6/80, Howitt to Morgan 3/22/80 in Stern, ed., 1930:424, 428.

21 Fison & Howitt 1880; LFMP: Fison to Howitt 3/26/80.

22 Fison & Howitt 1880:27; EBTP: Fison to Tylor, 8/17/79—Tylor 1879.

23 Fison & Howitt 1880:50–51, 76–95.

24 Ibid. 99–100; Fison to Morgan 10/7/80 in Stern, ed., 1930:434.

25 Fison to Morgan 4/10/79 in Stern, ed., 1930:419; Fison & Howitt 1880:361, 117, 139, 149, 321, 103—Lubbock 1870; H. Spencer 1874. See also Peel 1971:16.

26 Fison & Howitt 1880:103.

27 Fison & Howitt 1880:132–33, 319.

28 Ibid. 90; Fison to Morgan 1/6/79, 2/8/80 in Stern, ed., 1930:271, 427—cf. LFPC: Fison to Howitt 11/6/78; Fison 1879.

29 Fison & Howitt 1880:127–28, 332–34, 340; Fison to Morgan 1/27/79, 2/14/79 in Stern, ed., 1930:276, 278.

30 Fison & Howitt 1880:177–292, 297, 298.

31 Ibid. 303, 202; EBTP: Fison to Tylor 8/17/79.

32 Fison & Howitt 1880:312, 311.

33 Ibid. 326, 54; EBTP: Fison to Tylor 9/6/81; Fison & Howitt 1880:327, 147. See also Hodgen 1936; Stocking 1987b:162–63.

34 Fison to Morgan 6/13/81 in Stern, ed., 1930:441; Tylor 1880:256, 262–63—1881c; Howitt & Fison 1882, 1884; Howitt 1883a, 1883b, 1886, 1888, 1890, 1904. See also Frazer 1909a; M. H. Walker 1971.

35 EBTP: Fison to Tylor, 7/15/81, 12/27/82, 12/26/83. See also Stocking 1973a, 1987b.

36 LFPC: Fison to Howitt 12/16/78, 4/5/79—Hearn 1879.

37 LFPC: Fison to Howitt 1/17/79; EBTP: Fison to Tylor 7/15/81.

38 EBTP: Fison to Tylor 9/27/81, 1/16/80, 3/1/81.

39 EBTP: Fison to Tylor 9/27/81.

40 EBTP: Fison to Tylor 8/23/82.

41 EBTP: Fison to Tylor 9/29/93.

42 Darwin 1871:II, 362—Westermarck 1891. See also Stocking 1987b; this volume, 152.

43 EBTP: Fison to Tylor 10/18/89, 8/5/95; Fison 1892a:150–51—1892b, 1892c. See also Frazer 1909a:222.

44 Fison 1904:xiii, xviii.
45 See Beidelman 1974a; Warren 1967.
46 RHCP: miscellaneous biographical material; diary for 1859: 3/20/59. See also Stocking 1987a.
47 See Fox 1958:6; Armstrong 1900.
48 Patteson in Gutch 1971:171; Codrington in Fox 1958:16; Yonge 1874:II, 414; USPG: Codrington to Bullock 4/4/67. See also Clammer 1976; Sohmer 1988.
49 RHCP: Codrington to his aunt 10/2/70, n.d./71, 10/15/71. See also Docker 1970.
50 USPG: Codrington to Bullock 11/8/71; RHCP: Codrington to his aunt 11/10/71.
51 RHCP: Codrington to his aunt 2/2/72; Island Voyage Journal 7/25/72; Codrington to his aunt 6/16/76.
52 RHCP: Codrington to his aunt 10/15/71, 9/5/73, 8/8/71, 2/12/75, 1/5/76, 7/24/75.
53 RHCP: Codrington to his aunt 8/25/74, 10/2/70.
54 Yonge 1874:II, appendix I; Müller 1902:II, 320–21—Maine 1861, Müller 1856b, Tylor 1865. See also Clammer 1976; Stocking 1989.
55 RHCP: Codrington to Gerland 12/31/74; Codrington 1885:12—Waitz 1862–77.
56 RHCP: Codrington to his aunt 8/8/71; LFPC and RCLF, correspondence of Fison and Codrington.
57 RCLF: Codrington to Fison 9/29/77, 9/16/76; LFPC: Fison to Codrington 12/22/76—Codrington 1880.
58 LFPC: Fison to Codrington 3/30/81—EBTP: lecture roll book.
59 RHCP: "Diary in Mota" 1869; "For the Island Voyage" 1882; Codrington 1876; Marau 1894.
60 Codrington 1880:143, 1885:222, 140–41, 1876:31.
61 Codrington 1891:116–18.
62 Ibid. v–vii.
63 Ibid. vii, Codrington 1881:312.
64 Tylor 1871:428–29; Codrington 1881:313, 1891:123, 348.
65 JGFP: Codrington to Frazer 9/27/88, 12/4/88; EBTP: Codrington to Tylor 5/4/98—Frazer 1887a.
66 Müller in Codrington 1891:118–19.
67 RCLF: Codrington to Fison 3/22/72, 9/29/77.
68 Codrington 1891:68, 27–28, 20–21.
69 Müller 1885. See also Schrempp 1983; Crick 1976; Stocking 1989.
70 Codrington 1891:38; RHCP: Codrington to his aunt 2/17/76; Codrington 1891:1; Rivers 1914c:II, 578.
71 Gillen in Mulvaney & Calaby 1985:172. See also Elkin 1963; McKnight 1990; Mulvaney 1958.

2. Animism, Totemism, and Christianity: A Pair of Heterodox Scottish Evolutionists

1 Tylor 1888:256. See also Stocking 1987b.
2 See, among others, Turner 1974; Leach 1985.
3 McLennan 1866:282–83—1868, 1869. See also Schmidt 1987.
4 Müller in Stocking 1987b:60—McLennan 1869:422–23. See also Dorson 1955; Stocking 1987b:60, 306–8.
5 McLennan 1885:vi–vii.
6 Green 1946:vii; Lang 1908:127. See also De Cocq 1968; Duff-Cooper 1986; R. A. Jones 1984; Beidelman 1974b; Langstaff 1978; Wheeler-Barclay 1987.
7 Stevenson in Green 1946:178, 1; Lang 1905a:22; Buchan 1933:10; Green 1946:8, 11.
8 Lang in Green 1946:13; Lang 1905a:29. See also Crawford 1986:857; Turner 1981; Richter 1964.
9 Haggard 1926:I, 230. See also Crawford 1986:862; Salmond, ed., 1949:ix; Green 1946:241–59.
10 Lang in G. Gordon 1927:10—Haggard 1887; Lang & Pollock 1887. See also J. J. Gross 1969:137; Green 1946:168; Orel 1984:124–50; Heyck 1982; De Cocq 1968; Duff-Cooper 1986.
11 See Stocking 1987b; Dorson 1968a, ed., 1968b; Montenyohl 1987.
12 Dorson, ed., 1968b:I, 66; Lang 1905a:37–38, 1884:28, 1907b:1—Müller 1856a. See also Green 1946:68–69; Kitagawa & Strong 1985; Stocking 1987b.
13 Dorson 1968a:196, 206–7; Clodd 1916:11; Gomme 1890a:5—Clodd 1891, 1920; Gomme 1890b, 1892; Hartland 1890, 1909–10, 1921, 1924. See also Dorson 1955, 1968a:190–94, 202ff.
14 Lang 1884:2, 21–25, 53, 150, 211, 125.
15 Ibid. 212, 233, 236, 230–31—Müller 1882.
16 Hartland 1914:13.
17 Baker 1980:254. See also Gauld 1968; Cerullo 1982; Soffer 1978; Turner 1974.
18 Lang in Baker 1980:236; Lang in Stocking 1994:ix (cf. Lang 1888); Lang 1884:180, 211; Lang in Haggard 1926:II, 80, I, 228; Lang in Baker 1980:256. See also Baker 1980:402–5.
19 Lang in Green 1946:71, 112–13; Lang 1894:xiv–xv, 180, 77.
20 Lang 1894:338.
21 Lang 1898:1, 2.
22 Ibid. 3, 6–7, 15.
23 Ibid. 60, 62, 63, 64, 66–67.
24 Ibid. 73, 160.
25 Ibid. 172–73, 175, 181, 201, 214–16, 192–97, 274.
26 Ibid. 274, 280, 281–82, 294, 329.
27 Ibid. 291, 316, 66, 50–51; Clodd in Baker 1980:254.
28 Lang 1898:iii, 1907b:13—Tylor 1871. See also Stocking 1992a.
29 Freire-Marreco 1907; Stocking 1992b. See also Baker 1980:388–401; Stocking 1992a.
30 EBTP: Oxford University Press galleys. See also Stocking 1992a, 1987b.
31 Clodd in Baker 1980:400.

32 Tylor in Baker 1980:401; Lang 1907b:13, 11 (emphasis added), 14. See also Stocking 1987b:74–77.
33 W. R. Smith 1882:260–61. See also Black & Chrystal 1912:1–10; Frazer 1894.
34 Black & Chrystal 1912:14, 13, 19. See also Beidelman 1974b.
35 Black & Chrystal 1912:75, 80, 91, 88, 69, 118—W. R. Smith 1869. See also R. A. Jones 1984:54.
36 W. R. Smith 1869:151, 139, 157, 147, 142, 162. See also Black & Chrystal 1912:118.
37 Black & Chrystal 1912:116, 144–45—McLennan 1865.
38 Black & Chrystal 1912:129–30.
39 W. R. Smith 1875:634; Black & Chrystal 1912:194.
40 Black & Chrystal 1912:582–607, 350, 401. See also Riesen 1985.
41 Black & Chrystal 1912:354; W. R. Smith 1880b:482–83; General Assembly in Beidelman 1974b:21. See also Black & Chrystal 1912:361–451, 608–16.
42 W. R. Smith 1881:xi.
43 Ibid. 388, 239; Black & Chrystal 1912:417; W. R. Smith 1882:v. See also Beidelman 1974b:21–22.
44 W. R. Smith 1881:vi–vii, 1882:221, 263, 112, 126, 338, 314, 102, 224, 174, 368, 344, cf. 1868. See also Stocking 1987b:309–10.
45 WRSP: Journal 5/26/76; Black & Chrystal 1912:333—W. R. Smith 1880a.
46 W. R. Smith 1885:xix; Tylor 1888:256. See also Stocking 1987b:122, 197–208, 296.
47 W. R. Smith 1885:xix–xx—Fustel de Coulanges 1864.
48 W. R. Smith 1885:3–4. See also A. Kuper 1982.
49 W. R. Smith 1885:32, 33, 36, 62, 47, 85, 142, 205–6.
50 Ibid. 212, 215—McLennan 1865.
51 W. R. Smith 1885:217–18, 219.
52 Ibid. 252–53, 266, 270, 278—McLennan 1865.
53 W. R. Smith 1885:259, 266—1889.
54 W. R. Smith 1881:3–4; WRSP: McLennan to Gibson, 5/11/77, 7/1/79, 7/2/80; W. R. Smith 1889:v.
55 W. R. Smith 1889:26, vii. See also Black & Chrystal 1912:511–12, 525, 535.
56 W. R. Smith 1889; 439, 255, 260, 254, 258, 255, 28–29.
57 Ibid. 1—Rousseau 1755.
58 W. R. Smith 1889:273–74, 287, 90, 84, 121, 125, 122–24, 151, 165, 213–14—Frazer 1888. See also Ackerman 1987:62–63.
59 W. R. Smith 1889:312–13, 320; Smith in Beidelman 1974b:57; cf. W. R. Smith 1889:393.
60 W. R. Smith 1889:354, 367, 391.
61 Ibid. 395–96, 440, 1.
62 Tylor 1871:II, 448, 461, 480—1888:268. See also Evans-Pritchard 1933; Parsons 1937.
63 W. R. Smith 1889:85–86, 287, 154, 164, 449, 399, 391—Lang 1884. See also Stocking 1987b:190–97.
64 W. R. Smith 1889:59, 32, 35, 73–74, 2, 28—Lang 1884:17, 27; Tylor 1871:I, 1. See also Stocking 1987b:302–4, 310–11.

65 See Turner 1981:83, 121–23; 1974; Ackerman 1972:225–28, 1991; De Cocq 1968; Duff-Cooper 1986; R. A. Jones 1984.
66 See R. Needham 1974; De Cocq 1968:107; Marett 1929b; Brandiwie 1983.
67 Freud 1913:132–39, 142. See also Hughes 1958; Wallace 1983.
68 Durkheim in R. A. Jones 1981:185—Hubert & Mauss 1898:4–7; Evans-Pritchard 1965:51–53, 1981:69–81; Leach 1985:238–42. See also Beidelman 1974b.

3. From the Armchair to the Field: The Darwinian Zoologist as Ethnographer

1 BAAS 1874:iv; Tylor 1888:262, 258, 269—1884, 1885a. See also Hinsley 1981; Mark 1976.
2 BAAS 1887:173–74, 181–82. See also Gruber 1967.
3 BAAS 1887:174—E. F. Wilson 1887:183–84. See also Nock 1988; Stocking 1968b:133–60, ed., 1974c; Urry 1984a, 1993.
4 Tylor in Marett 1941:167—J. L. Myres in Grey et al. 1953:6. See also Van Keuren 1982; Kuklick 1991; Urry 1993; Stocking 1987b:262–69.
5 See Geison 1978.
6 WBSP: Spencer to H. Goulty 3/5/83, 11/25/83. See also Mulvaney & Calaby 1985:59, et passim.
7 See Mulvaney & Calaby 1985:52; Chapman 1985:35, 37.
8 EBTP: Spencer to Tylor 5/23/89; Horn in W. B. Spencer, ed., 1896:I, ix; WBSP: Howitt to Spencer 2/4/95.
9 WBSP: Gillen to Spencer 5/1/96, 9/22/95, 3/9/95, 1/31/96—Stirling 1896; Gillen 1896. See also Mulvaney & Calaby 1985:131.
10 WBSP: Gillen to Spencer 11/7/95, 12/20/95, 1/31/96, 6/5/96, 7/14/96.
11 WBSP: Gillen to Spencer 7/14/96, 8/n.d./96, 10/8/96, 2/23/97—Spencer & Gillen 1912:II, 268.
12 WBSP: Gillen to Spencer 2/9/97, 9/8/94; Spencer & Gillen 1899:135, 72; WBSP: Gillen to Spencer 7/30/97. See also Mulvaney & Calaby 1985:174.
13 WBSP: Gillen to Spencer 3/23/97, 2/9/97, 6/18/97. See also Mulvany & Calaby 1985:174.
14 WBSP: Gillen to Spencer 11/15/99, 4/3/98, 6/5/96, 2/18/01, 7/30/97, 10/22/97, 9/28/99.
15 Spencer & Gillen 1899:157, 456, 272, 158, 471, 470, 324, 169, 455, 137.
16 WBSP: Gillen to Spencer 7/30/97; Spencer & Gillen 1899:11–12, 1912:I, 6–7.
17 Spencer & Gillen 1899:118.
18 WBSP: Gillen to Spencer 9/10/97—Spencer & Gillen 1904, 1912; W. B. Spencer 1928; Marett & Penniman, eds., 1931. See also Mulvaney & Calaby 1985:408, 240–41, 360–61.
19 Marett in Marett & Penniman, eds., 1931:30; Malinowski 1913c; Spencer & Gillen 1899:265.
20 Spencer & Gillen 1899:56–57.
21 Ibid. 126.

22 Durkheim 1912:475, 472. See also R. A. Jones 1986; Lukes 1973.
23 Spencer & Gillen 1899:vi, 34–36, 121.
24 Foster in Quiggin 1942:33.
25 See Quiggin 1942; Geison 1978.
26 Haddon in Quiggin 1942:57, 60, 72.
27 Ibid. 80.
28 Haddon, ed., 1935:xi, 1901a:vii—Frazer 1887a. See also Kuklick n.d.; Bolger 1977.
29 ACHP: Haddon diary 1888.
30 ACHP: Haddon diary 1888; Haddon 1890. See also Beckett 1987.
31 Haddon in Stocking 1993e:8; ACHP: Haddon diary 1888; Haddon 1890:387; Haddon in BAAS 1895:16–17.
32 Haddon in Stocking 1993e:3–4; ACHP: undated fragment.
33 Haddon in Stocking 1993e:13–14. See also J. M. MacKenzie 1984:122–27.
34 ACHP: Huxley to Haddon 1/1/92.
35 Huxley in Quiggin 1942:93–94.
36 RAIA: Council minutes 3/21/93, 5/9/93. See also Stocking 1987b:261–62.
37 Haddon 1898:xxii; Hartland 1895a:513—Haddon & Browne 1893. See also Urry 1984b:83–101.
38 Haddon 1898:v.
39 ACHP: Haddon diary 1888.
40 ACHP: Haddon to Ellis 5/14/90; Haddon 1895:3, 74—Ellis 1939:180–82. See also Kuklick n.d.
41 Haddon 1895:319. See also Urry 1993:66–73; Stocking 1987b.
42 Haddon 1895:150, 12, 248, 180, 327, 332–33—Boas 1903, 1896. See also Stocking 1974b.
43 ACHP: Haddon to Geddes 1/4/97—Macalister 1896. See also Quiggin 1942: 110; Meller 1973; Sillitoe 1977; Urry 1993:75.
44 ACHP: Codrington to Haddon 4/9/90, Ray to Haddon 6/6/97—Haddon & Ray 1893.
45 Haddon 1895:300–305, 333—C. S. Myers 1923. See also Slobodin 1978; Langham 1981; Hearnshaw 1964.
46 ACHP: Rivers to Haddon 11/25/97—McDougall to Haddon 5/26/97, 12/5/97, Seligman to Haddon 10/26/97, 10/28/97, 11/14/97, Wilkin to Haddon 1/27/98; C. S. Myers 1936:216.
47 ACHP: Haddon to Hose, draft n.d., Haddon, receipts, expenditures.
48 Haddon 1901a:9–10, xiii–iv, et passim—ACHP: Haddon diary 1898; CSMF: diary 1898; CSMD. See also Sillitoe 1977: table 1.
49 Haddon 1901a:294, 396, 330—Hose 1927.
50 Evans-Pritchard 1950a:73; Radcliffe-Brown 1958b:153; ACHP: Myers to Haddon 1/10/99—ACHP and BMLP, passim. See also Sillitoe 1977; Jorion 1977.
51 Rivers 1908b:65, 1900:74–75; Rivers in Haddon 1901a:124–25; Rivers 1904: 126—G. W. Marshall 1866; FGP: Rivers to Galton 1/4/97; Rivers 1899. See also Schneider 1968, 1984; Howard 1981; Pilling 1952.
52 Rivers 1910:10, 2, 1900:82, 1910:96.
53 ACHP: Brown to Haddon 2/8/13—Rivers 1912a, 1913a.

54 Haddon 1901a:209—ed., 1901b, ed., 1903c, ed., 1904, ed., 1907, ed., 1908b, ed., 1912, ed., 1935.
55 Haddon in Urry 1993:75; Haddon 1895:vi—1906.
56 Haddon 1906. See also Stocking 1979b; Kuklick 1993, n.d.; and Myres 1929, who suggests Haddon's debt to French regional geography.
57 Haddon 1903a:15, 22, 1903b:229, 1906:188, 1910:3.
58 BMPL: Seligman to Malinowski 7/1/12.
59 Haddon to Frazer 10/25/99 in Urry 1993:79–81—ACHP: Haddon to Frazer 12/30/00; Ridgeway to Haddon 1/5/99; CBAS: passim. See also Gathercole 1977; Quiggin 1942; Haddon 1923; Hayter 1939; Fortes 1953.
60 Seligman to Haddon 3/10/19; Haddon 1901a:viii—ix, 1939; C. S. Myers 1909, 1936:218—McDougall 1905, 1908, 1920, 1921, 1930; Hose & McDougall 1912.
61 CSMF: Diary 1909; Haddon 1934:3—C. G. Seligman 1910; Seligman & Seligman 1911, 1932. See also Fortes 1941; R. W. Firth 1975c.
62 See this volume, 184–208, 235–44.
63 Wheeler 1926:vii; Hocart 1922; WHRP: Hocart to Rivers 4/16/09—AMHP; Jenness & Ballantyne 1920; Jenness 1922–23; Landtman 1927; Karsten 1923, 1932; Freire-Marreco 1916; Czaplička 1914, 1916; Layard 1942. See also Swazye 1960; MacClancy 1986.
64 AMHP. See also Stocking 1983:28–32; Richards 1939; Urry 1984a; and note 63, above.
65 ACHP: Landtman to Haddon 4/4/11, 8/28/10—Landtman 1927:453–61; Malinowski 1929c.
66 Landtman 1927:ix; Malinowski 1922a.
67 BAAS 1899:87–88. See also Stocking 1993b; Urry 1993:17–41.
68 BAAS 1912:iii–iv; Myres in Urry 1993:29.
69 BAAS 1912:186; Rivers 1912a:109, 124, 119.
70 Rivers 1912a:110–11, 112.
71 Ibid. 113, 123, 116, 125.
72 Rivers 1913a:5–6, 13, 10–11, 9–10, 7.
73 Ibid. 7, 5.

4. The Frazerian Moment: Evolutionary Anthropology in Disarray

1 Malinowski 1926b—Frazer 1910; Rivers 1911.
2 See Stocking 1968b:133–233, ed., 1974c; Barkan 1992; this volume, 243 & 381–82.
3 Haddon 1895, 1909c, 1911c. See also Langham 1981; Slobodin 1978; Leach 1984.
4 James to Miss Frances R. Morse 12/25/00 in H. James, ed., 1926:II, 138–40; Ackerman 1987:48—William James 1890, 1896, 1902. See also G. E. Myers 1986; Soffer 1978:135–161.
5 Frazer 1935:132; Downie 1970:18, 20, 21; Frazer in Ackerman 1987:188–89. See also Fraser 1990a:209–12; Ackerman 1987:5, 8–9; Downie 1940.

6 Frazer 1935:122–24. See also Ackerman 1987:13–16.
7 Frazer 1930:10, 66–67; Lilly Frazer in Ackerman 1987:144; Jackson 1881. See also Ackerman 1987:25–27; Fraser 1990a:34–38.
8 JGFP: Notebook on philosophy, 4/6/80—Ward 1885. See also Ackerman 1887:40–44; Fraser 1990a.
9 Frazer 1898. See also Ackerman 1987:53–58, passim; Fraser 1990a:39–43.
10 Frazer 1885:64, 70, 64, 76—Tylor 1871. See also Fraser 1990a:45.
11 Frazer 1886:3 (n. 3).
12 Frazer 1886:3, 41.
13 Galton ibid. 48, 49; Tylor ibid. 48; Frazer ibid. 50.
14 Frazer in Ackerman 1987:60–62. See also Ackerman 1987:172.
15 Smith in Ackerman 1987:63—Frazer 1887b, 1888.
16 Frazer 1888:86, 1910:I, viii.
17 Frazer 1887b:3–4.
18 Ibid. 31, 36, 37.
19 Ibid. 71, 78.
20 Ibid. 81, 82, 87.
21 See R. A. Jones 1984.
22 Frazer in Ackerman 1987:87–91.
23 Ibid. 88–89.
24 Ibid. 89–91—W. R. Smith 1889.
25 Frazer to Jackson 10/27/87 in Fraser 1990a:77; Frazer 1890:I, vii; Strabo in Fraser 1990a:1–2; Frazer:1890:I, 1—W. R. Smith 1887; Frazer 1885, 1886, 1887a. See also Fraser 1990a:1–6, 50–52, 75–79; cf. Ackerman 1987:93.
26 MCMA: 11/8/89. See also C. L. Morgan 1944:168–73.
27 Frazer 1890:I, viii, ix, x—Lang 1884:103, 1887. See also Dorson 1968a:202–57.
28 Frazer 1890:I, 3–4. See also Fraser 1990a:54; Geertz 1973.
29 Frazer 1890:I, 8–9; 1900:I, 9–62.
30 MCMA: Frazer to Macmillan 8/19/99; Frazer 1900:I, 9–10, 49, 49n, 62, 62n—Hartland 1895b:II, 55–116. See also Fraser 1990a:118–35; Ackerman 1987:164–69.
31 Frazer 1890:II, 338–39; 1900:III, 416n. See also Fraser 1990a:70–85; Hyman 1966:212–32.
32 Spencer to Frazer 7/12/97, Frazer to Spencer 9/15/98 in Marett & Penniman, eds., 1932:4–11, 24–29, esp. 29—Frazer 1901:201.
33 Frazer to Spencer 9/15/98 in Marett & Penniman, eds., 1932:4–11.
34 Spencer to Frazer 10/20/98, Frazer to Spencer 11/28/98 in Marett & Penniman, eds., 1932:31–37, 37–42, esp. 41—Frazer 1899.
35 Frazer 1910:IV, 57, 61–62.
36 Ibid. IV, 61–65, 69—Frazer 1905b:158–62.
37 JGFP: Tylor to Frazer 9/15/98; MCMA: Frazer to Macmillan 9/13/98—Tylor 1898.
38 Frazer 1888:86–87—Marett 1919:170.
39 Tylor 1871:II, 453; Frazer 1909b:154–55, 1908:170, 171. See also Hyman 1966:193–211; Hynes 1968; Dangerfield 1935; Stocking 1987b:186–237.
40 Marett 1919:173—MCMA: passim; Frazer 1938. See also Ackerman 1987:302; Filby 1958.

41 Frazer 1911b:I, x, 1913:I, xi, 1911b:I, viii. See also Marett 1919:173; Ackerman 1987:251–56; Hyman 1966; Manganaro 1992:18–67.
42 Marett 1919:173, 178; Downie 1970:21; Marett 1919:173. See also Vickery 1973:71; Beard 1992.
43 J. P. Bishop in Hyman 1966:253–54; Frazer 1911a:vi, viii. See also Ackerman 1987:239; Fraser 1990a:209–12, passim.
44 Ackerman 1987:257, 99. See also Beard 1992; Fraser, ed., 1990b; Vickery 1973.
45 Frazer in Evans-Pritchard 1950:72 (citing Ruth Benedict, who gave no source); Ackerman 1987:1—Marett, ed., 1908c.
46 Harrison in Ackerman 1991:93. See also Ackerman 1972; Stocking 1993c.
47 *Quarterly Review* in Ackerman 1987:329; Nutt ibid. 170, 173; Clodd ibid. 333—Tylor 1871.
48 Marett 1919:173, 176.
49 Seligman in Ackerman 1987:244–45; Frazer 1931a:9—Frazer 1905a; C. G. Seligman 1934; BMPY: Seligman to Malinowski 10/20/26; JGFP: Frazer to Roscoe, passim; Marett & Penniman, eds., 1932:22, 24; Junod 1912:I, 6. See also Hyman 1966:229–31.
50 Westermarck 1928:190—Frazer 1913:I, vi–vii.
51 Von Wright 1982:49; Westermarck 1891:4.
52 Westermarck 1927:22, 30, 35–36; Von Wright 1982:28—H. Spencer 1862. See also Stroup 1982a:25, 29–34, 1984.
53 Westermarck 1927:44, 45–46, 76. See also Hirn 1947.
54 Westermarck 1927:67–68, 1936:223—Darwin 1871; Haeckel 1868. See also Von Wright 1982:30.
55 Westermarck 1927:77–80—Darwin 1891. See also Stroup 1982a:39; Hirn 1947.
56 Wikman, ed., 1940:7; Wallace in Westermarck 1891:v–vi; Wikman, ed., 1940:9, 12.
57 Tylor 1891, 1896b:82.
58 Westermarck 1891:544, 335; Tylor 1891, 1896b:89, 93. See also Spain 1987.
59 Tylor 1891; Westermarck 1891:543, 41–43, 20, 546, 5. See also Stroup 1982a: 129–31; Stocking 1987b:145–85.
60 Westermarck 1891:2, 549–50, 1927:98–99.
61 Westermarck 1927:100; Westermarck in Stroup 1982a:131, 54—Westermarck 1927:127, 103—Darwin 1871; William James 1884. See also Von Wright 1982:35.
62 Shand 1914:13, 1, viii; Westermarck 1927:127, 101. See also Stroup 1982a:44.
63 Westermarck in Stroup 1982a:75; Westermarck 1927:145–46, 101, 194, 1926: I, v.
64 Westermarck 1927:235, 139, vi.
65 MCMA: Westermarck to Macmillan 7/21/01; Westermarck 1927:173, 158, 185, 170, 179, 239; Malinowski 1927a; K. Brown 1982:220.
66 Westermarck 1906–8:I, v; MCMA: Westermarck to Macmillan 2/15/07—Westermarck 1914, 1920, 1926, 1931, 1933.
67 Westermarck 1927:219; K. Brown 1982:222; Westermarck 1936:241, 1928: 191, 1906–8:I, 444–51, II, 607–10, 1914:370–76, 1926:I, 17, 1908. See also Stroup 1982a:126–28.

68 Westermarck 1906–8:I, 20, 4, 383, II, 81, 84, I:186ff., esp. 209.
69 Ibid. I, 73–74, II, 744, 746, II, 685, 696, Westermarck 1927:254—1931; Frazer 1900.
70 Ackerman 1987:207–14; Westermarck 1927:220, 283.
71 Galton in Abrams 1968:261; Geddes ibid. 266; Hobhouse ibid. 254. See also Halliday 1968; Caine 1963; J. P. Beveridge 1960:61, 92; Cole 1961:67–77; Abrams 1968: esp. 261, 266; Collini 1979: esp. 200; Searle 1976.
72 Westermarck 1927:197, 200–202.
73 Syllabus in Abrams 1968:111–12; Hobhouse, Wheeler, & Ginsberg 1915—EBTP: Anthropology lecture books 1885; Hobhouse 1906.
74 Branford in Abrams 1968:109–10; Branford in Halliday 1968:381; Collini 1979:1–5, 211, 249. See also Abrams 1968:130, 144; Halliday 1968:388, 394.
75 LSEA: 3/25/08—R. W. Firth 1963.
76 Durkheim & Fauconnet 1905:278–79; Durkheim in Stroup, ed., 1982b:xiii—Durkheim 1905. See also Pipping 1982.
77 W. R. Smith 1891; cf. Tylor 1891—Westermarck 1891.
78 Mauss, as reported in Dumont 1973; Marett 1941.
79 Marett 1941:61, 68, 323, 74, 81, 87, 84, 104—Lang 1884.
80 Marett 1941:115–16, 117—Tylor 1871.
81 Marett 1892:350. See also Buxton 1936a:5; Penniman 1936.
82 Marett 1941:299—1902, 1914:153–54, 163–64. See also Soffer 1978:135–61.
83 Marett 1941:146, 1914:viii, 1900:6, 3, 14–15, 28, 1914:xxxi.
84 Marett 1904:33–34, 35, 36, 37—Frazer 1900.
85 Marett 1904:37, 38–39, 41, 45.
86 Ibid. 48–49, 54, 50, 71.
87 Marett 1907:75, 77, 80, 83, 84, 97, 1941:165—1908b. See also Stocking 1974b.
88 Marett 1908b:103–4.
89 Marett 1941:163, 1908a.
90 Marett 1908a:124, 127, 129–30, 133, 135.
91 Ibid. 142, 138, 141, 143.
92 Marett in Ackerman 1987:225–28—Marett 1935; Marett & Penniman, eds., 1931, 1932.
93 Marett 1912:251, 255, 259—1941:202–7.
94 Marett 1941:272; Marett, ed., 1908c:5; Marett to Committee for Anthropology in Van Keuren 1982:237; OUCA: passim. See also Van Keuren 1982:216–40; Wallis 1957.
95 OUCA: passim; Frazer 1921:235; Evans-Pritchard 1933.
96 Marett 1927:173.
97 *London Times* 11/25/24, p. 14; Crawley 1902:I, x, xii, 1, xi—Hartland 1909. See also this volume, footnote on 28.
98 Crawley 1902:I, xii, 215, II, 260–61, et passim. See, in addition, the discussion of religion in Crawley 1907b, in which Shand and Marett also participated.
99 Lang in Baker 1980:258; Lang 1901a:206, 75.
100 Lang 1903:xi, 1. See also Duff-Cooper 1986; R. Needham 1974.
101 Lang 1903:3; J. J. Atkinson 1903:209; Lang 1903:166, 30.
102 Lang 1903:36, 57, 34–35.

103 Ibid. 100–101, 103, 129.
104 Ibid. 187–88, 68ff., 71, 76.
105 Ibid. 70, 6, 187. See, in addition, Lang 1905c, as well as his frequent short contributions to the journal *Man*.
106 Thomas 1906:63, 147.
107 Lang 1905b:xi, 1907a:209.
108 Lang 1898:45—Westermarck in Wheeler 1910:v–vi; Malinowski 1913c.
109 Van Gennep 1920; Frazer 1910.
110 Lévi-Strauss 1962:1—Goldenweiser 1910; Lubbock 1911.
111 Marett 1927:178—Clodd 1920; Durkheim 1912; Freud 1913; Hartland 1917, 1921, 1924.

5. The Revival of Diffusionist Ethnology: Rivers and the Heliolithic School

1 Rivers 1911:125—BAAS 1911.
2 Rivers 1911:120–22.
3 Ibid. 122, 124–25. See also W. D. Smith 1991.
4 Rivers 1911:123—Ratzel 1882. See also Stocking 1992c:327–49, 1973a.
5 Boas to Tylor 3/6/89 in Stocking, ed., 1974c:134. See also Stocking 1987b.
6 Tylor 1865:5, 1910—1896a.
7 Keane 1895:224.
8 Gomme 1892:vi, 15, 1896:627—Taylor 1890; Müller 1885, 1892; Boas 1896; cf. Marett 1917:72ff. See also De Caro 1982.
9 Haddon, ed., 1903c:v–vi; Mathew 1899:22—C. G. Seligman 1910; Seligman & Seligman 1932; Skeat & Blagden 1906:I, 19. See also Gulick 1988; this volume, 315.
10 G. E. Smith in Rivers 1926:x–xi—Waitz 1863. See also Slobodin 1978:78–79.
11 See Slobodin 1978:10–12; R. M. Young 1970:197–223.
12 McDougall 1903:195; Kuklick 1991:143.
13 Rivers 1901a:48–49, 70, 1901c:44–45, 47, 49, 57, 1901d:244.
14 Boas in Stocking, ed., 1974c:76; Rivers 1901a:93, 1901c:49, 57, 1905:391–96. Cf. Mandelbaum 1980:293. See also Hardin 1988:156–69.
15 Rivers 1908a:449. See also Slobodin 1978:31–35; Langham 1981:56–64.
16 Cf. Langham 1981:62.
17 Rivers 1900:78, 1904:139—L. H. Morgan 1871:144; Rivers 1907a.
18 Rivers 1906:v.
19 Ibid. 7–9. See also Mandelbaum 1980:295–96.
20 Crawley 1907a:462; Leach 1968:527; Rivers in A. Kuper 1988:153; Rivers 1906:v. See also Mandelbaum 1980:280–82, 194–95; Rooksby 1971:120; Emeneau 1941.
21 McLennan 1865:64, 71; Rivers 1906:2—W. E. Marshall 1873:225.
22 Rivers 1906:561, 546–47, 520.
23 Ibid. 548, 493, 541.
24 Ibid. 3, 329, 14, 356, 427.
25 Ibid. 453, 454, 455, 459, 4—529–32, 549.

26 Ibid. 442; Slobodin 1978:103; Rivers 1906:717.
27 Rivers 1907b:612, 617, 624—Boas 1896.
28 Fortes 1969:3–5.
29 L. H. Morgan 1871:10.
30 Ibid. 480, L. H. Morgan 1877:393; Rivers 1914b:95, 1907a. See also Langham 1981:90.
31 Rivers 1907a:176.
32 Ibid. 183, 189.
33 Ibid. 190, 192, Rivers 1901. See also Schneider 1968:12.
34 Kroeber 1909:175, 178.
35 Ibid. 180–81.
36 Rivers 1914b.
37 Ibid. 45, 47–48.
38 Ibid. 49, 53.
39 Ibid. 55, 57, 58, 61.
40 Ibid. 61–62, 63, 71. See also Slobodin 1978:144.
41 Rivers 1914b:81, 82, 88, 83, 87.
42 R. W. Firth 1968:22; Langham 1981:52, 340. See also Slobodin 1978:110; Service 1985:13–110.
43 L. White in Fortes 1969:9; Fortes 1969:23, 24; Rivers 1914b:95, 1910:9, 1914b:95, 1914c:I, 3–4. See also Schneider 1968, 1984.
44 See Trautman 1987; Stocking 1974a; Service 1985; Langham 1981:118–39.
45 Haddon 1908a; Rivers 1914c:I, 2, 3—Hocart 1922.
46 Rivers 1911:125–26.
47 Ibid. 126–27.
48 Ibid. 130.
49 See Stocking 1968b, 1989.
50 Rivers 1914c:II, 7; Rivers, as quoted in C. S. Myers 1923:165—Kroeber 1952:22–23, 47, 172–73—McDougall 1905, 1908; C. S. Myers 1909. See also Aberle 1960; Karpf 1932; Pear 1960; A. Kuper 1990; Hearnshaw 1964; Stocking 1968b.
51 Rivers 1913b:303.
52 Rivers 1914c:II, 3. See also Stocking 1976.
53 Rivers 1911:132, 134–35, 137.
54 Rivers 1912b, 1913b, 1913c.
55 Rivers 1914c:I, vi, II, 1, I, 20, et passim.
56 Ibid. I, 310, 299–303; cf. R. W. Firth 1936:xxviii.
57 Rivers 1914c:II, 121, 186–87, 192.
58 Ibid. II, 574, 205, 207, 214, 210.
59 Ibid. II, 579–80, 290, 407, 557, 581.
60 Ibid. II, 5, 8, 405, 272.
61 Ibid. II, 209, I, 182, II, 412–13.
62 Ibid. II, 430 (see also 61), 586, 589, 591.
63 Ibid. II, 591, 595. Rivers goes unmentioned in Adams, Van Gerven, & Levy 1978, and in Rouse 1986; cf., however, Brunton 1989, which takes Rivers' kava hypothesis very seriously.
64 Tylor 1910:119; Prichard in Stocking 1973a:lxii–lxiii; Prichard 1813:558;

Bryant in Stocking 1973a:xlii–xliii—Prichard 1819. See also Iversen 1961; Feldman & Richardson, eds., 1972:241–48.

65 Tylor 1871; McLennan 1869. See also Bernal 1987; Wortham 1971; Stocking 1987b; Van Riper 1993.

66 See Daniel 1950:174–77; Bratton 1968:80; Fagan 1975:357; Welch 1988; Drower 1985.

67 G. E. Smith 1938:114; Dawson, ed., 1938:114, 28, 18. See also Welch 1988: 145–46; Zuckerman, ed., 1973.

68 G. E. Smith 1927:141, 64. See also Zuckerman, ed., 1973:12, 18; Dart in Elkin & Macintosh, eds., 1974:29; F. Spencer 1990:172–73; Weiner in Zuckerman, ed., 1973:23–26; Keith 1950:326, 398.

69 G. E. Smith in Rivers 1923b:126n—G. E. Smith 1911. See also Dawson, ed., 1938:44.

70 G. E. Smith 1912:119, 1911:5, 8–9, 10–11.

71 G. E. Smith 1911:83, 64, 161ff., 1923:vi—Sergi 1901. See also Swan 1977.

72 G. E. Smith in Dawson, ed., 1938:52, 53.

73 W. J. Perry 1918:2; Dawson, ed., 1938:54; D. Watson in Dawson, ed., 1938:65; G. E. Smith 1915:25–28—Rivers 1915b. See also Dawson, ed., 1938:62; Langham 1981:351.

74 G. E. Smith 1915:1, 3, 7, 37, 69, 132–34, 24, 6, 7, v.

75 Ibid. 108, 12, 16; Rivers 1915b:167, 172, 1923b:122, 129, 1915a; G. E. Smith 1924.

76 JWPM; W. J. Perry 1918:3, 181, ix—Rivers 1914c:II, 577; Frazer 1900.

77 G. E. Smith 1919:1, vii–viii, 24, 113.

78 Ibid. 233–34, 76, 233—W. J. Perry 1923b.

79 W. J. Perry 1923b:vi–vii, 1923a.

80 W. J. Perry 1923a:127–28.

81 Ibid. 215, 406, 428, 414, 81, 96, 461, 501.

82 Ibid. 413, 467—Frazer 1900, 1910.

83 Hyman 1966:193; W. J. Perry 1923a:472, 466.

84 Ibid. 491.

85 Ibid. 154, 493, 492, 162, 488, 493, 495—W. J. Perry 1924; Rivers 1923b:81–95.

86 W. J. Perry 1923a. See also Massingham 1941:54–66; Elkin 1974a, 1974b; Langham 1981:160–99.

87 G. E. Smith 1923:201–2; Haddon 1924:183, 1925:53—1911c, 1920. See also Langham 1981:162.

88 Marett 1924a:108–9.

89 W. J. Perry 1923a:413, 103, 473—1923b.

90 C. G. Seligman 1913:637, 1927, 1934:60. See also Lyons 1983; Fortes 1941.

91 W. J. Perry 1935; G. E. Smith 1933:124, 179, 181—W. J. Perry 1923a. Cf. Stocking 1987b for a different interpretation of Tylor's religious and anthropological opinions. See also JWPM.

92 Fortes 1937; G. E. Smith 1922. Cf., however, the early 1970s attempt by C. E. Joel to revive heliolithic diffusion in the quarterly *New Diffusionist*.

93 Evans-Pritchard in R. Needham 1970:liii; Fortes, Leach in Daniel 1973:427, 432. See also Langham 1981:311–12; R. Needham 1970.

94 Hocart 1936:4. See also R. Needham 1970.

95 Hocart in Langham 1981:125, 340; AMHP: obituaries, reel 9.
96 AMHP: passim; personal communication from M. Sahlins.
97 Hocart 1912a:85, 1912b:267–68.
98 Hocart 1915a:115, 116, 120, 121, 124, 125.
99 Ibid. 125–26, 129–30.
100 Ibid. 134, 137.
101 Hocart 1915b:91–92—1916, 1918.
102 See R. Needham 1970:xix–xx; Malalgoda 1980; Morrison 1983a.
103 Copy of Hocart's preface provided by M. Sahlins. See also Stocking 1977b.
104 Hocart 1925b, 1925a—1926. See also Malalgoda 1980.
105 Hocart 1927:14, vi.
106 Ibid. v–vi, 32, 207, 201. See also Ackerman 1991.
107 Hocart 1927:v, 70, 99.
108 Ibid. 236, 134, 152.
109 Ibid. 5–6, 33, 55, 117, 200, 201, Hocart 1954:7. Cf. R. Needham 1970.
110 Hocart 1927:2, 1950:vi, 1929:105—1933, 1935.
111 Hocart 1950, 1952, 1954. See also R. Needham 1970.
112 Rivers 1911; A. Bennett 1922. See also Langham 1981:62–63.
113 See this volume, 268, 277–79, 304.
114 Hocart 1925b—Leach, Fortes in Daniel 1973:427–36; W. J. Perry 1935. See also Barkan 1992:48–49.
115 B. Z. Seligman 1925:58.
116 Stocking 1989:356–57.
117 Ibid., Stocking 1976.
118 Stocking 1989.
119 Ibid., Stocking 1987b, 1993b.
120 Malinowski 1926b:131.

6. From Fieldwork to Functionalism: Malinowski and the Emergence of British Social Anthropology

1 Dawson, ed., 1932:ix–xv; Frazer 1921—Malinowski 1922a. See also Ackerman 1987:258, 284, 288.
2 Frazer in Malinowski 1922a:viii–ix.
3 Malinowski to Frazer 10/25/17 in Ackerman 1987:267. See also Hyman 1966:201, 225.
4 Malinowski 1926d:93–94; JGFP: Malinowski to Frazer 5/25/23—Malinowski 1910.
5 Malinowski 1926d:146–47; Jarvie 1964:43–44; Malinowski 1967:289; Durkheim in Downie 1970:79; Malinowski 1923b:271; Frazer in Downie 1970:21—Frazer 1909b. See also Leach 1961, 1966.
6 Malinowski 1923b:274; ACHP: Malinowski to Haddon 5/25/16. See also R. J. Thornton 1992a, 1992b; Thornton & Skalnik, eds., 1993b.
7 Rivers 1912c:36–37, 42–43, 45—1923a, 1923b; Haddon & Bartlett 1922; Lévy-Bruhl 1910.
8 Rivers 1913b:303, 1916b:5, 4, 16, 7.
9 Rivers 1916b:18–19—1917b; Wallas 1908.

10 Pear 1960:231—Rivers 1914a; Smith & Pear 1917. See also Slobodin 1978:53; MacClancy 1986:52; Stone 1985.
11 Pear 1960:229, 231, 232.
12 Slobodin 1978:59; Rivers 1918:440. See also Showalter 1987.
13 Showalter 1987:67; Rivers 1923a:167, 172, 168.
14 Rivers 1917b:163, 165, 166, 167. See also Pulman 1986.
15 Head 1924:xlv; Rivers 1920a:v, 156, 119, 158—C. S. Myers 1923.
16 Rivers 1923a:5, 7, 11–12, 137–38, 144, 49, 126, 177, 153, 122, 32.
17 Rivers 1923a:128–33—1917a.
18 Rivers 1923a:85, 1917a:389, 406, 407–8, 1923a:94–95, 40–44—Trotter 1920.
19 Rivers 1923a:134, ed., 1922e:94–95—1920b, 1921, 1922d.
20 Rivers 1921:12, 20, 22.
21 Rivers 1922d:17, 19, 31–32.
22 Rivers 1919, 1922c.
23 Pear 1960:235. See also Hearnshaw 1964; Soffer 1978; Stocking 1986b.
24 C. G. Seligman 1924:13; Marett 1924b; RAIA: council minutes 2/19/24. See also Pulman 1989.
25 Kubica 1988:88–90; Thornton & Skalnik 1993a:9–16. See also Brooks 1985; F. Gross 1986; Jerschina 1988; Janik & Toulmin 1973; Średniawa 1981; Schorske 1980; Symmons 1958; Wayne 1985.
26 Mach 1895:15–16, 1905:120, 180. See also Stocking 1986a:31.
27 Malinowski 1908a:89; Mach 1905:96, 105, 120, 206, 210; Malinowski in Stocking 1986a:17. See also Gellner 1988; Paluch 1981; Flis 1988; Symmons 1959.
28 A. Micińska in Thornton & Skalnik, eds., 1993b:270 n. 13; Malinowski 1967:34—1904; Witkiewicz 1910. See also Thornton & Skalnik, eds., 1993a; Gerould 1981.
29 Malinowski 1908a:112. In the last phrase, I have used the translation of E. Martinek: "relation" instead of "attitude" (Malinowski 1908b:56–57).
30 Malinowski in Ellen et al., eds., 1988:203, 199, 204—Malinowski 1911; Frazer 1909b. See also Wayne 1985:532.
31 Malinowski 1912:209, 210, 221—1910, 1911–13; Frazer 1909b.
32 Malinowski 1913c:168, 19—Langlois & Seignobos 1898.
33 Malinowski 1913c:300, vi, 19, 214, 182.
34 Ibid. 308–9, 233.
35 Malinowski 1913a:285, 286; BMPY: Series II, box 27, folder 245—Malinowski 1915b; Durkheim 1912.
36 Malinowski 1915b, as translated in Symmons 1960:5—Malinowski 1914.
37 BMPL: Malinowski to Seligman 2/22/12; ACHP: Malinowski to Haddon 11/12/11; C. G. Seligman 1910:2, 24–25. See also Mulvaney 1989; R. W. Firth 1975c.
38 Malinowski 1967:8, 17; BMPL: Malinowski to Seligman 10/11/14—F. E. Williams, ed., 1939. See also West 1968:211–18.
39 Malinowski 1967:13, 25, 37, 40.
40 Ibid. 16, 31, 25, 41, 37—Saville 1912.
41 Malinowski 1915a:109—BAAS 1912. See also Payne 1981; K. MacKenzie 1974.

42 Malinowski 1967:49, 54–55, 62, 1915a:109, 273–75.
43 Malinowski 1915a:300, 1967:40, 73, 69, 1915a:282; Conrad 1902.
44 Malinowski 1967:13, 64; Malinowski in M. W. Young 1988a:19–20; Hunt in Laracy 1976:266—Malinowski 1915a: passim; BAAS 1912. See also Rowley 1958:287–91.
45 See Laracy 1976:265; Wayne 1985.
46 Malinowski in M. W. Young 1984:13, 15–17; Austen 1945:57; M. W. Young 1984:16. See also Julius 1960:5.
47 Rivers 1913a:7. See also Rodman & Cooper, eds., 1983.
48 Malinowski 1916:183; BMPL: Malinowski to Seligman 7/30/15, 9/24/15, 10/19/15; Malinowski 1967:259—C. G. Seligman 1910:664–65. See also Weiner 1976:33–34.
49 Leach 1965:viii–ix. See also Evans-Pritchard 1950a:74. Cf. Richards 1939b; Kaberry 1957; Urry 1984a:49.
50 Malinowski 1922a:1–25, 1967: passim.
51 Malinowski 1935a:I, 453, 325; WHRP: Malinowski to Rivers 10/15/15—Malinowski 1916.
52 Malinowski 1916:154, 271.
53 Jarvie 1964:44; Leach 1957:120; Malinowski 1916:236, 238—167, 208, 246, 264, 267. See also Panoff 1972:43–45; Leach 1967; Spiro 1982.
54 BMPY: Hancock to Malinowski 8/29/18—Malinowski 1935a:I, 452–82; ACHP: passim; WHRP: passim; BMPL: passim. See also Weiner 1976:xv–xvii, 8–11; Stocking 1977a.
55 Malinowski 1916:273–74, 241, 245, 252–53, 1926c:121. Cf. 1922a:24.
56 BMPY: Stirling to Malinowski 4/1/16, Malinowski to Lady Stirling n.d. See also Wayne 1985:333–34.
57 ACHP: Malinowski to Haddon 5/25/16; M. W. Young 1984:21–22; JGFP: Malinowski to Frazer 10/25/17.
58 Wax 1978:5, 8; Malinowski 1967:152, 1929d:32–33, 1935a:I, 41, 1929d:61. See also Weiner 1976; Fardon 1990a.
59 Malinowski 1967:291 (cf. 1935a:I, 181–87), 1967:276, 1935a:I, 86. See also Wax 1978:12; Malinowski 1967:276, 1922a:479.
60 Malinowski 1929d:282–83, 1967:234, 1922a:8 (cf. M. W. Young, ed., 1979:14–15), 1929d:187; R. Black 1957:279; Hogbin 1946; Malinowski 1967:157, 1922a:244, 1929d:373, et passim. Cf. Forge 1967; Nelson 1969.
61 Malinowski 1967:235, 140, 279, 250. See also K. MacKenzie 1974.
62 Hsu 1979:521; this volume, 35, 92–93, 102. See also Leach 1980; Rapport 1990; Stocking 1983:49.
63 Malinowski 1967:238, 154, 3, 103. See also Stocking 1968a, 1983:22–28, 1990.
64 Malinowski 1967:133, 68, 105, 110, 261, 159, 192, 202; BMPY: Khuner to Malinowski 8/17/18. See also Wayne 1985; Tuzin 1994.
65 EMP: Mayo to his wife [Dorothea] 3/21/16, Mayo to Dorothea Mayo 10/19/19; BMPY: Mayo to Malinowski 11/23/18; Malinowski 1967:218, 174, 253.
66 Malinowski 1967:265, 274, 279, 283, 288; BMPY: Malinowski to Stirling 6/12/18, Malinowski to Lady Stirling n.d., Malinowski to Seligman 6/21/18. See also Wayne 1985:534.
67 Malinowski 1967:192, 295, 291, 293, 298, 291, 297.

68 Ibid. 113–14, 256, 186.
69 Ibid. 273.
70 Ibid. 119, 181, 294, Malinowski 1925c:81.
71 Malinowski 1967:119—1912, 1927b. See also Stocking 1986a:26–27, 1991a: 253–54.
72 Malinowski 1967:255, 267, 1922b:214—Rivers, ed., 1922e.
73 Malinowski 1925a:205.
74 Malinowski 1967:280, 195, 230, 161, 286—1922a:232.
75 Malinowski 1967:155; Malinowski in R. W. Firth 1957a:6; BMPY: Malinowski to B. Seligman 6/12/18. See also Langham 1981:171–77; Kirschner 1968; Stocking, ed., 1991b.
76 Wayne 1985:535; Weickhardt 1989:105; Malinowski 1967:289; JGFP: Malinowski to Frazer 5/8/21. See also Strenski 1982.
77 Malinowski 1922a:3–4; BMPL: "Method" n.d. See also Clifford 1983.
78 Malinowski 1922a:2–25.
79 Ibid. 6, 13. See also Boon 1983; Clifford 1983; Payne 1981; Strenski 1982; R. J. Thornton 1985. Cf. Dauber 1995; Stocking 1995.
80 Malinowski 1922a:35, 4, 517, et passim; ACHP: Malinowski to Haddon 11/25/21. See also Hyman 1966:201, 225.
81 Malinowski 1922a:146, 289. See also Geertz 1988:73; Payne 1981:427; Burton 1988.
82 Malinowski 1922a:237, 376, 6, 409, 1967:242 (cf. 1922a:16), 1967:216.
83 Malinowski 1922a:295, 397, 60. See also Payne 1981:421, et passim; Strathern 1987:113–18; Geertz 1968.
84 Payne 1981:421.
85 Malinowski 1922a:34, 16, 481. See also Sontag 1966.
86 BMPL: "Method" n.d.; Malinowski 1935a:I, 452–82.
87 Malinowski 1926d:139–40, 1922a:6; 1926d:126, 101, 108, 107. See also Westermarck 1927:158; Panoff 1972:54.
88 ACHP: Malinowski to Haddon 10/10/22; Haddon 1922; BMPL: Seligman to Malinowski 8/5/31; LSEA: Mair to Seligman 11/8/23. See also R. W. Firth 1957a.
89 Malinowski in R. W. Firth 1963:4; BMPL: Seligman to Malinowski 8/30/21; LSEA: W. Beveridge to Registrar 1/12/23.
90 JGFP: Malinowski to Frazer 5/25/23. See also Wayne 1993.
91 JGFP: Malinowski to Frazer 5/25/23; Malinowski 1922a:513, 516–17; Mauss 1925. See also R. W. Firth, ed., 1957b:220–24; Parsons 1957.
92 Malinowski 1935a:I, xix, 1924b, 1926b:133—W. J. Perry 1923a.
93 BMPY: Series II, box 27, folder 256.
94 BMPY: Seligman to Malinowski 2/12/18 (see also B. Seligman to Malinowski 8/19/18), Malinowski to Seligman 1/21/19—Malinowski 1927b:6.
95 BMPY: Series II, box 27, folder 239. See also Pulman 1989.
96 BMPL: "Sociol. Excerpts"; Malinowski 1921b:108; BMPL: "Sociol. Excerpts," "Gen. Idea of Ksp. Book"; Malinowski 1923a:116. See also BMPY: Series II, box 26, folders 221, 258; Malinowski 1921b, 1924a.
97 *Psyche* 1921(2):97—Rivers 1922d. See also E. Jones 1959:230.
98 BMPY: W. Stallybrass to Malinowski 7/25/22; BMSC: notation in copy of

Freud 1922a:346; BMPY: Series I, box 10, folder 714; Series II, box 26, folder 217—Seligman to Malinowski 1/6/23; BMPL: O. Rank to Malinowski 2/5/34; Freud 1922b, 1913.

99 Malinowski 1923d:128.

100 Malinowski 1923a:115–16—Freud 1913.

101 ACHP: Clodd to Haddon 9/19/24, 10/22/24; Malinowski 1924c:296, 294–95, 300–301, 327—E. Jones 1924b; C. G. Seligman 1924, 1932; Flugel 1921.

102 Malinowski 1924c:297, 327–28, 329–30, 331—1925a.

103 E. Jones 1924a:169–70—Rank 1924. See also Karpf 1953:88.

104 Malinowski 1927b:147—Kroeber 1920b; Freud 1913.

105 Malinowski 1927b:173, 216–17, 210—1922c, 1924a.

106 Malinowski 1927b:195, 221, 222, 232.

107 Malinowski 1927b:155–57, 207–9; BMPY: Series II, box 26, folder 218; Malinowski 1944:22–23, 133. See also Lasswell 1931; Wallace 1983:138–40; Spiro 1982; Stocking 1986a; MacClancy 1986.

108 BMPL: passim.

109 BMPY: [Gardiner] to Malinowski 1/18/18; Malinowski 1923c:299, 308, 309, 315, 322, 313, 315, 328—1922a:24, 1921a, 1967:267; A. H. Gardiner 1919; Ogden & Richards 1923. See also J. R. Firth 1957.

110 Malinowski 1935a:II, 58, 1923b:272.

111 BMPY: Needham to Malinowski 8/17/24; A. J. Balfour in J. Needham, ed., 1925:5.

112 Malinowski 1925c:21, 35–36.

113 Ibid. 38, 39–40, 42, 45, 51, 57–65—Malinowski 1922b.

114 Malinowski 1925c:65, 74, 75, 77, 80, 83.

115 Ibid. 82.

116 Malinowski 1926c; Hartland 1924; Rivers 1924.

117 Malinowski 1926c:3, 11, 23, 25, 29–30, 64.

118 Ibid. 74, 76, 78, 80, 101, 114, 121, 123, 125.

119 Ibid. 128–29. See also R. J. Thornton 1992b.

120 Malinowski 1926b:131–33, 139.

121 Malinowski 1932:xxii–xxiii.

122 Malinowski 1931b:623, 627, 629, 645, 634, 1944. See also M. W. Young 1987:41.

123 Malinowski 1932:xxix–xxx; BMPL: Malinowski to B. Seligman 3/18/32.

124 BMPL: Malinowski memo to C. Seligman, n.d. [c. 1927].

125 Leach 1957:120—Malinowski 1944:175. See also Parsons 1957:53.

126 Nadel 1957:189; Hyman 1966:193; Malinowski 1936a:169.

127 BMPL: S. Schmalhausen to Malinowski 11/13/28—Malinowski 1928, 1929b, 1930a, 1926a. See also Lyons & Lyons 1986.

128 Leach 1984:4–8; Marett 1941:222, 223, 237—OUCA and CBAS: passim; Buxton 1924; Malinowski 1925b; Marett 1935. See also Urry 1987; Langham 1981:180; Morrison 1983.

129 See Kuklick 1991: 63, 54–57.

130 Richards 1957:18–20; R. W. Firth 1957a:8, 1981:106–7. See also Comaroff & Comaroff 1988.

131 BMPL: Malinowski to Seligman 9/5/31, Seligman to Malinowski 9/17/31.

132 BMPL: Malinowski to Seligman 9/5/31, Seligman to Malinowski 10/31/32, 1/6/33, 1/16/33.

7. From Cultural Psychology to Social Structure: Radcliffe-Brown and the Delimitation of Social Anthropology

1 BMPY: Malinowski to Seligman 1/21/19; BMPL: Malinowski to Mrs. [Janet] Mair 6/11/31—Rivers 1914c; Malinowski 1935a. See also Sanjek, ed., 1990.
2 BMPL: Sociological notes, 1920–25; Malinowski 1923d:98—1929d.
3 Malinowski 1913c:182, 202, 171, 172, 199.
4 BMPL: passim; Fortes 1957:162—Malinowski 1929a, 1930b.
5 WHRP: "Unpublished notes on Ambrym"—Rivers 1914c:II, 89, 478, 1923a, 1923b, 1924, 1926; Radcliffe-Brown 1929a, 1929b. See also Langham 1981:94–100; Stocking 1992a.
6 Langham 1981:100–117.
7 MacClancy 1986:53—Layard 1942.
8 Armstrong in Langham 1981:207. See also Urry 1987.
9 Barnard in Langham 1981:210.
10 Deacon in Langham 1981:214–15, 234. See also M. Gardiner 1984.
11 Deacon to Gardiner n.d., 10/29/26, in M. Gardiner 1984:37–39, 47; ACHP: Haddon to Radcliffe-Brown 3/21/27. See also Langham 1981:234.
12 Deacon 1927:327–29, 334, 335—Rivers 1914c:II, 67; ACHP: Radcliffe-Brown to Haddon 3/22/27, 5/2/27, 5/9/27, 5/23/27, 5/25/27, 6/14/27, 7/19/27, 7/29/27.
13 Haddon in Langham 1981:238; B. Z. Seligman 1927:351–52—ACHP: Radcliffe-Brown to Haddon 5/2/27, 5/9/27; Radcliffe-Brown 1929a, 1929b.
14 Malinowski 1930b:151–52, 163.
15 ACHP: Radcliffe-Brown to Haddon 5/9/27; Radcliffe-Brown 1927:348—ACHP: Deacon to Haddon 2/15/27; Radcliffe-Brown 1929a, 1929b.
16 R. W. Firth 1951a:480. See also Powdermaker 1966:42–43; Stanner 1956.
17 ACHP: Brown to Haddon 11/12/21; Radcliffe-Brown to Kroeber n.d./46 in Kelly 1983; BMPL: Radcliffe-Brown to Malinowski 12/31/29. See also R. W. Firth 1956:287; Fortes 1956:149.
18 Cambridge University 1901, 1902, 1904a, 1904b.
19 Singer 1984:69–84; Radcliffe-Brown 1958b:189; Radcliffe-Brown to Kroeber n.d./46 in Kelly 1983—Kropotkin 1902; Rivers 1906. See also R. Perry 1975; M. A. Miller 1976:164–73. Cf. Barnard 1992.
20 Radcliffe-Brown 1941:50; RHLP: Radcliffe-Brown to R. Lowie 5/6/38—ACHP: Temple to Haddon 3/16/06; Radcliffe-Brown 1932:407; RBPR: "String figures from the Andaman Islands."
21 ACHP: Brown to Haddon n.d., 8/10/06; [Radcliffe-]Brown 1922b:vii–viii, 1914a:41, 1932:72; RBPR. See also Tomas 1991:96–97.
22 E. G. Watson 1946:83–85; R. W. Firth 1956:290.
23 Radcliffe-Brown 1932:407–94, 1910b:36; Lang 1905b. See also Langham 1981:260.
24 Brown to Mauss 8/6/12 in Testart, ed., 1979:4—Collini 1978:35; Harrison 1912:125; Stocking 1984a.

25 Stocking 1984a:122–28—[Radcliffe-]Brown 1923b:20–21; Lévi-Strauss 1962: 58–59; Durkheim 1893.
26 [Radcliffe-]Brown 1922b:ix; Stocking 1984a.
27 OUCA: 1/27/09, 3/5/09; Marett & Penniman, eds., 1932:106–7; JGFP: Frazer to Marett 4/4/09; E. G. Watson 1946:105–6. See also Mulvaney & Calaby 1985:220.
28 See E. G. Watson 1946:106; Salter 1972; I. White 1981:207–8.
29 Radcliffe-Brown 1947:153; RBDB: Brown to Bates n.d.—[Radcliffe-]Brown 1910a.
30 Radcliffe-Brown 1930–31:46; Frazer 1910:I, xii; [Radcliffe-]Brown 1910c; RBDB: Brown to Bates n.d.; E. G. Watson 1946:109. See also R. Needham 1974; Eggan 1974; I. White 1981 (cf. R. Needham 1982).
31 Salter 1972:136, 140, 141; I. White 1981:195; E. G. Watson 1946:85, 106.
32 E. G. Watson 1946:106–10; Salter 1972:142. See also Eggan 1974.
33 See E. G. Watson 1946:121–25; I. White 1981:208.
34 Brown in I. White 1981:201, 202, 203, 207.
35 ACHP: Brown to Haddon 6/8/12; Bates in Salter 1972:147—[Radcliffe-]Brown 1914c. See also I. White 1981:204, 210.
36 I. White 1981:204, 197; Eggan 1974; Rivers 1916a:424—ACHP: Thomas to Rivers 4/14/16. Cf. R. Needham 1974, 1982.
37 [Radcliffe-]Brown 1913c:185; cf. 1930–31:46. The first phase of the Brown/Rivers correspondence continued until late in 1912; resumed the following summer, it continued into the early part of 1914. Because the letters are almost all undated, I have offered no citations in the paragraphs that follow. Langham (1981:373–74) refers to envelopes 12027, 12039, 12058, and 1220 of the Haddon collection, cited here as WHRP, in which most of the correspondence is contained. His reading differed substantially from my own, perhaps because he did not have access to Brown's critically important letter responding to Rivers' article on survivals (1913b), a copy of which was made available to me by Fred Eggan before its subsequent publication by Meyer Fortes ([Radcliffe-]Brown 1913a). See also Stocking 1984b.
38 Rivers 1911.
39 Howitt 1890; Siebert 1910; Durkheim 1912. See also Langham 1981:46, 41–42, 276–77.
40 WHRP: Rivers to Brown 7/12/12. Cf. Rivers 1914c:I, 7.
41 Rivers 1924:194–201.
42 Brown to Mauss 8/6/12 in Testart, ed., 1979; Durkheim 1895:89–124.
43 WHRP: Rivers to Brown 7/12/13; CUPC: Rivers to A. R. Waller 5/29/13; Rivers 1912d.
44 Rivers 1913a; McDougall 1905:1; [Radcliffe-]Brown 1913a:35–36.
45 [Radcliffe-]Brown 1913a:35–41.
46 Ibid. 43–45.
47 Ibid. 45–46. The version of this draft article published by Fortes omits a parenthesis inserted by Brown explaining the reason for its unfinished state.
48 Rivers in [Radcliffe-]Brown 1913a:33–34.
49 WHRP: Brown to Rivers n.d.—Rivers 1914b, 1914c.

50 WHRP: Brown to Rivers n.d.—Rivers 1914d; [Radcliffe-]Brown 1914b.
51 Rivers 1916b:4; [Radcliffe-]Brown 1923b.
52 [Radcliffe-]Brown 1923b.
53 ACHP: Brown to Haddon 10/12/19; Brown to W. Hoernlé 8/11/25 in Carstens, Klinghardt, & West, eds., 1987:189. See also Stanner 1956:117.
54 RBMF: 1913–14; Temple 1914.
55 ACHP: Brown to Haddon 4/6/14, 10/22/23—[Radcliffe-]Brown 1913b:139. See also Mulvaney & Calaby 1985:195, 388; R. W. Firth 1956:292.
56 ACHP: Brown to Haddon n.d., 10/12/19—Williamson 1924.
57 ACHP: Brown to Haddon 3/13/20, Haddon to Smuts 4/17/20, Brown to Haddon 6/27/21—[Radcliffe-]Brown 1925b. See also Hancock 1962.
58 E. A. Walker 1928:583; Union of South Africa 1922b:6; Marett in Schapera 1990:7; ACHP: Registrar to Haddon 5/20/21. See also Union of South Africa 1922a; E. A. Walker 1928:571–96; Hancock 1962. Cf. Schapera 1990; R. Gordon 1990; R. J. Thornton 1983, 1989.
59 ACHP: Brown to Haddon 11/12/21; RBMF: 1921–25—[Radcliffe-]Brown 1924a. See also R. Gordon 1990.
60 RBMF: 1921–25.
61 RBMF: 1921–25; [Radcliffe-]Brown 1922a:38–39.
62 Temple 1922:121, 126; cf., however, Temple 1923, 1925, 1929, in which Temple was more systematically critical of Brown's ethnography—[Radcliffe-] Brown 1922b.
63 [Radcliffe-]Brown 1922b:231 (cf. 263), 405; Durkheim 1912:13—Rivers 1906.
64 [Radcliffe-]Brown 1922b:324, 306, 235, 324, 316, 324, 235.
65 Ibid. 233–34.
66 Ibid. 241, 246, 250, 264, 276, 280, 277–28, 282, 315, 325, 326. See also Stanner 1956, 1985.
67 [Radcliffe-]Brown 1922b:377, 381, 382, 384–85.
68 Ibid. 393, 330, 396, 397, 393, 344, 376.
69 Ibid. 400, 401–2.
70 CUPC: Radcliffe-Brown to Roberts 9/14/32—[Radcliffe-]Brown 1923b, 1932; Rivers 1916b.
71 [Radcliffe-]Brown 1923b:125, 126, 127—1922b:407, 492–94.
72 [Radcliffe-]Brown 1923b:128–29.
73 Ibid. 131, 132, 133.
74 Ibid. 133, 134. Cf. Rivers 1916b:8–10.
75 [Radcliffe-]Brown 1923b:136, 138.
76 Ibid. 139, 146—Rivers 1914c.
77 Ibid. 140–41, 142–43; Kroeber 1920a—Lowie 1920.
78 [Radcliffe-]Brown 1923b:146–47.
79 ACHP: Brown to Haddon 11/12/21; Junod 1912:I, 1, 6, 253–58; [Radcliffe-] Brown 1924b. See also R. J. Thornton 1983, 1989.
80 Malinowski 1931c; Junod 1912:II, 540—Rivers 1914c:II, 155–60. See also Langham 1981:295–97.
81 [Radcliffe-]Brown 1924b:17–18.
82 Ibid. 18–21.
83 Ibid. 21–22, 23, 24; Smith & Dale 1920.

84 [Radcliffe-]Brown 1924b:25, 27–28, 30–31.
85 Fortes 1969:45–49. See also A. Kuper 1976.
86 BMPL: Brown to Malinowski 5/22/23; RBSN—L. H. Morgan 1877; Tylor 1871.
87 MFP: Hoernlé to Fortes 1/7/49; ACHP: Brown to Haddon 12/18/22; [Radcliffe-]Brown 1924b:16. See also Carstens, ed., 1985:xii; Carstens, Klinghardt, & West, eds., 1987; R. Gordon 1987.
88 WHRP: Brown to Rivers 3/20/22; Brown to Hoernlé 7/31/25, 11/7/25, Hoernlé to Haddon 2/3/26 in Carstens, Klinghardt, & West, eds., 1987:184–92—[Radcliffe-]Brown 1925a, 1925b. See also De Jong & Vermeulen 1989:289–90.
89 ACHP: Brown to Haddon 10/22/23; Hoernlé to Haddon 2/3/26 in Carstens, Klinghardt, & West, eds., 1987:190–91; Carstens, ed., 1985:xi—Hoernlé 1937. See also H. B. Kuper 1984:193–96.
90 See Elkin 1952:35–36; Mulvaney & Calaby 1985:372; Weickhardt 1989:128–29, 132; Legge 1971; Rowley 1966, 1958; Beloff 1970:296, 344.
91 ACHP: "Record of Proceedings." See also Peterson 1990.
92 ACHP: Masson to Haddon n.d. [1923?]; Smith in Elkin 1952:37; Spencer in Mulvaney & Calaby 1985:388. See also Langham 1981:288–89; this volume, 395.
93 ACHP: Radcliffe-Brown to Haddon 11/15/26. See also Stocking 1985b:191.
94 ACHP: Radcliffe-Brown to Haddon 7/29/27. See also Elkin 1938; Stocking 1982b.
95 ACHP: Radcliffe-Brown to Haddon 3/1/27, 6/14/27, 10/12/23.
96 Elkin 1956:240; ACHP: Radcliffe-Brown to Haddon 11/15/26— [Radcliffe-] Brown 1918, 1923a, 1930–31. See also R. W. Firth 1932; Elkin 1938, 1943a.
97 Radcliffe-Brown 1930–31:34, 42, 44–46—1913c. See also Elkin 1956:247, 1963:19–21.
98 Radcliffe-Brown 1930–31:46, 60.
99 Ibid. 206, 426.
100 Ibid. 426–27, 428, 434, 437.
101 Ibid. 440, 441—[Radcliffe-]Brown 1922b:307, 328; Rivers 1924:67.
102 Radcliffe-Brown 1930–31:435, 439, 445, 452, 1958b:189.
103 Radcliffe-Brown 1930–31:456; Elkin 1956:247. See also Fortes 1955, 1970.
104 Brown to Hoernlé 7/31/25 in Carstens, Klinghardt, & West, eds., 1987:184.
105 Radcliffe-Brown 1926:23, 1923b:20–21.
106 Radcliffe-Brown 1929c:399, 415, 1930b.
107 Radcliffe-Brown 1930b:122–23, 127, 131, 132—1922b; Durkheim 1912.
108 Stanner 1956:117; RBSN; Tax 1956; as well as other lecture notes in the possession of GWS.
109 RBMF: 11/4/27; ACHP: Radcliffe-Brown to Haddon 11/15/26, 3/1/27, 5/2/27, 5/9/27, 5/23/27; Radcliffe-Brown 1930a. See also Elkin 1970.
110 R. W. Firth 1956:296.
111 Wise 1985:97; Wedgwood in Wise 1985:100; Radcliffe-Brown 1931a:279.
112 Masson in Wise 1985:101; Wise 1985:101; RAC: Radcliffe-Brown to Day 10/3/32; ACHP: Radcliffe-Brown to Haddon 1/13/30. See also Elkin 1938, 1952:38–39, 1956, 1973. Cf. Wise 1985; Gray 1994.

113 Radcliffe-Brown in Stanner 1956:118; Radcliffe-Brown 1931b:87, 44–45, 54, 87—Stocking 1993a.
114 Radcliffe-Brown 1931b:51–52, 61, 65; ACHP: Radcliffe-Brown to Haddon 5/9/27.
115 Radcliffe-Brown 1931b:67–68, 71, 79, 44, 80, 75, 77; Stocking 1993a.
116 Radcliffe-Brown 1931b:93, 94.
117 Ibid. 81–83, 95.
118 Ibid. 87.
119 FCCP: Cole to A. Small 11/12/24; interview with Fred Eggan 3/27/68. See also R. B. Miller 1975; Darnell 1990; Stocking 1979a.
120 BMPL: Radcliffe-Brown to Malinowski 12/31/29. See also Chiao 1987; McMillan 1986; Stocking 1979a, 1993a; Eggan & Warner 1956.
121 UCDA: "Report on research" 5/n.d./34; Fred Eggan, seminar discussion 1971—Morgan 1871; Eggan, ed., 1937. See also Schusky 1989.
122 See Stocking 1976, 1985b, 1993a; McMillan 1986; Warner 1988.
123 Boas 1932:258; Stocking 1978; GWS interview with Sol Tax 5/12/71—Linton 1936.
124 Radcliffe-Brown 1935a:531, 535; Kroeber 1934:199–200.
125 Lesser 1935:394, 387—Kroeber 1935; Boas 1936.
126 Radcliffe-Brown 1935b:394, 396, 401, 402—Durkheim 1895.
127 Olson 1933:409; Radcliffe-Brown 1935c:47–48, 37, 43, 45, 47.
128 Fortes 1970:49–51, 1955:21–22; Radcliffe-Brown 1950:11, 1933a, 1933b. See also A. Diamond, ed., 1991:99–192; A. Kuper 1982.
129 Radcliffe-Brown 1937:x, ix, 3–4. See also Adler 1977.
130 Radcliffe-Brown 1937:14, et passim; RBUC. Cf. Singer 1984.
131 Radcliffe-Brown 1937:103, 106, 124, 108 (cf. 55, 60–61), 30–31; Fred Eggan, seminar discussion 1971. Cf. Stocking 1993a; Singer 1984.
132 Radcliffe-Brown 1937:33, 38, 79, 39, 141–48.
133 ACHP: Bateson to Haddon, n.d./36; BMPL: Malinowski to Coupland 7/2/36, Coupland to Malinowski 7/31/36, Radcliffe-Brown to Malinowski 12/10/36; OUCA; JLMP. See also Morrison 1984.
134 Redfield 1937; RRP: F. Setzler to Redfield 6/23/37. See also McMillan 1986: 115–20, 127, 130–32, 140–45, 185–87.
135 BMPL: Malinowski to Radcliffe-Brown 5/11/27; Radcliffe-Brown 1946—Malinowski 1931b; lecture notes in the possession of GWS.
136 Malinowski 1934a:xxxiii, xxxviii.
137 Radcliffe-Brown 1935d.
138 Malinowski 1935b; J. McAllister, personal communication 3/15/78; BMPL: Radcliffe-Brown to Malinowski 12/20/36.
139 JMLP: 1935–40, passim; Stocking 1985c.
140 Radcliffe-Brown 1938; BMPL: Malinowski to Radcliffe-Brown 1/29/38, H. Clark to Malinowski 4/22/38, Malinowski to Clark 5/5/38.
141 This account of the debate is based primarily on BMPY: Series II, box 12, folder 34. See also Stocking 1984b: 173–75.
142 Malinowski 1939:243—Radcliffe-Brown 1939, 1940a, 1922b. See also Homans 1941.
143 Malinowski & de la Fuente 1982; Radcliffe-Brown 1940b, 1941.

8. Anthropological Institutions, Colonial Interests, and the First Cohorts of Social Anthropologists

1 Cf. A. Kuper 1973, 1983; Jarvie 1964, 1974; Evans-Pritchard 1973a.
2 Lugard 1922:18, 618. See also Beloff 1970:347; K. Robinson 1965; Perham 1956, 1960; Mair 1936; Bull 1963; Nicolson 1969; Afigbo 1972.
3 See, among others, Asad, ed., 1973; Huizer & Mannheim, eds., 1979; Le-Clerc 1972; Loizos 1977; Stauder 1980.
4 See Fardon, ed., 1990b; Kuklick 1978, 1979; Pels & Salemink 1993; Stocking, ed., 1991b.
5 Malinowski 1939:243. See also Kuklick 1991; A. Kuper 1973, 1983; Lombard 1972; Stocking 1987b; Van Keuren 1982; Urry 1993.
6 Freire-Marreco 1907:395. See also Kuklick 1991:27–74; Van Keuren 1982.
7 See Stocking 1987b:238–73.
8 Tylor 1871:II, 453, 1885a:94; BAAS 1874. See also Reining 1952; Stocking 1971b, 1987b:266; Feuchtwang 1973; R. R. Atkinson 1973; Urry 1993:17–40; Stocking 1987b:258–61, 1993b; Coote 1987.
9 See Van Keuren 1982; Stocking 1987b:238–73.
10 See Stocking 1987b:238–73; Urry 1984b.
11 Aborigines Protection Society, in Stocking 1987b:242. See also Morris 1968; S. Firth 1982; Robinson & Gallagher 1961; Fieldhouse 1981; Porter 1968; Semmel 1960.
12 See Urry 1993:102–7; R. R. Atkinson 1973; Myres 1929:36.
13 Read in Haddon 1897:574—RAIA: Council minutes 2/23/97, 3/9/97, 5/11/97, 11/9/97, 11/23/97, 5/30/99; Read 1896, 1900, 1901. See also Myres 1929:38–41; Van Keuren 1982:133–40.
14 Keith 1917:25—RAIA: Council minutes 3/30/97; Kingsley 1897, 1898, 1900. See also Urry 1993:109; Flint 1963; Porter 1968:149–53, 240–54; Rich 1990:27–50.
15 *Man: A Monthly Record of Anthropological Science; Man* 7 (1907):111–12—RAIA: Council minutes, passim.
16 *Man* 3 (1903):70–74—Haddon 1900. See also Schapera 1934; R. Gordon 1990.
17 RAIA: Council minutes 3/10/08, 3/24/08, 5/8/08; ACHP: Ridgeway to W. Duckworth 3/12/09; OUCA: 3/6/08; Read 1906; Duckworth et al. 1906; *Man* 9 (1909):85–87; *JRAI* 38 (1908):489–92; Haddon 1909a. See also Collins 1972; Phillips n.d.; Urry 1993:110–12.
18 JLMP: Ridgeway to Myres 11/22/08, Myres to T. Joyce 3/13/08; Asquith in *Man* 9 (1909):87—RAIA: Council Memoranda on Establishment of Imperial Bureau of Anthropology; Council minutes 4/28/08, 4/13/09, 4/5/11, 5/23/11, 10/31/11.
19 J. W. Flood in Kuklick 1991:201; RAIA: Report of the Committee to Examine the Results of a Survey of Nigeria, 1910—Council minutes 1/26/10; Haddon 1909b; Seligman & Seligman 1932:xi. See also Lackner 1973.
20 Alex Fiddian in Kuklick 1991:199—Kuklick 1991:201; Thomas 1910, 1913, 1916.
21 ACHP: C. Hose to Haddon 5/21/14—CBAS n.d. See also Heussler 1962; Jeffries 1964; Wilkinson 1964.

22 Temple 1905:139. See also Morrison 1984:148–53; Kuklick 1991:196–99.
23 Temple et al. 1914:59, 1913; Temple 1914.
24 Temple et al. 1914:58, 63, 61, 68.
25 Marett in Temple et al. 1913:192. See also Kuklick 1991:68.
26 See Kuklick 1991:68, 152.
27 See Heussler 1962; Kuklick 1991; Morrison 1984; Pinney 1990; Cohn 1987.
28 Article 22 of the League of Nations, in Lugard 1922:62–63. See also Beloff 1970:314; Louis 1967:119–59; Morris 1978:213–15, 300, 302; Hynes 1990:337–52; J. M. MacKenzie 1984:111; Eddy & Schreuder 1988.
29 Edward Grigg in Beloff 1970:347. See also Rich 1990:50–69; Geiss 1974; Robinson 1965; Cain & Hopkins 1993.
30 Lugard 1922:618–19, 69, 73, 74, 79, 82—Woolf 1919. See also Perham 1960; Robinson 1965.
31 Lugard 1922:203, 205, 215, 217, 219, 617. Cf. note 2 above.
32 Lugard 1922:281, 418, 209, 139–40.
33 See Reining 1952:80–174; Forde 1953. Unfortunately, the source of "Humboldt's parrot" suffered a similar fate.
34 Rivers 1917c:302, 321; Murray 1920:41; Malinowski 1967:64. See also C. G. Seligman 1910:v–vi; Hays, ed., 1991:17–18, 24–25; Urry 1987; Elkin 1943b; Schapera 1990:6; Stocking 1982b; West 1979.
35 Meek 1937:ix—1925:I.v–viii, 1931a, 1931b; ACHP: Taylor to Haddon 11/21/27, A. Hunt to Haddon 11/19/20. See also Perham 1937; G. I. Jones 1974; Lackner 1973.
36 Rattray 1923:6–10—1913, 1927, 1929, 1932. See also Von Laue 1976; Wraith 1967.
37 See Kuklick 1991:227.
38 Meek 1925:I, 173, 219, II, 11–12, 62, 1931a:xi–xii, 1937:xiii–xv.
39 Rattray 1923:21, 86–87, 89, 90, 140, 1927:9–11, 1929:22, 285–86, 1932:xi–xx—Van Gennep 1909.
40 Rattray 1923:10, 287–93—1934; E. W. Smith 1927; Meek 1937:325–55. See also Kuklick 1991:228; Von Laue 1976.
41 Marett in Williams 1928b:ix; Williams 1928b:93, 99, 152–65—1923a, 1923b, 1928a; Rivers 1922b; Malinowski 1922b; Temple 1921.
42 Rattray 1927:vii.
43 Williams 1928b:79, 81, 86, 89–92.
44 Ibid. ix, 171, 193, 173, 195. Cf. Malinowski 1925c:69–90; Evans-Pritchard 1937; Lévi-Strauss 1949.
45 J. Needham, ed., 1925:19–84; Williams 1930. See also Kuklick 1991:203; Reining 1952:80–174.
46 RAIA: Joint Committee for Anthropological Research and Teaching, Smith to J. L. Myres 12/13/22, E. N. Fallaize to Myres 12/18/22—Temple 1921:150–55, 173–75; Myres 1929:48–50; Haddon 1921.
47 RAIA: Joint Committee . . . , passim. See also Heussler 1963:43–47; Kuklick 1991:50.
48 See Fisher 1978, 1980, 1986, 1993. Cf. Ahmad 1991; Stocking 1985b.
49 Ruml in Bulmer & Bulmer 1981:362. See also Haraway 1989:72, 389; Stocking 1985b.

50 See Barkan 1992, 1985; Stepan 1982; G. Jones 1980; Stocking 1968b.
51 Pitt-Rivers 1927:126, 193; RHLP: Malinowski to R. Lowie 3/22/29—Rivers 1922b.
52 See Fisher 1978:28–32; Langham 1981:182–85; Kuklick 1991:210–211; Stocking 1985b:184–85.
53 RAC: M. Grant to R. B. Fosdick 12/29/23—ACHP: "Ethnological Research in the Pacific," by Smith & Perry. See also Elkin 1938, 1952; Mulvaney 1989:206–9; Mulvaney & Calaby 1985:372–73; Stocking 1985b:186–88.
54 Malinowski in Stocking 1986c. See also Rowley 1958:47–49; Stocking 1991a: 253–55.
55 Malinowski 1922b:217, 216, 209, 214–15. See also Stocking 1991a:256–58.
56 Malinowski 1922b:209.
57 W. H. Beveridge 1960:24–25, 83–97; Oldham 1924. See also J. Harris 1977: 272; Bulmer & Bulmer 1981:394–97; Potter 1987:173; Neill 1964:456; Cell 1976:59–60; Bliss 1984; G. Bennett 1960.
58 E. W. Smith 1934:1–2—Lugard 1928. See also Cell 1976:67–71; Forde 1967; King 1971.
59 Stocking 1985b:191.
60 Wissler in Stocking 1985b:191; Oldham in Kuklick 1991:208.
61 RAC: J. Van Sickle diary 10/6/30. See also Kuklick 1991:211; Stocking 1985b: 193.
62 BMPL: notes on Lugard's *Dual Mandate*. See also Stocking 1991a:260–61.
63 BMPL: notes on Lugard; Malinowski 1929b:28; BMPL: n.d., "The state of Anthropology . . . in England"; Day to C. Seligman 6/24/29; "Report on the Conditions in the Rockfeller Interests"; Malinowski to Oldham 6/11/29; RAC: Day to Van Sickle 11/16/29—Malinowski to Day 8/3/29, Van Sickle to Day 12/23/29. See also Stocking 1985b:194–95.
64 RAC: Malinowski to Day 3/26/30; H. A. L. Fisher et al. to the President of the Rockefeller Foundation 3/28/30; BMPL: Mem. Presented to Rockefeller Foundation 3/30/30, Malinowski to Oldham 2/9/30.
65 BMPL: Malinowski to Oldham 9/17/30; RAC: Gunn diary 9/25/30, Foundation minutes 4/15/31. See also Kuklick 1991:209–15.
66 RAC: Radcliffe-Brown "Memo. on Anth. Res." 11/17/30. See also Stocking 1985b:196.
67 BMPL: Radcliffe-Brown to Malinowski 9/17/30, A. Richards to Malinowski n.d., Oldham to Malinowski 9/9/31, Radcliffe-Brown to Malinowski 9/27/31, 1/30/32, 5/25/32.
68 RAC: Day "Foundation's Interest in Cult. Anth." 7/30/31, Rockefeller Foundation Rept. 1931:249—Gunn, interview with Malinowski 3/4/31, Gunn to Day 12/7/31, 2/1/32, Day to Gunn 1/25/32. See also Stocking 1985b:197.
69 RAC: Outhwaite to Day 4/19/32, 6/10/32, Outhwaite "Anthropology in Europe," Outhwaite "Condensed Rept.," p. 23—Day to Gunn 1/25/32.
70 AAAP: Research Committee proceedings; UCDA: J. Cooper to F. Cole 1/25/33; UCBA: Cooper to Rockefeller Foundation 6/24/32; RAC: Outhwaite to Day 10/12/32; UCDA: Cooper to M. Mason 3/6/33; UCBA: Mason to Cooper 4/26/33. See also Stocking 1985b:199–200.
71 RAC: Warner to Day 9/15/33; BMPL: Malinowski to W. Beveridge 11/19/

32; RAC: "Verbatim notes, Princeton Conf." 10/29/32, Day to D. Stevens 11/24/33—Day to A. Gregg 12/19/34, Staff Conf. 3/8/34. See also Fisher 1993:134–35.

72 See Stocking 1985b:201–11; Kuklick 1991:212–13.

73 See Stocking 1985a, 1985b:179–83.

74 See Stocking 1985b:184–85, 203–4.

75 Ibid. 207–11.

76 RAC: Smith to Herrick 2/13/27; BMPL: Malinowski, draft memo, "Res. Needs in Soc. & Cult. Anth."; RAC: Radcliffe-Brown "Memo. on Anth. Res."

77 See Urry 1972; Kuklick 1991:182–241, 1993; Stocking 1983:30, 1993b; Anderson 1969; Leach 1984.

78 See Kuklick 1991:55–56; Massingham 1941:54–66; R. W. Firth 1988, 1993; Comaroff & Comaroff 1988; La Fontaine 1985; S. Ardner, ed., 1992; Colson 1986; J. Harris 1977:72–74, 470; Barnes 1988; Evans-Pritchard 1973b; Kenny 1987.

79 See Beckett 1989; Gray 1994; S. Ardener, ed., 1992; Lipset 1980; Wetherell & Carr-Gregg 1990. See also Association of Social Anthropologists 1969; Gacs et al., eds., 1989.

80 See Goody 1993; Fortes 1978; R. W. Firth 1975b; H. B. Kuper 1984; Matthews 1981; Salat 1983.

81 BMPL: Malinowski to T. Kittredge 8/15/35, Malinowski to D. Brackett 8/15/35, Malinowski to Beemer 12/15/34. See also Edgar, ed., 1992:10–18; R. Brown 1973.

82 See R. W. Firth 1957a:8, 1975a:2–4, 1981:123–25; H. B. Kuper 1984:198–200; Richards 1957:24–25.

83 See Stocking 1985b; Kuklick 1991:182–241; Robinson 1965; Geiss 1974; Rich 1990.

84 Richards 1932; GWS interview with Richards June 1973; BMPL: Lugard to Richards 7/27/29, Richards to Malinowski 8/1/29; Richards 1939a:398—BMPL: Mem. to R. Fdn. 3/30/30.

85 BMPL: Oldham to Malinowski 11/19/31, 1/22/32, 2/16/32, Malinowski to Oldham 2/5/32, Oldham to Malinowski 3/18/32, Malinowski to Firth 9/26/32, D. O. Masson to Malinowski 9/26/32.

86 RAC: Kittredge memo, talk with Oldham & Malinowski 10/24/32; H. B. Kuper 1984:199; GWS interview with Kuper 7/27/77—BMPL: Malinowski to Director (LSE), 3/19/34, 4/27/34.

87 BMPL: Malinowski to Lugard 12/7/36. See also Murray-Brown 1972:180.

88 Kenyatta 1938:xvii, 306—BMPL: unsigned to Malinowski 12/21/36.

89 BMPL: Seminar notes 5/6/33; RAC: Malinowski in Van Sickle diary 11/29/29; BMPL: Malinowski to Wilson 11/22/34.

90 Malinowski 1931a:999. See also Wendy James 1973; Rossetti 1985; Stocking 1991a:261–62.

91 Malinowski 1936b:481, 484, 498, 501.

92 BMPL: "African (Negro) Patriotism." See also Stocking 1991a:263–64.

93 BMPL: Malinowski to Oldham 10/25/34; Malinowski 1937:viii, 1938a:x, 1938b:xxii–xxiii—1941.

94 Malinowski 1938a:ix, 1934b:406.
95 Stocking 1991a:265–66. See also Rossetti 1985; Wendy James 1973.
96 Radcliffe-Brown 1931a:269; BMPL: Richards to Malinowski 9/26/31.
97 BMPL: Brown to Malinowski 11/7/29; Brown & Hutt 1935:v.
98 Young in R. Brown 1973:177, 178–79, 185, 187; M. Gluckman to R. Brown, 12/8/72 (provided to GWS by Gluckman); BMPL: Malinowski to Wilson 7/2/37.
99 BMPL: Wilson to Malinowski 7/23/37, 11/10/37; R. Brown 1973:191–92—Wilson & Wilson 1945.
100 Richards 1977b:277, 1977a; R. Brown 1979:531; Gluckman 1945:3, 7.
101 Gluckman in R. Brown 1979:534, 535, 539. See also R. W. Firth 1975b.
102 Richards 1977b:278, 1977a; R. W. Firth 1977, which has, however, little to say on his role in the Colonial Social Science Research Council.
103 GMP: Richards to Murray 1/11/27, 10/4/30, 5/9/34; BMPL: Richards to Malinowski n.d. [1931], 3/24/33; MHP: MacDonald to Hailey 4/18/40, Hailey to MacDonald 5/n.d./40—Richards to Lord Hailey & Mr. Caine 10/18/43. See also Lee 1967:16; Cell 1989; Richards 1977a; Jeffries, ed., 1964.
104 Richards 1944:292; Colonial Office 1944:8; JHHC: Richards to Hutton 10/4/43. See also Lee 1967; Jeffries, ed., 1964.
105 Hailey 1944:15; Forde 1953:853—R. W. Firth 1947.
106 Evans-Pritchard 1946:95; R. W. Firth 1949:138. See also Reining 1952; Grillo 1985.
107 R. W. Firth 1949:137.
108 Foreign Office 1947.
109 Schapera in Comaroff & Comaroff 1988:557; cf. H. B. Kuper 1984:198. See also Powdermaker 1966:42.
110 H. B. Kuper 1984:197–98; BMPL: Malinowski to Oldham 2/26/34, Malinowski to Fortes 3/11/36; BMPY: Fortes to Malinowski 4/1/36—GWS interview with Fortes 8/9/69. See also Fortes 1978:3–4; R. W. Firth 1983:58.
111 Malinowski 1938b:xiii; BMPL: Fortes to Malinowski 6/29/38. See also Wayne 1985.
112 Firth in A. Kuper 1973:94; Richards 1957:27–28.
113 BMPL: Bateson to Malinowski n.d., 1/16/36, 11/5/35; Bateson 1936. See also BMPL: Hocart to Malinowski 3/20/35.
114 Malinowski 1938b:xxxvi.
115 BMPL: Evans-Pritchard to Malinowski 11/25/28; Fortes 1978:2, 6–7; BMPL: Richards to Malinowski 11/6/31; Evans-Pritchard 1940. See also Stocking 1984b:167.
116 Fortes, seminar presentation, Univ. of Chicago, 10/16/73; GWS interview with Fortes and Gluckman 9/6/69—BMPL: Malinowski to Richards 1/6/31, Richards to Malinowski 9/4/31; Radcliffe-Brown 1940b, 1941. See also Barnes 1988:453; Goody 1993; R. W. Firth 1975b.
117 Fortes & Evans-Pritchard, eds., 1940:xi, 205, xv, vii; Malinowski 1938b. See also A. Kuper 1973:89–122, 1988:190–209.

Epilogue: Moment and Tradition in the History of British Social Anthropology

1 Fortes 1956:152.
2 ASAM: Minutes of Oxford Meeting 7/13–24/46—GWS interviews with Fortes and Gluckman 9/6/69, with Edmund Leach 4/11/69; RAIA: Council minutes, passim. See also Kuklick 1991:58–71.
3 ASAM: Minutes 7/13–24/46 and following. See also Tapper 1980; Ardener & Ardener 1965.
4 ASAM: Minutes 7/5–7/47—GWS interview with Forde 2/6/73; GWS interview with Fürer-Haimendorf 7/17/73. See also Fortes 1976; University College n.d.:7–8; Phillips n.d.:44–59; Association of Social Anthropologists 1969; A. Kuper 1973:150–51.
5 Commonwealth Universities Yearbook 1947, 1952.
6 ACHP: Bateson to the Wyse Electors 1/18/35, 1/3/37; Bateson to Haddon n.d. [1936].
7 ACHP: Haddon to Bateson 1/19/36, Bateson to Haddon 8/30/36—BMPL: Malinowski to G. Wilson 12/1/36; Morrison 1983b.
8 JHHC: "Post-War Training for the Colonial Service" 2/23/45, p. 5, Hutton to Evans-Pritchard 7/16/49; GWS interview with Evans-Pritchard 6/21/73. See also Heussler 1963; Barnes 1988:456.
9 See A. Kuper 1973:150–61.
10 Murdock 1949:vii, xv–xvi. See also Stocking 1976.
11 Murdock 1951. See also Stocking 1984b:131–35.
12 Murdock 1951:470; Radcliffe-Brown 1950.
13 Murdock 1951:467–72. See also L. A. White 1966.
14 R. W. Firth 1951a:475–80.
15 Ibid., 477, 474, 479, 481, 483, 488.
16 Murdock 1951:466, 472; R. W. Firth 1951a:480, 482.
17 A. Kuper 1973:164; Evans-Pritchard 1950b:146, 148, 152; E. W. Ardener 1971:449; Radcliffe-Brown 1958b:133–89; R. W. Firth 1951b; Nadel 1951. See also A. Kuper 1973, 1983; Danaher 1992a, 1992b; Stocking 1992a.
18 Murdock 1951; R. W. Firth 1951a; Radcliffe-Brown 1937. Although the institute's renaming was apparently the result of contingent institutional factors (P. Rivière, personal communication 11/1/91), this does not negate its symbolic significance.
19 GWS interviews with Evans-Pritchard 5/30/69, 5/2/73.
20 Stocking 1993b; Urry 1972; Coote 1987.
21 RAI 1951:v–vi, 36–62—BAAS 1929; R. W. Firth, personal communication 3/13/93.
22 RAI 1951:28, 58, 104, 134, 39.
23 "Notes and Queries: Foreword, Draft 1," May 1973; J. Benthall, personal communication 2/8/93. Cf. Stocking 1992a.
24 Ellen, ed., 1984:3–4. See also Urry 1984a.

References Cited

Sources are listed by the date of the original or historically relevant edition. In cases where another edition was consulted the place of publication is that of the later edition, the date of which is indicated in parentheses at the end of the entry.

Abbreviations

AA	*American Anthropologist*
ARA	*Annual Review of Anthropology*
RAI	[Royal] Anthropological Institute of Great Britain and Northern Ireland
BAAS	British Association for the Advancement of Science
CA	*Current Anthropology*
HAN	*History of Anthropology Newsletter*
HOA	*History of Anthropology*
JAI	*Journal of the Anthropological Institute*
JASO	*Journal of the Anthropological Society of Oxford*
JRAI	*Journal of the Royal Anthropological Institute*

Aberle, D. F.
1960 The influence of linguistics on early culture and personality theory. In G. Dole & R. Carneiro, eds., *Essays in the science of culture in honor of Leslie A. White,* 1–29. New York.
Abrams, Philip
1968 *The origins of British sociology, 1834–1914.* Chicago.
Ackerman, R. E.
1972 Jane Ellen Harrison: The early work. *Greek, Roman, and Byzantine Studies* 13:209–30.
1987 *J. G. Frazer: His life and work.* Cambridge, Eng.
1991 *The myth and ritual school: J. G. Frazer and the Cambridge Ritualists.* New York.
Adams, W. Y., D. P. Van Gerven, & R. S. Levy
1978 The retreat from migrationism. *ARA* 7:483–532.
Adler, M. J.
1977 *Philosopher at large: An intellectual autobiography.* New York.
Afigbo, A. E.
1972 *The warrant chiefs: Indirect rule in southeastern Nigeria, 1891–1929.* London.

Ahmad, Salma
1991 American foundations and the development of the social sciences between the wars: Comment on the debate between Martin Bulmer and Donald Fisher. *Sociology* 25:511–20.

Anderson, Perry
1969 Components of the national culture. In A. Cockburn & R. Blackburn, eds., *Student power: Problems, diagnosis, action*, 214–86. Harmondsworth, Eng.

Ardener, E. W.
1971 The new anthropology and its critics. *Man* 6:448–67.

Ardener, E. W., & Shirley Ardener
1965 A directory study of social anthropologists. *British Journal of Sociology* 16:295–314.

Ardener, Shirley
1992 Ed. *Persons and powers: Essays in commemoration of Audrey I. Richards, Phyllis Kaberry and Barbara E. Ward*. New York.

Armstrong, E. S.
1900 *The history of the Melanesian Mission*. London.

Asad, Talal
1973 Ed. *Anthropology and the colonial encounter*. London.

Association of Social Anthropologists
1969 *Register of members*. Morristown, Swansea, Eng.

Atkinson, J. J.
1903 *Primal law*. Bound with Lang 1903. London.

Atkinson, R. R.
1973 British anthropology and British colonialism up to the Second World War. Unpublished manuscript.

Austen, Leo
1945 Cultural changes in Kiriwina. *Oceania* 16:14–60.

Bachofen, J. J.
1861 *Das Mutterrecht*, as excerpted in *Myth, religion and mother right: Selected writings of J. J. Bachofen*, 69–207. Trans. Ralph Manheim. Princeton, (1967).

Baker, P. G.
1980 The mild anthropologist and the mission of primitive man: Sir Edward Tylor and the anthropological study of religion in the Victorian era. Doctoral dissertation, University of Cambridge.

Barkan, Elazar
1988 Mobilizing scientists against Nazi racism, 1933–1939. *HOA* 5:180–205.
1992 *The retreat of scientific racism: Changing concepts of race in Britain and the United States between the world wars*. Cambridge, Eng.

Barnard, Alan
1992 Through Radcliffe-Brown's spectacles: Reflections on the history of anthropology. *History of the Human Sciences* 5:1–20.

Barnes, J. A.
1988 Edward Evan Evans-Pritchard, 1902–1973. *Proceedings of the British Academy* 73:447–90.

Bateson, Gregory
1936 *Naven: A survey of the problems suggested by a composite picture of the culture of a New Guinea tribe drawn from three points of view.* 2nd ed. Stanford (1958).
Beard, Mary
1992 Frazer, Leach and Virgil: The popularity (and unpopularity) of *The Golden Bough. Comparative Studies in Society and History* 34:202–24.
Beckett, Jeremy
1987 *Torres Straits islanders: Custom and colonialism.* Cambridge, Eng.
1989 *Conversations with Ian Hogbin.* Oceania Monograph 35. Sydney.
Beidelman, T. O.
1974a Social theory and the study of Christian missions in Africa. *Africa* 44:235–49.
1974b *William Robertson Smith and the sociological study of religion.* Chicago.
Beloff, Max
1970 *Imperial sunset.* Vol. I, *Britain's liberal empire, 1897–1921.* New York.
Bennett, Arnold
1922 W. H. R. Rivers: Some recollections. *The New Statesman,* 17 June, pp. 290–91.
Bennett, George
1960 From paramountcy to partnership: J. H. Oldham and Africa. *Africa* 32:356–60.
Benthall, Jonathan
1990 Élargir le contexte de l'anthropologie: Comment a comencé *Anthropology Today.* In S. Devers, ed., *Pour Jean Malaurie: 102 témoignages en hommage à quarante ans d'études arctiques,* 751–57. Paris.
Bernal, Martin
1987 *Black Athena: The Afroasiatic roots of classical civilization.* Vol. 1, *The fabrication of ancient Greece, 1785–1985.* London.
Beveridge, J. P.
1960 *An epic of Clare Market: Birth and early days of the London School of Economics.* London.
Beveridge, W. H.
1960 *The London School of Economics and its problems, 1919–1937.* London.
Black, J. S., & G. W. Chrystal
1912 *The life of William Robertson Smith.* London.
Black, R.
1957 Dr. Bellamy of Papua. *Medical Journal of Australia* 2:189–97, 232–38, 279–84.
Blamires, W., & J. Smith
1886 *The early story of the Wesleyan Methodist Church in Victoria.* Melbourne.
Bliss, Kathleen
1984 The legacy of J. H. Oldham. *International Bulletin of Mission Research* 8:18–24.
Boas, Franz
1887 Museums of ethnology and their classification. In Stocking, ed., 1974c: 61–67.

1889a On alternating sounds. In Stocking, ed., 1974c:72–77.
1889b The aims of ethnology. As excerpted in Stocking, ed., 1974c:67–71.
1896 The limitations of the comparative method of anthropology. *Science* 4:901–8.
1903 The decorative art of the North American Indians. In 1940:546–63.
1911 Instability of human types. In G. Spiller, ed., *Papers on inter-racial problems*, 99–104. London.
1932 The aims of anthropological research. In 1940:243–59.
1936 History and science in anthropology: A reply. In 1940:305–11.
1940 *Race, language and culture.* New York.

Bolger, Peter
1977 Anthropology and history in Australia: The place of A. C. Haddon. *Journal of Australian Studies* 2:93–106.

Boon, J. A.
1982 *Other tribes, other scribes: Symbolic anthropology in the comparative study of cultures, histories, religions, and texts.* Cambridge, Eng.
1983 Functionalists write, too: Frazer/Malinowski and the semiotics of the monograph. *Semiotica* 46:131–49.

Bouquet, Mary
1993 Being British and being English: Disclosing a hidden ethnography from the British kinship classics in a mid-1980s Portuguese pedagogical setting. In H. Driessen, ed., *The politics of ethnographic reading and writing*, 8–39. Saarbrücken.

Brandiwie, E. B.
1983 *Wilhelm Schmidt and the origin of the idea of God.* Lanham, Md.

Bratton, F. G.
1968 *A history of Egyptian archaeology.* New York.

British Association for the Advancement of Science
1874 *Notes and queries on anthropology, for the use of travellers and residents in uncivilized lands.* London.
1887 Third report of the committee . . . investigating and publishing reports on the physical characters, languages, industry and social condition of the north-western tribes of the Dominion of Canada. *Report of the 57th Meeting*, 173–83.
1895 *Discussion: "On the contact of European and native civilizations" held at the meeting of the British Association, Ipswich.* [Pamphlet.]
1899 *Notes and queries on anthropology, or a guide to anthropological research for the use of travellers and others.* 3rd ed. London.
1911 Discussion on totemism. *Report of the 81st Meeting*, 504–8.
1912 *Notes and queries on anthropology.* 4th ed., ed. B. W. Freire-Marreco & J. L. Myres. London.
1923 Progress of anthropological teaching. *Report of the 91st Meeting*, 416–21.
1929 *Notes and queries on anthropology.* 5th ed. London.

Brooks, M. Z.
1985 Lucjan Malinowski and Polish dialectology. *Polish Review* 30:167–70.

Brown, A. R. See under Radcliffe-Brown.

Brown, G. G., & A. M. B. Hutt
1935 *Anthropology in action: An experiment in the Iringa Province, Tanganyika Territory*. London.
Brown, Kenneth
1982 The "curse" of Westermarck. In Stroup, ed., 1982b:219–59.
Brown, Richard
1973 Anthropology and colonial rule: The case of Godfrey Wilson and the Rhodes-Livingston Institute, Northern Rhodesia. In Asad, ed., 1973: 173–98.
1979 Passages in the life of a white anthropologist: Max Gluckman in Northern Rhodesia. *Journal of African History* 20:525–41.
Brunton, Ron
1989 *The abandoned narcotic: Kava and cultural instability in Melanesia*. Cambridge, Eng.
Buchan, John
1933 Andrew Lang and the Border. In Salmond, ed., 1949:3–22.
Bull, M.
1963 Indirect rule in northern Nigeria, 1906–1911. In K. Robinson & F. Madden, eds., *Essays in imperial government presented to Marjory Perham*, 47–87. Oxford.
Bulmer, Martin, & Joan Bulmer
1981 Philanthropy and social science in the 1920s: Beardsley Ruml and the Laura Spelman Rockefeller Memorial, 1922–29. *Minerva* 19:347–407.
Burton, John
1988 Shadows at twilight: A note on history and the ethnographic present. *Proceedings of the American Philosophical Society* 132:420–33.
Buxton, L. D. H.
1924 *Primitive labour*. London.
1936a Robert Ranulf Marett. In 1936b:3–8. London.
1936b Ed. *Custom is king*. London.
Cain, P. J., & A. G. Hopkins
1993 *British imperialism: Crisis and deconstruction, 1914–1990*. London.
Caine, Sidney
1963 *The history of the foundation of the London School of Economics and Political Science*. London.
Cambridge, University of
1901 Moral Science Tripos. In *Ordinances*, 74–82.
1902 List of lectures . . . for Moral Sciences, 1902–3. *Reporter*, 8 October, p. 29.
1904a List of lectures . . . for Moral Sciences, 1903–4. *Reporter*, 13 January, p. 353.
1904b List of lectures . . . for Moral Sciences, 1904–5. *Reporter*, 8 October, p. 25.
Carstens, P. W.
1985 Ed. *The social organization of the Nama and other essays by Winifred Hoernlé*. Johannesburg.
Carstens, P. W., Gerald Klinghardt, & Martin West
1987 Eds. *Trails in the thirstland: The anthropological field diaries of Winifred Hoernlé*. Cape Town.

Cell, J. W.
1976 Ed. *By Kenya possessed: The correspondence of Norman Leys and J. H. Oldham, 1918–1926*. Chicago.
1989 Lord Hailey and the making of the African survey. *African Affairs* 88:481–505.
Cerullo, J. J.
1982 *The secularization of the soul: Psychical research in modern Britain*. Philadelphia.
Chapman, W. R.
1985 Arranging ethnology: A. H. L. F. Pitt Rivers and the typological tradition. *HOA* 3:15–48.
Chiao, Chien
1987 Radcliffe-Brown in China. *Anthropology Today* 3(2):5–6.
Christopher, A. J.
1988 *The British Empire at its zenith*. London.
Clammer, J. R.
1976 *Literacy and social change: A case study of Fiji*. Leiden.
Clifford, James
1983 On ethnographic authority. In *The predicament of culture: Twentieth-century ethnography, literature, and art*, 21–54. Cambridge, Mass. (1988).
Clodd, Edward
1891 *Myths and dreams*. London.
1905 *Animism: The seed of religion*. London.
1916 *Memories*. London.
1920 *Magic in names*. London.
Codrington, R. H.
1876 *Melanesian Mission: The island voyage, 1875*. Ludlow, Eng.
1880 Notes on the customs of Mota, Banks Islands. *Transactions of the Royal Society of Victoria* 16:119–43.
1881 Religious beliefs and practices in Melanesia. *JAI* 10:261–316.
1885 *The Melanesian languages*. Oxford.
1891 *The Melanesians: Studies in their anthropology and folk-lore*. Oxford.
Cohn, B. S.
1987 *An anthropologist among the historians and other essays*. Delhi.
Cole, Margaret
1961 *The story of Fabian socialism*. Stanford.
Collini, Stephan
1978 Sociology and idealism in Britain, 1880–1920. *Archives Européenes de Sociologie* 19:3–50.
1979 *Liberalism and sociology: L. T. Hobhouse and political argument in England, 1880–1914*. Cambridge, Eng.
Collins, Robert
1972 The Sudan Political Service: A portrait of the "imperialists." *African Affairs* 71:293–303.
Colonial Office [Great Britain]
1944 *Colonial Research Committee 1st Annual Report, 1943–44*. London.
Colson, E. F.
1986 Lucy Mair. *Anthropology Today* 2(4):22–24.

Comaroff, Jean, & J. L. Comaroff
1988 On the founding fathers, fieldwork and functionalism: A conversation with Isaac Schapera. *American Ethnologist* 15:554–65.
1991 *Of revelation and revolution: Christianity, colonialism and consciousness in South Africa*. Chicago.
Commonwealth Universities Yearbook
1947 *The yearbook of the universities of the Commonwealth*. London.
1952 *The yearbook of the universities of the Commonwealth*. London.
Conrad, Joseph
1902 Heart of darkness. In *Youth: A narrative and two other stories*, 49–182. Edinburgh.
Coote, J.
1987 *Notes and Queries* and social relations: An aspect of the history of social anthropology. *JASO* 18:255–72.
Cowan, R. S.
1985 *Sir Francis Galton and the study of heredity in the nineteenth century*. New York.
Crawford, Robert
1986 Pater's *Renaissance*, Andrew Lang, and anthropological romanticism. *ELH* 53:849–79.
Crawley, E. A.
1902 *The mystic rose: A study of primitive marriage and of primitive thought in its bearing on marriage*. Enlarged ed. by T. Besterman. 2 vols. London (1965).
1907a An anthropologist among the Todas. *Nature* 75:462–63.
1907b The origin and function of religion. *Sociological Papers* 3:243–78.
Crick, Malcolm
1976 The philological anthropology of Friedrich Max Müller. In *Explorations in language and meaning*, 15–35. London.
Czaplička, M. A.
1914 *Aboriginal Siberia: A study in social anthropology*. Oxford.
1916 *My Siberian year*. New York.
Danaher, P. A.
1992a "R-B" and "E-P": Intellectual links between A. R. Radcliffe-Brown and E. E. Evans-Pritchard as revealed in their writings. Paper presented to the Australian Anthropological Society. Canberra.
1992b Structural-functionalism revisited: A. R. Radcliffe-Brown's influence on the writing of social anthropology in the 1940s and 1950s. B.A. thesis, Deakin University.
Dangerfield, G. B.
1935 *The strange death of liberal England*. New York (1961).
Daniel, G. E.
1950 *A hundred years of archaeology*. London.
1973 Elliot Smith, Egypt and diffusionism. In Zuckerman, ed., 1973:407–47.
Darnell, R. D.
1990 *Edward Sapir: Linguist, anthropologist, humanist*. Berkeley.
Dart, R. A.
1974 Sir Grafton Elliot Smith and the evolution of man. In Elkin & MacIntosh, eds., 1974:25–38.

Darwin, C. R.
1871 *The descent of man, and selection in relation to sex.* 2 vols. London.
1891 *Life and letters of Charles Darwin,* ed. Francis Darwin. 2 vols. London.
Dasent, G. W.
1859 *Popular tales from the Norse.* Edinburgh.
Dawson, W. R.
1932 Ed. *The Frazer Lectures, 1922–1932.* London.
1938 Ed. *Sir Grafton Elliot Smith: A biographical record by his colleagues.* London.
Dauber, Kenneth
1995 Bureaucratizing the ethnographer's magic. *CA* 36:75–95.
Deacon, A. B.
1927 The regulation of marriage in Ambrym. *JRAI* 57:325–42.
De Brigard, Emilie
1975 The history of ethnographic film. In T. H. H. Thoresen, ed., *Toward a science of man: Essays in the history of anthropology,* 33–64. The Hague.
De Caro, F. A.
1982 G. L. Gomme: The Victorian folklorist as ethnohistorian. *Journal of the Folklore Institute* 19:107–17.
De Cocq, A. P.
1968 *Andrew Lang: A nineteenth century anthropologist.* Tilburg.
De Jong, P. E., & H. F. Vermeulen
1989 Cultural anthropology at Leiden University: From encyclopedism to structuralism. In W. Otterspeer, ed., *Leiden oriental collections, 1850–1940,* 280–316. Leiden.
Diamond, Alan
1991 Ed. *The Victorian achievement of Sir Henry Maine: A centennial reappraisal.* Cambridge, Eng.
Diamond, Stanley
1980 Ed. *Anthropology: Ancestors and heirs.* The Hague.
Docker, E. W.
1970 *The blackbirders: The recruiting of South Seas labor for Queensland, 1863–1907.* Sydney.
Dorson, R. M.
1955 The eclipse of solar mythology. *Journal of American Folklore* 68:393–416.
1968a *The British folklorists: A history.* Chicago.
1968b Ed. *Peasant customs and savage myths: Selections from the British folklorists.* 2 vols. Chicago.
Douglas, M. T.
1975 If the Dogon . . . . In *Implicit meanings: Essays in anthropology,* 124–41. London.
1978 Judgments on James Frazer. *Daedalus* 107:151–64.
Dow, M. M.
1984 A biparametric approach to network autocorrelation: Galton's problem. *Sociological Methods and Research* 13:201–17.
Downie, R. A.
1940 *James George Frazer: The portrait of a scholar.* London.
1970 *Frazer and "The Golden Bough."* London.

Drake, St. C.
1959 The responsibility of men of culture for destroying the "Hamitic myth." Unpublished manuscript.
Drower, M. S.
1985 *Flinders Petrie: A life in archaeology*. Madison (1995).
Duckworth, W. L. H., et al.
1906 Anthropology at the universities. *Man* 6:85–86.
Duff-Cooper, Andrew
1986 Andrew Lang: Aspects of his work in relation to current social anthropology. *Folk-Lore* 97:186–205.
Dumont, L. C. J.
1973 Review of Hocart 1952. *Man* 8:128–29.
Durkheim, Emile
1893 *The division of labor in society*. Trans. G. Simpson. New York (1964).
1895 *The rules of sociological method*. Trans. S. Solovay & J. Mueller. New York (1964).
1905 On the relation of sociology to the social sciences and to philosophy. *Sociological Papers* 1:197–203.
1912 *The elementary forms of the religious life*. Trans. J. Swain. New York (1965).
Durkheim, Emile, & Paul Fauconnet
1905 Sociology and the social sciences. *Sociological Papers* 1:258–80.
Eddy, John, & Deryck Schreuder
1988 The Edwardian empire in transformation and "decline." In Eddy & Schreuder, eds., *The rise of colonial nationalism: Australia, New Zealand, Canada and South Africa first assert their nationalities, 1880–1914*, 19–62. Sydney.
Edgar, R. R.
1992 Ed. *An African American in South Africa: The travel notes of Ralph J. Bunche*. Athens, Ohio.
Edwards, Elizabeth
1992 *Anthropology and photography, 1860–1920*. New Haven.
Eggan, F. R.
1937 Ed. *Social anthropology of North American tribes*. Chicago (1955).
1974 Aboriginal sins. *Times Literary Supplement*, 13 December.
Eggan, F. R., & W. L. Warner
1956 Alfred Reginald Radcliffe-Brown, 1881–1955. *AA* 58:544–47.
Elkin, A. P.
1938 Anthropological research in Australia and the western Pacific, 1927–1937. *Oceania* 8:306–27.
1943a Anthropology and the peoples of the Southwest Pacific: The past, the present and future. *Oceania* 14:1–19.
1943b F. E. Williams: Government anthropologist, Papua (1922–1943). *Oceania* 14:91–103.
1952 The emergence of psychology, anthropology and education. In *One hundred years of the faculty of arts*, 21–40. Sydney.
1956 A. R. Radcliffe-Brown, 1880[*sic*]–1955. *Oceania* 26:239–51.
1963 The development of scientific knowledge of the Aborigines. In W. Stan-

ner & H. Sheils, eds., *Australian Aboriginal studies: A symposium of papers presented at the 1961 research conference,* 3–28. Melbourne.
1970 The journal *Oceania:* 1930–1970. *Oceania* 40:246–79.
1973 Dean of Australian anthropologists. *International Social Science Journal* 25:13–27.
1974a Elliot Smith and the diffusion of culture. In Elkin & MacIntosh, eds., 1974:139–59.
1974b Sir Grafton Elliot Smith: The man and his work—A personal testimony. In Elkin & MacIntosh, eds., 1974:8–15.
1975 R. H. Mathews. *Oceania* 46:1–24, 126–52, 206–34.

Elkin, A. P., & N. W. G. MacIntosh
1974 Eds. *Grafton Elliot Smith: The man and his work.* Sydney.

Ellen, R. F.
1984 Ed. *Ethnographic research: A guide to general conduct.* London.

Ellen, R. F., et al.
1988 Eds. *Malinowski between two worlds: The Polish roots of an anthropological tradition.* Cambridge, Eng.

Ellis, H. H.
1939 *My life: Autobiography of Havelock Ellis.* Boston.

Emeneau, M. B.
1941 Language and social forms: A study of Toda kinship terms and dual descent. In L. Spier, A. Hallowell, & S. Newman, eds., *Language, culture, and personality: Essays in memory of Edward Sapir,* 158–79. Menasha, Wis.

Evans-Pritchard, E. E.
1933 The intellectualist (English) interpretation of magic. *Bulletin of the Faculty of Arts* [Cairo] 1:1–21.
1937 *Witchcraft, oracles and magic among the Azande.* Oxford.
1940 *The Nuer: A description of the modes of livelihood and political institutions of a Nilotic people.* Oxford.
1946 Applied anthropology. *Africa* 16:92–98.
1950a Social anthropology. In 1962:1–134.
1950b Social anthropology: Past and present. In 1962:139–57.
1962 *Social anthropology and other essays.* New York.
1965 *Theories of primitive religion.* Oxford.
1970 Social anthropology at Oxford. *Man* 5:704.
1973a Fifty years of British anthropology. *Times Literary Supplement,* 6 July.
1973b Fragments of an autobiography. *New Blackfriars* 54:35–37.
1981 *A history of anthropological thought.* New York.

Evans-Pritchard, E. E., et al.
1934 Eds. *Essays presented to C. G. Seligman.* London.

Fagan, B. M.
1975 *The rape of the Nile: Tomb robbers, tourists, and archaeologists in Egypt.* New York.

Fardon, Richard
1990a Malinowski's precedent: The imagination of equality. *Man* 25:569–87.
1990b Ed. *Localizing strategies: Regional traditions of ethnographic writing.* Edinburgh.

Feldman, B. E., & R. D. Richardson
1972 Eds. *The rise of modern mythology: 1680–1860*. Bloomington, Ind.
Feuchtwang, S. D. R.
1973 The discipline and its sponsors. In Asad, ed., 1973:71–102.
Fieldhouse, D. K.
1981 *Colonialism, 1870–1945: An introduction*. New York.
Filby, P. W.
1958 Life with the Frazers. Typescript in Cambridge University Library.
Findlay, G. G., & W. W. Holdsworth
1921–24 *The history of the Wesleyan Methodist Missionary Society*. 5 vols. London.
Firth, J. R.
1957 Ethnographic analysis and language with reference to Malinowski's views. In R. W. Firth, ed., 1957b:93–118.
Firth, R. W.
1929 *Primitive economics of the New Zealand Maori*.
1932 Anthropology in Australia, 1926–32—and after. *Oceania* 3:1–12.
1936 *We, the Tikopia: A sociological study of kinship in primitive Polynesia*. Boston (1963).
1947 Social problems and research in British West Africa. *Africa* 17:77–92, 170–80.
1949 Anthropology and colonial affairs: Summary of contributions by Professors E. E. Evans-Pritchard and Raymond Firth to a special public meeting of the Institute, 5 July 1949. *Man* 49:137–38.
1951a Contemporary British social anthropology. *AA* 53:474–89.
1951b *Elements of social organization*. Boston (1961).
1956 Alfred Reginald Radcliffe-Brown, 1881–1955. *Proceedings of the British Academy* 42:287–302.
1957a Introduction: Malinowski as scientist and as man. In 1957b:1–14.
1957b Ed. *Man and culture: An evaluation of the work of Bronislaw Malinowski*. New York (1964).
1963 *A brief history (1913–63)*. [Pamphlet.] Department of Anthropology, London School of Economics. London.
1968 Rivers on Oceanic kinship. Introduction to reprint edition of Rivers 1914b:17–36.
1975a An appraisal of modern social anthropology. *ARA* 4:1–25.
1975b Max Gluckman. *Proceedings of the British Academy* 61:478–96.
1975c Seligman's contributions to Oceanic anthropology. *Oceania* 45:272–82.
1977 Whose frame of reference? One anthropologist's experience. *Anthropological Forum* 4:145–67.
1981 Bronislaw Malinowski. In S. Silverman, ed., *Totems and teachers: Perspectives on the history of anthropology*, 101–40. New York.
1983 Meyer Fortes: An appreciation. *Cambridge Anthropology* 8(2):52–68.
1988 An interview with David Parkin. *CA* 29:327–41.
1993 Raymond Firth on social anthropology. An interview with Declan Quigley. *Social Anthropology* 1:207–22.

Firth, Stewart
1982 *New Guinea under the Germans*. Melbourne.
Fisher, Donald
1978 The Rockefeller Foundation and the development of scientific medicine in Great Britain. *Minerva* 16:20–41.
1980 American philanthropy and the social sciences: The reproduction of a conservative ideology. In R. F. Arnove, ed., *Philanthropy and cultural imperialism: The foundations at home and abroad*, 233–68. Boston.
1986 Rockefeller philanthropy and British social anthropology. *Anthropology Today* 2(1):5–8.
1993 *Fundamental development in the social sciences: Rockefeller philanthropy and the United States Social Science Research Council*. Ann Arbor, Mich.
Fison, Lorimer
1879 Australian marriage laws. *JAI* 9:354–57.
1888 Appendix to Howitt 1888. *JAI* 18:68–70.
1892a Address by the president. *Report of the 4th Meeting of the Australasian Association for the Advancement of Science*, 144–53. Sydney.
1892b Group marriage and relationship. *Report of the 4th Meeting of the Australasian Association for the Advancement of Science*, 688–97. Sydney.
1892c The Nair polyandry and the Dieri Pirauru. *Report of the 4th Meeting of the Australasian Association for the Advancement of Science*, 717–20. Sydney.
1904 *Tales from old Fiji*. London.
Fison, Lorimer, & A. W. Howitt
1880 *Kamilaroi and Kurnai: Group-marriage and relationship* . . . Osterhout, N.B., Netherlands (1967).
1884 On the deme and the horde. *JAI* 14:142–69.
Flis, Andrejz
1988 Cracow philosophy of the beginning of the twentieth century and the rise of Malinowski's scientific ideas. In Ellen et al., eds., 1988:105–27.
Flint, J. E.
1963 Mary Kingsley—A reassessment. *Journal of African History* 4:95–104.
Flugel, J. C.
1921 *The psycho-analytic study of the family*. London (1939).
Forde, C. D.
1953 Applied anthropology in government: British Africa. In A. L. Kroeber, ed., *Anthropology today*, 841–65. New York.
1967 Anthropology and the development of African studies. *Africa* 37:389–406.
Foreign Office [Great Britain]
1947 *Report of the Interdepartmental Commission of Enquiry on Oriental, Slavonic, East European and African Studies*. London.
Forge, A. W.
1967 The lonely anthropologist. *New Society* 10:221–23.
Forrest, D. W.
1974 *Francis Galton: The life and work of a Victorian genius*. London.
Fortes, Meyer
1937 Review of W. J. Perry 1935. *Man* 37:70–71.

1941 Obituary of C. G. Seligman. *Man* 41:1–6.
1946 Applied anthropology. *Africa* 16:92–98.
1953 *Social anthropology at Cambridge since 1900.* Cambridge, Eng.
1955 Radcliffe-Brown's contributions to the study of kinship. *British Journal of Sociology* 6:16–30.
1956 Alfred Reginald Radcliffe-Brown, F.B.A., 1881–1955: A memoir. *Man* 56:149–53.
1957 Malinowski and the study of kinship. In R. W. Firth, ed., 1957b:157–88.
1968 C. G. Seligman. *International Encyclopedia of the Social Sciences* 14:159–162.
1969 *Kinship and the social order: The legacy of Lewis Henry Morgan.* Chicago.
1976 Cyril Daryll Forde, 1902–1973. *Proceedings of the British Academy* 62:459–83.
1978 An anthropologist's apprenticeship. *ARA* 7:1–30.

Fortes, Meyer, & E. E. Evans-Pritchard
1940 Eds. *African political systems.* London.

Fox, C. E.
1958 *Lord of the southern isles: Being the story of the Anglican mission in Melanesia.* London.

Frank, Katherine
1986 *A voyager out: The life of Mary Kingsley.* Boston.

Fraser, Robert
1990a *The making of "The Golden Bough": The origins and growth of an argument.* New York.
1990b Ed. *Sir James Frazer and the literary imagination.* New York.

Frazer, J. G.
1885 On Prytaneum, the temple of Vesta, the Vestals, perpetual fires. In 1931b:51–79.
1886 On certain burial customs, as illustrative of the primitive theory of the soul. In 1931b:3–50.
1887a *Questions on the manners, customs, religion, superstitions, etc. of uncivilized or semi-civilized peoples.* Privately printed.
1887b *Totemism.* In 1910:I, 1–87.
1888 Taboo. In 1931b:80–87.
1890 *The golden bough: A study in comparative religion.* 2 vols. London.
1894 William Robertson Smith. In *Sir Roger de Coverley and other literary pieces,* 194–209. London (1920).
1898 *Pausanias's description of Greece.* Trans. with commentary. 6 vols. London.
1899 The origin of totemism. In 1910:I, 89–138.
1900 *The golden bough: A study in magic and religion.* 3 vols. London.
1901 On some ceremonies of the central Australian tribes. In 1931b:198–204.
1905a *Lectures on the early history of kingship.* London.
1905b The beginnings of religion and totemism among the Australian aborigines. In 1910:I, 139–172.
1908 The scope of social anthropology: An inaugural lecture. In 1909b:159–76.
1909a Fison and Howitt. In *Sir Roger de Coverley and other literary pieces,* 210–59. London (1920).

1909b *Psyche's task: A discourse concerning the influence of superstition on the growth of institutions*. 2nd ed. (1913).
1910 *Totemism and exogamy: A treatise on certain early forms of superstition and society*. 4 vols. London.
1911a *Taboo and the perils of the soul*. [Part II of the 3rd ed. of *The golden bough*.] London.
1911b *The magic art and the evolution of kings*. 2 vols. [Part I of the 3rd ed. of *The golden bough*.] London.
1913 *Balder the beautiful: The fire-festivals of Europe and the doctrine of the external soul*. 2 vols. [Part VII of the 3rd ed. of *The golden bough*.] London.
1918 *Folklore in the Old Testament*. 3 vols. London.
1921 The scope and method of mental anthropology. In 1931b:234–51.
1930 *The growth of Plato's ideal theory: An essay*. London.
1931a Baldwin Spencer as anthropologist. In Marett & Penniman, eds., 1931: 1–13.
1931b *Garnered sheaves*. London.
1935 *Creation and evolution in primitive cosmologies and other pieces*. London.
1938 *Anthologia Anthropologica: The native races of Africa and Madagascar*, ed. R. A. Downie. London.

Freire-Marreco, B. W.
1907 A bibliography of Edward Burnett Tylor. In Rivers et al., eds., 1907:375–409.
1916 Cultivated plants. In W. W. Robbins, J. P. Harrington, and B. W. Friere-Marreco, *The ethnobotany of the Tewa Indians*, 76–118. Bureau of American Ethnology Bulletin 55. Washington, D.C.

Freud, Sigmund
1913 *Totem and taboo: Some points of agreement between the mental lives of savages and neurotics*. Trans. J. Strachey. New York (1950).
1922a *Drei Abhandlungen zur Sexualtheorie*. 5th ed. Leipzig.
1922b *Vorlesungen zur Einfühlung in die Psychoanalyse*. Vol. 3. Leipzig.

Fustel de Coulanges, N. D.
1864 *The ancient city: A study of the religion, laws and institutions of Greece and Rome*. Trans. W. Small. Garden City, N.Y. (n.d.).

Gacs, Ute, et al.
1989 Eds. *Women anthropologists: Selected biographies*. Urbana, Ill.

Galton, Francis
1883 *Inquiries into human faculty and its development*. London.

Gardiner, A. H.
1919 Some thoughts on the subject of language. *Man* 19:2–6.

Gardiner, Margaret
1984 *Footprints on Malekula: A memoir of Bernard Deacon*. Edinburgh.

Gathercole, P. W.
1977 Cambridge and the Torres Straits. *Cambridge Anthropology* 3(3):22–31.

Gauld, Alan
1968 *The founders of psychic research*. New York.

Geertz, Clifford
1968 Under the mosquito net. *New York Review of Books*, 14 September, pp. 12–13.

1973 Thick description: Toward an interpretive theory of culture. In *The interpretation of cultures: Selected essays*, 3–30. New York.
1988 *Works and lives: The anthropologist as author*. Stanford.

Geison, G. L.
1978 *Michael Foster and the Cambridge school of physiology: The scientific enterprise in late Victorian society*. Princeton.

Geiss, Imanuel
1974 *The Pan-African movement: A history of Pan-Africanism in America, Europe, and Africa*. Trans. A. Keet. New York.

Gellner, E. A.
1988 "Zeno of Cracow" or "Revolution at Nemi" or "The Polish revenge: a drama in three acts." In Ellen et al., eds., 1988:164–95.

Gerholm, Tomas, & Ulf Hannerz
1982 Eds. *The shaping of national anthropologies*. *Ethnos* 47(1–2).

Gerould, D. C.
1981 *Witkacy: Stanislaw Ignacy Witkiewicz as an imaginative writer*. Seattle.

Gillen, F. J.
1896 Notes on some manners and customs of the Aborigines of the Macdonnell Ranges belonging to the Arunta tribe. In W. B. Spencer, ed., 1896:IV, 162–86.

Gluckman, Max
1945 The seven-year research plan of the Rhodes-Livingstone Institute. *Human Problems in British Central Africa* 4:1–32.
1975 Anthropology and apartheid: The work of South African social anthropologists. In M. Fortes & S. Patterson, eds., *Studies in African social anthropology*, 21–39. London.

Goldenweiser, A. A.
1910 Totemism, an analytical study. *Journal of American Folklore* 23:178–298.

Gomme, G. L.
1890a *The handbook of folklore*. London.
1890b *The village community, with special reference to the origin and form of its survivals in Britain*. London.
1892 *Ethnology in folklore*. London.
1896 On the method of determining the value of folklore as ethnological data. In BAAS, *Report of the 66th Meeting*, 626–56.

Goody, J. R.
1993 Meyer Fortes, 1906–1983. *Proceedings of the British Academy* 80:275–87.

Gordon, George
1927 Andrew Lang. In Salmond, ed., 1949:10–21.

Gordon, Robert
1987 Remembering Agnes Winifred Hoernlé. *Social Dynamics* 13:68–72.
1988 Apartheid's anthropologists: The genealogy of Afrikaner anthropology. *American Ethnologist* 15:535–53.
1990 Early social anthropology in South Africa. *African Studies* 49:15–48.

Grattan, C. H.
1963 *The Southwest Pacific to 1900: A modern history: Australia, New Zealand, the islands, Antarctica*. Ann Arbor, Mich.

Gray, Geoffrey
1994 "Piddington's indiscretion": Ralph Piddington, the Australian National Research Council and academic freedom. *Oceania* 64:217–45.
Green, R. L.
1946 *Andrew Lang: A critical biography*. Leicester, Eng.
Greener, Leslie
1967 *The discovery of Egypt*. New York.
Grey, St. G., et al.
1953 *Anthropology at Oxford* [Proceedings of the 500th meeting of the Oxford University Anthropological Society]. Oxford.
Grillo, R. D.
1985 Applied anthropology in the 1980s: Retrospect and prospect. In R. D. Grillo & A. Rew, eds., *Social anthropology and development policy*, 1–36. London.
Grimshaw, A. D., & Keith Hart
1993 *Anthropology and the crisis of the intellectuals.* [Prickly Pear Pamphlet 1]. Cambridge, Eng.
Gross, Feliks
1986 Young Malinowski and his later years. *American Ethnologist* 13:556–70.
Gross, J. J.
1969 *The rise and fall of the man of letters: A study of the idiosyncratic and the humane in modern literature.* London.
Gruber, J. W.
1967 Horatio Hale and the development of American anthropology. *Proceedings of the American Philosophical Society* 111:5–37.
Gulick, J. M.
1988 W. W. Skeat and Malayan ethnography: An appreciation. *Journal of the Malaysian Branch of the Royal Asiatic Society* 61:117–52.
Gutch, John
1971 *Martyr of the islands: The life and death of John Coleridge Patteson*. London.
Haddon, A. C.
1890 The ethnography of the western tribes of the Torres Straits. *JAI* 19:297–440.
1895 *Evolution in art*. London.
1897 A plea for a bureau of ethnology for the British Empire. *Nature* 56:574–75.
1898 *The study of man*. London.
1900 A plea for the study of the native races in South Africa. *Nature* 63:157–159.
1901a *Head-hunters: Black, white, and brown*. London.
1901b Ed. *Reports of the Cambridge Anthropological Expedition to Torres Straits*. Vol. II, *Physiology and psychology*, Part 1. Cambridge, Eng.
1903a Anthropology: Its position and needs. *JAI* 33:11–23.
1903b The saving of vanishing data. *Popular Science Monthly* 62:222–29.
1903c Ed. *Reports of the Cambridge Anthropological Expedition to Torres Straits*. Vol. II, *Physiology and psychology*, Part 2. Cambridge, Eng.
1904 Ed. *Reports of the Cambridge Anthropological Expedition to Torres Straits*.

Vol. V, *Sociology, magic, and religion of the western islanders*. Cambridge, Eng.
1906 A plea for an expedition to Melanesia. *Nature* 74:187–88.
1907 Ed. *Reports of the Cambridge Anthropological Expedition to Torres Straits*. Vol. III, *Linguistics*. Cambridge, Eng.
1908a The Percy Sladen Trust expedition to Melanesia. *Nature* 78:393–94.
1908b Ed. *Reports of the Cambridge Anthropological Expedition to Torres Straits*. Vol. VI, *Sociology, magic and religion of the eastern islanders*. Cambridge, Eng.
1909a An Imperial Bureau of Ethnology. *Nature* 80:73–74.
1909b The anthropological survey of the Sudan. *Nature* 81:491.
1909c *The races of man and their distribution*. London.
1910 *The history of anthropology*. [With A. H. Quiggin.] London.
1911a The First Universal Races Congress. *Science* 34:304–6.
1911b The Universal Races Congress. London *Times*, 8 August, p. 6.
1911c *The wanderings of peoples*. Cambridge.
1912 Ed. *Reports of the Cambridge Anthropological Expedition to Torres Straits*. Vol. IV, *Arts and crafts*. Cambridge, Eng.
1920 Migrations of culture in British New Guinea. *JRAI* 50:237–80.
1921 *The practical value of ethnology*. London.
1922 Ceremonial exchange. *Nature* 110:472–74.
1923 *A brief history of the study of anthropology at Cambridge*. [Pamphlet.] Cambridge, Eng.
1924 Pearls as "Givers of life." *Man* 24:177–85.
1925 Pearls as "Givers of life." *Man* 25:51–53.
1934 An appreciation. In Evans-Pritchard et al., eds., 1934:1–4.
1935 Ed. *Reports of the Cambridge Anthropological Expedition to Torres Straits*. Vol. I, *General ethnography*. Cambridge, Eng.
1939 Obituary of Sydney Ray. *Man* 39:58–61.

Haddon, A. C., & F. C. Bartlett
1922 Obituary of W. H. R. Rivers. *Man* 22:97–103.

Haddon, A. C., & C. Browne
1893 The ethnography of the Aran Islands. *Proceedings of the Royal Irish Academy* 2:768–830.

Haddon, A. C., & Sidney Ray
1893 A study of the languages of the Torres Straits. *Proceedings of the Royal Irish Academy* 2:463–616.

Haeckel, Ernst
1868 *Natürliche Schöpfungsgeschichte*. Berlin.

Haggard, H. R.
1887 *She: A history of adventure*. London.
1926 *The days of my life: An autobiography*. 2 vols. London.

Haggard, H. R., & Andrew Lang
1890 *The world's desire*. London.

Hailey, W. M.
1938 *An African survey: A study of problems arising in Africa south of the Sahara*. London.

1944 The role of anthropology in colonial development. *Man* 44:10–16.
Halliday, Robert
1968 The sociological movement, the Sociological Society, and the genesis of academic sociology in Britain. *Sociological Review* 16:377–98.
Hammel, E. A.
1980 The comparative method in anthropological perspective. *Comparative Studies in Society and History* 22:145–55.
Hancock, W. K.
1962 *Smuts: The fields of force.* Cambridge, Eng.
Haraway, D. J.
1989 *Primate visions: Gender, race, and nature in the world of modern science.* New York.
Hardin, C. L.
1988 *Color for philosophers: Unweaving the rainbow.* Indianapolis.
Harris, José
1977 *William Beveridge: A biography.* Oxford.
Harris, Marvin
1980 History and ideological significance of the separation of social and cultural anthropology. In E. Ross, ed., *Beyond the myths of culture,* 391–407.
Harrison, Jane
1912 *Themis: A study of the social origins of Greek religion.* Cambridge, Eng.
Hartland, E. S.
1890 *The science of fairy tales.* London.
1895a Notes explanatory to the schedules. In BAAS, *Report of the 65th Meeting,* 513–18.
1895b *The Legend of Perseus: A study of tradition in story, custom, and belief.* Vol. II, *The life-token.* London.
1909–10 *Primitive paternity: The myth of supernatural birth in relation to the history of the family.* 2 vols. London.
1914 *Ritual and belief: Studies in the history of religion.* London.
1917 *Matrilineal kinship and the question of its priority.* American Anthropological Association Memoir IV(1). Lancaster, Pa.
1921 *Primitive society: The beginnings of the family and the reckoning of descent.* New York (1969).
1924 *Primitive law.* New York (1969).
Hays, T. E.
1991 Ed. *Ethnographic presents: Pioneering anthropologists in the Papua New Guinea highlands.* Berkeley.
Hayter, F. J.
1939 Museum of Archaeology and of Ethnology. The Faculty of Archaeology and Anthropology. Their inception and development in association with the Cambridge Antiquarian Society for 100 years from 1839 to 1939. Unpublished manuscript in the Museum of Archaeology and Anthropology, Cambridge, Eng.
Head, Henry
1924 William Halse Rivers Rivers, 1864–1922. *Proceedings of the Royal Society of London* 95:xliii–xlvii.

Hearn, W. E.
1879 *The Aryan household, its structure and development: An introduction to comparative jurisprudence*. London.
Hearnshaw, L. S.
1964 *A short history of British psychology, 1840–1940*. London.
Henson, Hilary
1974 *British social anthropologists and language: A history of separate development*. Oxford.
Heussler, Robert
1963 *Yesterday's rulers: The making of the British colonial service*. Syracuse, N.Y.
Heyck, T. W.
1982 *The transformation of intellectual life in Victorian England*. London.
Hinsley, C. M.
1981 *Savages and scientists: The Smithsonian Institution and the development of American anthropology, 1846–1910*. Washington, D.C.
Hirn, Yrjö
1947 Edward Westermarck and his English friends. *Transactions of the Westermarck Society* 1:39–51.
Hobhouse, L. T.
1906 *Morals in evolution: A study in comparative ethics*. London (1951).
Hobhouse, L. T., G. C. Wheeler, & Morris Ginsberg
1915 *The material culture of the simpler peoples*. Expanded ed. London (1931).
Hocart, A. M.
1912a A native Fijian on the decline of his race. *Hibbert Journal* 11:85–98.
1912b The psychological interpretation of language. *British Journal of Psychology* 5:267–79.
1915a Psychology and ethnology. *Folk-Lore* 26:115–37.
1915b Review of Rivers 1914c. *Man* 15:89–93.
1916 The common sense of myth. *AA* 18:307–18.
1918 A point of grammar and a study in method. *AA* 20:265–79.
1922 The cult of the dead in Eddystone Island. *JRAI* 52:71–112.
1925a Letter: Divine kings. *Man* 25:31–32.
1925b Review of W. J. Perry 1923a. *Indian Antiquary* 54:119–20.
1926 Archaeology. In H. W. Codrington, *A short history of Ceylon*, 183–89. London.
1927 *Kingship*. London.
1929 *Lau Islands, Fiji*. Bernice P. Bishop Museum Bulletin 62. Honolulu.
1933 *The progress of man: A short survey of his evolution, his customs and his works*. London.
1936 *Kings and councillors: An essay in the comparative anatomy of human society*. Reprint, ed. R. Needham; foreword by E. E. Evans-Pritchard. Chicago (1970).
1950 *Caste: A comparative study*. London.
1952 *The life-giving myth and other essays*, ed. Lord Raglan. London.
1954 *Social origins*. London.
Hodgen, M. T.
1936 *The doctrine of survivals: A chapter in the history of scientific method in the study of man*. London.

Hoernlé, A. W. T.
1937 The social organization of the Bantu-speaking peoples of South Africa. In Carstens, Klinghardt, & West, eds., 1985:90–114.

Hogbin, H. I.
1946 The Trobriand Islands, 1945. *Man* 46:72.

Homans, G. C.
1941 Anxiety and ritual: The theories of Malinowski and Radcliffe-Brown. *AA* 43:164–72.

Hose, Charles
1927 *Fifty years of romance and research, or a jungle-wallah at large*. London.

Hose, Charles, & William McDougall
1912 *The pagan tribes of Borneo: A description of their physical, moral and intellectual condition with some discussion of their ethnic relations*. 2 vols. London.

Howard, Catherine
1981 Rivers' genealogical method and the *Reports* of the Torres Straits Expedition. Seminar paper, University of Chicago.

Howitt, A. W.
1883a Some Australian beliefs. *JAI* 13:185–98.
1883b Some Australian ceremonies of initiation. *JAI* 13:432–59.
1886 On Australian medicine men. *JAI* 16:23–59.
1888 Further notes on the Australian class systems. *JAI* 18:31–70.
1890 The Dieri and other kindred tribes of Central Australia. *JAI* 20:30–104.
1904 *The native tribes of south-east Australia*. London.

Howitt, A. W., & Lorimer Fison
1882 From mother-right to father-right. *JAI* 12:30–46.
1884 On the deme and the horde. *JAI* 14:142–69.

Hsu, F. L.
1979 The cultural problem of the cultural anthropologist. *AA* 81:517–32.

Hubert, Henri, & Marcel Mauss
1898 *Sacrifice: Its nature and function*. Trans. W. Halls. Chicago (1964).

Hughes, H. S.
1958 *Consciousness and society: The reorientation of European social thought, 1890–1930*. New York.

Huizer, Gerrit, & Bruce Mannheim
1979 Eds. *The politics of anthropology: From colonialism and sexism toward a view from below*. The Hague.

Hyman, S. E.
1966 *The tangled bank: Darwin, Marx, Frazer and Freud as imaginative writers*. New York.

Hynes, S. L.
1968 *The Edwardian turn of mind*. Princeton.
1990 *A war imagined: The First World War and English culture*. London.

Iversen, Erik
1961 *The myth of Egypt and its hieroglyphs in European tradition*. Copenhagen.

Jackson, Henry
1881 Plato's later theory of ideas. *Journal of Philology* 10:132–50, 253–93.

James, Henry
1926 Ed. *Letters of William James*. 2 vols. Boston.

James, Wendy
1973 The anthropologist as reluctant imperialist. In Asad, ed., 1973:41–70.
James, William
1884 What is an emotion? *Mind* 9:188–205.
1890 *The principles of psychology.* 2 vols. New York.
1896 The will to believe. In *The will to believe and other essays in popular philosophy,* 1–31. New York (1903).
1902 *The varieties of religious experience.* New York.
Janik, Allan, & Stephen Toulmin
1973 *Wittgenstein's Vienna.* New York.
Jarvie, I. C.
1964 *The revolution in anthropology.* London.
1974 Review of A. Kuper 1973. *Philosophy of Social Science* 4:301–9.
Jeffries, C. J.
1964 Ed. *A review of colonial research, 1940–60.* London.
Jenness, Diamond
1922–23 *Life of the Copper Eskimo. Reports of the Canadian Arctic Expedition.* Vol. 12, *Southern party 1913–16.* Ottawa.
Jenness, Diamond, & Andrew Ballantyne
1920 *The northern D'Entrecasteaux.* Oxford.
Jerschina, Jan
1988 Polish culture of modernism and Malinowski's personality. In Ellen et al., eds., 1988:128–48.
Jones, Ernest
1924a Mother-right and the sexual ignorance of savages. In 1974:II, 145–73.
1924b Psycho-analysis and anthropology. In 1974:II, 114–44.
1959 *Free associations: Memories of a psycho-analyst.* New York.
1974 *Psycho-myth, psycho-history: Essays in applied psychoanalysis.* 2 vols. New York.
Jones, Greta
1980 *Social Darwinism and English thought: The interaction between biological and social theory.* Atlantic Highlands, N.J.
Jones, G. I.
1974 Social anthropology in Nigeria during the colonial period. *Africa* 44:280–89.
Jones, R. A.
1981 Robertson Smith, Durkheim, and sacrifice: An historical context for *The Elementary Forms of the Religious Life. Journal of the History of the Behavioral Sciences* 17:184–205.
1984 Robertson Smith and James Frazer on religion: Two traditions in British social anthropology. *HOA* 2:31–58.
1986 Durkheim, Frazer and Smith: The role of interests, analogies and exemplars in the development of Durkheim's sociology of religion. *American Journal of Sociology* 92:596–627.
Jorion, Paul
1977 Anthropological fieldwork: Forerunners and inventors. *Cambridge Anthropology* 3(2):22–25.

Julius, Charles
1960 Malinowski's Trobriand Islands. *Journal of Public Service* [Territory of Papua and New Guinea] 2:5–13, 57–64.

Junod, H. A.
1912 *The life of a South African tribe.* 2 vols. London (1962).

Kaberry, P. M.
1957 Malinowski's contribution to field-work methods and the writing of ethnography. In R. W. Firth, ed., 1957b:71–92.

Karpf, F. B.
1932 *American social psychology: Its origins, development and European background.* New York.
1953 *The psychology and psychotherapy of Otto Rank.* New York.

Karsten, Rafael
1923 *Blood revenge, war and victory feasts among the Jibaro Indians of eastern Ecuador.* Bureau of American Ethnology Bulletin 79. Washington, D.C.
1932 *Indian Tribes of the Argentine and Bolivian Chaco.* Helsinki.

Keane, A. H.
1895 *Ethnology.* London.

Keith, Arthur
1917 How can the Institute best serve the needs of anthropology? *JRAI* 47:12–30.
1950 *An autobiography.* London.

Kelly, Lawrence
1983 Structure, function and anarchy in Radcliffe-Brown. Paper presented to the Central States Anthropological Society, 8 April.

Kenny, Michael
1987 Trickster and mystic: The anthropological persona of E. E. Evans-Pritchard. *Anthropology and Humanism Quarterly* 12(1):9–15.

Kenyatta, Jomo
1938 *Facing Mount Kenya: The tribal life of the Gikuyu.* London.

King, Kenneth
1971 *Pan-Africanism and education: A study of race philanthropy and education in the southern states of America and East Africa.* Oxford.

Kingsley, M. H.
1897 *Travels in West Africa.* London.
1898 Liquor traffic with West Africa. *Fortnightly Review* 63:537–60.
1900 *West African Studies.* London.

Kirschner, Paul
1968 *Conrad: The psychologist as artist.* Edinburgh.

Kitagawa, J. M., & J. Strong
1985 Friedrich Max Müller and the comparative study of religion. In N. Smart et al., eds., *Nineteenth century religious thought in the West,* III:179–213. Cambridge, Eng.

Knight, R. P.
1786 *A discourse on the worship of Priapus, and its connection with the mystic theology of the ancients, . . . to which is added an essay* [by Thomas Wright, in 1865 edition] *on the worship of the generative powers during the Middle Ages of Western Europe.* Secaucus, N.J. (1974).

Köbben, A. J. F.
1952 The statistical method in social anthropology. *JRAI* 82:129–46.
Koepping, K.-P.
1985 *Adolf Bastian and the psychic unity of mankind.* Brisbane.
Kroeber, A. L.
1909 Classificatory systems of relationship. In 1952:175–81.
1915 Eighteen professions. *AA* 17:712–18.
1920a Review of Lowie 1920. *AA* 22:377–81.
1920b *Totem and taboo:* An ethnologic psychoanalysis. *AA* 22:48–55.
1934 Yurok and neighboring kin term systems. In 1952:196–201.
1935 History and science in anthropology. In 1952:63–66.
1952 *The nature of culture.* Chicago.
Kropotkin, Peter
1902 *Mutual aid.* London.
Kubica, Grażyna
1988 Malinowski's years in Poland. In Ellen et al., eds., 1988:88–104.
Kuklick, Henrika
1978 The sins of the fathers: British anthropology and African colonial administration. *Research in Sociology of Knowledge, Sciences and Art* 1:93–119.
1979 *The imperial bureaucrat: The colonial administrative service in the Gold Coast, 1920–1939.* Stanford.
1991 *The savage within: The social history of British anthropology, 1885–1945.* Cambridge, Eng.
1993 From the study to the verandah to the field. Paper presented to the American Anthropological Association, 19 November.
n.d. Islands in the Pacific: Darwinian biogeography and anthropological theory. Unpublished manuscript.
Kuper, Adam
1973 *Anthropologists and anthropology: The British school, 1922–1972.* London.
1976 Radcliffe-Brown, Junod, and the mother's brother in South Africa. *Man* 11:111–15.
1982 Lineage theory: A critical retrospect. *ARA* 11:71–95.
1983 *Anthropology and anthropologists: The modern British school.* London.
1988 *The invention of primitive society: Transformations of an illusion.* London.
1990 Psychology and anthropology: The British experience. *History of the Human Sciences* 3:397–413.
Kuper, H. B.
1984 Function, history, biography: Reflections on fifty years in the British anthropological tradition. *HOA* 2:192–213.
Lackner, Helen
1973 Colonial administration and social anthropology: Eastern Nigeria, 1920–1940. In Asad, ed., 1973:123–52.
La Fontaine, J. S.
1985 Ed. Audrey Richards: In memoriam. *Cambridge Anthropology* 10(1).
Landtman, Gunnar
1927 *The Kiwai Papuans of British New Guinea: A nature-born instance of Rousseau's ideal community.* London.

Lang, Andrew
1884 *Custom and myth*. London.
1887 *Myth, ritual, and religion*. 2 vols. London.
1888 *XXXII ballades in blue china*. London.
1894 *Cock Lane and common-sense*. London.
1898 *The making of religion*. London.
1901a *Magic and religion*. London.
1901b *Myth, ritual, and religion*. 2nd ed. 2 vols. London.
1903 *Social origins*. Bound with Atkinson 1903. London.
1905a *Adventures among books*. London.
1905b Introduction. In K. L. Parker, *The Euahlayi tribe: A study of Aboriginal life in Australia*, xi–xxvii. London.
1905c *The secret of the totem*. London.
1907a Australian problems. In Rivers et al., eds., 1907:203–18.
1907b Edward Burnett Tylor. In Rivers et al., eds., 1907:1–15.
1908 *The origins of religion*. London.
Lang, Andrew, & W. Pollock
1887 *He*. In R. Reginald & D. Menville, eds., *They: Three parodies of H. Rider Haggard's "She."* New York (1978).
Langham, Ian
1981 *The building of British social anthropology: W. H. R. Rivers and his Cambridge disciples in the development of kinship studies, 1898–1931*. Dordrecht.
Langlois, C. V., & Charles Seignobos
1898 *Introduction to the study of history*. Trans. G. G. Berry. New York (1926).
Langstaff, E. D.
1978 *Andrew Lang*. Boston.
Laracy, H. M.
1976 Malinowski at war, 1914–1918. *Mankind* 10:264–68.
Lasswell, H. D.
1931 A hypothesis rooted in the preconceptions of a single civilization tested by Bronislaw Malinowski. In S. Rice, ed., *Methods in social science*, 480–88. Chicago.
Layard, J. W.
1942 *Stone men of Malekula*. London.
Leach, E. R.
1957 The epistemological background to Malinowski's empiricism. In R. W. Firth, ed., 1957b:119–37.
1961 Golden bough or gilded twig? *Daedalus* 90:371–99.
1965 Introduction. In reprint edition of Malinowski 1935a:I, viii–xvii.
1966 On the "founding fathers." *CA* 7:560–67.
1967 Virgin birth. In RAI, *Proceedings*, 39–50.
1968 W. H. R. Rivers. In *International Encyclopedia of the Social Sciences* 13:526–28.
1980 On reading *A Diary in the Strict Sense of the Term:* Or the self-mutilation of Professor Hsu. *RAIN* 36:2–3.
1984 Glimpses of the unmentionable in the history of British social anthropology. *ARA* 13:1–23.

1985 Anthropology of religion: British and French schools. In N. Smart et al., eds., *Nineteenth century religious thought in the West*, III:215–62. Cambridge, Eng.

1990 Masquerade: The presentation of self in holi-day life. *Cambridge Anthropology* 13(3):47–69.

LeClerc, Gérard

1972 *Anthropologie et colonialisme: Essai sur l'histoire de l'africanisme*. Paris.

Lee, J. M.

1967 *Colonial development and good government: A study of the ideas expressed by the British official classes in planning decolonization, 1939–1964*. Oxford.

Legge, J. D.

1971 The Murray period: Papua 1906–40. In W. J. Hudson, ed., *Australia and Papua New Guinea*, 32–56. Sydney.

Leopold, Joan

1980 *Culture in comparative and evolutionary perspective: E. B. Tylor and the making of "Primitive Culture."* Berlin.

Lesser, Alexander

1935 Functionalism in social anthropology. *AA* 37:386–93.

Lévi-Strauss, Claude

1949 The sorcerer and his magic. In *Structural anthropology*, 167–85. New York (1963).

1962 *Totemism*. Trans. R. Needham. Boston (1963).

Lévy-Bruhl, Lucien

1910 *Les Fonctions mentales dans les sociétés inférieures*. Trans. L. Clare as *How natives think*. New York (1966).

Linton, Ralph

1936 *The study of man*. New York.

Lipset, David

1980 *Gregory Bateson: The legacy of a scientist*. Englewood Cliffs, N.J.

Loizos, Peter

1977 Personal evidence: Comments on an acrimonious argument. *Anthropological Forum* 4:137–44.

Lombard, Jacques

1972 *L'anthropologie britannique contemporaine*. Paris.

Louis, W. R.

1967 *Great Britain and Germany's lost colonies, 1914–1919*. Oxford.

Lowie, R. H.

1920 *Primitive society*. New York.

1947 Franz Boas, 1858–1942. *National Academy of Sciences, Biographical Memoirs* 24(9):305.

Lubbock, John (Lord Avebury)

1865 *Prehistoric times, as illustrated by ancient remains, and the manners and customs of modern savages*. London.

1870 *The origin of civilisation and the primitive condition of man*. London.

1871 On the development of relationships. *JAI* 1:1–29.

1911 *Marriage, totemism and religion: An answer to critics*. London.

Lugard, F. D.

1922 *The dual mandate in British tropical Africa*. London.

1928 The International Institute of African Languages and Cultures. *Africa* 1:1–12.

Lukes, Steven
1973 *Emile Durkheim: His life and work.* London.

Lyons, A. P.
1983 Hamites, cattle, and kingship: An episode in the history of diffusionist anthropology. Paper presented to the 11th International Congress of Anthropological and Ethnological Sciences.

Lyons, A. P., & H. D. Lyons
1986 Savage sexuality and secular morality: Malinowski, Ellis, Russell. *Canadian Journal of Anthropology* 5:51–64.

Macalister, Alexander
1896 Anthropology at the universities. *The Hospital* 1 February, p. 302.

MacClancy, Jeremy
1986 Unconventional character and disciplinary convention: John Layard, Jungian and anthropologist. *HOA* 4:49–71.

McDougall, William
1903 Cutaneous sensations. Muscular sense. Variations of blood pressure. In Haddon, ed., 1903c:189–95, 196–200, 201–204.
1905 *Physiological psychology.* London.
1908 *An introduction to social psychology.* Boston (1928).
1920 *The group mind.* London.
1921 *Is America safe for democracy?* New York.
1930 William McDougall. In C. Murchison, ed., *A history of psychology in autobiography,* I:191–223. Worcester, Mass.

Mach, Ernst
1895 *Popular scientific lectures.* Trans. T. J. McCormack. Chicago.
1905 *Knowledge and error: Sketches on the psychology of inquiry.* Trans. T. J. McCormack & P. Foulkes. Dordrecht (1976).

MacKenzie, J. M.
1984 *Propaganda and empire: The manipulation of British public opinion, 1880–1960.* Manchester.

MacKenzie, Kenneth
1974 Some British reactions to German colonial methods, 1885–1907. *Historical Journal* 17:165–75.

McKnight, David
1990 The Australian Aborigines in anthropology. In Fardon, ed., 1990b:42–70.

McLennan, J. F.
1865 *Primitive marriage,* ed. P. Rivière. Chicago (1970).
1866 Kinship in ancient Greece. In 1876a:233–309.
1868 Totem. *Chambers's Encyclopaedia.* Supplement, 753–54.
1869 The worship of plants and animals. *Fortnightly Review* 6:407–27; 7:194–216.
1876a *Studies in ancient history.* London.
1876b The classificatory system of relationships. In 1876a:329–407.
1885 *The patriarchal theory, based on the papers of the late John Ferguson McLennan,* ed. D. McLennan. London.

McMillan, R. A.
1986 The study of anthropology, 1931 to 1937, at Columbia University and the University of Chicago. Doctoral dissertation, York University.

Maine, H. S.
1861 *Ancient law, its connection with the early history of society and its relation to modern ideas.* London (1873).

Mair, L. P.
1936 *Native policies in Africa.* London.

Malalgoda, Kitsiri
1980 A. M. Hocart's archaeological and anthropological work in Ceylon. *Ceylon Studies Seminar,* Series no. 4, Serial no. 88.

Malinowski, Bronislaw
1904 Observations on Friedrich Nietzsche's *The Birth of Tragedy.* In Thornton & Skalnik, eds., 1993b:67–88.
1908a On the principle of the economy of thought. In Thornton & Skalnik, eds., 1993b:89–115.
1908b Ozasadzie ekonomii myslenia [On the principle of the economy of thought]. Trans. E. C. Martinek as M.A. thesis, University of Chicago (1985).
1910 Religion and magic: *The Golden Bough.* In Thornton & Skalnik, eds., 1993b:117–22.
1911 Review of *Kwartalnik Ethnograficny Ludowi. Folk-Lore* 22:382–85.
1911–13 Totemism and Exogamy. In Thornton & Skalnik, eds., 1993b:123–99.
1912 The economic aspect of the intichiuma ceremonies. In Thornton & Skalnik, eds., 1993b:209–27.
1913a Elementary forms of the religious life. In 1962:282–88.
1913b Review of Spencer & Gillen 1912. *Folk-Lore* 24:278–79.
1913c *The family among the Australian Aborigines.* New York (1963).
1914 A fundamental problem of religious sociology. In 1962:266–67.
1915a The natives of Mailu: Preliminary results of the Robert Mond research work in British New Guinea. In M. W. Young, ed., 1988b:78–331.
1915b *Wierzenia pierwotne i formy ustroju spotecznego* [Primitive beliefs and forms of social organization]. Polish Academy of Science, Cracow.
1916 Baloma: The spirits of the dead in the Trobriand Islands. In 1948:149–274.
1921a Classificatory particles in the language of Kiriwina. *Bulletin of the School of Oriental Studies* 1(4):33–78.
1921b Review of McDougall 1920. *Man* 21:106–9.
1922a *Argonauts of the western Pacific: An account of native enterprise and adventure in the archipelagoes of Melanesian New Guinea.* New York (1961).
1922b Ethnology and the study of society. *Economica* 2:208–19.
1922c Sexual life and marriage among primitive mankind. In 1962:117–22.
1923a Psycho-analysis and anthropology. In 1962:114–16.
1923b Science and superstition in primitive mankind. In 1962:268–74.
1923c The problem of meaning in primitive languages. In Ogden & Richards 1923:296–336.
1923d The psychology of sex and the foundations of kinship in primitive societies. *Psyche* 4:98–128.

1924a Instinct and culture in human and animal societies. *Nature* 114:79–82.
1924b New and old anthropology. *Nature* 113:299–301.
1924c Psychoanalysis and anthropology. *Psyche* 4:293–332.
1925a Complex and myth in mother-right. *Psyche* 5:194–216.
1925b Labour and primitive economics. *Nature* 116:926–30.
1925c Magic, science and religion. In 1948:17–92.
1926a Address on anthropology and social hygiene. In *Foundations of social hygiene*. London.
1926b Anthropology. *Encyclopaedia Britannica*. 13th ed. I:131–39.
1926c *Crime and custom in savage society*. Paterson, N.J. (1964).
1926d Myth in primitive psychology. In 1948:93–148.
1927a Anthropology in the westernmost Orient. *Nature* 120:867–68.
1927b *Sex and repression in savage society*. Cleveland (1965).
1927c *The father in primitive psychology*. New York (1966).
1928 The life of culture. In G. E. Smith et al., *Culture: The diffusion controversy*, 26–46. New York.
1929a Kinship. *Encyclopaedia Britannica*. 14th ed. In 1962:132–50.
1929b Practical anthropology. *Africa* 2:22–38.
1929c Review of Landtman 1927. *Folk-Lore* 40:109–12.
1929d *The sexual life of savages in northwestern Melanesia*. New York (n.d.).
1930a Parenthood, the basis of social structure. In V. H. Calverton & S. Schmalhausen, eds., *The new generation*, 113–68. New York.
1930b The impasse on kinship. In 1962:150–64.
1931a A plea for an effective colour bar. *Spectator* 146:999–1001.
1931b Culture. *Encyclopaedia of the Social Sciences* 4:621–45.
1931c The anthropology of Africa. *Nature* 127:655–57.
1932 Special foreword to the third edition. In *The sexual life of savages*, xix–xliv. London.
1934a Introduction. In H. I. Hogbin, *Law and order in Polynesia*, xvii–lxxii. London.
1934b Whither Africa? *International Review of Missions* 25:401–7.
1935a *Coral gardens and their magic*. 2 vols. Bloomington (1965).
1935b Primitive law. *Man* 35:55–56.
1936a Culture as a determinant of behavior. In 1962:167–95.
1936b Native education and culture contact. *International Review of Missions* 25:480–515.
1937 Introduction. In J. E. Lips, *The savage hits back*, vii–ix. New Haven.
1938a Introduction. In Kenyatta 1938:vii–xiii.
1938b The anthropology of changing cultures. In *Methods of study of culture contact in Africa*, vii–xxxviii. Memorandum XV of the International African Institute. London.
1939 The group and the individual in functional analysis. In 1962:233–45.
1941 Introduction. In I. Schapera, *Married life in an African tribe*, i–xvii. New York.
1944 *A scientific theory of culture and other essays*. New York (1960).
1948 *Magic, science and religion and other essays*. Garden City, N.Y. (1954).
1962 *Sex, culture and myth*. New York.

1967 *A diary in the strict sense of the term*. Trans. N. Guterman. New York.
Malinowski, Bronislaw, & Julio de la Fuente
1982 *Malinowski in Mexico: The economics of a Mexican market system*. London.
Man, E. H.
1885 *On the aboriginal inhabitants of the Andaman Islands*. London.
Mandelbaum, D. G.
1980 *The Todas* in time perspective. *Reviews in Anthropology* 7:279–302.
Manganaro, Marc
1992 *Myth, rhetoric and the voice of authority: A critique of Frazer, Eliot, Frye, and Campbell*. New Haven.
Marau, Clement
1894 *Story of a Melanesian deacon: Clement Marau*. Trans. R. H. Codrington. London.
Marett, R. R.
1892 The ethics of industrialism. *Economic Review* 2:342–50.
1900 Pre-animistic religion. In 1914:1–28.
1902 Origin and validity in ethics. In H. Sturt, ed., *Personal idealism: Philosophical essays by eight members of the University of Oxford*, 221–87. London.
1904 From spell to prayer. In 1914:29–72.
1907 Is taboo a negative magic? In 1914:75–98.
1908a A sociological view of comparative religion. In 1914:122–144.
1908b The conception of *mana*. In 1914:99–121.
1908c Ed. *Anthropology and the classics: Six lectures delivered before the University of Oxford*. New York (1966).
1912 The study of magico-religious facts. In BAAS 1912:251–61.
1914 *The threshold of religion*. 2nd ed. London.
1917 The psychology of culture-contact. In 1920:72–98.
1919 The interpretation of survivals. In 1920:168–95 [as "Magic or religion?"].
1920 *Psychology and folk-lore*. London.
1924a Anthropology [Review of W. J. Perry 1923a and other books]. *London Mercury* 9:107–9.
1924b Psychology and anthropology. In W. Brown, ed., *Psychology and the sciences*, 29–52. London.
1927 The diffusion of culture. In Dawson, ed., 1932:172–89.
1929a Anthropology. *Encyclopaedia Britannica*. 14th ed. 2:41–46.
1929b *The raw material of religion*. The Andrew Lang Lecture. Oxford.
1935 *Head, heart, and hands in human evolution*. London.
1936 *Tylor*. New York.
1941 *A Jerseyman at Oxford*. London.
Marett, R. R., & T. K. Penniman
1931 Eds. *Spencer's last journey: Being the journal of an expedition to Tierra del Fuego by the late Sir Walter Baldwin Spencer, with a memoir*. Oxford.
1932 Eds. *Spencer's scientific correspondence with Sir J. G. Frazer and others*. Oxford.
Mark, J. T.
1976 Frank Hamilton Cushing and an American science of anthropology. *Perspectives in American History* 10:449–86.

Marshall, G. W.
1866 Remarks on genealogy in connexion with anthropology. *Memoirs of the Anthropological Society of London* 2:68–73.
Marshall, W. E.
1873 *A phrenologist among the Todas; Or, the study of a primitive tribe in South India: History, character, customs, religion, infanticide, polyandry, language.* London.
Massingham, H. J.
1941 *Remembrance: An autobiography.* London.
Mathew, John
1899 *Eaglehawk and crow: A study of the Australian Aborigines including an inquiry into their origin and a survey of Australian languages.* London.
Mathews, R. H.
1905 *Ethnological notes on the Aboriginal tribes of New South Wales and Victoria.* Sydney.
Matthews, Z. K.
1981 *Freedom for my people: The autobiography of Z. K. Matthews: Southern Africa 1901 to 1968.* London.
Mauss, Marcel
1925 *The gift.* Trans. I. Cunnison. New York (1967).
Meek, C. K.
1925 *The northern tribes of Nigeria.* 2 vols. Oxford.
1931a *A Sudanese kingdom: An ethnographical study of the Jukun-speaking peoples of Nigeria.* London.
1931b *Tribal studies in Northern Nigeria.* 2 vols. London.
1937 *Law and authority in a Nigerian tribe: A study of indirect rule.*
Meller, H. E.
1973 Patrick Geddes: An analysis of his theory of civics, 1880–1904. *Victorian Studies* 16:291–315.
Merz, J. T.
1904 *A history of European thought in the nineteenth century.* Vol. I. New York (1965).
Miller, M. A.
1976 *Kropotkin.* Chicago.
Miller, R. B.
1975 Anthropology and institutionalization: Frederick Starr at the University of Chicago, 1892–1923. *Kroeber Anthropological Society Papers* 51–52.
Montagu, M. F. A.
1982 Edward Westermarck: Recollections of an old student in young age. In Stroup, ed., 1982b:63–70.
Montenyohl, E.
1987 Andrew Lang's training in folklore. *Folk-Lore* 98:180–82.
Morgan, C. L.
1944 *The House of Macmillan (1843–1943).* New York.
Morgan, L. H.
1871 *Systems of consanguinity and affinity of the human family.* Osterhout, N.B., Netherlands (1970).

1877 *Ancient society, or researches in the lines of human progress from savagery through barbarism to civilization*, ed. E. B. Leacock. Cleveland (1963).

Morris, J. H.

1968 *Pax Britannica: The climax of an empire*. New York.

1978 *Farewell to trumpets: An imperial retreat*. New York.

Morrison, Charles

1983a Hocart and Cambridge: Complaints of a colonial commissioner in Ceylon. *HAN* 10:9–13.

1983b The Hutton hiatus in Cambridge anthropology. Paper presented to the American Anthropological Association, 20 November.

1984 Three styles of imperial ethnography: British officials as anthropologists in India. *Knowledge and Society: Studies in the Sociology of Culture Past and Present* 5:141–69.

Müller, F. M.

1856a Comparative mythology. In *Chips from a German workshop*, II:1–140. New York (1876).

1856b *Outline dictionary for the use of missionaries*. London.

1882 *Lectures on the origin and growth of religion, as illustrated by the religions of India*. London.

1885 The savage. *Nineteenth Century* 17:109–32.

1892 On the untrustworthiness of anthropological evidence. In *Anthropological religion*, 413–35. London.

1902 *Life and letters of the Rt. Hon. Friedrich Max Müller*, ed. G. Müller. 2 vols. New York.

Mulvaney, D. J.

1958 The Australian Aborigines 1606–1929: Opinion and fieldwork. *Historical Studies, Australia and New Zealand* 8:131–51, 297–314.

1970 The anthropologist as tribal elder. *Mankind* 7:205–17.

1971 The ascent of aboriginal man: Howitt as anthropologist. In M. H. Walker 1971:285–312.

1989 Australian anthropology and the ANZAAS: "Strictly scientific and critical." In R. MacLeod, ed., *The commonwealth of science: ANZAAS and the scientific enterprise in Australia, 1888–1988*, 196–221. Melbourne.

Mulvaney, D. J., & J. H. Calaby

1985 *"So much that is new": Baldwin Spencer, 1860–1929*. Melbourne.

Murdock, G. P.

1949 *Social structure*. New York.

1951 British social anthropology. *AA* 53:465–73.

Murray, J. H. P.

1920 *Review of the Australian administration in Papua from 1907 to 1920*. Port Moresby.

Murray-Brown, Jeremy

1972 *Kenyatta*. London.

Myers, C. S.

1903 Hearing. Smell. Taste. Reaction-times. In Haddon, ed., 1903c:141–68, 169–85, 186–88, 205–223.

1909 *A text-book of experimental psychology*. London.

1923 The influence of the late W. H. R. Rivers. In Rivers 1923b:147–81.
1936 Charles Samuel Myers. In C. Murchison, ed., *A history of psychology in autobiography*, III:215–30. Worcester, Mass.

Myers, G. E.
1986 *William James: His life and thought*. New Haven.

Myres, J. L.
1929 The science of man in the service of the state. *JRAI* 60:19–52.

Nadel, S. F.
1951 *Foundations of social anthropology*. London.
1957 Malinowski on magic and religion. In R. W. Firth, ed., 1957b:189–208.

Needham, Joseph
1925 Ed. *Science, religion and reality*. New York.

Needham, Rodney
1967 *A bibliography of Arthur Maurice Hocart (1883–1939)*. Oxford.
1970 Editor's introduction. In reprint edition of Hocart 1936:ix–xcix.
1974 Surmise, discovery and rhetoric. In *Remarks and inventions: Sceptical essays about kinship*, 109–72. London.
1982 Kariera refutations. *Oceania* 51:123–38.

Neill, Stephen
1964 *Christian missions*. Harmondsworth, Eng.

Nelson, H. N.
1969 European attitudes in Papua, 1906–1914. In *The history of Melanesia*. 2nd Waigani Seminar. Canberra and Port Moresby.

Nicolson, I. F.
1969 *The administration of Nigeria, 1900–1960: Men, methods, and myth*. Oxford.

Nock, D.
1988 *A Victorian missionary and Canadian Indian policy: Cultural synthesis vs. cultural replacement*. Waterloo, Ont.

Ogden, C. K., & I. A. Richards
1923 *The meaning of meaning: A study of the influence of language upon thought and of the science of symbolism*. London.

Oldham, J. H.
1924 *Christianity and the race problem*. New York.

Olson, R. L.
1933 Clan and moiety in North America. *University of California Publications in American Archaeology and Ethnology* 33:351–422.

Orel, Harold
1984 *Victorian literary critics*. London.

Paluch, A. K.
1981 The Polish background of Malinowski's work. *Man* 16:276–85.

Panoff, Michel
1972 *Bronislaw Malinowski*. Paris.

Parsons, Talcott
1937 *The structure of social action: A study in social theory with special reference to a group of recent European writers*. New York.
1957 Malinowski and the theory of social systems. In R. W. Firth, ed., 1957b:53–70.

1970 On building social systems theory: A personal history. *Daedalus* 99:826–81.

Payne, H. C.

1981 Malinowski's style. *Proceedings of the American Philosophical Society* 125:416–40.

Pear, T. H.

1960 Some early relations between English ethnologists and psychologists. *JRAI* 90:227–37.

Peel, J. D. Y.

1971 *Herbert Spencer: The evolution of a sociologist*. New York.

Pels, Peter

1992 Anthropology and mission: Towards a historical analysis of professional identity. In R. Bonsen et al., eds., *The ambiguity of rapprochement: Reflections of anthropologists on their controversial relations with missionaries*, 77–100. Nijmegen, Netherlands.

Pels, Peter, & Oscar Salemink

1993 Ethnography as colonial practice: Five theses and a question. Draft document for symposium on "Colonial ethnographies: Writing, cultures, and historical contexts." Amsterdam.

Penniman, T. K.

1936 A bibliography of the scientific writings of R. R. Marett. In Buxton, ed., 1936b:303–25. London.

Perham, M. F.

1937 *Native administration in Nigeria*. London.

1956 *Lugard: The years of adventure, 1858–1898*. London.

1960 *Lugard: The years of authority, 1898–1945*. London.

Perry, R.

1975 Radcliffe-Brown and Kropotkin: The heritage of anarchism in British social anthropology. *Kroeber Anthropological Society Papers* (1978): 61–65.

Perry, W. J.

1918 *The megalithic culture of Indonesia*. Manchester.

1923a *The children of the sun: A study in the early history of civilization*. London.

1923b *The origin of magic and religion*. New York.

1924 *The growth of civilization*. London.

1935 *The primordial ocean: An introductory contribution to social psychology*. London.

Peterson, Nicolas

1990 "Studying man and man's nature": The history of the institutionalization of Aboriginal anthropology. *Australian Aboriginal Studies* 32:3–19.

Phillips, C. S., Jr.

n.d. *The school of Oriental and African Studies, University of London, 1917–1967: An introduction*. London.

Pilling, A. R.

1952 On the genealogical method in cultural anthropology. Unpublished manuscript.

Pinney, Christopher

1990 Colonial anthropology in the "laboratory of mankind." In C. A. Bayly, ed., *The Raj: India and the British, 1600–1947*, 252–63. London.

Pipping, K. G.
1982 The first Finnish sociologist. *Acta Sociologica* 25:347–57.

Pitt-Rivers, G. L. S.
1927 *The clash of culture and the contact of races: An anthropological and psychological study of the laws of racial adaptability with special reference to the depopulation of the Pacific and the government of subject races*. London.

Porter, Bernard
1968 *Critics of empire: British radical attitudes to colonialism in Africa, 1895–1914*. London.

Potter, Philip
1987 From missions to mission: Reflections on seventy-five years of the IRM. *International Review of Mission* 76:155–73.

Powdermaker, Hortense
1966 *Stranger and friend: The way of an anthropologist*. New York.

Prichard, J. C.
1813 *Researches into the physical history of man*, ed. G. W. Stocking, Jr. Chicago (1973).
1819 *An analysis of the Egyptian mythology: To which is subjoined a critical examination of the remains of Egyptian chronology*. London.

Pulman, Bertrand
1986 Aux origines du dêbat ethnologie/psychanalyse: W. H. R. Rivers (1864–1922). *L'Homme 100* 26(4):119–42.
1989 Aux origines du dêbat anthropologie/psychanalyse: Seligman (1873–1940). *Gradhiva* 6:35–49.

Quiggin, A. H.
1942 *Haddon the headhunter*. Cambridge, Eng.

Radcliffe-Brown, A. R.
1909 The religion of the Andaman Islanders. *Folk-Lore* 20:257–71.
1910a Marriage and descent, North Australia. *Man* 10:55–58.
1910b Peluga: A reply to Father Schmidt. *Man* 10:33–37.
1910c Study of native races [interview]. *The Western Australian*, 11 September.
1913a An unpublished paper by A. R. Radcliffe-Brown on "The study of social institutions," with a letter in reply by W. H. R. Rivers and an introduction by Meyer Fortes. *Cambridge Anthropology* 3(3, 1976–77):32–48.
1913b Australia. In W. Hutchinson, ed., *The customs of the world*. 2 vols. I:139–98. London.
1913c Three tribes of Western Australia. *JRAI* 43:143–94.
1914a Notes on the language of the Andaman Islands. *Anthropos* 9:36–52.
1914b The definition of totemism. *Anthropos* 9:622–30.
1914c Varieties of totemism in Australia. In BAAS, *Report of the 84th Meeting*, 532–33.
1918 Notes on the social organization of Australian tribes. Part I. *JRAI* 48:222–53.
1922a Some problems in Bantu sociology. *Bantu Studies* 1:38–46.
1922b *The Andaman Islanders: A study in social anthropology*. Cambridge, Eng.
1923a Notes on the social organization of Australian tribes. Part II. *JRAI* 53:424–47.

1923b The methods of ethnology and social anthropology. *South African Journal of Science* 20:124–47.
1924a Science and native problems: How to understand the Bantu. *Anthropology Today* 2(4):17–21 (August 1986).
1924b The mother's brother in South Africa. In 1952:15–31.
1925a Culture areas of Africa. *AA* 27:346–47.
1925b Native dolls in the Transvaal Museum. *Annals of the Transvaal Museum* 11:99–102.
1925c Review of three books by Leo Frobenius. *AA* 27:325–29.
1926 The rainbow-serpent myth of Australia. *JRAI* 56:19–25.
1927 The regulation of marriage in Ambrym. *JRAI* 57:343–48.
1929a A further note on Ambrym. *Man* 29:50–53.
1929b Bilateral descent. *Man* 29:199–200.
1929c Notes on totemism in Eastern Australia. *JRAI* 59:399–415.
1930a Editorial. *Oceania* 1:1–4.
1930b The sociological theory of totemism. In 1952:117–32.
1930–31 The social organization of Australian tribes. *Oceania* 1:(1–4):34–63, 207–46, 322–41, 426–56.
1931a Applied anthropology. *Report of the 20th Meeting of the Australian and New Zealand Association for the Advancement of Science, 1930,* 267–80. Brisbane.
1931b The present position of anthropological studies. In 1958:42–95.
1932 *The Andaman Islanders.* 2nd ed. Chicago.
1933a Primitive law. In 1952:212–19.
1933b Social sanctions. In 1952:205–11.
1935a Kinship terminologies in California. *AA* 37:530–35.
1935b On the concept of function in social science. *AA* 37:394–402.
1935c Patrilineal and matrilineal succession. In 1952:32–48.
1935d Primitive law. *Man* 35:47–48.
1937 *A natural science of society.* Chicago (1956).
1938 Motherhood in Australia. *Man* 38:14–15.
1939 Taboo. In 1952:133–52.
1940a On joking relationships. In 1952:90–104.
1940b On social structure. In 1952:188–204.
1941 The study of kinship systems. In 1952:49–89.
1946 Note on functional anthropology. *Man* 46:38–41.
1947 Australian social organization. *AA* 49:151–54.
1950 Introduction. In Radcliffe-Brown & Forde, eds., 1950:1–85.
1952 *Structure and function in primitive society.* New York (1965).
1958a *Method in social anthropology: Selected essays,* ed. M. N. Srinivas. Chicago.
1958b Social anthropology. In 1958a:133–89.

Radcliffe-Brown, A. R., & C. D. Forde
1950 Eds. *African systems of kinship and marriage.* London.

Ranger, T. O.
1976 From humanism to the science of man: Colonialism in Africa and the understanding of alien societies. *Transactions of the Royal Historical Society* 26:115–41.

Rank, Otto
1924 *Das Träuma der Geburt und sein Bedeutung für die Psychoanalyse.* Leipzig.

Rapport, Nigel
1990 "Surely everything has already been said about Malinowski's Diary!" *Anthropology Today* 6(1):5–9.
Rattray, R. S.
1913 *Hausa Folk-Lore, customs, proverbs, etc. collected and transliterated with English translation and notes.* 2 vols. New York (1969).
1923 *Ashanti.* London.
1927 *Religion and art in Ashanti.* London.
1929 *Ashanti law and constitution.* Oxford.
1932 *The tribes of the Ashanti hinterland.* 2 vols. Oxford.
1934 Present tendencies in African colonial government. *Journal of the African Society* 33:22–36.
Ratzel, Friedrich
1882 *Anthropo-Geographie, oder Gründzeuge der Anwendung der Erdkunde auf die Geschichte.* Stuttgart.
Read, C. H.
1896 An Imperial Bureau of Ethnology. In BAAS, *Report of the 66th Meeting,* 928.
1900 Presidential address. *JAI* 30:6-21.
1901 Presidential address. *JAI* 31:9–19.
1906 Anthropology at the universities. *Man* 6:56–59.
Redfield, Robert
1937 Introduction. In Eggan, ed., 1937:ix–xiv.
Reining, C. C.
1952 Applied anthropology in theory and practice. B. Litt. thesis, Oxford University.
Resek, Carl
1960 *Lewis Henry Morgan: American scholar.* Chicago.
Rich, P. B.
1984 "The baptism of a new era": The 1911 Universal Races Congress and the liberal ideology of race. *Ethnic and Racial Studies* 7:534–50.
1990 *Race and empire in British politics.* 2nd ed. Cambridge, Eng.
Richards, A. I.
1932 *Hunger and work in a savage society: A functional study of nutrition among the southern Bantu.*
1939a *Land, labour and diet in Northern Rhodesia: An economic study of the Bemba tribe.* London.
1939b The development of fieldwork methods in social anthropology. In F. C. Bartlett, ed., *The study of society,* 272–316. London.
1944 Practical anthropology in the lifetime of the International African Institute. *Africa* 14:289–301.
1957 The concept of culture in Malinowski's work. In R. W. Firth, ed., 1957b:15–32.
1977a The Colonial Office and the organization of social research. *Anthropological Forum* 4:168–89.
1977b The Rhodes-Livingstone Institute: An experiment in research, 1933–38. *African Social Research* 24:275–79.

Richter, Melvin
1964 *The politics of conscience: T. H. Green and his age*. Cambridge, Mass.
Riesen, R. A.
1985 *Criticism and faith in late Victorian Scotland: A. B. Davidson, William Robertson Smith, and George Adam Smith*. New York.
Risley, Herbert
1890 The study of ethnology in India. *JAI* 20:235–63.
Rivers, W. H. R.
1899 Two new departures in anthropological method. In BAAS, *Report of the 69th Meeting*, 879–80.
1900 A genealogical method of collecting social and vital statistics. *JAI* 30:74–82.
1901a Introduction. Vision. In Haddon, ed., 1901b:1–7, 9–132.
1901b On the function of the maternal uncle in Torres Straits. On the functions of the son-in-law and brother-in-law in Torres Straits. *Man* 1:107–9.
1901c Primitive colour vision. *Popular Science Monthly* 59:44–58.
1901d The colour vision of the natives of Upper Egypt. *JAI* 31:229–47.
1904 Genealogies. Kinship. In Haddon, ed., 1904:122–28, 129–52.
1905 Observations on the senses of the Todas. *British Journal of Psychology* 1:321–96.
1906 *The Todas*. Osterhout, N.B., Netherlands (1967).
1907a On the origin of the classificatory system of relationships. In 1924:175–94.
1907b The marriage of cousins in India. *Journal of the Royal Asiatic Society* 39:611–40.
1908a A human experiment in nerve division [with H. Head]. *Brain* 31:323–450.
1908b Genealogies. Kinship. The regulation of marriage. In Haddon, ed., 1908b:64–91, 92–101, 120–24.
1910 The genealogical method of anthropological inquiry. *Sociological Review* 3:1–12.
1911 The ethnological analysis of culture. In 1926:120–40.
1912a A general account of method. In BAAS 1912:108–27.
1912b The disappearance of the useful arts. In *Festkrift tillegnad Edvard Westermarck*, 109–30. Helsinki.
1912c The primitive conception of death. In 1926:36–50.
1912d The sociological significance of myth. *Folk-Lore* 23:307–31.
1913a Report on anthropological research outside America. In W. H. R. Rivers et al., *Reports upon the present condition and future needs of the science of anthropology*, 5–28. Washington, D.C.
1913b Survival in sociology. *Sociological Review* 6:293–305.
1913c The contact of peoples. In E. C. Quiggin, ed., *Essays and studies presented to William Ridgeway*, 474–92. Cambridge, Eng.
1914a Is Australian culture simple or complex? In 1926:58–66.
1914b *Kinship and social organization*. London (1968).
1914c *The history of Melanesian society*. 2 vols. Osterhout, N.B., Netherlands (1968).

1914d The terminology of totemism. *Anthropos* 9:640–46.
1915a Review of G. E. Smith 1915. *Journal of Egyptian Archaeology*. 2:256–57.
1915b The distribution of megalithic civilization. In 1926:167–72.
1916a Marriage. Mother-right. *Hastings' Encyclopaedia of Religion and Ethics* 8:423–32, 851–59.
1916b Sociology and psychology. In 1926:3–20.
1917a Dreams and primitive culture. *Bulletin of the John Rylands Library* 4:387–410.
1917b Freud's psychology of the unconscious. In 1920a:159–69.
1917c The government of subject peoples. In A. C. Seward, ed., *Science and the nation*, 302–28. Cambridge, Eng.
1918 Psycho-therapeutics. *Hastings' Encyclopaedia of Religion and Ethics* 10:433–40.
1919 Instinct and the unconscious [with contributions by C. Myers, C. Jung, G. Wallas, J. Drever, W. McDougall]. *British Journal of Psychology* 10:1–42.
1920a *Instinct and the unconscious: A contribution to a biological theory of the psycho-neuroses*. Cambridge, Eng.
1920b The dying-out of native races. *Lancet* 98:42–44, 109–11.
1921 Conservatism and plasticity. *Folk-Lore* 32:10–27.
1922a *History and ethnology*. London.
1922b The psychological factor. In 1922e:84–113.
1922c The relations of complex and sentiment [with contributions by A. Tausley, A. Shand, T. Pear, B. Hart, C. Myers]. *British Journal of Psychology* 13:107–48.
1922d The symbolism of rebirth. *Folk-Lore* 33:14–33.
1922e Ed. *Essays on the depopulation of Melanesia*. Cambridge, Eng.
1923a *Conflict and dream*. London.
1923b *Psychology and politics and other essays*. London.
1924 *Social organization*. London.
1926 *Psychology and ethnology*, ed. G. E. Smith. London.

Rivers, W. H. R., et al.
1907 Eds. *Anthropological essays presented to Edward Burnett Tylor in honour of his 75th birthday, Oct. 2 1907*. Oxford.

Roberts, Jeff
1993 Using global knowledge down the local. *Anthropology Today* 9(5):17–18.

Robinson, Kenneth
1965 *The dilemmas of trusteeship: Aspects of British colonial policy between the wars*. London.

Robinson, Ronald, & John Gallagher
1961 *Africa and the Victorians: The climax of imperialism*. Garden City, N.Y. (1968).

Rodman, Margaret, & Matthew Cooper
1983 Eds. *The pacification of Melanesia*. Ann Arbor, Mich.

Rooksby, R. L.
1971 W. H. R. Rivers and the Todas. *South Asia* 1:109–21.

Rossetti, Carlo
1985 Bronislaw Malinowski, the sociology of modern problems in Africa and the colonial situation. *Cahiers d'Études Africaines* 25:477–503.

Rouse, Irving
1986 *Migrations in prehistory: Inferring population movement from cultural remains*. New Haven.
Rousseau, J. J.
1755 *Discourse on the origin and foundations of inequality among men*. Amsterdam.
Rowley, C. D.
1958 *The Australians in German New Guinea, 1914–1921*. Melbourne.
1966 *The New Guinea villager: The impact of colonial rule on primitive society and economics*. New York.
1970 *The destruction of Aboriginal society*. Canberra.
Royal Anthropological Institute
1951 *Notes and queries on anthropology*. 6th ed. London.
Salat, Jana
1983 *Reasoning as enterprise: The anthropology of S. F. Nadel*. Trans. G. Quatember. Göttingen.
Salmond, J. B.
1949 Ed. *Concerning Andrew Lang: Being the Andrew Lang Lectures . . . 1927–1937*. Oxford.
Salter, Elizabeth
1972 *Daisy Bates*. New York.
Sanjek, Roger
1990 Ed. *Fieldnotes: The makings of anthropology*. Ithaca, N.Y.
Saville, W. J.
1912 A grammar of the Mailu language. *JRAI* 42:397–436.
Schapera, Isaac
1934 The present state and future development of ethnographic research in South Africa. *Bantu Studies* 8:219–342.
1990 The appointment of Radcliffe Brown to the chair of social anthropology at the University of Cape Town. *African Studies* 49:1–14.
Schirbel, Gabriele
1991 *Structuren des Internationalismus: First Universal Races Congress, London 1911*. Münster.
Schmidt, Francis
1987 Polytheisms: Degeneration or progress? *History and Anthropology* 3:9–60.
Schneider, D. M.
1968 Rivers and Kroeber in the study of kinship. In reprint edition of Rivers 1914b:7–16.
1984 *A critique of the study of kinship*. Ann Arbor, Mich.
Schorske, C. E.
1980 *Fin-de-siècle Vienna: Politics and culture*. New York.
Schrempp, Gregory
1983 The re-education of Friedrich Max Müller: Intellectual apapropriation and epistemological antimony in mid-Victorian evolutionary thought. *Man* 18:90–110.
Schusky, Ernest
1989 Fred Eggan: Anthropologists full circle. *American Ethnologist* 16:142–57.

Searle, G. R.
1976 *Eugenics and politics in Britain, 1900–1914*. Leyden.

Seligman, B. Z.
1925 Problems of social organization. *Man* 25:53–59.
1927 Bilateral descent and the formation of marriage classes. *JRAI* 57:349–75.

Seligman, C. G.
1910 *The Melanesians of British New Guinea*. Cambridge, Eng.
1913 Some aspects of the Hamitic problem in the Anglo-Egyptian Sudan. *JRAI* 43:593–705.
1924 Anthropology and psychology: A study of some points of contact. *JRAI* 54:13–46.
1927 Review of Rivers 1926. *Nature* 120:685–87.
1932 Anthropological perspective and psychological theory. *JRAI* 62:193–228.
1934 *Egypt and Negro Africa: A study in divine kingship*. London.

Seligman, C. G., & B. Z. Seligman
1911 *The Veddas*. Osterhout, N.B., Netherlands (1969).
1932 *Pagan tribes of the Nilotic Sudan* London.

Semmel, Bernard
1960 *Imperialism and social reform: English social-imperial thought, 1895–1914*. Garden City, N.Y. (1968).

Sergi, Guiseppe
1901 *The Mediterranean race: A study of the origin of European peoples*. London.

Service, E. R.
1985 *A century of controversy: Ethnological issues from 1860 to 1960*. Orlando, Fla.

Shand, A. F.
1914 *The foundations of character: Being a study of the tendencies of the emotions and sentiments*. London.

Shapin, Steven
1992 Discipline and bounding: The history and sociology of science as seen through the externalism-internalism debate. *History of Science* 30:332–69.

Shipman, Pat
1994 *The evolution of racism: Human differences and the use and abuse of science*. New York.

Showalter, Elaine
1987 Rivers and Sassoon: The inscription of male gender anxieties. In M. Higonnet et al., eds., *Behind the lines: Gender and the two world wars*, 61–69. New Haven.

Siebert, Otto
1910 Sagen und Sitten der Dieri. *Globus* 97(3):44–50.

Sillitoe, Paul
1977 To Mer, Mabuiag, Muralug, and Moresby: The Torres Straits Expedition. *Cambridge Anthropology* 3(2):1–21.

Singer, M. B.
1984 A neglected source of structuralism: Radcliffe-Brown, Russell, and Whitehead. *Semiotica* 48(1–2):11–96.

Skeat, W. W., & C. O. Blagden
1906 *Pagan races of the Malay Peninsula*. London (1966).

Slobodin, R. R.
1978 *W. H. R. Rivers.* New York.
Smith, E. W.
1927 *The golden stool: Some aspects of the conflict of cultures in modern Africa.* London.
1934 The story of the Institute: The first seven years. *Africa* 7:1–27.
Smith, E. W., & A. M. Dale
1920 *The Ila-speaking peoples of Northern Rhodesia.* 2 vols. New Hyde Park, N.Y. (1968).
Smith, G. E.
1911 *The ancient Egyptians and their influence upon the civilisation of Europe.* London.
1912 Presidential address to the anthropological section. *Nature* 90:118–26.
1915 *The migrations of early culture: A study of the significance of the geographical distribution of the practice of mummification as evidence of the migrations of peoples and the spread of certain customs and beliefs.* Manchester.
1919 *The evolution of the dragon.* Manchester.
1922 Anthropology. *Encyclopaedia Britannica.* ("New Volumes" [12th ed.]). 30:143–54.
1923 *The ancient Egyptians and the origin of civilization.* London.
1924 Preface. In C. E. Fox, *The threshold of the Pacific,* v–vi. London.
1927 *The evolution of man: Essays.* 2nd ed. London.
1933 *The diffusion of culture.* London.
1938 Fragments of autobiography. In Dawson, ed., 1938:113–22.
Smith, G. E., Bronislaw Malinowski, et al.
1927 *Culture: The diffusion controversy.* New York.
Smith, G. E., & T. H. Pear
1917 *Shell shock and its lessons.* Manchester.
Smith, W. D.
1991 *Politics and the sciences of culture in Germany, 1840–1920.* Oxford.
Smith, W. R.
1868 Prophecy and personality: A fragment. In 1912:97–108.
1869 The work of the Theological Society. In 1912:137–162.
1875 Bible. *Encyclopaedia Britannica.* 9th ed. 2:634–48.
1880a A journey in the Hejâz. In 1912:484–600.
1880b Animal tribes in the Old Testament. In 1912:455–83.
1880c Hebrew language and literature. *Encyclopaedia Britannica.* 9th ed. 11:594–602.
1881 *The Old Testament in the Jewish church: A course of lectures on biblical criticism.* 2nd ed. London (1908).
1882 *The prophets of Israel and their place in history to the close of the eighth century B.C.* New York (1892).
1885 *Kinship and marriage in early Arabia.* Boston (n.d.).
1887 Review of E. Renan, *Histoire du Peuple d'Israël.* In 1912:608–22.
1889 *Lectures on the religion of the Semites: The fundamental institutions.* New York (1957).
1891 Review of Westermarck 1891. *Nature* 44:270–71.

1912 *Lectures and essays of William Robertson Smith,* ed. J. S. Black & G. W. Chrystal. London.

Smyth, R. B.
1878 *The Aborigines of Victoria with notes relating to the habits of the natives of other parts of Australia and Tasmania.* 2 vols. Melbourne.

Sohmer, S. H.
1988 "A selection of fundamentals": The intellectual background of the Melanesian Mission of the Church of England, 1850–1914. Doctoral dissertation, University of Hawaii.

Soffer, R. N.
1978 *Ethics and society in England: The revolution in the social sciences, 1870–1914.* Berkeley.

Sontag, Susan
1966 The anthropologist as hero. In E. N. Tayes & T. Tayes, eds., *Claude Lévi-Strauss: The anthropologist as hero,* 184–97. Cambridge, Mass.

Spain, D. H.
1987 The Westermarck-Freud incest theory debate: An evaluation and reformulation. *CA* 28:623–35.

Spencer, Frank
1990 *Piltdown: A scientific forgery.* London.

Spencer, Herbert
1862 *First principles.* London.
1874 *Descriptive sociology: Lowest races, Negrito races, and Malayo-Polynesian races.* London.

Spencer, W. B.
1896 Ed. *Report on the work of the Horn scientific expedition to central Australia.* 4 vols. London.
1928 *Wanderings in wild Australia.* 2 vols. London.

Spencer, W. B., & F. J. Gillen
1899 *The native tribes of Central Australia.* New York (1968).
1904 *The northern tribes of Central Australia.* London.
1912 *Across Australia.* 2 vols. London.

Spiro, M. E.
1982 *Oedipus in the Trobriands.* Chicago.

Średniawa, B.
1981 The anthropologist as a young physicist: Bronislaw Malinowski's apprenticeship. *Isis* 72:613–20.

Srinivas, M. N.
1973 Itineraries of an Indian social anthropologist. *International Social Science Journal* 25:129–48.

Stanner, W. E.
1956 A. R. Radcliffe-Brown. *Kroeber Anthropological Society Papers* 13:116–25.
1985 Radcliffe-Brown's ideas on "social value." *Social Analysis* 17:113–25.

Stauder, Jack
1980 Great Britain: Functionalism abroad. A theory in question. In S. Diamond, ed., 1980.

Stepan, N. L.
1982 *The idea of race in science: Great Britain 1800–1960.* London.

Stern, B. J.
1930 Ed. Selections from the letters of Lorimer Fison and A. W. Howitt to Lewis Henry Morgan. *AA* 32:257–79, 419–53.
Stigler, S. M.
1986 *The history of statistics: The measurement of uncertainty before 1900.* Cambridge, Mass.
Stipe, C. E.
1980 Anthropologists versus missionaries: The influence of presuppositions. *CA* 21:165–79.
Stirling, E. C.
1896 Anthropology. In W. B. Spencer, ed., 1896:IV, 1–161.
Stocking, G. W., Jr.
1968a Empathy and antipathy in the heart of darkness. *Journal of the History of the Behavioral Sciences* 4:189–94.
1968b *Race, culture and evolution: Essays in the history of anthropology.* New York.
1968c Tylor, Edward Burnett. *International Encyclopedia of the Social Sciences* 10:170–77.
1971a Animism in theory and practice: E. B. Tylor's unpublished "Notes on spiritualism." *Man* 6:88–104.
1971b What's in a name? The origins of the Royal Anthropological Institute, 1837–1971. *Man* 6:369–90.
1973a From chronology to ethnology: James Cowles Prichard and British anthropology, 1800–1850. In reprint edition of Prichard 1813, ix–cx.
1973b Notes on manuscript sources in British anthropology. *HAN* 1(1):2–5.
1974a Some problems in the understanding of nineteenth-century cultural evolutionism. In R. Darnell, ed., *Readings in the history of anthropology,* 407–25. New York.
1974b The basic assumptions of Boasian anthropology. In 1974c:1–20.
1974c Ed. *The shaping of American anthropology, 1883–1911: A Franz Boas reader.* New York.
1976 Ideas and institutions in American anthropology: Thoughts toward a history of the interwar period. In 1992c:114–77.
1977a Contradicting the doctor: Billy Hancock and the problem of baloma. *HAN* 4(1):4–7.
1977b The aims of Boasian ethnography: Creating the materials for traditional humanistic scholarship. *HAN* 4(2):4–5.
1978 The problems of translation between paradigms: The 1933 debate between Ralph Linton and Radcliffe-Brown. *HAN* 5(1):7–9.
1979a *Anthropology at Chicago: Tradition, discipline, department.* Chicago.
1979b "The intensive study of limited areas": Toward an ethnographic context for the Malinowskian innovation. *HAN* 6(2):9–12.
1982a Afterword: A view from the center. In Gerholm & Hannerz, eds., 1982:172–86.
1982b Gatekeeper to the field: E. W. P. Chinnery and the ethnography of the New Guinea mandate. *HAN* 9(2):3–12.
1983 The ethnographer's magic: Fieldwork in British anthropology from Tylor to Malinowski. In 1992c:12–59.

1984a Comparative sociology at Cambridge sociology in 1910 [ed. with introduction by G. W. S.]. *HOA* 2:106–30.
1984b Radcliffe-Brown and British social anthropology. *HOA* 2:131–91.
1985a Essays on museums and material culture. *HOA* 3:3–14.
1985b Philanthropoids and vanishing cultures: Rockefeller funding and the end of the museum era in Anglo-American anthropology. In 1992c:178–211.
1985c "Yours affectionately, Rex"—Radcliffe-Brown during and after World War II. *HAN* 12(2):3–11.
1986a Anthropology and the science of the irrational: Malinowski's encounter with Freudian psychoanalysis. *HOA* 4:13–49.
1986b Essays on culture and personality. *HOA* 4:3–12.
1986c Why does a boy "sign on"?—Malinowski's first statement on practical anthropology. *HAN* 13(2):6–9.
1987a Codrington, R. H. *Encyclopedia of Religion* 3:558.
1987b *Victorian anthropology*. New York.
1989 Paradigmatic traditions in the history of anthropology. In 1992c:342–61.
1990 Malinowski's diary redux: Entries for an index. *HAN* 17(1):3–10.
1991a Maclay, Kubary, Malinowski: Archetypes from the dreamtime of anthropology. In 1992c:211–75.
1991b Ed. *Colonial situations: Essays on the contextualization of anthropological knowledge. HOA* 8.
1992a *Books unwritten, turning points unmarked: Notes for an anti-history of anthropology*. Skomp Lecture, Indiana University Department of Anthropology. Bloomington, Ind.
1992b Charting the progress of animism: E. B. Tylor on "The common religion of mankind." *HAN* 19(1):3–10.
1992c *The ethnographer's magic and other essays in the history of anthropology*. Madison.
1993a Margaret Mead and Radcliffe-Brown: Society, social system, cultural character, and the idea of culture, 1931–35. *HAN* 20(2):3–11.
1993b Reading the palimpsest of inquiry: *Notes and Queries* and the history of British social anthropology. Huxley Memorial Lecture. Unpublished manuscript.
1993c Review of Ackerman 1991 and Kuklick 1991. *Victorian Studies* 36:232–33.
1993d The camera eye as I witness [review of Edwards 1992]. *Visual Anthropology* 6:211–18.
1993e The red-paint of British aggression, the gospel of ten-per-cent, and the cost of maintaining our ascendancy: A. C. Haddon on the need for an Imperial Bureau of Ethnology. *HAN* 20(1):3–15.
1994 Edward Burnett Tylor and the mission of primitive man. Introduction to *The collected works of Edward Burnett Tylor,* I:ix–xxvi. London.
1995 Comments on Dauber 1995. *CA* 36:89–91.

Stolcke, Verena
1993 And the locals in the global? An outsider's view. *Anthropology Today* 9(5):16–17.

Stone, M.
1985 Shellshock and the psychologists. In W. F. Bynum, R. Porter, & M. Shepherd, eds., *The anatomy of madness*, 2:242–71. London.

Strathern, Marilyn
1987 Out of context: The persuasive fictions of anthropology. In M. Manganaro, ed., *Modernist anthropology: From fieldwork to text*, 80–130. Princeton (1990).
1993 Audrey Isabel Richards, 1899–1984. *Proceedings of the British Academy* 82:439–53.

Strauss, D. J., & Martin Orans
1975 Mighty sifts: A critical appraisal of solutions to Galton's problem and a partial solution. *CA* 16:573–94.

Strehlow, T. G. H.
1971 *Songs of Central Australia*. Sydney.

Strenski, Ivan
1982 Malinowski: Second positivism, second romanticism. *Man* 17:266–71.

Stroup, Timothy
1982a *Westermarck's ethics*. Åbo, Finland.
1982b Ed. *Edward Westermarck: Essays on his life and works*. Helsinki.
1984 Edward Westermarck: A reappraisal. *Man* 19:575–92.

Swan, D. A.
1977 Sir Grafton Elliot Smith on "the Negro race." *Mankind Quarterly* 17:283–93.

Swayze, Nancy
1960 *Canadian portraits: Jenness, Barbeau, Wintemberg: The man hunters*. Toronto.

Symmons[-Symonolewicz], Konstantin
1958 Bronislaw Malinowski: An intellectual profile. *Polish Review*. 3(4):55–76.
1959 Bronislaw Malinowski: Formative influences and theoretical evolution. *Polish Review* 4(4):18–45.
1960 The origin of Malinowski's theory of magic. *Polish Review* 5(4):1–9.

Tapper, N.
1980 ASA: A professional association? *Royal Anthropological Institute News* 36:6–7.

Tax, Sol
1956 Primitive religion. Notes on the lectures of A. R. Radcliffe-Brown, Winter 1932. *Anthropology Tomorrow* 4(2):3–41.

Taylor, Isaac
1890 *The origin of the Aryans: An account of the prehistoric ethnology and civilisation of Europe*. London.

Temple, R. C.
1905 The practical value of anthropology. *Indian Antiquary* 34:132–44.
1914 *Anthropology as a practical science: Address delivered at meetings of the British Association at Birmingham, the Antiquarian Society of Cambridge, and the Anthropological Society of Oxford*. London.
1921 "Tout savoir, tout pardonner." An appeal for an Imperial School of Applied Anthropology. [With discussion.] *Man* 21:150–55, 173–75.

1922 A revolutionary theory of social anthropology. *Man* 22:121–27.
1923 Remarks on the Andaman Islanders and their country (I and II). *Indian Antiquary* 52:151–57, 216–24.
1925 Remarks on the Andaman Islanders and their country (III and IV). *Indian Antiquary* 54:21–29, 46–55, 81–94.
1929 Remarks on the Andaman Islanders and their country. *Indian Antiquary* 58:1–48.

Temple, R. C., et al.
1913 Suggestions for a school of applied anthropology. *Man* 13:185–92.
1914 Anthropological teaching in the universities. *Man* 14:57–72.

Testart, Alain
1979 Ed. Lettres de Radcliffe-Brown à Mauss. *Études durkheimiennes* 4:2–7.

Thomas, N. W.
1906 *Kinship organisations and group marriage in Australia*. London (1966).
1910 *Anthropological report on the Edo-speaking peoples of Nigeria*. London.
1913 *Anthropological report on the Ibo-speaking peoples of Nigeria*. London.
1916 *Anthropological report on Sierra Leone*. London.

Thornton, A. P.
1959 *The imperial idea and its enemies: A study in British power*. Garden City, N.Y. (1968).

Thornton, R. J.
1983 Narrative ethnography in Africa, 1850–1920: The creation and capture of an appropriate domain for anthropology. *Man* 18:502–20.
1985 "Imagine yourself set down": Mach, Conrad, Frazer, Malinowski and the role of imagination in ethnography. *Anthropology Today* 1(5):7–14.
1989 Capture by description: Writing ethnography in southern Africa, 1845–1900. Unpublished manuscript.
1992a Life in the perspective of science: Malinowski and the birth of functionalism from the spirit of Central Europe, or Zarathustra in the London School of Economics. Paper presented at the 8th Triennial Conference of the International Society for the Study of Time.
1992b The chains of reciprocity: The impact of Nietzsche's *Genealogy* on Malinowski's *Crime and Custom in Savage Society*. *Polish Sociological Bulletin* 1(97):19–34.

Thornton, R. J., & Peter Skalnik
1993a Introduction: Malinowski's reading, writing, 1904–1914. In 1993b:1–64.
1993b Eds. *The early writings of Bronislaw Malinowski*. Cambridge, Eng.

Titchener, E. B.
1916 On ethnological tests of sensation and perception, with special reference to tests of color vision and tactile discrimination described in the Reports of the Cambridge Anthropological Expedition to Torres Straits. *Proceedings of the American Philosophical Society* 55:204–36.

Tomas, David
1991 Tools of the trade: The production of ethnographic observations in the Andaman Islands, 1858–1922. *HOA* 7:75–108.

Trautman, T. R.
1987 *Lewis Henry Morgan and the invention of kinship*. Berkeley.

Trotter, W. M.
1920 *Instincts of the herd in peace and war.*
Turner, F. M.
1974 *Between science and religion: The reaction to scientific naturalism in late Victorian England.* New Haven.
1981 *The Greek heritage in Victorian Britain.* New Haven.
Tuzin, Donald
1994 The forgotten passion: Sexuality and anthropology in the ages of Victoria and Bronislaw. *Journal of the History of the Behavioral Sciences* 29:114–37.
Tylor, E. B.
1861 *Anuahac, or Mexico and the Mexicans, ancient and modern.* London.
1865 *Researches into the early history of mankind and the development of civilization.* 2nd ed. London (1870).
1871 *Primitive culture: Researches into the development of mythology, philosophy, religion, language, art, and custom.* 2 vols. London (1873).
1873 Primitive society. *Contemporary Review* 21:701–18; 22:53–72.
1878 Review of L. H. Morgan 1877. *Academy* 14:67–68.
1879 Remarks on Australian marriage laws. *JAI* 9:354.
1880 Anniversary address. *JAI* 9:443–99.
1881a *Anthropology: An introduction to the study of man and civilization.* London.
1881b Obituary of J. F. M'Lennan. *Academy* 20:9–10.
1881c Review of Fison & Howitt 1880. *Academy* 19:264–66.
1884 American aspects of anthropology. In BAAS, *Report of the 54th Meeting,* 899–910.
1885a How the problems of American anthropology look to the English anthropologist. *Transactions of the Anthropological Society of Washington* 3:81–94.
1885b Review of McLennan 1885. *Academy* 28:67–68.
1888 On a method of investigating the development of institutions, applied to laws of marriage and descent. *JAI* 18:245–72.
1891 Review of Westermarck 1891. *Academy* 40:288–89.
1892 On the limits of savage religion. *JAI* 21:283–301.
1893 On the Tasmanians as representatives of palaeolithic man. *JAI* 23:141–52.
1896a On American lot-games, as evidence of Asiatic intercourse before the time of Columbus. *International Archiv für Ethnographie* 9:55–67.
1896b The matriarchal family system. *Nineteenth Century* 40:81–96.
1898 Remarks on totemism, with special reference to some modern theories respecting it. *JAI* 28:138–48.
1910 Anthropology. *Encyclopaedia Britannica.* 11th ed. 2:108–19.
Union of South Africa.
1922a Report of the martial law inquiry judicial commission. Pretoria.
1922b Report of the Native Affairs Commission for the year 1921. Cape Town.
University College, London.
n.d. *University College London: A survey, 1950–1955.* London.

Urry, James
1972 *Notes and Queries on Anthropology* and the development of field methods in British anthropology, 1870–1920. In 1993:17–40.
1984a A history of field methods. In Ellen, ed., 1984; 35–61.
1984b Englishmen, Celts, and Iberians: The ethnographic survey of the United Kingdom, 1892–1899. In 1993:83–101.
1987 W. E. Armstrong and social anthropology at Cambridge, 1922–1926. *Man* 20:412–33.
1993 *Before social anthropology: Essays on the history of British anthropology*. Chur, Switzerland.

Van Gennep, Arnold
1909 *The rites of passage*. Trans. M. Vizedom & G. Caffee. Chicago (1961).
1920 *L'État actuel du probleme totemique*. Paris.

Van Keuren, D. K.
1982 Human science in Victorian Britain: Anthropology in institutional and disciplinary formation, 1863–1908. Doctoral dissertation, University of Pennsylvania.

Van Riper, A. B.
1993 *Men among mammoths: Victorian science and the discovery of human prehistory*. Chicago.

Vaughn, J. H., Jr.
1980 A reconsideration of divine kingship. In I. Karp & C. Bird, eds., *Explorations in African systems of thought*, 120–42. Bloomington, Ind.

Vickery, J. B.
1973 *The literary impact of "The Golden Bough."* Princeton.

Von Laue, Theodore
1976 Anthropology and power: R. S. Rattray among the Ashanti. *African Affairs* 75:33–54.

Von Wright, G. H.
1982 The origin and development of Westermarck's moral philosophy. In Stroup, ed., 1982b:25–62.

Waitz, Theodor
1862–77 *Anthropologie der Naturvölker*. [Completed by G. Gerland.] 6 vols. Leipzig.
1863 *Introduction to Anthropology*. Vol. I. Ed. J. F. Collingwood. London.

Walker, E. A.
1928 *A history of South Africa*. London.

Walker, M. H.
1971 *Come wind, come weather: A biography of Alfred Howitt*. Melbourne.

Wallace, E., R., IV
1983 *Freud and anthropology: A history and appraisal*. New York.

Wallas, Graham
1908 *Human nature in politics*. London.

Wallis, W. D.
1957 Anthropology in England early in the present century. *AA* 59:781–90.

Ward, James
1885 Psychology. *Encyclopaedia Britannica*. 9th ed. 20:37–85.

Warner, M. H.
1988 *W. Lloyd Warner: Social anthropologist*. New York.
Warren, M. A. C.
1967 *Social history and Christian mission*. London.
Watson, E. G.
1946 *But to what purpose? The autobiography of a contemporary*. London.
Watson, Graham
1984 The social construction of boundaries between social and cultural anthropology in Britain and North America. *Journal of Anthropological Research* 40:351–67.
Wax, M. L.
1978 Tenting with Malinowski. *American Sociological Review* 47:1–13.
Wayne Malinowska, Helena
1985 Bronislaw Malinowski: The influence of various women on his life and works. *American Ethnologist* 12:529–40.
1993 An Anglo-Polish couple on the Ritten, or, an ideal place to live. Unpublished manuscript.
Welch, W. M.
1988 *No country for a gentleman: British rule in Egypt, 1883–1907*. New York.
Weickhardt, Len
1989 *Masson of Melbourne: The life and time of David Orme Masson*. Parkville, Victoria, Australia.
Weiner, A. B.
1976 *Women of value, men of renown: New perspectives in Trobriand Island exchange*. Austin, Texas.
West, F. J.
1968 *Hubert Murray: The Australian proconsul*. Melbourne.
1979 Ernest William Pearson Chinnery (1887–1972). *Australian Dictionary of Biography (1891–1939)* 7:639–40.
Westermarck, E. A.
1891 *The history of human marriage*. London.
1906–8 *The origin and development of moral ideas*. 2 vols. London.
1908 The killing of the divine king. *Man* 8:22–24.
1914 *Marriage ceremonies in Morocco*. London.
1920 *The belief in spirits in Morocco*. Åbo.
1926 *Ritual and belief in Morocco*. 2 vols. London.
1927 *Memories of my life*. Trans. A. Barwell. New York.
1928 The study of popular sayings. In Dawson, ed., 1932:190–212.
1931 *Wit and wisdom in Morocco: A study in native proverbs*. New York.
1933 *Pagan survivals in Mohammedan civilisation*. London.
1936 Methods in social anthropology. *JRAI* 46:223–48.
Wetherell, David, & Charlotte Carr-Gregg
1990 *Camilla: C. H. Wedgwood, 1901–1955, a life*. Kensington, New South Wales.
Wheeler, G. C.
1910 *The tribe, and intertribal relations in Australia*. London.
1926 *Mono-Alu folklore, Bougainville Straits, Western Solomon Islands*. London.

Wheeler-Barclay, Marjorie
1987 The science of religion in Britain, 1860–1915. Doctoral dissertation, Northwestern University.

White, Isobel
1981 Mrs. Bates and Mr. Brown: An examination of Rodney Needham's allegations. *Oceania* 51:103–210.

White, L. A.
1966 The social organization of ethnological theory. *Rice University Studies* 52(4).

Wikman, K. R.
1940 Ed. Letters from Edward B. Tylor and Alfred Russel Wallace to Edward Westermarck. *Acta Academia Aboensis Humaniora* 13:1–22.

Wilkinson, Rupert
1964 *Gentlemanly power: British leadership and the public school tradition, a comparative study in the making of rulers.* Oxford.

Williams, F. E.
1923a The collection of curios and the preservation of native culture. *Anthropology: Report number 3.* Port Moresby.
1923b The vailala madness and the destruction of native ceremonies in the gulf division. *Anthropology: Report number 4.* Port Moresby.
1928a Native education: The language of instruction and intellectual education. *Anthropology: Report number 9.* Port Moresby.
1928b *Orokaiva magic.* Oxford.
1930 *Orokaiva society.* London.
1939 Ed. The reminiscences of Ahuia Ova. *JRAI* 69:11–44.

Williams, T. R., & James Calvert
1859 *Fiji and the Fijians,* ed. G. S. Rowe. New York.

Williamson, R. W.
1924 *The social and political systems of central Polynesia.* Cambridge, Eng.

Wilson, E. F.
1887 Report on the Blackfoot tribes. In BAAS, *Report of the 57th Meeting,* 183–97.

Wilson, Godfrey, & M. H. Wilson
1945 *The analysis of social change, based on observations in Central Africa.* Cambridge (1968).

Wise, Tiger
1985 *The self-made anthropologist: A life of A. P. Elkin.* Sydney.

Witkiewicz, S. I.
1910 *The 622 downfalls of Bungo; or, the demonic woman.* Excerpted & translated in D. Gerould, ed., *The Witkiewicz reader,* 52–74. Evanston, Ill. (1992).

Wolfe, Patrick
1994 White man's flour: Imperialism and an appropriated anthropology. Doctoral dissertation, University of Melbourne.

Woolf, Leonard
1919 *The empire and commerce in Africa: A study in economic imperialism.* London.

Wortham, J. D.
1971 *The genesis of British Egyptology, 1549–1906.* Norman, Okla.

Wraith, R. E.
1967 *Guggisberg*. London.

Wright, T. V.
1991 The fieldwork photographs of Jenness and Malinowski and the beginnings of modern anthropology. *JASO* 22:41–58.

Yonge, C. M.
1874 *Life of John Coleridge Patteson*. 2nd ed. 2 vols. London.

Young, M. W.
1979 Ed. *The ethnography of Malinowski: The Trobriand Islands, 1915–18*. London.
1984 The intensive study of a restricted area: or, why did Malinowski go to the Trobriand Islands? *Oceania* 55:1–26.
1987 The ethnographer as hero: The imponderabilia of Malinowski's everyday life in Mailu. *Canberra Anthropology* 10(2):32–50.
1988a Editor's introduction. In 1988b: 1–76.
1988b Ed. *Malinowski among the Magi: "The natives of Mailu."* London.

Young, R. M.
1970 *Mind, brain and adaptation in the nineteenth century: Cerebral localization and its biological context from Gall to Ferrier*. Oxford.

Zuckerman, Solly
1973 Ed. *The concepts of human evolution: A symposium held to mark the centenary of the birth of Sir Grafton Elliot Smith, FRS*. Symposia of the Zoological Society of London, 34.

Manuscript Sources

In writing this book I have drawn on correspondence and other manuscript materials (some of them in printed form) in a number of archives, which are listed here alphabetically, according to the acronyms used in the notes. (See also Stocking 1973b.) Because many of these collections were consulted more than twenty years ago, and were then uncatalogued, or have since been reorganized (or relocated), in general I have not made use of any system of catalogue references, but have simply cited by correspondent and date, or in some instances by file title. Scholars consulting these materials today will no doubt wish to make use of such finding aids as are now available.

AAAP	American Anthropological Association Papers, National Anthropological Archives, Smithsonian Institution, Washington, D.C.
ACHP	Alfred C. Haddon Papers, Cambridge University Library, Cambridge, Eng.
AKP	Arthur Keith Papers, Royal College of Surgeons, London.
ALKP	A. L. Kroeber Papers, Bancroft Library, University of California, Berkeley.
AMHP	A. M. Hocart Papers, Alexander Turnbull Library, Wellington, New Zealand (nine reels, microfilm, 1970). An index of these is included in R. Needham 1967.
ASAM	Minutes of the Association of Social Anthropologists, made available to me in 1969 by Peter Lloyd, University of Sussex.
BMPL	Bronislaw Malinowski Papers, London School of Economics.
BMPY	Bronislaw Malinowski Papers, Yale University Library.
BMSC	Bronislaw Malinowski personal volumes, University of California, Santa Cruz.
CBAS	Cambridge University Board of Anthropological Studies minutes, etc., in the Museum of Archaeology and Anthropology, Cambridge, Eng.
CSMF	Charles G. Seligman Papers, in the possession of Meyer Fortes at the time of consultation.
CSAI	Seligman manuscripts in the archives of the Royal Anthropological Institute.
CSMD	Manuscript diary of Charles Myers, 1898, in the possession of Brig. Gen. Edmund Myers, Broadwell, Glos., Eng.
CUPC	Correspondence files, Cambridge University Press.

EBTP	Edward B. Tylor Papers, Pitt Rivers Museum, Oxford.
EMP	Elton Mayo Papers, Harvard Business School, Cambridge, Mass.
FCCP	Fay-Cooper Cole Papers, Regenstein Library, University of Chicago.
FGP	Francis Galton Papers, University College, London.
GMP	Gilbert Murray Papers, Bodleian Library, Oxford.
JGFP	Typed copies of J. G. Frazer's letters in the Trinity College Library, Cambridge, Eng.
JHHC	John Henry Hutton correspondence, Museum of Archaeology and Anthropology, Cambridge, Eng.
JLMP	John Linton Myres Papers, Bodleian Library, Oxford.
JWPM	Manuscript biography of William Perry, by C. E. Joel, made available to me by Mrs. Margaret Harkness.
LFMM	Lorimer Fison, letters printed in the *Wesleyan Missionary Notices*, Methodist Missionary Society, London.
LFPC	Typed copies of material from the letter books of Lorimer Fison in the Tippett Collection, St. Mark's Library, Canberra, made available to me by Mark Francillon.
LFPM	Lorimer Fison, Miscellaneous Papers on Fiji, a microfilm copy of materials in the Pacific Manuscripts Bureau, Research School of Pacific Studies, Australian National University.
LHMP	Lewis Henry Morgan Papers, University of Rochester Library.
LSEA	Archives of the London School of Economics.
MCMA	The Macmillan Archive, British Museum, London.
MFP	Personal manuscripts in the possession of the late Meyer Fortes.
MHP	Lord Malcolm Hailey Papers, Rhodes House, Oxford.
OUCA	Records of the Oxford University Committee on Anthropology, Bodleian Library.
RAC	Archives of the Laura Spelman Rockefeller Memorial and the Rockefeller Foundation, in the Rockefeller Archive Center, North Tarryton, N.Y.
RAIA	Archives of the Royal Anthropological Institute, London.
RBDB	Letters of A. R. Brown to Daisy Bates, Battye Library, Perth, Australia.
RBMF	Clippings of Radcliffe-Brown, in the possession of the late Meyer Fortes.
RBPR	Materials of A. R. Brown in the Pitt Rivers Museum, Oxford.
RBSN	Notes on the lectures of A. R. Brown taken by Isaac Schapera, in the Institute of Social Anthropology, Oxford.
RBUC	Typescript, corrected version of the opening section of Radcliffe-Brown 1937, Regenstein Library, University of Chicago.
RCLF	Typed copies of letters from Robert Codrington to Lorimer Fison in the Fison Papers, Tippett Collection, St. Mark's Library, Canberra, made available to me by Mark Francillon.
RHCP	Robert Henry Codrington Papers, Rhodes House, Oxford.
RHLP	Robert Lowie Papers, Bancroft Library, University of California, Berkeley.

RRP	Robert Redfield Papers, Regenstein Library, University of Chicago.
UCBA	University of California, Berkeley, Department of Anthropology Papers, Bancroft Library, Berkeley.
UCDA	University of Chicago Department of Anthropology Papers, Regenstein Library, University of Chicago.
USPG	Letters of Codrington and Patteson, United Society for the Propagation of the Gospel, London.
WBSP	Letters of Walter Baldwin Spencer, Pitt Rivers Museum, Oxford.
WHRP	William Rivers Papers, in the Haddon Papers, Cambridge University Library, Cambridge, Eng.
WRSM	William Robertson Smith Papers, Cambridge University Library, Cambridge, Eng.

Oral Sources

Aside from casual conversations in the course of collegial interaction at various academic venues—including the University of Chicago, Cambridge University, the London School of Economics, Oxford University, and three meetings of the Association of Social Anthropologists (1969, 1984, 1993)—I have had extended conversations with a number of participants in this history (or their relatives or associates) or have been present at seminars in which they offered reminiscences. They include Gregory Bateson, Beatrice Blackwood, Miles Burkitt, Geoffrey Bushnell, Fred Eggan, Edward Evan Evans-Prichard, Raymond Firth, Daryll Forde, Meyer Fortes, Reo Fortune, Maurice Freedman, Max Gluckman, Jack Goody, Ernest Haddon, Margaret Harkness (daughter of William Perry), Christoph von Fürer-Haimendorf, Hilda Kuper, John Layard, Phyllis Kaberry, Edmund Leach, Peter Lloyd, Lucy Mair, Edmund Myers, Cynthia Pike (daughter of A. R. Radcliffe-Brown), Julian Pitt-Rivers, A. H. Quiggin, Audrey Richards, Isaac Schapera, M. N. Srinivas, Sol Tax, Helena Wayne Malinowska, and Monica Wilson.

Index